Through the Prism of Difference

Readings on Sex and Gender

Through the Prism of Difference

Readings on Sex and Gender

Edited by

MAXINE BACA ZINN
Michigan State University

PIERRETTE HONDAGNEU-SOTELO
University of Southern California

MICHAEL A. MESSNER
University of Southern California

ALLYN AND BACON

Boston   London   Toronto   Sydney   Tokyo   Singapore

Editor-in-Chief, Social Sciences: Karen Hanson
Series Editor: Sarah Dunbar
Editorial Assistant: Jennifer Jacobson
Marketing Manager: Karon Bowers
Sr. Editorial Production Administrator: Susan McIntyre
Editorial Production Service: Ruttle, Shaw & Wetherill, Inc.
Composition Buyer: Linda Cox
Manufacturing Buyer: Megan Cochran
Cover Administrator: Linda Knowles

Library of Congress Cataloging-in-Publication Data

Through the prism of difference : readings on sex and gender / edited
  by Maxine Baca Zinn, Pierrette Hondagneu-Sotelo, Michael A. Messner.
       p.   cm.
    Includes bibliographical references (p.).
    ISBN 0-205-26415-8
    1. Sex role.   I. Zinn, Maxine Baca, [date]   II. Hondagneu-
Sotelo, Pierrette.   III. Messner, Michael A.
HQ1075.T49   1996
305.3–dc20   96-43746
                                                                 CIP

Printed in the United States of America
10 9 8 7 6 5 4 3 2 1   03 02 01 00 99 98 97

CONTENTS

Preface   ix

Introduction: Sex and Gender through the Prism of Difference   1

Part One
Perspectives on Sex, Gender, and Difference   9

Chapter 1   Sex and Gender: The Challenge of Difference

1. Judith Lorber, "Believing Is Seeing: Biology as Ideology"   13
2. Maxine Baca Zinn and Bonnie Thornton Dill, "Theorizing Difference
   from Multiracial Feminism"   23
3. Edna Acosta-Belén and Christine E. Bose, "Colonialism, Structural Subordination,
   and Empowerment: Women in the Development Process in Latin America
   and the Caribbean"   30
4. Barrie Thorne, "Children and Gender: Constructions of Difference"   39
5. Carol B. Stack, "Different Voices, Different Visions: Gender, Culture,
   and Moral Reasoning"   51
6. Pierrette Hondagneu-Sotelo and Michael A. Messner, "Gender Displays
   and Men's Power: The 'New Man' and the Mexican Immigrant Man"   58

Chapter 2   Studying across Difference

7. Margaret L. Andersen, "Studying across Difference: Race, Class, and Gender
   in Qualitative Research"   70
8. Kath Weston, "Fieldwork in Lesbian and Gay Communities"   79
9. Steven J. Gold, "A White Guy among Vietnamese Women"   86

Part Two
Bodies   91

Chapter 3   Embodiments of Control and Resistance

10. Becky Wangsgaard Thompson, "'A Way Outa No Way': Eating Problems among
    African American, Latina, and White Women"   93
11. Thomas J. Gerschick and Adam Stephen Miller, "Coming to Terms: Masculinity
    and Physical Disability"   104

Chapter 4   Violence

12. Jack C. Straton, "The Myth of the 'Battered Husband Syndrome'"   118
13. Beth E. Richie and Valli Kanuha, "Battered Women of Color in Public Health Care
    Systems: Racism, Sexism, and Violence"   121

14. Tim Beneke, "Men on Rape"   130
15. Nancy A. Matthews, "Surmounting a Legacy: The Expansion of Racial Diversity in a Local Anti-Rape Movement"   136
16. Michael A. Messner, "When Bodies Are Weapons"   146

Chapter 5   Reproductive Politics

17. Debbie Nathan, "Abortion Stories on the Border"   151
18. Rayna Rapp, "Constructing Amniocentisis: Maternal and Medical Discourses"   154
19. Barbara Katz Rothman, "On 'Surrogacy'"   164

Part Three
Sexualities   171

Chapter 6   Sexual Relations, Intimacy, and Power

20. Deborah L. Tolman, "Doing Desire: Adolescent Girls' Struggles for/with Sexuality"   173
21. Robert Staples, "Anita Hill, Sexual Harassment, and Gender Politics in the Black Community"   186
22. Cynthia Enloe, "It Takes More Than Two: The Prostitute, the Soldier, the State, and the Entrepreneur"   193

Chapter 7   Sexuality and Identity

23. Marilyn Frye, "Lesbian 'Sex'"   205
24. Joseph Carrier, "Miguel: Sexual Life History of a Gay Mexican American"   210
25. Evelyne Accad, "Sexuality and Sexual Politics: Conflicts and Contradictions for Contemporary Women in the Middle East"   221

Part Four
Identities   231

Chapter 8   Defining the Self through Difference

26. Slavenka Drakulic, "A Letter from the United States—the Critical Theory Approach"   233
27. Michael S. Kimmel, "Judaism, Masculinity and Feminism"   237
28. Gloria Anzaldúa, "La Conciencia de la Mestiza: Towards a New Consciousness"   240
29. Anastasia Higginbotham, "Chicks Goin' at It"   249

Part Five
Families   255

Chapter 9   Constructing Motherhood and Fatherhood

30. Nancy Scheper-Hughes, "(M)Other Love: Culture, Scarcity, and Maternal Thinking"   257

31. Patricia Hill Collins, "The Meaning of Motherhood in Black Culture and Black Mother–Daughter Relationships"   264

32. Denise A. Segura, "Working at Motherhood: Chicana and Mexican Immigrant Mothers and Employment"   276

33. Ralph LaRossa, "Fatherhood and Social Change"   291

Chapter 10   Work and Families

34. David D. Gilmore, "Men and Women in Southern Spain: 'Domestic Power' Revisited"   303

35. M. Patricia Fernández Kelly, "Delicate Transactions: Gender, Home, and Employment among Hispanic Women"   313

36. Nazli Kibria, "Culture, Social Class, and Income Control in the Lives of Women Garment Workers in Bangladesh"   323

37. Elizabeth Higginbotham and Lynn Weber, "Moving Up with Kin and Community: Upward Social Mobility for Black and White Women"   337

Part Six
Public Institutions: Work and Education   347

Chapter 11   Constructing Gender in Workplaces

38. Peter M. Nardi, "The Social World of Magicians: Gender and Conjuring"   349

39. Rosemary Pringle, "Male Secretaries"   357

40. Patti A. Giuffre and Christine L. Williams, "Boundary Lines: Labeling Sexual Harassment in Restaurants"   372

41. Karen J. Hossfeld, "'Their Logic against Them': Contradictions in Sex, Race, and Class in Silicon Valley"   388

42. Teresa Amott, "Shortchanged: Restructuring Women's Work"   401

43. Esther Ngan-Ling Chow, "Asian American Women at Work"   408

Chapter 12   Negotiating Gender in Schools

44. R. W. Connell, "Disruptions: Improper Masculinities in Schooling"   418

45. Wendy Luttrell, "'Becoming Somebody': Aspirations, Opportunities, and Womanhood"   431

Part Seven
Ideology   441

Chapter 13   Competing Ideas and Images

46. Manning Marable, "The Black Male: Searching beyond Stereotypes"   443

47. Stan Denski and David Sholle, "Metal Men and Glamour Boys: Gender Performance in Heavy Metal"   450

48. Clara Sue Kidwell, "Indian Women as Cultural Mediators"   457

Part Eight
Change and Politics   465

Chapter 14   Patriarchal Bargains: The Contradictions of Cultural Changes

49. Deniz Kandiyoti, "Bargaining with Patriarchy"   467
50. Pierrette Hondagneu-Sotelo, "Overcoming Patriarchal Constraints: The Reconstruction of Gender Relations among Mexican Immigrant Women and Men"   477
51. Tracy Bachrach Ehlers, "Debunking Marianismo: Economic Vulnerability and Survival Strategies among Guatemalan Wives"   486
52. Judith Stacey and Susan Elizabeth Gerard, "'We Are Not Doormats': The Influence of Feminism on Contemporary Evangelicals in the United States"   498

Chapter 15   Social Movements: Communities and the State

53. Mary Pardo, "Mexican American Women Grassroots Community Activists: 'Mothers of East Los Angeles'"   509
54. Cheryl Townsend Gilkes, "Building in Many Places: Multiple Commitments and Ideologies in Black Women's Community Work"   515
55. Helen Icken Safa, "Women's Social Movements in Latin America"   528

Chapter 16   Visions of the Future

56. Audre Lorde, "Age, Race, Class, and Sex: Women Redefining Difference"   539
57. Walter L. Williams, "Benefits for Nonhomophobic Societies: An Anthropological Perspective"   545
58. bell hooks and Cornel West, "Breaking Bread"   554

Credits   559

PREFACE

Over the past 25 years, texts and readers intended for use in women's studies and gender studies courses have changed and developed in important ways. In the 1970s and into the early 1980s, many courses and texts focused almost exclusively on women as a relatively undifferentiated category. Two developments have broadened the study of women. First, in response to criticisms by women of color and by lesbians that heterosexual, White middle-class feminists had tended to "falsely universalize" their own experiences and issues, courses and texts on gender began in the 1980s to systematically incorporate race and class diversity. And simultaneously, as a result of feminist scholars' insistence that gender be studied as a relational construct, more concrete studies of men and masculinity began to emerge in the 1980s.

This book reflects this belief that race, class, and sexual diversity among women and men should be central to the study of gender. But this collection adds an important new dimension that will broaden the frame of gender studies. By including some articles that are based on research in countries outside the United States, in nonindustrial societies, and among immigrant groups, we hope that *Through the Prism of Difference* will contribute to a transcendence of the often myopic, U.S.-based, and Eurocentric focus in the study of sex, and gender. The inclusion of these perspectives is not simply useful for illuminating our own cultural blind spots; it also begins to demonstrate how, as the twentieth century comes to a close, gender relations are increasingly centrally implicated in current processes of globalization.

Because the amount of high-quality research on sex and gender has expanded so dramatically in the past decade, the most difficult task in assembling this collection was deciding *what* to include. We would especially like to acknowledge Margaret L. Andersen for her contributions. We thank our faculty and staff colleagues in the Department of Sociology and the Program for the Study of Women and Men in Society at the University of Southern California and in the Department of Sociology and the Julian Samora Research Institute at Michigan State University for their generous support and assistance.

Other people contributed their labor to the development of this book. We are grateful to our research assistants, Faye Linda Wachs of the University of Southern California and Barbara A. Wells of Michigan State University, who contributed invaluable groundwork. Nancy Mezey and Darcel Smith of Michigan State University also provided assistance on this project.

We acknowledge the helpful criticism and suggestions made by those who reviewed earlier drafts of the manuscript: Claire Renzetti of St. Joseph's University, Rachel K. Jones of Tulane University, Virginia Powell of Beloit College, and Beth Hess of County College of Morris. Our editor at Allyn and Bacon, Karen Hanson, has always been helpful, encouraging, and, above all, patient. Jennifer Jacobson was an efficient and professional editorial assistant as the book moved into production.

Finally, we would like to thank our families for their love and support as we worked on this book. Prentice Zinn and Gabrielle Cobbs are now intellectuals and activists in their own right. They provide inspiration through their fierce commitment to bridging scholarship and practice. Miles Hondagneu-Messner and Sasha Hondagneu-Messner continually challenge the neatness of Mike and Pierrette's image of social life. Life with a seven-year-old and a three-year-old is less a neat rainbow shining through a stable prism than it is a kaleidoscope of constantly shifting moments and meanings. We do hope, though, that the kind of work that is collected in this book will eventually help them, and their generation, make sense of the world and move that world into more peaceful, humane, and just directions.

Through the Prism of Difference

Readings on Sex and Gender

Introduction

Sex and Gender through
the Prism of Difference

"Men can't cry." "Women are victims of patriarchal oppression." "After divorces, single mothers are downwardly mobile, often moving into poverty." "Men don't do their share of housework and childcare." "Professional women face barriers such as sexual harassment and a 'glass ceiling' that prevent them from competing equally with men for high-status positions and high salaries." "Heterosexual intercourse is an expression of men's power over women." Sometimes, the students in our sociology and gender studies courses balk at these kinds of generalizations, and they are right to do so. After all, some men are more emotionally expressive than some women, some women have more power and success than some men, some men do their share—or more—of housework and childcare, and some women experience sex with men as both pleasurable and empowering. Indeed, contemporary gender relations are complex, changing in various directions, and so we need to be wary of simplistic, if handy, slogans that seem to sum up the essence of relations between women and men.

On the other hand, we think it is a tremendous mistake to conclude that "all individuals are totally unique and different" and that therefore all generalizations about social groups are impossible or inherently oppressive. In fact, we are convinced that it is this very complexity, this multifaceted nature of contemporary gender relations that fairly begs for a sociological analysis of gender. In the title of this book, we use the image of "the prism of difference" to illustrate our approach to developing this sociological perspective on contemporary gender relations. *The American Heritage Dictionary* defines *prism,* in part, as "a homogeneous transparent solid, usually with triangular bases and rectangular sides, used to produce or analyze a continuous spectrum." Imagine a ray of light, which to the naked eye appears to be only one color, refracted through a prism onto a white wall. To the eye, the result is not an infinite, disorganized scatter of individual colors. Rather, the refracted light displays an order, a structure of relationships among the different colors—a rainbow. Similarly, we use the "prism of difference" in this book to analyze a continuous spectrum of people, to show how gender is organized and experienced differently when refracted through the prism of sexual, racial/ethnic, social class, physical abilities, age, and national citizenship differences.

EARLY WOMEN'S STUDIES: CATEGORICAL VIEWS OF "WOMEN" AND "MEN"

Taken together, the articles in this book present a case to show that it is possible to make good generalizations about women and men. But these generalizations should be drawn carefully, by always asking the questions "*which* women?" and "*which* men?". Scholars of sex and gender have not always done this. In the 1960s and 1970s, women's studies focused on the differences *between* women and men rather than *among* women and men. The very concept of gender, women's studies scholars demonstrated, is based on socially defined difference between women and men. From the macro level of social institutions, such as the economy, politics, and religion, to the micro level of interpersonal relations, distinctions between women and men structure social relations. Defining differences between males and females is the essence of gender. It is also the basis of men's power and domination. Understanding this was profoundly illuminating. Knowing that difference produced domination enabled women to name, analyze, and set about changing their victimization.

In the 1970s, riding the wave of a resurgent feminist movement, colleges and universities began to develop women's studies courses that aimed first and foremost to make women's lives visible. The texts that were developed for these courses tended to stress the things that women shared under patriarchy: having the responsibility for housework and childcare, the experience or fear of men's sexual violence, a lack of formal or informal access to education, exclusion from high-status professional and managerial jobs, political office, and religious leadership positions (Brownmiller, 1975; Kanter, 1977).

Attention to the study of women in society offered new ways of seeing the world. But the 1970s approach was limited in several ways. Thinking of gender primarily in terms of differences between women and men led scholars to overgeneralize about both. The concept of patriarchy led to a dualistic perspective of male privilege and female subordination. Women and men were cast as opposites. Each was treated as a homogeneous category with common characteristics and experiences. This approach *essentialized* women and men. Essentialism, simply put, is the notion that female and male attributes are categorically and universally different. From this perspective, male control and coercion of women produced conflict between the sexes. The feminist insight originally introduced by Simone De Beauvoir in 1953—that women, as a group, had been socially defined as the "other" and that men had constructed themselves as the subjects of history, while constructing women as their objects—fueled an energizing sense of togetherness among many women. As college students read books like *Sisterhood Is Powerful* (Morgan, 1970) many of them joined organizations that fought, with some success, for equality and justice for women.

THE VOICES OF "OTHER" WOMEN

Although this view of women as an oppressed "other" was empowering for certain groups of women, some women began to claim that the feminist view of universal sisterhood ignored and marginalized their major concerns. It soon became apparent that treating women as a group united in its victimization by patriarchy was biased by too narrow a focus on the experiences and perspectives of women from more privileged social groups. "Gender" was treated as a generic category, uniformly applied to all women. Ironically, this analysis, which was meant to unify women, instead produced divisions between and among them. The concerns projected as "universal" were removed from the realities of many women's lives. For example, it became a matter of faith in second-wave feminism that women's liberation would be accomplished by breaking down the "gendered public-domestic split." Indeed, the feminist call for women to move out of the kitchens and into the workplaces resonated in the experiences of many of the college-educated White women who were inspired by Betty Friedan's 1963 book, *The Feminine Mystique*. But the idea that women's movement into workplaces was itself empowering or liberating seemed absurd or irrelevant to many working-class women and women of color. They were already working for wages, as had many of their mothers and grandmothers, and did not consider access to jobs and public life as "liberating." For many of these women, liberation had more to do with organizing in workplaces—often alongside men—for better pay, decent benefits, and policies that broke down occupational segregation by gender or race. The feminism of the 1970s did not seem to address these issues.

As more and more women analyzed their own experiences, they began to address the power relations creating differences among women and the part that privileged women played in the oppression of others. For many women of color, working-class women, lesbians, and women in contexts outside the United States (especially women in non-Western societies), the focus on male domination was a distraction from other oppressions. Their own experiences could support neither a unitary theory of gender nor an ideology of universal sisterhood. As a result, finding common ground in a universal female victimization was never a priority for many groups of women.

Challenges to gender stereotypes soon emerged. Women of varied races, classes, national origins, and sexualities insisted that the concept of gender be broadened to take their differences into account (Baca Zinn et al., 1986; Hartmann, 1976; Rich, 1980; Smith, 1977). Many women began to argue that their lives are affected by their location in a number of different hierarchies: as African Americans, Latinas, Native Americans, or Asian Americans in the race hierarchy; as young or old in the age hierarchy; as heterosexual or homosexual in the sexual orientation hierarchy; and as women outside the United States in subordinated geopolitical contexts. These arguments made it clear that women were not victimized by gender alone but by the historical and systematic denial of rights and privileges based on other differences as well.

MEN AS GENDERED BEINGS

As the voices of "other" women in the mid- to late 1970s began to challenge and expand the parameters of women's studies, a new area of scholarly inquiry was beginning to stir—a critical examination of men and masculinity. To be sure, in those early years of gender studies, the major task was to conduct studies and develop courses about the lives of women and, by doing so, to begin to correct centuries of scholarship that rendered women's lives, problems, and accomplishments invisible. But the core idea of feminism—that "femininity" and women's subordination is a social construction—logically led to an examination of the social construction of "masculinity" and men's power. Many of the first scholars to undertake this task were psychologists who were concerned with looking at the social construction of "the male sex role" (e.g., Pleck, 1981). By the late 1980s, there was a growing interdisciplinary collection of studies of men and masculinity, much of it produced by social scientists (Brod, 1987; Kaufman, 1987; Kimmel, 1987; Kimmel & Messner, 1989).

Reflecting developments in women's studies, the scholarship on men's lives tended to develop three themes: First, what we think of as "masculinity" is not a fixed, biological essence of men but, rather, a social construction that shifts and changes over time as well as between and among various national and cultural contexts. Second, power is central to understanding gender as a relational construct, and the dominant definition of masculinity is largely about expressing difference from—and superiority over—anything considered "feminine." Third, there is no singular "male sex role." Rather, at any given time there are various masculinities. R. W. Connell (1987, 1995) has been among the most articulate advocates of this perspective. Connell argues that hegemonic masculinity (the dominant form of masculinity at any given moment) is constructed in relation to femininities *as well as* in relation to various subordinated or marginalized masculinities. For example, in the United States, various racialized masculinities (e.g., as represented by African American men, Latino immigrant men, etc.) have been central to the construction of hegemonic (White, middle class) masculinity. As Hondagneu-Sotelo and Messner (in this book) argue, this "othering" of racialized masculinities helps to shore up the material privileges that have been historically connected to hegemonic masculinity. When viewed this way, we can better understand hegemonic masculinity as part of a system that includes gender as well as racial, class, sexual, and other relations of power.

The new literature on men and masculinities also begins to move us beyond the simplistic, falsely categorical, and pessimistic view of men as simply a privileged sex class. When race, social class, sexual orientation, physical abilities, and immigrant or national status are taken into account, we can see that in some circumstances "male privilege" is partly—sometimes substantially—muted (Kimmel & Messner, 1995). Although it is unlikely that we will soon see a "men's movement" that aims to undermine the power and privileges that are connected with hegemonic masculinity, when we begin to look at "masculinities" through the prism of difference, we can see similarities and possible points of coalition between and among certain groups of women and men. Certain kinds of changes in gender relations—for instance, a national family leave policy for working parents—might serve as a means of uniting particular groups of women and men.

GENDER IN INTERNATIONAL CONTEXTS

It is an increasingly accepted truism that late twentieth-century increases in transnational trade, international migration, and global systems of production and communication have diminished both the power of nation-states and the significance of national borders. A much more ignored issue is the extent to which gender relations—in the United States and elsewhere—are increasingly linked to patterns of global economic restructuring. Decisions made in corporate headquarters located in Los Angeles, Tokyo, or London may have immediate repercussions in how women and men thousands of miles away organize their work, community, and family lives (Sassen, 1991). It is no longer possible to study gender relations without attention to global processes and inequalities. Scholarship on gender in third-world contexts has moved from liberal concerns for the impact of development policies on women (Boserup, 1970) to more critical perspectives that acknowledge how international labor and capital mobility are transforming gender relations (Fernandez-Kelly, this volume; Ward, 1990), to theoretical debates on third-world feminism (Mohanty, 1991), and to analyses of women and post-Cold War political alignments (Enloe, 1993).

Around the world, women's paid and unpaid labor is key to global development strategies. Yet it would be a mistake to conclude that gender is molded from the "top down." What happens on a daily basis in families and workplaces simultaneously constitutes and is constrained by structural transnational institutions. For instance, in the second half of the twentieth century young, single women, many of them from poor rural areas, have been recruited for work in export assembly plants along the U.S.–Mexico border, in East and Southeast Asia, in Silicon Valley, in the Caribbean, and in Central America. While the profitability of these multinational factories depends, in part, on management's ability to manipulate the young women's ideologies of gender, the women—as suggested by various shopfloor ethnographies and by Karen Hossfeld's article in this volume—do not respond passively or uniformly, but they actively resist, challenge, and accommodate. At the same time, the global dispersion of the assembly line has concentrated corporate facilities in many U.S. cities, making available myriad managerial, administrative, and clerical jobs for college-educated women. Women's paid labor is used at various points along this international system of production. Yet one need not be employed in these industries to be affected by them. A high probability exists that the clothing you are wearing and the computer you use originated in multinational corporate headquarters and in assembly plants scattered around third-world nations. And if these items were actually manufactured in the United States, they were probably assembled by Latin American and Asian-born women.

Worldwide, international labor migration and refugee movements are creating new types of multiracial societies. While these developments are often discussed and analyzed with respect to racial differences, gender typically remains absent from these discussions. As several commentators have noted, the White feminist movement in the United States has not addressed issues of immigration and nationality. Gender, however, has been fundamental in shaping immigration policies (Chang, 1994; Hondagneu-Sotelo, 1994). Direct labor recruitment programs generally solicit either male or female labor (e.g., Filipina nurses, Mexican male farm workers), national disenfranchisement has particular repercussions for women and men, and current immigrant laws are based on gendered notions of what constitutes "family unification." As Chandra Mohanty suggests, "analytically these issues are the contemporary metropolitan counterpart of women's struggles against colonial occupation in the geographical third world" (1991: 23). Moreover, immigrant and refugee women's daily lives often challenge familiar feminist paradigms. The occupations where immigrant and refugee women concentrate—paid domestic work, informal sector street vending, assembly or industrial piecework performed in the home—often blur the ideological distinction between work and family and between the public and domestic spheres.

FROM PATCHWORK QUILT TO PRISM

All of these developments—the voices of "other" women, the study of men and masculinities, and the examination of gender in transnational contexts—have helped redefine the study of gender. By working to develop knowledge that is inclusive of the experiences of all groups, new insights about gender have begun to emerge. Examining gender in the context of other differences makes it clear that nobody experiences themselves as solely gendered. Instead, gender is "intertwined with other identities, and forms of difference, involving race, ethnicity, class, sexual preference, religion, and politics to name a few" (Ginsberg & Tsing, 1990: 5).

By the mid-1980s, thinking about gender had entered a new stage, which was more carefully grounded in the experiences of diverse groups of women and men. This perspective is a general way of looking at women and men and understanding their locations in the social order. Gender is no longer viewed simply as a matter of two opposite categories of people—males and females—but as a range of relationships of power among differently situated people. Because centering on difference is a radical challenge to the conventional gender framework, it raises several concerns. Does the recognition that gender can be understood only contextually (meaning that there is no singular "gender" per se) make women's studies and men's studies newly vulnerable to critics in the academy? Does the immersion in difference throw us into a whirlwind of "spiraling diversity" (Hewitt, 1992: 316), where multiple identities and locations shatter the categories "women" and "men"?

Throughout the book, we take a position directly opposed to a pluralism without analytic worth. We believe that the categories "woman" and "man" have multiple meanings. However, this does not reduce gender to a "postmodern kaleidoscope of lifestyles. Rather, it points to the *relational* character of gender" (Connell, 1992: 736). Not only are masculinity and femininity relational, but different masculinities are interconnected and different femininities are interconnected through the structure of gender relations and through other social structures such as race, class, and nation. Groups are created in their relationships with each other. The meaning of *woman* is defined by the existence of women of different races and classes. For example, being a White woman in the United States is defined "by the existence of subordinated colored women. American Indian culture and thus American Indian individuals have been changed by relations with European-American settlers, soldiers, and governments" (Gordon, 1991: 106).

Just as masculinity and femininity each depend on the definition of the other to produce domination, differences *among* women and *among* men also involve relationships of domination and subordination. Some women derive benefits from their race and their class while they are simultaneously restricted by gender. In other words, such women are subordinated by patriarchy, yet race and class intersect to create for them privileged opportunities, choices, and ways of living. They may even use their race and class advantage to minimize some of the consequences of patriarchy and to oppose other women. Similarly, one can become a man in opposition to other men. For example, "the relation between heterosexual and homosexual men is central, carrying heavy symbolic freight. To many people, homosexuality is the *negation* of masculinity.... Given that assumption, antagonism toward homosexual men may be used to define masculinity" (Connell, 1992: 736).

Analyzing the multiple constructions of gender does not mean just studying groups of women and groups of men as different. It is clearly time to go beyond what we call the "patchwork quilt" phase in the study of women and men—that is, the phase in which we have acknowledged the importance of examining differences within constructions of gender, but do so largely by collecting together a study here on African American women, a study there on gay men, a study on working class Chicanas, and so forth. This patchwork quilt approach too often amounts to no more than "adding difference and stirring." The result may be a lovely mosaic, but like a patchwork quilt, it still tends to overemphasize boundaries rather than highlight bridges of interdependency. In addition, this approach too often does not explore the ways that social constructions of femininities and masculinities are based on and reproduce relations of power. In short, we think that the substantial quantity of research that has been done on various groups and subgroups needs to be analyzed within a framework that emphasizes differences and inequalities, not as discrete areas of separation but as interrelated bands of color that together make up a spectrum.

A recent spate of sophisticated sociological theorizing along these lines has introduced some useful ways of thinking about difference in relational terms. Patricia Hill Collins (1990) has suggested that we think of race, class, and gender as a socially structured "matrix of domination"; R. W. Connell and his colleagues have pressed us to think of multiple differences not in simple additive ways, but rather as they "abrade, inflame, amplify, twist, negate, dampen, and complicate each other" (Kessler et al., 1985). Similarly, Maxine Baca Zinn and Bonnie Thornton Dill (in this volume) have suggested that we consider a body of theory and practice they call "multiracial feminism" as a means of coming to grips with the relations between various systems of inequality.

These are the kinds of concerns that we had in mind in putting together this collection. We sought individual articles that explored intersections or axes in the matrix of domination by comparing different groups. We brought together articles that explored the lives of people who experience the daily challenges of multiple marginality (e.g., Black lesbians, immigrant women) or the often paradoxical realities of those who may identify simultaneously with a socially marginalized or subordinated identity (e.g., gay, poor, physically disabled, Latino) along with a socially dominant identity (e.g., man, white, professional class). When we could not find articles that directly compared or juxtaposed categories or groups, we attempted to juxtapose two or three articles that, together, explored difference and similarities between groups. To this end, we have added a fifth dimension to the now commonly accepted "race/class/gender/sexuality" matrix: national origin. Reflecting a tendency in U.S. sociology in general, courses on sex and gender have been far too U.S.-focused and Eurocentric. Focusing on the construction of gender in nonindustrial societies or the shifting relations of gender among immigrant groups challenges and broadens our otherwise narrow assumptions about the constraints and possibilities facing contemporary women and men.

We hope this book contributes to the beginnings of a new generation of scholarship in the study of sex and gender—one that moves beyond the patchwork quilt approach that lists or catalogs differences, to an approach that takes up the challenge of exploring the relations of power that structure these differences. Gloria Anzaldua (1990), a Chicana lesbian and feminist, uses the border as a metaphor to capture the spatial, ethnic, class, and sexual transitions traversed in one's lifetime. She states in a poem that, "To survive the borderlands you must live *sin fronteras*" (without borders). Breaking down, reassessing, and crossing the borders that divide the patches on the quilt—both experientially and analytically—is key to the difficult task of transforming knowledge about gender. Looking at the various prisms that organize gender relations, we think, will contribute to the kind of bridge-building that is needed to construct broad-based coalitions to push for equality and social justice in the twenty-first century.

REFERENCES

Anzaldua, Gloria. 1990. "To Live in the Borderlands Means You." Pp. 194–195 in Gloria Anzaldua, *Borderlands La Frontera: The New Mestiza.* San Francisco, CA: Spinsters/Aunt Lute.

Baca Zinn, M., Weber Cannon, L., Higginbotham, E., & Thornton Dill, B. 1986. "The Costs of Exclusionary Practices in Women's Studies," *Signs: Journal of Women in Culture and Society 11:* 290–303.

Boserup, Ester. 1970. *Woman's Role in Economic Development.* London: George Allen & Unwin.

Brod, Harry. (ed.). 1987. *The Making of Masculinities: The New Men's Studies.* Boston: Allen & Unwin.

Brownmiller, Susan. 1975. *Against Our Will: Men, Women, and Rape.* New York: Simon and Schuster.

Chang, Grace. 1994. "Undocumented Latinas: The New 'Employable Mothers.'" Pp. 259–285 in Evelyn Nakano Glenn, Grace Chang, and Linda Rennie Forcey, (eds.) *Mothering, Ideology, Experience, and Agency.* New York and London: Routledge.

Collins, Patricia Hill. 1990. *Black Feminist Thought: Knowledge, Consciousness, and the Politics of Empowerment.* Boston: Unwin Hyman.

Connell, R. W. 1987. *Gender and Power.* Stanford, CA: Stanford University Press.

Connell, R. W. 1992. "A Very Straight Gay: Masculinity, Homosexual Experience, and the Dynamics of Gender," *American Sociological Review 57:* 735–751.

Connell, R. W. 1995. *Masculinities.* Berkeley: University of California Press.

De Beauvoir, Simone. 1953. *The Second Sex.* New York: Knopf.

Enloe, Cynthia. 1993. *The Morning After: Sexual Politics at the End of the Cold War.* University of California Press.

Friedan, Betty. 1963. *The Feminine Mystique.* New York: W. W. Norton.

Ginsberg, Faye & Anna Lowenhaupt Tsing. 1990. *Uncertain Terms.* Boston: Beacon Press.

Gordon, Linda. 1991. "On Differences," *Genders* (Spring): 91–111.

Hartmann, Heidi. 1976. "Capitalism, Patriarchy, and Job Segregation by Sex," *Signs 1:* (3), part 2, Spring: 137–67.

Hewitt, Nancy A. 1992. "Compounding Differences," *Feminist Studies 18:* 313–326.

Hondagneu-Sotelo, Pierrette. 1994. *Gendered Transitions: Mexican Experiences of Immigration.* Berkeley: University of California Press.

Kanter, Rosabeth Moss. 1977. *Men and Women of the Corporation.* New York: Basic Books.

Kessler, Sandra, Dean J. Ashenden, R. W. Connell, & Gary W. Dowsett. 1985. "Gender Relations in Secondary Schooling," *Sociology of Education* 58: 34–48.

Kaufman, Michael. 1987. *Beyond Patriarchy: Essays by Men on Pleasure, Power, and Change.* Toronto: Oxford University.

Kimmel, Michael S. (ed.). 1987. *Changing Men: New Directions in Research on Men and Masculinity.* Newbury Park, CA: Sage.

Kimmel, Michael S., & Michael A. Messner (eds.). 1989. *Men's Lives.* New York: Macmillan.

Mohanty, Chandra Talpade. 1991. "Cartographies of Struggle: Third World Women and the Politics of Feminism." Pp. 51–80 in Chandra Talpade Mohanty, Ann Russo, & Lourdes Torres (eds.). *Third World Women and the Politics of Feminism.* Bloomington: Indiana University Press.

Morgan, Robin. 1970. *Sisterhood Is Powerful: An Anthology of Writings from the Women's Liberation Movement.* New York: Vintage Books.

Pleck, Joseph H. 1981. *The Myth of Masculinity.* Cambridge, MA: M. I. T. Press.

Rich, Adrienne. 1980. "Compulsory Heterosexuality and Lesbian Existence," *Signs 5:* 631–60.

Sassen, Saskia. 1991. *The Global City: New York, London, Tokyo.* Princeton, N.J.: Princeton University Press.

Smith, Barbara. 1977. *Toward a Black Feminist Criticism.* Freedom, CA: Crossing Press.

Ward, Kathryn. 1990. "Introduction and Overview." Pp. 1–22 in Kathryn Ward (ed.), *Women Workers and Global Restructuring.* Ithaca, N.Y.: International Labor Relations Press, Cornell University.

PART ONE

Perspectives on Sex, Gender, and Difference

Chapter 1   Sex and Gender: The Challenge of Difference

Chapter 2   Studying across Difference

Are women and men or boys and girls really different, or do we just think and act as though they are different? In other words, are gender differences and inequalities rooted in biology, or are they socially constructed? Today, these questions are rarely answered with simplistic, pat answers. And the questions that gender scholars are asking have also grown more complex. Are these differences constant over time, historically invariant? If women and men are different, then are women—as a group—similar to one another? Do White women share experiences similar to those of women of color? The readings in this opening part reflect a sampling of recent gender scholarship in the social sciences. They tackle tricky questions of differences between women and men, as well as issues of differences among groups of women and among groups of men.

In recent years the concept of "difference feminism" has crept into the vocabulary of women's studies. Difference feminism arose in opposition to liberal feminists who sought women's equality by appealing to the logic of sameness. If women and men are inherently similar, liberal feminists argued, then according to meritocratic principles, women deserve the same treatment and opportunities that men receive. Difference feminists sought women's equality by appealing to the logic of difference. By acknowledgment, and even sometimes underscoring biological, emotional, and social differences between women and men, they argued that women cannot rely on men's strategies to achieve equality.

While difference feminism highlights differences between women and men, another line of thinking questions the basis of difference and equality between women and men. In the first reading, Judith Lorber goes right to the heart of both sexist thinking and difference feminism by questioning what is generally taken for granted: physical, bodily difference between women and men. She deconstructs "the making" of gendered bodies and deftly shows that physiological differences remain meaningless without substantial scaffolding composed of social meanings and practices. A complex ongoing social apparatus is required to transform physiological differences into gender inequality.

In contrast to difference feminism's premise of a unitary, implied sameness in the category "women" or "men," the second reading by Maxine Baca Zinn and Bonnie Thornton Dill questions this universalism. Here, the authors focus on differences of race and class between women. They analyze the development of this scholarship, noting both the tensions and the benefits, as they explore theories and concepts of multiracial feminism. A key insight is recognition of the ways in which the differences between women are historically and socially constructed and the ways in which they intersect.

While there is increasing recognition of racial and class differences, most women's studies scholarship in the United States remains plagued by a very provincial view, one that fails to acknowledge the lives of women outside the United States. This seems especially odd when one considers how closely tied are the past and the future of women in the United States with the women who live in the southern portion of the Americas. Edna Acosta-Belén and Christine Bose explore the legacies of these ties. While differences between U.S. and Latin American women are rooted in distinct histories of colonization, women in general share characteristics with colonies: they both share structured subordination and serve as poor non-wage and low-wage producers.

The remaining readings in Chapter 1 bring different points of critique to the categorical "difference" lens applied to women and men. The article by Barrie Thorne raises important theoretical and methodological questions for scholarship that highlights differences between and within the sexes. Ethnographic research of children in elementary schools leads Thorne to question the "dualistic models of sex differences." She persuasively argues the merits of a more fluid and contextually situated view of gender relations. In the subsequent article on moral reasoning among African American youth, Carol Stack directly challenges the "difference" findings of Carol Gilligan. Her critique points to the importance of considering race, class, and culture in any sweeping generalization that might be made about young women and men. And in the final reading in Chapter 1, Pierrette Hondagneu-Sotelo and Michael Messner look at differences between hegemonic masculinities, characterized by class and race privileges, and the marginalized masculinities of Mexican, working class, undocumented immigrant men. The authors note that popular "common sense" views of masculinity and "machismo" typically fail to distinguish between gender display and structural power.

Chapter 2 turns to questions about research itself. Where shall research on gender come from? Who should study gender and under what conditions? Can men study women? Can women study men? Can "outsiders" comprehend the subjectivity of women and men who are different from themselves, or are "insiders" better qualified to conduct research with those of the same gender, race, and sexual orientation? How do the experiences of those who have historically been intellectual outsiders shape their view of social reality?

Questions about insiders and outsiders have been the subject of much debate in the social sciences. As more researchers adopt qualitative approaches to capture the nuances of everyday life and as they become more sensitive to difference, questions about social location and research are among the most important issues in feminist scholarship. We are discovering just how much different identities and different locations matter in the production of knowledge.

Knowledge changes when it is produced by people who are differently positioned in the social order. Many intellectuals who are outside the dominant society have used their marginality as a location from which to see aspects of gender within their own groups that were once obscure from more privileged vantage points. Their unique perspectives offer powerful correctives to mainstream distortions about gender relations in subordinated groups. Yet, all researchers can cross the boundaries of their locations to study women and men whose experiences are underrepresented in the literature on gender.

Chapter 2 considers the question, "What difference does difference make in doing gender research?" Margaret L. Andersen draws on her field research in a Black community for lessons in studying groups different from one's own. She encourages White scholars to develop research practices that acknowledge the race, class, and gender relations in which all research activities are situated. Kath Weston then demonstrates the distinct advantages that accompanied her insider status in recruiting lesbians and gay men for her research on family and kinship. Finally, Steven J. Gold discusses the ways in which his position as a "knowledgeable outsider" enabled him to bridge the divisions of gender, nationality, language, and ethnicity in his field research among Vietnamese women.

Believing Is Seeing

Biology as Ideology

JUDITH LORBER

Until the eighteenth century, Western philosophers and scientists thought that there was one sex and that women's internal genitalia were the inverse of men's external genitalia: the womb and vagina were the penis and scrotum turned inside out (Laqueur 1990). Current Western thinking sees women and men as so different physically as to sometimes seem two species. The bodies, which have been mapped inside and out for hundreds of years, have not changed. What has changed are the justifications for gender inequality. When the social position of all human beings was believed to be set by natural law or was considered God-given, biology was irrelevant; women and men of different classes all had their assigned places. When scientists began to question the divine basis of social order and replaced faith with empirical knowledge, what they saw was that women were very different from men in that they had wombs and menstruated. Such anatomical differences destined them for an entirely different social life from men.

In actuality, the basic bodily material *is* the same for females and males, and except for procreative hormones and organs, female and male human beings have similar bodies (Naftolin and Butz 1981). Furthermore, as has been known since the middle of the nineteenth century, male and female genitalia develop from the same fetal tissue, and so infants can be born with ambiguous genitalia (Money and Ehrhardt 1972). When they are, biology is used quite arbitrarily in sex assignment. Suzanne Kessler (1990) interviewed six medical specialists in pediatric intersexuality and found that whether an infant with XY chromosomes and anomalous genitalia was categorized as a boy or a girl depended on the size of the penis— if a penis was very small, the child was categorized as a girl, and sex-change surgery was used to make an artificial vagina. In the late nineteenth century, the presence or absence of ovaries was the determining criterion of gender assignment for hermaphrodites because a woman who could not procreate was not a complete woman (Kessler 1990, 20).

Yet in Western societies, we see two discrete sexes and two distinguishable genders because our society is built on two classes of people, "women" and "men." Once the gender category is given, the attributes of the person are also gendered: Whatever a "woman" is has to be "female"; whatever a "man" is has to be "male." Analyzing the social processes that construct the categories we call "female and male," "women and men," and "homosexual and heterosexual" uncovers the ideology and power differentials congealed in these categories (Foucault 1978). This article will use two familiar areas of social life—sports and technological competence—to show how myriad physiological differences are transformed into similar-appearing, gendered social bodies. My perspective goes beyond accepted feminist views that gender is a cultural overlay that modifies physiological sex differences. That perspective assumes either that there are two fairly similar sexes distorted by social practices into two genders with purposefully different characteristics or that there are two sexes whose essential differences are rendered unequal by social practices. I am arguing that bodies differ in many ways physiologically, but they are completely transformed by social practices to fit into the salient categories of a society, the most pervasive of which are "female" and "male" and "women" and "men."

Neither sex nor gender are pure categories. Combinations of incongruous genes, genitalia, and hormonal input are ignored in sex categorization, just as combinations of incongruous physiology, identity, sexuality, appearance, and behavior are ignored in the social construction of gender statuses. Menstruation, lactation, and gestation do not demarcate women from men. Only some women are pregnant and then only some of the time; some women do not have a uterus or ovaries. Some women have stopped menstruating temporarily, others have reached menopause, and some have had hysterectomies. Some women breastfeed some of the time, but some men lactate (Jaggar 1983, 165fn). Menstruation, lactation, and gestation are individual experiences of womanhood (Levesque-Lopman 1988), but not determinants of the social category "woman," or even "female." Similarly, "men are not always spermproducers, and in fact, not all sperm producers are men. A male-to-female transsexual, prior to surgery, can be socially a woman, though still potentially (or actually) capable of spermatogenesis" (Kessler and McKenna [1978] 1985, 2).

When gender assignment is contested in sports, where the categories of competitors are rigidly divided into women and men, chromosomes are now used to determine in which category the athlete is to compete. However, an anomaly common enough to be found in several women at every major international sports competition are XY chromosomes that have not produced male anatomy or physiology because of a genetic defect. Because these women are women in every way significant for sports competition, the prestigious International Amateur Athletic Federation has urged that sex be determined by simple genital inspection (Kolata 1992). Transsex-

uals would pass this test, but it took a lawsuit for Renée Richards, a male-to-female transsexual, to be able to play tournament tennis as a woman, despite his male sex chromosomes (Richards 1983). Oddly, neither basis for gender categorization—chromosomes nor genitalia—has anything to do with sports prowess (Birrell and Cole 1990).

In the Olympics, in cases of chromosomal ambiguity, women must undergo "a battery of gynecological and physical exams to see if she is 'female enough' to compete. Men are not tested" (Carlson 1991, 26). The purpose is not to categorize women and men accurately, but to make sure men don't enter women's competitions, where, it is felt, they will have the advantage of size and strength. This practice sounds fair only because it is assumed that all men are similar in size and strength and different from all women. Yet in Olympics boxing and wrestling matches, men are matched within weight classes. Some women might similarly successfully compete with some men in many sports. Women did not run in marathons until about twenty years ago. In twenty years of marathon competition, women have reduced their finish times by more than one-and-one-half hours; they are expected to run as fast as men in that race by 1998 and might catch up with men's running times in races of other lengths within the next 50 years because they are increasing their fastest speeds more rapidly than are men (Fausto-Sterling 1985, 213–18).

The reliance on only two sex and gender categories in the biological and social sciences is as epistemologically spurious as the reliance on chromosomal or genital tests to group athletes. Most research designs do not investigate whether physical skills or physical abilities are really more or less common in women and men (Epstein 1988). They start out with two social categories ("women," "men"), assume they are biologically different ("female," "male"), look for similarities among them and differences between them, and attribute what they have found for the social categories to sex differences (Gelman, Collman, and

Maccoby 1986). These designs rarely question the categorization of their subjects into two and only two groups, even though they often find more significant within-group differences than between-group differences (Hyde 1990). The social construction perspective on sex and gender suggests that instead of starting with the two presumed dichotomies in each category—female, male; woman, man—it might be more useful in gender studies to group patterns of behavior and only then look for identifying markers of the people likely to enact such behaviors.

WHAT SPORTS ILLUSTRATE

Competitive sports have become, for boys and men, as players and as spectators, a way of constructing a masculine identity, a legitimated outlet for violence and aggression, and an avenue for upward mobility (Dunning 1986; Kemper 1990, 167–206; Messner 1992). For men in Western societies, physical competence is an important marker of masculinity (Fine 1987; Glassner 1992; Majors 1990). In professional and collegiate sports, physiological differences are invoked to justify women's secondary status, despite the clear evidence that gender status overrides physiological capabilities. Assumptions about women's physiology have influenced rules of competition; subsequent sports performances then validate how women and men are treated in sports competitions.

Gymnastic equipment is geared to slim, wiry, prepubescent girls and not to mature women; conversely, men's gymnastic equipment is tailored for muscular, mature men, not slim, wiry prepubescent boys. Boys could compete with girls, but are not allowed to; women gymnasts are left out entirely. Girl gymnasts are just that—little girls who will be disqualified as soon as they grow up (Vecsey 1990). Men gymnasts have men's status. In women's basketball, the size of the ball and rules for handling the ball change the style of play to "a slower, less intense, and less exciting modification of the 'regular' or men's game" (Watson 1987,

441). In the 1992 Winter Olympics, men figure skaters were required to complete three triple jumps in their required program; women figure skaters were forbidden to do more than *one*. These rules penalized artistic men skaters and athletic women skaters (Janofsky 1992). For the most part, Western sports are built on physically trained men's bodies:

> *Speed, size, and strength seem to be the essence of sports. Women* are *naturally inferior at "sports" so conceived.*
> *But if women had been the historically dominant sex, our concept of sport would no doubt have evolved differently. Competitions emphasizing flexibility, balance, strength, timing, and small size might dominate Sunday afternoon television and offer salaries in six figures. (English 1982, 266, emphasis in original)*

Organized sports are big businesses and, thus, who has access and at what level is a distributive or equity issue. The overall status of women and men athletes is an economic, political, and ideological issue that has less to do with individual physiological capabilities than with their cultural and social meaning and who defines and profits from them (Messner and Sabo 1990; Slatton and Birrell 1984). Twenty years after the passage of Title IX of the U.S. Civil Rights Act, which forbade gender inequality in any school receiving federal funds, the *goal* for collegiate sports in the next five years is 60 percent men, 40 percent women in sports participation, scholarships, and funding (Moran 1992).

How access and distribution of rewards (prestigious and financial) are justified is an ideological, even moral, issue (Birrell 1988, 473–76; Hargreaves 1982). One way is that men athletes are glorified and women athletes ignored in the mass media. Messner and his colleagues found that in 1989, in TV sports news in the United States, men's sports got 92 percent of the coverage and women's sports 5 percent, with the rest mixed or gender-neutral (Messner, Duncan, and Jensen

1993). In 1990, in four of the top-selling newspapers in the United States, stories on men's sports outnumbered those on women's sports 23 to 1. Messner and his colleagues also found an implicit hierarchy in naming, with women athletes most likely to be called by first names, followed by Black men athletes, and only white men athletes routinely referred to by their last names. Similarly, women's collegiate sports teams are named or marked in ways that symbolically feminize and trivialize them—the men's team is called Tigers, the women's Kittens (Eitzen and Baca Zinn 1989).

Assumptions about men's and women's bodies and their capacities are crafted in ways that make unequal access and distribution of rewards acceptable (Hudson 1978; Messner 1988). Media images of modern men athletes glorify their strength and power, even their violence (Hargreaves 1986). Media images of modern women athletes tend to focus on feminine beauty and grace (so they are not really athletes) or on their thin, small, wiry androgynous bodies (so they are not really women). In coverage of the Olympics,

> loving and detailed attention is paid to pixie-like gymnasts; special and extended coverage is given to graceful and dazzling figure skaters; the camera painstakingly records the fluid movements of swimmers and divers. And then, in a blinding flash of fragmented images, viewers see a few minutes of volleyball, basketball, speed skating, track and field, and alpine skiing, as television gives its nod to the mere existence of these events. (Boutilier and SanGiovanni 1983, 190)

Extraordinary feats by women athletes who were presented as mature adults might force sports organizers and audiences to rethink their stereotypes of women's capabilities, the way elves, mermaids, and ice queens do not. Sports, therefore, construct men's bodies to be powerful; women's bodies to be sexual. As Connell says,

> The meanings in the bodily sense of masculinity concern, above all else, the superiority of men to women, and the exaltation of hegemonic masculin-

> ity over other groups of men which is essential for the domination of women. (1987, 85)

In the late 1970s, as women entered more and more athletic competitions, supposedly good scientific studies showed that women who exercised intensely would cease menstruating because they would not have enough body fat to sustain ovulation (Brozan 1978). When one set of researchers did a yearlong study that compared 66 women—21 who were training for a marathon, 22 who ran more than an hour a week, and 23 who did less than an hour of aerobic exercise a week—they discovered that only 20 percent of the women in any of these groups had "normal" menstrual cycles every month (Prior et al. 1990). The dangers of intensive training for women's fertility therefore were exaggerated as women began to compete successfully in arenas formerly closed to them.

Given the association of sports with masculinity in the United States, women athletes have to manage a contradictory status. One study of women college basketball players found that although they "did athlete" on the court—pushing, shoving, fouling, hard running, fast breaks, defense, obscenities and sweat" (Watson 1987, 441), they "did woman" off the court, using the locker room as their staging area:

> While it typically took fifteen minutes to prepare for the game, it took approximately fifteen minutes after the game to shower and remove the sweat of an athlete, and it took another thirty minutes to dress, apply make-up and style hair. It did not seem to matter whether the players were going out into the public or getting on a van for a long ride home. Average dressing time and rituals did not change. (Watson 1987, 443)

Another way women manage these status dilemmas is to redefine the activity or its result as feminine or womanly (Mangan and Park 1987). Thus women bodybuilders claim that "flex appeal is sex appeal" (Duff and Hong 1984, 378).

Such a redefinition of women's physicality affirms the ideological subtext of sports that physical strength is men's prerogative and justifies men's physical and sexual domination of women (Hargreaves 1986; Messner 1992, 164–72; Olson 1990; Theberge 1987; Willis 1982). When women demonstrate physical strength, they are labeled unfeminine:

> It's threatening to one's takeability, one's rape-ability, one's femininity, to be strong and physically self-possessed. To be able to resist rape, not to communicate rapeability with one's body, to hold one's body for uses and meanings other than that can transform what being a woman means. (MacKinnon 1987, 122, emphasis in original)

Resistance to that transformation, ironically, was evident in the policies of American women physical education professionals throughout most of the twentieth century. They minimized exertion, maximized a feminine appearance and manner, and left organized sports competition to men (Birrell 1988, 461–62; Mangan and Park 1987).

DIRTY LITTLE SECRETS

As sports construct gendered bodies, technology constructs gendered skills. Meta-analysis of studies of gender differences in spatial and mathematical ability have found that men have a large advantage in ability to mentally rotate an image, a moderate advantage in a visual perception of horizontality and verticality and in mathematical performance, and a small advantage in ability to pick a figure out of a field (Hyde 1990). It could be argued that these advantages explain why, within the short space of time that computers have become ubiquitous in offices, schools, and homes, work on them and with them has become gendered: Men create, program, and market computers, make war and produce science and art with them; women microwire them in computer factories and enter data in computerized offices; boys play games, socialize, and commit crimes with

computers; girls are rarely seen in computer clubs, camps, and classrooms. But women were hired as computer programmers in the 1940s because

> the work seemed to resemble simple clerical tasks. In fact, however, programming demanded complex skills in abstract logic, mathematics, electrical circuitry, and machinery, all of which . . . women used to perform in their work. Once programming was recognized as "intellectually demanding," it became attractive to men. (Donato 1990, 170)

A woman mathematician and pioneer in data processing, Grace M. Hopper, was famous for her work on programming language (Perry and Greber 1990, 86). By the 1960s, programming was split into more and less skilled specialties, and the entry of women into the computer field in the 1970s and 1980s was confined to the lower-paid specialties. At each stage, employers invoked women's and men's purportedly natural capabilities for the jobs for which they were hired (Cockburn 1983, 1985; Donato 1990; Hartmann 1987; Hartmann, Kraut, and Tilly 1986; Kramer and Lehman 1990; Wright et al. 1987; Zimmerman 1983).

It is the taken-for-grantedness of such everyday gendered behavior that gives credence to the belief that the widespread differences in what women and men do must come from biology. To take one ordinarily unremarked scenario: In modern societies, if a man and woman who are a couple are in a car together, he is much more likely to take the wheel than she is, even if she is the more competent driver. Molly Haskell calls this taken-for-granted phenomenon "the dirty little secret of marriage: the husband-lousy-driver syndrome" (1989, 26), Men drive cars whether they are good drivers or not because men and machines are a "natural" combination (Scharff 1991). But the ability to drive gives one mobility; it is a form of social power.

In the early days of the automobile, feminists co-opted the symbolism of mobility as emancipation: "Donning goggles and dusters, wielding tire irons and tool kits, taking the wheel, they announced their intention to move beyond the bounds of women's place" (Scharff 1991, 68). Driving enabled them to campaign for women's suffrage in parts of the United States not served by public transportation, and they effectively used motorcades and speaking from cars as campaign tactics (Scharff 1991, 67–88). Sandra Gilbert also notes that during World War I, women's ability to drive was physically, mentally, and even sensually liberating:

> For nurses and ambulance drivers, women doctors and women messengers, the phenomenon of modern battle was very different from that experienced by entrenched combatants. Finally given a chance to take the wheel, these post-Victorian girls raced motorcars along foreign roads like adventurers exploring new lands, while their brothers dug deeper into the mud of France.... Retrieving the wounded and the dead from deadly positions, these once-decorous daughters had at last been allowed to prove their valor, and they swooped over the wastelands of the war with the energetic love of Wagnerian Valkyries, their mobility alone transporting countless immobilized heroes to safe havens. (1983, 438–39)

Not incidentally, women in the United States and England got the vote for their war efforts in World War I.

SOCIAL BODIES AND THE BATHROOM PROBLEM

People of the same racial ethnic group and social class are roughly the same size and shape—but there are many varieties of bodies. People have different genitalia, different secondary sex characteristics, different contributions to procreation, different orgasmic experiences, different patterns of illness and aging. Each of us experiences our bodies differently, and these experiences change as we grow, age, sicken, and die. The bodies of pregnant and nonpregnant women, short and tall people, those with intact and functioning limbs and those whose bodies are physically challenged are all different. But the salient categories of a so-

ciety group these attributes in ways that ride roughshod over individual experiences and more meaningful clusters of people.

I am not saying that physical differences between male and female bodies don't exist, but that these differences are socially meaningless until social practices transform them into social facts. West Point Military Academy's curriculum is designed to produce leaders, and physical competence is used as a significant measure of leadership ability (Yoder 1989). When women were accepted as West Point cadets, it became clear that the tests of physical competence, such as rapidly scaling an eight-foot wall, had been constructed for male physiques—pulling oneself up and over using upper-body strength. Rather than devise tests of physical competence for women, West Point provided boosters that mostly women used—but that lost them test points—in the case of the wall, a platform. Finally, the women themselves figured out how to use their bodies successfully. Janice Yoder describes this situation:

> I was observing this obstacle one day, when a woman approached the wall in the old prescribed way, got her fingertips grip, and did an unusual thing: she walked her dangling legs up the wall until she was in a position where both her hands and feet were atop the wall. She then simply pulled up her sagging bottom and went over. She solved the problem by capitalizing on one of women's physical assets: lower-body strength. (1989, 530)

In short, if West Point is going to measure leadership capability by physical strength, women's pelvises will do just as well as men's shoulders.

The social transformation of female and male physiology into a condition of inequality is well illustrated by the bathroom problem. Most buildings that have gender-segregated bathrooms have an equal number for women and for men. Where there are crowds, there are always long lines in front of women's bathrooms but rarely in front of men's bathrooms. The cultural, physiological, and demographic combinations of clothing, frequency of urination, menstruation, and child care add up to generally greater bathroom use by women than men. Thus, although an equal number of bathrooms seems fair, equity would mean more women's bathrooms or allowing women to use men's bathrooms for a certain amount of time (Molotch 1988).

The bathroom problem is the outcome of the way gendered bodies are differentially evaluated in Western cultures: Men's social bodies are the measure of what is "human." Gray's *Anatomy,* in use for 100 years, well into the twentieth century, presented the human body as male. The female body was shown only where it differed from the male (Laqueur 1990, 166–67). Denise Riley says that if we envisage women's bodies, men's bodies, and human bodies "as a triangle of identifications, then it is rarely an equilateral triangle in which both sexes are pitched at matching distances from the apex of the human" (1988, 197). Catharine MacKinnon also contends that in Western society, universal "humanness" is male because

> *virtually every quality that distinguishes men from women is already affirmatively compensated in this society. Men's physiology defines most sports, their needs define auto and health insurance coverage, their socially defined biographies define workplace expectations and successful career patterns, their perspectives and concerns define quality in scholarship, their experiences and obsessions define merit, their objectification of life defines art, their military service defines citizenship, their presence defines family, their inability to get along with each other—their wars and rulerships—define history, their image defines god, and their genitals define sex. For each of their differences from women, what amounts to an affirmative action plan is in effect, otherwise known as the structure and values of American society. (1987, 36)*

THE PARADOX OF HUMAN NATURE

Gendered people do not emerge from physiology or hormones but from the exigencies of the social order, mostly, from the need for a reliable division of the work of food production and the social (not physical) reproduction of new members. The moral imperatives of religion and cultural representations reinforce the boundary lines among genders and ensure that what is demanded, what is permitted, and what is tabooed for the people in each gender is well-known and followed by most. Political power, control of scarce resources, and, if necessary, violence uphold the gendered social order in the face of resistance and rebellion. Most people, however, voluntarily go along with their society's prescriptions for those of their gender status because the norms and expectations get built into their sense of worth and identity as a certain kind of human being and because they believe their society's way is the natural way. These beliefs emerge from the imagery that pervades the way we think, the way we see and hear and speak, the way we fantasize, and the way we feel. There is no core or bedrock human nature below these endlessly looping processes of the social production of sex and gender, self and other, identity and psyche, each of which is a "complex cultural construction" (Butler 1990, 36). The paradox of "human nature" is that it is *always* a manifestation of cultural meanings, social relationships, and power politics—"not biology, but culture, becomes destiny" (Butler 1990, 8).

Feminist inquiry has long questioned the conventional categories of social science, but much of the current work in feminist sociology has not gone beyond adding the universal category "women" to the universal category "men." Our current debates over the global assumptions of only two categories and the insistence that they must be nuanced to include race and class are steps in the direction I would like to see feminist research go, but race and class are *also* global categories (Collins 1990; Spelman 1988). Deconstructing sex, sexuality, and gender reveals many possible categories embedded in the social experiences and social practices of what Dorothy Smith calls the "everyday/everynight world" (1990, 31–57). These emergent categories group some people together for comparison with other people without prior assumptions about who is like whom. Categories can be broken up and people regrouped differently into new categories for comparison. This process of discovering categories from similarities and differences in people's behavior or responses can be more meaningful for feminist research than discovering similarities and differences between "females" and "males" or "women" and "men" because the social construction of the conventional sex and gender cate-

gories already assumes differences between them and similarities among them. When we rely only on the conventional categories of sex and gender, we end up finding what we looked for—we see what we believe, whether it is that "females" and "males" are essentially different or that "women" and "men" are essentially the same.

REFERENCES

Birrell, Susan J. 1988. Discourses on the gender/sport relationship: From women in sport to gender relations. In *Exercise and sport science reviews.* Vol. 16, edited by Kent Pandolf New York: Macmillan.

Birrell, Susan J., and Sheryl L. Cole. 1990. Double fault: Renée Richards and the construction and naturalization of difference. *Sociology of Sport Journal* 7:1–21.

Boutilier, Mary A., and Lucinda SanGiovanni. 1983. *The sporting woman.* Champaign, IL: Human Kinetics.

Brozan, Nadine. 1978. Training linked to disruption of female reproductive cycle. *New York Times,* 17 April.

Butler, Judith. 1990. *Gender trouble: Feminism and the subversion of identity.* New York and London: Routledge & Kegan Paul.

Carlson, Alison. 1991. When is a woman not a woman? *Women's Sport and Fitness* March:24–29.

Cockburn, Cynthia. 1983. *Brothers: Male dominance and technological change.* London: Pluto.

———. 1985. *Machinery of dominance: Women, men and technical know-how.* London: Pluto.

Collins, Patricia Hill. 1990. *Black feminist thought: Knowledge, consciousness, and the politics of empowerment.* Boston: Unwin Hyman.

Connell, R. W. 1987. *Gender and power.* Stanford, CA: Stanford University Press.

Donato, Katharine M. 1990. Programming for change? The growing demand for women systems analysts. In *Job queues, gender queues: Explaining women's inroads into male occupations,* written and edited by Barbara F. Reskin and Patricia A. Roos. Philadelphia: Temple University Press.

Duff, Robert W., and Lawrence K. Hong, 1984. Self-images of women bodybuilders. *Sociology of Sport Journal* 2:374–80.

Dunning, Eric. 1986. Sport as a male preserve: Notes on the social sources of masculine identity and its transformations. *Theory, Culture and Society* 3:79–90.

Eitzen, D. Stanley, and Maxine Baca Zinn. 1989. The deathleticization of women: The naming and gender marking of collegiate sport teams. *Sociology of Sport Journal* 6:362–70.

English, Jane. 1982. Sex equality in sports. In *Feminity, masculinity, and androgyny,* edited by Mary Vetterling-Braggin. Boston: Littlefield, Adams.

Epstein, Cynthia Fuchs. 1988. *Deceptive distinctions: Sex, gender and the social order.* New Haven, CT: Yale University Press.

Fausto-Sterling, Anne. 1985. *Myths of gender: Biological theories about women and men.* New York: Basic Books.

Fine, Gary Alan. 1987. *With the boys: Little League baseball and preadolescent culture.* Chicago: University of Chicago Press.

Foucault, Michel. 1978. *The history of sexuality: An introduction.* Translated by Robert Hurley. New York: Pantheon.

Gelman, Susan A., Pamela Collman, and Eleanor E. Maccoby. 1986. Inferring properties from categories versus inferring categories from properties: The case of gender. *Child Development* 57:396–404.

Gilbert, Sandra M. 1983. Soldier's heart: Literary men, literary women, and the Great War. *Signs: Journal of Women in Culture and Society* 8:422–50.

Glassner, Barry. 1992. Men and muscles. In *Men's lives,* edited by Michael S. Kimmel and Michael A. Messner. New York: Macmillan.

Hargreaves, Jennifer A., ed. 1982. *Sport, culture, and ideology.* London: Routledge & Kegan Paul.

———. 1986. Where's the virtue? Where's the grace? A discussion of the social production of gender relations in and through sport. *Theory, Culture, and Society* 3:109–21.

Hartmann, Heidi I., ed. 1987. *Computer chips and paper clips: Technology and women's employment.* Vol. 2. Washington, DC: National Academy Press.

Hartmann, Heidi I., Robert E. Kraut, and Louise A. Tilly, eds. 1986. *Computer chips and paper clips: Technology and women's employment.* Vol. 1. Washington, DC: National Academy Press.

Haskell, Molly. 1989. Hers: He drives me crazy. *New York Times Magazine,* 24 September, 26, 28.

Hudson, Jackie. 1978. Physical parameters used for female exclusion from law enforcement and athletics. In *Women and sport: From myth to reality,* edited by Carol A. Oglesby. Philadelphia: Lea and Febiger.

Hyde, Janet Shibley. 1990. Meta-analysis and the psychology of gender differences. *Signs: Journal of Women in Culture and Society* 16:55–73.

Jaggar, Alison M. 1983. *Feminist politics and human nature.* Totowa, NJ: Rowman & Allanheld.

Janofsky, Michael. 1992. Yamaguchi has the delicate and golden touch. *New York Times,* 22 February.

Kemper, Theodore D. 1990. *Social structure and testosterone: Explorations of the socio-biosocial chain.* Brunswick, NJ: Rutgers University Press.

Kessler, Suzanne J., 1990. The medical construction of gender: Case management of intersexed infants. *Signs: Journal of Women in Culture and Society* 16:3–26.

Kessler, Suzanne J., and Wendy McKenna. [1978] 1985. *Gender: An ethnomethodological approach.* Chicago: University of Chicago Press.

Kolata, Gina. 1992. Track federation urges end to gene test for femaleness. *New York Times,* 12 February.

Kramer, Patricia E., and Sheila L. Lehman. 1990. Mismeasuring women: A critique of research on computer ability and avoidance. *Signs: Journal of Women in Culture and Society* 16:158–72.

Laqueur, Thomas. 1990. *Making sex: Body and gender from the Greeks to Freud.* Cambridge, MA: Harvard University Press.

Levesque-Lopman, Louise. 1988. *Claiming reality: Phenomenology and women's experience.* Totowa, NJ: Rowman & Littlefield.

MacKinnon, Catharine. 1987. *Feminism unmodified.* Cambridge, MA: Harvard University Press.

Majors. Richard. 1990. Cool pose: Black masculinity in sports. In *Sport, men and the gender order: Critical feminist perspectives,* edited by Michael A.

Messner and Donald F. Sabo. Champaign, IL: Human Kinetics.

Mangan, J. A., and Roberta J. Park. 1987. *From fair sex to feminism: Sport and the socialization of women in the industrial and post-industrial eras.* London: Frank Cass.

Messner, Michael A. 1988. Sports and male domination: The female athlete as contested ideological terrain. *Sociology of Sport Journal* 5:197–211.

———. 1992. *Power at play: Sports and the problem of masculinity.* Boston: Beacon Press.

Messner, Michael A., Margaret Carlisle Duncan, and Kerry Jensen. 1993. Separating the men from the girls: The gendered language of televised sports. *Gender & Society* 7:121–37.

Messner, Michael A., and Donald F. Sabo, eds. 1990. *Sport, men, and the gender order: Critical feminist perspectives.* Champaign, IL: Human Kinetics.

Molotch, Harvey. 1988. The restroom and equal opportunity. *Sociological Forum* 3:128–32.

Money, John, and Anke A. Ehrhardt. 1972. *Man & woman, boy & girl.* Baltimore, MD: Johns Hopkins University Press.

Moran, Malcolm. 1992. Title IX: A 20-year search for equity. *New York Times* Sports Section, 21, 22, 23 June.

Naftolin, F., and E. Butz, eds. 1981. Sexual dimorphism. *Science* 211:1263–1324.

Olson, Wendy. 1990. Beyond Title IX: Toward an agenda for women and sports in the 1990s. *Yale Journal of Law and Feminism* 3:105–51.

Perry, Ruth, and Lisa Greber. 1990. Women and computers: An introduction. *Signs: Journal of Women in Culture and Society* 16:74–101.

Prior, Jerilynn C., Yvette M. Yigna, Martin T. Shechter, and Arthur E. Burgess. 1990. Spinal bone loss and ovulatory disturbances. *New England Journal of Medicine* 323:1221–27.

Richards, Renée, with Jack Ames. 1983. *Second serve.* New York: Stein and Day.

Riley, Denise. 1988. *Am I that name? Feminism and the category of women in history.* Minneapolis: University of Minnesota Press.

Scharff, Virginia. 1991. *Taking the wheel: Women and the coming of the motor age.* New York: Free Press.

Slatton, Bonnie, and Susan Birrell. 1984. The politics of women's sport. *Arena Review* 8.

Smith, Dorothy E. 1990. *The conceptual practices of power: A feminist sociology of knowledge.* Toronto: University of Toronto Press.

Spelman, Elizabeth. 1988. *Inessential woman: Problems of exclusion in feminist thought.* Boston: Beacon Press.

Theberge, Nancy. 1987. Sport and women's empowerment. *Women's Studies International Forum* 10:387–93.

Vecsey, George. 1990. Cathy Rigby, unlike Peter, did grow up. *New York Times* Sports Section, 19 December.

Watson, Tracey. 1987. Women athletes and athletic women: The dilemmas and contradictions of managing incongruent identities. *Sociological Inquiry* 57:431–46.

Willis, Paul. 1982. Women in sport in ideology. In *Sport, culture, and ideology,* edited by Jennifer A. Hargreaves. London: Routledge & Kegan Paul.

Wright, Barbara Drygulski et al., eds. 1987. *Women, work, and technology: Transformations.* Ann Arbor: University of Michigan Press.

Yoder, Janice D. 1989. Women at West Point: Lessons for token women in male-dominated occupations. In *Women: A feminist perspective,* edited by Jo Freeman. 4th ed. Palo Alto, CA: Mayfield.

Zimmerman, Jan, ed. 1983. *The technological woman: Interfacing with tomorrow.* New York: Praeger.

2

Theorizing Difference from Multiracial Feminism

MAXINE BACA ZINN
BONNIE THORNTON DILL

Women of color have long challenged the hegemony of feminisms constructed primarily around the lives of white middle-class women. Since the late 1960s, U.S. women of color have taken issue with unitary theories of gender. Our critiques grew out of the widespread concern about the exclusion of women of color from feminist scholarship and the misinterpretation of our experiences,[1] and ultimately "out of the very discourses, denying, permitting, and producing difference."[2] Speaking simultaneously from "within and against" *both* women's liberation and antiracist movements, we have insisted on the need to challenge systems of domination,[3] not merely as gendered subjects but as women whose lives are affected by our location in multiple hierarchies.

Recently, and largely in response to these challenges, work that links gender to other forms of domination is increasing. In this article, we examine this connection further as well as the ways in which difference and diversity infuse contemporary feminist studies. Our analysis draws on a conceptual framework that we refer to as "multiracial feminism."[4] This perspective is an attempt to go beyond a mere recognition of diversity and difference among women to examine structures of domination, specifically the importance of race in understanding the social construction of gender. Despite the varied concerns and multiple intellectual stances which characterize the feminisms of women of color, they share an emphasis on race as a primary force situating genders differently. It is

the centrality of race, of institutionalized racism, and of struggles against racial oppression that link the various feminist perspectives within this framework. Together, they demonstrate that racial meanings offer new theoretical directions for feminist thought.

TENSIONS IN CONTEMPORARY DIFFERENCE FEMINISM

Objections to the false universalism embedded in the concept "woman" emerged within other discourses as well as those of women of color.[5] Lesbian feminists and postmodern feminists put forth their own versions of what Susan Bordo has called "gender skepticism."[6]

Many thinkers within mainstream feminism have responded to these critiques with efforts to contextualize gender. The search for women's "universal" or "essential" characteristics is being abandoned. By examining gender in the context of other social divisions and perspectives, difference has gradually become important—even problematizing the universal categories, "women" and "men." Sandra G. Harding expresses the shift best in her claim that "there are no gender relations *per se,* but only gender relations as constructed by and between classes, races, and cultures."[7]

Many feminists now contend that difference occupies center stage as *the* project of women studies today.[8] According to one scholar, "difference has replaced equality as the central concern of feminist theory."[9] Many have welcomed the change, hailing it as a major revitalizing force in U.S. feminist theory.[10] But if *some* priorities within mainstream feminist thought have been refocused by attention to difference, there remains an "uneasy alliance"[11] between women of color and other feminists.

If difference has helped revitalize academic feminisms, it has also "upset the apple cart," and introduced new conflicts into feminist studies.[12] For example, in a recent and widely discussed essay, Jane Rowland Martin argues that the current preoccupation with difference is leading feminism into dangerous traps. She fears that in giving privileged status to a predetermined set of analytic categories (race, ethnicity, and class), "we affirm the existence of nothing but difference." She asks, "How do we know that for us, difference does not turn on being fat, or religious, or in an abusive relationship?"[13]

We, too, see pitfalls in some strands of the difference project. However, our perspectives take their bearings from social relations. Race and class difference are crucial, we argue, not as individual characteristics (such as being fat) but insofar as they are primary organizing principles of a society which locates and positions groups within that society's opportunity structures.

Despite the much-heralded diversity trend within feminist studies, difference is often reduced to mere pluralism; a "live and let live" approach where principles of relativism generate a long list of diversities which begin with gender, class, and race and continue through a range of social structural as well as personal characteristics.[14] Another disturbing pattern, which bell hooks refers to as "the commodification of difference," is the representation of diversity as a form of exotica, "a spice, seasoning that livens up the dull dish that is mainstream white culture."[15] The major limitation of these approaches is the failure to attend to the power relations that accompany difference. Moreover, these approaches ignore the inequalities that cause some characteristics to be seen as "normal" while others are seen as "different" and thus, deviant.

Maria C. Lugones expresses irritation at those feminists who see only the *problem* of difference without recognizing *difference*.[16] Increasingly, we find that difference *is* recognized. But this in no way means that difference occupies a "privileged" theoretical status. Instead of using difference to rethink the category of women, difference is often a euphemism for women who differ from the traditional norm. Even in purporting to accept difference, feminist pluralism often creates a social reality that reverts to universalizing women:

> *So much feminist scholarship assumes that when we cut through all of the diversity among women created by differences of racial classification, ethnicity, social class, and sexual orientation, a "universal truth" concerning women and gender lies buried underneath. But if we can face the scary possibility that no such certainty exists and that persisting in such a search will always distort or omit someone's experiences, with what do we replace this old way of thinking? Gender differences and gender politics begin to look very different if there is no essential woman at the core.*[17]

WHAT IS MULTIRACIAL FEMINISM?

A new set of feminist theories have emerged from the challenges put forth by women of color. Multiracial feminism is an evolving body of theory and practice informed by wide-ranging intellectual traditions. This framework does not offer a singular or unified feminism but a body of knowledge situating women and men in multiple systems of domination. U.S. multiracial feminism encompasses several emergent perspectives developed primarily by women of color: African Americans, Latinas, Asian Americans, and Native Americans, women whose analyses are shaped by their unique perspectives as "outsiders within"—marginal intellectuals whose social locations provide them a particular perspective on self and society.[18] Although U.S. women of color represent many races and ethnic backgrounds—with different histories and cultures—our feminisms cohere in their treatment of race as a basic social division, a structure of power, a focus of political struggle and hence a fundamental force in shaping women's and men's lives.

This evolving intellectual and political perspective uses several terms. While we adopt the label "multiracial," other terms have been used to describe this broad framework. For example, Chela Sandoval refers to "U.S. Third World feminisms,"[19] while other scholars refer to "indigenous feminisms." In their theory text-reader, Alison M. Jagger and Paula M. Rothenberg adopt the label "multicultural feminism."[20]

We use "multiracial" rather than "multicultural" as a way of underscoring race as a power system that interacts with other structured inequalities to shape genders. Within the U.S. context, race, and the system of meanings and ideologies which accompany it, is a fundamental organizing principle of social relationships.[21] Race affects all women and men, although in different ways. Even cultural and group differences among women are produced through interaction within a racially stratified social order. Therefore, although we do not discount the importance of culture, we caution that cultural analytic frameworks that ignore race tend to view women's differences as the product of group-specific values and practices that often result in the marginalization of cultural groups which are then perceived as exotic expressions of a normative center. Our focus on race stresses the social construction of differently situated social groups and their varying degrees of advantage and power. Additionally, this emphasis on race takes on increasing political importance in an era where discourse about race is governed by color-evasive language[22] and a preference for individual rather than group remedies for social inequalities. Our analyses insist upon the primary and pervasive nature of race in contemporary U.S. society while at the same time acknowledging how race both shapes and is shaped by a variety of other social relations.

In the social sciences, multiracial feminism grew out of socialist feminist thinking. Theories about how political economic forces shape women's lives were influential as we began to uncover the social causes of racial ethnic women's

subordination. But socialist feminism's concept of capitalist patriarchy, with its focus on women's unpaid (reproductive) labor in the home failed to address racial differences in the organization of reproductive labor. As feminists of color have argued, "reproductive labor has divided along racial as well as gender lines, and the specific characteristics have varied regionally and changed over time as capitalism has reorganized."[23] Despite the limitations of socialist feminism, this body of literature has been especially useful in pursuing questions about the interconnections among systems of domination.[24]

Race and ethnic studies was the other major social scientific source of multiracial feminism. It provided a basis for comparative analyses of groups that are socially and legally subordinated and remain culturally distinct within U.S. society. This includes the systematic discrimination of socially constructed racial groups and their distinctive cultural arrangements. Historically, the categories of African American, Latino, Asian American, and Native American were constructed as both racially and culturally distinct. Each group has a distinctive culture, shares a common heritage, and has developed a common identity within a larger society that subordinates them.[25]

We recognize, of course, certain pitfalls inherent in an uncritical use of the multiracial label. First, the perspective can be hampered by a biracial model in which only African Americans and Whites are seen as racial categories and all other groups are viewed through the prism of cultural differences. Latinos and Asians have always occupied distinctive places within the racial hierarchy, and current shifts in the composition of the U.S. population are racializing these groups anew.[26]

A second problem lies in treating multiracial feminism as a single analytical framework, and its principle architects, women of color, as an undifferentiated category. The concepts "multiracial feminism," "racial ethnic women," and "women of color" homogenize quite different experiences and can falsely universalize experiences across race, ethnicity, sexual orientation, and age.[27] The feminisms created by women of color exhibit a plurality of intellectual and political positions. We speak in many voices, with inconsistencies that are born of our different social locations. Multiracial feminism embodies this plurality and richness. Our intent is not to falsely universalize women of color. Nor do we wish to promote a new racial essentialism in place of the old gender essentialism. Instead, we use these concepts to examine the structures and experiences produced by intersecting forms of race and gender.

It is also essential to acknowledge that race itself is a shifting and contested category whose meanings construct definitions of all aspects of social life.[28] In the United States it helped define citizenship by excluding everyone who was not a white, male property owner. It defined labor as slave or free, coolie or contract, and family as available only to those men whose marriages were recognized or whose wives could immigrate with them. Additionally, racial meanings are contested both within groups and between them.[29]

Although definitions of race are at once historically and geographically specific, they are also transnational, encompassing diasporic groups and crossing traditional geographic boundaries. Thus, while U.S. multiracial feminism calls attention to the fundamental importance of race, it must also locate the meaning of race within specific national traditions.

THE DISTINGUISHING FEATURES OF MULTIRACIAL FEMINISM

By attending to these problems, multiracial feminism offers a set of analytic premises for thinking about and theorizing gender. The following themes distinguish this branch of feminist inquiry.

First, multiracial feminism asserts that gender is constructed by a range of interlocking inequalities, what Patricia Hill Collins calls a "matrix of domination."[30] The idea of a matrix is that several fundamental systems work with and through each other. People experiences race, class, gender, and sexuality differently depending upon their social location in the structures of race, class, gender,

and sexuality. For example, people of the same race will experience race differently depending upon their location in the class structure as working class, professional managerial class, or unemployed; in the gender structure as female or male; and in structures of sexuality as heterosexual, homosexual, or bisexual.

Multiracial feminism also examines the simultaneity of systems in shaping women's experience and identity. Race, class, gender, and sexuality are not reducible to individual attributes to be measured and assessed for their separate contribution in explaining given social outcomes, an approach that Elizabeth Spelman calls "pop-bead metaphysics," where a woman's identity consists of the sum of parts neatly divisible from one another.[31] The matrix of domination seeks to account for the multiple ways that women experience themselves as gendered, raced, classed, and sexualized.

Second, multiracial feminism emphasizes the intersectional nature of hierarchies at all levels of social life. Class, race, gender, and sexuality are components of both social structure and social interaction. Women and men are differently embedded in locations created by these cross-cutting hierarchies. As a result, women and men throughout the social order experience different forms of privilege and subordination, depending on their race, class, gender, and sexuality. In other words, intersecting forms of domination produce *both* oppression *and* opportunity. At the same time that structures of race, class, and gender create disadvantages for women of color, they provide unacknowledged benefits for those who are at the top of these hierarchies—whites, members of the upper classes, and males. Therefore, multiracial feminism applies not only to racial ethnic women but also to women and men of all races, classes, and genders.

Third, multiracial feminism highlights the relational nature of dominance and subordination. Power is the cornerstone of women's differences.[32] This means that women's differences are *connected* in systematic ways.[33] Race is a vital element in the pattern of relations among minority and white women. As Linda Gordon argues, the very meanings of being a white woman in the United States have been affected by the existence of subordinated women of color; "They intersect in conflict and in occasional cooperation, but always in mutual influence."[34]

Fourth, multiracial feminism explores the interplay of social structure and women's agency. Within the constraints of race, class, and gender oppression, women create viable lives for themselves, their families, and their communities. Women of color have resisted and often undermined the forces of power that control them. From acts of quiet dignity and steadfast determination to involvement in revolt and rebellion, women struggle to shape their own lives. Racial oppression has been a common focus of the "dynamic of oppositional agency" of women of color. As Chandra Talpade Mohanty points out, it is the nature and organization of women's opposition which mediates and differentiates the impact of structures of domination.[35]

Fifth, multiracial feminism encompasses wide-ranging methodological approaches, and like other branches of feminist thought, relies on varied theoretical tools as well. Ruth Frankenberg and Lata Mani identify three guiding principles of inclusive feminist inquiry: "building complex analyses, avoiding erasure, specifying location."[36] In the last decade, the opening up of academic feminism has focused attention on social location in the production of knowledge. Most basically, research by and about marginalized women has destabilized what used to be universal categories of gender. Marginalized locations are well-suited for grasping social relations that remained obscure from more privileged vantage points. Lived experience, in other words, creates alternative ways of understanding the social world and the experience of different groups of women within it. Racially informed standpoint epistemologies have provided new topics, fresh questions, and new understandings of women and men. Women of color have, as Norma Alarcón argues, asserted ourselves as sub-

jects, using our voices to challenge dominant conceptions of truth.[37]

Sixth, multiracial feminism brings together understandings drawn from the lived experiences of diverse and continuously changing groups of women. Among Asian Americans, Native Americans, Latinas and Blacks are many different national cultural and ethnic groups. Each one is engaged in the process of testing, refining, and reshaping these broader categories in its own image. Such internal differences heighten awareness of and sensitivity to both commonalities and differences, serving as a constant reminder of the importance of comparative study and maintaining a creative tension between diversity and universalization.

DIFFERENCE AND TRANSFORMATION

Efforts to make women's studies less partial and less distorted have produced important changes in academic feminism. Inclusive thinking has provided a way to build multiplicity and difference into our analyses. This has lead to the discovery that race matters for everyone. White women, too, must be reconceptualized as a category that is multiple defined by race, class, and other differences. As Ruth Frankenberg demonstrates in a study of whiteness among contemporary women, all kinds of social relations, even those that appear neutral, are, in fact, racialized. Frankenberg further complicates the very notion of a unified white identity by introducing issues of Jewish identity.[38] Therefore, the lives of women of color cannot be seen as a *variation* on a more general model of white American womanhood. The model of womanhood that feminist social science once held as "universal" is also a product of race and class.

When we analyze the power relations constituting all social arrangements and shaping women's lives in distinctive ways, we can begin to grapple with core feminist issues about how genders are socially constructed and constructed differently. Women's difference is built into our study of gender. Yet this perspective is quite far removed from the atheoretical pluralism implied in much contemporary thinking about gender.

Multiracial feminism, in our view, focuses not just on differences but also on the way in which differences and domination intersect and are historically and socially constituted. It challenges feminist scholars to go beyond the mere recognition and inclusion of difference to reshape the basic concepts and theories of our disciplines. By attending to women's social location based on race, class, and gender, multiracial feminism seeks to clarify the structural sources of diversity. Ultimately, multiracial feminism forces us to see privilege and subordination as interrelated and to pose such questions as, How do the existences and ex-

periences of all people—women and men, different racial-ethnic groups, and different classes— shape the experiences of each other? How are those relationships defined and enforced through social institutions that are the primary sites for negotiating power within society? How do these differences contribute to the construction of both individual and group identity? Once we acknowledge that all women are affected by the racial order of society, then it becomes clear that the insights of multiracial feminism provide an analytical framework, not solely for understanding the experiences of women of color but for understanding *all* women, and men, as well.

NOTES

1. Maxine Baca Zinn, Lynn Weber Cannon, Elizabeth Higginbotham, and Bonnie Thornton Dill, "The Costs of Exclusionary Practices in Women's Studies," *Signs* 11, (winter, 1986): 290–303.
2. Chela Sandoval, "U.S. Third World Feminism: The Theory and Method of Oppositional Consciousness in the Postmodern World," *Genders* (spring, 1991): 1–24.
3. Ruth Frankenberg and Lata Mani, "Cross Currents, Crosstalk: Race, 'Postcoloniality' and the Politics of Location," *Cultural Studies* 7 (May, 1993): 292–310.
4. We use the term "multiracial feminism" to convey the multiplicity of racial groups and feminist perspectives.
5. A growing body of works on difference in feminist thought now exists. Although we cannot cite all of the current work, the following are representative: Michèle Barrett, "The Concept of Difference," *Feminist Review* 26 (July, 1987): 29–42; Christina Crosby, "Dealing With Difference," in *Feminists Theorize the Political,* ed. Judith Butler and Joan W. Scott (New York: Routledge, 1992): 130–43; Elizabeth Fox-Genovese, "Difference, Diversity, and Divisions in an Agenda for the Women's Movement" in *Color, Class, and Country: Experiences of Gender,* ed. Gay Young and Bette J. Dickerson (London: Zed Books, 1994): 232–48; Nancy A. Hewitt, "Compounding Differences," *Feminist Studies* 18 (summer 1992): 313–26; Maria C. Lugones, "On the Logic of Feminist Pluralism," in *Feminist Ethics* ed. Claudia Card (Lawrence: University of Kansas Press, 1991), 35–44; Rita S. Gallin and Anne Ferguson, "The Plurality of

Feminism: Rethinking 'Difference,'" in *The Woman and International Development Annual* (Boulder: Westview Press, 1993), 3: 1–16; and Linda Gordon, "On Difference," *Genders* 10 (spring, 1991): 91–111.
6. Susan Bordo, "Feminism, Postmodernism, and Gender Skepticism," in *Feminism/Postmodernism,* ed. Linda J. Nicholson (London: Routledge, 1990), 133–56.
7. Sandra G. Harding, *Whose Science? Whose Knowledge? Thinking from Women's Lives* (Ithaca: Cornell University Press, 1991), 179.
8. Crosby, 131.
9. Fox-Genovese, 232.
10. Faye Ginsberg and Anna Lowenhaupt Tsing, Introduction to *Uncertain Terms, Negotiating Gender in American Culture* ed. Faye Ginsberg and Anna Lowenhaupt Tsing (Boston: Beacon Press, 1990), 3.
11. Sandoval, 2.
12. Sandra G. Morgan, "Making Connections: Socialist-Feminist Challenges to Marxist Scholarship," in *Women and a New Academy: Gender and Cultural Contexts,* ed. Jean F. O'Barr (Madison: University of Wisconsin Press, 1989), 149.
13. Jane Rowland Martin, "Methodological Essentialism, False Difference, and Other Dangerous Traps," *Signs* 19 (spring, 1994): 647.
14. Barrett, 32.
15. bell hooks, *Black Looks: Race and Representation* (Boston: South End Press, 1992), 21.
16. Lugones, 35–44.

17. Patricia Hill Collins, Foreword to *Women of Color in U.S. Society,* ed. Maxine Baca Zinn and Bonnie Thornton Dill (Philadelphia: Temple University Press, 1994), xv.

18. Patricia Hill Collins, "Learning from the Outsider Within: The Sociological Significance of Black Feminist Thought," *Social Problems* 33, (December, 1986): 514–532.

19. Sandoval, 1.

20. Alison M. Jagger and Paula S. Rothenberg, *Feminist Frameworks: Alternative Theoretical Accounts of the Relations between Women and Men.* 3d ed. (New York: McGraw Hill, 1993).

21. Michael Omi and Howard Winant, *Racial Formation in United States: From the 1960s to the 1980s,* 2d ed. (New York: Routledge, 1994).

22. Ruth Frankenberg, *The Social Construction of Whiteness: White Women, Race Matters* (Minneapolis: University of Minnesota Press, 1993).

23. Evelyn Nakano Glenn, "From Servitude to Service Work: Historical Continuities in the Racial Division of Paid Reproductive Labor," *Signs* 18, (autumn, 1992): 3. See also Bonnie Thornton Dill, "Our Mothers' Grief: Racial-Ethnic Women and the Maintenance of Families," *Journal of Family History* 13, no. 4 (1988): 415–31.

24. Morgan, 146.

25. Maxine Baca Zinn and Bonnie Thornton Dill, "Difference and Domination," in *Women of Color in U.S. Society,* 11–12.

26. See Omi and Winant, 53–76, for a discussion of racial formation.

27. Margaret L. Andersen and Patricia Hill Collins, *Race, Class, and Gender: An Anthology* (Belmont, Calif.: Wadsworth, 1992), xvi.

28. Omi and Winant.

29. Nazli Kibria, "Migration and Vietnamese American Women: Remaking Ethnicity," in *Women of Color in U.S. Society,* 247–61.

30. Patricia Hill Collins, *Black Feminist Thought: Knowledge, Consciousness, and the Politics of Empowerment* (Boston: Unwin Hyman, 1990).

31. Elizabeth Spelman, *Inessential Women: Problems of Exclusion in Feminist Thought* (Boston: Beacon Press, 1988).

32. Several discussions of difference make this point. See Baca Zinn and Dill, 10; Gordon, 106; and Lynn Weber, in the "Symposium on West and Fenstermaker's 'Doing Difference,'" *Gender & Society* 9 (August 1995): 515–19.

33. Glenn, 10.

34. Gordon, 106.

35. Chandra Talpade Mohanty, "Cartographies of Struggle: Third World Women and the Politics of Feminism," in *Third World Women and the Politics of Feminism,* ed. Chandra Talpade Mohanty, Ann Russo, and Lourdes Torres (Bloomington: Indiana University Press, 1991), 13.

36. Frankenberg and Mani, 307.

37. Norma Alarçon, "The Theoretical Subject(s) of *This Bridge Called My Back* and Anglo American Feminism," in *Making Face, Making Soul, Haciendo Caras: Creative and Critical Perspectives by Women of Color,* ed. Gloria Anzaldua, (San Francisco: Aunt Lute, 1990), 356.

38. Frankenberg. See also Evelyn Torton Beck, "The Politics of Jewish Invisibility," *NWSA Journal* (fall 1988): 93–102.

3

Colonialism, Structural Subordination, and Empowerment

Women in the Development Process in Latin America and the Caribbean

EDNA ACOSTA-BELÉN
CHRISTINE E. BOSE

... This chapter introduces a theoretical framework for the study of women in the development process, with a focus on Latin America and the Caribbean which stresses that the basic paradigm of power relationships, established during the era of imperialist expansion between Europe and its New World colonial territories, and between women and men, has not varied significantly since then. These relations are still recreated through contemporary mechanisms. Much too often development projects promoted by Western countries have, in the long run, better served their own interests than those of their intended beneficiaries. As a result, contrary to expectations, growth and prosperity still elude most Latin American and Caribbean countries. In addition, if we examine the international economic crisis of the 1980s, the determining role of gender is illustrated, since women's unpaid or underpaid labor was at the core of new development programs and policies and a crucial part of this phase of capitalist expansion....

UNDERSTANDING THIRD WORLD DEVELOPMENT

Development is an all-encompassing word used to summarize the overriding concerns and aspirations of advanced capitalist nations and their inter-national agencies in undertaking initiatives and generating responses to a whole range of critical problems faced by what they categorized as the poor, "underdeveloped" countries of the world.[1] These chronic conditions include famine and malnutrition, displacement and homelessness, unemployment and underemployment, disease, the destruction of the environment, and political repression and violence. Survival problems remain historical constants for much of Latin America, the Caribbean, and the rest of the Third World, the outcome of the cumulative effects of the unequal and dependent relationships maintained for centuries. It has been accurately noted that "development would not exist without underdevelopment, wealth would not exist without poverty, and the domination of men would not exist without the subjection and submissiveness of women" (Mies et al. 1988, 3)....

Not surprisingly, most of the development strategies and policies for Latin America and the Caribbean have been formulated from the ideological and economic perspectives and interests of the industrialized Western nations. Such plans are generally applied across the board, with scant attention to the specific national needs and realities of the territories they are intended to transform. Their overall failure is frequently attributed to the remnants of archaic forces that still loom over developing nations and supposedly keep them suspended in time, rather than to the misguided nature of the development projects. In reality, Latin American and Caribbean nations are faced with continued profound internal inequalities, the inability to meet the basic needs of their populations, rampant inflation, national deficits, and an unfavorable and vulnerable position in the international economy, exacerbated by foreign debt problems. These problems dispute the paternalistic tenets of most development policies. Although development agencies have begun to be more attentive to specific national needs, they are far from discarding profit-centered development in favor of people-centered programs. . . .

Industrialization and modernization projects have tended to rely on foreign investment, commercialization, and manufacturing for export rather than local consumption (Sen and Grown 1987). As a result, the development process has meant, to a large extent, the "denationalizing" of many Third World economies, because foreign industrial capital frequently interferes with or restricts the autonomy of local governments, as well as the capacity of national industries to compete in the world market. In addition, in order to promote their economies, these nations frequently become dependent on single-commodity export trade, leaving them extremely vulnerable to the fluctuations and perils of global markets. Such dependent, as opposed to self-sufficient, development strategies have been the norm rather than the exception.

A pioneering model for export-led industrialization projects in developing nations was Operation Bootstrap, an industrialization program introduced in Puerto Rico in 1948. Palmira N. Ríos's case study (1990) of Puerto Rico's industrialization process documents the resulting increased demand for female labor in the manufacturing sector. Although local governments of developing countries try to promote male-dominated industries, which they see as providing more stable jobs and higher wages than those where women workers predominate, Ríos's study shows that the foreign labor needs of multinationals are being met primarily by women.

Development policies and projects that are implemented from outside, without careful consideration of national infrastructures, internal human and natural resources, or needs for reform, can increase inequality in Latin America, the Caribbean, and other Third World regions. Agricultural development, for instance, without the precondition of agrarian reform and more equitable land distribution, has tended to benefit wealthy landowners rather than poor peasants. Moreover, it has often stimulated peasant migration from rural areas to towns and cities, disrupting the lives of families and entire communities. In some areas of Latin America and the Caribbean it is the women who were driven out of agricultural pursuits and forced to migrate, whereas in some African countries men have moved to towns and cities in search of jobs and left women to do agricultural work (Boserup 1970).

GENDER AND DEVELOPMENT

A quick perusal of international data demonstrates that almost without exception, women *everywhere* in the world are worse off than men. On the whole, women have less power and money and more work and responsibility (Seager and Olson 1986, 7; Young, Fort, and Danner forthcoming). When the United Nations proclaimed International Women's Year in 1975, the data it released showed that women were performing two-thirds of the world's work and receiving only 10 percent of all income, while owning only 1 percent of the means of production (Bennholdt-Thomsen 1988b). The picture becomes even more distressing when we consider the enormous socioeconomic disparities between the highly industrialized and developing nations. First World nations constitute only one-fourth of the world's population, but they receive four-fifths of the income (Brandt Report 1980). . . .

It is difficult to address gender issues in the developing countries of Latin America and the Caribbean without recognizing that they are inextricably linked to a global capitalist and patriarchal model of accumulation and hence to the history of imperialist expansion and colonialism (Saffioti 1978; Mies et al. 1988). Although it is not always self-evident, both women and colonies have served as the foundations of industrial development of the economically dominant Western nations.

Colonialism, born in the fifteenth century—the gateway to discovery, exploration, and conquest—was to become the mainspring of European industrial development. Since the "discovery" of their existence by European settlers, primarily from Spain, Portugal, Great Britain, France, and the Netherlands, territories in the New World have served as the major sources of precious metals, labor, raw materials, and food products to support the commerce, consumption, and economic development of what are today's industrialized nations. The basis for the ascendancy of capitalism in Europe was the colonial exploitation of its overseas empires. Although the nature of colonization varied from one region of the world to another, the system was based on extracting the wealth of the new lands by using the labor of both the subjugated indigenous populations and that of the displaced and enslaved African populations to support the lavish lives of European aristocracies and the consumption needs of a rising bourgeoisie (Saffioti 1978; Etienne and Leacock 1980). The wealth and natural resources of the colonies were the essence of European mercantilist capitalism and, at a later stage, of its industrial revolution. The manufactured goods produced in European factories with the colonies' raw materials and labor found their way back into colonial markets. With some variations, this cycle has essentially perpetuated itself through the centuries.

In the Americas the United States emerged as a new colonial power to substitute for the Spanish, consolidating itself in the nineteenth century through the pursuit of its Manifest Destiny policies of territorial expansion and the Monroe Doctrine (1823), aimed at reducing European presence and influence in the hemisphere. After its Civil War (1861–65) the United States was determined to become the major economic and geopolitical power in the Americas.

In the twentieth century capitalism entered its new monopoly and multinational stages of development, and the neocolonial relations developed then still link the colonizing and colonized countries into a global economic network. The unequal relationship that has kept Latin American and Caribbean nations dependent helps explain the continuing internal turmoil and clamor for change emanating from most of these nations today.

It is quite evident in the colonial literature that from the beginning of the European monarchies' imperial expansion, the adventurers, missionaries, and officials who came to the New World had little regard for any patterns of communal and egalitarian relationships among the native populations subjugated during the colonial enterprise. In many precolonial societies women's position and participation in productive activities was parallel to that of men, rather than subservient (Saffioti 1978; Etienne and Leacock 1980). The imposition of European patriarchal relationships that presupposed the universal subordination of women in many instances deprived indigenous women of property and personal autonomy and restricted the productive functions and any public roles they might have played before colonization (Saffioti 1978; Etienne and Leacock 1980; Nash 1980)....

...Feminist researchers are now paying attention to those previously ignored sectors of working women essential to Third World economies. For instance, historical studies on the New World colonial experience are beginning to examine the contribution of African enslaved women in both the productive and reproductive spheres and in those areas that made their experience so different from that of black men (Morrissey 1989; Bush 1990).

Several other key studies attempt to document the diverse roles and activities of women in the productive sphere. Elsa M. Chaney and Mary

Garcia Castro (1989) describe the contemporary search of household domestic workers in Latin America and the Caribbean for a class identity, demanding both respect for their labor and legal recognition of their rights. The authors argue that these women are striving for identification as workers rather than as *muchachas* (serving girls). Ximena Bunster, Elsa M. Chaney, and Ellan Young (1985) produced a compelling study of rural, mostly indigenous, women in Peru who migrate to the cities and towns, where they find their greatest employment opportunities are as street vendors and servants. These two occupations account for one-third of all employed women in Latin America....

Through some of the studies mentioned, we can see why the feminist critique of development paradigms was a major factor in the emergence of women's studies as a field of academic inquiry in Latin American and Caribbean higher education institutions during the 1980s. A significant body of scholarship has emerged and programmatic initiatives are being undertaken in spite of limited institutional resources and support, bureaucratic barriers, and the quasi-"subversive" character and implications of feminism, which in these countries is often regarded as a Western penetration that threatens traditional cultural values and sex roles.[2]...

Women and the Economic Crisis of the 1980s

...According to June Nash and María Patricia Fernández Kelly (1983), the 1980s' international crisis, compared by some to the Great Depression, reflects a new relationship between less developed and highly industrialized countries based on the geographic dispersion of the various stages of manufacturing production by large corporations. Attracted by low-cost labor, tax exemptions, and lax production restrictions, transnational corporate capital is radically altering the international workforce. These changes are also causing substantial transformations of families and community structures worldwide.

The growing integration of the world system of production no longer is based on the exploitation of primary sources but on offshore production, or the transfer of assembly plants, primarily in electronics, apparel, and textiles, from core to peripheral or semiperipheral countries. Nash (1983) has shown how industrial plant closings and decline in blue-collar employment in the United States are linked to the emergence of a new, cheaper industrial force in the Third World, now in direct competition with the First World labor force.

Many of the hidden aspects of offshore production occur in export processing zones. In a study of *maquiladoras* (subsidiaries of multinational corporations) on the U.S.–Mexico border, Fernández Kelly (1983) confirms that these industries are encouraging the use of young women's labor. As a development strategy, the *maquiladoras* exacerbate unemployment and underemployment and increase sex segregation in the labor force. Women's alternatives are not substantially improved because these companies offer no job security, provide minimal possibilities for advancement, and frequently expose workers to hazardous conditions. In fact, the families of women working in *maquiladoras* generally are poorer than other migrant households where the women work in service or commerce jobs (Young and Fort forthcoming). Thus, transnational corporations have contributed to the growing proletarianization of Latin American women, aptly described as working on the global assembly line.

This new international division of labor has had considerable economic and political impact on Latin American and Caribbean nations, since it keeps them at the mercy of external economic interests that determine what and how they will produce. To worsen an already detrimental situation, multinational corporations frequently generate economic havoc by moving their operations to a new port with more advantageous incentives when their "industrial peace" is threatened by labor activism or when they seek increased profit margins.

One continuing concern of both the developing and advanced capitalist nations is the increasing amount of women's poverty worldwide, associated with the rise in female-headed households. Whereas in North America and a large part of the Caribbean such households are primarily created by divorce or childbirth out of wedlock, in most Latin American countries the origin lies more in household splits due to migration of one partner from rural to urban areas or even out of the country in search of work, and in the case of several Central American countries war and violence have created large numbers of widows. The attention paid to this feminization of poverty since the 1980s' economic crisis partly stems from the increased visibility and effectiveness of women's movements around the world. Poor women in Latin America have used their responsibilities as mothers and domestic workers not only to enter the formal and informal economies but as the basis for political demands.... Their organizing and advocacy on behalf of the survival of their children and families have made them as potentially explosive as the former colonies in which they live.

Women as a Last Colony

The conceptualization of women as a last colony, advanced by the work of German feminist scholars Mies, Bennholdt-Thomsen, and Werlhof (1988), has provided a valuable new interpretative model for feminist research on Third World issues. This framework underscores the convergences of race, class, and gender and recognizes one complex but coherent system of oppression. It also allows us to see that the patterns of sexism are compounded by a layer of oppression, shared by Third World men and women, brought about by the colonizing experience.

Werlhof (1988a, 25) argues that the relationship of Third World subsistence workers of both genders to First World multinationals in some ways resembles the relationship between men and women worldwide. Women and colonies are both low-wage and nonwage producers, share structural subordination and dependency, and are overwhelmingly poor. Werlhof contends that in response to its

accumulation crisis, capitalism is now implicitly acknowledging that the unpaid labor of women in the household goes beyond the reproductive sphere into the production of commodities. Nevertheless, housewives are frequently and explicitly excluded from what is defined as the economy in order to maintain the illusion of the predominance of the male wage worker. The problems with this definition are increasingly obvious, as many Latin American and Caribbean households, using multiple income strategies, rely on women's informal economy activities or subsistence work.

Mies et al. (1988, 7) indicates there are actually three tiers in the capitalist pyramid of exploitation: (1) the holders of capital, (2) wage workers (mostly white men or the traditional proletariat) and nonwage workers (mostly women), and (3) housewives and subsistence producers (men and women) in the colonial countries. Using this model, both Werlhof (1988a) and Bennholdt-Thomsen (1988a) argue that the new international trend in the division of labor is toward the "housewifization" (*Hausfrauisierung*) of labor, namely, labor that exhibits the major characteristics of housework, and away from the classical proletariat whose labor is now being replaced. Of course, the housewife role entails different things across nations, ranging from cooking, cleaning, washing, and taking care of children and the elderly, to grinding maize, carrying water, or plowing the family plot. The determining factor is always whether or not these tasks are performed for wages.

EMPOWERMENT
Women Organizing for Change

Women are not passive victims in the socioeconomic processes that maintain their lower status. Instead, they are developing creative ways in which to resist the new forms of subordination. Latin American activists expect that changes in sexist practice and ideology can be obtained during economic crises—an experience quite different from that of feminists in the core capitalist countries whose achievements were made in the context of improving material conditions. In Latin America and the Caribbean various types of resistance, solidarity, and collective action are used by women in diverse geographic regions and under different sociopolitical structures, a pattern that is beginning to be recognized in comparative studies of women's movements (Margolis 1993).

Although Latin American women's subsistence activities as peasant producers can be seen as similar to the unpaid housework of women in Europe and the United States, the resultant political strategies are different...perhaps because of the class differences between them. In First World countries women have responded to cutbacks in government services to families by entering the paid labor force, especially in the service industry, and by taking over the tasks of eldercare and childcare. In Latin America and the Caribbean nations, though some women do create micro-enterprises..., take jobs in export processing zones, or enter the service sector, the vast majority respond to the breakdown of their subsistence economy by organizing collective meals, health cooperatives, mothers' clubs, neighborhood water-rights groups, or their own textile and craft collectives, which produce goods both for street vending and for international markets. Thus, rather than *privatizing* their survival problems, these women *collectivize* them and form social-change groups based on social reproduction concerns. In these new terms, the political discourse and arena of struggle is not worker exploitation and control of the means of production but rather moral persuasion to place demands on the state for rights related to family survival.

Many Latin American women activists contend that their traditional roles as wives and mothers are the basis for these collective actions on behalf of their families. Although most of the groups are composed of poor women, they do not organize either explicitly on a class basis or at the workplace. Instead, they organize at a neighborhood level around a broad list of issues that they redefine as women's concerns, such as running water or transportation for squatter communities. Some feminist scholars argue that this approach

constitutes a movement of women but not necessarily a feminist movement; others feel these tactics represent a form of working-class feminism that promotes consciousness of how gender shapes women's lives (Sternback et al. 1992). Safa notes that this approach, which emphasizes women's traditional roles, is clearly different from European or U.S. women's movements, which are viewed as seeking participation in the public sphere based on the elimination (rather than the retention) of most gender distinctions....

Urban organizing is not the only form of empowerment. Indigenous and peasant women in rural areas find that agricultural issues are often paramount. Women's development-related activism in this setting includes struggles over land tenure, actions of landlords, and plantation working conditions—issues that link community and labor—as well as cultural concerns related to ethnic identity and survival of indigenous peoples (Chinchilla 1993). Norma Stoltz Chinchilla indicates that women's rural organizing has changed since the 1960s, when women were involved in housewives' committees, such as those of the Bolivian miners; in the 1980s more women participated in independent peasant organizations such as Mexican *ejidos* or other agrarian reform unions.

Other forms of resistance include women's participation in revolutionary movements. Not surprisingly, women on the left retained a commitment to changing the social relations of production, and many were critiqued for subordinating gender to class concerns. Early organizers saw themselves as engaged in a double militancy, carrying out both political and feminist activism in separate organizations (Sternbach et al. 1992). Nicaragua stands as an exception in that period and an example of how feminism has the potential to strengthen class struggle without being reduced by it, as exhibited in the Sandanista call for links between the women's movement and working-class organizations such as unions (Chinchilla 1990).

In many other Latin American countries the Catholic church, the left, and traditional political parties are seen as major obstacles to women's empowerment, necessitating considerable grass-roots women's organizing. The result is a change in the concept of double militancy: instead of bringing class analysis to the women's movement, feminists try to bring a gender analysis to their political party, union, job, or neighborhood organization (Sternbach et al. 1992). Nancy Saporta Sternbach et al. argue that this change is reflected in the debates that occurred during the series of five feminist *Encuentros* held in Latin America, beginning in Bogotá, Colombia, in 1981 and culminating in San Bernardo, Argentina, in 1990....

These brief examples give a sense of the wide range of alternatives used by women in Latin America and the Caribbean to achieve a measure of empowerment in the context of capitalist dependency and development....

CONCLUSION

If we accept the premise that the layer of subordination experienced by *any* woman because of her gender is in many ways comparable to that of any colonial subject (male or female), then, for women in Latin America, the Caribbean, and other Third World areas who historically share the commonality of the colonial experience, gender represents a compounding factor of their oppression, just as race or ethnicity does for women of color living in First World countries or indigenous, mestizo, and black populations in Latin America and the Caribbean. The concept of women as a last colony thus becomes a compelling metaphor of liberation and should be an integral part of any human rights struggle. Ultimately, therefore, we see a pressing need to focus on a worldwide project of gender decolonization that calls for profound reformulations and restructuring of the existing power relations between women and men at the domestic and societal levels....

Although feminists share a universal struggle against gender subordination and for egalitarian relations, the experiences of Latin American and Caribbean women, with their compounding layers of oppression, will continue to generate a wide diversity of feminist and women's movements. Women are striving to decolonize gender through collective action reflected in the creation of worker organizations in agriculture and export processing zones, neighborhood groups challenging the state to deliver services, cultural affirmation and human rights struggles of indigenous peoples, and feminist research and activist groups, all working in the context of the agendas of international aid organizations and transnational corporations. These movements represent articulated responses from women of all classes, races, ethnicities, and nationalities who, in the midst of their socioeconomic and political difficulties, are carrying the struggle for liberation and equality forward on a variety of fronts, ranging from the home and within the family, to their communities and governments, to their international quests for peace, human rights, and a healthy environment, but most of all, for the possibility of a more just society.

NOTES

1. The term *underdevelopment* was commonly used in most of the literature before the mid-1960s. Third World intellectuals, in particular, considered the term to be value-laden and based on the notion that the Western industrialized nations were more qualified for setting the development norms and standards for the rest of the world. Beginning in the 1970s the terms *developing* or *Third World nations* have been more widely acceptable.

2. The emergence of women's studies programs in Latin American and Caribbean higher education institutions was a phenomenon of the 1980s. Among the programs established in these regions are the ones at El Colegio de México, the University of Costa Rica, the Universidad Nacional at Heredia (Costa Rica), the Confederación Universitaria Centroamericana (CSUCA), the University of Puerto Rico, the University of Buenos Aires, and the University of the West Indies.

REFERENCES

Acosta-Belén, Edna. 1986. "Puerto Rican Women in Culture, History, and Society." In *The Puerto Rican Woman: Perspectives on Culture, History, and Society,* ed. Edna Acosta-Belén, 1–29. New York: Praeger.

Bennholdt-Thomsen, Veronika. 1988a. "'Investment in the Poor': An Analysis of World Bank Policy." In *Women: The Last Colony,* ed. Maria Mies, Veronika Bennholdt-Thomsen, and Claudia von Werlhof, 51–63. London: Zed.

———. 1988b. "Why Do Housewives Continue to be Created in the Third World Too?" In *Women: The Last Colony,* ed. Maria Mies, Veronika Bennholdt-Thomsen, and Claudia von Werlhof, 159–167. London: Zed.

Blauner, Robert. 1972. *Racial Oppression in America.* New York: Harper and Row.

Bose, Christine E. 1987. "Devaluing Women's Work: The Undercount of Women's Employment in 1900 and 1980." In *Hidden Aspects of Women's Work.* ed. Christine Bose, Roslyn Feldberg, and Natalie Sokoloff, 95–115, New York: Praeger.

Boserup, Ester. 1970. *Woman's Role in Economic Development.* New York: St. Martin's Press.

Brandt Report. 1980. *North-South: A Programme for Survival.* London: Pan World Affairs.

Bunster, Ximena, Elsa M. Chaney, and Ellan Young. 1985. *Sellers and Servants: Working Women in Lima, Peru.* New York: Praeger.

Bush, Barbara. 1990. *Slave Women in Caribbean Society.* Kingston, Jamaica: Heinemann; Bloomington: Indiana University Press; London: James Currey.

Chaney, Elsa M., and Mary Garcia Castro, eds. 1989. *Muchachas No More: Household Workers in Latin America and the Caribbean.* Philadelphia: Temple University Press.

Chinchilla, Norma Stoltz. 1990. "Revolutionary Popular Feminism in Nicaragua: Articulating Class, Gender, and National Sovereignty." *Gender and Society* 4 (3): 370–397.

———. 1993. "Gender and National Politics: Issues and Trends in Women's Participation in Latin America Movements." In *Researching Women in Latin America and the Caribbean,* ed. Edna Acosta-Belén and Christine E. Bose, 37–54. Boulder Colo.: Westview.

Deere, Carmen Diana. 1987. "The Latin American Agrarian Reform Experience." In *Rural Women and State Policy: Feminist Perspectives on Latin American Agricultural Development,* ed. Carmen Diana Deere and Magdalena León, 165–190. Boulder, Colo.: Westview.

Etienne, Mona, and Eleanor Leacock, eds. 1980. *Women and Colonization: Anthropological Perspectives.* New York: Praeger.

Fernández Kelly, M. Patricia. 1983. *For We Are Sold, I and My People: Women and Industry in Mexico's Frontier.* Albany: State University of New York Press.

Genovese, Eugene. 1965. *The Political Economy of Slavery.* New York: Pantheon.

Kardam, Nüket. 1991. *Bringing Women In: Women's Issues in International Development Programs.* Boulder, Colo.: Lynne Reinner.

Leacock, Eleanor. 1990. "Montagnais Women and the Jesuit Program for Colonization." In *Women and Colonization: Anthropological Perspectives,* ed. Mona Etienne and Eleanor Leacock, 25–42. New York: Praeger.

Margolis, Diane Rothbard. 1993. "Women's Movements around the World: Cross-Cultural Comparisons." *Gender & Society* 7 (3): 379–399.

Mies, Maria, Veronika Bennholdt-Thomsen, and Claudia von Werlhof. 1988. *Women: The Last Colony.* London: Zed.

Morrissey, Marietta. 1989. *Slave Women in the New World: Gender Stratification in the Caribbean.* Lawrence: University of Kansas Press.

Nash, June. 1980. "Aztec Women: The Transition from Status to Class in Empire and Colony." In *Women and Colonization: Anthropological Perspectives,* ed. Mona Etienne and Eleanor Leacock, 134–148. New York: Praeger.

———. 1983 "The Impact of the Changing International Division of Labor on Different Sectors of the Labor Force." In *Women, Men, and the International Division of Labor,* ed. June Nash and María Patricia Fernández Kelly, 3–38. Albany: State University of New York Press.

Nash, June, and María Patricia Fernández Kelly, eds. 1983. *Women, Men, and the International Division of Labor.* Albany: State University of New York Press.

Ríos, Palmira. 1990. "Export-Oriented Industrialization and the Demand for Female Labor: Puerto Rican Women in the Manufacturing Sector, 1952–1980." *Gender & Society* 4 (3): 321–337.

Saffioti, Heleieth I. B. 1978. *Women in Class Society.* New York: Monthly Review.

Seager, Joni, and Ann Olson. 1986. *Women in the World: An International Atlas.* New York: Simon and Schuster.

Sen, Gita, and Caren Grown. 1987. *Development, Crises, and Alternative Visions.* New York: Monthly Review.

Stallings, Barbara, and Robert Kaufman, eds. 1989. *Debt and Democracy in Latin America.* Boulder, Colo.: Westview.

Sternback, Nancy Saporta, Marysa Navarro-Aranguren, Patricia Chuchryk, and Sonia E. Alvirez. 1992. "Feminisms in Latin America: From Bogotá to San Bernardo." *Signs: Journal of Women in Culture and Society* 17 (2): 393–434.

Werlhof, Claudia von. 1988a. "Women's Work: The Blind Spot in the Critique of Political Economy." In *Women: The Last Colony,* ed. Maria Mies, Veronika Bennholdt-Thomsen, and Claudia von Werlhof. 13–26. London: Zed.

———. 1988b. "The Proletarian Is Dead: Long Live the Housewife!" In *Women: The Last Colony,* ed. Maria Mies, Veronika Bennholdt-Thomsen, and Claudia von Werlhof, 168–181. London: Zed.

Young, Gay, and Luci Fort, Forthcoming. "Household Responses to Economic Change: Migration and Maquila Work in Northern Mexico." *Social Science Quarterly.*

Young, Gay, Lucia Fort, and Mona Danner. Forthcoming. "Moving from 'The Status of Women' to 'Gender Inequality': Conceptualization, Social Indicators, and an Empirical Application." *Gender & Society.*

4

Children and Gender
Constructions of Difference

BARRIE THORNE

When I first began observing in elementary schools as an ethnographer with gender on my mind, events like the following drew me and my notetaking like a magnet:

> On the playground, a cluster of children played "girls-chase-the-boys" or "boys-chase-the-girls" (they used both names). Boys and girls were by definition on different sides. In the back-and-forth of chasing and being chased, they used gender terms ("I'm gonna get that girl"; "Let's go after those boys") rather than individual names for members of the other side.
>
> In a combined fourth-and-fifth-grade classroom the teacher introduced a math game organized as girls against boys; she would write addition and subtraction problems on the board, and a member of each team would race to be the first to write the correct answer. As the teacher wrote two scorekeeping columns headed "Beastly Boys" and "Gossipy Girls," several boys yelled out, "Noisy girls! Gruesome girls!" while some of the girls laughed. As the game proceeded, the girls sat in a row on top of their desks; sometimes they moved collectively, pushing their hips or whispering, "Pass it on." The boys stood along the wall, several reclining against desks. When members of either group came back victorious from the front of the room, they would do the "giving five" hand-slapping ritual with their team members.

On such occasions—when gender divisions were highlighted and "the girls" and "the boys" were defined as separate, opposing groups—I felt I was at the heart of children's gender relations.

But these moments are not the whole of social life in elementary schools; at other times boys and girls interacted in relaxed rather than bounded and antagonistic ways. An example from the same fourth-and-fifth-grade classroom:

> A student teacher had listed various activities on the board and asked students to choose one and sign up for it. Three boys and two girls had chosen to tape record a radio play. The teacher told them they could rehearse in the back of the room. They moved from their desks, settled in chairs at a round table (seated girl-boy-girl-boy-boy), and took turns leaning into the microphone and reading from the script. Now and then they stopped to talk and argue as a group.

I had to press myself to record the details of this situation; it seemed less juicy, less ripe for gendered analysis than the chasing sequence, the math game, or a same-gender group. This disparity in my perception of its relevance led me to ponder our frameworks for thinking about children and gender. These frameworks, which emphasize oppositional dichotomies, neatly fit situations in which boys and girls are organized as separate, bounded groups, and they obscure more relaxed, mixed-gender encounters. What kinds of frameworks can more fully account for the complexity of children's gender relations?

Is it "in the nature" of children that we should gear up different questions for them than we do for adults? Feminist scholarship has mostly centered upon the lives and experiences of adults; it has either ignored children, seen them as objects of adult (primarily women's) labor, or confined discussion of them to questions of "socialization" and "development."[1] In the last two decades our frameworks for thinking about adults and gender have moved beyond unexamined dualisms toward greater complexity. But when we focus on children, we tend to think in more simplistic ways— perhaps one reason for the lingering power of dualisms.[2]

THE DUALISTIC MODEL OF SEX DIFFERENCES

Most of the research on children and gender involves a search either for individual or for group sex differences. Both approaches conceptualize gender in terms of dualisms.

Studies in the "individual sex differences" tradition typically set out to explore possible statistical correlations between individual sex/gender (usually understood as an unproblematic male/female dichotomy) and a specific piece of behavior or measure of personality. The pieces that have been studied range widely, including such personality traits as self-esteem, intellectual aptitudes like verbal or spatial ability, such motivational structure as need for affiliation, and specific behavior, for example, the amount of time spent in rough-and-tumble play. Extensive research has studied whether parents and teachers interact (for example, touch or talk) differently with girls and boys. Sex difference studies specify and gauge behavior (for example, with tests of spatial ability or measures of time spent in rough-and-tumble play or talking with a teacher), aggregate across many individuals, and then look for statistically significant correlations by sex.[3]

The results of sex difference research are always a matter of statistical frequency, for sex/gender differences are never absolutely dichotomous. But where statistically significant differences are found, the language of frequency quickly slides into a portrayal of dualism ("boys engage in more rough-and-tumble play than girls"; "girls have greater verbal ability than

boys"; "boys receive more teacher attention"). Many writers have cautioned against translating statistical complexity into a discourse of "the pinks and the blues," the tellingly dichotomous title of a popular television documentary on sex difference among children.[4] They have noted other related pitfalls in the sex difference approach, such as a bias toward reporting difference rather than similarity and a failure to distinguish statistical significance from the size of an effect.

But dichotomous portrayals may be unavoidable when one's basic strategy is to compare males and females. Individual sex categories[5]— female/male, woman/man, girl/boy—divide the population in half and are marked and sustained by daily social practices of gender display and attribution.[6] Sex difference research treats these categories as relatively unproblematic and continues binary framing with distinctions like similarity versus difference. Recent proposals to use phrases like "sex similarities and differences" or "sex-related differences," provide at best awkward and ambiguous tools for grasping the complexities of gender.

Although the situation is gradually beginning to change, sociologists and anthropologists have largely ceded the study of children to psychologists, who in turn have relegated the study of children to specialists in child development. The social science literature on children and gender reflects this division of labor. The focus has been more on individuals than on social relations, and the favored methods—laboratory experiments, observations organized around preset categories— strip human conduct from the contexts in which it is given meaning.

Group Differences

When psychologists, sociologists, and anthropologists of gender have studied the social relations of children, they have primarily relied on a model of group differences that is founded on the prevalence of gender separation in children's friendships and daily encounters. Every observational study of children's interactions in preschools, elementary schools, and junior high schools in the United States has found a high degree of gender separation in seating choices and in the groups children form.[7] In a study of sixth- and seventh-graders in a middle school whose enrollment was half Black and half white, Schofield found that while racial separation among the students was extensive, gender separation was even greater.[8]

After documenting widespread gender separation in children's social relations, most researchers have compared the separate worlds of boys and girls. The result is a by now familiar litany of generalized contrasts, usually framed as a series of dualisms: boys' groups are larger, and girls' groups are smaller ("buddies" versus "best friends"); boys play more often in public, and girls in more private places; boys engage in more rough-and-tumble play, physical fighting, and overt physical conflict than do girls; boys play more organized team sports, and girls engage in more turn-taking play; within same-gender groups, boys continually maintain and display hierarchies, while girls organize themselves into shifting alliances.[9]

There are problems with this separate worlds approach. Much of the literature, like that on individual sex differences, suffers from androcentrism: the "boys' world" is usually described first (as above) and more extensively; the less richly articulated "girls' world" seems explicitly (as in Lever's study)[10] or implicitly lacking.[11] Even where efforts are made to revalue the "girls' world" (as in Gilligan's reframing of Lever's work)[12] and to give both poles equal weighting, people still construe children's gender relations as polarities. The convention of separate worlds compresses enormous complexity into a series of contrasts: public/private, large/small, competitive/cooperative. It suggests a Victorian world of separate spheres writ small and contemporary.

Gender separation among children is not so total as the separate worlds rendering suggests, and the amount of separation varies by situation. For example, Luria and Herzog found that in a

nursery school in Massachusetts two-thirds of playgroups were same-gender (one-third were mixed); 80 percent of playground groups of fifth- and sixth-graders in a public elementary school were same-gender (20 percent were mixed); in a private school, 63 percent of playground groups were same-gender (37 percent were mixed).[13] For many children in the United States, gender separation is more extensive on school playgrounds than in other daily settings. Girls and boys interact frequently in most elementary school classrooms, since adults organize much of the activity and usually rely on criteria other than gender. Children often report engaging in more cross-gender play in neighborhoods and in families than they do on school playgrounds; in these less populous situations they may have to cross gender and age categories to find playmates, and there are fewer witnesses to tease girls and boys who choose to be together.[14]

The occasions when girls and boys are together are as theoretically and socially significant as when they are apart, yet the literature on children's gender relations has largely ignored interaction between them. In much of the research on children's group life, "gender" has first been located in the separation of boys and girls and then in comparisons of same-gender groups.[15] Comparing groups of girls with groups of boys not only neglects the occasions when they are together but also ignores the complex choreography of separation and integration in children's daily interactions. Frequency counts provide snapshots of single moments, but they cannot teach us about the social processes by which gender is used—or overridden or ignored—as a basis for group formation.[16]

Finally, in relying on a series of contrasts to depict the whole, the separate worlds approach exaggerates the coherence of same-gender interactions and glosses extensive variation among boys and among girls. Characterizations of the "boys' world" suffer from a distortion akin to the "Big Man Bias" in anthropological ethnographies in which male elites are equated with men in general.[17] Larger, bonded groups of boys figure prominently in Joffe's ethnographic description of the "male subculture" of a preschool, Best's description of boys in an elementary school, Everhart's ethnography of a junior high and Cusick's of a high school, and Willis' study of working-class "lads" in a vocational secondary school in England.[18] Other less popular, disruptive, dominant, or socially visible boys—and girls (who remain invisible in the majority of school ethnographies)—appear at the edges of these portrayals, but their standpoints and experiences are voiced only indirectly. (Cusick reports that as a participant-observer he avoided "isolates"; "I was there to do a study not to be a friend to those who had no friends.")[19]

In the fourth-and-fifth-grade class in which I was a participant-observer,[20] a relatively stable group of four to six boys (often joined by a girl who successfully crossed gender boundaries) sat together in the classroom and the lunchroom and moved around the playground as a group, playing the team sports of every season. Because of the group's size, physicality, and social dominance, it *seemed* to be the core of the "boys' world" in that classroom—one more instance of the familiar generalization that boys are organized into "flocks" or "gangs." But other fourth-and-fifth-grade boys did not fit the model. Three of them were loners who avoided sports, preferred to stay indoors, and hung out at the edges of the playground. Three more were involved in an intense dyad-into-triad pattern similar to the social organization often generalized as typical of girls' friendships.[21] Two boys were recent immigrants from Mexico, spoke little English, were marginal in most classroom interaction, and on the playground often joined six to ten other Spanish-speaking, nonbilingual children in an ongoing game of dodgeball that was more mixed in gender and age than any other recurring playground group.

Depictions of girls' social relations have also masked considerable variation. While the fourth-and-fifth-grade girls I observed often used a language of "best friends" (dyads and triads did figure centrally in their social relationships), they

also regularly organized into groups of five to seven doing "tricks" on the bars or playing jump rope. Hughes, who observed on an upper-middle-class school playground, and Goodwin, who observed Black children ages ten to thirteen in an urban neighborhood, also found that girls constructed larger groups and complex social networks.[22] Girls' social relations are usually depicted as more cooperative than those of boys, but ethnographers have documented patterns of dispute and competition in girls' interactions with one another, including ritual insults that are often said to be typical of boys.[23] Boys' social relations are usually claimed to be more hierarchical than girls', but type of activity affects mode of interaction. The group of neighborhood girls Goodwin studied constructed hierarchies when they played house (a form of pretend play that, tellingly for children's representations of families, involved continual marking of dominance).[24] But when the girls engaged in a task activity like making rings from the rims of glass bottles, their interactions were more collaborative and egalitarian.

FROM DUALISMS TO GENDER AS FLUID AND SITUATED

Instead of scrambling to describe girls (or girls' groups) in contrast to boys', we are beginning to develop more varied and complex ways of thinking about children and gender. This shift of interpretive conventions has been furthered by the work of anthropologists, folklorists, and sociologists, who are more prone than developmental psychologists to start with social relations and to emphasize social contexts and meanings.

Conceptualizing gender in terms of social relations breaks with the relatively static equation of gender with dichotomous difference. An emphasis on social relations is well developed in studies of social class and ethnicity. But what Connell calls "categoricalism" has hounded the study of gender: reliance on relatively unexamined, dichotomous sex (or gender) categories—male/female, woman/man, boy/girl—as tools of analysis.[25] I have already discussed this problem in sex difference research. It is also a problem in the use of gender as an untheorized binary variable,[26] and—coming from a quite different intellectual and political context—in feminist theories that take "women" and "men" as unproblematic categories.[27]

At the level of basic social categories, gender does operate more dualistically than class, race, or ethnicity. Our culture has only two sex categories, and every person is permanently assigned to one or the other with very few attempts to switch. In every situation each individual displays, and others attribute to her or him, characteristics associated with one or the other of the two categories.[28] The workings of social class and race and ethnic categories seem from the start to be far more complex and contingent than gender. Social class and ethnic categories are multiple, sometimes ambiguous, and may vary by situation. A person's social class or ethnicity may not be readily apparent, nor (as is the case with gender) do we always feel a need to know the class or ethnicity of those with whom we interact.

The distinctive features of sex categories lie behind what Wallman calls "the peculiar epistemology of sex"—the deep hold of dualisms on our ways of thinking about gender.[29] But dichotomous sex categories are only one part of the organizational and symbolic processes of gender. The two categories woman and man have multiple and changing meanings, as ethnographies of "femininities" and "masculinities" suggest.[30]

Shifting the level of analysis from the individual to social relations and from sex categories to the variable social organization and symbolic meanings of gender further unravels dichotomous constructions. When the topic is gender, there is no escaping the theme of difference. But the presence, significance, and meanings of differences are refocused when one asks about the social relations that construct differences—and diminish or undermine them.

How is gender made more or less salient in different situations? In specific social contexts, how do the organization and meanings of gender take shape in relation to other socially constructed divisions like age, race, and social class? How do children in varied positions (for example, popular, marginal, or more or less involved in teen culture) navigate and experience a given set of gender relations? By emphasizing variable social contexts and multiple standpoints and meanings, these questions open a more fluid and situated approach to gender.

Social Contexts and the Relative Salience of Gender

Much of the research on children and gender has neglected the importance of social context. Children have been pulled from specificity and fixed by abstract stages of development. Studies of individual sex differences often generalize about girls versus boys without attending to variations in society and culture. A different perspective emerges when one shifts from individuals to group life, with close attention to social contexts.

Earlier I contrasted situations where gender is highly salient with those in which its importance is muted. When children play "boys-chase-the-girls," gender is basic to the organization and symbolism of the encounter. Group gender boundaries are charged with titillating ambiguity and danger,[31] and girls and boys become by definition separate teams or sides.

The idea of *borderwork,* used by Barth to analyze ethnic relations,[32] can also be used to conceptualize social relations maintained across yet based upon and strengthening gender boundaries. When girls and boys are organized as opposing sides in a math contest or in cross-gender chasing, members of both sides may express solidarity within their gender and playful and serious antagonism to the other. But borderwork is also asymmetric. Boys invade girls' games and scenes of play much more than girls invade boys'. Boys control far more playground space than girls. Girls are more often defined as polluting and boys as running the risk of contamination (for example, girls are more often defined as giving "cooties").[33] Difference is related to dominance in children's gender group arrangements, and the workings of power are complex. Girls do not always passively accept their devaluation, but sometimes challenge and derogate boys. They guard their play and respond angrily to invasions; they complain to adults.[34]

Moments of separation and of bounded interaction evoke perceptions of difference by participants and by the experts who observe them. In everyday life in schools, children and adults talk about the different "natures" of girls and boys primarily to justify exclusion or separation and in situations of gender conflict. Two examples from my field notes:

> *A group of sixth-grade girls grabbed the football from the ongoing play of a group of boys [this was one of the few occasions when I saw a group of girls invade a group of boys on the playground]. The boys complained to the playground aide. She responded, "Why won't you let the girls play?" The boys replied, "They can't tackle; when we tackle 'em they cry."*
>
> *During lunchtime an aide who was frazzled by problems of discipline told the third-grade girls and boys they had to sit at separate tables. One girl turned to another and said, half in jest and half in earnest, "The boys are naughty and we're good."*

Gender-marked moments seem to express core truths: that boys and girls are separate and fundamentally different as individuals and as groups. They help sustain a sense of dualism in the face of enormous variation and complex circumstances. But the complexities are also part of the story. In daily school life many situations are organized along lines other than gender, and girls and boys interact in relaxed and non-gender-marked ways. For example, children often play handball and dodgeball in mixed groups; girls and boys sometimes sit together and converse in relaxed ways in classrooms, the cafeteria, or the library. Collective projects, like the radio play described earlier, often draw girls and boys together and diminish the salience of gender.

Children's gender relations can be understood only if we map the full array of their interactions—occasions when boys and girls are together as well as those when they separate (Goffman coined the apt phrase "with-then-apart" to describe the periodic nature of gender segregation).[35] To grasp the fluctuating significance of gender in social life, we must examine encounters where gender seems largely irrelevant as well as those where it is symbolically and organizationally central.

Broadening the site of significance to include occasions where gender is both unmarked and marked is one of several analytic strategies that I believe can provide fuller understanding of children's gender relations. Our conceptual frameworks are whetted on the marked occasions. Extensive gender separation or organizing an event as boys against the girls sets off contrastive thinking and feeds an assumption of gender as dichotomous difference. By also seeing other contexts as relevant to gender, we can situate the equation of gender with dualism more accurately and understand something of the hold that conceptualization has on us in the thrall of our culture. By developing a sense of the whole and attending to the waning as well as the waxing of gender salience, we can specify not only the social relations that uphold but also those that undermine the construction of gender as binary opposition. We can also gain a more complex understanding of the dynamics of power.

Multiple Differences

In specific social contexts, complex interactions among gender and such other social divisions as age, race, ethnicity, social class, and religion are another source of multiplicity. General terms like *intersecting differences* obscure the complex, sometimes contradictory dynamics of concrete situations. The range of possibilities is better evoked by Connell and colleagues, who observe that different social divisions and forms of inequality may "abrade, inflame, amplify, twist, dampen, and complicate each other."[36]

In the world of elementary schools, age is a more formally institutionalized social division than gender. Being in the first, fourth, or sixth grades determines daily activities and the company one keeps. Different grades may be allocated separate turfs in the lunchroom and the playground, and those who venture out of their age-defined territory may be chastised. In some situations children unite on the basis of age, which then becomes more salient than gender. One day a much disliked teacher who was on yard duty punished a fourth-grader for something he didn't do. He was very upset, and others from his classroom who were playing in the vicinity and witnessed or heard about the incident perceived a great injustice. Girls and boys talked about the situation in mixed clusters and joined as a group to argue with the adult.

Adults (including sociological observers) who work in schools are accorded privileges denied to children. They are not confined to specific lines, seats, and tables; they can move more freely through space; and they have institutionalized authority. Teachers and aides sometimes use their authority to construct and enhance gender divisions among children, as in the cases of the teacher who organized girls and boys into separate teams for classroom contests and the noontime aide who ordered boys and girls to sit at different tables. But adult practices also undermine gender separation between children in schools. In the United States there is a long tradition of mixed-gender public elementary schools, with girls and boys sharing a curriculum and with an ideology of treating everyone the same and of attending to individual needs. Some structural pressures run against separating girls and boys in daily school life, especially in classrooms.[37] Adult practices work in both directions, sometimes separating and sometimes integrating boys and girls. Overall, however, school-based observers have found that less gender separation takes place among children when adults control a situation than when children have more autonomy.[38]

When children have constructed sharp gender boundaries, few of them attempt to cross. But adults claim the privilege of freelancing. In the schools I studied, when boys and girls sat at separate tables in school cafeterias, teachers and aides of both genders sat at either table, and the pres-

ence of an adult sometimes created a wedge for more general mixed seating. When the fourth-and-fifth-graders drew names for a winter holiday gift exchange, they decided (in a discussion punctuated by ritual gender antagonism) that girls would give to girls and boys to boys. The teacher decided that she would draw with the boys and suggested that the aide and I (both women) draw with the girls. Our adult status altered the organization of gender.

A mix of age, gender, and ethnicity contributed to the marginalization of two Latino boys in the fourth-and-fifth-grade classroom. The boys were recent immigrants from Mexico and spoke very little English. They sat in a back corner of the classroom and sometimes worked at a side table with a Spanish-speaking aide. The other children treated them as if they were younger, with several girls who sat near them repeatedly monitoring the boys' activities and telling them what to do. When the children were divided by gender, other boys repeatedly maneuvered the Latino boys and another low-status boy into sitting next to girls. These spatial arrangements drew upon a gender meaning—an assumption that being by girls is contaminating—to construct ethnic subordination and marginality.

Gender display may symbolically represent and amplify social class divisions. The students in the two schools I studied were largely working class, but within that loose categorization children's different economic circumstances affected how they looked, especially the girls. It was easier to spot girls from impoverished families than boys because the girls' more varied clothing was less adaptable (as in the case of a mismatched top and bottom) than the T-shirts and jeans the boys wore. Girls' hairstyles were also more varied and complex, providing material for differentiated display of style and grooming, and grooming standards were more exacting for girls than for boys. A fifth-grade girl whose unkempt hair and mismatched old clothing marked her impoverished background was treated like a pariah, while the most popular girl had many well-matched outfits and a well-groomed appearance. The top and bottom rungs of girls' popularity (positions partly shaped by social class) were defined by heterosexual meanings when children teased about a particular boy "liking" or "goin' with" a specific girl. The teasers most frequently named either the most popular girl or the pariah as targets of a boy's liking—the most and least probable and polluting targets of desire.

Attention to the dynamics of social contexts helps situate gender in relationship to other lines of difference and inequality. The meanings of gender are not unitary but multiple, and sometimes contradictory.

Multiple Standpoints

Exploring varied standpoints on a given set of gender relations is another strategy for deconstructing a too coherent, dichotomous portrayal of girls' groups versus boys' groups and for developing a more complex understanding of gender relations. Children who are popular or marginal, those defined as troublemakers or good students, and those who are more or less likely to cross gender boundaries have different experiences of the same situations. Their varied experiences—intricately constructed by and helping to construct gender, social class, ethnicity, age, and individual characteristics—provide multiple vantage points on the complexity of children's social worlds.

An array of social types, including the bully, the troublemaker, the sissy, the tomboy, and the isolate populates both fictional and social science literature on children in schools. If we shift from types to processes, we can get a better hold on the experiences these terms convey. For example, the terms tomboy and sissy take complicated social processes—changing gender boundaries and a continuum of crossing—and reify them into individual essences or conditions (for example, "tomboyism"). Crossing involves definition, activity, and the extent to which a child has a regular place in the other gender's social networks. Boys who frequently seek access to predominantly female groups and activities ("sissies") are more often ha-

rassed and teased by both boys and girls. But girls who frequently play with boys ("tomboys") are much less often stigmatized, and they continue to maintain ties with girls, a probable reason that, especially in the later years of elementary school, crossing by girls is far more frequent than crossing by boys.[39]

When girls are accepted in boys' groups and activities without changing the terms of the interactions (one girl called it being a "buddy"), gender becomes low. Heterosexual idioms, which mark and dramatize gender difference, pose a threat to such acceptance; one can't be a "buddy" and "goin' with" at the same time. The fifth-grade girl who was "buddies" with a group of boys navigated the field of gender relations and meanings very differently than did girls who frequently initiated heterosexual chasing rituals. Unitary notions like the girls' world and girls versus boys are inadequate for this sort of analysis. Instead, one must grapple with multiple standpoints, complex and even contradictory meanings, and the varying salience of gender.

ETHNOGRAPHIES OF SCHOOLING

In developing a contextual and deconstructive approach to understanding gender and children's worlds, I have been influenced by the work of other ethnographers, whose methods bring sensitivity to social contexts and to the construction of meanings. Ethnographers of education who work within "social reproduction theory" (asking how schools reproduce inequalities, mostly of social class and gender) have emphasized students' varying subcultures, some more conforming and some created in opposition to the official structure of schools. In an ethnographic study of working class "lads" in a vocational school in England, Willis gave attention to gender as well as to social class (the primary focus of this tradition anchored in Marxist theories).[40] Resisting the middle-class authority of the school, the lads created an oppositional culture of aggression and joking tied to the working class "masculine" subculture of factory workers. The lads' subculture, different from that of more conforming boys, helped reproduce their class position.

Recent research within this tradition has finally moved girls from the periphery more toward the center of attention. In a study of fifth-graders in U.S. schools, Anyon analyzed strategies related to social class that girls used both to resist and to accommodate institutionalized attempts to enforce femininity.[41] For example, some girls used exaggerated feminine behavior to resist work assignments; those who were "discipline problems" rebelled both against the school and against expectations of them as girls.

Connell and his colleagues, who have studied girls and boys of different social classes in high schools in Australia, use the plural notions *masculinities* and *femininities* to articulate an array of subcultures and individual styles or types of identity.[42] (I find it problematic that they mix, rather than carefully distinguishing, individual and group levels of analysis.) They conceptualize gender and class as "structuring processes" and argue that each school has a "gender regime," constructing, ordering, and arbitrating between different kinds of masculinity and femininity. "The gender regime is in a state of play rather than a permanent condition."[43]

These studies are important in part because they break with the pervasive determinism of conventional "sex-role socialization" literature on gender and schools. Instead of simply "being socialized" (the imagery of children in much feminist literature), girls and boys are granted agency in constructing culture and resisting it as well as in adapting to dominant ideologies. By positing a complex and plural approach to gender, these ethnographies also challenge simplistic dualisms like "the male role versus the female role" or "girls' groups versus boys' groups."

But for all their value, these conceptualizations leave unresolved some of the issues I raised earlier. They analyze gender primarily by emphasizing separation between boys and girls and comparing the dynamics and subcultures of same-gender groups. While the groups and subcultures are multiple, a sense of deep division (separate worlds) between girls and boys persists. How far such divisions may vary by situation or subculture is not made clear. Dualistic assumptions poke through the multiplicity.

A second problem with Connell's work is that while the plural masculinities and femininities seem useful, the patterns these ethnographers describe sometimes seem more classificatory (an ever-finer grid for fixing gender) than anchored in a close analysis of social processes. By what criteria should a given pattern of interaction be seen as constructing a femininity or a masculinity, that is, as being relevant to the organization and meanings of gender? Some "social reproduction" ethnographers like Everhart largely ignore gender in their analyses of students' everyday interactions.[44] Others, for example, Anyon and Connell and his colleagues, refer the entire field of interaction to notions of gender.[45] This variation points to a more general question. Is gender always relevant? Do some parts of social life transcend it? If our challenge is to trace the threading of gender (and gender inequalities) through the complexity of social life, how can we determine when and how to invoke gendered interpretations?

These difficult questions suggest the need for finer conceptual tuning. In every situation we display and attribute core sex categories: gender does have ubiquitous relevance. But there is wide variation in the organization and symbolism of gender. Looking at social context shifts analysis from fixing abstract and binary differences to examining the social relations and contexts in which multiple differences are constructed, undermined, and given meaning.

This contextual approach to gender—questioning the assumption that girls and boys (and men and women) have different "essential natures" best understood in terms of opposition—clearly resonates with deconstructive, postmodernist tendencies in feminist thought.[46] I reached a deconstructive approach not by way of French theorists, however, but through the contextual and interpretive methods of ethnography.

Feminists have been more deconstructive and aware of multiplicities in thinking about adults than in thinking about children. We refer children's experiences to development and socialization, while granting adults a much broader scene of action. One way around that conceptual double standard is extending to children the frameworks (in this case, a fluid and contextual approach to gender) also used in analyzing the world of adults.

In following that path, however, I have slid across a project that awaits close attention: grappling with differences of age, which, like gender, involve complex interactions of biology and culture. We should turn our critical attention to the dualism adult/child as well as to gender dualisms.

NOTES

1. See Barrie Thorne, "Re-Visioning Women and Social Change: Where Are the Children?" *Gender & Society* 1 (1987): 85–109. The invisibility of children in feminist and sociological thought can be documented by reviewing scholarly journals. Ambert analyzed issues of eight widely-read sociology journals published between 1972 and 1983. At the top of the journals in the proportion of space devoted to children, *Journal of Marriage and Family* had only 3.6 percent and *Sociology of Education* only 6.6 percent of articles on children. The index for the first ten years of the feminist journal *SIGNS* has one entry under "child development," one under "child care," and four under "childbirth." See Anne-Marie Ambert, "Sociology of Sociology: The Place of Children in North American Sociology," in Peter Adler and Patricia A. Adler, eds., *Sociological Studies of Child Development* (Greenwich, Conn.: JAI, 1986) 1:11–31.

2. See M. Z. Rosaldo, "The Use and Abuse of Anthropology: Reflection on Feminism and Cross-Cultural Understanding," *SIGNS* 5 (1980): 389–417.

3. For reviews of some of the research on sex differences see Eleanor Maccoby and Carol Jacklin, *The Psychology of Sex Differences* (Stanford: Stanford University Press, 1974), and Jere E. Brophy and Thomas L. Good, *Teacher-Student Relations* (New York: Holt, Reinhart, 1974).

4. For example, see Carol Jacklin, "Methodological Issues in the Study of Sex-Related Differences," *Developmental Review* 1 (1981): 266–73; Maccoby and Jacklin, *Psychology of Sex Differences;* and Maureen C. McHugh, Randi Daimon Keoske, and Irene Hanson Frieze, "Issues to Consider in Conducting Nonsexist Psychological Research," *American Psychologist* 41 (1986): 879–90.

5. Here is the inevitable footnote on terminology, one more example of the definitional fiddling so prevalent in the social science literature on sex and gender. This perpetual fiddling reflects our ongoing efforts to locate subject matter, to construct appropriate levels of analysis, and to grapple with difficult problems such as how to weigh and simultaneously grasp the biological and the cultural. I am currently persuaded that: (1) we should conceptually distinguish biological sex, cultural gender, and sexuality (desire), but (2) we should not assume that they are easily separable. One of our central tasks is to clarify their complex, often ambiguous relationships—kept alive in the term "sex/gender system" (a term first put forward in Gayle Rubin, "The Traffic in Women: Notes on the 'Political Economy' of Sex," in Rayna R. Reiter, ed., *Toward an Anthropology of Women* [New York: Monthly Review Press, 1975], 157–210). We should muse about why, after all our careful distinctions, we so easily slip into interchangeable use of *sex, gender,* and *sexual.*

The phrase *sex category* refers to the core, dichotomous categories of individual sex and gender (female/male; girl/boy; woman/man)—dualisms riddled with complexities of biology/culture and age/gender. While these categories appear to be rockbottom and founded in biology—hence "sex" category—they are deeply constructed by cultural beliefs and by social practices of gender display and attribution. *Gender* still seems serviceable as an all-purpose term linked with other words for finer conceptual tuning, e.g., "gender identity," "gender ideology," "the social organization of gender." In my discussion of "sex difference" research I use "sex" rather than "gender" because that has been the (perhaps telling) verbal practice of that tradition.

6. See Suzanne J. Kessler and Wendy McKenna, *Gender: An Ethnomethodological Approach* (New York: John Wiley, 1978); Erving Goffman, "The Arrangement between the Sexes," *Theory and Society* 4 (1977): 301–36; Spencer E. Cahill, "Language Practices and Self-Definition: The Case of Gender Identity Acquisition,"

Sociological Quarterly 287 (1987): 295–311; and Candace West and Don H. Zimmerman, "Doing Gender," *Gender & Society* 1 (1987): 125–51.

7. See reviews in Marlaine E. Lockheed, "Sex Equity in Classroom Organization and Climate," in Susan B. Klein, ed., *Handbook for Achieving Sex Equity through Education* (Baltimore: Johns Hopkins University Press, 1985), 189–217; and Eleanor Maccoby, "Social Groupings in Childhood: Their Relationship to Prosocial and Antisocial Behavior in Boys and Girls," in Dan Olweus, Jack Block, and Marian Radke-Yarrow, eds., *Development of Antisocial and Prosocial Behavior* (San Diego: Academic, 1985), 263–84.

8. Janet Schofield, *Black and White in School* (New York: Praeger, 1982).

9. See reviews in Daniel N. Maltz and Ruth A. Borker, "A Cultural Approach to Male-Female Miscommunication," in John J. Gumperz, ed., *Language and Social Identity* (New York: Cambridge University Press, 1983), 195–216; Barrie Thorne, "Girls and Boys Together...But Mostly Apart: Gender Arrangements in Elementary Schools," in Willard W. Hartup and Zick Rubin, eds., *Relationships and Development* (Hillsdale, N.J.: Lawrence Erlbaum, 1986), 167–84; and Maccoby, "Social Groupings."

10. Janet Lever, "Sex Differences in the Games Children Play," *Social Problems* 23 (1976): 478–87.

11. The invisibility and marginalization of girls in the extensive British literature on "youth subcultures" was first noted in Angela McRobbie and Jenny Garber, "Girls and Subcultures," in S. Hall and T. Jefferson, eds., *Resistance through Rituals* (London: Hutchinson, 1976).

12. Lever, "Sex Differences"; Carol Gilligan, *In a Different Voice* (Cambridge: Harvard University Press, 1982): 9–11.

13. Zella Luria and Eleanor Herzog, "Gender Segregation across and within Settings" (unpublished paper presented at 1985 annual meeting of the Society for Research in Child Development, Toronto).

14. Most observational research on the gender relations of preadolescent children in the United States has been done in schools. Goodwin's research on children in an urban neighborhood is a notable exception. See Marjorie Harness Goodwin, *Conversational Practices in a Peer Group of Urban Black Children* (Bloomington: Indiana University Press, in press).

15. Two decades ago there was a reverse pattern in research on adult interaction, at least in the literature on sociolinguistics and small groups. "Gender" was assumed to "happen" when men and women were together, not when they were separated. It took feminist effort to bring same-gender relations, especially among women (a virtually invisible topic in traditional research on communication), into that subject matter (see Barrie Thorne, Cheris Kramarae, and Nancy Henley, eds., *Language, Gender and Society* [Rowley, Mass.: Newbury House, 1983]). These inverse ways of locating gender—defined by the genders separating for children and by their being together for adults—may reflect age-based assumptions. In our culture, adult gender is defined by heterosexuality, but children are (ambivalently) defined as asexual. We load the interaction of adult men and women with heterosexual meaning, but we resist defining children's mixed-gender interaction in those terms. Traditional constructions of children and gender exemplify and ideal of latency.

16. See Barrie Thorne, "An Analysis of Gender and Social Groupings," in Laurel Richardson and Verta Taylor, eds., *Feminist Frontiers* (Reading, Mass.: Addison-Wesley, 1983), 61–63; and idem, "Girls and Boys Together," 170–71.

17. Sherry B. Ortner, "The Founding of the First Sherpa Nunnery, and the Problem of 'Women' as an Analytic Category," in Vivian Patraka and Louise Tilly, eds., *Feminist Re-Visions* (Ann Arbor: University of Michigan Women's Studies Program, 1984).

18. Carole Joffe, "As the Twig Is Bent," in Judith Stacey, Susan Bereaud, and Joan Daniels, eds., *And Jill Came Tumbling After* (New York: Dell, 1974), 79–90; Raphaela Best, *We've All Got Scars* (Bloomington: Indiana University Press, 1983); Robert B. Everhart, *Reading, Writing and Resistance* (Boston: Routledge & Kegan Paul, 1983); Philip A. Cusick, *Inside High School* (New York: Holt, Reinhart and Winston, 1973).

19. Cusick, *Inside High School,* 168.

20. I was a participant-observer in two different elementary schools—for eight months in a largely working class school in California (there were about 500 students, 5 percent Black, 20 percent Hispanic, and 75 percent white), and for three months in a school of similar size, class, and racial/ethnic composition in Michigan. Most of the examples in this paper come from the California school, where I focused primarily on fourth- and fifth-graders. For further reports from this work, see my "Gender and Social Groupings"; "Girls and Boys Together"; and "Crossing the Gender Divide: What 'Tomboys' Can Teach Us about Processes of Gender Separation among Children" (unpublished pa-

per presented at 1985 meeting of the Society for Research on Child Development, Toronto). See also Barrie Thorne and Zella Luria, "Sexuality and Gender in Children's Daily World," *Social Problems* 33 (1986): 176–90.

21. See Thorne and Luria, "Sexuality and Gender," 182–84.

22. Linda A. Hughes, "Beyond the Rules of the Game: Girls' Gaming at a Friends' School (unpublished Ph.D. diss., University of Pennsylvania Graduate School of Education, 1983); Goodwin, *Conversational Practices.*

23. Marjorie Harness Goodwin and Charles Goodwin, "Children's Arguing," in Susan Philips, Susan Steele, and Christina Tanz, eds., *Language, Gender, and Sex in Comparative Perspective* (Cambridge: Cambridge University Press, 1988).

24. Goodwin, *Conversational Practices.*

25. R. W. Connell, "Theorising Gender," *Sociology* 12 (1985): 260–72. Also see R. W. Connell, *Gender and Power* (Stanford: Stanford University Press, 1987).

26. See Judith Stacey and Barrie Thorne, "The Missing Feminist Revolution in Sociology," *Social Problems* 32 (1985): 301–16.

27. This problem is analyzed in Connell, "Theorising Gender" and *Gender and Power;* Hester Eisenstein, *Contemporary Feminist Thought* (Boston: G. K. Hall, 1984); Jane Flax, "Postmodernism and Gender Relations in Feminist Theory," *SIGNS* 12 (1987): 621–43; Bell Hooks, *Feminist Theory: From Margin to Center* (Boston: South End, 1984); and Sylvia J. Yanagisako and Jane F. Collier, eds., *Gender and Kinship: Essays toward a Unified Analysis* (Stanford: Stanford University Press, 1987).

28. West and Zimmerman, "Doing Gender."

29. Sandra Wallman, "Epistemologies of Sex," in Lionel Tiger and Heather T. Fowler, eds., *Female Hierarchies* (Chicago: Aldine, 1978). Also see Nancy Chodorow, "Feminism and Difference: Gender, Relation, and Difference in Psychoanalytic Perspective," *Socialist Review* 46 (1979): 51–70; Rosaldo, "Use and Abuse of Anthropology"; and Yanagisako and Collier, "Feminism, Gender, and Kinship."

30. See Paul Willis, *Learning to Labor* (New York: Columbia University Press, 1977); and R. W. Connell, D. J. Ashenden, S. Kessler, and G. W. Dowsett, *Making the Difference: Schools, Families, and Social Division* (Boston: Allen & Unwin).

31. On the charged nature of socially constructed boundaries, see Mary Douglas, *Purity and Danger* (New York: Praeger, 1966).

32. Frederik Barth, *Ethnic Groups and Boundaries* (Boston: Little, Brown, 1969).

33. See Thorne, "Girls and Boys Together," 174–75.

34. In an ethnographic study of multiracial school in England, Fuller found that girls of varied social classes and ethnicities had somewhat different ways of responding to boys' efforts to control and devalue them. See Mary Fuller, "Black Girls in a London Comprehensive," in Rosemary Deem, eds., *Schooling for Women's Work* (London: Routledge & Kegan Paul, 19980), 52–65.

35. Goffman, "The Arrangement between the Sexes," 316. The phrase "sex (or gender) segregation among children" has been in widespread use, but as William Hartup suggested in comments at the 1985 meeting of the Society for Research in Child Development, the term *segregation* implies separation far more total and sanctioned than in most social relations among children in the United States.

36. R. W. Connell et al., *Making the Difference,* 182.

37. See David Tyack and Elisabeth Hansot, "Gender in American Public Schools: Thinking Institutionally," *SIGNS* 13 (1988): 741–60. British schools have institutionalized extensive gender separation, described in Sara Delamont, "The Conservative School? Sex Roles at Home, at Work and at School," in Stephen Walker and Len Barton, eds., *Gender, Glass and Education* (Sussex: Falmer, 1983): 93–105.

38. See Luria and Herzog, "Gender Segregation," and Thorne, "Girls and Boys Together."

39. For a fuller analysis, see Thorne, "Crossing the Gender Divide."

40. Willis, *Learning to Labor.*

41. Joan Anyon, "Intersections of Gender and Class: Accommodation and Resistance by Working-Class and Affluent Females to Contradictory Sex-Role Ideologies," in Walker and Len Barton, eds. *Gender, Class and Education,* 1–19.

42. Connell et al., *Making the Difference;* S. Kessler, D. J. Ashenden, R. W. Connell, and G. W. Dowsett, "Gender Relations in Secondary Schooling," *Sociology of Education* 58 (1985): 34–48.

43. Kessler et al., "Gender Relations," 42.

44. Everhart, *Reading, Writing and Resistance.*

45. Anyon, "Intersections of Gender and Class"; Connell et al., *Making the Difference.*

46. On feminist postmodernism, see Flax, "Postmodernism and Gender Relations"; Sandra Harding, *The Science Question in Feminism* (Ithaca: Cornell University Press, 1986); and Toril Moi, *Sexual/Textual Politics* (London: Methuen, 1985).

5

Different Voices, Different Visions
Gender, Culture, and Moral Reasoning

CAROL B. STACK

A great debate stirred my undergraduate college seminar, "Women and Justice." At midsemester, William Jones, an honors student from a rural, Southern, African-American community, stood up and addressed the class. "What," he questioned, "is gender all about?" With some reluctance, he continued. "If Carol Gilligan is right, my brothers and I were raised to be girls as much as boys, and the opposite goes for my sisters. We were raised in a large family with a morality of care as well as justice. We were raised to be responsible to kin, and to be able to face injustices at an early age. Sisters, brothers, it doesn't make a difference. Carol Gilligan should come visit my home town!"

I learn a great deal from teaching. The summer following that course I revisited families I had come to know in rural Carolina counties, bringing William's challenge to Gilligan's scholarship back home. Those observations and the debates that followed in class paralleled my own curiosity, and our collaborative hunch proved true. This chapter reports the results of my own study of the culture of gender, echoing William's question, "What is gender all about?"

Do women and men tend to see moral problems from different horizons? According to some researchers, two moral visions shape our ways of assessing these questions. Carol Gilligan argues in her book, *In a Different Voice,* that "care reasoning," which compels us to respond to those in need, and "justice reasoning," which dictates that we treat others fairly, represent separate moral orientations.[1] In her view, these are not opposites but different modes of apprehending human dilem-

mas. Gilligan's subsequent research suggests that these moral perspectives originate in the dynamics of early childhood relationships, solidify in adolescence, and are reproduced in the resolution of moral conflicts throughout the life course.[2]

Feminist scholars are indebted to Gilligan and her colleagues, who have brought the voice of care to moral reasoning and to our understanding of the social construction of gender. Nevertheless, as Gilligan's observations confirm, the cross-cultural construction of gender remains relatively unexplored. During the course of my study of African-American return migration to rural Southern homeplaces,[3] moral voices of both justice and care emerged from my interviews with adults and twelve- and thirteen-year-old boys and girls. However, their responses are strikingly different from the gender configurations in Gilligan's published findings.

In my research, I became interested in the vocabulary of gender and gendered discourse surrounding this return migration movement. Influenced by Gilligan's work on moral reasoning, and puzzled by the absence of reference to race and class, I chose to collect working-class adolescent and adult narratives on moral reasoning in addition to my own ethnographic research on return migration, which involved structured observation and the collection of narratives and life histories.[4] I asked these young people and adults about dilemmas similar to the difficult choices examined in Gilligan's studies. The people I interviewed were return migrants—men, women, and children who had moved back to rural Southern homeplaces. The experiences of those I interviewed differ from those of African-Americans who never left the South, and from long-term and recent dwellers in many cities in the United States. Indeed, this work does not generalize from a specific group to all African-Americans.

This study argues that moral reasoning is negotiated with respect to individual or group location within the social structure. Gender is one, but only one, of the social categories—including, among many, class, culture, racial and ethnic formation, and region—that shape the resources within which we construct morality. My goal is to contextualize gender differences in constructing moral lives within the setting of my current research on return migration, as a modest challenge to explanations that fail to situate gender differences.[5] In this chapter I report the responses of fifteen adults and eighty-seven adolescents, borrowing the orientations of "care" and "justice" in order to bring the issue of gendered strategies in moral reasoning into the race, culture, and socioeconomic context.[6]

Situating the construction of gender across race, culture, and historical conditions transforms our thinking about moral reasoning. The creation of gender roles within specific historical and socioeconomic situations is a creative process, one better viewed as mobile than static. Gender construction is negotiated among members of specific communities, for example, as they respond to situations of institutionalized oppression and/or racial stratification. As an anthropologist concerned with the construction of gender, it has been my hypothesis that gender relationships are improvised against local and global political, economic, and familial affiliations, which are always in transition. My perspective registers serious objections to frameworks built on polarities or fixed oppositions, especially notions that create an illusory sense of "universal" or "essential" gender differences.[7]

Historically, gender as an analytic category has unfolded from early depictions of sex differences and the range of sex roles, to an examination of how gender constructs politics and how politics, class, and race construct gender.[8] Anthropological studies of gender have moved from particular, to universal, and, in this chapter, to contextual. Feminist scholars emerge from this experience with a subtle category of analysis constructed from the concrete, deeply rooted in relationships of power, class, race, and historical circumstance.

Data from my earlier research in urban Black communities in the 1970s,[9] and from my studies of the return migration of African-Americans from the Northeast to the rural South,[10] suggest new notions about the nexus of gender, race, and class relations. Class, racial formation,[11] and economic systems within rural Southern communities create a context in which African-Americans— women and men, boys and girls—experience their relationship to production, employment, class, and material and economic rewards in strikingly similar ways, rather than the divergent ways predicted by theorists of moral reasoning. It is from the vantage point of over twenty years of research on the African-American family that I situate my contributions to Carol Gilligan's discourse on moral voices.[12] I focus on gender as a social relation and suggest that it is negotiated along changing axes of difference.[13]

Although philosophers have debated Gilligan's distinction between care and justice reasoning, as well as her methods of interpreting and coding narratives or moral reasoning, in this chapter I will not challenge such concerns. This present undertaking is narrower in scope. The research does not disentangle methodological issues surrounding Gilligan and her critics,[14] or enter debates on moral reasoning or moral stages of development. It does, however, question the validity of universal gender differences.

On separate occasions several adults and adolescents who had returned home to rural Southern communities worked with me on this research by constructing scenarios of difficult choices they face in their own lives. The dilemmas constructed by local community members approximate Gilligan and colleagues' most current procedures, in which they ask people to talk about a situation where they were unsure what the right thing to do was, and they had to make a choice.[15] I chose to elicit culturally relevant dilemmas rather than employing the classic "Heinz dilemma" (whether Heinz should steal drugs for his dying wife) used by Gilligan. In Gilligan's current, more open-ended approach, people respond to a dilemma of their own making. What is important in this style of research is not the specific nature of the dilemma but what people say about it.

An intriguing aspect of my study of Black return migration is the cyclical migration of children. They accompany parents or extended kin, or journey alone along well-worn paths between their families' home bases in the North and in the South. Many of the parents of these children had participated in cyclical migrations and dual residences. Today, dual patterns of residence are common for young Black children whose kinship ties extend across state lines and regions of the country.[16] Their homes are in both city and countryside; their schooling is divided between public schools in Harlem, Brooklyn, or Washington, D.C., and country schools in the South. Their cyclical patterns of residence are common knowledge to school administrators, teachers, and social workers in their communities. I have been interested in how children experience their own migration, especially in light of the vivid descriptions they have given me of the tough choices they are asked to make. Straddling family ties in the North and South, and loyalties and attachments across the generations, children face real-life dilemmas over where to reside and with whom, and over what defines their responsibility to others. Their dilemmas dramatize cultural aspects of migration.

Several twelve- and thirteen-year-olds helped me construct a dilemma from the real-life situations they had described to me. One child suggested that we put the dilemma in the form of a "Dear Abby" letter, since the "Dear Abby" column is popular reading in the local community. Eighty-seven children of the North-South return migration responded to the following dilemma:

Dear Abby:

I am 12 and my brother is 10. My mother wants us to go and stay with her in New York City, and my grandparents want us to stay here in New Jericho with them. What should we do?

Love, Sally

The way children resolved the "Dear Abby" dilemma and personalized their responses reflects children's experiences as participants in this migration trend. From what children "told" "Dear Abby," and from complementary life histories, we began to understand how these boys and girls perceived their lives and constructed their roles—gender, among others—as family members caught in the web of cultural, economic, and historical forces. Their responses were infused with both a sense of responsibility to those in need and an attempt to treat others fairly.

Jimmy wrote:

I think I should stay with the one that needs my help the most. My grandmother is unable to do for herself and I should stay with her and let my mother come to see me.

Sarah wrote:

I should talk to my parents and try to get them to to understand that my grandparents cannot get around like they used to. I want to make an agreement to let my brother go to New York and go to school, and I'll go to school down here. In the summer I will go and be with my parents and my brother can come down home.

Helen wrote:

I should stay with my grandparents because for one reason, there are many murderers up North, and my grandparents are old and need my help around the house.

A group of adults who had returned to Southern homeplaces, women and men between the ages of twenty-five and forty, designed the "Clyde Dilemma":

> Clyde is very torn over a decision he must make. His two sisters are putting pressure on him to leave Washington, D.C., and go back home to take care of his parents. His mother is bedridden and his father recently lost a leg from sugar. One of his sisters has a family and a good job up North, and the other just moved there recently to get married. Clyde's sisters see him as more able to pick up and go back home since he is unmarried and works part-time—although he keeps trying to get a better job. What should Clyde do?

People deeply personalized their responses as they spoke of experiences within their own extended families. James Hopkins recalled, "Three of us rotated to keep my father at home," and he went on to remind me that "you must love a human being, not a dollar." Molly Henderson, who moved back in 1979, said, "Family should take care of family. It's a cycle. Someone has to do it, and it is Clyde's turn." Sam Henderson, Molly's uncle, told me, "You must take care of those who took care of you. Clyde's next in line, it's his turn." And Sam Hampton said, "He has no alternative." Others repeated, "It's not so hard if everybody helps" or "Family is the most important sacrifice we can make."

FINDINGS

My findings pay particular attention to class differences as well as the formation of ethnic and racial consciousness. They contrast dramatically with Gilligan's observations that while girls and women turn equally to justice and care reasoning, boys and men far less often turn to care reasoning, especially as they grow older.[17] All of the responses to the dilemmas were coded and analyzed for fifteen adults and eighty-seven adolescents (forty-two girls, forty-five boys), according to the recoded guidelines of Gilligan and colleagues. Gilligan has a separate category termed

TABLE 1   Justice and Care Reasoning Among Adolescents, by Gender

	Boys (N = 45)	Girls (N = 42)
Justice only	42% (19)	43% (18)
Care only	31% (14)	31% (13)
Justice and Care	27% (12)	26% (11)

"both," which I will call "mixed" (as in a mixture that cannot be separated into constituents). In the final analysis, my results do not differ whether "mixed" is dropped or is counted as both justice and care. As shown in Table 1, the presence of justice as a reason (with or without care) is not different for boys versus girls. Likewise, the presence of care as a reason (with or without justice) is not different for boys versus girls (Pearson Chi-square test). Table 2 shows that the same conclusions are obtained for adult men versus women (Fisher exact test).

The patterns of percentages are virtually identical for boys and girls, with justice higher than care in each group. The percentage was also nearly the same for boys and girls who used both.

The adult women articulated both kinds of reasoning (care and justice) more than men did. There is no real difference between men and women in justice reasoning. Notice that only one (and that one a man) of fifteen of the adults used care reasoning alone.

The contextualization of moral reasoning in this study presents a configuration of gender dif-

TABLE 2   Justice and Care Reasoning Among Adults, by Gender

	Men (N = 7)	Women (N = 8)
Justice only	43% (3)	37.5% (3)
Care only	14% (1)	.0%
Justice and Care	43% (3)	62.5% (5)

ferences and similarities strikingly different from Gilligan's results. Among African-American families returning to the South, adolescents and adults are close to identical when their discourse is coded for care and justice reasoning. This suggests that situating gender difference in the context of class and race transforms our thinking about moral reasoning.

MORAL KNOWLEDGE, SOCIAL ACTION, AND GENDER

Two questions arise from these results. First, in contrast to Gilligan's findings, why the convergence between African-American male and female responses? How and why do these similarities exist? Second, what is the relationship between moral reasoning and the ways in which men and women carry out their lives and conduct social actions?

This research substantiates findings from my earlier studies of dependency relationships experienced by both African-American males and females. In many aspects of their relationship to work, to social institutions, and to political conditions, Black women and other women of color affirm the similar circumstances that encircle their lives and the lives of men. In *Talking Back,* an essay on feminist thinking, bell hooks argues the oversimplicity of viewing women as victims and men as dominators; women can be agents of domination, and men and women are both oppressed and dominated.[18] Such realities do not discount the role of sexism in public and private lives or the participation of oppressed men in the domination of others. However, data from my study of return migration suggest that the shared experience that informs the construction of self and the formation of identity among return migrants produces a convergence in the vocabulary of rights, morality, and the social good.

A collective social conscience manifests itself in several strategies across the life course. From an early age girls and boys become aware of the tyranny of racial and economic injustice. By the age of twelve or thirteen, children are aware of the workplace experiences of their parents, of sexual favors rural women must offer to keep their jobs in Southern mills and processing plants, of threats to the sanity and dignity of kin. Women and men who return to the South are imbued with a sense of both memory and history. Those who return home confront their past, and engage in a collective negotiation with social injustice. They carry back with them a mission or desire to fight for racial justice as they return to what they refer to as "my testing ground." They define themselves as "community" or as "race persons"—those who work for the good of the race.

These men and women also share a care orientation. Those who return to rural Southern communities find refuge across the generations in their Southern families. Both men and women are embedded in their extended families; they similarly experience tensions between their individual aspirations and the needs of kin. These tensions surface as a morality of responsibility; they are voiced loud and clear in the Clyde dilemma, and in life histories I collected during the course of my research.

Parallels in the experiences of men and women with reference to external forces that shape their lives, suggest that under these conditions there is a convergence between Black men and women of all ages in their construction of themselves in relationship to others. The way both men and women describe themselves indicates a sense of identity deeply connected to others—to borrow Wade Nobles's language, an "extended self." Individuals perceive their obligations within the context of a social order anchored in others rather than in an individualist focus on their personal welfare.[19] In more than 1,000 pages of self-narratives that I collected during the course of the study of return migration, people affirmed, with force and conviction, the strength of kinship ties to their rural Southern families. Over and over they emphasized, "Family is the most important sacrifice." Family ties entail intricate dependencies for Black men and women, especially for those on the edge of poverty.

Likewise, the interviews with children revealed a collective social conscience and a profound sensitivity among young people to the needs of their families. The children's voices tell a somber story of the circumstances and material conditions of their lives. Their expectations about where they will live in the coming year conform to the changing needs and demands of other family members, old and young, and family labor force participation.

The construction of gender, as Black and other feminist researchers of color have emphasized, is shaped by the experience of sex, race, class, and consciousness.[20] Future research on the construction of gender must contribute another dimension to the construction of feminist theory. It should provide a critical framework for analysis of gender consciousness, and a cautionary reminder to those theorists who argue that gender is universally shared and experienced.

My treatment of the results of coding data on care and justice reasoning among African-Americans returning to the South has startling results. Taken out of context, and compared with Gilligan's early findings, it would appear that, in contrast to the Harvard studies, gender configures fewer differences in ways of knowing among this specific group of African-Americans. But what is the relationship between ways of knowing and ways of acting?

My five-year study of African-American return migration to the rural South makes it clear that in any study we must examine multiple levels of analysis. Looking beyond the coding, the men and women who received similar scores on justice and care reasoning produced remarkably different gendered strategies for action. In their assumption of the work of kinship, the roles of wage earners and caretakers, and in their political actions, men and women in these rural Southern communities differed.

Particularly striking are gendered strategies of political action. In their battle to subvert an op-pressive social order, the men who return as adults to their Southern homeplaces work principally within the local Black power structure, avoiding confrontation with the near-at-hand White power structure. When they challenge existing mores, they confront the Black male hierarchy within local landowning associations or the church. The social order women discover upon their return is a male symbolic order both within the local Black community and in relation to the local white community. Women find themselves struggling between contradictory forces of the old South and their own political missions. They face a race and gender system in which they are drawn into dependencies emerging from male structures in the local Black community. But these women, unlike the men who return, take action to circumvent this race/gender hierarchy as well as the local patronage systems. They create public programs, such as Title XX Day Care and Head Start, by creating an extensive statewide network of support in the public and private sectors. These women build community bases by carrying out their struggle in a public domain outside the jurisdiction of the local public power structure. Male preachers, politicians, and power brokers also reproduce dependency relationships between Blacks and Whites. While men participate in public spheres within their local Black communities, women bypass local black and white male structures, moving within a wider, regionally defined public domain.

There is a disjunction across race, culture, class, and gender between the study of moral voices—what people say—and observations of how people conduct themselves—what they do—as they are situated in familiar places and public spaces. We must always study, side by side, both discourse and course of action. This brings us face to face with the difference between interpretative studies of moral voices and ethnographies of gender that situate moral reasoning in everyday activity. Cross-disciplinary differences in feminist methodologies reinforce the importance within feminist scholarship of "talking back" to one another.

NOTES

1. Carol Gilligan, *In a Different Voice: Psychological Theory and Women's Development,* (Cambridge, Mass.: Harvard University Press, 1982).
2. Carol Gilligan and Grant Wiggins, "The Origins of Morality in Early Childhood Relationships," in *The Emergence of Morality,* ed. Jerome Kagan and Sharon Lamb (Chicago: University of Chicago Press, 1987).
3. Carol B. Stack, *The Proving Ground: African-Americans Reclaim the Rural South,* (New York: Pantheon, in press).
4. Between 1975 and 1980, 326,000 black individuals returned to a ten-state region of the South.
5. I am grateful to Nancy Chodorow for her view that this chapter addresses gender differentiation and gender strategies rather than gender construction.
6. Carol B. Stack, "The Culture of Gender Among Women of Color," *Signs* 12, no. 1 (Winter 1985): 321–324.
7. Laura Nader, 1989. "Orientalism, Occidentalism, and the Control of Women," *Cultural Dynamics* 2, no. 3 (1989): 323.
8. Joan W. Scott, "Gender: A Useful Category of Historical Analysis," *American Historical Review* 91, no. 5 (December 1986): 1053–1075.
9. Carol B. Stack, *All Our Kin: Strategies for Survival in a Black Community* (New York: Harper & Row, 1974).
10. Stack, *The Proving Ground.*
11. Michael Omi and Howard Winant, *Racial Formation in the United States* (New York: Routledge and Kegan Paul, 1986).
12. Gilligan, *In a Different Voice.*
13. Teresa de Lauretis, "Eccentric Subjects: Feminist Theory and Historical Consciousness," unpublished MS, University of California at Santa Cruz.
14. Linda K. Kerber, Catherine G. Greeno, Eleanor E. Maccoby, Zella Luria, Carol B. Stack, and Carol Gilligan, "In a Different Voice: An Interdisciplinary Forum," *Signs* 12, no. 1 (Winter 1985): 304–333.
15. Jane Atanuchi, private communication.
16. Carol B. Stack and John Cromartie, "The Journeys of Children," unpublished MS.
17. Carol Gilligan, "Women's Place in Man's Life Cycle," *Harvard Educational Review* 49, no. 4 (1979): 413–446; and *In a Different Voice.*
18. bell hooks (Gloria Watkins), *Talking Back: Thinking Feminist, Thinking Back* (Boston: South End Press, 1989), esp. p. 20.
19. Vernon Dixon, "World Views and Research Methodology," in L. M. King, Vernon Dixon, and W. W. Nobles, eds., *African Philosophy: Assumptions and Paradigms for Research on Black Persons* (Los Angeles: Fanon Center, 1976).
20. Bonnie Thornton Dill, "The Dialectics of Black Womanhood," in *Feminism and Methodology,* ed. Sandra Harding (Bloomington: Indiana University Press, 1987).

6

Gender Displays and Men's Power

The "New Man" and the Mexican Immigrant Man

PIERRETTE HONDAGNEU-SOTELO
MICHAEL A. MESSNER

In our discussions about masculinity with our students (many of whom are white and upper-middle class), talk invariably turns to critical descriptions of the "macho" behavior of "traditional men." Consistently, these men are portrayed as "out there," not in the classroom with us. Although it usually remains an unspoken subtext, at times a student will actually speak it: Those men who are still stuck in "traditional, sexist, and macho" styles of masculinity are Black men, Latino men, immigrant men, and working-class men. They are not us; we are the New Men, the Modern, Educated, and Enlightened Men. The belief that poor, working-class, and ethnic minority men are stuck in an atavistic, sexist "traditional male role," while White, educated middle-class men are forging a more sensitive egalitarian "New," or "Modern male role," is not uncommon. Social scientific theory and research on men and masculinity, as well as the "men's movement," too often collude with this belief by defining masculinity almost entirely in terms of gender display (i.e., styles of talk, dress, and bodily comportment), while ignoring men's structural positions of power and privilege over women and the subordination of certain groups of men to other men (Brod, 1983–1984).

In this chapter, we will contrast the gender display and structural positions of power (in both public and domestic spheres of life) of two groups of men: class-privileged White men and Mexican immigrant men. Our task is to explore and explicate some links between contemporary men's gender displays and men's various positions in a social structure of power.

THE "NEW MAN" AS IDEOLOGICAL CLASS ICON

Today there is a shared cultural image of what the New Man looks like: He is a White, college-educated professional who is a highly involved and nurturant father, "in touch with" and expressive of his feelings, and egalitarian in his dealings with women. We will briefly examine two fragments of the emergent cultural image of the contemporary New Man: the participant in the mythopoetic men's movement and the New Father.[1] We will discuss these contemporary images of men both in terms of their larger cultural meanings and in terms of the extent to which they represent any real shift in the ways men live their lives vis-à-vis women and other men. Most important, we will ask if apparent shifts in the gender displays of some White, middle-class men represent any real transformations in their structural positions of power and privilege.

ZEUS POWER AND THE MYTHOPOETIC MEN'S MOVEMENT

A recently emergent fragment of the cultural image of the New Man is the man who attends the weekend "gatherings of men" that are at the heart of Robert Bly's mythopoetic men's movement. Bly's curious interpretations of mythology and his highly selective use of history, psychology, and anthropology have been soundly criticized as "bad social science" (e.g., Connell, 1992a; Kimmel, 1992; Pelka, 1991). But perhaps more important than a critique of Bly's ideas is a sociological interpretation of why the mythopoetic men's movement has been so attractive to so many predominantly White, college-educated, middle-class, middle-aged men in the United States over the past decade. (Thousands of men have attended Bly's gatherings, and his book was a national best-seller.) We speculate that Bly's movement attracts these men *not* because it represents any sort of radical break from "traditional masculinity" but precisely because it is so congruent with shifts that are already taking place within current constructions of hegemonic masculinity. Many of the men who attend Bly's gatherings are already aware of some of the problems and limits of narrow conceptions of masculinity. A major preoccupation of the gatherings is the poverty of these men's relationships with their fathers and with other men in workplaces. These concerns are based on very real and often very painful experiences. Indeed, industrial capitalism undermined much of the structural basis of middle-class men's emotional bonds with each other as wage labor, market competition, and instrumental rationality largely supplanted primogeniture, craft brotherhood, and intergenerational mentorhood (Clawson, 1989; Tolson, 1977). Bly's "male initiation" rituals are intended to heal and reconstruct these masculine bonds, and they are thus, at least on the surface, probably experienced as largely irrelevant to men's relationships with women.

But in focusing on how myth and ritual can reconnect men with each other and ultimately with their own "deep masculine" essences, Bly manages to sidestep the central point of the feminist critique—that men, as a group, benefit from a structure of power that oppresses women as a group. In ignoring the social structure of power,

Bly manages to convey a false symmetry between the feminist women's movement and his men's movement. He assumes a natural dichotomization of "male values" and "female values" and states that feminism has been good for women in allowing them to reassert "the feminine voice" that had been suppressed. But Bly states (and he carefully avoids directly blaming feminism for this), "the masculine voice" has now been muted—men have become "passive...tamed...domesticated." Men thus need a movement to reconnect with the "Zeus energy" that they have lost. "Zeus energy is male authority accepted for the good of the community" (Bly, 1990, p. 61).

The notion that men need to be empowered *as men* echoes the naïveté of some 1970s men's liberation activists who saw men and women as "equally oppressed" by sexism (e.g., Farrell, 1975). The view that everyone is oppressed by sexism strips the concept of oppression of its political meaning and thus obscures the social relations of domination and subordination. Oppression is a concept that describes a relationship between social groups; for one group to be oppressed, there must be an oppressor group (Freire, 1970). This is not to imply that an oppressive relationship between groups is absolute or static. To the contrary, oppression is characterized by a constant and complex state of play: Oppressed groups both actively participate in their own domination and actively resist that domination. The state of play of the contemporary gender order is characterized by men's individual and collective oppression of women (Connell, 1987). Men continue to benefit from this oppression of women, but, significantly, in the past 25 years, women's compliance with masculine hegemony has been counterbalanced by active feminist resistance.

Men do tend to pay a price for their power: They are often emotionally limited and commonly suffer poor health and a life expectancy lower than that of women. But these problems are best viewed not as "gender oppression," but rather as the "costs of being on top" (Kann, 1986). In fact, the shifts in masculine styles that we see among some relatively privileged men may be interpreted as a sign that these men would like to stop paying these costs, but it does not necessarily signal a desire to cease being "on top." For example, it has become commonplace to see powerful and successful men weeping in public—Ronald Reagan shedding a tear at the funeral of slain U.S. soldiers, basketball player Michael Jordan openly crying after winning the NBA championship. Most recent, the easy manner in which the media lauded U.S. General Schwartzkopf as a New Man for shedding a public tear for the U.S. casualties in the Gulf War is indicative of the importance placed on *styles of masculine gender display* rather than the institutional *position of power* that men such as Schwartzkopf still enjoy.

This emphasis on the significance of public displays of crying indicates, in part, a naive belief that if boys and men can learn to "express their feelings," they will no longer feel a need to dominate others. In fact, there is no necessary link between men's "emotional inexpressivity" and their tendency to dominate others (Sattel, 1976). The idea that men's "need" to dominate others is the result of an emotional deficit overly psychologizes a reality that is largely structural. It does seem that the specific type of masculinity that was ascendent (hegemonic) during the rise of entrepreneurial capitalism was extremely instrumental, stoic, and emotionally inexpressive (Winter & Robert, 1980). But there is growing evidence (e.g., Schwartzkopf) that today there is no longer a neat link between class-privileged men's emotional inexpressively and their willingness and ability to dominate others (Connell, 1991b). We speculate that a situationally appropriate public display of sensitivity such as crying, rather than signaling weakness, has instead become a legitimizing sign of the New Man's power.[2]

Thus relatively privileged men may be attracted to the mythopoetic men's movement because, on the one hand, it acknowledges and validates their painful "wounds," while guiding them to connect with other men in ways that are both nurturing and mutually empowering.[3] On the other hand, and unlike feminism, it does not confront men with the reality of how their own privileges are based on the continued subordination of women and other men. In short, the mythopoetic men's movement may be seen as facilitating the reconstruction of a new form of hegemonic masculinity—a masculinity that is less self-destructive, that has revalued and reconstructed men's emotional bonds with each other, and that has learned to feel good about its own Zeus power.

THE NEW FATHER

In recent years Western culture has been bombarded with another fragment of the popular image of the New Man: the involved, nurturant father. Research has indicated that many young heterosexual men do appear to be more inclined than were their fathers to "help out" with housework and child care, but most of them still see these tasks as belonging to their wives or their future wives (Machung, 1989; Sidel, 1990). Despite the cultural image of the "new fatherhood" and some modest increases in participation by men, the vast majority of child care, especially of infants, is still performed by women (Hochschild, 1989; La Rossa, 1988; Lewis, 1986; Russell, 1983).

Why does men's stated desire to participate in parenting so rarely translate into substantially increased involvement? Lynn Segal (1990) argues that the fact that men's apparent attitudinal changes have not translated into widespread behavioral changes may be largely due to the fact men that may (correctly) fear that increased parental involvement will translate into a loss of their power over women. But she also argues that increased paternal involvement in child care will not become a widespread reality unless and until the structural preconditions—especially economic equality for women—exist. Indeed, Rosanna Hertz (1986) found in her study of upper-middle class "dual career families" that a more egalitarian division of family labor sometimes developed as a rational (and constantly negotiated) response to a need to maintain his career, her career, and the family. In other words, career and pay equality for women was a structural precondition for the development of equality between husbands and wives in the family.

However, Hertz notes two reasons why this is a very limited and flawed equality. First, Hertz's sample of dual-career families in which the women and the men made roughly the same amount of money is still extremely atypical. In two-income families, the husband is far more likely to have the higher income. Women are far more likely than men to work part-time jobs, and among full-time workers, women still earn about 65 cents to the male dollar and are commonly segregated in lower paid, lower status, dead-end jobs (Blum, 1991; Reskin & Roos, 1990). As a result, most women are not in the structural position to be able to bargain with their husbands for more egalitarian divisions of labor in the home. As Hochschild's (1989) research demonstrates, middle-class women's struggles for equity in the home are often met by their husbands' "quiet resistance," which sometimes lasts for years. Women are left with the choice of either leaving the relationship (and suffering not only the emotional upheaval, but also the downward mobility, often into poverty, that commonly follows divorce) or capitulating to the man and quietly working her "second shift" of family labor.

Second, Hertz observes that the roughly egalitarian family division of labor among some upper-middle class dual-career couples is severely shaken when a child is born into the family. Initially, new mothers are more likely than fathers to put their careers on hold. But eventually many resume their careers, as the child care and much of the home labor is performed by low-paid employees, almost always women, and often immigrant women and/or women of color. The construction of the dual-career couple's "gender equality" is thus premised on the family's privileged position within a larger structure of social inequality. In other words, some of the upper-middle class woman's gender oppression is, in effect, bought off with her class privilege, while the man is let

off the hook from his obligation to fully participate in child care and housework. The upper-middle class father is likely to be more involved with his children today than his father was with him, and this will likely enrich his life. But given the fact that the day-to-day and moment-to-moment care and nurturance of his children is still likely to be performed by women (either his wife and/or a hired, lower-class woman), "the contemporary revalorisation of fatherhood has enabled many men to have the best of both worlds" (Segal, 1990, p. 58). The cultural image of the New Father has given the middle-class father license to choose to enjoy the emotional fruits of parenting, but his position of class and gender privilege allow him the resources with which he can buy or negotiate his way out of the majority of second shift labor.

In sum, as a widespread empirical reality, the emotionally expressive, nurturant, egalitarian New Man does not actually exist; he is an ideological construct, made up of disparate popular images that are saturated with meanings that express the anxieties, fears, and interests of relatively privileged men. But this is not to say that some changes are not occurring among certain groups of privileged men (Segal, 1990). Some men are expressing certain feelings that were, in the past, considered outside the definition of hegemonic masculinity. Some men are reexamining and changing their relationships with other men. Some men are participating more—very equitably in some cases, but marginally in many others—in the care and nurturance of children. But the key point is that when examined within the context of these men's positions in the overall structure of power in society, these changes do not appear to challenge or undermine this power. To the contrary, the cultural image of the New Man and the partial and fragmentary empirical changes that this image represents serve to file off some of the rough edges of hegemonic masculinity in such a way that the possibility of a happier and healthier life for men is created, while deflecting or resisting feminist challenges to men's institutional power and privileges. But because at least verbal acceptance of the "New Woman" is an important aspect of this reconstructed hegemonic masculinity, the ideological image of the New Man requires a counterimage against which to stand in opposition. Those aspects of traditional hegemonic masculinity that the New Man has rejected—overt physical and verbal displays of domination, stoicism and emotional inexpressivity, overt misogyny in the workplace and at home—are now increasingly projected onto less privileged groups of men: working-class men, gay body-builders, Black athletes, Latinos, and immigrant men.

MEXICAN IMMIGRANT MEN

According to the dominant cultural stereotype, Latino men's "machismo" is supposedly characterized by extreme verbal and bodily expressions of aggression toward other men, frequent drunkenness, and sexual aggression and dominance expressed toward normally "submissive" Latinas. Manuel Peña's (1991) research on the workplace culture of male undocumented Mexican immigrant agricultural workers suggests that there is a great deal of truth to this stereotype. Peña examined the Mexican immigrant male's participation in *charritas coloradas* (red jokes) that characterize the basis of the workplace culture. The most common basis of humor in the *charritas* is sexualized "sadism toward women and symbolic threats of sodomy toward other males" (Paredes, 1966, p. 121).

On the surface, Peña argues, the constant "half-serious, half playful duels" among the men, as well as the images of sexually debased "perverted wenches" and "treacherous women" in the *charritas,* appear to support the stereotype of the Mexican immigrant male group as being characterized by a high level of aggressive masculine posturing and shared antagonisms and hatred directed toward women. But rather than signifying a fundamental hatred of women, Peña argues that these men's public displays of machismo should be viewed as a defensive reaction to their oppressed class status:

As an expression of working-class culture, the folklore of machismo can be considered a realized signifying system [that] points to, but simultaneously displaces, a class relationship and its attendant conflict. At the same time, it introduces a third element, the gender relationship, which acts as a mediator between the signifier (the folklore) and the signified (the class relationship). (Peña, 1991, p. 40)

Undocumented Mexican immigrant men are unable to directly confront their class oppressors, so instead, Peña argues, they symbolically displace their class antagonism into the arena of gender relations. Similar arguments have been made about other groups of men. For instance, David Collinson (1988) argues that Australian male blue-collar workers commonly engage in sexually aggressive and misogynist humor, as an (ultimately flawed) means of bonding together to resist the control of management males (who are viewed, disparagingly, as feminized). Majors and Billson (1992) argue that young black males tend to embody and publicly display a "cool pose," an expressive and often sexually aggressive style of masculinity that acts as a form of resistance to racism. These studies make important strides toward building an understanding of how subordinated and marginalized groups of men tend to embody and publicly display styles of masculinity that at least symbolically resist the various forms of oppression that they face within hierarchies of intermale dominance. These studies all share the insight that the public faces of subordinated groups of men are *personally and collectively constructed performances of masculine gender display.* By contrast, the public face of the New Man (his "sensitivity," etc.) is often assumed to be one-and-the-same with who he "is," rather than being seen as a situationally constructed public gender display.

Yet in foregrounding the oppression of men by men, these studies risk portraying aggressive, even misogynist, gender displays primarily as liberatory forms of resistance against class and racial oppression (e.g., Mirandé, 1982). Though these studies view microlevel gender display as constructed within a context of structured power relations, macrolevel gender relations are rarely viewed as a constituting dynamic within this structure. Rather gender is commonly viewed as ... an effect of the dominant class and/or race relations. What is obscured, or even drops out of sight, is the feminist observation that masculinity itself is a form of domination over women. As a result, women's actual experiences of oppression and victimization by men's violence are conspicuously absent from these analyses, thus leaving the impression that misogyny is merely a symbolic displacement of class (or race) antagonism. What is needed, then, is an examination of masculine gender display and power within the context of intersecting systems of class, race, and gender relations (Baca Zinn, Cannon, Higgenbotham, & Dill, 1986; Collins, 1990). In the following section we will consider recent ethnographic research on Mexican immigrant communities that suggests that gender dynamics help to constitute the immigration process and, in turn, are reconstituted during and following the immigrant settlement process.

THE RHETORIC OF RETURN MIGRATION AS GENDER DISPLAY

Mexican immigrant men who have lived in the United States for long periods of time frequently engage in the rhetoric of return migration. These stated preferences are not necessarily indicative of what they will do, but they provide some telling clues to these men's feelings and perceptions about their lives as marginalized men in the United States. Consider the following statements:[4]

I've passed more of my life here than in Mexico. I've been here for thirty-one years. I'm not putting down or rejecting this country, but my intentions have always been to return to Mexico ... I'd like to retire there, perhaps open a little business. Maybe I could buy and sell animals, or open a restaurant. Here I work for a big company, like a slave, always watching the clock. Well I'm bored with that.

I don't want to stay in the U.S. anymore. [Why not?] Because here I can no longer find a good job. Here, even if one is sick, you must report for work. They don't care. I'm fed up with it. I'm tired of working here too. Here one must work daily, and over there with my mother, I'll work for four, maybe five months, and then I'll have a four or five month break without working. My mother is old and I want to be with the family. I need to take care of the rancho. Here I have nothing, I don't have my own house, I even share the rent! What am I doing here?

I would like to return, but as my sons are born here, well that is what detains me here. Otherwise, I would go back to Mexico ... Mexico is now in a very inflationary situation. People come here not because they like it, but because the situation causes them to do so, and it makes them stay here for years and years. As the song says, this is a cage made of gold, but it is still a cage.

These statements point to disappointments with migration. In recent years, U.S.-bound migration has become institutionalized in many areas of Mexico, representing a rite of passage for many young, single men (Davis, 1990; Escobar, Gonzalez de la Rocha, & Roberts, 1987). But once in the United States the accomplishment of masculinity and maturity hinges on living up to the image of a financially successful migrant. If a man returns home penniless, he risks being seen as a failure or a fool. As one man explained: "One cannot go back without anything, because people will talk. They'll say 'oh look at this guy, he sacrificed and suffered to go north and he has nothing to show for it.'"

Although most of these men enjoyed a higher standard of living in the United States than in Mexico, working and settling in the United States significantly diminished their patriarchal privileges. Although the men compensated by verbally demonstrating their lack of commitment to staying in the United States, most of these men realized that their lives remained firmly anchored in the United States and that they lacked the ability to return. They could not acquire sufficient savings in the public sphere to fund return migration, and in the domestic sphere, they did not command enough authority over their wives or children, who generally wished to remain in the United States, to coerce the return migration of their families. Although Mexican immigrant men blamed the terms of U.S. production as their reason for wanting to return to Mexico, we believe that their diminished patriarchal privileges significantly fueled this desire to return.[5] Here, we examine the diminution of patriarchy in three arenas: spatial mobility, authority in family decision-making processes, and household labor.

Mexican immigrant men, especially those who were undocumented and lacked legal status privileges, experienced limited spatial mobility in their daily lives and this compromised their sense of masculinity (Rouse, 1990). As undocumented immigrants, these men remained fearful of apprehension by the Immigration Naturalization Service and by the police.[6] In informal conversations, the men often shared experiences with police harassment and racial discrimination. Merely "looking Mexican," the men agreed, was often cause for suspicion. The jobs Mexican immigrant men commonly took also restricted their spatial mobility. As poor men who worked long hours at jobs as gardeners, dishwashers, or day laborers, they had very little discretionary income to afford leisure activities. As one man offered, "Here my life is just from work to the home, from work to the home."

Although the men, together with their families, visited parks, shops, and church, the public spaces open to the men alone were typically limited to street corners and to a few neighborhood bars, pool halls, and doughnut shops. As Rouse (1990) has argued, Mexican immigrant men, especially those from rural areas, resent these constrictions on their public space and mobility and attempt to reproduce public spaces that they knew in Mexico in the context of U.S. bars and pool halls. In a California immigrant community Rouse observed that "men do not come to drink alone or to meet with a couple of friends...they move from table to table, broadening the circuits of in-

formation in which they participate and modulating social relationships across the widest possible range." Although these men tried to create new spaces where they might recapture a public sense of self, the goal was not so readily achieved. For many men, the loss of free and easy mobility signified their loss of publicly accorded status and recognition. One man, a junkyard assembler who had worked in Mexico as a rural *campesino* (peasant), recalled that in his Mexican village he enjoyed a modicum of public recognition: "I would enter the bars, the dances, and when I entered everyone would stand to shake my hand as though I were somebody—not a rich man, true, but I was famous. Wherever you like, I was always mentioned. Wherever you like, everyone knew me back there." In metropolitan areas of California, anonymity replaced public status and recognition.

In Mexico many of these men had acted as the undisputed patriarchs in major family decision-making processes, but in the United States they no longer retained their monopoly on these processes. When families were faced with major decisions—such as whom to seek for legal help, whether or not to move to another town, or the decision to lend money or make a major purchase—spousal negotiation replaced patriarchal exertions of authority. These processes did not go uncontested, and some of the decision-making discussions were more conflictual than harmonious, but collaboration, not domination, characterized them.

This trend toward more egalitarian patterns of shared authority often began with migration. In some families, men initially migrated north alone, and during their absences, the women acted decisively and autonomously as they performed a range of tasks necessary to secure family sustenance. Commentators have referred to this situation as one in which "thousands of wives in the absence of their husbands must 'take the reigns'" (Mummert, 1988, p. 283) and as one in which the wives of veteran migrants experience "a freedom where woman command" (*una libertad donde mujeres mandan*) (Baca & Bryan, 1985). This trend toward more shared decision making continued after the women's migration and was also promoted by migration experiences as well as the relative increase in women's and the decrease in men's economic contributions to the family (Hondagneu-Sotelo, 1992). As the balance of relative resources and contributions shifted, the women assumed more active roles in key decision-making processes. Similar shifts occurred with the older children, who were now often reluctant to subordinate their earnings and their autonomy to a patriarchal family hierarchy. As one man somewhat reluctantly, but resignedly, acknowledged: "Well, each person orders one's self here, something like that...Back there [Mexico], no. It was still whatever I said. I decided matters."

The household division of labor is another arena that in some cases reflected the renegotiation of patriarchal relations. Although most families continued to organize their daily household chores along fairly orthodox, patriarchal norms, in some families—notably those where the men had lived for many years in "bachelor communities" where they learned to cook, iron, and make tortillas—men took responsibility for some of the housework. In these cases, men did part of the cooking and housework, they unself-consciously assumed the role of host in offering guests food and beverages, and in some instances, the men continued to make tortillas on weekends and special occasions. These changes, of course, are modest if judged by ideal standards of feminist egalitarianism, but they are significant when compared to patriarchal family organization that was normative before immigration.

This movement toward more egalitarian divisions of labor in some Mexican immigrant households cannot be fully explained by the men's acquisition of household skills in bachelor communities. (We are reminded, for instance, of several middle-class male friends of ours who lived in "bachelor" apartments during college, and after later marrying, conveniently "forgot" how to cook, wash clothes, and do other household chores.) The acquisition of skills appears to be a necessary, but

not a sufficient, condition for men's greater household labor participation in reunited families.

A key to the movement toward greater equality within immigrant families was the change in the women's and men's relative positions of power and status in the larger social structure of power. Mexican immigrant man's public status in the United States is very low, due to racism, insecure and low-paying jobs, and (often) illegal status. For those families that underwent long periods of spousal separation, women often engaged in formal- or informal-sector paid labor for the first time, developed more economic skills and autonomy, and assumed control over household affairs. In the United States nearly all of the women sought employment, so women made significant economic contributions to the family. All of these factors tend to erode men's patriarchal authority in the family and empower women to either directly challenge that authority or at least renegotiate "patriarchal bargains" (Kandiyoti, 1988) that are more palatable to themselves and their children.

Although it is too hasty to proclaim that gender egalitarianism prevails in interpersonal relations among undocumented Mexican immigrants, there is a significant trend in that direction. This is indicated by the emergence of a more egalitarian household division of labor, by shared decision-making processes, and by the constraints on men's and expansion of women's spatial mobility. Women still have less power than men, but they generally enjoy more than they previously did in Mexico. The stereotypical image of dominant macho males and submissive females in Mexican immigrant families is thus contradicted by actual research with these families.

MASCULINE DISPLAYS AND RELATIVE POWER

We have suggested that men's overt public displays of masculine bravado, interpersonal dominance, misogyny, embodied strength, and so forth are often a sign of a lack of institutional power and privilege, vis-à-vis other men. Though it would be a mistake to conclude that Mexican immigrant men are not misogynist (or, following Peña, that their misogyny is merely a response to class oppression), there is considerable evidence that their actual relations with women in families—at least when measured by family divisions of labor and decision-making processes—are becoming more egalitarian than they were in Mexico. We have also argued that for more privileged men, public displays of sensitivity might be read as signs of class/race/gender privilege and power over women and (especially) over other men (see Table 1 for a summary comparison of these two groups)....

In complex, stratified societies where the standards of hegemonic masculinity are that a man should control resources (and other people), men who do not have access to these standards of masculinity thus tend to react with displays of toughness, bravado, "cool pose," or "hombre" (Baca Zinn, 1982). Marginalized and subordinated men, then, tend to overtly display exaggerated embodiments and verbalizations of masculinity that can be read as a desire to express power over others within a context of relative powerlessness. By contrast, many of the contemporary New Man's highly celebrated public displays of sensitivity can be read as a desire to project an image of egalitarianism within a context where he actually enjoys considerable power and privilege over women and

other men. Both groups of men are "displaying gender," but the specific forms that their masculine displays take tend to vary according to their relative positions in (a) the social structure of men's overall power relationship to women and (b) the social structure of some men's power relationships with other men.

CONCLUSION

We have argued for the importance of viewing microlevel gender displays of different groups of men within the context of their positions in a larger social structure of power. Too often critical discussions of masculinity tend to project atavistic hypermasculine, aggressive, misogynist masculinity onto relatively powerless men. By comparison, the masculine gender displays of educated, privileged New Men are too often uncritically applauded, rather than skeptically and critically examined. We have suggested that when analyzed within a structure of power, the gender displays of the New Man might best be seen as strategies to reconstruct hegemonic masculinity by projecting aggression, domination, and misogyny onto subordinate groups of men. Does this mean that all of men's changes today are merely symbolic and ultimately do not contribute to the types of changes in gender relations that feminists have called for? It may appear so, especially if social scientists

TABLE 1   Comparison of Public and Domestic Gender Displays of White, Class-Privileged Men and Mexican Immigrant Men

	PUBLIC		DOMESTIC	
	Power/Status	*Gender Display*	*Power/Status*	*Gender Display*
White, class-privileged men	High, built into position	"Sensitive," little overt misogyny	High, based on public status/ high income	"Quiet control"
Mexican immigrant men	Low (job status, pay, control of work, legal rights, public status)	"Hombre": verbal misogyny, embodied toughness in work/peer culture	Contested, becoming more egalitarian	Exaggerated symbols of power and authority in family

continue to collude with this reality by viewing shifts in styles of hegemonic masculinity as indicative of the arrival of a New Man, while viewing marginalized men as Other—as atavistic, traditional men. Instead, a critical/feminist analysis of changing masculinities in the United States might begin with a focus on the ways that marginalized and subordinated masculinities are changing.

This shift in focus would likely accomplish three things: First, it would remove hegemonic masculinity from center stage, thus taking the standpoints of oppressed groups of men as central points of departure. Second, it would require the deployment of theoretical frameworks that examine the ways that the politics of social class, race, ethnicity, and sexuality interact with those of gender (Baca Zinn, Cannon, Higgenbotham, & Dill, 1986; Collins, 1990; Harding, 1986; Hondagneu-Sotelo, 1992; Messner, 1990). Third, a sociology of masculinities that starts from the experience of marginalized and subordinated men would be far more likely to have power and politics—rather than personal styles or lifestyles—at its center. This is because men of color, poor and working-class men, immigrant men, and gay men are often in very contradictory positions at the nexus of intersecting systems of domination and subordination. In short, although they are oppressed by class, race, and/or sexual systems of power, they also commonly construct and display forms of masculinity as ways of resisting other men's power over them, as well as asserting power and privilege over women. Thus, to avoid reverting to the tendency to view masculinity simply as a defensive reaction to other forms of oppression, it is crucial in such studies to keep women's experience of gender oppression as close to the center of analysis as possible. This sort of analysis might inform the type of progressive coalition building that is necessary if today's changing masculinities are to contribute to the building of a more egalitarian and democratic world.

NOTES

1. This section of the chapter is adapted from Messner (1993).
2. It is significant, we suspect, that the examples cited of Reagan, Jordan, and Schwartzkopf publicly weeping occurred at moments of *victory* over other men in war and sport.
3. Our speculation on the class and racial bias of the mythopoetic men's movement and on the appeal of the movement to participants is supported, in part, by ongoing (but as yet unpublished) research by sociologist Michael Schwalbe. Schwalbe observes that the "wounds" of these men are very real, because a very high proportion of them are children of alcoholic parents and/or were victims of childhood sexual abuse or other forms of violence. Many are involved in recovery programs.

4. Material in this section is drawn from Hondagneu-Sotelo's study of long-term undocumented immigrant settlers, based on 18 months of field research in a Mexican undocumented immigrant community. See Hondagneu-Sotelo, (1992) *Gendered Transitions: Mexican Experiences of Immigrants.* Berkeley: University of California Press.
5. For a similar finding and analysis in the context of Dominican immigrants in New York City, see Pessar (1986).
6. This constraint was exacerbated by passage of the Immigration Reform and Control Act of 1986, which imposed employer sanctions and doubly criminalized undocumented immigrants' presence at the workplace.

REFERENCES

Baca, R., & Bryan, D. (1985). Mexican women, migration and sex roles. *Migration Today, 13,* 14–18.

Baca Zinn, M. (1982). Chicano men and masculinity. *Journal of Ethnic Studies, 10,* 29–44.

Baca Zinn, M., Cannon, L. W., Higginbotham, E., & Dill, B. T. (1986). The costs of exclusionary practices in woman's studies. *Signs: Journal of Women in Culture and Society, 11,* 290–303.

Blum, L. M. (1991). *Between feminism and labor: The significance of the comparable worth movement.* Berkeley: University of California Press.

Bly, R. (1990). *Iron John: A book about men.* Reading, MA: Addison-Wesley.

Brod, H. (1983–1984). Work clothes and leisure suits: The class basis and bias of the men's movement. *Changing Men, 11,* 10–12, 38–40 (Winter).

Brod, H. (Ed.). (1987). *The making of masculinities: The new men's studies.* Boston: Allen & Unwin.

Clawson. M. A. (1989). *Constructing brotherhood: Class, gender, and fraternalism.* Princeton, NJ: Princeton University Press.

Collins, P. H. (1990). *Black feminist thought: Knowledge, consciousness, and the politics of empowerment.* Boston: Unwin Hyman.

Collinson, D. L. (1988). "Engineering humor": Masculinity, joking and conflict in shop-floor relations. *Organization Studies, 9,* 181–199.

Coltrane, S. (1992). The micropolitics of gender in nonindustrial societies. *Gender & Society, 6,* 86–107.

Connell, R. W. (1987). *Gender and power.* Stanford, CA: Stanford University Press.

Connell, R. W. (1991a). Live fast and die young: The construction of masculinity among young working-class men on the margin of the labour market. *Australian & New Zealand Journal of Sociology, 27,* 141–171.

Connell, R. W. (1991b). *Men of reason: Themes of rationality and change in the lives of the men in the new professions.* Unpublished paper.

Connell, R. W. (1992a). Drumming up the wrong tree. *Tikkun, 7,* 517–530.

Connell, R. W. (1992b). Masculinity, violence, and war. In M. S. Kimmel & M. A. Messner (Eds.), *Men's lives* (2nd ed., pp. 176–182). New York: Macmillan.

Davis, M. (1990). *Mexican voices, American dreams: An oral history of Mexican immigration to the United States.* New York: Henry Holt.

Escobar, A. L., Gonzalez de la Rocha, M., & Roberts, B. (1987). Migration, labor markets, and the international economy: Jalisco, Mexico and the United States. In J. Eades (Ed.), *Migrants, workers, and the social order* (pp. 42–64) London: Tavistock.

Farrell, W. (1975). *The liberated man.* New York: Bantam.

Freire, P. (1970). *Pedagogy of the oppressed.* New York: Herder & Herden.

Harding, S. (1986). *The science question in feminism.* Ithaca, NY: Cornell University Press.

Henley, N. M. (1977). *Body politics: Power, sex, and nonverbal communication.* Englewood Cliffs, NJ: Prentice Hall.

Hertz, R. (1986). *More equal than others: Women and men in dual career marriages.* Berkeley: University of California.

Hochschild. A. (1989). *The second shift: Working parents and the revolution at home.* New York: Viking.

Hondagneu-Sotelo, P. (1992). Overcoming patriarchal constraints: The reconstruction of gender relations among Mexican immigrant women and men. *Gender & Society, 6,* 393–415.

Kandiyoti, D. (1988). Bargaining with patriarchy. *Gender & Society, 2,* 274–290.

Kann, M. E. (1986). The costs of being on top. *Journal of the National Association for Women Deans, Administrators, & Counselors, 49,* 29–37.

Kaufman, M. (Ed.). (1987). *Beyond patriarchy: Essays by men on pleasure, power, and change.* Toronto: Oxford University Press.

Kimmel, M. S. (1992). Reading men: Men, masculinity, and publishing. *Contemporary Sociology, 21,* 162–171.

La Rossa, R. (1998). Fatherhood and social change. *Family Relations, 37,* 451–457.

Lewis, C. (1986). *Becoming a father.* Milton Keynes, UK: Open University Press.

Lyman, P. (1987). The fraternal bond as a joking relation: A case study of the role of sexist jokes in male group bonding. In M. Kimmel (Ed.), *Changing men: New directions in research on men and masculinities* (pp. 148–163). Newbury Park, CA: Sage.

Machung, A. (1989). Talking career, thinking job: Gender differences in career and family expectations of Berkeley seniors. *Feminist Studies, 15.*

Majors, R., & Billson, J. M. (1992). *Cool pose: The dilemmas of black manhood in America.* New York: Lexington.

Martin, P. Y., & Hummer, R. A. (1989). Fraternities and rape on campus. *Gender & Society, 3,* 457–473.

Messner, M. A. (1990). Men studying masculinity: Some epistemological questions in sport sociology. *Sociology of Sport Journal, 7,* 136–153.

Messner, M. A. (1992). *Power at play: Sports and the problem of masculinity.* Boston: Beacon.

Messner, M. A. (1993). "Changing men" and feminist politics in the U.S. *Theory & Society, 22,* 723–737.

Mirandé, A. (1982). Machismo: Rucas, chingasos y chagaderas. *De Colores: Journal of Chicano Expression and Thought, 6*(1/2), 17–31.

Mummert, G. (1988). Mujeres de migrantes y mujeres migrantes de Michoacán: Nuevo papeles para las que se quedan y para las que se van. In T. Calvo & G. Lopez (Eds.), *Movimientos de población en el occident de Mexico* (pp. 281–295). Mexico, DF: Centre de'etudes mexicaines and centroamericaines and El colegio de Mexico.

Paredes, A. (1966). The Anglo-American in Mexican folklore. In R. B. Browne & D. H. Wenkelman (Eds.), *New voices in American studies.* Lafayette, IN: Purdue University Press.

Pelka, F. (1991). Robert Bly and Iron John: Bly romanticizes history, trivializes sexist oppression and lays the blame for men's "grief" on women. *On the Issues, 19,* 17–19, 39.

Peña, M. (1991). Class, gender and machismo: The "treacherous woman" folklore of Mexican male workers. *Gender & Society, 5,* 30–46.

Pessar, P. (1986). The role of gender in Dominican settlement in the United States. In J. Nash & H. Safa (Eds.). *Women and change in Latin America* (pp. 273–294). South Hadley, MA: Bergin & Garvey.

Reskin, B. F., & Roos, P. A. (1990). *Job queues, gender queues: Explaining women's inroads into male occupations.* Philadelphia: Temple University Press.

Rouse, R. (1990, March 14). *Men in space: Power and the appropriation of urban form among Mexican migrants in the United States.* Paper presented at the Residential College, University of Michigan, Ann Arbor.

Russell, G. (1983). *The changing role of fathers.* London: University of Queensland.

Sabo, D. F. (1985). Sport, patriarchy, and male identity: New questions about men and sport. *Arena Review, 9,* 1–30.

Sattel, J. W. (1976). The inexpressive male: Tragedy or sexual politics? *Social Problems, 23,* 469–477.

Segal, L. (1990). *Slow motion: Changing masculinities, changing men.* New Brunswick, NJ: Rutgers University.

Sidel, R. (1990). *On her own: Growing up in the shadow of the American dream.* New York: Penguin.

Tolson, A. (1977). *The limits of masculinity: Male identity and women's liberation.* New York: Harper & Row.

Winter, M. F., & Robert, E. R. (1980). Male dominance, late capitalism, and the growth of instrumental reason. *Berkeley Journal of Sociology, 25,* 249–280.

Studying across Difference
Race, Class, and Gender in Qualitative Research

MARGARET L. ANDERSEN

Sociological studies of race have often been distorted by having been centered in the perspectives and experiences of dominant group members. This has resulted both from the exclusion of African American, Latino, and Native American people from the general frameworks of sociology and from the application of ethnocentric concepts to the study of racial-ethnic groups. As Ladner (1973), among others, points out:

> Blacks have always been measured against an alien set of norms. As a result they have been considered to be a deviation from the ambiguous white middle-class model, which itself has not always been clearly defined. This inability or refusal to deal with Blacks as a part and parcel of the varying historical and cultural contributions to the American scene has, perhaps, been the reason sociology has excluded the Black perspective from its widely accepted mainstream theories. (p. xxiii)

Like its sister discipline, women's studies, Black studies seeks to build more inclusive research through incorporating the experiences and perspectives of traditionally excluded groups. One way to accomplish this has been to encourage studies of race and ethnic relations by minority scholars themselves, on the assumption that they are better able to understand the nuances of racial oppression. This assumption is best stated by Blauner and Wellman (1973):

> There are certain aspects of racial phenomena, however, that are particularly difficult, if not impossible, for a member of the oppressing group to grasp empirically and formulate conceptually. These barriers are existential and methodological as well as political and ethical. We refer here to the nuances of culture and group ethos; to the meaning of oppression and especially psychic relations; to what is called the Black, the Mexican-American, the Asian and the Indian experience. (p. 329)

Blauner and Wellman's argument underscores the point that research occurs in the context of power relationships, both between the researcher and research subjects and in the society at large. As they point out:

> Scientific research does not exist in a vacuum. Its theory and practice reflect the structure and values of society. In capitalist America, where massive inequalities in wealth and power exist between classes and racial groups, the processes of social research express both race and class oppression. The control, exploitation, and privilege that are generic components of social oppression exist in the relation of researchers to researched, even though their manifestations may be subtle and masked by professional ideologies. (pp. 314–315)

This position, largely articulated during the early 1970s in sociological writing, poses important questions about the social construction of knowledge about race and ethnic relations. Particularly, the question is raised; How can White scholars contribute to our understanding of the experiences of racial groups? Can dominant groups comprehend the experiences of outsiders and, if so, under what conditions and with which methodological practices?

Doing research in minority communities poses unique methodological problems for members of both minority and majority groups. Baca Zinn (1979), a Chicana sociologist, has described the methodological problems she faces when doing research on Chicano families. She directly acknowledges that her relationships with research subjects are never equal and that, as a researcher, she cannot alter the political context in which research takes place. She argues that minority scholars may generate questions that are different from those asked by majority group researchers. Minority scholars are also less likely to experience distrust, hostility, and exclusion within minority communities. At the same time, however, the accountability and commitment of minority scholars to the communities they study pose unique problems for their research practice. In a different context, Cannon, Higginbotham, and Leung (1988) have shown that qualitative studies are also easily biased by the greater willingness of white middle-class subjects to participate in research. Because dominant groups have less reason to expect they will be exploited by researchers, they are more likely to volunteer as research subjects.

The problems of doing research within minority communities are compounded by the social distance imposed by class and race relations when interviewers are White and middle-class and those being interviewed are not. For White scholars wanting to study race relations, these conclusions in the research literature are daunting. How can White scholars elicit an understanding of race relations as experienced by racial minorities? How can White scholars study those who have been historically subordinated without further producing sociological accounts distorted by the political economy of race, class, and gender?

John Gwaltney, a blind Black anthropologist who studied the experiences and beliefs of people in his hometown community, has written eloquently about the obstacles white researchers should expect when doing research in Black communities. The Black men and women he interviewed strongly expressed their mistrust of White social scientists. They reported, "I wouldn't want to talk to any anthropologist or sociologist or any of those others if they were White because whatever I said they would write down what they felt like, so I might just as well save my breath" (quoted in Gwaltney, 1980, p. xxv). Another said, "We know White folks but they do not know us, and that's just how the Lord planned the thing.... Now they are great ones for begging you to tell them what you really think. But you know, only a fool would really do that" (p. 102). Given these problems, how can White researchers study Black and Latino subjects or, for that matter, how can men study women? Although the focus in this chapter is on studying across racial differences, the theoretical discussion applies to the relationship between any dominant group researcher and his or her minority group subjects.

Feminist scholars have argued that members of subordinated groups have unique viewpoints on their own experiences and on the society as a whole. Known as standpoint theorists, these scholars argue that race, class, and gender are origins of, as well as objects of, sociological knowledge. According to this literature, a feminist standpoint is distinct from a perspective or bias because it "preserve[s] the presence of the active and experiencing subject" (D. E. Smith, 1987, p. 105). Standpoint theorists understand that researchers and their subjects are located in specific social-historical settings. Because there is a social relationship between researchers and their research subjects, research cannot be construed as a process of eliminating the presence of the researcher. Yet, the claim of objectivity often assumes that the researcher has no presence or that to be objective is to remove oneself from the situation at hand. Considering this argument, feminist standpoint theorists have argued that research must be seen in context. Politically engaged standpoints are not simply the result of biological identity. Rather, standpoints are achieved; they are not inherent in one's race, sex, or class. But how are such standpoints accomplished by dominant group members wanting to construct liberating knowledge about race, class, and gender relations?

Standpoint theorists argue that those who maintain an interest in reproducing racist and sexist relations are least able to see the social construction of race, class, and gender relations. Indeed, "there are some perspectives on society from which, however well-intentioned one may be, the real relations of humans with each other and with the natural world are not visible" (Hartsock, 1983, p. 285). Feminist standpoint theorists draw from Marxist theory the idea that material life structures and sets limits on the understanding of social relations; thus the vision of the ruling class, race, and gender is partial, because it not only structures the material relations in which all are forced to participate, but also takes for granted the labor, indeed the very existence, of oppressed groups.

Patricia Hill Collins (1986) argues that the marginality of Black feminist scholars gives them distinctive analyses of race, class, and gender. She sees Black feminist scholars as best generating Black feminist theory, but also suggests that all intellectuals can learn to read their personal and cultural biographies as significant sources of knowledge. As "outsiders within," Black feminist scholars use the tension in their cultural identities to generate new ways of seeing and new sociological insights. Likewise, majority group scholars can develop and utilize tensions in their own cultural identities to enable them to see different aspects of minority group experiences and to examine critically majority experiences and beliefs.

This understanding recasts earlier arguments that only minority scholars can produce knowledge about racial-ethnic groups. It suggests that White scholars doing research on race and ethnicity should examine self-consciously the influence of institutional racism and the way it shapes the formulation and development of their research, rather than assume a color-blind stance. This is a fundamentally different posture from that advocated by the norms of "unbiased, objective" scientific research, in which one typically denies the influence of one's own status (be it race, gender, class, or other social status) in the shaping of knowledge. It requires that we see ourselves as "situated in the action of our research" (Rapp, 1983), examining our own social location, not just that of those we study.

Elsewhere I have argued that White feminist scholars can transform their teaching and thinking through centering their thoughts in the experience of women of color (Andersen, 1988). Feminist scholarship has shown that moving previously excluded groups to the center of our research and teaching produces more representative accounts of society and culture. Building more inclusive ways of seeing requires scholars to take multiple views of their subjects, abandoning the idea that there is a singular reality that social science can discover. Minority group members have insights about and interpretations of their experiences that are likely different from those generated by White scholars. The question is not whether White scholars should write about or attempt to know the experience of people of color, but whether their interpretations should be taken to be the most authoritative (Hooks, 1989). Furthermore, how, in constructing sociological analyses, can dominant group members examine their own racial identities and challenge the societal system of racial stratification in which what they observe is situated?

THE SETTING

These issues are examined, here in the context of a community study of race relations. In this study, I (a White scholar) wanted to know how changes in the political economy of race relations were experienced by African Americans in this community. What meaning do African Americans in this community give to their experience? And how do they define the class, race system in which they live? I studied a small community with a historically rigid racial division of labor and a history of paternalism persistently defining contemporary relations between Whites and Blacks—hardly a social structure conducive to the trust and empathy desirable for building a sociological research project. I entered this project knowing the particular limitations that my own racial status would create.

The community is located on the Eastern Shore of Maryland—a peninsula on the eastern shore of the Chesapeake Bay. The community appears prosperous and alluring and in many ways seems to be an ideal American town. There is a central village green. Church spires are the highest points in the city skyscape, and the main street is dotted with chic boutiques. Those who walk on the streets seem to know each other; they stop to chat and, in their conversations, they inquire about each other's families and exchange news about others in town.

Because this is a waterfront community, it can also be approached by boat. On the shore, one sees expensive waterfront estates—so many of them that one might wonder how so many people became so rich. Many of these estates are invisible from land; from the bay, their long docks can be seen—many with multiple yacht slips. Sailboats fill the rivers and coves surrounding this town, and motor yachts twice the size of the average American home (and full of more than the usual amenities) are common. One of these yachts displays a flag at the bow: "He who dies with the most toys wins!"

Yet there is a dual reality here—one hidden in small, all-Black hamlets that do not, in many cases, even appear on the road maps and that do not front the bay waters, as do the privileged acres of the rich. The dual reality is perhaps no better described than by Frederick Douglass, himself a slave 150 years ago on the estate of Edward Lloyd, the Eastern Shore's largest slaveholder. The sailing ships that contemporary visitors today covet and admire were, to Douglass, symbols of the oppression of Black people. Standing on the shores of the Chesapeake, he wrote, "Those beautiful vessels, robed in white and so delightful to the eyes of freemen, were to me so many shrouded ghosts to terrify and tor-

ment me with thoughts of my wretched condition" (Douglass, 1962, p. 125).

Sociological descriptions of the county in which the Eastern Shore lies reveal great inequality in the experiences of Whites and Blacks living here. Slightly more than one-third of Black persons live below the poverty line, compared with less than 5% of White families.[1] (Nationally, 16.1% of Black families in the same year lived in poverty.) Median income for White families here in 1980 was approximately $21,000; for Black families, it was less than $7,500—only 35% of White family income. (Nationally, Black family income in 1980 was 60.2% of White family income.) Inequality between Whites and Blacks in this county is further demonstrated by the skewed character of income distribution. Nearly 40% of Black households in this county have incomes less than $5,000 per year (nationally, this figure is 2.5%), compared with less than 13% for White households. No Black households in this county have incomes higher than $35,000, and only 2% have incomes between $25,000 and $35,000, compared with one-fourth of White households.

The persistence of such striking inequality on the Eastern Shore, with its historical past based on a plantation economy, makes it a region rich for sociological study. Less than 100 miles from Philadelphia, Baltimore, and Washington, D.C., the region seems like an anachronism in that the yachts, fashionable shops, and luxury automobiles are clearly symbolic of contemporary class relations, but the juxtaposition of rurally segregated Black communities and paternalistic relations between Whites and Blacks evokes a strong feeling that the past is still present. The Eastern Shore remains predominantly rural, agricultural, and geographically isolated. It is here that slavery originated in the United States, although slavery is more typically associated with states further south. Until 1790, two-thirds of the slave population lived around the Chesapeake Bay, where tobacco and wheat crops dominated production. In 1660, Maryland was the first state to enact laws defining slavery as a legitimate institution. Now, former plantations are owned by elites and, in some cases, multinational corporations. Patterns of residential segregation are characteristic of the living arrangements between Whites and Blacks.

Two questions framed my research on the Eastern Shore: What has been the experience of African Americans in this community? and What are their understandings of how race relations have changed in their lifetimes? Pursuing the answers to these questions demanded data different from those that could be gathered through secondary sources. My questions were both historical and qualitative, each involving different methodological problems that ultimately will shape what is known from this study. The absence of firsthand accounts reflecting on and describing African American experience in this community limits sociological understanding of the development and persistence of racism. The methodological problems posed by the historical analysis are similar to those posed by contemporary qualitative research. Historians have been overly dependent on historical records left by members of the dominant group, usually elites. Other available historical documents are typically those left by philanthropists or government agencies, documents often characterized by images of Black Americans as pathological (Uya, 1981).

Although I used primary historical evidence from archival and personal documents to understand the historical experience of African Americans in this community, contemporary accounts of race relations through the eyes of Black Americans are rare. This is precisely the kind of information that the literature suggests is most inaccessible to white researchers. Wondering whether I could reliably collect such information, I proceeded to do field research and to conduct extended interviews with low-income, elderly (mostly in their 80s) women, both Black and White, who had little formal schooling. As a White, middle-aged, middle-class researcher, I knew I was crossing not only racial boundaries but also those of class, age, and education. Because of the high degree of racial and class segregation in this community, these bound-

aries seemed potentially even more clearly marked. Ideally, I could have hired Black interviewers to conduct these interviews, but without research funding, this was impossible.

INTERVIEWING ACROSS RACE AND CLASS

The subjects for this study were poor elderly women, both Black and White—women whose lives have perhaps been the most distorted by social scientific research. These are women whose experiences have been underrepresented, at best, in the social science literature. More typically, they are excluded and ignored in sociological studies, even though their lives provide a rich portrait of the fabric of social life and, especially, race, class, and gender relations. My interviews with these women reveal that the scientific framework of social science research actually obstructs the formation of relationships essential to achieving an understanding of these women's lives.

The interviews were designed to produce open-ended oral histories of the women's work and family histories and their perceptions of how relations between Whites and Blacks in their community had changed over the course of their lifetimes. Although qualitatively based, interviews are typically guided by the same principles of detachment and neutrality characteristic of quantitative research analyses. As Oakley (1981) has argued, conventional reports of interview data typically include the following information about the interviews: how many there were, how long they were, how they were recorded, and whether the questions followed a standard format. Researchers typically do not report the characteristics of interviewers, nor do they discuss interviewees' feelings about being interviewed, the quality of the interaction between the interviewer and interviewee, or the reception and hospitality extended to the interviewer. Routine methodological instructions tell interviewers to control the interview by directing their questions and the answers of those with whom they are speaking. This method of research procedure is, as Oakley argues, fundamentally hierarchical. It manipulates those being interviewed as objects of study and suggests that there should be minimal human contact and no emotional involvement between the research subject and the researcher. In fact, researchers are warned that the

> interview is designed to minimize the local, concrete, immediate circumstances of the particular encounter, including the respective personalities of the participants.... As an encounter between these two particular people the typical interview has no meaning; it is conceived in a framework of other, comparable meanings, between other couples, each recorded in such fashion that elements of communication in common can be easily isolated from more idiosyncratic qualities. (Benney & Hughes, 1970, pp. 196–197; quoted in Oakley, 1981, p. 32)

Oakley concludes that sociologists are routinely instructed to interview research subjects by manipulating them as objects of study. According to conventional methodology, the best data are those that are produced through minimal human contact and minimal interrelationship. Researchers are admonished not to get too emotionally involved with subjects. Such a method assumes the passivity of respondents and forces them to adapt to the situation as defined by the interviewer. Moreover, researchers are told never to inform interviewees of their own beliefs and values.

My research suggests that this conventional methodological approach is counter to that required for White scholars to produce more inclusive and less partial and distorted accounts of race, class, and gender relations. To begin with, it is impossible even to count the exact number of interviews in my project and to report the amount of time they took. Many of the women included in this research refused to be interviewed formally, but were willing to talk with me for hours. One woman asked that the tape recorder be turned off at various places in our conversation. With the tape recorder off, she spoke freely about information she thought should remain confidential, although it revealed important, yet sensitive,

information about race and gender relationships in the community. Another woman told me her long and intriguing life history and talked openly about class and race relations in the community, but refused to be taped. We sat in my car for most of an afternoon, in subfreezing winter temperatures. Other important information and ideas in this project came from many days and hours of informal discussion with these women at the local senior center. Thus the field research for the project and the actual interviews blur, with no exact number of interviews to be reported, but, nonetheless, with these conversations/interviews providing rich data about race and gender relations in this community.

As found in other work on race and ethnic relations, the women in this study were savvy to the potentially exploitive character of academic research. Many told stories about past researchers who had come to study them but who had not, in their eyes, done a very good job. They talked at length about what was wrong with the researchers' approaches, personalities, and attitudes. They scoffed at the presumption of many researchers that they could come to this community and learn about women's lives from a distance. The women also clearly understood that the research was more important to me than it was to them. They knew it would have little effect on them, and it would not change their lives. They made themselves helpers for my purposes, but did not let themselves be exploited. Moreover, within their accounts of previous research projects were clues about the grounds on which they would trust me—despite the clear differences between us.

Several talked at length about how my "personality" made them more trusting, open, and willing to speak with me. These comments made me think about what I was doing—consciously and unconsciously—to elicit their reported trust. Primarily, I did not pose myself as an expert in their lives. Quite the contrary, I introduced myself as someone who was interested in learning about them particularly because their lives were unreported and undervalued by teachers and scholars.

Most responded by being honored that someone was going to "write a book about them." One woman reported talking with her daughter following the interview, saying how helpful it had been because now she and her family were talking about their racial histories. She said, "I really liked talking with you. You know it's helpful to us talking about our backlives. It helps you start to think about your backlife. You talk plain and understanding. It helps me think about my backlife."

Most of these women thought of themselves as "just ordinary." When they were reluctant to be interviewed, it was often because they did not understand why anyone would take an interest in them. Defining their experience as important to know and understand, especially in a context where their age, class, gender, and, in some cases, race left them undervalued, increased the cooperation and rapport I was able to generate with them. More important, for many, seeing their life as of interest to a "teacher" affirmed them and made them feel positively valued. Throughout the process of meeting and interviewing them, I was reminded of the humility with which I had to work. I could not assume the role of expert, and I needed to be willing to talk about my life as a woman and as a White person in my conversations with them. It was important that I did not think of them as victims of racial, sexual, and class oppression, but wanted to learn how they valued their own experience. I was actually aided by the fact that I had no research funding and was not representing an agency. Although in some ways the research suffered from my being unable to hire Black interviewers, it also was important to the women that the research was not sponsored by any organization. They particularly wanted assurance that I was not from the Social Security Administration—a key agency in their own feelings of economic dependence and frustration with bureaucracy.

As other field researchers have found, engaging myself in their world was critical to my research. I was an active volunteer in the senior center that these women regularly attended. Although it was difficult for me to contribute as much time as I did, given other demands on my time as a scholar-teacher, my participation in the center reassured the women of my commitment to them. During the interviews, many talked explicitly about the fact that I spent so many hours there and worked with them on their projects. I was careful to disengage from my role as a professional scholar-teacher while at the center, sharing in their activities, including senior exercises, music, and crafts.

My participation in the everyday activities of the women's culture, both in the center and in their homes, greatly facilitated this research. I threaded needles for those with failing eyesight, glued sequins on pipe-cleaner butterflies in preparation for an annual yard sale, delivered sandwiches during the yard sale, helped make Christmas ornaments and pottery, and discussed cooking, knitting, sewing, and crafts. Often, while doing these things, the women provided the most telling comments on their relationships with each other, their pasts, their feelings about their community, their families, and their work. During these times, I also learned how the women felt; their conversations were filled with emotion, humor, gossip, and play.

In sum, what seems to have made these interviews possible was my direct violation of the usual admonitions to social science researchers. During the interviews, I answered questions about myself, my background, my family, and my ideas. In the interviews and during the field research, the women and I exchanged our feelings and ideas about many of the subjects we were discussing. At times, I showed the emotion I felt during very moving moments in their accounts of their experiences.

Other feminist and qualitative research shows that emotion, the engagement of self, and the relationship between the knower and the known all guide research, just as they guide social action. For example, in her book *Street Woman,* on women's crime, Miller (1986) writes of being afraid, intimidated, and uncomfortable, and, as she learned more about the women's lives, angry and depressed. But she concludes, "For reasons I do not know, these emotions, as paralyzing as they could have been, were rather motivating forces with regard to the research" (p. 189). In my project, despite my trepidations about crossing class, race, and age lines, I was surprised by the openness and hospitality with which I was greeted, I am convinced that the sincerity of these women's stories emanated not only from their dignity and honor, but also from my willingness to express how I felt, to share my own race and gender experiences, and to deconstruct the role of expert as I proceeded through this research.

CONCLUSION

Some of the methodological practices that emerged in this research are common to more qualitative research methods. For example, qualitative researchers have typically noted the importance of rapport in establishing good research relations. But, as Reinharz (1983) has suggested, research is an act of self-discovery, as well as a process of learning about others. Self-examination of my own privilege as a White scholar facilitated this research project, allowing me to challenge the arrogance that the stance of White privilege creates. Although the structure of sociology as a profession discourages such engaged work, I am convinced that this self-reflective method of constructing knowledge is more compelling and reliable than standard, detached ways of knowing. I know that my understanding of these women's lives will always be partial, incomplete, and distorted. I also know that the Black women did not likely report the same things to me as they would have to a Black interviewer, but that does not make their accounts any less true. If the task of sociology is to understand the multiple intersections between social structure and biographies, then the many ways in which we see ourselves and our relationships to others should be part of sociological accounts.

Feminist scholars have argued that the reconstruction of knowledge from a feminist standpoint necessitates studying the world from the perspective of women (McIntosh, 1983, 1988). Because androcentric scholarship has imposed on sociological observations categories, concepts, and theories originating in the lives of men from dominant groups, we have created an incomplete and distorted knowledge of social life. Studying women on their own terms is more likely to engage the subjective self—that of both the actor and the researcher. Yet, when our research remains too tightly bound by the framework of scientific methodology, we miss much of the texture and nuance in social relationships.

Feminist discussions of research methodology have focused on discovering the social relationship between the knower and the known, arguing that the attempt at scientific neutrality obfuscates and denies this relationship (Harding, 1986). Contrary to the scientific image of the knower as a neutral and objective party, feminist epistemologists have argued that the relationship between the researcher and her subjects is a social relationship, and is bound by the same patterns of power relations found in other social relationships.

My study with the women of the Eastern Shore, as well as the above discussion, suggests that we should develop research practices that acknowledge and take as central the class, race, and gender relations in which researchers and research subjects are situated. At the same time, we should question assumptions that the knower is the ultimate authority on the lives of those whom she or he studies. We should not assume that White scholars are unable to generate research with people of color as research subjects, but we must be aware that to do so, White scholars must work in ways that acknowledge and challenge White privilege and question how such privilege may shape research experiences. Developing analyses that are inclusive of race, class, and gender also requires that discussions of race, class, and gender be thoroughly integrated into debates about research process and the analysis of data. This requires an acknowledgment of the complex, multiple, and contradictory identities and realities that shape our collective experience. As whites learn to see the world through the experiences of others, a process that is itself antithetical to the views of privileged

groups, we can begin to construct more complete and less distorted ways of seeing the complex relations of race, class, and gender.

NOTES

1. Data are taken from 1980 U.S. Census materials. Because the respondents were promised anonymity, data are given in approximate terms so as not to disclose the exact identity of the town.

REFERENCES

Andersen, M. L. (1988). Moving our minds: Studying women of color and re-constructing sociology. *Teaching Sociology, 15,* 123–132.

Baca Zinn, M. (1979). Field research in minority communities: Ethical, methodological and political observations by an insider. *Social Problems, 27,* 209–219.

Blauner R., & Wellman, D. (1973). Toward the decolonization of social research. In J. Ladner (Ed.), *The death of white sociology.* New York: Vintage.

Cannon, L. W., Higginbotham, E., & Leung, M. A. (1988). Race and class bias in qualitative research on women. *Gender & Society, 2,* 449–662.

Collins, P. H. (1986). Learning from the outsider within: The sociological significance of Black feminist thought. *Social Problems, 33,* 14–32.

Douglass, F. (1962). *The life and times of Frederick Douglass.* New York: Collier.

Gwaltney, J. (1980). *Drylongso: A self-portrait of Black America.* New York: Random House.

Harding, S. (1986). *The science question in feminism.* Ithaca, NY: Cornell University Press.

Hartsock, N. (1983). The feminist standpoint: Developing the ground for a specifically feminist historical materialism. In S. Harding & M. Hintakka (Eds.), *Discovering reality: Feminist perspectives on epistemology, metaphysics, methodology, and philosophy of science* (pp. 283–310). Dordrecht, Netherlands: D. Reidel.

Ladner, J. A. (Ed.). (1973). *The death of white sociology.* New York: Random House.

Miller, E. (1986). *Street woman.* Philadelphia: Temple University Press.

McIntosh, P. (1983). *Interactive phases of curriculum revision* (Working Paper). Wellesley, MA: Wellesley College, Center for Research on Women.

Oakley, A. (1981). Interviewing women. In H. Roberts (Ed.), *Doing feminist research* (pp. 30–61). New York: Routledge & Kegan Paul.

Rapp, R. (1983). *Anthropology: The science of man?* Address presented at the University of Delaware.

Reinharz, S. (1983). Experiential analysis: A contribution to feminist research. In G. Bowles & R. R. Duelli-Klein (Ed.), *Theories of woman's studies* (pp. 162–191). New York: Routledge & Kegan Paul.

Smith, D. E. (1987). *The everyday world as problematic: A feminist sociology.* Boston: Northeastern University Press.

Uya, O. E. (1981). Using federal archives: Some problems in doing research. In R. L. Clark (Ed.), *Afro-American history sources for research* (pp. 19–29). Washington, DC: Howard University Press.

Fieldwork in Lesbian and Gay Communities

KATH WESTON

This study addresses a deceptively simple set of questions: What is all this talk about gay families? Where did those families come from, and why should they appear now?...

The fieldwork that provides the basis for my analysis was conducted in the San Francisco Bay Area during 1985–1986, with a follow-up visit in 1987. San Francisco is a port city with a large and extremely diverse population of lesbians and gay men, as well as a history of gay immigration that dates at least to World War II (D'Emilio 1989). A wave of lesbian and gay immigrants arrived in the Bay Area during the 1970s, when young people of all sexualities found themselves attracted by employment opportunities in the region's rapidly expanding service sector (FitzGerald 1986). Some came for the work, some for the climate, and some to be a part of "gay mecca." Others, of course, grew up in California.

Several San Francisco neighborhoods—Folsom, Polk Street, the Castro, Bernal Heights, parts of the Tenderloin, and increasingly the Mission— were recognized even by heterosexual residents as areas with high concentrations of gay men and/or lesbians.

The third tour bus in as many hours rolls through the Castro. I watch from behind the plate glass window of the donut shop, trying to imagine this neighborhood, so symbolic of "gay America," through tourist eyes. Every television reporter who covers AIDS seems to station herself somewhere on this block. The Castro used to be a place where gay men could come to cruise and enjoy one another, objects (if not always subjects) for themselves. Nowadays, says the man sitting next to me, when you see those buses coming around, you feel like you're in a museum or a zoo or something.

With its unique history and reputation as a gay city, San Francisco hardly presents a "typical" lesbian and gay population for study. Yet the Bay Area proved to be a valuable field site because it brought together gay men and lesbians from very different colors and classes, identities and backgrounds. One estimate for 1980 put San Francisco's combined self-identified lesbian, gay, and bisexual population at 17 percent. Of those who placed themselves in one of these categories, 30 percent were women and 70 percent were men (DeLeon and Brown 1980). Lesbians were a visible presence on both sides of the bay. In contrast to many smaller cities, the region supported an abundance of specialized organizations aimed at particular sectors of the gay population, from groups for people over or under a certain age to associations of individuals who played music or enjoyed hiking. With its multicultural population, the Bay Area also hosted a variety of social organizations, political groups, and informal gathering places for gay people of color.

Among lesbians and gay men in the country at large, San Francisco is known as a place that allows people to be relatively open about their sexual identities. Carol Warren (1977) has emphasized the need to be especially protective of re-spondents' identities when working with gay people, in light of the social stigmatization of ho-mosexuality. Although I follow anthropological tradition by using pseudonyms throughout this study, I feel it is important to note that the vast majority of participants expressed a willingness to have their real names appear in print. Fear of los-ing employment and a desire to protect children's identities were the reasons offered by the few who requested assurances of anonymity. Unlike many studies of gay men and lesbians, this one assigns surnames to participants. In a Western context, in-troducing strangers by given names alone para-doxically conveys a sense of intimacy while subtly withholding individuality, respect, and full adult status from research participants. Because the same qualities are routinely denied to lesbians and gay men in society at large, the use of only first names can have the unintended consequence of perpetuating heterosexist assumptions.

While we sit at the bar watching women play pool, Sharon Vitrano is telling me about her expe-rience walking home through the Tenderloin after one of the annual Gay Pride Parades. As she and a woman friend approached a group of men in front of a Mom-and-Pop grocery store, the two stopped walking arm in arm. On her mind, she says, were the tensions growing out of San Fran-cisco's rapid gentrification, and escalating street violence linked to perceptions of gay people as wealthy real estate speculators. To Sharon's sur-prise and delight, one of the men shouted out, "Go ahead, hold hands! It's your day!"

In addition to the long hours of participant-observation so central to anthropological field-work, my analysis draws on 80 in-depth interviews conducted while in the field. Interview participants were divided evenly between women and men, with all but two identifying themselves as lesbian or gay. Random sampling is clearly an impossibil-ity for a population that is not only partially hidden or "closeted," but also lacks consensus as to the

criteria for membership (Morin 1977; NOGLSTP 1986). In general, I let self-identification be my guide for inclusion. Determined to avoid the race, class, and organizational bias that has character-ized so many studies of gay men and lesbians, I made my initial connections through personal con-tacts developed over the six years I had lived in San Francisco previous to the time the project got underway. The alternative—gaining entree through agencies, college classes, and advertisements—tends to weight a sample for "joiners," profes-sional interviewees, the highly educated, persons with an overtly political analysis, and individuals who see themselves as central (rather than mar-ginal) to the population in question.

By asking each person interviewed for names of potential participants, I utilized techniques of friendship pyramiding and snowball sampling to arrive at a sample varied in race, ethnicity, class, and class background. While the Bay Area is per-haps more generally politicized than other regions of the nation, the majority of interview partici-pants would not have portrayed themselves as po-litical activists. Approximately 36 percent were people of color; of the 64 percent who were White, 11 (or 14 percent of the total) were Jewish. Slightly over 50 percent came from working-class backgrounds, with an overlapping 58 percent em-ployed in working-class occupations at the time of the interview.

At the outset I had intended to arrange second interviews with a portion of the sample, but de-cided instead to seek informal contexts for follow-up that would allow me to interact with partici-pants as part of a group. Most of the direct quota-tions in this study are drawn from interviews, but some arose during dinner table conversations, birthday parties, a night out at a bar, or asides dur-ing a ball game. I strove not to select interview participants on the basis of the kind of experiences they claimed to have had. Individuals' character-izations of their personal histories ran the gamut from "boring" to "incredible," but I found these assessments a completely unreliable index of in-terest from an anthropological point of view.

Out of 82 people contacted, only two turned down my request for an interview. A few individuals made an effort to find me after hearing about the study, but most were far from self-selecting. The vast majority demanded great persistence and flexibility in scheduling (and rescheduling) on my part to convince them to participate. I believe this persistence is one reason this study includes voices not customarily heard when lesbians and gay men appear in the pages of books and journals: people who had constructed exceedingly private lives and could scarcely get over their disbelief at allowing themselves to be interviewed, people convinced that their experiences were uneventful or unworthy of note, people fearful that a researcher would go away and write an account lacking in respect for their identities or their perceptions.

To offset the tendency of earlier studies to focus on the White and wealthier sectors of lesbian and gay populations, I also utilized theoretic sampling. From a growing pool of contacts I deliberately selected people of color, people from working-class backgrounds, and individuals employed in working-class occupations.

What a busy day for a Friday, I think to myself, sinking into a chair after three back-to-back interviews. At the first apartment, stacks of papers had covered every counter, table, desk, and anything else approximating a flat surface. Before the interview began, Bernie Margolis, a Jewish man in his sixties, insisted on showing me his picture gallery. In one frame, a much younger Bernie stood next to Martin Luther King, Jr.; others held snapshots of children from a previous marriage and distinguished service awards from a variety of community organizations. Before I left, he asked me to proofread a political leaflet. From his Mission district flat I traveled up to the Fillmore to meet Rose Ellis, an African-American woman in her thirties. Laid off from her construction job, she was cooking a batch of blackeyed peas and watching soap operas when I arrived. After the interview, Rose asked me to play back part of the

tape through her roommate's stereo system—so that she could hear what her voice sounded like. A little later I hurried home to interview Annie Sorenson, a young white woman who described herself as a "lesbian virgin" with few gay or lesbian friends. From the vantage point of an easy chair reflecting back upon the day, my initial reaction is to wonder what these three people are doing in the same book.

In any sample this diverse, with so many different combinations of identities, theoretic sampling cannot hope to be "representative." To treat each individual as a representative of his or her race, for instance, would be a form of tokenism that glosses over the differences of gender, class, age, national origin, language, religion, and ability which crosscut race and ethnicity. At the same time, I am not interested in these categories as demographic variables, or as reified pigeonholes for people, but rather as identities meaningful to participants themselves. I concentrate here on the interpretive links participants made (or did not make) between sexual identity and other aspects of who they considered themselves to be, always with the awareness that identical symbols can carry very different meanings in different contexts. The tables in the appendix present demographic information on the interview sample, but—since this is not a statistically oriented study—merely to illustrate its diversity and provide descriptive information about participants.

Despite my efforts to incorporate differences, the sample remains weak in several areas, most notably the age range (which tends to cluster around the twenties and thirties), the inclusion of relatively few gay parents, and a bias toward fairly high levels of education. Given the age-, gender-, and race-segregated structure of gay institutions and social organization, these results may partially have been a function of my own situation and identities. I was in my late twenties at the time of the study, had no children, and usually ran out of boxes to check when asked to number my years of education on forms or surveys. But the sample's deficiencies also indicate my emphasis during fieldwork, since its composition does not reflect other aspects of identity as a White woman from a working-class background. I made the greatest effort to achieve breadth in the areas of present class, class background, and race/ethnicity.

In retrospect, I wish I had added age to this list of priorities. Judging from the gay men and lesbians in older age cohorts that I did interview, people who came out before the social movements of the 1950s–1970s may possess distinctive perspectives on the issue of disclosing their sexual identities to others, including relatives (cf. Hall 1978). Although those movements affected people of all ages who lived through that time period, older interview participants often cast their experiences in a comparative framework, distinguishing between what it meant to pursue same-sex erotic relations "then" and "now." Life experiences had made many acutely aware of the negative social and economic consequences that can follow from disclosure of a lesbian or gay identity. In her study of lesbians over 60, Monika Kehoe (1989) found that women who had married before they claimed a lesbian identity were likely to have maintained close ties with blood relatives (especially female kin) after coming out. Yet some of the same women had suffered ostracism at the hands of their heterosexual adult children.

To date there is conflicting evidence regarding the relationship between lesbian or gay identity and aging. Both the older gay men studied by Raymond Berger (1982b) and Kehoe's survey respondents reported loneliness and isolation, but their responses may have reflected the loneliness experienced by many people in the United States following retirement or the death of a partner. Further research needs to be conducted on the development of friendship networks among gay people over time, particularly given the high value historically placed on friendship by both lesbians and gay men. Do those networks expand, contract, or maintain their size as individuals grow older? Do gay people look more often to friendships, as opposed to other types of social

relations, for support and assistance as they age? Are older gay men and lesbians participating in the discourse on gay families to the same extent as their younger counterparts? Since most existing studies compare lesbians to heterosexual women and gay men to heterosexual men within their respective age cohorts, there is also a need for research that contrasts the experiences of older lesbians and gay men.

"Are you a lesbian? Are you gay?" Every other day one of these questions greets my efforts to set up interviews over the telephone. Halfway through my fieldwork, I remark on this concern with the researcher's identity while addressing a course in anthropological field methods. "Do you think you could have done this study if you weren't a lesbian?" asks a student from the back of the classroom. "No doubt," I reply, "but then again, it wouldn't have been the same study."

As late as 1982, Raymond Berger experienced difficulty locating lesbians of any class, color, or creed for a study of older gay people. Concluding that lesbians had little in the way of a visible public community, he gave up and confined his book to men. While gay male institutions may be more apparent to the eye, lesbians have their own (actually quite accessible) organizations and establishments, most well-documented in local community newspapers. My point here is that lesbians remained invisible *to Berger;* for me, as a woman, finding male participants proved more of a challenge. Recent work in cultural anthropology has stressed the importance of recognizing the researcher as a positioned subject (Mintz 1979; Rosaldo 1989). In my case, being a woman also influenced how I spent my time in the field: I passed more hours in lesbian clubs and women's groups than gay men's bars or male gyms.

Once I started to gain referrals, my lesbian identity clearly helped me lay claim to those bywords that anthropologists like to apply to relationships in the field when information is forthcoming: "trust" and "rapport." Many participants mentioned that they would not have talked to me had I been straight, and one or two cited "bad experiences" of having had their words misinterpreted by heterosexual researchers. In interviews with me people devoted relatively little time to addressing anti-gay stereotypes, and spoke freely about subjects such as butch/fem, gay marriage, sadomasochism (s/m), and drag queens—all topics controversial among gay men and lesbians themselves. Occasionally, of course, the larger context of eventual publication would intrude, and individuals would qualify their statements.

Presumptions of a common frame of reference and shared identity can also complicate the anthropologist's task by leaving cultural notions implicit, making her work to get people to state, explain, and situate the obvious. To study one's own culture involves a process of making the familiar strange, more the province of the poet or phenomenologist than of fieldworkers traveling abroad to unravel what seems puzzling about other societies. Early in the research my daily routine was structured by decisions about what to record. Everything around me seemed fair game for notes: one day I was living a social reality, the next day I was supposed to document it. Unlike anthropologists who have returned from the field to write ethnographies that contain accounts of reaching "their" island or village, I saw no possibility of framing an arrival scene to represent the inauguration of my fieldwork, except perhaps by drawing on the novelty of the first friend who asked (with a sidelong glance), "Are you taking notes on this?" My task could not even be characterized as an exploration of "strangeness inside the familiar," a phrase used by Frances FitzGerald (1986) to describe her investigation of the gay Castro district. For me, doing fieldwork among gay and lesbian San Franciscans did not entail uncovering some "exotic" corner of my native culture but rather discovering the stuff of everyday life.

After three rings I put aside the interview I've been transcribing and reluctantly head for the phone. It's my friend Mara calling for the first time in months. With a certain embarrassment, she tells me about the affair she's been having with a man. Everything is over now, she assures me, maintaining that the affair has no wider implications for her lesbian identity. "The reason I'm calling," she says half in jest, "is that I need an anthropologist. How would you like to ghostwrite a book about this whole thing? I'm going to call it My Year Among the Savages."

During interviews I used coming-out stories as a point of departure for investigating issues of identity and relationships with blood or adoptive relatives. Such narratives are customarily related to and for other lesbians and gay men rather than for the benefit of a heterosexual audience. Coming-out stories had the advantage of representing a category meaningful to participants themselves, a category so indigenous that one woman asked, "Do you want the 33 or the 45 rpm version?" Making new acquaintances was one type of occasion that often called for telling a coming-out story, and it seemed to me at times that my role as interviewer began to blend with the role of "lesbian friend of a friend."

In New York to do research at the Lesbian Herstory Archives, I notice that local news programs are dominated by coverage of the Statue of Liberty Restoration project. "Miss Liberty" and "Lady Liberty," the newscasters call her. To people in the United States, "Mrs. Liberty" would sound like a joke.

A note on terminology is apropos here. I frequently refer to "lesbians and gay men" to remind readers of gendered differences and to undermine the all too common assumption that findings about gay men hold equally for lesbians. At times, however, I employ "gay" and "gay people" as generic terms that embrace both women and men. In the Bay Area, women themselves held different opinions regarding the application of these terms. Those who had come out in association with the

women's movement were inclined to call themselves lesbians and reserve the word "gay" for
men. Younger women, women who maintained
social ties to gay men, and women with less connection to lesbian-feminism, were more apt to describe themselves as gay. In certain contexts a
broad range of people employed "gay" as a contrasting parallel to the categories "straight" and
"heterosexual."

Readers may also notice the conspicuous absence of the term "American" throughout the text.
A Latino participant playfully suggested the mod-
ifier "United Statesian" as a substitute that would
demonstrate respect for residents of Central and
South America—as well as Canada, Mexico, and
the Caribbean—who also reside in the Americas
name. I have elected to avoid such summary terms
altogether, not only in deference to the linguistic
claims of other peoples, but also because the label
"American" is so bound up with nationalist sentiment ("the American way") that it defies limitation to a descriptive reference.

I have interchanged "African-American" with
"Black," "Native American" with "American Indian," and "Mexican-American" with "Chicano"
and "Chicana." Preference for one or the other of
these terms varied with regional origin, generation, political involvement, and personal likes or
dislikes. In many contexts people referred to more
specific racial and ethnic identities (Cuban-Amer-
ican rather than Hispanic, Chinese-American
rather than Asian-American). Occasionally, however, they appealed to a collective racial identity
defined vis-à-vis the socially dominant categories

"White" or "Anglo." "Minorities" is clearly unsat-
isfactory for describing this collectivity, since
White people represent the numerical minority in
many parts of the Bay Area, not to mention the
world as a whole. I employ "people of color" for
lack of a better term, although the phrase remains
problematic. Racial identity and skin tone do not
always correspond to the color symbolism used to
depict race in the United States. The term "people
of color" can also reinforce racist perceptions of
White as the unmarked, and so more generically
human, category. White, of course, is also a color,
and white people are as implicated in race relations as anyone else in this society.

Defining class is always a vexed issue, especially in the United States, where class consciousness is often absent or superseded by other
identities (Jackman and Jackman 1983). Rayna
Rapp (1982) has astutely observed that class is a
process, not a position or a place. Class in this
sense cannot be indexed by income or plotted
along a sociological continuum from "upper" to
"lower." Nevertheless, to convey the range of the
interview sample, I have organized a rough classification of participants based on occupation (or
parents' occupations, in the case of class background), following a Marxist interpretation of
class as a relation to processes of production.
Where the term "middle class" appears in the text,
it is always in quotation marks to indicate its
status as an indigenous term used by people I encountered during fieldwork, rather than an analytic category of my own choosing.

REFERENCES

Berger, Raymond M. 1982a. "The Unseen Minority:
Older Gays and Lesbians." *Social Work* 27(3):
236–242.
———. 1982b. *Gay and Gray: The Older Homosexual
Man.* Urbana: University of Illinois Press.
D'Emilio, John. 1989. "Gay Politics, Gay Community:
San Francisco's Experience." In Martin Bauml
Duberman, Martha Vicinus, and George Chauncey

Jr., eds., *Hidden From History: Reclaiming the
Gay and Lesbian Past,* pp. 456–473. New York:
New American Library.
DeLeon, Richard and Courtney Brown. 1980. "Prelimi-
nary Estimates of Size of Gay/Bisexual Population
in San Francisco Based on Combined Data from
January and June S.F. Charter Commission Sur-
veys." Mimeograph.

FitzGerald, Frances. 1986. *Cities on a Hill: A Journey Through Contemporary American Cultures.* New York: Simon & Schuster.

Hall, Marny. 1978. "Lesbian Families: Cultural and Clinical Issues." *Social Work* 23(4):380–385.

Kehoe, Monika. 1989. *Lesbians Over 60 Speak for Themselves.* New York: Harrington Park Press.

Jackman, Mary R. and Robert W. Jackman. 1983. *Class Awareness in the United States.* Berkeley: University of California Press.

Mintz, Sidney W. 1979. "The Anthropological Interview and the Life History." *Oral History Review* 17:18–26.

Morin, Stephen F. 1977. "Heterosexual Bias in Psychological Research on Lesbianism and Male Homosexuality." *American Psychologist* 32:629–637.

National Organization of Gay & Lesbian Scientists & Technical Professionals (NOGLSTP). 1986. "Measuring the Gay and Lesbian Population." Pamphlet.

Rapp, Rayna. 1982. "Family and Class in Contemporary America: Notes Toward an Understanding of Ideology." In Barrie Thorne with Marilyn Yalom, eds., *Rethinking the Family,* pp. 168–187. New York: Longman.

———. 1987. "Toward a Nuclear Freeze? The Gender Politics of Euro-American Kinship Analysis." In Jane Fishburne Collier and Sylvia Junko Yanagisako, eds., *Gender and Kinship: Essays Toward a Unified Analysis,* pp. 119–131. Stanford: Stanford University Press.

Rosaldo, Michelle Z. 1983. "The Shame of Headhunters and the Autonomy of Self." *Ethos* 11(3):135–151.

———. 1984. "Toward an Anthropology of Self and Feeling." In Richard Shweder and Robert Levine, eds., *Culture Theory: Essays on Mind, Self, and Emotion,* pp. 137–157. New York: Cambridge University Press.

Warren, Carol A. B. 1974. *Identity and Community in the Gay World.* New York: Wiley.

———. 1977. "Fieldwork in the Gay World: Issues in Phenomenological Research." *Journal of Social Issues* 33(4):93–107.

A White Guy among Vietnamese Women

STEVEN J. GOLD

Between 1982 and 1990, I conducted participant observation research within the Vietnamese community of California. This article discusses some of the dynamics involved as I, a native-born, heterosexual, White male, who knows only a few words of Vietnamese, studied Vietnamese women. While each research interaction engaged a multiplicity of identities, those of gender, nationality, language, citizenship status, age, and social class certainly loom large in determining the kinds of interactions that transpired during the course of my research.

In retrospect, the key factors that shaped my relations with Vietnamese women were tenure in the United States and social class. I tended to develop much better rapport with women who had been in the United States a considerable period of time and were well educated. I found that I was able to reduce social gaps by being a good listener and referring to common interests and experiences. In contrast, I had much less interaction with recently arrived and less educated women.

My interactions with Vietnamese women were shaped by the type of fieldwork roles through which I contacted them. Despite their relatively recent settlement in the United States, the Vietnamese are marked by a great deal of diversity in terms of class, social origins, religion, ethnicity, and patterns of settlement. Accordingly, to develop a well-rounded picture of the Vietnamese community, I used several strategies to contact various types of refugees.

To meet recently arrived refugees, I worked as an English teacher. Obtaining referrals from a church-based volunteer agency, I visited a network of Vietnamese households on a weekly basis

for a year and a half in Oakland. To learn about the resettlement system and its clients, I served for two years as a resettlement worker, first as a volunteer and later for pay, in two San Francisco Vietnamese-oriented resettlement agencies. Finally, as a college professor, I was invited by the Asian students at my institution (many of whom were Vietnamese) to be the faculty advisor of their association.

To increase my access to these communities, I conducted more than sixty in-depth interviews with refugees and others who were knowledgeable about them. I concentrated on interviewing community leaders and activists, resettlement staff, and the self-employed. Finally, I attended numerous refugee community events, spent time in refugee neighborhoods, and reviewed popular and ethnic media reports and academic literature regarding Vietnamese refugees. In several cases, I developed friendly relations with the Vietnamese refugees with whom I worked, and we shared meals, parties, weekend trips, home visits, and daily interaction in the course of work and school (Gold 1992).

GENDER AND PATTERNS OF INTERACTION IN VIETNAMESE HOMES

Most of my visits to refugees' homes in the capacity of volunteer English teacher involved interactions with males. This was due to both demographics and social practices. Demographically, the Vietnamese boat people who arrived in the United States during the late 1970s and early 1980s were a disproportionately male population. In 1981, 55 percent of Southeast Asian refugees in the United States were male (ORR 1983, table 8). (In Vietnam, men were subject to being drafted into the Vietnamese army—among the largest in the world at that time—and were conscripted into various work programs that involved their forcible removal to remote "New Economic Zones.") In addition, among many Vietnamese, social activities are highly segregated by sex. Following a relatively common double standard, men are free to maintain an active social life, while women—especially those not married—are encouraged to remain at home. Hence, the household networks I encountered were male in composition, and my contact with women members of these households was often limited.

For example, one household that I visited regularly for over a year included four adult men and a junior-high-aged girl, Lien, the sister of two of the men. Because of her age and full-time attendance in school, Lien could speak English better than any of the male household members. (I knew this because her brothers showed me essays she had written.) However, I had virtually no contact with Lien. When I would visit their home, she would often be at another apartment, and when I invited the family to visit my house, Lien did not come. This pattern was fairly common. Often, when I visited refugees' homes, women would stay in the kitchen or a back bedroom. Similarly when I would visit a coffee shop or restaurant with a group of refugees, I would be accompanied by males alone. I was never sure if my lack of interaction with women was the choice of the women themselves or due to the prerogative of the male household members.

This rule was not always the case, however. The Nguyen family of Oakland often invited along their cousin Debbie—a high school student from San Jose—when we got together on weekends. Debbie was well adapted to American culture and spoke English virtually without an accent. As the most Americanized member of her extended family, Debbie was well suited to play the role of cultural intermediary between the Nguyens and me.

Forms of typical "male bonding"—including viewing pictures of women, friendly competition, and shared interest in technology and mechanics—functioned as a social lubricant and basis for solidarity in my interactions with recently arrived Vietnamese men (Berger 1972). Several young refugees displayed "pin-ups" of American actresses and Hong Kong starlets in their apartments. The Ung brothers taught me about animals and numbers, which, in Chinese and Vietnamese culture, are symbolic of sexual prowess. Refugees often referred to these carnal topics in a good-natured and informal manner. Some friendly competition also took place: solving puzzles and riddles, playing the guitar, or competing at carnival games. Finally, we regularly discussed typically male mechanical interests—cars, auto repair, electronic equipment, and the like—as a means of maintaining a social atmosphere and bridging cultural boundaries.

Further, because these refugees were generally better at playing the guitar, competing at carnival games, and solving puzzles than I, this allowed some equalization of our social ranks in which I, as a native-born, White, middle-class male acting within the role of "teacher," had greater status than they. Another way in which male refugees were able to enhance their status was by inviting me to Vietnamese restaurants, friends' homes, or social events—where I was the outsider—and refusing to allow me to pay for food. These gender-based patterns of sociability that I shared with recently arrived Vietnamese men seemed to minimize the effects of social class in our development of social relations. Among women, those with whom I generally developed the best rapport were middle class and long settled in the States. However, my closest relations with Vietnamese men were with the recently arrived and working-class refugees with whom I spent a great deal of time.

ACKNOWLEDGING GENDER AND RACE CONFLICTS THROUGH TEASING AND DISCUSSION

Vietnamese culture is influenced by Confucianism and, as such, has a very strong element of patriarchy. At the same time, the Vietnamese tradition is rich with strong women. In fact, the original Vietnamese anticolonists were women: the Trung sisters who began the nation's fight against the Chinese over two millennia ago (Vinh ND; Marr 1971). Further, the decades of war encountered by Vietnam since the early 1950s meant that men were often absent, opening certain nontraditional opportunities and responsibilities for women. Reflecting this pattern, as Nazli Kibria notes in *Family Tightrope* (1993), Vietnamese gender relations in the United States involve a complexly interwoven arrangement of male dominance and women's empowerment.

In social settings, this is manifested as Vietnamese women frequently make joking or teasing comments about their use of various techniques to subvert patriarchy and take advantage of male vanity (a kind of sociability based on gender difference roughly analogous to the bonding drawing on common gender as discussed above). Such jokes often depict women's manipulation of several men to reduce the influence of any single man over them. For example, upon showing some Vietnamese women with whom I worked a photograph of my wife, one chided, "She's good looking—she can get a better boyfriend than you."

At other times, Vietnamese women referred to the inequalities they faced in a more direct manner, discussing the social injustices—based on race, class, gender, and ideology—within their own community and the conflicts they have encountered with the individuals, agencies, and social groups of American society. They sometimes described their status as women, foreigners, and minorities in a society dominated by native-born, White men.

A job placement worker in a resettlement agency was among the most outspoken in her expressions of hostility toward what she sarcastically called "the great White American." She would jest about the similarity of her Vietnamese name—Bich—to the American epithet, suggesting that she would not be a meek, deferential, and compliant woman. Nor would she tolerate what

she felt to be ethnic discrimination. For example, she spoke at length of the damage done to her community by stereotypes promoted by the American mass media saying, "Don't let them do it to us." Apparently Bich's outspoken attitude embarrassed some of her Vietnamese coworkers (men and women alike), as they would usually apologize after her outbursts.

Vietnamese women were often politically sophisticated. At the same time, many described their ability to tolerate the conflicts and abuses inherent in resettlement work as rooted in religious faith. Such was the case of Minh, a long-established refugee who was one of only a handful of Vietnamese women in California to direct a resettlement agency. She described her reactions to constantly being "the token woman," saying that she was frequently the sole female present in a meeting of refugee leaders. Minh described how male Vietnamese community leaders thought of her as a man and told her so, leaving her puzzled as to whether she had been complimented or insulted. She shook her head as she told me that even her own son (whom she had brought to the States after becoming a war widow in the 1960s) initially doubted her ability to run an agency.

SHARING COMMON CONCERNS IN RESETTLEMENT WORK

Through my research and my employment in resettlement agencies, I became knowledgeable about important issues, concerns, and personalities in the Vietnamese refugee community. When I worked with or interviewed Vietnamese women like Minh who shared these concerns, our common interests offered a means of bridging some of the gaps implied by gender, nationality—status, language, and ethnicity. Many had attended universities and knew of Asian American scholars and community leaders with whom I was familiar, so we shared many common points on which to base our relationships.

In some cases, women as well as men enjoyed discussing community matters with someone such as myself, who was knowledgeable about the community but at the same time not as immediately affected by the complex of political conflicts and loyalties within it. For example, Mai, a social service worker, asserted that she felt more comfortable interacting with non-Vietnamese resettlement staff, whether Asian American, Latino, or White, male or female, than she did with Vietnamese resettlement staff.

NEUTRALIZATION BY REFERRING TO THE SHARED IMMIGRANT EXPERIENCE

One way I learned to address the gap between myself and refugees was by pointing out my own family's relatively recent immigrant heritage. In interviews and casual discussion, I would tell refugees that my grandparents had come to the United States as immigrants and that my parents grew up in an environment similar to the one they occupied—in immigrant tenements, my mother's family working in the garment business, and my father's family living behind a small grocery store—Jewish shopkeepers in a hostile Irish neighborhood.

Interestingly, many Vietnamese have developed a degree of empathy with American Jews, thus offering a basis for connection. Mimi, who peppered her conversation with Yiddish expressions, told me that she identified with Jews because, like Vietnamese, they are refugees, members of a minority group, value education, have suffered religious persecution, and emphasize self-employment. Many Vietnamese have met Jews because they are well represented among the ranks of resettlement workers, and a fair proportion have been resettled by HIAS (The Hebrew Immigrant Aid Society). (From 1979–1991, over 20,000 Southeast Asian Refugees have been resettled by HIAS and thousands more received resettlement aid from Jewish agencies and service providers [HIAS 1995; ORR 1983: 58].) Finally, the representative of an Orange County Vietnamese association told me that some refugees see a prophetic parallel between their own group's experience of exile from Vietnam and the story of the Jews' exile from and eventual return to Israel.

TEACHER AND STUDENT ROLES

Vietnamese culture values education and therefore, the teacher-student relationship is well understood and highly valued. In fact, rapport was facilitated by my status as a graduate student and, later, as a professor. In the course of fieldwork, Vietnamese women often adopted the "teacher" role, informing me about their jobs in resettlement agencies and offering their opinions on the larger community. During my early period of volunteer work in a San Francisco resettlement agency, Tuy, my Chinese-Vietnamese supervisor, would sometimes laugh with her colleagues at my endless and sometimes naive questions about resettlement work. Similarly, a Vietnamese college administrator generously helped me with translation and terminology and took me to several Vietnamese restaurants in the San Gabriel Valley.

Later, as a professor, I developed close relations as a teacher and adviser with Vietnamese students. In contrast to students of other ethnic backgrounds, who tend to downplay differences in hierarchy between faculty and students, Vietnamese were especially interested in involving me as an adviser. I was offered deference and attention but was also requested to provide extensive advice, direct independent studies, provide job references, and the like. It was one of these women students who explicitly invited me to be the adviser of the college's Asian student association. Interestingly, during the several years that I was adviser to the Asian Students' Association, they also had an Asian woman faculty member as co-adviser. Apparently, they felt that the combination of a White man and an Asian woman was ideal for their group.

CONCLUSIONS

Class and assimilation were crucial features in shaping my interactions with Vietnamese refugee women. Generally, I was able to develop good rapport with Vietnamese women who were familiar with American life, spoke English, and shared common concerns involving education and the nature of the Vietnamese community in the United States. On the other hand, I had much less contact with recently arrived Vietnamese women and those who were less educated. My relations among recently arrived Vietnamese tended be within male networks, and only a few of the women who were part of these networks were open to interacting with me. For insights into this group of Vietnamese women, I had to rely on the comments of middle-class Vietnamese women, recently arrived men, or the scholarship of women colleagues, such as Kibria (1993) (Gold and Kibria 1992).

In conclusion, differences of gender, nationality, class, and language shaped the nature of my research on Vietnamese women. As a male, I simply lacked access to many female refugees. Concurrently, however, shared involvement in male-oriented interests allowed me to develop rapport with Vietnamese men despite our vastly distinct cultural and linguistic origins and class status. Further, because I was seen as a "knowledgeable outsider," women resettlement workers often felt relatively comfortable in describing their perspectives to me and were able to share confidences that would not have been extended to co-ethnics. In all of these ways, the social categories to which I belong and the relationship between my status and that of the refugees with whom I was doing fieldwork significantly affected my access to and interpretations of this population. Personal and group characteristics, which originate in the larger social structure, influence the nature and findings of social research.

REFERENCES

Berger, John. (1972). *Ways of Seeing*. London: BBC.

Gold, Steven. (1992). *Refugee Communities: A Comparative Field Study*. Newbury Park, CA: Sage.

Gold, Steven, and Nazli Kibria. (1993). "Vietnamese Refugees and Blocked Mobility," *Asian and Pacific Migration Journal*, 2 (1): 27–56.

HIAS. (1995). Statistical Report.

Kibria, Nazli. (1993). *Family Tightrope: The Changing Lives of Vietnamese Americans*. Princeton, N.J.: Princeton University Press.

Marr, David G. (1971). *Vietnamese Anticolonialism 1885–1925*. Berkeley: University of California Press.

ORR (Office of Refugee Resettlement). (1983). Report to Congress: Refugee Resettlement Program.

Vinh, Pham Kim. (ND). *The Vietnamese Culture: An Introduction*. Solana Beach, CA: PM Enterprises.

PART TWO

Bodies

Chapter 3   Embodiments of Control and Resistance

Chapter 4   Violence

Chapter 5   Reproductive Politics

The old Freudian dictum that "biology is destiny," that women's and men's different *social* positions and activities are simply reflections of *natural* differences between the sexes, is deeply grounded in our cultural assumptions. But this belief does not stand up to critical scrutiny. First, even when we acknowledge that there are some average differences between women's and men's bodies (e.g., on average, men have a higher muscle-to-fat ratio than women do), average differences are not categorical differences (e.g., some women are more muscular than some men). Second, average bodily differences between women and men do not necessarily translate into particular social structures or practices. In fact, recent research in the sociology of the body shows a dynamic, reciprocal relationship between bodies and their social environments. For examples, boys and men have been encouraged and rewarded for "building" muscular bodies, whereas girls and women have been discouraged or punished for this. Even among today's fitness-conscious young women, most feel that "too much muscle" is antithetical to attractiveness. These social beliefs and practices result in more muscular male bodies and "slimmed" or "toned" female bodies that, together, appear to reflect "natural" differences.

In short, average bodily differences between women and men are at least as much a *result* of social beliefs and practices as they are a cause. In fact, since the early 1970s, many feminists have pointed to patriarchal control over women's bodies (e.g., sexual control, rape and other forms of violence, medical control of women reproduction, the imposition of commercial fashions and narrow beauty standards, cultural beliefs about food and an obsession with thinness) as a major locus of men's control over women. In short, many feminists argued that social inequalities were predicated on men's assertion of their own will through the objectification and exploitation of women's bodies. This is a power-ful observation that informed a great deal of fruitful feminist organizing around issues like girls' and women's eating disorders, rape crisis centers, and women's shelters against do-mestic violence. But as the two articles in Chapter 3 demonstrate, the view of women as disempowered body-objects and men as empowered body-subjects tends to overgeneral-ize about a more complex reality. Becky Wangsgaard Thompson's article shows that women's eating problems tend to reflect coping and survival strategies that vary signifi-cantly among African American, Latina, and White women. And Thomas J. Gerschick and Adam Stephen Miller's analysis of physically disabled men shows how a marginal-ized group of men relates to dominant conceptions of masculinity that stress physical strength and independence.

Men's violence against other men on the streets and in wars has historically been more visible than men's violence against women. Only very recently have we begun to understand the extent of men's violence against women and the more general implications of this violence for gender relations. Together, the articles in Chapter 4 explore several di-mensions of the relationship between gender and violence. Jack Straton draws on recent studies to dispel the "myth of the battered husband," and Beth E. Richie and Valli Kanuha discuss the particular issues and barriers that battered women of color have faced in the public health care system. Next, Tim Beneke draws from his own research with convicted rapists to dispel popular rape myths, and Nancy Matthews's article discusses the crucial importance of expanding racial diversity in the antirape movement. Finally, Michael Messner examines male athletes' violence against other men and its broader significance for gender relations.

Chapter 5 focuses on a hotly debated area of body politics: abortion and reproduc-tion. First, Debbie Nathan's description of abortion around the Texas–Mexico border re-veals the dangers and risks associated with abortion when it is limited or outlawed by state or national law. The subsequent two articles raise troubling questions about the impact and rapid adoption of new reproductive technologies. Rayna Rapp examines amniocente-sis and raises critical questions about the shifting definitions of motherhood and abortion among women of different racial/ethnic and social class backgrounds. And finally, Bar-bara Katz Rothman examines the implications of artificial insemination and surrogate motherhood. Rothman's suggestion that surrogacy allows some "upper class women [to] have some of the privileges of patriarchy" introduces a difficult but crucial question into feminist discourse about bodies, power, and social equality.

"A Way Outa No Way"

Eating Problems among African-American, Latina, and White Women

BECKY WANGSGAARD THOMPSON

Bulimia, anorexia, binging, and extensive dieting are among the many health issues women have been confronting in the last 20 years. Until recently, however, there has been almost no research about eating problems among African-American, Latina, Asian-American, or Native American women, working-class women, or lesbians.[1] In fact, according to the normative epidemiological portrait, eating problems are largely a white, middle-, and upper-class heterosexual phenomenon. Further, while feminist research has documented how eating problems are fueled by sexism, there has been almost no attention to how other systems of oppression may also be implicated in the development of eating problems.

In this article, I reevaluate the portrayal of eating problems as issues of appearance based in the "culture of thinness." I propose that eating problems begin as ways women cope with various traumas including sexual abuse, racism, classism, sexism, heterosexism, and poverty. Showing the

interface between these traumas and the onset of eating problems explains why women may use eating to numb pain and cope with violations to their bodies. This theoretical shift also permits an understanding of the economic, political, social, educational, and cultural resources that women need to change their relationship to food and their bodies.

EXISTING RESEARCH ON EATING PROBLEMS

There are three theoretical models used to explain the epidemiology, etiology, and treatment of eating problems. The biomedical model offers important scientific research about possible physiological causes of eating problems and the physiological dangers of purging and starvation (Copeland 1985; Spack 1985). However, this model adopts medical treatment strategies that may disempower and traumatize women (Garner 1985; Orbach 1985). In addition, this model ignores many social, historical, and cultural factors that influence women's eating patterns. The psychological model identifies eating problems as "multidimensional disorders" that are influenced by biological, psychological, and cultural factors (Garfinkel and Garner 1982). While useful in its exploration of effective therapeutic treatments, this model, like the biomedical one, tends to neglect women of color, lesbians, and working-class women.

AUTHOR'S NOTE: The research for this study was partially supported by an American Association of University Women Fellowship in Women's Studies. An earlier version of this article was presented at the New England Women's Studies Association Meeting in 1990 in Kingston, Rhode Island. I am grateful to Margaret Andersen, Liz Bennett, Lynn Davidman, Mary Gilfus, Evelynn Hammonds, and two anonymous reviewers for their comprehensive and perceptive comments on earlier versions of this article.

The third model, offered by feminists, asserts that eating problems are gendered. This model explains why the vast majority of people with eating problems are women, how gender socialization and sexism may relate to eating problems, and how masculine models of psychological development have shaped theoretical interpretations. Feminists offer the culture of thinness model as a key reason why eating problems predominate among women. According to this model, thinness is a culturally, socially, and economically enforced requirement for female beauty. This imperative makes women vulnerable to cycles of dieting, weight loss, and subsequent weight gain, which may lead to anorexia and bulimia (Chernin 1981; Orbach 1978, 1985; Smead 1984).

Feminists have rescued eating problems from the realm of individual psychopathology by showing how the difficulties are rooted in systematic and pervasive attempts to control women's body sizes and appetites. However, researchers have yet to give significant attention to how race, class, and sexuality influence women's understanding of their bodies and appetites. The handful of epidemiological studies that include African-American women and Latinas casts doubt on the accuracy of the normative epidemiological portrait. The studies suggest that this portrait reflects which particular populations of women have been studied rather than actual prevalence (Andersen and Hay 1985; Gray, Ford, and Kelly 1987; Hsu 1987; Nevo 1985; Silber 1986).

More important, this research shows that bias in research has consequences for women of color. Tomas Silber (1986) asserts that many well-trained professionals have either misdiagnosed or delayed their diagnoses of eating problems among African-American and Latina women due to stereotypical thinking that these problems are restricted to white women. As a consequence, when African-American women or Latinas are diagnosed, their eating problems tend to be more severe due to extended processes of starvation prior to intervention. In her autobiographical account of her eating problems, Retha Powers (1989), an Af-

rican-American woman, describes being told not to worry about her eating problems since "fat is more acceptable in the Black community" (p. 78). Stereotypical perceptions held by her peers and teachers of the "maternal Black woman" and the "persistent mammy-brickhouse Black woman image" (p. 134) made it difficult for Powers to find people who took her problems with food seriously.

Recent work by African-American women reveals that eating problems often relate to women's struggles against a "simultaneity of oppression" (Clarke 1982; Naylor 1985; White 1991). Byllye Avery (1990), the founder of the National Black Women's Health Project, links the origins of eating problems among African-American women to the daily stress of being undervalued and overburdened at home and at work. In Evelyn C. White's (1990) anthology, *The Black Woman's Health Book: Speaking for Ourselves,* Georgiana Arnold (1990) links her eating problems partly to racism and racial isolation during childhood.

Recent feminist research also identifies factors that are related to eating problems among lesbians (Brown 1987; Dworkin 1989; Iazzetto 1989; Schoenfielder and Wieser 1983). In her clinical work, Brown (1987) found that lesbians who have internalized a high degree of homophobia are more likely to accept negative attitudes about fat than are lesbians who have examined their internalized homophobia. Autobiographical accounts by lesbians have also indicated that secrecy about eating problems among lesbians partly reflects their fear of being associated with a stigmatized illness ("What's Important" 1988).

Attention to African-American women, Latinas, and lesbians paves the way for further research that explores the possible interface between facing multiple oppressions and the development of eating problems. In this way, this study is part of a larger feminist and sociological research agenda that seeks to understand how race, class, gender, nationality, and sexuality inform women's experiences and influence theory production.

METHODOLOGY

I conducted 18 life history interviews and administered lengthy questionnaires to explore eating problems among African-American, Latina, and White women. I employed a snowball sample, a method in which potential respondents often first learn about the study from people who have already participated. This method was well suited for the study since it enabled women to get information about me and the interview process from people they already knew. Typically, I had much contact with the respondents prior to the interview. This was particularly important given the secrecy associated with this topic (Russell 1986; Silberstein, Striegel-Moore, and Rodin 1987), the necessity of women of color and lesbians to be discriminating about how their lives are studied, and the fact that I was conducting across-race research.

To create analytical notes and conceptual categories from the data, I adopted Glaser and Strauss's (1967) technique of theoretical sampling, which directs the researcher to collect, analyze, and test hypotheses during the sampling process (rather than imposing theoretical categories onto the data). After completing each interview transcription, I gave a copy to each woman who wanted one. After reading their interviews, some of the women clarified or made additions to the interview text.

Demographics of the Women in the Study

The 18 women I interviewed included 5 African-American women, 5 Latinas, and 8 White women. Of these women, 12 are lesbian and 6 are heterosexual. Five women are Jewish, 8 are Catholic, and 5 are Protestant. Three women grew up outside of the United States. The women represented a range of class backgrounds (both in terms of origin and current class status) and ranged in age from 19 to 46 years old (with a median age of 33.5 years).

The majority of the women reported having had a combination of eating problems (at least two of the following: bulimia, compulsive eating, anorexia, and/or extensive dieting). In addition, the particular types of eating problems often changed during a woman's life span. (For example, a woman might have been bulimic during adolescence and anorexic as an adult.) Among the women, 28 percent had been bulimic, 17 percent had been bulimic and anorexic, and 5 percent had been anorexic. All of the women who had been anorexic or bulimic also had a history of compulsive eating and extensive dieting. Of the women, 50 percent were compulsive eaters and dieters (39 percent) or compulsive eaters (11 percent) but had not been bulimic or anorexic.

Two-thirds of the women have had eating problems for more than half of their lives, a finding that contradicts the stereotype of eating problems as transitory. The weight fluctuation among the women varied from 16 to 160 pounds, with an average fluctuation of 74 pounds. This drastic weight change illustrates the degree to which the women adjusted to major changes in body size at least once during their lives as they lost, gained, and lost weight again. The average age of onset was 11 years old, meaning that most of the women developed eating problems prior to puberty. Almost all of the women (88 percent) consider themselves as still having a problem with eating, although the majority believe they are well on the way to recovery.

THE INTERFACE OF TRAUMA AND EATING PROBLEMS

One of the most striking findings in this study was the range of traumas the women associated with the origins of their eating problems, including racism, sexual abuse, poverty, sexism, emotional or physical abuse, heterosexism, class injuries, and acculturation.[2] The particular constellation of eating problems among the women did not vary with race, class, sexuality, or nationality. Women from various race and class backgrounds attributed the origins of their eating problems to sexual abuse, sexism, and emotional and/or physical abuse.

Among some of the African-American and Latina women, eating problems were also associated with poverty, racism, and class injuries. Heterosexism was a key factor in the onset of bulimia, compulsive eating, and extensive dieting among some of the lesbians. These oppressions are not the same nor are the injuries caused by them. And certainly, there are a variety of potentially harmful ways that women respond to oppression (such as using drugs, becoming a workaholic, or committing suicide). However, for all these women, eating was a way of coping with trauma.

Sexual Abuse

Sexual abuse was the most common trauma that the women related to the origins of their eating problems. Until recently, there has been virtually no research exploring the possible relationship between these two phenomena. Since the mid-1980s, however, researchers have begun identifying connections between the two, a task that is part of a larger feminist critique of traditional psychoanalytic symptomatology (DeSalvo 1989; Herman 1981; Masson 1984). Results of a number of incidence studies indicate that between one-third and two-thirds of women who have eating problems have been abused (Oppenheimer et al. 1985; Root and Fallon 1988). In addition, a growing number of therapists and researchers have offered interpretations of the meaning and impact of eating problems for survivors of sexual abuse (Bass and Davis 1988; Goldfarb 1987; Iazzetto 1989; Swink and Leveille 1986). Kearney-Cooke (1988) identifies dieting and binging as common ways in which women cope with frequent psychological consequences of sexual abuse (such as body image disturbances, distrust of people and one's own experiences, and confusion about one's feelings). Root and Fallon (1989) specify ways that victimized women cope with assaults by binging and purging: bulimia serves many functions, including anesthetizing the negative feelings associated with victimization. Iazzetto's innovative study (1989), based on in-depth interviews and art therapy ses-

sions, examines how a woman's relationship to her body changes as a consequence of sexual abuse. Iazzetto discovered that the process of leaving the body (through progressive phases of numbing, dissociating and denying) that often occurs during sexual abuse parallels the process of leaving the body made possible through binging.

Among the women I interviewed, 61 percent were survivors of sexual abuse (11 of the 18 women), most of whom made connections between sexual abuse and the beginning of their eating problems. Binging was the most common method of coping identified by the survivors. Binging helped women "numb out" or anesthetize their feelings. Eating sedated, alleviated anxiety, and combated loneliness. Food was something that they could trust and was accessible whenever they needed it. Antonia (a pseudonym) is an Italian-American woman who was first sexually abused by a male relative when she was four years old. Retrospectively, she knows that binging was a way she coped with the abuse. When the abuse began, and for many years subsequently, Antonia often woke up during the middle of the night with anxiety attacks or nightmares and would go straight to the kitchen cupboards to get food. Binging helped her block painful feelings because it put her back to sleep.

Like other women in the study who began binging when they were very young, Antonia was not always fully conscious as she binged. She described eating during the night as "sleep walking. It was mostly desperate—like I had to have it." Describing why she ate after waking up with nightmares, Antonia said, "What else do you do? If you don't have any coping mechanisms, you eat." She said that binging made her "disappear," which made her feel protected. Like Antonia, most of the women were sexually abused before puberty; four of them before they were five years old. Given their youth, food was the most accessible and socially acceptable drug available to them. Because all of the women endured the psychological consequences alone, it is logical that they coped with tactics they could do alone as well.

One reason Antonia binged (rather than dieted) to cope with sexual abuse is that she saw little reason to try to be the small size girls were supposed to be. Growing up as one of the only Italian Americans in what she described as a "very WASP town," Antonia felt that everything from her weight and size to having dark hair on her upper lip were physical characteristics she was supposed to hide. From a young age she knew she "never embodied the essence of the good girl. I don't like her. I have never acted like her. I can't be her. I sort of gave up." For Antonia, her body was the physical entity that signified her outsider status. When the sexual abuse occurred, Antonia felt she had lost her body. In her mind, the body she lived in after the abuse was not really hers. By the time Antonia was 11, her mother put her on diet pills. Antonia began to eat behind closed doors as she continued to cope with the psychological consequences of sexual abuse and feeling like a cultural outsider.

Extensive dieting and bulimia were also ways in which women responded to sexual abuse. Some women thought that the men had abused them because of their weight. They believed that if they were smaller, they might not have been abused. For example when Elsa, an Argentine woman, was sexually abused at the age of 11, she thought her chubby size was the reason the man was abusing her. Elsa said, "I had this notion that these old perverts liked these plump girls. You heard adults say this too. Sex and flesh being associated." Looking back on her childhood, Elsa believes she made fat the enemy partly due to the shame and guilt she felt about the incest. Her belief that fat was the source of her problems was also supported by her socialization. Raised by strict German governesses in an upper-class family, Elsa was taught that a woman's weight was a primary criterion for judging her worth. Her mother "was socially conscious of walking into places with a fat daughter and maybe people staring at her." Her father often referred to Elsa's body as "shot to hell." When asked to describe how she felt about her body when growing up,

Elsa described being completely alienated from her body. She explained,

> Remember in school when they talk about the difference between body and soul? I always felt like my soul was skinny. My soul was free. My soul sort of flew. I was tied down by this big bag of rocks that was my body. I had to drag it around. It did pretty much what it wanted and I had a lot of trouble controlling it. It kept me from doing all the things that I dreamed of.

As is true for many women who have been abused, the split that Elsa described between her body and soul was an attempt to protect herself from the pain she believed her body caused her. In her mind, her fat body was what had "bashed in her dreams." Dieting became her solution, but, as is true for many women in the study, this strategy soon led to cycles of binging and weight fluctuation.

Ruthie, a Puerto Rican woman who was sexually abused from 12 until 16 years of age, described bulimia as a way she responded to sexual abuse. As a child, Ruthie liked her body. Like many Puerto Rican women of her mother's generation, Ruthie's mother did not want skinny children, interpreting that as a sign that they were sick or being fed improperly. Despite her mother's attempts to make her gain weight, Ruthie remained thin through puberty. When a male relative began sexually abusing her, Ruthie's sense of her body changed dramatically. Although she weighed only 100 pounds, she began to feel fat and thought her size was causing the abuse. She had seen a movie on television about Romans who made themselves throw up and so she began doing it, in hopes that she could look like the "little kid" she was before the abuse began. Her symbolic attempt to protect herself by purging stands in stark contrast to the psychoanalytic explanation of eating problems as an "abnormal" repudiation of sexuality. In fact, her actions and those of many other survivors indicate a girl's logical attempt to protect herself (including her sexuality) by being a size and shape that does not seem as vulnerable to sexual assault.

These women's experiences suggest many reasons why women develop eating problems as a consequence of sexual abuse. Most of the survivors "forgot" the sexual abuse after its onset and were unable to retrieve the abuse memories until many years later. With these gaps in memory, frequently they did not know why they felt ashamed, fearful, or depressed. When sexual abuse memories resurfaced in dreams, they often woke feeling upset but could not remember what they had dreamed. These free floating, unexplained feelings left the women feeling out of control and confused. Binging or focusing on maintaining a new diet were ways women distracted or appeased themselves, in turn, helping them regain a sense of control. As they grew older, they became more conscious of the consequences of these actions. Becoming angry at themselves for binging or promising themselves they would not purge again was a way to direct feelings of shame and self-hate that often accompanied the trauma.

Integral to this occurrence was a transference process in which the women displaced onto their bodies painful feelings and memories that actually derived from or were directed toward the persons who caused the abuse. Dieting became a method of trying to change the parts of their bodies they hated, a strategy that at least initially brought success as they lost weight. Purging was a way women tried to reject the body size they thought was responsible for the abuse. Throwing up in order to lose the weight they thought was making them vulnerable to the abuse was a way to try to find the body they had lost when the abuse began.

Poverty

Like sexual abuse, poverty is another injury that may make women vulnerable to eating problems. One woman I interviewed attributed her eating problems directly to the stress caused by poverty. Yolanda is a Black Cape Verdean mother who began eating compulsively when she was 27 years old. After leaving an abusive husband in her early 20s, Yolanda was forced to go on welfare. As a single mother with small children and few financial resources, she tried to support herself and her children on $539 a month. Yolanda began binging in the evenings after putting her children to bed.

Eating was something she could do alone. It would calm her, help her deal with loneliness, and make her feel safe. Food was an accessible commodity that was cheap. She ate three boxes of macaroni and cheese when nothing else was available. As a single mother with little money, Yolanda felt as if her body was the only thing she had left. As she described it,

> I am here, [in my body] 'cause there is no where else for me to go. Where am I going to go? This is all I got...that probably contributes to putting on so much weight cause staying in your body, in your home, in yourself, you don't go out. You aren't around other people...You hide and as long as you hide you don't have to face...nobody can see you eat. You are safe.

When she was eating, Yolanda felt a momentary reprieve from her worries. Binging not only became a logical solution because it was cheap and easy but also because she had grown up amid positive messages about eating. In her family, eating was a celebrated and joyful act. However, in adulthood, eating became a double-edged sword. While comforting her, binging also led to weight gain. During the three years Yolanda was on welfare, she gained seventy pounds.

Yolanda's story captures how poverty can be a precipitating factor in eating problems and highlights the value of understanding how class inequalities may shape women's eating problems. As a single mother, her financial constraints mirrored those of most female heads of households. The dual hazards of a race- and sex-stratified labor market further limited her options (Higginbotham 1986). In an article about Black women's health, Byllye Avery (1990) quotes a Black woman's explanation about why she eats compulsively. The woman told Avery,

> I work for General Electric making batteries, and, I know it's killing me. My old man is an alcoholic. My kid's got babies. Things are not well with me. And one thing I know I can do when I come home is cook me a pot of food and sit down in front of the TV and eat it. And you can't take that away from me until you're ready to give me something in its place. (P. 7)

Like Yolanda, this woman identifies eating compulsively as a quick, accessible, and immediately satisfying way of coping with the daily stress caused by conditions she could not control. Connections between poverty and eating problems also show the limits of portraying eating problems as maladies of upper-class adolescent women.

The fact that many women use food to anesthetize themselves, rather than other drugs (even when they gained access to alcohol, marijuana, and other illegal drugs), is partly a function of gender socialization and the competing demands that women face. One of the physiological consequences of binge eating is a numbed state similar to that experienced by drinking. Troubles and tensions are covered over as a consequence of the body's defensive response to massive food intake. When food is eaten in that way, it effectively works like a drug with immediate and predictable effects. Yolanda said she binged late at night rather than getting drunk because she could still get up in the morning, get her children ready for school, and be clearheaded for the college classes she attended. By binging, she avoided the hangover or sickness that results from alcohol or illegal drugs. In this way, food was her drug of choice since it was possible for her to eat while she continued to care for her children, drive, cook, and study. Binging is also less expensive than drinking, a factor that is especially significant for poor women. Another woman I interviewed said that when her compulsive eating was at its height, she ate breakfast after rising in the morning, stopped for a snack on her way to work, ate lunch at three different cafeterias, and snacked at her desk throughout the afternoon. Yet even when her eating had become constant, she was still able to remain employed. While her patterns of eating no doubt slowed her productivity, being drunk may have slowed her to a dead stop.

Heterosexism

The life history interviews also uncovered new connections between heterosexism and eating problems. One of the most important recent feminist contributions has been identifying compulsory heterosexuality as an institution which truncates opportunities for heterosexual and lesbian women (Rich 1986). All of the women interviewed for this study, both lesbian and heterosexual, were taught that heterosexuality was compulsory, although the versions of this enforcement were shaped by race and class. Expectations about heterosexuality were partly taught through messages that girls learned about eating and their bodies. In some homes, boys were given more food than girls, especially as teenagers, based on the rationale that girls need to be thin to attract boys. As the girls approached puberty, many were told to stop being athletic, begin wearing dresses, and watch their weight. For the women who weighed more than was considered acceptable, threats about their need to diet were laced with admonitions that being fat would ensure becoming an "old maid."

While compulsory heterosexuality influenced all of the women's emerging sense of their bodies and eating patterns, the women who linked heterosexism directly to the beginning of their eating problems were those who knew they were lesbians when very young and actively resisted heterosexual norms. One working-class Jewish woman, Martha, began compulsively eating when she was 11 years old, the same year she started getting clues of her lesbian identity. In junior high school, as many of her female peers began dating boys, Martha began fantasizing about girls, which made her feel utterly alone. Confused and ashamed about her fantasies, Martha came home every day from school and binged. Binging was a way she drugged herself so that being alone was tolerable. Describing binging, she said, "It was the only thing I knew. I was looking for a comfort." Like many women, Martha binged because it softened painful feelings. Binging sedated her, lessened her anxiety, and induced sleep.

Martha's story also reveals ways that trauma can influence women's experience of their bodies. Like many other women, Martha had no sense of herself as connected to her body. When I asked Martha whether she saw herself as fat when she was growing up she said, "I didn't see myself as fat. I didn't see myself. I wasn't there. I get so sad about that because I missed so much." In the literature on eating problems, *body image* is the term that is typically used to describe a woman's experience of her body. This term connotes the act of imagining one's physical appearance. Typically, women with eating problems are assumed to have difficulties with their body image. However, the term body image does not adequately capture the complexity and range of bodily responses to trauma experienced by the women. Exposure to trauma did much more than distort the women's visual image of themselves. These traumas often jeopardized their capacity to consider themselves as having bodies at all.

Given the limited connotations of the term body image, I use the term *body consciousness* as a more useful way to understand the range of bodily responses to trauma.[3] By body consciousness I mean the ability to reside comfortably in one's body (to see oneself as embodied) and to consider one's body as connected to oneself. The disruptions to their body consciousness that the women described included leaving their bodies, making a split between their body and mind, experiencing being "in" their bodies as painful, feeling unable to control what went in and out of their bodies, hiding in one part of their bodies, or simply not seeing themselves as having bodies. Binging, dieting, or purging were common ways women responded to disruptions to their body consciousness.

Racism and Class Injuries

For some of the Latinas and African-American women, racism coupled with the stress resulting from class mobility related to the onset of their eating problems. Joselyn, an African-American woman, remembered her White grandmother telling her she would never be as pretty as her cousins because they were lighter skinned. Her grandmother often humiliated Joselyn in front of others, as she made fun of Joselyn's body while she was naked and told her she was fat. As a young child,

Joselyn began to think that although she could not change her skin color, she could at least try to be thin. When Joselyn was young, her grandmother was the only family member who objected to Joselyn's weight. However, her father also began encouraging his wife and daughter to be thin as the family's class standing began to change. When the family was working class, serving big meals, having chubby children, and keeping plenty of food in the house was a sign the family was doing well. But, as the family became mobile, Joselyn's father began insisting that Joselyn be thin. She remembered, "When my father's business began to bloom and my father was interacting more with White businessmen and seeing how they did business, suddenly thin became important. If you were a truly well-to-do family, then your family was slim and elegant."

As Joselyn's grandmother used Joselyn's body as territory for enforcing her own racism and prejudice about size, Joselyn's father used her body as the territory through which he channeled the demands he faced in the white-dominated business world. However, as Joselyn was pressured to diet, her father still served her large portions and bought treats for her and the neighborhood children. These contradictory messages made her feel confused about her body. As was true for many women in this study, Joselyn was told she was fat beginning when she was very young even though she was not overweight. And, like most of the women, Joselyn was put on diet pills and diets before even reaching puberty, beginning the cycles of dieting, compulsive eating, and bulimia.

The confusion about body size expectations that Joselyn associated with changes in class paralleled one Puerto Rican woman's association between her eating problems and the stress of assimilation as her family's class standing moved from poverty to working class. When Vera was very young, she was so thin that her mother took her to a doctor who prescribed appetite stimulants. However, by the time Vera was eight years old, her mother began trying to shame Vera into dieting. Looking back on it, Vera attributed her mother's change of heart to competition among extended family members that centered on "being White, being successful, being middle class,... and it was always, 'Ay Bendito. She is so fat. What happened?'"

The fact that some of the African-American and Latina women associated the ambivalent messages about food and eating to their family's class mobility and/or the demands of assimilation while none of the eight White women expressed this (including those whose class was stable and changing) suggests that the added dimension of racism was connected to the imperative to be thin. In fact, the class expectations that their parents experienced exacerbated standards about weight that they inflicted on their daughters.

EATING PROBLEMS AS SURVIVAL STRATEGIES

Feminist Theoretical Shifts

My research permits a reevaluation of many assumptions about eating problems. First, this work challenges the theoretical reliance on the culture-of-thinness model....

Establishing links between eating problems and a range of oppressions invites a rethinking of both the groups of women who have been excluded from research and those whose lives have been the basis of theory formation. The construction of bulimia and anorexia as appearance-based disorders is rooted in a notion of femininity in which White middle- and upper-class women are portrayed as frivolous, obsessed with their bodies, and overly accepting of narrow gender roles. This portrayal fuels women's tremendous shame and

guilt about eating problems—as signs of self-centered vanity. This construction of White middle- and upper-class women is intimately linked to the portrayal of working-class White women and women of color as their opposite: as somehow exempt from accepting the dominant standards of beauty or as one step away from being hungry and therefore not susceptible to eating problems. Identifying that women may binge to cope with poverty contrasts the notion that eating problems are class bound. Attending to the intricacies of race, class, sexuality, and gender pushes us to rethink the demeaning construction of middle-class femininity and establishes bulimia and anorexia as serious responses to injustices.

Understanding the link between eating problems and trauma also suggests much about treatment and prevention. Ultimately, their prevention depends not simply on individual healing but also on changing the social conditions that underlie their etiology. As Bernice Johnson Reagon sings in Sweet Honey in the Rock's song "Oughta Be a Woman," "A way outa no way is too much to ask/ too much of a task for any one woman" (Reagon 1980).[4] Making it possible for women to have healthy relationships with their bodies and eating is a comprehensive task. Beginning steps in this direction include insuring that (1) girls can grow up without being sexually abused, (2) parents have adequate resources to raise their children, (3) children of color grow up free of racism, and (4) young lesbians have the chance to see their reflection in their teachers and community leaders. Ultimately, the prevention of eating problems depends on women's access to economic, cultural, racial, political, social, and sexual justice.

NOTES

1. I use the term *eating problems* as an umbrella term for one or more of the following: anorexia, bulimia, extensive dieting, or binging. I avoid using the term eating disorder because it categorizes the problems as individual pathologies, which deflects attention away from the social inequalities underlying them (Brown 1985).

However, by using the term *problem* I do not wish to imply blame. In fact, throughout, I argue that the eating strategies that women develop begin as logical solutions to problems, not problems themselves.

2. By trauma I mean a violating experience that has long-term emotional, physical, and/or spiritual conse-

quences that may have immediate or delayed effects. One reason the term *trauma* is useful conceptually is its association with the diagnostic label Post Traumatic Stress Disorder (PTSD) (American Psychological Association 1987). PTSD is one of the few clinical diagnostic categories that recognizes social problems (such as war or the Holocaust) as responsible for the symptoms identified (Trimble 1985). This concept adapts well to the feminist assertion that a woman's symptoms cannot be understood as solely individual, considered outside of her social context, or prevented without significant changes in social conditions.

3. One reason the term *consciousness* is applicable is its intellectual history as an entity that is shaped by social context and social structures (Delphy 1984; Marx 1964). This link aptly applies to how the women described their bodies because their perceptions of themselves as embodied (or not embodied) directly relate to their material conditions (living situations, financial resources, and access to social and political power).

4. Copyright © 1980. Used by permission of Songtalk Publishing.

REFERENCES

American Psychological Association. 1987. *Diagnostic and statistical manual of mental disorders.* 3rd ed. rev. Washington, DC: American Psychological Association.

Andersen, Arnold, and Andy Hay. 1985. Racial and socioeconomic influences in anorexia nervosa and bulimia. *International Journal of Eating Disorders* 4:479–87.

Arnold, Georgiana. 1990. Coming home: One Black woman's journey to health and fitness. In *The Black women's health book: Speaking for ourselves,* edited by Evelyn C. White. Seattle, WA: Seal Press.

Avery, Byllye Y. 1990. Breathing life into ourselves: The evolution of the National Black Women's Health Project. In *The Black women's health book: Speaking for ourselves,* edited by Evelyn C. White. Seattle, WA: Seal Press.

Bass, Ellen, and Laura Davis. 1988. *The courage to heal: A guide for women survivors of child sexual abuse.* New York: Harper & Row.

Brown, Laura S. 1985. Women, weight and power: Feminist theoretical and therapeutic issues. *Women and Therapy* 4:61–71.

———. 1987. Lesbians, weight and eating: New analyses and perspectives. In *Lesbian psychologies,* edited by the Boston Lesbian Psychologies Collective. Champaign: University of Illinois Press.

Chernin, Kim. 1981. *The obsession: Reflections on the tyranny of slenderness.* New York: Harper & Row.

Clarke, Cheryl. 1982. *Narratives.* New Brunswick, NJ: Sister Books.

Copeland, Paul M. 1985. Neuroendocrine aspects of eating disorder In *Theory and treatment of anorexia nervosa and bulimia: Biomedical sociocultural and psychological perspectives,* edited by Steven Wiley Emmett. New York: Brunner/Mazel.

Delphy, Christine. 1984. *Close to home: A materialist analysis of women's oppression.* Amherst: University of Massachusetts Press.

DeSalvo, Louise. 1989. *Virginia Woolf: The impact of childhood sexual abuse on her life and work.* Boston, MA: Beacon.

Dworkin, Sari H. 1989. Not in man's image: Lesbians and the cultural oppression of body image. In *Loving boldly: Issues facing lesbians,* edited by Ester D. Rothblum and Ellen Cole. New York: Harrington Park Press.

Garfinkel, Paul E, and David M. Garner. 1982. *Anorexia nervosa: A multidimensional perspective.* New York: Brunner/Mazel.

Garner, David. 1985. Iatrogenesis in anorexia nervosa and bulimia nervosa. *International Journal of Eating Disorders* 4:701–26.

Glaser, Barney G., and Anselm L. Strauss. 1967. *The discovery of grounded theory. Strategies for qualitative research.* New York: Aldine DeGruyter.

Goldfarb, Lori. 1987. Sexual abuse antecedent to anorexia nervosa, bulimia and compulsive overeating: Three case reports. *International Journal of Eating Disorders* 6:675–80.

Gray, James, Kathryn Ford, and Lily M. Kelly. 1987. The prevalence of bulimia in a Black college population. *International Journal of Eating Disorders* 6:733-40.

Herman, Judith. 1981. *Father-daughter incest.* Cambridge, MA: Harvard University Press.

Higginbotham, Elizabeth. 1986. We were never on a pedestal: Women of color continue to struggle with poverty, racism and sexism. In *For crying out loud,* edited by Rochelle Lefkowitz and Ann Withorn. Boston: MA: Pilgrim Press.

Hsu, George. 1987. Are eating disorders becoming more common in Blacks? *International Journal of Eating Disorders* 6:113–24.

Iazzetto, Demetria. 1989. When the body is not an easy place to be: Women's sexual abuse and eating problems. Ph.D. diss., Union for Experimenting Colleges and Universities, Cincinnati, Ohio.

Kearney-Cooke, Ann. 1988. Group treatment of sexual abuse among women with eating disorders. *Women and Therapy* 7:5–21.

Marx, Karl. 1964. *The economic and philosophic manuscripts of 1844.* New York: International.

Masson, Jeffrey. 1984. *The assault on the truth: Freud's suppression of the seduction theory.* New York: Farrar, Strauss & Giroux.

Naylor, Gloria. 1985. *Linden Hills.* New York: Ticknor & Fields.

Nevo, Shoshana. 1985. Bulimic symptoms: Prevalence and ethnic differences among college women. *International Journal of Eating Disorders* 4:151–68.

Oppenheimer, R., K. Howells, R. L. Palmer, and D. A. Chaloner. 1985. Adverse sexual experience in childhood and clinical eating disorders: A preliminary description. *Journal of Psychiatric Research* 19:357–61.

Orbach, Susie. 1978. *Fat is a feminist issue.* New York: Paddington.

———. 1985. Accepting the symptom: A feminist psychoanalytic treatment of anorexia nervosa. In *Handbook of psychotherapy for anorexia nervosa and bulimia,* edited by David M. Garner and Paul E. Garfinkel. New York: Guilford.

Powers, Retha. 1989. Fat is a Black women's issue. *Essence,* Oct., 75, 78, 134, 136.

Reagon, Bernice Johnson. 1980. Oughta be a woman. On Sweet Honey in the Rock's album, *Good News.* Music by Bernice Johnson Reagon; lyrics by June Jordan. Washington, DC: Songtalk.

Rich, Adrienne. 1986. Compulsory heterosexuality and lesbian existence. In *Blood, bread and poetry.* New York: Norton.

Root, Maria P. P., and Patricia Fallon. 1988. The incidence of victimization experiences in a bulimic sample. *Journal of Interpersonal Violence* 3:161–73.

———. 1989. Treating the victimized bulimic: The functions of binge-purge behavior. *Journal of Interpersonal Violence* 4:90–100.

Russell, Diana E. 1986. *The secret trauma: Incest in the lives of girls and women.* New York: Basic Books.

Schoenfielder, Lisa, and Barbara Wieser, eds. 1983. *Shadow on a tightrope: Writings by women about fat liberation.* Iowa City, IA: Aunt Lute Book Co.

Silber, Tomas. 1986. Anorexia nervosa in Blacks and Hispanics. *International Journal of Eating Disorders* 5:121–28.

Silberstein, Lisa, Ruth Striegel-Moore, and Judith Rodin. 1987. Feeling fat: A woman's shame. In *The role of shame in symptom formation,* edited by Helen Block Lewis. Hillsdale, NJ: Lawrence Erlbaum.

Smead, Valerie. 1984. Eating behaviors which may lead to and perpetuate anorexia nervosa, bulimarexia, and bulimia. *Women and Therapy* 3:37–49.

Spack, Norman. 1985. Medical complications of anorexia nervosa and bulimia. In *Theory and treatment of anorexia nervosa and bulimia: Biomedical sociocultural and psychological perspectives,* edited by Steven Wiley Emmett. New York: Brunner/Mazel.

Swink, Kathy, and Antoinette E. Leveille. 1986. From victim to survivor: A new look at the issues and recovery process for adult incest survivors. *Women and Therapy* 5:119–43.

Trimble, Michael. 1985. Post-traumatic stress disorder: History of a concept. In *Trauma and its wake: The study and treatment of post-traumatic stress disorder,* edited by C. R. Figley. New York: Brunner/Mazel.

What's important is what you look like. 1988. *Gay Community News,* July, 24–30.

White, Evelyn C., ed. 1990. *The Black women's health book: Speaking for ourselves.* Seattle, WA: Seal Press.

———. 1991. Unhealthy appetites. *Essence,* Sept., 28, 30.

Coming to Terms

Masculinity and Physical Disability

THOMAS J. GERSCHICK
ADAM STEPHEN MILLER

Men with physical disabilities are marginalized and stigmatized in American society. The image and reality of men with disabilities undermines cultural beliefs about men's bodies and physicality. The body is a central foundation of how men define themselves and how they are defined by others. Bodies are vehicles for determining value, which in turn translates into status and prestige. Men's bodies allow them to demonstrate the socially valuable characteristics of toughness, competitiveness, and ability (Messner 1992). Thus, one's body and relationship to it provide a way to apprehend the world and one's place in it. The bodies of men with disabilities serve as a continual reminder that they are at odds with the expectations of the dominant culture. As anthropologist Robert Murphy (1990: 94) writes of his own experiences with disability:

> *Paralytic disability constitutes emasculation of a more direct and total nature. For the male, the weakening and atrophy of the body threaten all the cultural values of masculinity: strength, activeness, speed, virility, stamina, and fortitude.*

This article seeks to sharpen our understanding of the creation, maintenance, and recreation of gender identities by men who, by birth, accident, or illness, find themselves dealing with a physical disability. We examine two sets of social dynamics that converge and clash in the lives of men with physical disabilities. On the one side, these men must deal with the presence and pressures of hegemonic masculinity, which demands strength. On the other side, societal members perceive people with disabilities to be weak.

For the present study, we conducted in-depth interviews with ten men with physical disabilities in order to gain insights into the psychosocial aspects of men's ability to come to terms with their physical and social condition. We wanted to know how men with physical disabilities respond to the demands of hegemonic masculinity and their marginalization. For instance, if men with disabilities need others to legitimate their gender identity during encounters, what happens when others deny them the opportunity? How do they reconcile the conflicting expectations associated with masculinity and disability? How do they define masculinity for themselves, and what are the sources of these definitions? To what degree do their responses contest and/or perpetuate the current gender order? That is, what are the political implications of different gender identities and practices? In addressing these questions, we contribute to the growing body of literature on marginalized and alternative gender identities.

We will first discuss the general relationship between physical disability and hegemonic masculinity. Second, we will summarize the methods used in this study. Next, we will present and discuss our central findings. Finally, we discuss how the gender identities and life practices of men with disabilities contribute to the politics of the gender order.

HEGEMONIC MASCULINITY AND PHYSICAL DISABILITY

Recently, the literature has shifted toward understanding gender as an interactive process. Thus, it is presumed to be not only an aspect of what one *is,* but more fundamentally it is something that one *does* in interaction with others (West and Zimmerman 1987). Whereas previously, gender was thought to be strictly an individual phenomenon, this new understanding directs our attention to the interpersonal and institutional levels as well. The lives of men with disabilities provide an instructive arena in which to study the interactional nature of gender and its effect on individual gender identities.

In *The Body Silent,* Murphy (1990) observes that men with physical disabilities experience "embattled identities" because of the conflicting expectations placed on them as men and as people with disabilities. On the one side, contemporary masculinity privileges men who are strong, courageous, aggressive, independent and self-reliant (Connell 1987). On the other side, people with disabilities are perceived to be, and treated as, weak, pitiful, passive, and dependent (Murphy 1990). Thus, for men with physical disabilities, masculine gender identity and practice are created and maintained at the crossroads of the demands of contemporary masculinity and the stigmatization associated with disability. As such, for men with physical disabilities, being recognized as masculine by others is especially difficult, if not impossible, to accomplish. Yet not being recognized as masculine is untenable because, in our culture, everyone is expected to display an appropriate gender identity (West and Zimmerman 1987).

METHODS

This research was based on in-depth interviews with ten men. Despite the acknowledged problem of identity management in interviews, we used this method because we were most interested in the subjective perceptions and experiences of our informants. To mitigate this dynamic, we relied on probing questions and reinterviews. Informants were located through a snowball sample, utilizing friends and connections within the community of people with disabilities. All of our informants were given pseudonyms, and we further protected their identity by deleting nonessential personal detail. The age range of respondents varied from sixteen to seventy-two. Eight of our respondents were white, and two were African American. Geographically, they came from both coasts and the Midwest. All were "mobility impaired," and most were para- or quadriplegics. Given the small sample size and the modicum of diversity within it, this work must necessarily be understood as exploratory.

We interviewed men with physical disabilities for three primary reasons. First, given the diversity of disabilities and our modest resources, we had to bound the sample. Second, mobility impairments tend to be more apparent than other disabilities, such as blindness or hearing loss, and people respond to these men using visual clues. Third, although the literature in this area is scant, much of it focuses on men with physical disabilities.

Due to issues of shared identities, Adam did all the interviews. Interviews were semistructured and tape-recorded. Initial interviews averaged approximately an hour in length. Additionally, we contacted all of our informants at least once with clarifying questions and, in some cases, to test ideas that we had. These follow-ups lasted approximately thirty minutes. Each informant received a copy of his interview transcript to ensure that we had captured his perspective accurately. We also shared draft copies of this chapter with them and incorporated their insights into the current version.

There were two primary reasons for the thorough follow-up. First, from a methodological standpoint, it was important for us to capture the experience of our informants as fully as possible. Second, we felt that we had an obligation to allow them to control, to a large extent, the representation of their experience.

Interviews were analyzed using an analytic induction approach (Denzin 1989; Emerson 1988; Katz 1988). In determining major and minor patterns of masculine practice, we used the responses to a series of questions including, What is the most important aspect of masculinity to you? What would you say makes you feel most manly or masculine? Do you think your conception of masculinity is different from that of able-bodied men as a result of your disability? If so, how and why? If not, why not? Additionally, we presented our informants with a list of characteristics associated with prevailing masculinity based on the work of R. W. Connell (1987, 1990a, 1990b, 1991) and asked them to rate their importance to their conception of self. Both positive and negative responses to this portion of our questionnaire guided our insight into how each man viewed his masculinity. To further support our discussion, we turned to the limited academic literature in this area. Much more helpful were the wide range of biographical and autobiographical accounts of men who have physical disabilities (see, for instance, Murphy 1990; Callahan 1989; Kriegel 1991; Hahn 1989; and Zola 1982).

Finally, in analyzing the data we were sensitive to making judgments about our informants when grouping them into categories. People with disabilities are shoehorned into categories too much as it is. We sought to discover what was common among their responses and to highlight what we perceived to be the essence of their views. In doing so, we endeavored to provide a conceptual framework for understanding the responses of men with physical disabilities while trying to be sensitive to their personal struggles.

DISABILITY, MASCULINITY, AND COMING TO TERMS

While no two men constructed their sense of masculinity in exactly the same way, there appeared to be three dominant frameworks our informants used to cope with their situations. These patterns can be conceived of in relation to the standards inherent in dominant masculinity. We call them the three Rs: *reformulation,* which entailed men's redefinition of hegemonic characteristics on their

own terms; *reliance,* reflected by sensitive or hypersensitive adoptions of particular predominant attributes; and *rejection,* characterized by the renunciation of these standards and either the creation of one's own principles and practices or the denial of masculinity's importance in one's life. However, one should note that none of our interviewees *entirely* followed any one of these frameworks in defining his sense of self. Rather, for heuristic reasons, it is best to speak of the major and minor ways each man used these three patterns. For example, some of our informants relied on dominant standards in their view of sexuality and occupation but also reformulated the prevailing ideal of independence.

Therefore, we discuss the *primary* way in which these men with disabilities related to hegemonic masculinity's standards, while recognizing that their coping mechanisms reflected a more complex combination of strategies. In doing so, we avoid "labeling" men and assigning them to arbitrary categories.

Reformulation

Some of our informants responded to idealized masculinity by reformulating it, shaping it along the lines of their own abilities, perceptions, and strengths, and defining their manhood along these new lines. These men tended not to contest these standards overtly, but—either consciously or unconsciously—they recognized in their own condition an inability to meet these ideals as they were culturally conceived.

An example of this came from Damon, a seventy-two-year-old quadriplegic who survived a spinal-cord injury in an automobile accident ten years ago. Damon said he always desired, and had, control of his life. While Damon required round-the-clock personal care assistants (PCAs), he asserted that he was still a very independent person:

> *I direct all of my activities around my home where people have to help me to maintain my apartment, my transportation, which I own, and direction in*

where I go. I direct people how to get there, and I tell them what my needs will be when I am going and coming, and when to get where I am going.

Damon said that his sense of control was more than mere illusion; it was a reality others knew of as well. This reputation seemed important to him:

People know from Jump Street that I have my own thing, and I direct my own thing. And if they can't comply with my desire, they won't be around.... I don't see any reason why people with me can't take instructions and get my life on just as I was having it before, only thing I'm not doing it myself. I direct somebody else to do it. So, therefore, I don't miss out on very much.

Hegemonic masculinity's definition of independence privileges self-reliance and autonomy. Damon required substantial assistance: indeed, some might term him "dependent." However, Damon's reformulation of the independence ideal, accomplished in part through a cognitive shift, allowed him to think otherwise.

Harold, a forty-six-year-old polio survivor, described a belief and practice akin to Damon's. Also a quadriplegic, Harold similarly required PCAs to help him handle daily necessities: Harold termed his reliance on and control of PCAs "acting through others":

When I say independence can be achieved by acting through other people, I actually mean getting through life, liberty, and the pursuit of happiness while utilizing high-quality and dependable attendant-care services.

As with Damon, Harold achieved his perceived sense of independence by controlling others. Harold stressed that he did not count on family or friends to do favors for him, but *employed* his PCAs in a "business relationship" he controlled. Alternatives to family and friends are used whenever possible because most people with disabilities do not want to burden or be dependent on their families any more than necessary (Murphy 1990).

Social class plays an important role here. Damon and Harold had the economic means to afford round-the-clock assistance. While none of our informants experienced economic hardship, many people with disabilities depend on the welfare system for their care, and the amount and quality of assistance they receive make it much more difficult to conceive of themselves as independent.

A third man who reformulated predominant demands was Brent, a forty-five-year-old administrator. He told us that his paraplegic status, one that he had lived with since he was five years old, had often cast him as an "outsider" to society. This status was particularly painful in his late adolescence, a time when the "sexual revolution" was sweeping America's youth:

A very important measure of somebody's personhood—manhood—was their sexual ability.... What bothers me more than anything else is the stereotypes, and even more so, in terms of sexual desirability. Because I had a disability, I was less desirable than able-bodied people. And that I found very frustrating.

His experiences led him to recast the hegemonic notion that man's relations with a partner should be predominantly physical. As a result, he stressed the importance of emotional relations and trust. This appeared to be key to Brent's definition of his manhood:

For me, that is my measure of who I am as an individual and who I am as a man—my ability to be able to be honest with my wife. Be able to be close with her, to be able to ask for help, provide help. To have a commitment, to follow through, and to do all those things that I think are important.

As Connell (1990a) notes, this requires a capacity to not only be expressive, but also to have feelings worth expressing. This clearly demonstrates a different form of masculine practice.

The final case of reformulation came from Robert, a thirty-year-old survivor of a motorcycle accident. Able-bodied for much of his life, Robert's accident occurred when he was twenty-four, leaving him paraplegic. Through five years of intensive physical therapy, he regained 95 percent of his original function, though certain effects linger to this day.

Before his accident, Robert had internalized many of the standards of dominant masculinity exemplified by frequenting bars, leading an active sex life, and riding a motorcycle. But, if our research and the body of autobiographical works from men with physical disabilities has shown anything, it is that coming to terms with a disability eventually changes a man. It appeared to have transformed Robert. He remarked that, despite being generally "recovered," he had maintained his disability-influenced value system:

> I judge people on more of a personal and character level than I do on any physical, or I guess I did; but, you know, important things are guys that have integrity, guys that are honest about what they are doing, that have some direction in their life and know... peace of mind and what they stand for.

One of the areas that Robert said took the longest to recover was his sexuality—specifically, his confidence in his sexual ability. While Robert said sexual relations were still important to him, like Brent he reformulated his previous, largely hegemonic notion of male sexuality into a more emotionally and physically egalitarian model:

> I've found a whole different side to having sex with a partner and looking at satisfying the partner rather than satisfying myself; and that has taken the focus off of satisfying myself, being the big manly stud, and concentrating more on my partner. And that has become just as satisfying.

However, reformulation did not yield complete severance from prevailing masculinity's standards as they were culturally conceived. For instance, despite his reformulative inclinations, Robert's self-described "macho" attitude continued in some realms during his recovery. He, and all others we interviewed, represented the complexity of gender identities and practices; no man's masculinity fell neatly into any one of the three patterns.

For instance, although told by most doctors that his physical condition was probably permanent, Robert's resolve was unyielding. "I put my blinders on to all negative insight into it and just totally focused on getting better," he said. "And I think that was, you know, a major factor on why I'm where I'm at today." This typified the second pattern we identified—reliance on hegemonic masculinity's standards. It was ironic, then, that Robert's tenacity, his never-ending work ethic, and his focused drive to succeed were largely responsible for his almost-complete recovery. While Robert reformulated much of his earlier sense of masculinity, he still relied on this drive.

Perhaps the area in which men who reformulate most closely paralleled dominant masculinity was the emphasis they placed on their occupation. Our sample was atypical in that most of our informants were professionally employed on a full-time basis and could, therefore, draw on class-based resources, whereas unemployment among people with disabilities is very high. Just as societal members privilege men who are accomplished in their occupation, Harold said he finds both "purpose," and success, in his career:

> No one is going to go through life without some kind of purpose. Everyone decides. I wanted to be a writer. So I became a writer and an observer, a trained observer.

Brent said that he drew much of his sense of self, his sense of self-esteem, and his sense of manhood from his occupational accomplishments. Initially, Brent denied the importance of the prevailing ideal that a man's occupational worth was derived from his breadwinner status:

> It is not so important to be the breadwinner as it is to be competent in the world. You know, to have a career, to have my name on the door. That is what is most important. It is that recognition that is very important to me.

However, he later admitted that being the breadwinner still was important to him, although he denied a link between his desires and the "stereotypical" conception of breadwinner status. He maintained that "it's still important to me, because I've always been able to make money." Independence, both economic and physical, were important to all of our informants.

Rejection of hegemonic ideals also occurred among men who primarily depended on a reformulative framework. Harold's view of relationships with a partner dismissed the sexually powerful ideal: "The fact of the matter is that I'm not all that upset by the fact that I'm disabled and I'm a male. I mean, I know what I can do." We will have more to say about the rejection of dominant conceptions of sexuality later.

In brief summary, the subset of our informants whose primary coping pattern involved reformulation of dominant standards recognized their inability to meet these ideals as they are culturally conceived. Confident in their own abilities and values, and drawing from previous experience, they confronted standards of masculinity on their own terms. In doing so, they distanced themselves from masculine ideals.

Reliance

However, not all of the men with physical disabilities we interviewed depended on a reformulative approach. We found that many of our informants *were* concerned with others' views of their masculinity and with meeting the demands of hegemonic masculinity. They primarily used the second pattern, reliance, which involves the internalization of many more of the ideals of predominant masculinity, including physical strength, athleticism, independence, and sexual prowess. Just as some men depended on reformulation for much of their masculine definition, others, despite their inability to meet many of these ideals, relied on them heavily. As such, these men did not seem to be as comfortable with their sense of manhood; indeed, their inability to meet society's standards bothered them very much.

This subset of our informants found themselves in a double bind that left them conflicted. They embraced dominant conceptions of mascu-

linity as a way to gain acceptance from themselves and from others. Yet, they were continuously reminded in their interactions with others that they were "incomplete." As a result, the identity behind the facade suffered; there were, then, major costs associated with this strategy.

The tension between societal expectations and the reality of men with physical disabilities was most clearly demonstrated by Jerry, a sixteen-year-old who had juvenile rheumatoid arthritis. While Jerry was physically able to walk for limited distances, this required great effort on his part; consequently, he usually used a wheelchair. He was concerned with the appearance of his awkward walking. "I feel like I look a little, I don't know, more strange when I walk," he said.

The significance of appearance and external perception of manliness is symptomatic of the difficulty men with physical disabilities have in developing an identity and masculinity free of others' perceptions and expectations. Jerry said:

> I think [others' conception of what defines a man] is very important, because if they don't think of you as one, it is hard to think of yourself as one; or, it doesn't really matter if you think of yourself as one if no one else does.

Jerry said that, particularly among his peers, he was not perceived as attractive as the able-bodied teenagers; thus, he had difficulty in male-female relations beyond landing an occasional date. "[The girls believe] I might be a 'really nice person,' but not like a guy per se," he said. "I think to some extent that you're sort of genderless to them." This clearly represents the emasculation and depersonalization inherent in social definitions of disability.

However, Jerry said that he faced a more persistent threat to his autonomy—his independence and his sense of control—from others being "uncomfortable" around him and persisting in offering him assistance he often did not need. This made him "angry," though he usually did not refuse the help out of politeness. Thus, with members of his social group, he participated in a "bargain": they would socialize with him as long as he remained in a dependent position where they could "help" him.

This forced, situational passivity led Jerry to emphasize his autonomy in other areas. For instance, Jerry avoided asking for help in nearly all situations. This was directly tied to reinforcing his embattled manhood by displaying outward strength and independence:

> If I ever have to ask someone for help, it really makes me like feel like less of a man. I don't like asking for help at all. You know, like even if I could use some, I'll usually not ask just because I can't, I just hate asking.... [A man is] fairly self-sufficient in that you can sort of handle just about any situation, in that you can help other people, and that you don't need a lot of help.

Jerry internalized the prevailing masculine ideal that a man should be independent; he relied on that ideal for his definition of manhood. His inability to meet this ideal—partly through his physical condition, and partly from how others treated him—threatened his identity and his sense of manhood, which had to be reinforced even at the expense of self-alienation.

One should not label Jerry a "relier" simply because of these struggles. Being only sixteen years of age—and the youngest participant in our study—Jerry was still developing his sense of masculinity; and, as with many teenagers both able-bodied and disabled, he was trying to fit into his peer group. Furthermore, Jerry will continue to mature and develop his self-image and sense of masculinity. A follow-up interview in five years might show a degree of resolution to his struggles.

Such a resolution could be seen in Michael, a thirty-three-year-old manager we interviewed, who also internalized many of the standards of hegemonic masculinity. A paraplegic from an auto accident in 1977, Michael struggled for many years after his accident to come to terms with his condition.

His struggles had several sources, all tied into his view of masculinity's importance. The first was that, before his accident, he accepted much of the dominant conception of masculinity. A high-school student, farm hand, and football and track star at the time, Michael said that independence, relations with the women he dated, and physical strength were central to his conception of self.

After his accident, Michael's doctors told him there was a 50-50 chance that he would regain the ability to walk, and he clung to the hope. "I guess I didn't understand it, and had hope that I would walk again," he said. However, he was "depressed" about his situation, "but not so much about my disability, I guess. Because that wasn't real yet."

But coming home three months after his accident didn't alleviate the depression. Instead, it heightened his anxiety and added a new component—vulnerability. In a span of three months, Michael had, in essence, his sense of masculinity and his security in himself completely stripped away. He was in an unfamiliar situation; and far from feeling strong, independent, and powerful, he felt vulnerable and afraid: "No one," he remarked, "can be prepared for a permanent disability."

His reliance on dominant masculinity, then, started with his predisability past and continued during his recovery as a coping mechanism to deal with his fears. The hegemonic standard Michael strove most to achieve was that of independence. It was central to his sense of masculinity before and at the time of our interview. Indeed, it was so important that it frustrated him greatly when he needed assistance. Much like Jerry, he refused to ask for it:

> I feel that I should be able to do everything for myself and I don't like it.... I don't mind asking for things that I absolutely can't do, like hanging pictures, or moving furniture, or having my oil changed in my car; but there are things that I'm capable of doing in my chair, like jumping up one step. That I feel like I should be able to do, and I find it frustrating when I can't do that sometimes. ... I don't like asking for [help I don't think I need]. It kind of makes me mad.

When asked if needing assistance was "un-manly," Michael replied, "There's probably some of that in there." For both Michael and Jerry, the independence ideal often led to risk-taking behavior in order to prove to themselves that they were more than their social definition.

Yet, much like Robert, Michael had reformulated his view of sexuality. He said that his physical sexuality made him "feel the most masculine"—apparently another reliant response with a stereotypical emphasis on sexual performance. However, it was more complicated. Michael said that he no longer concentrated on pleasing himself, as he did when able-bodied, but that he now had a more partner-oriented view of sexuality. "I think that my compensation for my feeling of vulnerability is I've overcompensated by trying to please my partner and leave little room to allow my partner to please me.... Some of my greatest pleasure is exhausting my partner while having sex." Ironically, while he focused more on his partner's pleasure than ever before, he did so at his own expense; a sense of balancing the needs of both partners was missing.

Thus, sex served multiple purposes for Michael—it gave him and his partner pleasure; it reassured his fears and his feelings of vulnerability; and it reconfirmed his masculinity. His sexuality, then, reflected both reliance and reformulation.

While independence and sexuality were both extremely important to Scott, a thirty-four-year-old rehabilitation engineer, he emphasized a third area for his sense of manhood—athletics. Scott served in the Peace Corps during his twenties, working in Central America. He described his life-style as "rigorous" and "into the whole sports thing," and used a mountain bike as his primary means of transportation and recreation. He was also an avid hockey player in his youth and spent his summers in softball leagues.

Scott acquired a polio-like virus when he was twenty-five years old that left him permanently paraplegic, a situation that he did not initially accept. In an aggressive attempt to regain his physical ability, and similar to Robert, Scott obsessively attacked his rehabilitation

...thinking, that's always what I've done with all the sports. If I wasn't good enough, I worked a little harder and I got better. So, I kept thinking my

walking isn't very good now. If I push it, it will get better.

But Scott's athletic drive led not to miraculous recovery, but overexertion. When ordered by his doctors to scale back his efforts, he realized he could not recover strictly through tenacity. At the time of our interview, he was ambivalent about his limitations. He clearly did not feel like a failure: "I think that if I wouldn't have made the effort, I always would have wondered, could I have made a difference?" Following the athlete's code of conduct, "always give 110 percent," Scott attacked his recovery. But when his efforts were not enough—when he did not "emerge victorious"—he accepted it as an athlete would. Yet, his limitations also frustrated him at times, and in different areas.

For example, though his physical capacity was not what it was, Scott maintained a need for athletic competition. He played wheelchair basketball and was the only wheelchair-participant in a city softball league. However, he did not return to hockey, the sport he loved as a youngster; in fact, he refused to even try the sled-based equivalent.

Here was Scott's frustration. His spirit of athleticism was still alive, but he lamented the fact that he could not compete exactly as before:

[I miss] the things that I had. I played hockey: that was my primary sport for so many years. Pretty much, I did all the sports. But, like, I never played basketball; never liked basketball before. Which is why I think I can play now. See, it would be like the equivalent to wheelchair hockey. Some friends of mine have talked to me about it, [but] I'm not really interested in that. Because it wouldn't be real hockey. And it would make me feel worse, rather that better.

In this respect, Scott had not completely come to terms with his limitations. He still wanted to be a "real" athlete, competing in the same sports, in the same ways, with the same rules, with others who shared his desire for competition. Wheelchair hockey, which he derogatorily referred to as "gimp hockey," represented the antithesis of this for him.

Scott's other responses added to this emphasis. What he most disliked about having a disability was "that I can't do the things that I want to be able to do," meaning he could not ride his bike or motorcycle, he could not play "real" hockey, and he was unable to live a freewheeling, spontaneous life-style. Rather, he had to plan ahead of time where he went and how he got there. The frustration caused by having to plan nearly every move was apparent in almost all of our interviews.

However, on the subject of independence, Scott said "I think I'm mostly independent," but complained that there were some situations where he could not meet his expectations and had to depend on his wife. Usually this was not a "major issue," but "there's still times when, yeah, I feel bad about it; or, you know it's the days where she doesn't feel like it, but she kind of has to. That's what bothers me the most, I guess." Thus, he reflected the general desire among men with disabilities not to be a burden of any kind on family members.

Much of the time, Scott accepted being "mostly independent." His reliance on the ideals of athleticism and independence played a significant part in his conception of masculinity and self. However, Scott learned, though to a limited degree, to let go of some of his previous ideals and to accept a different, reformulated notion of independence and competition. Yet, he could not entirely do so. His emphasis on athletics and independence was still strong, and there were many times when athletics and acceptance conflicted.

However, one should stop short of a blanket assessment of men with disabilities who rely on hegemonic masculinity standards. "Always" is a dangerous word, and stating that "men who rely on hegemonic standards are *always* troubled" is a dangerous assumption. An apparent exceptional case among men who follow a reliant pattern came from Aaron, a forty-one-year-old paraplegic. Rather than experiencing inner turmoil and conflict, Aaron was one of the most upbeat individuals we interviewed. Aaron said that, before his 1976 accident, he was "on top of the world," with a successful business, a commitment to ath-

letics that included basketball shoot-arounds with NBA prospects, and a wedding engagement. Indeed, from the time of his youth, Aaron relied on such hegemonic standards as sexuality, independence, athleticism, and occupational accomplishment.

For example, when asked what masculinity meant to him before his accident, Aaron said that it originally meant sexual conquest. As a teen, he viewed frequent sexual activity as a "rite of passage" into manhood.

Aaron said he had also enjoyed occupational success, and that this success was central to his definition of self, including being masculine. Working a variety of jobs ranging from assembly-line worker to white-collar professional, Aaron said, "I had been very fortunate to have good jobs, which were an important part of who I was and how I defined myself."

According to Aaron, much of his independence ideal came from his father. When his parents divorced, Aaron's father explained to him that, though he was only five, he would have to be "the man of the house." Aaron took this lesson to heart, and strived to fulfill this role both in terms of independence and providing for the family. "My image of manhood was that of a provider," he said, "one who was able to make a contribution to the financial stability of the family in addition to dealing with the problems and concerns that would come up."

His accident, a gunshot wound injuring his spinal cord, left him completely dependent. Predictably, Aaron could not immediately cope with this. "My whole self-image itself was real integrally tied up with the things I used to do," he said. "I found my desire for simple pleasures to be the greatest part of the pain I had to bear."

His pain increased when he left the hospital. His fiancee had left him, and within two years he lost "everything that was important to me"—his house, his business, his savings, most of his friends, and even, for a while, his hope.

However, much as with Robert, Aaron's resiliency eventually turned his life around. Just as he hit bottom, he began telling himself that "if you hold on long enough, if you don't quit, you'll get through it." Additionally, he attacked his therapy with the vengeance he had always devoted to athletics. "I'd never been confronted with a situation in my entire life before that I was not able to overcome by the efforts of my own merit," he said. "I took the same attitude toward this."

Further, he reasserted his sexuality. Though he then wore a colostomy bag, he resumed frequent sexual intercourse, taking the attitude that "this is who I was, and a woman was either going to have to accept me as I was, or she's got to leave me f—— alone."

However, he realized after those five years that his hard work would not be rewarded nor would he be miraculously healed. Figuring that "there's a whole lot of life that I need to live, and this wasn't the most efficient way to live it," he bought a new sport wheelchair, found a job, and became involved in wheelchair athletics. In this sense, a complex combination of all three patterns emerged in Aaron as reliance was mixed with reformulation and rejection.

Furthermore, his soul-searching led him to develop a sense of purpose in his life, and a reason for going on:

[During my recovery] I felt that I was left here to enrich the lives of as many people as I could before I left this earth, and it gave me a new purpose, a new vision, a new mission, new dreams.

Tenacity, the quest for independence, athletics, and sexual activity carried Aaron through his recovery. Many of these ideals, which had their source in his father's teachings, remained with him as he continued to be active in athletics (everything from basketball to softball to scuba diving), to assert his sexuality, and to aim for complete autonomy. To Aaron, independence, both physical and financial, was more than just a personal ideal; it was one that should be shared by all people with disabilities. As such, he aspired to be a role model for others:

The work that I am involved in is to help people gain control over their lives, and I think it's vitally

important that I walk my talk. If...we hold ourselves out to be an organization that helps people gain control over their lives, I think it's vitally important for me as the CEO of that organization to live my life in a way that embodies everything that we say we're about.

Clearly, Aaron was not the same man he was before his disability. He said that his maturity and his experience with disability "made me stronger," and that manhood no longer simply meant independence and sexual conquest. Manhood also meant

...being responsible for one's actions; being considerate of another's feelings; being sensitive to individuals who are more vulnerable than yourself to what their needs would be; standing up on behalf and fighting for those who cannot speak out for themselves, fight for themselves. It means being willing to take a position and be committed to a position, even when it's inconvenient or costly to take that point of view, and you do it only because of the principle involved.

This dovetailed significantly with his occupation, which was of great importance to him. But as alluded to above, Aaron's emphasis on occupation cannot be seen as mere reliance on the hegemonic conception of occupational achievement. It was more a reformulation of that ideal from self-achievement to facilitating the empowerment of others.

Nevertheless, Aaron's struggle to gain his current status, like the struggle of others who rely on hegemonic masculinity's standards, was immense. Constructing hegemonic masculinity from a subordinated position is almost always a Sisyphean task. One's ability to do so is undermined continuously by physical, social, and cultural weakness. "Understandably, in an effort to cope with this stress (balancing the demands for strength and the societal perception of weakness)," writes political scientist Harlan Hahn, "many disabled men have tended to identify personally and politically with the supposed strength of prevalent concepts of masculinity rather than with their disability" (1989: 3). To relinquish masculinity under these circumstances is to court gender annihilation, which is untenable to some men. Consequently, relying on hegemonic masculinity becomes more understandable (Connell 1990a: 471).

Rejection

Despite the difficulties it presents, hegemony, including that related to gender, is never complete (Janeway 1980, Scott 1985). For some of our informants, resistance took the form of creating alternative masculine identities and subcultures that provided them with a supportive environment. These men were reflected in the final pattern: rejection. Informants who followed this pattern did not so much share a common ideology or set of practices; rather, they believed that the dominant conception of masculinity was wrong, either in its individual emphases or as a practice. One of these men developed new standards of masculinity in place of the ones he had rejected. Another seemingly chose to deny masculinity's importance, although he was neither effeminate or androgynous. Instead, they both emphasized their status as "persons," under the motto of "people first." This philosophy reflected a key tenet of the Disability Rights Movement.

Alex, a twenty-three-year-old, first-year law student, survived an accident that left him an incomplete quadriplegic when he was fourteen. Before that time, he felt he was an outsider at his private school because he eschewed the superficial, athletically oriented, and materialistic atmosphere. Further, he said the timing of the accident, when many of his peers were defining their social roles, added to this outsider perspective, in that it made him unable to participate in the highly social, role-forming process. "I didn't learn about the traditional roles of sexuality, and whatever the rules are for such behavior in our society, until later," he said. "Because of my physical characteristics, I had to learn a different set of rules."

Alex described himself as a "nonconformist." This simple moniker seemed central to his conception of selfhood and masculinity. Alex, unlike

men who primarily reformulate these tenets, rejected the attitudinal and behavioral prescriptions of hegemonic masculinity. He maintained that his standards were his own—not society's—and he scoffed at commonly held views of masculinity.

For example, Alex blamed the media for the idea that men must be strong and attractive, stating "The traditional conception is that everyone has to be Arnold Schwartzenegger…[which] probably lead[s] to some violence, unhappiness, and things like that if they [men] don't meet the standards."

As for the importance of virility and sexual prowess, Alex said "There is a part of me that, you know, has been conditioned and acculturated and knows those [dominant] values"; but he sarcastically laughed at the notion of a man's sexual prowess being reflected in "making her pass out," and summed up his feelings on the subject by adding, "You have to be willing to do things in a nontraditional way."

Alex's most profound rejection of a dominant ideal involved the importance of fathering, in its strictest sense of the man as impregnator:

> There's no reason why we (his fiancee and himself) couldn't use artificial insemination or adoption. Parenting doesn't necessarily involve being the male sire. It involves being a good parent…. Parenting doesn't mean that it's your physical child. It involves responsibility and an emotional role as well. I don't think the link between parenthood is the primary link with sexuality. Maybe in terms of evolutionary purposes, but not in terms of a relationship.

Thus, Alex rejected the procreation imperative encouraged in hegemonic masculinity. However, while Alex took pride at overtly rejecting prevailing masculinity as superficial and silly, even he relied on it at times. Alex said he needed to support himself financially and would not ever want to be an emotional or economic "burden" in a relationship. On one level, this is a common concern for most people, disabled or not. But on another level, Alex admitted that it tied in to his sense of masculinity:

If I was in a relationship and I wasn't working, and my spouse was, what could be the possible reasons for my not working? I could have just been fired. I could be laid off. Who knows what happened? I guess . . . that's definitely an element of masculinity, and I guess I am just as influenced by that as, oh, as I guess as other people, or as within my definition of masculinity. What do you know? I have been caught.

A different form of rejection was reflected in Leo, a fifty-eight-year-old polio survivor. Leo, who had striven for occupational achievement since his youth, seemed to value many hegemonic traits: independence, money-making ability, and recognition by peers. But he steadfastly denied masculinity's role in shaping his outlook.

Leo said the most important trait to him was his mental capacity and intelligence, since that allowed him to achieve his occupational goals. Yet he claimed this was not related to the prevailing standard. Rather, it tied into his ambitions from before his disability and his willingness to do most anything to achieve his goals.

Before we label him "a rejector," however, note that Leo was a believer in adaptive technology and personal assistance, and he did not see a contradiction between using personal-care assistants and being independent. This seemed to be a reformulation, just as with Damon and Harold but when we asked Leo about this relation to masculinity, he flatly denied any connection.

Leo explained his renunciation of masculinity by saying "It doesn't mean a great deal . . . it's not how I think [of things]." He said that many of the qualities on our list of hegemonic characteristics were important to him on an individual level but did not matter to his sense of manhood. Leo maintained that there were "external" and "internal" reasons for this.

The external factors Leo identified were the Women's and Disability Rights Movements. Both provided support and alternatives that allow a person with a disability the freedom to be a person, and not (to use Leo's words) a "strange bird." Indeed, Leo echoed the call of the Disability Rights

Movement when he described himself as a "person first." In this way, his humanity took precedence and his gender and his disability became less significant.

Also, Leo identified his background as a contributing factor to his outlook. Since childhood, he held a group of friends that valued intellectual achievement over physical performance. In his youth, Leo said he was a member of a group "on the college route." He remained in academia.

Internally, his view of masculinity came from maturity. He had dealt with masculinity and related issues for almost sixty years and reached a point at which he was comfortable with his gender. According to him, his gender conceptions ranged across all three patterns. This was particularly evident in his sexuality. When younger, he relied on a culturally valued, genital sexuality and was concerned with his potency. He wanted to "be on top," despite the physical difficulties this presented him. At the time of our interview, he had a reformulated sexuality. The Women's Movement allowed him to remain sexually active without worrying about "being on top." He even rejected the idea (but not necessarily the physical condition) of potency, noting that it was "even a funny word—potent—that's power."

Further, his age allowed Leo to let go of many of the expectations he had for himself when younger. For instance, he used to overcompensate with great physical activity to prove his manhood and to be "a good daddy." But, he said, he gradually learned that such overcompensation was not necessary.

The practice of "letting go," as Leo and many of our other informants had done, was much like that described by essayist Leonard Kriegel (1991) who, in a series of autobiographical essays, discussed the metaphor of "falling into life" as a way of coping with a disability and masculinity. Kriegel described a common reaction to coping with disability; that is, attempting to "overcome" the results of polio, in his case, by building his upper-body strength through endless hours of exercise. In the end, he experienced premature arthritis in his shoulders and arms. The metaphor of giving up or letting go of behavioral expectations and gender practices as a way to gain greater strength and control over one's life was prevalent among the men who primarily rejected dominant masculinity. As Hahn notes, this requires a cognitive shift and a change in reference group as well as a source of social support:

> I think, ironically, that men with disabilities can acquire strength by acknowledging weakness. Instead of attempting to construct a fragile and ultimately phony identity only as males, they might have more to gain, and little to lose, both individually and collectively by forging a self-concept about the concept of disability. Certainly this approach requires the exposure of a vulnerability that has been a primary reason for the elaborate defense mechanisms that disabled men have commonly employed to protect themselves (1989:3).

Thus, men with disabilities who rejected or renounced masculinity did so as a process of deviance disavowal. They realized that it was societal conceptions of masculinity, rather than themselves, that were problematic. In doing so, they were able to create alternative gender practices.

SUMMARY AND CONCLUSION

The experiences of men with physical disabilities are important, because they illuminate both the insidious power and limitations of contemporary masculinity. These men have insider knowledge of what the subordinated know about both the gender and social order (Janeway 1980). Additionally, the gender practices of some of these men exemplify alternative visions of masculinity that are obscured but available to men in our culture. Finally, they allow us to elucidate a process of paramount importance: How men with physical disabilities find happiness, fulfillment, and a sense of self-worth in a culture that has, in essence, denied them the right to their own identity, including their own masculinity.

Based on our interviews, then, we believe that men with physical disabilities depend on at least three patterns in their adjustment to the double bind associated with the demands of hegemonic masculinity and the stigmatization of being disabled. While each of our informants used one pattern more than the others, none of them depended entirely on any one of the three.

To judge the patterns and practices associated with any form of masculinity, it is necessary to explore the implications for both the personal life of the individual and the effect on the reproduction of the societal gender order (Connell 1990a). Different patterns will challenge, comply, or actively support gendered arrangements.

The reliance pattern is reflected by an emphasis on control, independence, strength, and concern for appearances. Men who rely on dominant conceptions of masculinity are much more likely to internalize their feelings of inadequacy and seek to compensate or overcompensate for them. Because the problem is perceived to be located within oneself rather than within the social structure, this model does not challenge, but rather perpetuates, the current gender order.

A certain distancing from dominant ideals occurs in the reformulation pattern. But reformulation tends to be an independent project, and class-based resources play an important role. As such, it doesn't present a formidable challenge to the gender order. Connell (1990a: 474) argues that this response may even modernize patriarchy.

The rejection model, the least well represented in this article, offers the most hope for change. Linked closely to a sociopolitical approach that defines disability as a product of interactions between individuals and their environment, disability (and masculinity) is understood as socially constructed.

Members of the Disability Rights Movement, as a result, seek to reconstruct masculinity through a three-prong strategy. First, they focus on changing the frame of reference regarding who defines disability and masculinity, thereby changing the social-construction dynamics of both. Second, they endeavor to help people with disabilities be more self-referent when defining their identities. To do that, a third component must be implemented: support structures, such as alternative subcultures, must exist. If the Disability Rights Movement is successful in elevating this struggle to the level of collective practice, it will challenge the legitimacy of the institutional arrangements of the current gender order.

In closing, there is much fruitful work to be done in the area of masculinity and disability. For instance, we should expect men with disabilities to respond differently to the demands associated with disability and masculinity due to sexual orientation, social class, age of onset of one's disability, race, and ethnicity. However, *how* and *why* gender identity varies for men with disabilities merits further study. We hope that this work serves as an impetus for others to take up these issues.

REFERENCES

Callahan, John. 1989. *Don't Worry, He Won't Get Far on Foot.* New York: Vintage Books.

Connell, R. W. 1991. "Live Fast and Die Young: The Construction of Masculinity among Young Working-Class Men on the Margin of the Labor Market." *The Australian and New Zealand Journal of Sociology,* Volume 27, Number 2, August, pp. 141–171.

————. 1990a. "A Whole New World: Remaking Masculinity in the Context of the Environmental Movement." *Gender & Society,* Volume 4, Number 4, December, pp. 452–478.

————. 1990b. "An Iron Man: The Body and Some Contradictions of Hegemonic Masculinity," In *Sport, Men, and the Gender Order,* Michael Messner and Donald Sabo, eds. Champaign, IL: Human Kinetics Publishers, Inc., pp. 83–96.

————. 1987. *Gender and Power: Society, the Person, and Sexual Politics.* Stanford, CA: Stanford University Press.

Denzin, Norman. 1989. *The Research Act: A Theoretical Introduction to Sociological Methods.* Englewood Cliffs, NJ: Prentice-Hall.

Emerson, Robert. 1988. "Introduction." In *Contemporary Field Research: A Collection of Readings,* Robert Emerson, ed. Prospect Heights, IL: Waveland Press, pp. 93–107.

Hahn, Harlan. 1989. "Masculinity and Disability." *Disability Studies Quarterly,* Volume 9, Number 3, pp. 1–3.

Janeway, Elizabeth. 1980. *Powers of the Weak.* New York: Alfred A. Knopf.

Katz, Jack. 1988. "A Theory of Qualitative Methodology: The Social System of Analytic Fieldwork." In *Contemporary Field Research: A Collection of Readings,* Robert Emerson, ed. Prospect Heights, IL: Waveland Press, pp. 127–148.

Kriegel, Leonard. 1991. *Falling into Life.* San Francisco: North Point Press.

Messner, Michael A. 1992. *Power at Play: Sports and the Problem of Masculinity.* Boston: Beacon Press.

Murphy, Robert F. 1990. *The Body Silent.* New York: W. W. Norton.

Scott, James C. 1985. *Weapons of the Weak: Everyday Forms of Peasant Resistance.* New Haven: Yale University Press.

West, Candace, and Don H. Zimmerman. 1987. "Doing Gender." *Gender & Society,* Volume 1, Number 2, June, pp. 125–151.

Zola, Irving Kenneth. 1982. *Missing Pieces: A Chronicle of Living with a Disability.* Philadelphia: Temple University Press.

The Myth of the
"Battered Husband Syndrome"

JACK C. STRATON

The most recurrent backlash against women's safety is the myth that men are battered as often as women. Suzanne Steinmetz (1978) created this myth with her 1977 study of 57 couples, in which four wives were seriously beaten *but no husbands were beaten.* By a convoluted thought process (Pagelow, 1985) she concluded that her finding of zero battered husbands implied that men just don't report abuse and therefore 250,000 American husbands (Steinmetz, 1977) are battered each year by their wives (*Time Magazine,* 1978), a figure that exploded to 12 million in the subsequent media feeding frenzy (Storch, 1978).

Men have never before been shy in making their needs known, so it is peculiar that in 17 years, this supposedly huge contingent of "battered men" has never revealed itself in the flesh. Could it be that it simply does not exist? Indeed, a careful analysis of domestic violence, using everything from common experience to medical studies to U.S. National Crime Survey data, show that only three (Gaquin, 1977/1978) to four (Schwartz, 1987) percent of interspousal violence involves attacks on men by their female partners.

In the myth's latest incarnation, Katherine Dunn (The New Republic, August 1, 1994) is unable to counter these hard scientific data so she turns to disputed sociological studies by Murray Straus and associates (Straus & Gelles, 1986; Straus, Gelles, & Schwartz, 1980, p. 36) for "proof" that violence rates are almost equal. She first implies that these studies are unassailable by calling the authors "two of the most respected researchers in the field of domestic violence." She then cynically attempts to undercut Straus's critics by labeling them as "advocacy groups." In fact, Straus's critics are unimpeachable scientists of both genders, such as Emerson and Russell Dobash (1981) and Edward Gondolf (1988) who say his studies are *bad science,* with findings and conclusions that are contradictory, inconsistent, and unwarranted (Dobash & Dobash, 1981; Pleck et al., 1978; Pagelow, 1980; Saunders, 1988).

There are three major flaws in Straus's work. The first is that he used a set of questions that cannot discriminate between intent and effect (Dobash, Dobash, Wilson, & Daly, 1992; Jackson, 1988; Newton & Gildman, 1983). This so-called Conflict Tactics Scale (or CTS) equates a woman pushing a man in self-defense to a man pushing a woman down the stairs (Jackson, 1988). It labels a mother as violent if she defends her daughter from the father's sexual molestation. It combines categories such as "hitting" and "trying to hit" despite the important difference between them (Pagelow, 1985, p. 178).

Because it looks at only one year, this study equates a single slap by a woman to a man's 15-year history of domestic terrorism. Even Steinmetz herself says the CTS studies ignore the difference between a slap that stings and a punch that causes permanent injury (Steinmetz, 1980). Indeed, after analyzing the results of the U.S. National Crime Surveys, sociologist Martin Schwartz concluded that 92% of those seeking medical care from a private physician for injuries received in a spousal assault are women (Schwartz, 1987). The NCS study shows that one man is hospitalized for injuries received in a spousal assault for every 46 women hospitalized (Saunders, 1988).

Even if we ignore all of the previously mentioned flaws in Straus's CTS studies, they are bad science on a second set of grounds. Straus interviewed only one partner, but other studies (Szinovacz, 1983; Jouriles & O'Leary, 1985) that independently interviewed both partners found that their accounts of the violence did not match. Also, a study by Richard Gelles and John Harrop (1991) using the CTS failed to find any difference in self-reporting of violence against children by step-parents versus birth-parents—in vivid contrast to the actual findings that a step-parent is up to 100 times more likely to assault a small child than is a birth parent (Daly & Wilson, 1988; Dobash et al., 1992). Any research technique that contains a 10,000 percent systematic error is totally unreliable.

In fact, a third independent case can be made against Straus's study. It excluded incidents of violence that occur after separation and divorce, yet these account for 75.9 percent of spouse-on-spouse assaults, with a male perpetrator 93.3 percent of the time, according to the U.S. Department of Justice (1984). The Straus study relied on self-reports of violence by one member of each household, yet men who batter typically under-report their violence by 50 percent (Edleson & Brygger, 1986). Finally, the CTS does not include sexual assault as a category although more women are raped by their husbands than beaten only (Russell, 1990, p. 90). Adjusting Straus's own statistics to include this reality makes the ratio of male to female spousal violence more than sixteen to one.

Police and court records persistently indicate that women are 90 to 95 percent of the victims of reported assaults (Dobash et al., 1992). Promoters of the idea that women are just as abusive as men suggest that these results may be biased because the victims were self-reporting. But Schwartz's analysis of the 1973–1982 U.S. National Crime Surveys shows that men who are assaulted by their spouses actually call the police more often than women who were assaulted by their spouses (Schwartz, 1987). In any case, criminal victimization surveys using random national samples are free of any reporting bias. They give similar results:

- The 1973–81 U.S. National Crime Survey, including over a million interviews, found that only 3 to 4% of marital assaults involved attacks on men by their female partners (Gaquin, 1977/1978; Schwartz, 1987).
- The 1981 and 1987 Canadian surveys (Solicitor General of Canada, 1985; Sacco & Johnson, 1990) found that the number of assaults of males was too low to provide reliable estimates.
- The 1982 and 1984 British surveys found that women accounted for all of the victims of marital assaults (Worrall & Pease).

This is not to say that men are not harmed in our society, but most often men are harmed by other men. Eighty-seven percent of men murdered in the U.S. are killed by other men (U.S. Department of Justice, 1991, p. 17). Those doing the killing in every major and minor war in this and previous centuries have mostly been men! Instead of attempting to undercut services for the enormous number of women who are terrorized by their mates, those who claim to care for men had better address our real enemies: ourselves.

Of course we must have compassion for those relatively few men who are harmed by their wives and partners, but it makes logical sense to focus our attention and work on the vast problem of male violence (96 percent of domestic violence) and not get side-tracked by the relatively tiny (4 percent) problem of male victimization. The biggest concern, though, is not the wasted effort on a false issue, it is the fact that batterers, like O. J. Simpson, who think *they* are the abused spouses, are very dangerous during separation and divorce. In one study of spousal homicide, over half of the male defendants were separated from their victims (Bernard et al., 1982). Arming these men with warped statistics to fuel their already warped world view is unethical, irresponsible, and quite simply lethal.

REFERENCES

Bernard, G. W., Vera, H., Vera, M. I., & Newman, G. (1982). Till death do us part: A Study of spouse murder. *Bulletin of the American Academy of Psychiatry and the Law, 10.*

Daly, M., & Wilson, M. (1988). Evolutionary social psychology and family homicide. *Science, 242,* 519–524.

Dobash, R. E., & Dobash, R. P. (1981). The case of wife beating. *Journal of Family Issues, 2,* 439–470.

Dobash, R. E., Dobash, R. P., Wilson, M., & Daly, M. (1992). The myth of sexual symmetry in marital violence. *Social Problems, 39,* 71–91.

Edleson, J., & Brygger, M. (1986). Gender differences in reporting of battering incidences. *Family Relations 35,* 377–382.

Gaquin, D. A. (1977/1978). Spouse abuse: Data from the National Crime Survey. *Victimology, 2,* 632–643.

Gelles. R. J., & Harrop, J. W. (1991). The risk of abusive violence among children with nongenetic caretakers. *Family Relations, 40,* 78–83.

Gondolf, E. G. (1988). (Letter). *Social Work, 32,* 190.

Jackson, J. (1988). (Letter). *Social Work, 32,* 189–190.

Jouriles, E. N., & O'Leary, K. D. (1985). Interspousal reliability of marital violence. *Journal of Consulting and Clinical Psychology, 53,* 419–421 (as analyzed in Dobash et al., 1992).

Newton, P., & Gildman, G. (1983). *Defining domestic violence: Violent episode or violent act?* Paper presented at the American Sociological Association Conference, Detroit, Illinois.

Pagelow, M. (1980, November). *Double victimization of battered women.* Presented at the meeting of the American Society of Criminology, San Francisco.

Pagelow, M. D. (1985). The "battered husband syndrome": Social problem or much ado about little. In N. Johnson (Ed.), *Marital violence* (Sociological Review Monograph, 31, pp. 172–195). London: Routledge & Kegan Paul.

Pleck, E., Pleck, J. H., Grossman, M., & Bart, P. B. (1978). The Battered Date Syndrome: A comment on Steinmetz' article. *Victimology, 2,* 680–684.

Russell, D. E. H. (1990). *Rape in marriage.* Bloomington, IN: Indiana University Press.

Sacco, V. F., & Johnson, H. (1990). *Patterns of criminal victimization.* Ottawa: Statistics Canada.

Saunders, D. G. (1988). Other "truths" about domestic violence: A reply to McNeely and Robinson-Simpson. *Social Work, 32,* 179–183.

Schwartz, M. D. (1987). Gender and injury in spousal assaults. *Sociological Focus, 20,* 61–75.

Solicitor General of Canada. (1985). Female victims of crime. *Canadian Urban Victimization Survey Bulletin* No. 4. Ottawa: Programs Branch/Research and Statistics Group.

Steinmetz, S. (1977). Wifebeating, husbandbeating: A comparison of the use of physical violence to resolve marital fights. In M. Roy (Ed.), *Battered women* (pp. 63–72). New York: Van Nostrand Reinhold.

Steinmetz, S. K. (1978). The battered husband syndrome. *Victimology, 2,* 499–509.

Steinmetz, S. K. (1980). Women and violence: Victims and perpetrators. *American Journal of Psychotherapy, 34,* 334–350.

Storch, G. (1978, August 7). Claim of 12 million battered husbands takes a beating. *Miami Herald,* p. 16.

Straus, M. A., & Gelles, R. J. (1986). Societal change and change in family violence from 1975 to 1985 as revealed by two national surveys. *Journal of Marriage and the Family, 48,* 465–479.

Straus, M. A., Gelles, R. J., & Steinmetz, S. (1980). *Behind closed doors: Violence in the American family.* New York: Doubleday.

Szinovacz, M. E. (1983). Using couple data as a methodological tool: The case of marital violence. *Journal of Marriage and the Family, 45,* 633–644.

Time Magazine. (1978, March 20). *The battered husbands,* p. 69.

U.S. Department of Justice, Bureau of Justice Statistics. (1984, April). *Family Violence,* p. 4.

U.S. Department of Justice. (1991). *Crime in the United States: Uniform Crime Reports.* Washington, DC: Author.

Worrall, A., & Pease. K. (1986). *Patterns in criminal homicide: Evidence from the 1982 British crime survey.* Philadelphia: University of Pennsylvania Press.

Battered Women of Color
in Public Health Care Systems
Racism, Sexism, and Violence

BETH E. RICHIE
VALLI KANUHA

INTRODUCTION

The problems of rape, battering, and other forms of violence against women have existed throughout history. Only recently have these experiences, traditionally accepted as natural events in the course of women's lives, received significant attention as major social problems (Schechter 1985). For many years there was a tendency for both human service providers and public policy research to focus only on the individual lives of women, children, and men who are damaged or lost due to domestic violence. This narrow focus on individual victims and perpetrators involved in domestic violence rather than on an examination of the role social institutions play in the maintenance of violence against women represents one of the major gaps in our analysis of this pervasive social issue. Paradoxically, the very institutions which have been constructed for the protection and care of the public good—such as the criminal justice system, religious organizations, hospitals, and health care agencies—have long sanctioned disparate and unequal attention to women in society (Lewin and Olesen 1985). Only through a critique of these historically patriarchal and often sexist institutions will we comprehend domestic violence as more than individual acts of violence by perpetrators against victims.

Another equally problematic gap in contemporary analysis and study of violence against women exists with regard to race and ethnicity, i.e., how individual and institutional racism affects the lives of women of color who are battered. With a few notable exceptions, there is very little research on the ways that traditional responses of societal institutions to violence against women are complicated by racism and, therefore, how battered women of color are systematically at a disadvantage when seeking help in most domestic violence situations (Rios 1985). The result is that battered women who are African-American, Latina, Asian/Pacific Islander, East Indian, Native-American, and members of other communities of color are vulnerable to abuse not only from their partners, but from insensitive, ineffective institutions as well.

This chapter will address an important factor which is often ignored in our understanding and analysis of domestic violence. While our increasing knowledge of battered women is usually applied in the context that "all women are vulnerable to male violence," the emphasis of this discussion will be on those differential social, economic, and cultural circumstances that render women of color, in particular, vulnerable to male violence at both individual and institutional levels. In addition, this article will focus specifically on the experiences of battered women of color within the health care system, including hospitals, clinics, and public health agencies. As will be described in later sections, many women of color rely significantly on public health institutions not only for ongoing preventive health care and crisis intervention services, but, more importantly, as a viable access point for other services and institutions, e.g., public welfare, housing assistance, legal advice, and so on. Thus the emphasis of this chapter is on the relationship between health care institutions and battered women of color, although similar critiques could be made about the inadequate response of other public institutions (such as religious organizations or the criminal justice system) to battered women of color. Finally, this essay will discuss some effective strategies and programs which address the unique and complex issues affecting women of color who are battered.

BALANCING OUR MULTIPLE LOYALTIES: SPECIAL CONSIDERATIONS FOR WOMEN OF COLOR AND VICTIMS OF DOMESTIC VIOLENCE

In order to understand the special circumstances and tensions experienced by battered women of color it is important to understand the interface of gender inequality, sexism, and racism as they affect women both in their racial/ethnic communities and in society at large. Because of the powerful effects of a violent relationship, many battered women are required, either overtly or covertly, to balance the often conflicting needs and expectations of their batterers, their communities, and the larger society. These conflicting expectations, rules, and loyalties often compromise the strategies which are available to liberate women of color from violent relationships. This discussion will serve as a foundation for examining the compound effects of oppression which many women of color face even prior to entering the health care system for medical treatment of and protection from domestic violence.

Communities of color in this country have historically been devastated by discriminatory and repressive political, social, and economic policies. It is commonplace to associate high infant mortality, school drop-out rates, criminality, drug abuse,

and most other indices of social dysfunction with African-American, Latino, Native-American, and other non-European ethnic groups (Perales and Young 1988). Even among the "model minorities," Asians and Pacific Islanders, groups of new immigrants as well as their assimilated relatives have shown increased rates of HIV and AIDS, mental health problems, and other negative cofactors which are in part attributable to their status as non-majority (non-White) people in the United States (Chua-Eoan 1990).

Most everyone, from historians to social scientists to politicians, whether conservative or radical, considers racism to be a significant, if not the primary, cause of this disproportionate level of social deterioration among communities of color (Steinberg 1989). While the dynamics of racism have often been studied from a macro-perspective, comparing the effects of race discrimination on particular ethnic groups vis-à-vis society at large, the differential effects of racism on women versus men of color has not been given due attention. In order to adequately understand any analysis of the combined effects of racism, sexism, and battering, a consideration of gender-based tension within communities of men and women of color, separate from and related to the predominant White society, is required.

There are many stereotypes about women of color which affect not only our understanding of them as women, but particularly our analysis of and sensitivity to them with regard to domestic violence. For example, many portrayals of women of color espouse their inherent strengths as historical, matriarchal heads of households (Rudwick and Rudwick 1971). While this stereotype of women of color as super homemakers, responsible family managers, and unselfish nurturers may be undisputed, such attributions do not mean that all (or most) women of color are therefore empowered and supported in their various family roles or have positions of leadership within their ethnic communities. Many women of color with whom we work state that they face the burden either of having to be overly competent and successful or having to avoid the too-often painful reality of becoming "just another one of those horror stories or pitiful statistics on the front page of the newspaper." For women of color who are experiencing domestic violence, the implicit community and societal expectation to be strong and continue to care for themselves and their families results in their denying not only the actual existence of battering in their lives, but the extent and nature of that abuse (Richie 1992). For example, one Korean woman who was repeatedly punched around her head and face by her husband reported that she used cosmetics extensively each day when she went to Mass with her husband, in order to assure protection of her own, as well as her husband's, dignity among their church and neighborhood friends. When she went to work as a typist in a White business, she was especially careful not to disclose evidence of her abuse, in order to protect both herself and her husband from her co-workers' judgments that "there was something wrong with Korean people."

While public policy makers are concerned about the rapidly escalating crime rate in this country, many leaders in cities predominated by communities of color are becoming increasingly concerned about the profile of those convicted for crimes, i.e., young boys and men of color. The predominance of men of color in correctional facilities (close to 90 percent of the penal population in some cities) has polarized everyone, from scholars to community leaders to policy makers. While most mainstream legislators and public health officials are reluctant to discuss it publicly, there is a rising belief that men of color are inherently problematic and socially deviant. More progressive analysts have ascribed criminal behavior among nonwhite males to historically racist social conditions that are reinforced by criminal, legal, and penal systems which disproportionately arrest and convict men of color at least in part because of their skin color (Kurtz 1990).

There are no equally concerned dialogues about how women of color continue to be victims of crime more often than white women and about the disparate treatment they receive from not only racist, but sexist social systems. An African-American woman who works with battered women as a court advocate states unequivocally that battered women of color are usually treated less respectfully by prosecutors and judges than the white women with whom she works. In addition, when this same court advocate has raised this disparity with her African-American brothers and male friends in her community, she is often derided as being "one of those White women's libbers" who has betrayed "her own" by working on a problem like domestic violence, which will further stigmatize and destroy the men of color who are charged with battering. Unfortunately, this dialectic of the comparable oppression of women and men of color has resulted in a troubling silence about the needs of women of color and led to counterproductive discussions between women and men of color about the meaning and significance of domestic violence, specifically, and sexism in general.

For a battered woman of color who experiences violence at the hands of a man of color from her own ethnic group, a complex and troublesome dynamic is established that is both enhanced and compromised by the woman's relationship to her community. She is battered by another member of her ethnic community, whose culture is vulnerable to historical misunderstanding and extinction by society at large. For the battered woman, this means that she may be discriminated against in her attempt to secure services *while at the same time* feeling protective of her batterer, who might also be unjustly treated by such social institutions as the police and the judicial system. Most battered women of color are acutely aware of how the police routinely brutalize men of color, how hospitals and social services discriminate against men of color, and the ways men of color are more readily labeled deviant than White men. In one Midwestern city, anecdotal reports from court and police monitors have shown that men of color awaiting arraignment for domestic violence charges frequently arrive in court with bruises supposedly inflicted by police officers. One Indian woman stated that when she saw her husband in court the morning after a battering incident, he looked just as bad as she did, with black eyes and bruises about his face. Feeling pity for him, she refused to testify, and upon release he told her of being beaten by police while being transported between the jail and the court house. Although the existence of police brutality is unfortunately not a new phenomenon, it is certainly compromised and complicated in the context of domestic violence, *especially* for men and women of color who are seeking help from this already devastating problem. For battered women of color, seeking help for the abuse they are experiencing always requires a tenuous balance between care for and loyalty to themselves, their batterers, and their communities.

The situation is further complicated by the fact that communities of color have needed to prioritize the pressing social, economic, and health problems which have historically plagued their people and neighborhoods. Because of sexism, the particular concerns of women typically do not emerge at the top of the list. The values of family stability, community self-determination, and protection of one's racial and ethnic culture are often seen as incompatible with addressing the needs of battered women within communities of color. Most of us who have worked in the domestic violence movement are well aware of the gross misconceptions that battering is just a woman's issue or that domestic violence in communities of color is not as serious as other problems. The most dangerous consequence, for battered women of color, however, is that they are often entrapped by these misconceptions and misguided loyalties and thus remain in the confines of violent and abusive households (Richie 1985).

While credit for a broad-based societal response to the problem of violence against women must be given to the feminist movement and its successful grassroots organizing in the mid-1970s, another process of "split loyalties" has emerged, compromising the analysis regarding battered women of color. Those women of color who identify themselves as activists, feminists, and organiz-

ers within the battered women's movement often face an additional barrier among their feminist peers when raising issues related to the particular dynamics of domestic violence and race/ethnicity (Hooks 1984). Many White feminists and the organizations they have created become very threatened when women of color, with their concomitant expanded analysis of battering and racism, have moved into leadership roles. Many women of color in the violence against women movement have challenged the long-standing belief of many White feminists that sexism is the primary, if not the only, cause of women's oppression. In a reform movement which has had such a significant impact on the values, behaviors, and subsequent policies regarding women and violence, the reluctance or inability to integrate an understanding of violence against women with other forms of oppression (such as racism, classism, ageism) in addition to sexism has been disappointing (Davis 1985). A more significant concern, though, is the effect of limited analysis on women and children of color who are seeking refuge and safety from both hostile partners and social institutions outside the battered women's movement.

In summary, our understanding of women of color who are battered must be considered against the political, social, and cultural backdrop of their racial and ethnic communities; within the framework of institutional responses that are historically based in racism and other prejudices; and against the background of the feminist agenda, which has been primarily responsible for galvanizing all of the above to address this pervasive social issue. It is in this context that we turn to an examination of the particular influence, concerns, and barriers of the health care system in dealing with battered women of color.

BATTERED WOMEN OF COLOR: HEALTH PROBLEMS AND HEALTH CARE

Women who are battered are often seriously hurt; their physical and psychological injuries are life-threatening and long-lasting. In one-third of all battering incidents, a weapon is used, and 40 percent result in the need for emergency medical attention (Stark 1977). Research suggests that one-third of all adult female suicide attempts can be associated with battering, and 25 percent of all female homicide victims die at the hands of their husbands or boyfriends (Browne 1987). More women are injured in their homes by their spouses or male partners each year than by accidents or illnesses (FBI 1982).

It is not surprising, therefore, that most battered women report their first attempt to seek help is from a health care institution, even before contacting the police (Stark 1977). This is especially true in communities of color, where police response is likely to be sporadic, at best (Davis 1985). Yet research indicates that of those battered women using the emergency room for acute treatment of injuries related to an abusive incident, only one in ten was identified as battered (McLeer and Amwar 1989). Similar findings have been cited for women using ambulatory care settings. A random sample of women seeking health maintenance visits at neighborhood health clinics revealed that 33 percent were battered women and less than 10 percent received safety information or counseling for domestic violence (Richie 1985). The following story of Yolanda (a pseudonym) illustrates the role of health facilities in the lives of battered women.

> Yolanda is a forty-six-year old who receives primary health care from a neighborhood health clinic. She uses the services of the walk-in clinic two or more times each month, complaining of discomfort, sleeplessness and fatigue. Yolanda never mentions that her boyfriend abuses her, but her clinic visits correspond directly with the pattern of his alcohol binges. The staff of the clinic know about her boyfriend's mistreatment, because he sometimes comes to the clinic drunk and will threaten her if she does not leave with him.

For Yolanda, the clinic symbolizes a safe, public place of refuge. From her experience, she knows it is legitimate to seek assistance when one is sick, and she trusts health authorities to take care of her

needs. Health providers lose an important opportunity for intervention when they do not offer assistance to Yolanda, especially since they have clear evidence that her boyfriend is violent toward her. She, in turn, feels that the violence must be hidden and that it is a source of shame, since her health care providers do not acknowledge it or offer to help.

For many battered women of color, the unresponsiveness of most health care institutions is symbolic of the overall reality of social disenfranchisement and deterioration in poor, nonwhite communities across the United States. While lack of quality, affordable housing is a major problem for many people of color, the majority of the homeless are women of color and their children (Perales and Young 1988). The drug epidemic, particularly crack and heroin use, has had a significant impact on violence against women. There is growing anecdotal evidence to suggest that battered women are often forced to use drugs as part of the pattern of their abuse, yet there is a serious lack of treatment programs for women, particularly poor women with children (Chavkin 1990). The spread of HIV and AIDS among many women of color has been compounded by the HIV infection rate among children of HIV-positive mothers. Many women with HIV report that negotiating for safer sex or clean needles is difficult when they are controlled by violent, coercive partners.

With regard to women and the social problems of drugs, homelessness, and AIDS, most public health officials have been quick to label women as the criminals, rather than the victims of a society that is disintegrating before our very eyes. When we add to the above the battering, rape, and psychological abuse of those same women who are homeless, drug addicted, and HIV-positive, it is clear that the health care system can be either a vehicle for assistance or a significant barrier for women who are seeking protection from a myriad of health and social problems.

The experience of Ana illustrates the interrelatedness that can occur between domestic violence, drug use, HIV infection, and the chronic and acute need for health care. Ana's husband was an injection drug user who had battered her severely throughout their ten-year marriage. He had been very ill for a period of months and had tested positive for HIV. Ana was already pregnant when her husband was tested, but he insisted that she carry through with the pregnancy. She was battered twice in the four months since she had gotten pregnant, and after one incident she was unable to get out of bed for two days. Her husband Daniel reportedly was concerned about the baby and took her to the emergency room of their local hospital. During the triage interview, the ER (Emergency Room) nurse noticed the tension between Ana and Daniel but was uncomfortable addressing it. The nurse later reported that she did not want to offend them by suggesting that they appeared to be having "marriage problems" because they were Hispanic, and she understood that Hispanics were embarrassed about discussing such matters with health professionals. After being admitted for observation, Ana began to complain of increased pains in her abdomen. After five days in the hospital, Ana hemorrhaged and lost her baby. At that time, she discovered that she had been tested for HIV and was seropositive. She returned home to a distraught and angry husband, who blamed the baby's death on her. She was beaten again and returned to the ER once more.

Ana's case illustrates one of the most troubling examples of the interface between health care and violence against women. With the long-standing lack of adequate and accessible prenatal care for poor women of color, pregnant women of color who are battered are especially vulnerable. Research indicates that 20 percent of all women who are battered experience the first incident during pregnancy (McFarlane 1989). The situation for pregnant battered women is further complicated by the troubling legal trend to hold women accountable for any damage inflicted upon a fetus in utero. If a pregnant woman is battered and the fetus is harmed, she may be criminally liable for not leaving the abusive relationship. Not surprisingly, in most recent "fetal death" cases across the country, the women who are most severely punished are women of color (Pollitt 1990).

As the health care system has labored under increased social and economical stress, specialized programs for women and for certain communities have also been curtailed. For battered women of color this trend has specific and dangerous affects. With a steady increase in immigrants from Central America, South America, and the Caribbean, battered women who do not have legal status in this country are destined to remain invisible and underserved. Because of their undocumented status and other significant barriers (such as language and cultural differences), many battered women of color are denied assistance by the same organizations established to protect them, e.g., public welfare, legal advocacy, and health clinics (Kanuha 1987). One battered women's program specifically targeted to serve Caribbean women and their children reports that battered women who must use hospital services for their injuries often have to borrow Medicaid cards from other women in order to conceal their undocumented status. Staff from this same program describe the difficulty that one undocumented woman had even getting out of the house, much less to the hospital, as her batterer was rightfully suspicious that reports of his criminal behavior would also jeopardize *his* illegal status.

Most hospital-based crisis intervention programs do not have multi-lingual or multi-cultural staff who are trained in and sensitive to the special issues of women of color. For example, reliance on translators to communicate with non-English speaking women effectively compromises the confidentiality and protection of battered women who are immigrants, from small ethnic communities, or who must use their own family members as translators to describe painful and private incidents of violence in the home. There are numerous stories of women of color receiving insensitive treatment by health care staff who attribute domestic violence to stereotypes such as "I've heard you Latins have hot tempers" or "Asian women are so passive, it really explains why they get beaten by their husbands."

Finally, if a battered woman of color is also a lesbian, differently abled, or from any other group that is already stigmatized, her access to quality care from health providers may be further compromised. One battered lesbian who was an African American described a physician who was continually incredulous about her claims that a "pretty girl like her" would be beaten by her female lover. In fact, she stopped going to the hospital for emergency attention, even though she had no other health insurance, because she was angry at such homophobic treatment and therefore became increasingly reluctant to use the services of that hospital.

As long as health care institutions continue to be the primary, and usually first, access point for battered women of color, we must require them to institute ongoing training, education, and specialized programs, and to hire culturally knowledgeable staff to address the particular needs of this special group of women.

THE RESPONSE OF WOMEN OF COLOR

Despite the philosophical and political contradictions and the practical barriers described in the previous sections, women of color have actively and creatively challenged the discriminatory, institutional practices of health care and crisis intervention services. Against extremely difficult economic, cultural, and political odds, battered women of color and their advocates have initiated a broad-based response to violence against women in communities of color. Aspects of this response will be summarized in the remainder of the chapter.

One of the most significant developments in response to domestic violence in communities of color has been the creation of grassroots crisis intervention services by and for women of color. The majority of these programs have been organized autonomously from White women, privileging the analysis and experience of women of color by assuming the cultural, historical, and linguistic norms of Asian/Pacific Islander, Latin, African-American, Native-American and other nonwhite cultures. Typically located in neighborhoods and communities of color, these programs have a strong emphasis on community organization and public education. While many of these programs struggle for financial support and recognition from mainstream public health agencies and feminist organizations, they endure in great part because they are grounded in a community-based approach to problem solving.

The Violence Intervention Program for Latina women and their children in the community of East Harlem and the Asian Womens' Center in Chinatown are good examples of community-based programs in New York City. Refugee Women In Development (REFWID), in Washington, D.C., has a domestic violence component, as does Arco Iris, a retreat center for Native-American women and other women of color who have experienced violence in Arkansas. In Minnesota, women of color have created a statewide battered women's coalition called Black, Indian, Hispanic and Asian Women In Action (BIHA). In California, California Women Of Color Against Domestic Violence organizes and publishes a newsletter, "Out Loud," and women of color from seven southern states have created The Southeast Women Of Color Task Force Against Domestic Violence. Nationally, the members of the Women Of Color Task Force of the National Coalition Against Domestic Violence have provided national leadership training and technical assistance on the issues of battering and women of color, and their task force has served as a model for the development of programs for battered women of color across the country.

In addition to providing crisis intervention and emergency shelter services to battered women, these community-based programs and statewide coalitions for women of color are involved in raising the issue of battering within other contexts of social justice efforts. Representatives of grassroots battered women's programs are often in leadership roles on such issues as reproductive freedom, immigration policy, lesbian rights, criminal justice reform, homelessness, AIDS policy, and other issues that affect women of color. The National

Black Women's Health Project in Atlanta is a good example of this.

Finally, in the past several years there has been a proliferation of literature on violence against women by scholars and activists who are women of color. Seal Press's New Leaf Series published Evelyn C. White's *Chain, Chain Change: For Black Women Dealing With Physical And Emotional Abuse* and Myrna Zambrano's *Mejor Sola Que Mal Acompanada.* Another good example of analysis by and for battered women of color is a publication by the Center For Domestic And Sexual Violence in Seattle, *The Speaking Profits Us: Violence Against Women Of Color,* a collection of papers edited by Mary Violet Burns. Kitchen Table, Women of Color Press in Albany, New York, has been a leader in publishing writing by women of color, addressing the issue of violence against women in the Freedom Organizing pamphlet series and in many other works (Smith 1985).

By providing direct crisis intervention services, educating communities of color, advocating on broader feminist and social justice issues and publishing culturally relevant resources, Asian/Pacific Islanders, Latinas, Native-Americans, African Americans, Caribbeans, and other women of color have demonstrated a strong commitment to addressing violence against women. Our contributions have significantly enhanced both the conventional research on battered women and the progressive work of the battered women's movement, challenging the accepted analysis that violence against women has equivalent effects on all women. We must continue to develop community-based programs that are culturally relevant and responsive to the complexity of experiences faced by women of color, including inadequate health care, unemployment, homelessness, a failing educational system, and violence. Equally important, we must continue to work within our own cultures to challenge those traditions, assumptions, and values that reinforce male domination and ignore women's needs. In so doing, the struggle to end violence against women of color will include individual liberation as well as social reform. For us, the most compelling motivation for continuing this effort comes from the courage, commitment, and endurance that battered women of color have shown in their personal and collective struggles. On a daily basis they persist in defying the limits that violence, sexism, and racism impose on their lives. Our response must be to let their stories challenge and inspire us—women of color, battered women, White women, and men alike—to work actively to end individual and institutional violence against women.

NOTE

The women described in this essay are referred to anonymously or by pseudonyms to protect their safety and privacy. Their stories are both composites and individual accounts of women with whom the authors have worked.

REFERENCES

Browne, A. 1987. *When Battered Women Kill.* New York: Free Press.

Cazenave, N., and M. Straus. 1979. "Race, Class Network Embeddedness and Family Violence: A Search For Potent Support Systems." *Journal of Comparative Family Studies* 10:281–299.

Chavkin, W. 1990. "Drug Addiction and Pregnancy: Policy Crossroads." *American Journal of Public Health* 80 (4):483–87.

Chua-Eoan, H. 1990. "Strangers in Paradise." *Time* (April). 135:32–35.

Davis, A. 1985. *Violence against Women and the Ongoing Challenge to Racism.* Latham, N.Y.: Kitchen Table Press.

Federal Bureau of Investigation. 1982. *Uniform Crime Reports.* Washington, D.C.: Department of Justice.

Flitcraft, A. 1977. "Battered Women: An Emergency Room Epidemiology with Description of a Clinical Syndrome and Critique of Present Therapeutics." Doctoral Thesis, Yale University School Of Medicine. New Haven: Yale University.

Hooks, B. 1984. *Feminist Theory: From Margin to Center.* Boston: South End Press.

Kanuha, V. 1987. "Sexual Assault in Southeast Asian Communities: Issues in Intervention." *Response* 10:3–4.

Kurtz, H. 1990. "Jail City: Behind Bars with New York's 20,000 Inmates." *New York Magazine.* April 23, 1990.

Lewin, E., and F. Olesen, eds. 1985. *Women, Health and Healing: Towards a New Perspective.* New York: Travistock Publications.

McFarlane, J. 1989. "Battering During Pregnancy: Tip of an Iceberg Revealed." *Women and Health* 15 (3):69–84.

McLeer, S., and R. Amwar. 1989. "A Study of Battered Women Presenting in an Emergency Department." *American Journal of Public Health.* 79 (1):65–66.

Perales, C., and L. Young, eds. 1988. *Too Little Too Late: Dealing with the Health Needs of Women in Poverty.* New York: Harrington Press.

Pollitt, K. 1990. "A New Assault on Feminism." *Nation.* 250:409–11.

Richie, B. 1985. "Battered Black Women: A Challenge for the Black Community." *Black Scholar,* 16:40–44.

Richie, B. 1992. "An Exploratory Study of the Link between Gender Identity Development, Violence Against Women, and Crime among African-American Battered Women." Ph.D. diss., The Graduate School and University Center, City University of New York.

Rios, E. 1985. "Double Jeopardy: Cultural and Systemic Barriers Faced by the Latina Battered Woman." Unpublished paper presented at the New York Women against Rape Conference, New York.

Rudwick, B., A. Meier, and E. Rudwick, eds. 1971. *Black Matriarchy: Myth or Reality.* Belmont, Calif.: Wadsworth Press.

Schechter, S. 1985. *Women and Male Violence.* Boston: South End Press.

Smith, B., ed. 1985. *Home Girls: A Black Feminist Anthology.* Latham, N.Y.: Kitchen Table Press.

Stark, E., A. Flintcraft and W. Frazier. 1977. "Medicine and Patriarchal Violence: The Social Construction of a 'Private Event.'" *International Journal of Health Services.* 9 (3): 461–94.

Steinberg, S. 1989. *The Ethnic Myth: Race, Ethnicity, and Class in America.* Boston: Beacon Press.

White, E. 1985. *Chain, Chuin Change: For Black Women Dealing with Physical and Emotional Abuse.* Seattle: Seal Press.

Zambrano, M. 1985. *Mejor Sola Que Mal Acompanada: Para la Mujer Golpeada/ For the Latina in an Abusive Relationship.* Seattle: Seal Press.

Men on Rape

TIM BENEKE

Rape may be America's fastest growing violent crime; no one can be certain because it is not clear whether more rapes are being committed or reported. It *is* clear that violence against women is widespread and fundamentally alters the meaning of life for women; that sexual violence is encouraged in a variety of ways in American culture; and that women are often blamed for rape.

Consider some statistics:

- In a random sample of 930 women, sociologist Diana Russell found that 44 percent had survived either rape or attempted rape. Rape was defined as sexual intercourse physically forced upon the woman, or coerced by threat of bodily harm, or forced upon the woman when she was helpless (asleep, for example). The survey included rape and attempted rape in marriage in its calculations (personal communication).
- In a September 1980 survey conducted by *Cosmopolitan* magazine to which over 106,000 women anonymously responded, 24 percent had been raped at least once. Of these, 51 percent had been raped by friends, 37 percent by strangers, 18 percent by relatives, and 3 percent by husbands. Ten percent of the women in the survey had been victims of incest. Seventy-five percent of the women had been "bullied into making love." Writer Linda Wolfe, who reported on the survey, wrote in reference to such bullying: "Though such harassment stops short of rape, readers reported that it was nearly as distressing."
- An estimated 2–3 percent of all men who rape outside of marriage go to prison for their crimes.[1]

- The F.B.I. estimates that if current trends continue, one woman in four will be sexually assaulted in her lifetime.[2]
- An estimated 1.8 million women are battered by their spouses each year.[3] In extensive interviews with 430 battered women, clinical psychologist Lenore Walker, author of *The Battered Woman,* found that 59.9 percent had also been raped (defined as above) by their spouses. Given the difficulties many women had in admitting they had been raped, Walker estimates the figure may well be as high as 80 or 85 percent (personal communication). If 59.9 percent of the 1.8 million women battered each year are also raped, then a million women may be raped in marriage each year. And a significant number are raped in marriage without being battered.
- Between one in two and one in ten of all rapes are reported to the police.[4]
- Between 300,000 and 500,000 women are raped each year outside of marriage.[5]

What is often missed when people contemplate statistics on rape is the effect of the *threat* of sexual violence on women. I have asked women repeatedly, "How would your life be different if rape were suddenly to end?" (Men may learn a lot by asking this question of women to whom they are close.) The threat of rape is an assault upon the meaning of the world; it alters the feel of the human condition. Surely any attempt to comprehend the lives of women that fails to take issues of violence against women into account is misguided.

Through talking to women, I learned: *The threat of rape alters the meaning and feel of the night.* Observe how your body feels, how the night feels, when you're in fear. The constriction in your chest, the vigilance in your eyes, the rubber in your legs. What do the stars look like? How does the moon present itself? What is the difference between walking late at night in the dangerous part of a city and walking late at night in the country, or safe suburbs? When I try to imagine what the threat of rape must do to the night, I think of the stalked, adrenalated feeling I get walking late at night in parts of certain American cities. Only, I remind myself, it is a fear different from any I have known, a fear of being raped.

It is night half the time. If the threat of rape alters the meaning of the night, it must alter the meaning and pace of the day, one's relation to the passing and organization of time itself. For some women, the threat of rape at night turns their cars into armored tanks, their solitude into isolation. And what must the space inside a car or an apartment feel like if the space outside is menacing?

I was running late one night with a close woman friend through a path in the woods on the outskirts of a small university town. We had run several miles and were feeling a warm, energized serenity.

"How would you feel if you were alone?" I asked.

"Terrified!" she said instantly.

"Terrified that there might be a man out there?" I asked, pointing to the surrounding moonlit forest, which had suddenly been transformed into a source of terror.

"Yes."

Another woman said, "I know what I can't do and I've completely internalized what I can't do. I've built a viable life that basically involves never leaving my apartment at night unless I'm directly going some place to meet somebody. It's unconsciously built into what it occurs to women to do." When one is raised without freedom, one may not recognize its absence.

The threat of rape alters the meaning and feel of nature. Everyone has felt the psychic nurturance of nature. Many women are being deprived of that nurturance, especially in wooded areas near cities. They are deprived either because they cannot experience nature in solitude because of threat, or because, when they do choose solitude in nature, they must cope with a certain subtle but nettlesome fear.

Women need more money because of rape and the threat of rape makes it harder for women to earn money. It's simple: if you don't feel safe walking at night, or riding public transportation, you need a car. And it is less practicable to live in cheaper, less secure, and thus more dangerous neighborhoods if the ordinary threat of violence that men experience, being mugged, say, is compounded by the threat of rape. By limiting mobility at night, the threat of rape limits where and when one is able to work, thus making it more difficult to earn money. An obvious bind: women need more money because of rape, and have fewer job opportunities because of it.

The threat of rape makes women more dependent on men (or other women). One woman said: "If there were no rape I wouldn't have to play games with men for their protection." The threat of rape falsifies, mystifies, and confuses relations between men and women. If there were no rape, women would simply not need men as much, wouldn't need them to go places with at night, to feel safe in their homes, for protection in nature.

The threat of rape makes solitude less possible for women. Solitude, drawing strength from being alone, is difficult if being alone means being afraid. To be afraid is to be in need, to experience a lack; the threat of rape creates a lack. Solitude requires relaxation; if you're afraid, you can't relax.

The threat of rape inhibits a woman's expressiveness. "If there were no rape," said one woman, "I could dress the way I wanted and walk the way I wanted and not feel self-conscious about the responses of men. I could be friendly to people. I wouldn't have to wish I was ugly. I wouldn't have to make myself small when I got on the bus. I wouldn't have to respond to verbal abuse from men by remaining silent. I could respond in kind."

If a woman's basic expressiveness is inhibited, her sexuality, creativity, and delight in life must surely be diminished.

The threat of rape inhibits the freedom of the eye. I know a married couple who live in Manhattan. They are both artists, both acutely sensitive and responsive to the visual world. When they walk separately in the city, he has more freedom to look than she does. She must control her eye movements lest they inadvertently meet the glare of some importunate man. What, who, and how she sees are restricted by the threat of rape.

The following exercise is recommended for men.

> *Walk down a city street. Pay a lot of attention to your clothing; make sure your pants are zipped, shirt tucked in, buttons done. Look straight ahead. Every time a man walks past you, avert your eyes and make your face expressionless. Most women learn to go through this act each time we leave our houses. It's a way to avoid at least some of the encounters we've all had with strange men who decided we looked available.[6]*

To relate aesthetically to the visual world involves a certain playfulness, spirit of spontaneous exploration. The tense vigilance that accompanies fear inhibits that spontaneity. The world is no longer yours to look at when you're afraid.

I am aware that all culture is, in part, restriction, that there are places in America where hardly anyone is safe (though men are safer than women virtually everywhere), that there are many ways to enjoy life, that some women may not be so restricted, that there exist havens, whether psychic, geographical, economic, or class. But they are *havens,* and as such, defined by threat.

Above all, I trust my experience: no woman could have lived the life I've lived the last few years. If suddenly I were restricted by the threat of rape, I would feel a deep, inexorable depression. And it's not just rape; it's harassment, battery, Peeping Toms, anonymous phone calls, exhibitionism, intrusive stares, fondlings—all contributing to an atmosphere of intimidation in women's lives. And I have only scratched the surface; it would take many carefully crafted short stories to begin to express what I have only hinted at in the last few pages. I have not even touched upon what it might mean for a woman to be sexually assaulted. Only women can speak to that. Nor have I suggested how the threat of rape affects marriage.

Rape and the threat of rape pervade the lives of women, as reflected in some popular images of our culture.

"SHE ASKED FOR IT"— BLAMING THE VICTIM[7]

Many things may be happening when a man blames a woman for rape.

First, in all cases where a woman is said to have asked for it, her appearance and behavior are taken as a form of speech. "Actions speak louder than words" is a widely held belief; the woman's actions—her appearance may be taken as action—are given greater emphasis than her words; an interpretation alien to the woman's intentions is given to her actions. A logical extension of "she asked for it" is the idea that she wanted what happened to happen; if she wanted it to happen, she *deserved* for it to happen. Therefore, the man is not to be blamed. "She asked for it" can mean either that she was consenting to have sex and was not really raped, or that she was in fact raped but somehow she really deserved it. "If you ask for it, you deserve it," is a widely held notion. If I ask you to beat me up and you beat me up, I still don't deserve to be beaten up. So even if the notion that women asked to be raped had some basis in reality, which it doesn't, on its own terms it makes no sense.

Second, a mentality exists that says: a woman who assumes freedoms normally restricted to a man (like going out alone at night) and is raped is doing the same thing as a woman who goes out in the rain without an umbrella and catches a cold. Both are considered responsible for what happens to them. That men will rape is taken to be a legitimized given, part of nature, like rain or snow. The view reflects a massive abdication of responsibility for rape on the part of men. It is so much easier to think of rape as natural than to acknowledge one's part in it. So long as rape is regarded as natural, women will be blamed for rape.

A third point. The view that it is natural for men to rape is closely connected to the view of women as commodities. If a woman's body is regarded as a valued commodity by men, then of course, if you leave a valued commodity where it can be taken, it's just human nature for men to take it. If you left your stereo out on the sidewalk, you'd be asking for it to get stolen. Someone will just take it. (And how often men speak of rape as "going out and *taking* it.") If a woman walks the streets at night, she's leaving a valued commodity, her body, where it can be taken. So long as women are regarded as commodities, they will be blamed for rape.

Which brings us to a fourth point. "She asked for it" is inseparable from a more general "psychology of the dupe." If I use bad judgment and fail to read the small print in a contract and later get taken advantage of ("screwed" or "fucked over") then I deserve what I get; bad judgment makes me liable. Analogously, if a woman trusts a man and goes to his apartment, or accepts a ride hitchhiking, or goes out on a date and is raped, she's a dupe and deserves what she gets. "He didn't *really* rape her" goes the mentality—"he merely took advantage of her." And in America it's okay for people to take advantage of each other, even expected and praised. In fact, you're considered dumb and foolish if you don't take advantage of other people's bad judgment. And so, again, by treating them as dupes, rape will be blamed on women.

Fifth, if a woman who is raped is judged attractive by men, and particularly if she dresses to look attractive, then the mentality exists that she attacked him with her weapon so, of course, he counter-attacked with his. The preview to a popular movies states: "She was the victim of her own *provocative beauty.*" Provocation: "There is a line which, if crossed will *set me off* and I will lose control and no longer be responsible for my behavior. If you punch me in the nose then, of course, I will not be responsible for what happens: you will have provoked a fight. If you dress, talk, move, or act a certain way, you will have provoked me to rape. If your appearance *stuns* me, *strikes* me, *ravishes* me, *knocks me out*, etc., then I will not be held responsible for what happens; you will have asked for it." The notion that sexual

feeling makes one helpless is part of a cultural abdication of responsibility for sexuality. So long as a woman's appearance is viewed as a weapon and sexual feeling is believed to make one helpless, women will be blamed for rape.

Sixth, I have suggested that men sometimes become obsessed with images of women, that images become a substitute for sexual feeling, that sexual feeling becomes externalized and out of control and is given an undifferentiated identity in the appearance of women's bodies. It is a process of projection in which one blurs one's own desire with her imagined, projected desire. If a woman's attractiveness is taken to signify one's own lust and a woman's lust, then when an "attractive" woman is raped, some men may think she wanted sex. Since they perceive their own lust in part projected onto the woman, they disbelieve women who've been raped. So long as men project their own sexual desires onto women, they will blame women for rape.

And seventh, what are we to make of the contention that women in dating situations say "no" initially to sexual overtures from men as a kind of pose, only to give in later, thus revealing their true intentions? And that men are thus confused and incredulous when women are raped because in their sexual experience women can't be believed? I doubt that this has much to do with men's perceptions of rape. I don't know to what extent women actually "say no and mean yes"; certainly it is a common theme in male folklore. I have spoken to a couple of women who went through periods when they wanted to be sexual but were afraid to be, and often rebuffed initial sexual advances only to give in later. One point is clear: the ambivalence women may feel about having sex is closely tied to the inability of men to fully accept them as sexual beings. Women have been traditionally punished for being openly and freely sexual; men are praised for it. And if many men think of sex as achievement of possession of a valued commodity, or aggressive degradation, then women have every reason to feel and act ambivalent.

These themes are illustrated in an interview I conducted with a 23 year old man who grew up in

Pittsburgh and works as a file clerk in the financial district of San Francisco. Here's what he said:

"Where I work it's probably no different from any other major city in the U.S. The women dress up in high heels, and they wear a lot of makeup, and they just look really *hot* and really sexy, and how can somebody who has a healthy sex drive not feel lust for them when you see them? I feel lust for them, but I don't think I could find it in me to overpower someone and rape them. But I definitely get the feeling that I'd like to rape a girl. I don't know if the actual act of rape would be satisfying, but the *feeling* is satisfying.

"These women look so good, and they kiss ass of the men in the three-piece suits who are *big* in the corporation, and most of them relate to me like 'Who are *you?* Who are *you* to even *look* at?' They're snobby and they condescend to me, and I resent it. It would take me a lot longer to get to first base than it would somebody with a three-piece suit who had money. And to me a lot of the men they go out with are superficial assholes who have no real feelings or substance, and are just trying to get ahead and make a lot of money. Another thing that makes me resent these women is thinking, 'How could she want to hang out with somebody like that? What does that make her?'

"I'm a file clerk, which makes me feel like a nebbish, a nurd, like I'm not making it, I'm a failure. But I don't really believe I'm a failure because I know it's just a phase, and I'm just doing it for the money, just to make it through this phase. I catch myself feeling like a failure, but I realize that's ridiculous."

What Exactly Do You Go through When You See These Sexy, Unavailable Women?
"Let's say I see a woman and she looks really pretty and really clean and sexy, and she's giving off very feminine, sexy vibes. I think, 'Wow, I would love to make love to her,' but I know she's not really interested. It's a tease. A lot of times a woman knows that she's looking really good and she'll use that and flaunt it, and it makes me feel like she's laughing at me and I feel *degraded.*

"I also feel dehumanized, because when I'm being teased I just turn off, I cease to be human. Because if I go with my human emotions I'm going to want to put my arms around her and kiss her, and to do that would be unacceptable. I don't like the feeling that I'm supposed to stand there and take it, and not be able to hug her or kiss her; so I just turn off my emotions. It's a feeling of humiliation, because the woman has forced me to turn off my feelings and react in a way that I really don't want to.

"If I were actually desperate enough to rape somebody, it would be from wanting the person, but it would be a very spiteful thing, just being able to say, 'I have power over you and I can do anything I want with you,' because really I feel that *they* have power over *me* just by their presence. Just the fact that they can come up to me and just melt me and make me feel like a dummy makes me want revenge. They have power over me so I want power over them. . . .

"Society says that you have to have a lot of sex with a lot of different women to be a real man. Well, what happens if you don't? Then what are you? Are you half a man? Are you still a boy? It's ridiculous. You see a whiskey ad with a guy and two women on his arm. The implication is that real men don't have any trouble getting women."

How Does It Make You Feel toward Women to See All These Sexy Women in Media and Advertising Using Their Looks to Try to Get You to Buy Something?
"It makes me hate them. As a man you're taught that men are more powerful than women, and that men always have the upper hand, and that it's a man's society; but then you see all these women and it makes you think, 'Jesus Christ, if we have all the power how come all the beautiful women are telling us what to buy?' And to be honest, it just makes me hate beautiful women because they're using their power over me. I realize they're being used themselves, and they're doing it for money. In *Playboy* you see all these beautiful women who look so sexy and they'll be giv-

ing you all these looks like they want to have sex so bad; but then in reality you know that except for a few nymphomaniacs, they're doing it for the money; so I hate them for being used and for using their bodies in that way.

"In this society, if you ever sit down and realize how manipulated you really are it makes you pissed off—it makes you want to take control. And you've been manipulated by women, and they're a very easy target because they're out walking along the streets, so you can just grab one and say, 'Listen, you're going to do what I want you to do,' and it's an act of revenge against the way you've been manipulated.

"I know a girl who was walking down the street by her house, when this guy jumped her and beat her up and raped her, and she was black and blue and had to go to the hospital. That's beyond me. I can't understand how somebody could do that. If I were going to rape a girl, I wouldn't hurt her. I might *restrain* her, but I wouldn't *hurt* her. . . .

"The whole dating game between men and women also makes me feel degraded. I hate being put in the position of having to initiate a relationship. I've been taught that if you're not aggressive with a woman, then you've blown it. She's not going to jump on *you,* so *you've* got to jump on *her.* I've heard all kinds of stories where the woman says, 'No! No! No!' and they end up making great love. I get confused as hell if a woman pushes me away. Does it mean she's trying to be a nice girl and wants to put up a good appearance, or does it mean she doesn't want anything to do with you? You don't know. Probably a lot of men think that women don't feel like real women unless a man tries to force himself on her, unless she brings out the 'real man,' so to speak, and probably too much of it goes on. It goes on in my head that you're complimenting a woman by actually staring at her or by trying to get into her pants. Lately, I'm realizing that when I stare at women lustfully, they often feel more threatened than flattered."

NOTES

1. Such estimates recur in the rape literature. See *Sexual Assault* by Nancy Gager and Cathleen Schurr, Grosset & Dunlap, 1976, or *The Price of Coercive Sexuality* by Clark and Lewis, The Women's Press, 1977.
2. *Uniform Crime Reports,* 1980.
3. See *Behind Closed Doors* by Murray J. Strauss and Richard Gelles, Doubleday, 1979.
4. See Gager and Schurr (above) or virtually any book on the subject.
5. Again, see Gager and Schurr, or Carol V. Horos, *Rape,* Banbury Books, 1981.
6. From "Willamette Bridge" in *Body Politics* by Nancy Henley, Prentice-Hall, 1977, p. 144.
7. I would like to thank George Lakoff for this insight.

15

Surmounting a Legacy
The Expansion of Racial Diversity in a
Local Anti-Rape Movement

NANCY A. MATTHEWS

The anti-rape movement in Los Angeles originated from collectivist feminism and feminist social work networks. Between 1973 and 1980, five grassroots-led rape crisis organizations were started, including the Los Angeles Commission on Assaults Against Women (LACAAW), the Pasadena YWCA Rape Crisis Center and Hotline, the East Los Angeles Rape Hotline (ELA), the Center for the Pacific-Asian Family, and the San Fernando Valley Rape Crisis Service. While the bilingual, Latina-run East Los Angeles hotline and the multilingual Pacific-Asian hotline brought some women of color into the movement, very few Black women were involved, and the predominantly Black areas of the county (South Central Los Angeles) were virtually unserved. Since 1980, when the California Office of Criminal Justice Planning began funding rape crisis services, the state has promoted a relatively conservative, social service approach to this work. Yet ironically, during these years, state money also furthered one of the more progressive goals of the American anti-rape movement, to become multiracial and multicultural and to expand services to all women.

This article examines the problem of racial and ethnic diversity in the Los Angeles anti-rape movement, shows how racial diversity in the local movement was facilitated by the state's involvement in establishing two new Black rape crisis centers in the mid-1980s, and explores the consequences for race relations in the anti-rape movement in the United States.

FEMINISM, RACE, AND RAPE

The predominance of Whites, problematic for the American feminist movement as a whole, also affected the anti-rape movement. Despite collectivist feminist roots in the civil rights movement and the new left of the 1960s, the women's liberation movement in the United States remained dominated by White and middle-class women (Ferree and Hess 1985). Evans (1979) attributes this narrowness to the historic conjunction of the birth of feminism within the new left just when the Black movement was becoming separatist.

Many Black women who were interested in feminism in the early 1970s agreed with Black Panther Kathleen Cleaver that Black and White women would have to work in separate organizations, coming together in coalitions, because the problems each group of women faced were different enough that they could not be solved in the same organizations (Giddings 1984, p. 311). Thus the early anti-rape movement in the United States arose in a context of the distrust Black women felt of White feminism and the beginnings of Black feminism. This legacy, combined with the general level of racism in American society, has made multiracial organizing, feminist or otherwise, difficult.

Long before the anti-rape movement, the issues of race and rape were linked in the United States. From the 1880s through the 1950s, lynchings of Black men were justified on the basis of their threat to White women's virtue. Although Ida B. Wells investigated over 700 lynchings and found that accusations of rape had been made in less than one-third, the myth of Black men's proclivity for rape became ingrained in our culture (Davis 1981; Giddings 1984; Hooks 1981) and was manipulated to keep both Black men and White women in their places. Lynching, rather than rape, became the focus of Black women's activism against violence.

Incidents that linked race and rape caused further disjuncture between White feminists and Blacks in the current feminist movement in the United States. First, as the nationalist phase of the Black movement crested, several male leaders, most notably Eldridge Cleaver in *Soul on Ice* (1968), called for the raping of White women as a political act. Second, Susan Brownmiller, in her eagerness to prove the seriousness of rape, echoed the racist justification of lynching in her pathbreaking book *Against Our Will* (1975), perpetuating the "myth of the Black rapist" (Davis 1981). Rather than confront the issue of rape, even when Black women were raped by Black men, a special issue of *Ebony* magazine on Black-on-Black crime omitted rape (Bart and O'Brien 1985, p. 90).

In 1973, Roz Pulitzer, a Black member of the Manhattan (New York) Women's Political Caucus, which was lobbying on rape issues, said she did not expect Black women to get very involved in the issue. Like Kathleen Cleaver, she felt that "the splits between the concerns of White women and our concerns was so great that strategically we had to have a Black organization to give the women's movement credibility in our own communities. Every group must go through its period of self-identity" (New York Radical Feminists 1974, p. 243). However, Pulitzer, who had been instrumental in forming a Mayor's Task Force on Rape in New York City in 1973, hoped that Black women would take what White women had

learned and use it to set up rape counseling and public education in the Black community.

In Los Angeles, it took more than 10 years to happen, and when it did, the impetus came not from grass-roots Black feminist groups, but Black community organizations responding to the state's call for proposals. This study of the expansion of racial diversity in the Los Angeles anti-rape movement is based primarily on oral-history interviews with participants since its beginning in the early 1970s through 1988 and with officials in the California Office of Criminal Justice Planning (OCJP). I conducted 35 interviews between 1987 and 1989 with women who were known as leaders, formal and informal. The interviews took from one to three hours and covered the participant's experience in rape crisis work, her account and perceptions of historical events, and explanations of how the organizations worked. Movement documents, in particular the monthly minutes of the Southern California Rape Hotline Alliance from 1979 to 1988, supplemented the oral accounts.

WOMEN OF COLOR AND THE LOS ANGELES ANTI-RAPE MOVEMENT

The early 1980s were a period of increasing awareness of racial and ethnic issues in the U.S. anti-rape movement. Although there were relatively few women of color in the movement in California, the formation of the Southern California Rape Hotline Alliance and the statewide Coalition of Rape Crisis Centers brought them together and provided the forum in which to raise issues about doing rape crisis work among Black, Latina and Chicana, Asian, and Native American women. The Coalition's Women of Color Caucus brought together women of color in southern California.

The East Los Angeles Rape Hotline, founded in 1976, was the earliest, and one of the few anti-rape organizations that was not predominantly White. It was founded by Latina women concerned about providing bilingual and culturally appropriate services in the largely Latino, Chicano, and Mexicano area of east Los Angeles county. As one of the few bilingual hotlines of any kind, it was kept busy with all kinds of community services, not just rape crisis work. Its connection to the other local anti-rape organizations waxed and waned over the years until 1979, when the Alliance grew and the statewide Coalition provided a forum for meeting other women of color in the movement.

Another ethnically based rape hotline also existed by the late 1970s, although it was less connected to the Los Angeles anti-rape movement. In 1978, Nilda Rimonte started a project to provide rape crisis services to Pacific and Asian immigrant women in Los Angeles. Although Rimonte participated in the Alliance regularly, the Center for the Pacific-Asian Family, as the hotline she founded was called, was not a grassroots organization to the same extent as other hotlines. Because it was set up to serve many language groups (Vietnamese, Korean, Laotian, Cambodian, Filipino, and others), counselors were generally staff members. They also ran a battered women's shelter, so the rape hotline was only one project of the organization. Nevertheless, Rimonte was a central figure in raising ethnic and racial issues in the California anti-rape movement.

By 1982, racism had become a central issue in the movement and in groups' disputes with the state funding agency. Santa Cruz Women Against Rape was defunded (Mackle, Pernell, Shirchild, Baratta, and Groves 1982) and later that year, the East Los Angeles Rape Hotline was audited by the OCJP. Although the organization was told that the OCJP planned "to very carefully scrutinize all rape crisis centers receiving funds" (Alliance Minutes, June 12, 1982), the fact that it was singled out seemed to carry racist overtones. Hotlines had also begun to treat racism as a serious topic in counselor training and the Women of Color Caucus had begun meeting regularly.

The National Coalition Against Sexual Assault (NCASA) had also begun to pay attention to racial diversity. Beverly Smith, a nationally known Black feminist, was a keynote speaker at its 1984 conference and tried to transform the

historic connection between race and rape into a positive one by comparing the two crimes rather than setting them in opposition to each other. She made the analogy that "lynching is to racism as rape is to sexism," suggesting that the cultural context makes such acts possible (Roth and Baslow 1984, p. 56).

By 1983, the Women of Color Caucus had made a connection between OCJP funding criteria and problems of rape crisis centers serving Third World people. According to Alliance minutes of January 15, 1983, Emilia Bellone and Teresa Contreras noted that state allocations were based primarily on the number of victims served by particular programs. In addition, the state allocated funds for "new and innovative" programs, encouraging new grant proposals, while money was most needed for basic services, community education, and outreach. An Alliance committee prepared a position paper asking the OCJP to revise its funding allocation criteria. Their central criticism was that using the number of victims served as the only criterion caused "inequities in the distribution of funds, which especially handicaps ethnic minority rape crisis centers":

> One concern stems from the fact that in order to provide rape crisis services in ethnic minority communities, a great deal of time and effort has to go into doing strong outreach and community education. Although in recent years there has been a marked increase in awareness and information about sexual assault for the general public, much of this has not permeated ethnic minority communities. Many factors affect this—language barriers, racism, distrust of educators and the media, etc. (Position Paper 1983, p. 1)

The paper goes on to point out several related problems: traditional coping strategies among some cultures that discourage going outside the family for help, the need for materials to be translated to reach nonassimilated people, and the extra hours of work required both for outreach in ethnic communities and to provide adequate services to individual survivors. They linked class issues with those of race and ethnicity:

Typically, more time must be spent with a survivor who has fewer personal resources. These survivors tend to be ethnic minority women. Often, a non-assimilated ethnic minority survivor requires translating and interpreting, transportation, overnight shelter for herself and possibly children, and counseling to significant others in addition to the usual counseling and advocacy services. So, if a rape crisis center serves a predominantly ethnic minority population, the "average" number of hours of service provided to each survivor is much higher than for a center that serves a predominantly White population. (Position Paper 1983, p. 2)

Grant proposals for "innovative" programs had been the only strategy centers had to increase funding for special outreach. A major issue for the East Los Angeles Rape Hotline was how to include families, especially the men, in their services, which was essential in order to gain legitimacy in the Latino community. In 1983, through a grant for innovative projects from the OCJP, they produced a *fotonovela* about a family in which a teenage girl has been sexually assaulted by her uncle. The story line upholds the cultural value placed on the family, but modifies it so that the young girl's integrity is not sacrificed. They also had an innovative theater program for education in rape prevention. These programs were successful for reaching their community, but were costly to the organization in the time spent creating new programs, and did not solve the problem of more money for basic services.

Although the Alliance committee that wrote the position paper did not get a direct response, Marilyn Peterson, the Branch Manager of the Sexual Assault Program at the OCJP began pursuing avenues of additional money for "high crime" and "minority" areas. The OCJP studied the rates of rape reported by police agencies and rape crisis centers in communities across the state, assuming that the rate of underreporting was consistent. They then surveyed the availability of services in the community by district attorneys' offices, law enforcement, hospitals, family service agencies, and so on. In addition to a high crime rate, the

poverty rate was factored in, because areas with few resources tend to have fewer social services. According to Peterson, the survey was a necessary formality—a bureaucratic justification for what she already knew was needed. The target money was awarded to some of the existing rape crisis centers in Los Angeles, but its most significant effect in the county was the establishment of two new programs located in predominantly Black areas, South Central Los Angeles and Compton. Women in these areas could theoretically use one of the existing hotlines, but geographical distance made providing in-person services such as hospital accompaniment more difficult. The primarily White hotlines did sparse outreach to the Black community. Furthermore, women of color in the anti-rape movement were developing a theory of service provision that recognized that women in crisis were most likely to feel comfortable and use services if they were provided by someone like themselves (Dubrow et al. 1986; Kanuha 1987; Lum 1988; Rimonte 1985). This notion reflects the influence of the peer-counseling roots of rape crisis work as well as increasing awareness of cultural issues. For outreach to succeed, it was important for services like rape crisis to be *of* the community, which the White hotlines were not. Thus homogeneous organizations of different ethnic groups were more effective.

CONSEQUENCES OF FUNDING: A DIFFERENT APPROACH

The first of the new hotlines, the Rosa Parks Sexual Assault Crisis Center, began in late 1984, in anticipation of the target funding. Avis Ridley-Thomas, who was instrumental in its founding, was at the nexus of several networks that led to the founding of Rosa Parks. She had been working for the new Victim Witness Assistance Program out of the city attorney's office since 1980. Because of her work there, she had been recommended by Assembly woman Maxine Waters to be on the State Sexual Assault Services Advisory Committee (SAC), which advised the OCJP on funding for rape crisis services, training for prosecutors, and funding for research. Ridley-Thomas became chair of the committee, which at first had very little money to give out. Hers was another voice, in addition to those of the Alliance members, raising the issue of underfunding of minority areas. It was clear from her knowledge of South Central Los Angeles that this area had the highest rate of reported sexual assault in the state and no community-provided services.

A longtime activist in the Black community, she tried to organize women's groups to take on rape crisis services as a project, but none that she approached felt they could do that in addition to their other work. She and her husband, Mark Ridley-Thomas, who was the director of the local branch of the Southern Christian Leadership Conference (SCLC), applied for and received an OCJP grant to start a rape crisis service. Thus Avis Ridley-Thomas's position in the funding agency, her involvement in service provision to victims, and her relationship to SCLC converged to create a place for the new service.

The Compton YWCA was the second new organization to start a rape crisis program in a predominantly Black community. When the OCJP called for proposals for target funding, the city's police chief encouraged the YWCA director, Elaine Harris, to apply for it. Compton, one of the small cities that compose Los Angeles county, is located south of South Central Los Angeles. Although the rate of home ownership is high, so are the poverty and crime rates. As in many of the economically abandoned areas of the county, gangs are an important source of social identity for young people, which, combined with their involvement in drug dealing, has created a violent environment. The Compton YWCA has struggled to be a community resource in this context. In addition to traditional programs ranging from fitness to music, it offers a minority women's employment program, a job board, a support group for single parents, a food program for needy families, drug diversion counseling, and a support group for families of incarcerated people. With crime and vio-

lence a major social and political issue in the community, the organization had a cooperative relationship with the police, which led to the application for target funding. The YWCA had numerous resources, including experience with grant proposal writing, that could be enlisted in starting the Sexual Assault Crisis Program.

How these two new rape crisis programs were started differed markedly from the existing anti-rape organizations, which had consequences for the nature of the movement and relationships between the new organizations and the older ones in the Alliance and the Coalition. All of the older organizations had been founded out of some kind of grassroots process and with some connection to the wider feminist movement of the 1970s. The stands on feminism differed among the older organizations, but because they were founded in the midst of vibrant feminist activism, they associated what they were doing with the women's movement at some level. The Rosa Parks and Compton programs, by contrast, were founded with substantial state funding and without strong links to contemporary feminism.

Their parent organizations were not simply social service agencies. Both SCLC and the YWCA were progressive organizations with grass-roots origins, but had long since become established and "becalmed" (Zald and Ash 1966), with hierarchical leadership and bureaucratic structures. The women who were hired to direct the sexual assault programs were social service administrators, not activists. Nevertheless, many of the women who worked in the new organizations were drawn by the opportunity to work with Black women. As Joan Crear, a staff member at Rosa Parks, said:

> Personally, I got involved because I was very much interested in women's issues, in particular Black women, and I didn't feel that there was a forum in my community for them. I know there was resistance to the whole notion of violence, women's issues, feminism, and I wanted to work in an environment that advocated on behalf of Black women. As for the Rosa Parks Center, it seemed like a good place to start, and I envisioned the cen-

ter as a place where eventually, while we're funded to deal with sexual assault, that it's very difficult to separate sexual assault from just what it means to be a woman in the universe, so it gave me an avenue to do that kind of work.

Similarly, Monica Williams, director of the Compton YWCA program, said:

I had a genuine concern for women's issues and rights and moreover, I think I had a real concern for living, since I live in this community [Compton] now, a real concern for Black women. I think our image has always been of strong and persevering and you can take it all, and it doesn't make a difference, and I started to notice that most of the women who were assaulted, that it wasn't a priority for them, that they couldn't see that they were hurting, too. And that usually their first concern was their children, or their home or their husband, or how'm I going to make ends meet, so for me it's just, it's a challenge.

Drawn by their interest in combining working with Black women and working for the Black community, and influenced by the articulated feminism of the women they met through the Alliance, these women began to see themselves as feminists, but the primary interpretive framework in their organizations was community service.

The community action framework, very much a part of the mission of both parent organizations, provided a rationale within which to fit rape crisis services, which replaced the feminist impetus of the older groups. SCLC linked the rape crisis service with their philosophy of nonviolence. The YWCA had a long history of programs to help women and girls in crisis, and many Ys around the country sponsored rape crisis services. Additionally, the emphasis of the target grants on racial and ethnic inequity in service and funding resonated with the national YWCA imperative adopted in 1970 and used in much of their literature: "to thrust our collective power as a women's movement toward the elimination of racism wherever it exists and by any means necessary."

Despite these ideological frames, the new centers were more influenced by the OCJP's defi-nition of rape crisis work than the older anti-rape organizations. Founded with OCJP grants, they had not gone through the grass-roots stage of scraping together precious resources from their communities and therefore did not have independent community roots. As a consequence of their dependence on the OCJP, they were more bureaucratized from the beginning and less suspicious of the OCJP, in contrast to the contentious history that members of the Alliance had with the agency, but similar to the feelings of many less radical rape crisis people around the state. (See Rodriguez [1988] and Schecter [1982] for accounts of similar splits in the battered women's shelter movement between those who resisted conventional bureaucratic organization and those who accepted it.)

Nevertheless, the community context in which the new services were provided posed contradictions with the state's bureaucratic concerns and practices. The special grants that led to the founding of Rosa Parks and Compton were intended to adjust for problems in the delivery of services, such as "hazardous working conditions, an absence of complementary service providers or agencies, high cost of providing services, lack of alternative funding sources, geographical and/or economic conditions; and unmet need for culturally and/or ethnically appropriate services" (OCJP Guidelines 1987, p. 33). These new organizations were therefore encouraged to design programs that met the basic guidelines *and* the specific needs of their communities. The sponsoring organizations, the YWCA and SCLC, were both practiced at responding to their communities and developed rape crisis programs with emphases that differed from other anti-rape programs. For example, the Rosa Parks staff set up support groups to deal with the intertwined problems of incest and alcoholism.

The ways the Compton women served their community despite standardized guidelines was an even sharper contrast. There, rape crisis workers confronted the reality of gangs on a daily basis as part of the context of the community they served.

For example, to avoid confrontations among participants, they had to monitor what colors the young women wore to educational and support group meetings. Some of the women they counseled were survivors of gang-related rapes. Because basic survival was often the presenting problem of the women served, they evolved a broader approach to support and counseling. As the director said:

> A woman may come in or call in for various reasons. She has no place to go, she has no job, she has no support, she has no money, she has no food, she's been beaten, and after you finish meeting all those needs, or try to meet all those needs, then she may say, by the way, during all this, I was being raped. So the immediate needs have to be met. So that makes our community different than other communities. A person wants their basic needs first. It's a lot easier to discuss things when you're full. So that we see people who, when they come in with their children, and their children are running around and the person is on edge, we may find out that she just hasn't eaten in a few days. And we may have to pool together money and give her everybody's lunch, or take them to lunch, and days later, maybe months later, the person will say, by the way, I did come in because I was raped, but since you brought up . . . the other things, I do need a place to stay, and I do need a job, and I can't go to the police. So . . . needs are different.

Approaching rape crisis work in such a holistic way did not conform to the requirements of the bureaucracy that provided the funding. In spite of this director's positive view of the OCJP, she also expressed frustration that very labor-intensive work was often not counted toward funding:

> A lot of what we do cannot be documented. That there's no place on that form for this woman called and she's standing outside with three kids and she don't have no place to go. [Because the form asks about] rape! So you know you just, it's almost like you end up having this group that's so concerned that it's very difficult for us when a woman calls and says she's battered, not to tell her to come here for counseling, even though that's not what we're supposed to do. When she says, but I'm right

up the street, I don't want to go to the shelter, I just want to talk to somebody, and a staff person like Irma or Roslyn will spend hours with this person and afterwards come in and say, god she's feeling better, and I think this, and I'm going to take her over to the shelter, and . . . it fits no place. It's just something you did. It was an "information and referral."

These "special service delivery problems," as the OCJP *Guidelines* (1987) puts it, are also different from the kind of issues other rape crisis centers face, largely because of this center's location in a relatively impoverished community in which services are scarce.

NEED FOR INNOVATIVE OUTREACH

The challenge of successful outreach to ethnically and racially diverse communities was one of the issues that prompted the Alliance position paper. Getting clients was more than a simple issue of publicity and involved changing the cultural ethic about seeking help. The ELA and Pacific-Asian rape hotlines had faced this problem for years, and women at the hotlines in the Black communities tackled it anew. Despite the high rates of sexual assault in these communities, there was no mobilized citizens' group demanding services. Once the services were funded, women from both Rosa Parks and Compton had to work on legitimizing the idea of seeking a support group or therapy from the outside, a relatively new idea in the Black community. Joan Crear of Rosa Parks explained:

> In our community confidentiality, whether it's rape or anything else, is really the key; a community where things don't go outside your family; you know, have a history of family taking care, says don't tell. . . . [I]n terms of picking up and using a hotline, when we're doing education, it's not just about rape, it's about . . . you can call us, we won't tell anybody, we'll keep your secrets. Also in a community where you talk about gang violence, you have people that are afraid. It's really difficult when I talk to a teenager and she's been raped by a gang member. I don't want to . . . tell her to tell

the police necessarily, 'cause she's scared for her brother, you know, and she's scared for her family.

Ethnographic studies of Black communities have illuminated the extent of informal networks among members of even the poorest communities that provide both material and emotional support (e.g., Liebow 1967; Stack 1974), but the pursuit of more formal support through counseling is new. Avis Ridley-Thomas, founder of Rosa Parks, talked about the pressure to "strain up"—be tough and take the hard knocks—which militates against seeking outside help with emotional or psychological problems. Williams elaborated:

I think we work on empowerment a lot more because of the community we serve. That it's difficult for a person to sit in a group and talk about their rape and the rapist and go through all of the psychological changes without first understanding that they have some other problems too. So that what's been helpful is for Black women to see other Black women to say I understand what it's like, to have to worry about the kids and him.... [T]he former sources of support are gone. That now you see more of us putting children in childcare and daycare, whereas before we had mothers and sister and aunts, and you know, the extended family. So that now, we're kind of [little rueful laugh] socialized a little more, so that we're running into the same things that other people are running into. We say we're stressed. Before we just said life was tough.

The emergence of an ethic to protect victim's rights was a bridge by which rape crisis services came to Black communities. Competition between the Sexual Assault and Victim-Witness Programs within OCJP led Marilyn Peterson to look for creative ways to increase rape crisis funding, and the target grants were one such strategy that succeeded. Despite this internal competition, victims' rights was a significant factor in Black communities' receptivity to rape crisis services.

The movement for victim's rights helped legitimize the culture of therapy. Because people of color are more likely to be victims of violent crime in the United States, much of the outreach by the newly established victim-witness programs

in the early 1980s was to Blacks, according to Avis Ridley-Thomas. Seeking help for emotional traumas became more acceptable, not only in state supported services, but also in grass-roots victim's groups. While these groups are only loosely connected to the rape crisis organizations, they contributed to a climate in which reaching and helping sexual assault victims was less alien than it might have been earlier.

RACISM, HOMOPHOBIA, AND FEMINISM

The dynamics of interpersonal racism in the Los Angeles anti-rape movement are intertwined in a complex way with differences of political perspective and homophobia. Although the anti-rape movement had become more diverse, the dominant subculture within the local movement is (White) feminism, strongly influenced by a lesbian perspective. The combination of feminist jargon and political viewpoints and the high number of lesbians in leadership positions create an alienating environment for many of the Black women in the anti-rape movement. Although White activists are ideologically predisposed to accept women of color because they believe it is right, their theory about what women of color should be—that is, they should be radical because they are oppressed—does not always fit with reality. Black women hired to work in rape crisis centers have tended to identify with the social service orientation, thus the more conservative side of the movement, which creates tension with the more politically radical women who have dominated the Alliance.

Racial and political differences are compounded by homophobia. Homosexuality is even more hidden in the American Black community than in the general society. Blacks are not alone in the anti-rape movement in their discomfort with the openly lesbian presence; dissension has also surfaced in the statewide Coalition, often between centers outside the major urban areas, which tend to be more conservative, and those from Los Angeles and the Bay Area. However, locally, because a substantial number of the White women are lesbians and most of the Black women are heterosexual, the overlap of racial and sexuality differences exaggerates the schism. Both sides feel they have a moral cause for offense when someone from the other side is inadvertently racist or homophobic.

Despite the fact that all of the centers include these topics in their volunteer and staff training, these tensions affect both interpersonal interactions and organizational processes. Differences in life-style lead to divergent concerns. For example, several Black women mentioned that they wished there were support in the Alliance for dealing with husbands and families while working in rape crisis. This concern for intimate others was shared by heterosexual White women, but not by lesbians, because their partners were less likely to be threatened by their work with survivors of male violence. Lesbians, expecting Black women to be homophobic, sometimes have challenged and tested their sexuality. Even differences of style separated women: for example, the convention of dressing up in the Black community and of dressing down in White feminist circles.

Black women, like some Chicana women earlier, have also felt marginalized by being outside the shared reference system of White feminists. As Teresa Contreras of ELA put it:

> I'm fairly sure that some of us felt threatened by the jargon, the politics, the feminist politics, and the real assertiveness of the women involved in the rape crisis movement, and their confrontational style was totally contrary to the Chicano style.

In interviews, some Black women noted that they did not really understand what "feminism" was and yet felt expected to know and support its precepts. Being thrown into the Alliance and the Coalition where this was the political vocabulary could be intimidating and alienating. Over time, however, some have come to put the name "feminist" to their own positions. Joan Crear, for example, was tentatively identifying herself as a feminist at the time I interviewed her, after working in the anti-rape movement for over two years. She said:

> It has become important for me to say "I'm a feminist" to other women in my community, but I work on a definition where it doesn't sound like it's such a big thing, because I believe that most women, or a lot of women are under... some of the things that feminism encompasses.... [F]or me it means to want to be or to demand to share power in relationships, so I don't know if that's an appropriate term, because when I think about sharing power within relationships I have to look at that in terms of sharing power with my children, my boss, whether male or female, and so it means...I take responsibility for things that happen in my life.... I see myself as an adult woman, as an adult.

Not all women of color live in South Central or East Los Angeles, so the existence of the ethnically based rape crisis centers is only one step toward serving all women and having a multiracial movement. The predominantly White hotlines in Los Angeles are still concerned about recruiting women of color, but face a dilemma when that goal conflicts with maintaining their integrity on feminism and homophobia. But according to Rochelle Coffey, director of the Pasadena hotline, the existence of the Black hotlines has helped give the predominantly White hotlines credibility with women of color in other parts of the county.

CONCLUSION

Whether states co-opt or facilitate social movements is historically contingent on particular political forces (Tilly 1978), and in the historical period described here, both processes occurred. Without state funding, the new Black anti-rape organizations might not exist. But their founding also resulted in the further infusion of a bureaucratic orientation into the anti-rape movement, because the new organizations bear the stamp of their origins. However, there is also a new source of resistance, in addition to the feminists, to the state's demands. The commitment of Rosa Parks and Compton to "serve their community" means that they make demands back to the state to shift its policies so that service is possible.

Despite conflicts, women in the Alliance, Black and White, lesbian and heterosexual, work together. The predictions from the early 1970s that women of color would need to establish their own organizations in order to become active in feminist causes seems to be borne out. Racially and ethnically homogeneous organizations have contributed more to diversifying the movement than integration within organizations. They successfully work together in mixed coalitions when they have powerful common interests, but independent bases.

REFERENCES

Bart, Pauline and Patricia H. O'Brien. 1985. *Stopping Rape: Successful Survival Strategies.* New York: Pergamon.

Brownmiller, Susan. 1975. *Against Our Will: Men, Women, and Rape.* New York: Bantam.

Cleaver, Eldridge. 1968. *Soul on Ice.* New York: Dell.

Davis, Angela. 1981. *Women, Race, and Class.* New York: Random House.

Dubrow, Gail et al. 1986. "Planning to End Violence Against Women: Notes from a Feminist Conference at UCLA." *Women and Environments* 8:4–27.

Evans, Sara. 1979. *Personal Politics.* New York: Vintage Books.

Ferree, Myra Marx and Beth B. Hess. 1985. *Controversy and Coalition: The New Feminist Movement,* Boston: Twayne.

Giddings, Paula. 1984. *When and Where I Enter: The Impact of Black Women on Race and Sex in America.* New York: Bantam.

Hooks, Bell. 1981. *Ain't I a Woman: Black Women and Feminism.* Boston: South End Press.

Kanuha, Valli. 1987. "Sexual Assault in Southeast Asian Communities: Issues in Intervention." *Response* 10:4–6.

Liebow, Elliot. 1967. *Tally's Corner.* Boston: Little, Brown.

Lum, Joan. 1988. "Battered Asian Women." *Rice* (March):50–52.

Mackle, Nancy, Deanne Pernell, Jan Shirchild, Consuelo Baratta, and Gail Groves. 1982. "Dear Aegis: Letter from Santa Cruz Women Against Rape." *Aegis: Magazine on Ending Violence Against Women* 35:28–30.

New York Radical Feminists. 1974. *Rape: The First Sourcebook for Women,* edited by Noreen Connell and Cassandra Wilson. New York: New American Library.

Office of Criminal Justice Planning. 1987. *California Sexual Assault Victim Services and Prevention Program Guidelines.* Sacramento: State of California.

Rimonte, Nilda. 1985. Protocol for the Treatment of Rape and Other Sexual Assault. Los Angeles County Commission for Women.

Rodriguez, Noelie Maria. 1988. "Transcending Bureaucracy: Feminist Politics at a Shelter for Battered Women." *Gender & Society* 2:214–27.

Roth, Stephanie and Robin Baslow. 1984. "Compromising Positions at Anti-Rape Conference." *Aegis: Magazine on Ending Violence Against Women* 38: 56–58.

Schecter, Susan. 1982. *Women and Male Violence: The Visions and Struggles of the Battered Women's Movement.* Boston: South End Press.

Southern California Rape Hotline Alliance. 1982. Minutes.

———. 1983. "Position Paper." Drafted by Emilia Bellone and Nilda Rimonte for the Committee to Develop OCJP Position Paper.

Stack, Carol. 1974. *All Our Kin: Strategies for Survival in a Black Community.* New York: Harper & Row.

Tilly, Charles. 1978. *From Mobilization to Revolution.* Reading, MA: Addison-Wesley.

Zald, Mayer N. and Roberta Ash. 1966. "Social Movement Organizations: Growth, Decay and Change." *Social Forces* 44:327–41.

16

When Bodies Are Weapons

MICHAEL A. MESSNER

In many of our most popular spectator sports, winning depends on the use of violence. To score and win, the human body is routinely turned into a weapon to be used against other bodies, causing pain, serious injury, and even death. How do we interpret the social meaning of this violence? Is it socially learned behavior that serves to legitimize masculine power over women? Commentators—both apologists and critics—have made sweeping statements about sports and violence, but their analyses rarely take into account the meanings of violence in sports to the athletes themselves. We can begin to understand the broader social meanings of violence in sports by listening to the words of former athletes.

With the possible exception of the boxer in the ring, perhaps the one position in modern sports that requires the most constant physical aggressiveness is that of lineman in U.S. football. While TV cameras focus primarily on those few who carry, throw, catch, and kick the ball, the majority of the players on the field are lined up a few inches apart from each other. On each play they snarl, grunt, and curse; at the snap of the ball they slam their large and heavily armored bodies into each other. Blood, bruises, broken bones, and concussions often result.

Marvin Upshaw, now thirty-six years old, was a lineman in professional football for nine years. He seemed a bit stung when I asked him how he could submit to such punishment for so many years:

> *You know, a lot of people look at a lineman and they say, "Oh, man, you gotta be some kinda* ani-mal *to get down there and beat on each other like that." But it's just like a woman giving birth. Everybody says, you know, "That's a great accomplishment; she must be really beautiful." And I do, too—I think it's something that's an act of God, that's unreal. But she hasn't done nothing that she wasn't built* for. *See what I'm saying? Now here I am, 260, 270 pounds, and that's my position. My physical self helped me.... That's what I'm built for. Just like a truck carrying a big Caterpillar: you see the strain, but that's what it's built for. So as far as that being a real big accomplishment, it is, but it's not. That's all you were built for.*

BORN OR BUILT?

Upshaw's comparisons of the aggressive uses of his body in football with a woman giving birth and with a truck are telling. These comparisons exemplify one of the major paradoxes in men's construction of meaning surrounding the use of their bodies as weapons. On the one hand, many of the men I interviewed explained their aggression and violence as natural: to them, repeated bone-crunching collisions with other men are simply "an act of God," "like a woman giving birth." On the other hand, they know that their bodies are, like trucks, "built" by human beings to do a specific job. Time after time I have heard former athletes, almost in the same breath, talk of their "natural" and "God-given" talent *and* of the long hours, days, and years of training and sacrifice that went into developing their bodies and their skills. "I was a natural," said MacArthur Lane, a former professional football star. "Just about every hour of the day when I wasn't sleeping or eating, I'd be on the playground competing."

Similarly, Jack Tatum, who in his years with the Oakland Raiders was known as the Assassin for his fierce and violent "hits" on opposing receivers, described himself as a "natural hitter." But his descriptions of his earliest experiences in high school football tell a different story. Though he soon began to develop a reputation as a fierce defensive back, hitting people bothered him at first:

> When I first started playing, if I would hit a guy hard and he wouldn't get up, it would bother me. [But] when I was a sophomore in high school, first game, I knocked out two quarterbacks, and people loved it. The coach loved it. The more you play, the more you realize that it is just a part of the game— somebody's gonna get hurt. It could be you, it could be him—most of the time it's better if it's him.

Tatum's words suggest that the routine use of violence against others to achieve an athletic goal doesn't come naturally at all, but may require a good deal of encouragement from others. Recent studies of young ice hockey players corroborate this: the combination of violent adult athletic role models and rewards from coaches, peers, and the community for the willingness to successfully use violence creates a context in which violence becomes normative behavior. Young males who earn reputations as aggressive "hitters" often gain a certain status in the community and among their peers, thus anchoring (at least temporarily) what otherwise might be insecure masculine identities.

TWO INFAMOUS "HITS"

What happens when legitimate ("legal") aggression results in serious injury, as it so often does in sports? Both Jack Tatum and Ray Fosse, a former professional baseball player, were involved in frighteningly violent collisions, each of which resulted in serious injury. In each incident, the play was "legal"—no penalty was issued by officials. Each incident also stimulated a lively public con-troversy concerning violence in sports. These two men's remembrances are instructive in connecting the athlete's experiences of violence in sports with the larger social meanings surrounding such public incidents.

By the time Jack Tatum got to the pros, he had become the kind of fearsome hitter that coaches dream of. Though he took pride in the fact that he was not a "dirty" player (i.e., his hits were within the rules), he was perhaps too good at his craft. Intimidation was the name of the game, but there was growing concern within football and in the sports media that Jack Tatum's "knockouts" were too brutal. In 1978, Tatum delivered one of his hits to an opposing wide receiver, Darryl Stingley. Stingley's neck was broken in two places, and he would never walk again. Suddenly, Tatum was labeled as part of a "criminal element" in the National Football League. Tatum was confused, arguing that this had been a "terrible accident," but was nevertheless simply a "routine play" which was "within the rules."

> I guess the thing that mystified me was that I could play for nine years and one guy gets hurt and then everybody comes down on me, you know. It's just like for nine years I've been playing the game the wrong way. But I've made All-Pro, I've been runner-up for Rookie of the Year, I've got all the honors playing exactly the same way. So, you know, it just kind of mystified me as to why there was just all of a sudden this stuff because a guy got hurt. It wasn't the first time a guy got paralyzed in football, so it really wasn't that unusual.

Ray Fosse received a violent hit from Pete Rose in the 1970 Major League Baseball All-Star game, while 60 million people watched on television. In the twelfth inning, Pete Rose was steaming around third base; he needed only to touch home plate in order to score the winning run. Fosse's job as catcher was to block the plate with his body and hope that the ball arrived in time for him to catch it and tag Rose out. Rose arrived a split second before the ball, and, looking a lot like a football player delivering a hit, drove his body straight at Fosse and touched the plate safely. Fosse's shoulder was separated, and despite his youth he never fully regained the powerful home-run swing he had demonstrated earlier that summer. Again, a serious injury had resulted from a technically legal play. Rose was seen by some as a hero, but others criticized him, asking if it was right for him to hurt someone else simply to score a run in what was essentially an exhibition game. Rose seemed as mystified by these questions as Jack Tatum had been. "I play to win," responded Rose. "I just did what I had to do."

When I interviewed Fosse years later, well into his retirement, he lamented the effect of the injury but saw it not as the result of a decision by Pete Rose but rather as "part of the game." It was fate that had broken his body—not a person. In fact, he felt nothing but respect for Rose:

> *I never once believed that he hit me intentionally. He's just a competitor, and I only wish that every other major-league ball player played as hard as he did.... But I would say that that was the beginning of a lot of pain and problems for me....*

There is clearly a contextual morality in Tatum's and Fosse's constructions of meaning surrounding these two violent collisions. The rules of the game provide a context that frees the participants from the responsibility for moral choices. As long as the participants play by the rules, they not only feel that they should be free from moral criticism, but also understand that they are entitled to "respect"—that form of emotionally distant connection with others that is so important to traditional masculine identity. Flagrant rule-violators, most athletes believe, are "violent" and deserve to be penalized; others, like Tatum and Rose, are "aggressive competitors" deserving of respect. But this distinction is shaken when serious injury results from "legal" actions, and public scrutiny raises questions about the athletes' personal morality. Both Tatum and Fosse appear mystified by the public perspective on events in terms of individual choice or morality. They just play by the rules.

THE PRICE ATHLETES PLAY

There is another painful paradox in today's organized combat sports. Top athletes, who are popularly portrayed as models of good physical conditioning and health, suffer from a very high incidence of permanent injuries, alcoholism, drug abuse, obesity, and heart problems when they retire. The way athletes are taught to regard their bodies as machines and weapons with which to annihilate opponents often results in their using violence against their own bodies. Partly for this reason, former professional football players in the United States have an average life-expectancy of about fifty-six years—roughly fifteen years shorter than the overall average life-expectancy of U.S. males. Football, of course, is especially brutal, but baseball has had its share of casualties, too. Ray Fosse's interview with me seemed to be an almost endless chronicle of injuries and surgeries. "When someone got injured," he explained, "we had a saying: 'Throw dirt on it, spit on it, go play.'"

Not only professional athletes parade their injuries this way. Nearly every former athlete I interviewed, amateur or professional, told at least one story of an injury that disabled him, at least for a time. Many had incurred serious injuries that had permanently harmed their health. Although most wore these injuries with pride, like badges of masculine status, athletes also grudgingly acknowledged that their healthy bodies were a heavy price to pay for glory. But for them to question their decisions to "give up" their bodies would ultimately mean questioning the entire system of rules through which they had successfully established relationships and a sense of identity. Instead, former athletes usually rationalized their own injuries as "part of the game." They claimed that their pain contributed to the development of their character and ultimately gained them the respect of others.

Clearly, heavy personal costs are paid by those who participate in violent organized sports. And, because of poverty, institutionalized racism and lack of other career options, it is poor and ethnic minority males who are disproportionately channeled into athletic careers—and especially into the more dangerous positions within the combat sports. Males from more privileged backgrounds often play sports in school, but because they face a wider range of educational and career choices they often choose to leave sports at a relatively early age. Young men from poor and nonwhite backgrounds face a constricted range of options. Lacking other resources and choices, they may see sports as the one legitimate context in which a youngster from a disadvantaged background can establish a sense of masculine identity in the world.

SPORTS VIOLENCE
AND GENDER RELATIONS

With the twentieth century decline in the practical need for physical strength in work and in warfare, representations of the muscular male body as strong, virile, and powerful have taken on increasingly important ideological significance in gender relations. Indeed, the body plays such a central role in the construction of contemporary gender relations because it is so closely associated with the natural. Yet, to develop their bodies for competition, athletes spend a tremendous amount of time exercising and weight-training, and sometimes even use illegal and dangerous drugs, such as steroids. Though an athletic body is popularly thought of as natural, it is nevertheless the product of social practice.

The embodiment of culturally dominant forms of masculinity entails the imbedding of force and skill in the body. Through this process, men's power over women comes to appear as though it is natural. Sports are an important organizing institution for the embodiment of dominant masculinity. Sports suppress natural (sex) similarities, construct differences, and then, largely through the media, weave a structure of symbol and interpretation around these differences which naturalizes them. Several theorists have suggested that the major

ideological salience of sports as mediated spectacle may lie not so much in violence as it does in the opportunity sports give male spectators to identify with the muscular male body. Morse, in a fascinating analysis of the use of slow-motion instant replays in football, argues that the visual representation of violence is transformed by slow motion replays into gracefulness (Morse 1983). The salient social meanings of these images of male power and grace lie not in identification with violence, Morse argues, but rather, in narcissistic and homoerotic identification with the male body. Perhaps the violence represents a denial of the homoeroticism in sports.

Violence in sports may play another important social role—that of constructing differences among men. Whereas males from lower socioeconomic and ethnic minority backgrounds disproportionately pursue careers in violent sports, privileged men are likelier, as Woody Guthrie once suggested, to commit violence against others "with fountain pens." But with the exception of domestic violence against women and children, physical violence is rarely a part of the everyday lives of these men. Yet violence among men may still have important ideological and psychological meaning for men from privileged backgrounds. There is a curious preoccupation among middle-class males with both movie characters who are working-class tough guys, and with athletes who are fearsome "hitters" and who heroically "play hurt." These tough guys of the culture industry are both heroes, who "prove" that "we men" are superior to women, and the "other" against whom privileged men define themselves as "modern." The "tough guys" are, in a sense, contemporary gladiators sacrificed so that elite men can have a clear sense of where they stand in the intermale pecking order. Ironically, although many young black males are attracted to sports as a milieu in which they can find respect, to succeed in sports they must become intimidating, aggressive, and violent. Television images—like that of Jack Tatum "exploding" Darryl Stingley—become symbolic "proof" of the racist belief that black males are naturally more violent and aggressive. Their marginalization as men—signified by their engaging in the very violence that makes them such attractive spectacles—contributes to the construction of culturally dominant (White, upper- and middle-class) masculinity.

REFERENCES

Morse, M. 1983. "Sport on Television: Replay and Display," pp. 44–66. In *Regarding Television: Critical Approaches,* ed. E. A. Kaplan. Los Angeles: University Publications of America.

17

Abortion Stories on the Border

DEBBIE NATHAN

"Your period's late?" The clerk at Ciudad Juarez's Benavides Pharmacy offers a customer syringes of female hormones. "Inject this twice," she advises. Down the street, at the market where El Pasoans and tourists buy party piñatas, herbalists hawk bags of leaves and bark. "Guaranteed to bring on your period if you're less than three months overdue," one vendor says.

In Mexico, with few exceptions, abortion is a crime. State law governing the city of Juarez, for instance, declares that a woman convicted of having an illegal abortion can be imprisoned for as long as five years, and her abortionist for three.

Nevertheless, before the U.S. Supreme Court legalized abortion in 1973, American women flocked to Mexico to end their pregnancies. Black market abortions were easy to get then; and though most still offered today are medically risky, they remain available.

Texas already prohibits Medicaid funding of abortion and restricts techniques used to abort "viable fetuses" older than 20 weeks. After the Supreme Court ruled on the Webster case, Texas was considered one of 22 states likely to further limit or even outlaw abortion. Should this happen, the Mexican border may once again become an abortion underground option for many American women.

Elizabeth Canfield, a Planned Parenthood counselor in Albuquerque, New Mexico, worked from 1968 to 1971 with Clergy Counseling Service for Problem Pregnancies in Los Angeles. The group referred American women to abortionists in Mexican border cities, especially Juarez.

"Juarez had many abortionists," Canfield said. "Most were physicians; others were laypeople trained by doctors. They charged $160 to $200 to do an early abortion, and millions of dollars were being made. Everybody had relationships with the cop on the beat. Enormous payoffs were taking place—they couldn't conceive of the U.S. referrers not wanting a kickback."

A woman who went to Mexico for an abortion entered a James Bond world, Canfield says. "You needed to carry your money inside your bra. You couldn't ever say 'abortion,' just something like 'Liz sent me.'"

"Though some black market abortion providers were very humanitarian," Canfield says, "they were all doing it for the money." Even back-up services, like airlines, cleaned up—whether intentionally or not. She recalls, for instance, one U.S. travel agent who "didn't want to know anything about what we were doing when we made reservations through her. One day she called me and said, 'You won't believe this, but we received an award for selling the most three-day weekends to Mexico.' Her boss kept asking how it was that so many of her clients wanted to go there. She was mortified!" Canfield remembers.

After abortion was legalized in the United States, the Mexican black market dissolved. Mexican women of means, however, can still find doctors who will occasionally provide discreet early abortions, says Dr. Francisco Urango Vallarta, former director of the Autonomous University's medical school in Chihuahua City, about 225 miles beyond the border.

"It's illegal, of course, so no one is going to routinely do the procedure and thus earn a reputation as an abortionist," Urango says. "But occasionally, a doctor will, say, fall behind on his car payments. Then he may do one." The procedure of choice, Urango says, is the dilatation and curettage (D&C) procedure, scraping the pregnant patient's uterus under the pretext of checking for diseases. The D&C automatically causes abortion.

Many Mexican doctors who favor abortion rights but are reluctant to break the law refer their patients to U.S. clinics such as Reproductive Services in El Paso. Reproductive Services does 2,500 abortions annually, and a quarter of the patients are from Mexico. Most are middle- and upper-class women seeking medically safe abortions.

Those Mexican women with neither connections nor money to cross the border must rely on cheap home or drugstore remedies. As indigent American women did in the United States before abortion was legalized, many Mexicans trying to end their pregnancies drink tea made of herbs such as thyme, rue, or cedar bark, sold at herb markets. Or they use synthetic chemicals. At a Mexican pharmacy one doesn't need prescriptions to buy hormone injections and drugs to make the uterus contract so as to expel the fetus. If such measures aren't successful, a Mexican woman may apply caustic chemicals or pay midwives or nurses, nicknamed "stork scarers," to stick catheters through her cervix.

These methods are often ineffective and dangerous. The Mexican Social Security Institute reported almost 60,000 cases of abortion-related complications in 1988. Of those, at least 100 resulted in massive infections or hemorrhaging that led to death. Indeed, in Mexico, illegal abortion is considered the second most common cause of maternal mortality (after childbirth). Even so, the country's federal Health Secretariat estimates that at least 500,000 of the procedures are performed annually.

In Ciudad Juarez, Dr. Carlos Cano Vargas, Assistant Chief of Obstetrics and Gynecology at the city's General Hospital, believes many of the 350 miscarriages his department sees annually are really illegal abortions.

"But it's hard to prove," he says, "because everyone conceals it. The pharmacy drugs leave no traces. Infection can happen after a natural miscarriage too, so that's no proof either. You may see caustic chemical lesions or a catheter, but that's very rare. A woman can be on her death bed and usually won't admit anything. In six years I've seen only two cases of obvious abortions. For every verifiable one in Juarez, there are countless more covered up."

Delia is a pseudonym for a Juarez woman whose abortion would have gone unnoticed last year had it not been botched. The 26-year-old is the mother of three preschoolers; her husband is a "twin plant" factory worker, earning about $40 per week. When their youngest child was six months old, Delia found herself pregnant again. She is taciturn but matter-of-fact while describing what happened next.

"We couldn't afford another child, so I took hormone shots from the drugstore and rue tea from the herb market. Nothing worked. Then a friend told me about a nurse abortionist. For $350,000 pesos (at the time about $200) she put a catheter up me that she was going to remove next day. But at night I got such a high fever that my husband insisted I go to a clinic. If only I'd known how to take out the catheter! Because when the doctor saw it in me he got really mad and called the police. They came and interrogated me, but of course I wouldn't tell them where the nurse was.

"The police made the clinic detain me for three days. Later at the station I was interrogated again for four hours. Finally, the detectives left the room and I just walked out. I hid at my mother's house for a few days but the police never came back."

"Oh yes," Delia said, "it's very common for women here to get abortions. If you know the pharmacist you can get the injections, and there are lots of abortionists. A lot of my friends have had abortions. Most already have children."

Delia's abortion was reported in the local Mexican press—complete with her name and address—on the police blotter page, along with stories about gang leaders, robbers and rapists. She was never indicted, however.

"It is hard to prosecute these cases," shrugs State Police Chief Investigator Saul Oscar Osollo. Delia's was one of only about five abortions reported to the Juarez police each year, he said.

Some Mexican women with botched abortions are luckier than Delia—they make it to El Paso, where health care providers like Reproductive Services do mop-up duty. Once, says clinic director Patti Pagels, "We suctioned a woman's uterus and found rubber bands in it. The patient was from Juarez. We told her we weren't going to report it, but she wouldn't admit having done anything."

Another recent patient, a 17-year-old, "came in already 16 or 17 weeks pregnant. The lab work indicated she was perfectly healthy; but—this is how fast the infection sets in—next day when she returned, a faucet of green, rancid pus was coming out of her vagina. We immediately gave her 2000 milligrams of tetracycline. An hour later she was blue and shivering—she couldn't swallow and her temperature was 104.5. She ended up spending five days on antibiotics at Thomason (El Paso's county hospital)."

"She told us she'd gone to somebody in Juarez who'd stuck something up her. It scared me! I thought, 'What if she hadn't come here? How long would she have waited to tell her parents?'"

"Death from septic abortion is horrible," Pagels says. "My God, nobody should ever have to die like that."

Elizabeth Canfield, recalling her work two decades ago referring American women to Mexican abortionists, predicts that if abortions are outlawed in Texas, women will travel to other states where they remain legal. But if a change in the law results in ready availability of abortion in Mexican cities, Americans along the border may go south as they did in the past.

Canfield keeps in touch with a former Juarez abortionist. "He's now a law enforcement officer," she said. "He told me recently that if things ever get tough again in this country, he'll help us again."

18

Constructing Amniocentesis
Maternal and Medical Discourses

RAYNA RAPP

*When we walked into the doctor's office, both my husband and I were
crying. He looked up and said, "What's wrong? Why are you in tears?"
"It's the baby, the baby is going to die," I said. "That isn't a baby," he
said firmly. "It's a collection of cells that made a mistake."*
—Leah Rubinstein, White housewife, 39

The language of biomedical science is powerful.
Its neutralizing vocabulary, explanatory syntax,
and distancing pragmatics provide universal descriptions of human bodies and their life processes that appear to be pre-cultural or non-
cultural. But as the field of medical anthropology
constantly reminds us, bodies are also and always
culturally constituted, and their aches, activities,
and accomplishments are continuously assigned
meanings. While the discourse of biomedicine
speaks of the inevitable march of scientific and
clinical progress, its practices are constantly open
to interpretation. Its hegemonic definitions routinely require acceptance, transformation, or contestation from the embodied "objects" whose
subjectivity it so powerfully affects.

The necessary contest over the meaning assigned embodied experiences is particularly clear
in the field of reproductive health care, where consumer movements, women's health activism, and
feminist scholars have sharply criticized biomedical practices. Public accusations against the demeaning and controlling nature of gynecological
and obstetrical health care have led to dramatic results. Over the last 20 years, such criticisms have
influenced the reform of medical services, occasionally encouraged the development of alternative health practices, and often inspired women to
advocate for themselves and others. Contests over
the means and meanings of women's reproductive
health services are, thus, an ongoing part of
American social and institutional life. These conflicts reflect the complex hierarchies of power,
along which both providers and consumers of
health care are organized. They cannot easily be
resolved because the practices of biomedicine are
at once emancipatory and socially controlling, essential for healthy survival yet essentializing of
women's lives.

Reproductive medicine and its feminist critique thus share a central concern with the problem of female identity. In both discourses, as
throughout much of American culture, motherhood stands as a condensed symbol of female
identity. Changes in sexual practices, pregnancy,
and birth are widely believed to be transforming
the meaning of "womanhood" itself. This connection between women's reproductive patterns and a
notion of female gender is longstanding: cries of
alarm have been raised for over a century concerning the future of "the sex" as birth control practices spread, as abortion was criminalized and

medicalized, as childbirth moved from the hands of female lay practitioners to male professionals, and as a discourse of explicitly female sexual pleasure became articulated. There is, of course, great diversity in women's experiences with medical care in general, and the medicalization of sexual activity and reproduction in particular. Yet, the image of "womanhood" as a central symbol in American culture has often been constructed as if motherhood were its stable, and uniform core, threatened by external changes in technology, education, labor force participation, medicine, and the like.

This shared and shifting object of embodied gender is revealed when we examine what have come to be called "the new reproductive technologies," dramatic and well-publicized interventions into fertility, conception, and pregnancy management and screening. Biomedical claims about the NRTs are usually framed in the available language of neutral management of female bodies to insure progress; feminist critiques are often enunciated as protection of women's core experiences against intrusion by "technodocs." Both discourses are fraught with old assumptions about the meaning of pregnancy, itself an archetypically liminal state. And both discourses are shot through with contradictions and possibilities for the health care providers, pregnant women, and feminist commentators who currently must make sense of the rapid routinization of new reproductive technologies.

This article presents an analysis of amniocentesis, one of the new reproductive technologies.[1] My examples are drawn from an ongoing field study of the social impact and cultural meaning of prenatal diagnosis in New York City, where I have observed more than 250 intake interviews in which genetic counselors interact with pregnant patients; interviewed over 70 current users and refusers of amniocentesis; collected stories of 30 women who received what is so antiseptically referred to as a "positive diagnosis" (i.e., that something was wrong with their fetus), and participated and interviewed in a support group for parents of children with Down syndrome, the most com-

monly diagnosed chromosome abnormality, and the condition for which pregnant women are most likely to seek amniocentesis.[2]

In New York City, unlike many other parts of the United States, prenatal diagnosis is funded by both medicaid and the City's Health Department, so it is available to a population of women whose ethnic, class, racial and religious backgrounds are as diverse as the City itself. The City's cytogenetic laboratory through which I work reaches a population of pregnant women who are approximately one-third Hispanic, one-third African-American, and one-third White, according to the racial/ethnic categories provided by both the City and State Health Departments. But these categories undoubtedly conceal as much as they reveal. At the present time, "Hispanic" includes Puerto Ricans and Dominicans long familiar with City services and the "new migrants" of Central America, many of whom are drawn from rural backgrounds, are desperately poor, and often undocumented, as well as middle-class, highly educated Colombians and Ecuadorians who may be experiencing downward mobility through migration. African-Americans include fourth-generation New Yorkers, women whose children circle back and forth between the City and rural Alabama, and Haitians who have lived in Brooklyn only a few months. "White" encompasses Ashkenazi and Sephardic Jews, Irish, Italian and Slavic Catholics, Episcopalian and Evangelical Protestants, as if being neither Black nor Brown placed them in a homogenized racial category. The categories themselves thus freeze a "racial map," which ignores the historic complexity of identity endemic to New York, and many other urban areas in contemporary America. Despite any understanding of the historic processes by which such a map has been created and promulgated, it is nearly impossible to escape its sociological boundaries when conducting and describing fieldwork in New York City.

My interviews and observations are tuned to the tension between the universal abstract language of reproductive medicine, and the personal experiences pregnant women articulate in telling their amniocentesis stories. Differences among women are revealed in their reasons for accepting or refusing the test; their images of fetuses and of disabled children; and the meaning of abortion in their lives. My working assumption is that a conflict of discourses necessarily characterizes the arena of reproductive technology, where nothing is stable: scientific "information," popular struggles both feminist and anti-feminist, and the shifting meaning of maternity and womanhood for individuals and communities with diverse ethnic, racial relgious, sexual, and migration histories are all currently under negotiation. . . .

THE LANGUAGE OF TESTING

Women use very different language and reasons in describing their acceptance or refusal of the test. When I first began interviewing middle-class pregnant women about their amniocentesis decisions, it was hard for me to hear their cultural constructions, for, like my own, they mirrored the progressive message of science. Most (but not all) middle-class women, a disproportionately White group, accepted the test with some variant of this statement:

> I always knew I'd have amnio. Science is there to make life better, so why not use its power? Bill and I really want a child, but we don't want a baby with Down's, if we can avoid it.
>   (Susan Klein, White accountant, 37)

But even white, middle-class women often express ambivalence and they do so in a language intricately intertwined with the language of medicine itself. Their fears and fantasies reflect thoughts that both question and sustain the dominant discourse itself, for example:

> I cried for two days after I had the test. I guess I was identifying with universal motherhood, I felt like my image of my womb had been shattered. It still feels like it's in pieces, not like such a safe place as before. I guess technology gives us a certain kind of control, but we have to sacrifice something in return. I've lost my brash confidence that my body just produces healthy babies all by itself,

> naturally, and that if it doesn't, I can handle whatever comes along as a mother.
>   (Carola Mirsky, White school teacher, 39)

The low-income African-American women with whom I talked were far less likely to either accept, or be transformed by, the medical discourse of prenatal diagnosis. American Black women who had grown up in the South, especially the rural South, often described alternate, non-medical agendas in their use of amniocentesis, invoking other systems for interpreting bodily states, including pregnancy. Dreams, visions, healing sessions, root work and herbal teas could be used to reveal the state of a specific pregnancy. One such woman, who at 27 became the mother of a Down syndrome baby, told me she had been refused amniocentesis in five city hospitals, always because of her young age. When I asked why she had wanted the test, she described a dream which recurred throughout the pregnancy:

> So I am having this boy baby. It is definitely a boy baby. And something is wrong, I mean, it just is not right. Sometimes, he is missing an arm, and sometimes, it's a leg. Maybe it's a retarded baby. You can't really tell, it's all covered in hair. Once or twice, they give him to my husband and say, 'look at your son, take him the way he is.' As if the way he is isn't all right. I tried to get that test to make peace with that dream (Q: would you have had an abortion if you'd had the test?) Oh, no. The whole thing was going back to the dreams . . . just so's I could say, 'this baby is the baby in the dreams' and come to peace with it.
>   (May Norris, African-American hospital orderly, 27)

Another African-American woman, pregnant with a fourth, unexpected child at the age of 42, had this to say:

> So I was three months pregnant before I knew I was pregnant, just figured it was change of life. The clinic kept saying no, and it's really the same signs, menopause and pregnancy, you just feel that lousy. So when they told me I was pregnant I thought about abortion, I mean, maybe I figured I was too old for this. But in my neighborhood a lot of Caribbean women have babies, a lot of them are

late babies. So I got used to it. But the clinic doctor was freaked out. He sent me for genetic counseling. Counseling? I thought counseling meant giving reassurance, helping someone accept and find their way. Wisdom, help, guidance, you know what I mean. This lady was a smart lady, but right away she started pullin' out pictures of mongoloids. So I got huffy: 'I didn't come here to look at pictures of mongoloids,' I says to her. So she got huffy and told me it was about mongoloids, this counseling. So we got more and more huffy between us, and finally, I left. Wasn't gonna sit and listen to that stuff. By the time I got myself to the appointment (for the test) I'd been to see my healing woman, a healer, who calmed me down, gave me the reassurance I needed. I knew everything was gonna be ok. Oh, I wouldn't have had an abortion that late in the game. I just got helped out by the healer woman, so I could wait out the results of that test without too much fussin'.

(Naiumah Foster, school teacher, 43)

And among women whose background includes no prior encounter with the scientific description of amniocentesis, the test may be accepted out of the desire to avoid the suffering of children; a respect for the authority of doctors (or the conflated image of genetic counselors in white coats); or simple curiosity. One recently arrived Salvadoran, now working as a domestic, told me, for example, that she wanted the test because science had such miraculous powers to show you what God had in store. This mixing of religious and secular discourses is no less awed (and awesome!) than that of the native-born professional woman who told me she wanted her test to be an advancement to science. She knew it was the only way geneticists could legally obtain amniotic fluid for their research, to which she ardently wished to make a contribution. Both women characterized amniocentesis as a path of enlightenment, but their motivations for its use differed sharply. The one characterized it in terms of God's grace; the other in light of scientific progress....

When I first began observing counseling sessions, it was easy for me to share the psychological lingo many counselors use privately, in evaluating patients' motives for accepting or re-

jecting the test. A discourse of fluent Freudian phrases is used by counselors trained in psychological-psychoanalytic thinking, as well as in human genetics. Women may easily be labelled "denying," "regressed," "passive," or "fatalistic" when their choices are seen as irrational to professionals trained to balance empathy against epidemiological statistics. Such labels, however, reduce social phenomena and cultural contexts to individual idiosyncrasies. I have often observed communication gaps, negotiated decisions, and situations of multiple meaning, which cannot be understood when reduced to a model of individual decision-making. When a Puerto Rican garment worker, aged 39, who is a Charismatic Catholic, replied to the offer of "the needle test," "No, I take this baby as God's love, just the way it is, Hallelujah," one genetics counselor felt hard pressed to understand what was going on. It was easier to fall back upon individualizing psycho-speak than to acknowledge the complexity of the patient's cultural life, which profoundly influenced her choices. When a Hungarian-born artist, 38, refused amniocentesis because "it wouldn't be done in my country until 40, and besides, we are all very healthy," I observed a genetics counselor probe extensively into genealogy, and finally discover one possibly Ashkenazi Jewish grandparent. Because of this, the counselor was able to recommend Tay-Sacks screening. Visibly shaken, the pregnant woman agreed. In instances such as these, the hegemonic discourse of science encounters cultural differences of nationality, ethnicity, or religion and often chooses to reduce them to the level of individual defensiveness. Yet what is being negotiated (or not negotiated, in the first example) is the power of scientific technology to intersect and rewrite the languages previously used for the description of pregnancies, fetuses, and family problems.

WHAT IS SEEN

Whether they accepted or refused amniocentesis, virtually all the women with whom I spoke had undergone a sonogram by the mid-trimester of pregnancy. My data on images of fetuses have been collected in light of the powerful restructuring of experience and understanding this piece of obstetrical technology has already accomplished. Several native Spanish-speaking women (both poor and middle-class) described their fetuses in nontechnological imagery: "it's a liquid baby, it won't become a solid baby until the seventh month"; "it's like a little lizard in there, I think it has a tail"; "it's a cauliflower, a bunch of lumps growing inside me." Their relative autonomy from technological imagery may be due as much to having recently emigrated from countries and regions where hospital-based prenatal care is both less common and less authoritative, as to anything inherently "Hispanic."

Most women were fascinated with the glimpses they received of the fetal beating heart; its imagery fits nicely into a range of Christian symbols. And several were also impressed by the fetal brain, which is measured during sonography. Heart and brain, feeling and intellect, are already subjects of prenatal speculation among women for whom fetal imaging has been objectified.

Most women born in the United States, whatever their ethnic and class background, invoked the visual language of sonography and its popular interpretation to answer my query, "Tell me what the pregnancy feels and looks like to you now?" For one it was "a little space creature, alone in space,"[6] for another it was "a creature, a tiny formed baby creature, but because its eyes are closed, it is only a half baby." Another woman told me that as her pregnancy progressed, she felt the fetus' image becoming more finely tuned in, like a television picture coming into better focus. White middle-class women (especially those having a first baby) frequently spoke of following fetal development in books which included week-by-week sonograms. Thus, technological imagery is reproduced in text as well as image, available to be studied privately, at home, as well as in public, medical facilities. Learning about what the technology can do, and about what the baby appears to be, proceed simultaneously.

Poorer women were unlikely to have such primers, but they, too, had been bombarded by the visualization of fetuses (and amniocentesis, with its attendant moral dilemmas) in the popular media. When asked where they first learned about amniocentesis, many Hispanic and White working class women mentioned three episodes of "Dallas" in which prenatal diagnosis plays a large part, and one African-American woman said she knew about Down syndrome "because the Kennedys had one" in a story she'd read in the *National Enquirer.* In the weeks following a Phil Donahue show devoted to Down syndrome children and their families, clinic patients spoke with great interest about that condition. Increasingly, health care providers must confront the popularization of their technologies, with all its attendant benefits and distortions, in their interviews with patients....

Because amniocentesis was explicitly developed to probe for chromosome-based disabilities and confront a woman with the choice to end or continue her pregnancy based on its diagnostic powers, my interview schedule includes questions about the images of disabled fetuses women carry and disabled children they might raise. Here, too, television and magazine representations of disability loom large. One Peruvian factory worker who had lived in New York for 14 years spoke of them as Jerry kids (a reference to Jerry Lewis' telethons—an image hotly contested by the disability rights movement). A White working-class woman who had adopted two disabled children told this story about arriving at her maternal choices watching the telethons:

> *Ever since I was a little girl, I always watched those telethons, I always knew it was a shame, a crying shame that no one loved those kids enough. So when I was a teenager, I got to be a candy-striper, and I worked with kids in wheelchairs, and I always knew I'd adopt them before I'd have them for myself. I'm not afraid of problems. I've got a daughter with spina bifida, and they said she'd be a vegetable. Fat chance! My other one's gonna be mentally retarded. I can handle it. I learned these kids need love on the telethon.*
> (Lisa Feldman, White home maker, 26)

Most women in my sample could recall someone in their own childhood or community who had a child with Down syndrome. Their memories invoke mothers intensely involved and devoted. Many described positive relationships that women had with their mentally retarded children. And some even talked about the hidden benefits of having a "permanent child" as the mother herself grew older, and became widowed. Most middle-class women, however, drew a contrast between themselves and those Down syndrome mothers they had encountered:

> It's too much work. There's a certain kind of relationship I want to have with my child, and it isn't like that one, that's so dependent, forever. I wouldn't be any good at it, I'd resent my child.
> (Ilene Cooper, White college professor, 40)

> Oh, I know I'd work really hard at it, I'd throw myself into it, but I'm afraid I'd lose myself in the process. I wouldn't be like her, she was a really great mother, so self-sacrificing.
> (Laura Forman, White theatre producer, 35)

> My aunt was terrific. But she stayed home. I know I'm going back to work after this baby is born, and I can't imagine what it would take to do it her way.
> (Susan Klein, White accountant, 37)

What accompanied these she/me distinctions in the discourse of White, middle-class women was a running battle over the question of selfishness and self-actualization, a problem linked to the central importance of "choice" as a cultural value and strategy. This is a subject to which I will return below.

Working class and low-income African-American women were no less concerned about the possible diagnosis of Down syndrome, but they often saw their decision-making as taking place within networks of support. One low-income African-American single mother expressed strong anti-abortion sentiments, but requested the test. Had the results been positive, she intended to move home to Georgia, where her mother would help her to raise a baby with health problems. A Black secretary married to a Black plumber chose to end her third pregnancy after a prenatal diagnosis of Down Syndrome. When I asked her how she'd made the decision, and who had given her

advice, support or criticism, she described the active involvement of clergy and community members in the church to which she belonged.

Among many Hispanic women, mostly working-class and low-income (both those choosing and refusing amniocentesis), the image of mothering a disabled child conjured less ambivalence than among White, middle-class women. Friends and relations with sickly children were recalled, and testimonies about the sacrificial qualities of maternity were offered. There was often a conflation of maternal and child suffering, including this madonnalike image:

> When they told me what the baby would suffer, I decided to abort. But it was Easter, so I couldn't do it, I just couldn't do it until His suffering was ended. Then my child could cease to suffer as well.
> (Lourdes Ramirez, Dominican house cleaner, 41)

THE MEANING OF ABORTION

The meaning of abortion loomed large in the consciousness of pregnant women discussing amniocentesis. All women could articulate reasons for and against late abortion after a prenatal diagnosis of a serious condition. These included the evaluation of the child's suffering; the imagined effects of a disabled baby on other siblings and on the parents themselves; the sense of responsibility for having brought a baby into the world who might never grow to "independence"; and, sometimes, the "selfishness" of wanting one's own life to be free of the burdens a disabled child is thought to impose. For Hispanic women, fear of the child's suffering was most salient, followed closely by the effects its birth would have on other children. They were, in principle, more accepting of the sacrifices they imagined disabled children to call forth from their mothers. It is hard to disentangle ethnicity, language, class and religion in these responses. As one Honduran domestic worker awaiting amniocentesis results told me:

> Could I abort if the baby was going to have that problem? God would forgive me, surely, yes, I could abort. Latin Catholics, we are raised to fear God, and to believe in His love and forgiveness.

Now, if I were Evangelical, that's another story. It's too much work, being Evangelical. My sisters are both Evangelicals, they go to Church all the time. There's no time for abortion for them.

(Maria Acosta, 41)

Many Hispanic women reported having had early, multiple abortions and did not discuss the procedure as morally problematic. Yet many also identified *late* abortion as a sin, because quickening has occurred. In this case, a set of subtle and differentiated female experiences is being developed as popular theology.

Low-income African-American women weighed nonmedical agendas in deciding to accept amniocentesis and possibly consider abortion: confirmation of dreams, prior omens and use of healers all figured in the stories they told about why the test might be of use to them. Many low-income Hispanic women appear wrapped up in intertwined images of maternal and child suffering. White middle-class women seem most vulnerable to the abortion controversy currently raging in our national, political culture. Virtually all of the women I interviewed from this group, whether Catholic, Jewish, or Protestant, provided critical exegeses on the tension between "selfishness" and "self-actualization." Again and again, in assessing the possibility or the reality of aborting a disabled fetus, women questioned whether that decision would be selfish. Their concerns revealed something of the limits of self-sacrifice that mothers are alleged to embody.

I share a lot of the feelings of the Right-to-Life Movement. I've always been shocked by the number of abortion clinics, the number of abortions, in this city. But when it was my turn, I was grateful to find the right doctor. He helped me to protect my own life, and that's a life, too.

(Mary Fruticci, White home maker, 44)...

Several White, middle-class women articulated a different discourse, one which confronted selfishness with an implicit critique of medical technology, and nostalgia for a lost and imagined maternity:

The whole time they were doing more sonograms, checking the chromosomes, confirming their diagnosis, that whole time I kept thinking, "I'll keep the baby, I'll go to the hospital, I'll nurse right there. Who knows, in a year, two years, this baby might get better." I just kept romancing that, wanting to believe that I could be that kind of mother.

(Jamie Steiner, White health educator, 33)...

For some, the critique of technological reasoning is more explicit:...

I was hoping I'd never have to make this choice, to become responsible for choosing the kind of baby I'd get, the kind of baby we'd accept. But everyone, my doctor, my parents, my friends, everyone urged me to come for genetic counseling and have amniocentesis. Now, I guess I'm having a modern baby. And they all told me I'd feel more in control. But I guess I feel less in control. It's still my baby, but only if it's good enough to be our baby, if you see what I mean.

(Nancy Smithers, White lawyer, 36)

Why are White middle-class women so self-critical and ambivalently technological? Three themes contextualize their concerns.

The first is that the material conditions of motherhood really are changing, dramatically so, within these women's lifetimes. White women who "have careers" and postpone babies are directing their lives differently than the women in the communities from whom they learned to mother. Unlike African-American women, for whom working mothers are longstanding community figures, and motherhood is a culturally public role, and unlike many Hispanic respondents, who painted images of sacrificial motherhood, for White middle-class women, individual self-development looms large as a cultural goal.

While *all* Americans prize "choice" as a political and cultural value, large scale changes in education, labor-force participation, postponed marriage and childbirth have enabled many White middle-class women to maintain at least an illusion of control over their lives to a degree unprecedented for other groups. Their relative freedom from unwanted pregnancies and child illness and death is easily ascribed to advances in medical science. Medical technology transforms their "choices" on an individual level, allowing them, like their male partners, to imagine voluntary limits to their commitments to children.

But it does not transform the world of work, social services, media, and the like on which a different sense of maternity and the "private" sphere would depend. Moreover, that "private" sphere and its commitment to childbearing is now being enlarged to include men. Fathers, too, can now be socially created during the pregnancy, through birth-coaching, and early bonding. These new fathers may also claim the right to comment on women's motives for pregnancy and abortion in powerful ways.

Individually, White middle-class women may be "becoming more like men," freer than ever before to enter hegemonic realms of the culture from which they were formerly barred, but at the price of questioning and altering their traditional gender identity.[4] Modern, high-technological maternity is part of the gender relations now under negotiation, and may belong to new, emergent traditions. But it presently lies in an ambivalent terrain, a kind of "no man's land" between the technological claims to liberation through science, and the feminist recovery and romance with nurturance as a valuable activity.

A second reason for White middle-class women's ambivalence about prenatal diagnosis and abortion may well be, paradoxically, their close connection with the benefits and burdens of the increasing medicalization of pregnancy. While "everybody" now undergoes pregnancy sonograms, not everybody is as committed as this group to the medical discourse, and its images in pregnancy primers. For them, a paradoxical separation and reconnection to fetuses appears to be underway. On the one hand, they can "see" their fetuses in pictures and on medical screens. This allows for the "early bonding" which runs rampant through the parenting and obstetrical literature. But a seen fetus is also a separate fetus, one to whom one connects as a "maternal environment,"

in obstetrical language, and as a "sanctuary" in the words of The Silent Scream.[9] Paradoxically, White middle-class women are both better served by reproductive medicine, and also more controlled by it, than women of less privileged groups. They are likely to be educated in the same institutions in which doctors are produced, and their own language closely mirrors medical speech and its critique in both the Right-to-Life's discourse of "selfishness" and mainstream feminism's "self-actualization."

A third reason for complex and contradictory feelings about abortion is not confined to White middle-class women, although the cultural and medical importance of individualism may make them particularly vulnerable to its effects. This reason concerns the shifting historical ground on which abortion practices rest. That point was dramatically made to me in one amniocentesis story:

For three weeks, we tried to develop further information on oomphaloceles and satellites on the chromosomes, and the whole time, my mother kept saying, "why are you torturing yourselves, why don't you just end it now, why do you need to know more?" She'd had an abortion between her two pregnancies. And my mother-in-law had even had a late abortion when she first got to this country, and she kept saying the same thing: "I put away one, just do it, and get it over with." And I was so conflicted, and also so angry. So finally I turned on my mother and asked her, "How can you be so insensitive, it's such a hard decision for us, you can't just dismiss this." And as we talked, I realized how different their abortions were from mine. They were illegal. You've got to remember that, they were illegal. They were done when you worried about the stigma of getting caught, and maybe, getting sick. But you didn't think about the fetus, you thought about saving your own life.
(Jamie Steiner, White health educator, 33)

Illegal abortions were dangerous and expensive. They were performed under the shadow of death—maternal, not fetal. Morbidity and mortality from the complications of abortion dropped sharply after 1973, in the wake of Roe v. Wade.

Indeed, "Abortion related deaths have decreased by 73 percent" within a decade of abortion decriminalization.[10] Criminal prosecution, morbidity and mortality were the fears attached to illegal abortions but not "selfishness." A variety of social forces, including medical reform and feminist political organization, led to abortion law reform. On the heels of its success, the Right-to-Life movement was quickly organized. We cannot really understand the talk of "selfishness" articulated by middle-class women, and used against all women, until we locate the meaning of abortion at the intersection of culture, politics, technology, and social change.[11]

Science speaks a universal language of progress. But women express their diverse consciousness and practices in polyglot, multicultural languages. When women speak about the medical-ization of reproduction, what they tell us must be placed in its historical, social context. Amniocentesis and other new reproductive technologies open a Pandora's box of powerful knowledge, constructed through scientific and medical practices. But messages sent are not necessarily messages received. New technologies fall onto older cultural terrains, where women interpret their options in light of prior and contradictory meanings of pregnancy and childbearing. Any serious understanding of how "motherhood" is changing under the influence of the New Reproductive Technologies depends on realizing women's stratified diversity. Otherwise, it will reproduce the vexing problem of the false universalization of gender which feminism itself initially promised to transcend.

NOTES

1. Support for the field research on which this article is based was provided by the National Science Foundation, the National Endowment for the Humanities, the Rockefeller Foundation's "Program in Changing Gender Roles," and the Institute for Advanced Study. I thank them all. I am especially grateful to the many health care providers who shared their experiences with me, and allowed me to observe them at work, and to the hundreds of pregnant women and their supporters who shared their amniocentesis stories with me. Where individual illustrations are provided in the text, all names have been changed to protect confidentiality.

2. Additional reports on the fieldwork from which this article is drawn can be found in "Moral Pioneers: Women, Men and Fetuses on a Frontier of Reproductive Technology," *Women & Health* 13 (1987): 101–116; "The Powers of Positive Diagnosis: Medical and Maternal Discourses on Amniocentesis," in Karen Michaelson, ed. *Childbirth in America: Anthropological Perspectives* (South Hadley, Mass.: Bergin & Garvey, 1988); "Chromosomes and Communication: The Discourse of Genetic Counseling," *Medical Anthropology Quarterly* 2 (1988): 121–142; and "Accounting for Amniocentesis," in Shirley Lindenbaum and Margaret Lock, eds., *Analysis in Medical Anthropology* (New York: Cambridge University Press, forthcoming).

3. See Ann Oakley, *The Captured Womb* (Oxford, England: Blackwell, 1984), ch. 7, for an interesting discussion of how medical technology bypasses and reconstructs knowledge of fetuses, which excludes the perceptions of pregnant women.

4. Religiously framed anti-abortion sentiments were expressed more often among Evangelicals than Catholics, at least among Hispanics and Caribbean Blacks. At the same time, many Hispanic Pentecostals and Charismatic Catholics, and Black Seventh Day Adventists accept amniocentesis in City clinics. It is important to distinguish official Church theology from local practices, including the discursive resources, social networks, and strategies particular church membership may provide.

5. Amniocentesis adds an increase of one-third of one percent to the miscarriage rate. This is considered statistically insignificant, but as genetic counselors are quick to point out, no risk is insignificant when assessing a given pregnancy, rather than simply constructing statistics. And prior reproductive history powerfully shapes how this statistic is interpreted.

6. Barbara Katz Rothman, *The Tentative Pregnancy* (New York: Viking Penguin, 1986), 114, provides an excellent discussion of the implications of sonography for maternal/fetal separation. Rosalind Petchesky has

written a powerful critique of the history and hegemony of fetal images in "Fetal Images: the Power of Visual Culture in the Politics of Reproduction," *Feminist Studies* 13 (1987): 263–292. See Oakley, *The Captured Womb,* for a history of sonography. . . .

8. Faye Ginsburg, "Dissonance and Harmony: The Symbolic Function of Abortion in Activists' Life Stories," in The Personal Narratives Group, ed., *Interpreting Women's Lives* (Bloomington, Ind.: Indiana University Press, 1989).

9. Again, see Rosalind Petchesky, "Fetal Images . . ."

10. Rosalind Petchesky, *Abortion and Woman's Choice* (Boston: Northeastern University Press, 1984), 157.

11. See Faye Ginsburg, *Contested Lives: The Abortion Debate in an American Community* (Berkeley & Los Angeles, Calif: University of California Press, 1989) for an excellent analysis of these historical intersections.

19

On "Surrogacy"

BARBARA KATZ ROTHMAN

A QUESTION OF POLICY

The first thing to bear in mind is that surrogate motherhood is not a new procreative technology. The business of "surrogacy" has nothing to do with scientific progress, and everything to do with marketing. The procreative technology used is artificial insemination. Artificial insemination with donor sperm has been used in human beings for over a hundred years. The "technologies" involved are the technology of masturbation, and of the turkey baster or its equivalent.

It is important to remember that is the case, because we are sometimes overwhelmed with the developments of the new procreative technology, as with our other technologies. Sometimes we think— and sometimes we are encouraged to think—that there is nothing we can do to halt "progress." If science can produce "test-tube babies," how can we ever stop it? And if our new knowledge gives us these new powers, should we even want to stop it?

These are important questions. But they are not the questions of surrogate motherhood. Surrogate motherhood was not brought to us by the march of scientific progress. It was brought to us by brokers, by people who saw a new market and went after it. And the market is something we know we *can* control, and often *should* control.

When artificial insemination was introduced, it was used to support the traditional family structure, husbands and wives having and raising babies. In earlier times, when couples were unable to start a pregnancy, it was most often assumed to be the fault of the wife, and in some cultures husbands had the recourse of divorce. With expand-

ing knowledge, infertility was shown to be sometimes a problem in the husband's body. Wives were not given the recourse of divorce under these circumstances, and artificial insemination became a way of maintaining the intact husband-wife unit. Wives were not encouraged to take a "surrogate," a substitute lover, but rather doctors used semen, given anonymously, to impregnate wives....

Social fatherhood is the key issue here. What makes a woman a mother has always been quite obvious. But what makes a man a father has been subject to some question. The formula our society (along with many others) has arrived at is that fatherhood is determined by the man's relationship to the child's mother. A man married to a woman is the recognized father of her children. This way of reckoning fatherhood builds on two things: the obvious and unquestioned nature of biological motherhood, and the traditional patriarchal relationship of men and their wives. This is a way of acknowledging parenthood that is based on relationships: the relationship of the woman to her baby as it grows within, and the relationship of the man to the woman.

And so it stood for over a hundred years: artificial insemination was a way of managing male infertility that kept the patriarchal family intact, that allowed children to be born to a couple, children who would be truly theirs, to bring into the world together, to raise and to cherish together.

So what changed? For one thing, infertility appears to be more of a social problem: the actual rates of infertility may or may not be rising, but societal concern certainly is. For another, the supply of babies available for adoption has dropped dramatically. Young women, faced with unwanted pregnancies, have been given choices: the choice of abortion and the choice of raising a child without a husband. Infertile couples can no longer benefit, no matter how innocently, from the tragedies of young mothers. Our attitude toward infertility has also changed—and this may indeed be an indirect result of scientific progress. Progress against infertility has become a newspaper and television staple. Remember the excitement that surrounded the first in vitro baby, the first American in vitro baby, the first in vitro twins, and so on. The first in vitro quints were the cover story of *People* magazine in 1988. The idea began to be generated that infertility was curable, if only a couple tried hard enough, saw enough doctors, went through enough procedures. The reality is something quite different. Only 10 percent of those couples attempting in vitro fertilization will have a baby. There is a 90 percent failure rate with that technology.

What we have done is to create a population of desperate, heartbroken infertile people: people who cannot find babies to adopt, who have "tried everything" and cannot get pregnant, people who have devoted years of their lives to trying, one way or another, to get a baby.

The medical technology has enabled the couple to sort out "whose fault" the infertility is. When it is the husband who is infertile, the use of insemination with donor sperm remains a solution, enabling the couple to have a pregnancy and the much-wanted baby. When it is the wife who is infertile, the pressures mount on the woman to feel guilt at not being able to "give her husband" a child. A baby is what they want more than anything. And he could have one, if not for her.

It is in this context that the marketing of "surrogate" motherhood developed. Brokers entered the scene, telling the couple that they can indeed have a baby, and it will be "his" baby. "Surrogate motherhood" was sold as a solution to the tragedy of infertility and a way of resolving women's guilt at their own infertility. For couples who had spent untold thousands of dollars on medical treatments, the thousands more for surrogacy contracts may have seemed a bargain. For people without these many thousands of dollars, infertility remains unsolved. While attention has focused on the infertility of wealthy Whites, in fact infertility, like virtually all illness and disability, is class and race related. Poor people and people of color are much more likely to be infertile.

With this new use of artificial insemination, the relationships of the parties involved changed totally. The relationship of the mother to her baby within her no longer counts. The baby has become a commodity, something a woman can produce and sell. She is encouraged to think of the baby as no more hers than a factory worker thinks of the car he works on as his. The relationship of the father to the mother no longer counts: it will cease to exist as motherhood is made anonymous, handled by brokers and doctors. The relationships that will count are that of the father to his sperm donation and that of the market: the contracts and the fees. What makes a man a father is not his relationship to the mother, we are told, but that it is his sperm and his money.

The brokers tell us that this is not baby selling: how can a man buy his own baby? they ask. And true enough, how can someone buy something which is already his? But what makes the baby his? If the sperm donor in more traditional artificial insemination came up to the couple a year later, said he had had an accident and was now infertile, and would like to have their baby, he would have no right to it. If he offered them money, he would not be buying that which is his, but that which is theirs: producing a semen sample does not make a man a social father, does not make that his baby. Is it then his intention that makes the child his? The fathers in the surrogacy cases do not donate their sperm. They are not donating or giving or selling. They are buying. Then how is this different from any other example of baby buying and selling? The answer is it is not.

If we legalize surrogacy arrangements, then to buy a baby one will need sperm and money.

Couples—or just men—who have both can buy babies. But what of lesbian couples? And what of men without adequate sperm? Many cases of infertility involve both partners. What of a couple desperate to have a baby in which the wife cannot carry a pregnancy and the husband has insufficient sperm, or carries a deadly disease? Sperm, too, is for sale: we literally have sperm banks. If we permit surrogate motherhood for the situation of men who produce their "own" sperm, then what of the men who must buy sperm? Broker Noel Keane says he is prepared to make such arrangements. Once sperm is purchased, the owners of the sperm can use that sperm as their "own" to make their "own" baby with a surrogate. We are going to find ourselves selling babies in "kit" form, purchasing the pieces and services separately: sperm here, an egg there, a rented uterus somewhere else. This is of course a "slippery slope" kind of argument— once you permit some people to buy some babies under some conditions, it is very hard to justify any given person not being allowed to purchase a baby under other circumstances.

So surrogacy is baby selling. As Angela Holder has said, "If I order a widget from a widget maker, and I pay cash money for that widget, and a widget is delivered to me, I defy you to tell me I have not bought a widget."

And what would be wrong with simply opening up a market economy in babies? Others have argued eloquently what the problems are with baby selling, and we have as a society accepted those arguments. Some things, we have felt, should simply not be sold—and certainly not people. One of the strongest arguments against baby selling is that we know that if we allowed babies to be sold, some people would be put under great pressure to sell their babies. This is the same reason that we do not allow organs to be sold from living people, even when we know that lives might actually be saved. If we allowed some people to sell, say, a kidney, we know that some might feel forced to do so. And so now and again someone with much money dies for lack of an organ that he or she was willing to buy and someone else

was willing to sell because such a sale, such a contract, even if arguably in the best interests of the parties involved, would be against the best interests of the society as a whole. I believe that "surrogacy" presents a situation parallel to organ selling, and that the same arguments apply.

I began by saying that surrogacy is not a result of new procreative technology, but must be understood entirely as a marketing strategy. Let me now amend that slightly. Most of the surrogate motherhood cases that reach the courts and the media are based on the old technology of artificial insemination. But some are using a newer technology. We must consider what these new developments in procreative technology will mean for the future of surrogacy contracts.

The new technologies are varied, but share in common the use of genetic material from one woman to create a pregnancy in the body of another woman. There are several ways this can be done. An egg from one woman can be removed, fertilized in vitro (in glass), and put into the body of another woman. Some in vitro fertilization clinics are doing this for women who want to become mothers but cannot produce eggs. Other women, who produce "extra" eggs, donate those eggs for the use of infertile women who cannot produce their own eggs. Sometimes the donors are other women in the program who are ovulating well, sometimes they are hired egg donors, and sometimes they are friends or relatives of the infertile woman. Whether donated or purchased, genetic material from outside of the couple is used to enable a woman and her husband to have a pregnancy and share in the birthing and rearing of a baby. The situation is most closely analogous to artificial insemination with donated or purchased sperm.

Another way that this same thing can be accomplished is by allowing fertilization to take place within the body of the woman who is donating the egg. A fertilized egg, what some call a pre-embryo or pre-implantation embryo, is moved from the donor and placed within the body of the woman who will be the mother. This, too, is much like artificial insemination. Some months later we look at a pregnant woman and her husband expecting their child. In these situations of embryo transfer or egg donation, like the situation of artificial insemination with donor sperm, genetic material from outside the couple is used to create the pregnancy, but social parenthood, from the point of early pregnancy on, is shared within the couple.

That then is the technology. And what of the marketing? Like the marketing of artificial insemination, egg donations can also be turned around and used to create a pregnancy not within the family, but in a hired woman, leading to the ultimate purchase of a baby.

With this technology, it is not necessary for the "surrogate" to be genetically related to the baby she bears. So one marketing strategy is to hire a woman to carry a pregnancy for a woman who can produce eggs but not carry a pregnancy for herself. Now something challenging happens to our thinking: we are forced to confront the question of what makes a woman a mother. Is it the egg, or is it the pregnancy? In the cases mentioned above, where a woman is unable to create an egg, the transfer of the egg or embryo left the pregnant woman the social mother: it was the pregnant woman who intended to be the mother, who not only intended to bear and birth the child, but to raise the child as well. But if we hire a woman to carry the pregnancy, who then is the mother? Is it the egg donor, or the pregnant woman?

In one court decision involving such a case, the egg donor was named as the mother, and the name of the pregnant woman—the gestational mother—was not put on the birth certificate. This is of course analogous to the marketing of surrogate motherhood with the old technology of artificial insemination. Relationships are discounted, and the genetic tie as well as the exchange of money are given primacy. We are asked to accept the idea that the mother is the person who owned the egg and paid for the service, just as we are asked to accept the man who owned the sperm and paid for the services as the father.

But for which women are these substitutes available? Who can afford to hire substitutes for the various parts of mothering? The situation today is exactly what it has been historically: women of privilege, wealthy or fairly wealthy women, hiring the services of poor, or fairly poor, women. Upper-class women can have some of the privileges of patriarchy. Upper-class women can have, can buy, some of the privileges of their paternity, using the bodies of poorer women to "bear them offspring." And upper-class women can, as they so often have, be bought off with these privileges, and accept men's world view as their own. And so we have women, right along with men, saying that what makes a child one's own is the seed, the genetic tie, the "blood." And the blood they mean is not the real blood of pregnancy and birth, not the blood of the pulsing cord, the bloody show, the blood of birth, but the metaphorical blood of the genetic tie.

This opens up an enormous new profit potential for the brokers in the surrogacy market. The technologies of egg and embryo transfer, were surrogate motherhood contracts made enforceable, could be used to drive costs down and keep profits up for the baby brokers. As it stands now, the brokers are limited in their use of surrogate mothers. Because the women are genetically related to the babies they produce, the father-purchasers want only certain kinds of women: intelligent, attractive, and most assuredly of the same race as the couple. Since it is predominantly White couples who have the $25,000 and up that the brokers charge, and since it is particularly White babies that are in scarce supply for adoption, what brokers need are intelligent, attractive, healthy White women to act as surrogates. In our society, such women can command some money for their services, not enormous sums compared, say, to what corporate executives, or for that matter truck drivers, get, but at this moment the going rate is $10,000 to the mother.

But what will happen if the new technology allows brokers to hire women who are not related genetically to the babies that are to be sold? Like the poor and non-White women who are hired to do other kinds of nurturing and caretaking work, these mothers can be paid very little, with few benefits, and no long-term commitment. The same women who are pushing White babies in strollers, White old folks in wheelchairs, can be carrying White babies in their bellies. Poor, uneducated third world women and women of color from the United States and elsewhere, with fewer economic alternatives, can be hired more cheaply. They can also be controlled more tightly. With a legally supported surrogate motherhood contract, and with the new technology, the marketing possibilities are enormous—and terrifying. . . .

I used to envision "baby farms" located in third world countries, supplying babies to American purchasers. But now I wonder: most European countries have outlawed surrogacy-for-hire. In the United States, as long as one state permits it, if we have no national legislation barring it, the business can be legally established. Remember, in the most famous surrogacy case, that of Baby M, both the Sterns and the Whiteheads lived in New Jersey, the broker lived in Michigan, the clinic was located in New York, and the adoption was slated to go through Florida. If just one state exists for the legal paperwork, it may be the third world women of America—the women of our inner-city ghettos—who grow babies for "export." It is in the United States that the rights of rich people to buy are most deeply held.

The time to stop such nightmare visions is now. We stop it by not acknowledging the underlying principle of surrogate contracts, by not accepting the very concept of "surrogacy" for motherhood. A surrogate is a substitute. In some human relations, we can accept no substitutes. Any pregnant woman is the mother of the child she bears. Her gestational relationship establishes her motherhood. We will not accept the idea that we can look at a woman, heavy with child, and say the child is not hers. The fetus is part of the woman's body, regardless of the source of the egg and sperm. Biological motherhood is not a service, not a commodity, but a relationship. Motherhood can remain obvious. If a woman is carrying a baby, then it is her baby and she is its mother. Of course it is true that a mother, any mother, can abdicate her motherhood, can give away a baby. But it is hers to give. And if we were to allow the selling of babies, then it is hers to sell, or refuse to sell.

And what can we do with fatherhood? How can we protect the relationship between a father and his child? What will make a man a father? One possibility is to stay with the model that we had: a father can continue to take his fatherhood from his relationship with the mother of the child. In a married couple, the father can continue to be, as hitherto, the husband of the mother.

That is not a perfect solution to the troubling question of fatherhood. It gives, in some ways, too much power to women over men's procreation. And it gives, in other ways, too much power to men over women's procreation. But this is not a new problem. We are not struggling here with questions of science and new technology. Here we are struggling with age-old questions of relationships, of family, of how we are bound together. We have not found perfect ways of dealing with these issues in all of history. But we have, in this society, been clear in rejecting the use of money in these relationships. We have said that in our society husbands and wives, mothers and fathers, and babies are not for sale. Nothing in the new procreative technology need change that.

Those engaged in surrogacy brokering tell us that if we do not bring surrogacy into the open market, it, like adoption, will continue to exist in "gray-" or black-market forms. And they are probably right. Preventing the open sale of babies has not prevented couples from having to spend much money on getting babies, nor has it prevented brokers from making money out of matching babies to adopters.

I do not disagree with the brokers over acknowledging the problem, but over choosing the solution. There are grave costs to any form of open market in baby selling. If we wish to legalize baby selling, let us acknowledge what we are doing, and offer the appropriate protections to the parties involved. If we choose to allow a woman to sell her baby, so be it. But let us recognize that it is indeed *her* baby that she is selling. And if we do not wish to permit baby selling, then there is nothing in the new procreative technology that forces us to do so. We do not have to give the support of the state and of the courts to a view of babies as purchasable commodities or motherhood as a salable service. . . .

PART THREE

Sexualities

Chapter 6 Sexual Relations, Intimacy, and Power

Chapter 7 Sexuality and Identity

The women's movement reawakened during the late 1960s and early 1970s during a sexual revolution that was telling youth "if it feels good, do it!" In this context an initial impulse of second-wave feminism was for women to reclaim sexual pleasure for themselves. But soon, some feminists began to argue that "sexual liberation" had simply freed men to objectify and exploit women more. As studies began to illuminate the widespread realities of rape, sexual harassment in work places, and sexual exploitation of women in prostitution, it became more and more clear that, for women, sexuality was a realm of danger, rather than pleasure. As a result, by the mid to late 1970s, feminist activism focused more and more on anti-rape and anti-pornography efforts.

By the mid-1980s, other feminists—often younger women, women of color, or lesbian or bisexual women—began to criticize the radical feminist preoccupation with the centrality of male heterosexuality and pornography in women's oppression. And by the early 1990s many younger feminists sought to reclaim sexual pleasure as a realm of empowerment for women. In the first article of Chapter 6, Deborah Tolman argues that cultural factors that frame adolescent girls' sexuality as dangerous tend to divert them from discovering and using their sexual desires in empowering ways. Next, in a challenging discussion of the significance of the Anita Hill/Clarence Thomas sexual harassment debates, Robert Staples argues that the ways in which sexuality and gender relations are defined in many African American communities tend to conflict with the way that a predominantly middle-class and White feminist movement have come to define "sexual harassment." Finally, Cynthia Enloe's research demonstrates how female prostitutes on U.S. military bases are doing more than "sex work"—they are also serving as mediators between foreign soldiers and local men. In short, the commodification of women's sexuality provides key linkages in men's worlds, even across national and cultural boundaries.

The articles in Chapter 7 explore the area of sexual identity. It is widely accepted among scholars today that the idea that there are distinct sexual "types" of people like "the homosexual" and "the heterosexual" is a very modern construction. But it is also well known that social constructions have real consequences. Modern medical and scientific discourses may have created "the homosexual" with the goal of controlling "deviant" character types and normalizing "the heterosexual," but starting mostly in the 1970s men and women who identified as "gay" and "lesbian" drew strength from their shared identities. From this strength, they challenged prevailing cultural attitudes, customs, and laws.

In addition to challenging prejudice and discrimination, the existence of a movement of gay, lesbian, and bisexual people potentially raises critical questions about "normal" heterosexual practices. For instance, Marilyn Frye's article on "Lesbian 'Sex'" starts with empirical observations made by some sexologists that point to low levels of sexual activity by lesbian couples. She then shifts the inquiry away from the question of "how often" to the more difficult question of what does it mean to be "doing it"?—and Frye creatively redirects this question toward taken-for-granted assumptions about "straight sex." Next, through a fascinating biographical sketch of a gay Mexican American man, Joseph Carrier challenges stereotypes about "the gay male." When we take into account cultural differences—for instance, those between Mexican and Anglo, or even between Mexican and U.S.-born Chicanos—it becomes clear that the term "gay man" does not mean the same thing to all people in all contexts. Finally, Evelyne Accad examines current problems faced by women in the Middle East and argues convincingly that assertions of women's sexual identities are of key importance in the move to overcome male domination within the context of movements for national sovereignty.

20

Doing Desire

Adolescent Girls' Struggles for/with Sexuality

DEBORAH L. TOLMAN

In order to perpetuate itself, every oppression must corrupt or distort those various sources of power within the culture of the oppressed that can provide energy for change. For women, this has meant suppression of the erotic as a considered source of power and information within our lives. (Lorde 1984, 53)

Recent research suggests that adolescence is the crucial moment in the development of psychological disempowerment for many women (e.g., Brown and Gilligan 1992; Gilligan 1990). As they enter adolescence, many girls may lose an ability to speak about what they know, see, feel, and experience evident in childhood as they come under cultural pressure to be "nice girls" and ultimately "good women" in adolescence. When their bodies take on women's contours, girls begin to be seen as sexual, and sexuality becomes an aspect of adolescent girls' lives; yet "nice" girls and "good" women are not supposed to be sexual outside of heterosexual, monogamous marriage (Tolman 1991). Many girls experience a "crisis of connection," a relational dilemma of how to be oneself and stay in relationships with others who may not want to know the truth of girls' experiences (Gilligan 1989). In studies of adolescent girls' development, many girls have demonstrated the ironic tendency to silence their own thoughts and feelings for the sake of relationships, when what they think and feel threatens to be disruptive (Brown and Gilligan 1992). At adolescence, the energy needed for resistance

to crushing conventions of femininity often begins to get siphoned off for the purpose of maintaining cultural standards that stand between women and their empowerment. Focusing explicitly on embodied desire, Tolman and Debold (1993) observed similar patterns in the process of girls learning to look at, rather than experience, themselves, to know themselves from the perspective of men, thereby losing touch with their own bodily feelings and desires. It is at this moment in their development that many women will start to experience and develop ways of responding to their own sexual feelings. Given these realities, what are adolescent girls' experiences of sexual desire? How do girls enter their sexual lives and learn to negotiate or respond to their sexuality?

Despite the real gains that feminism and the sexual revolution achieved in securing women's reproductive rights and increasing women's sexual liberation (Rubin 1990), the tactics of silencing and denigrating women's sexual desire are deeply entrenched in this patriarchal society (Brown 1991). The Madonna/whore dichotomy is alternately virulent and subtle in the cultures of adolescents (Lees 1986; Tolman 1992). Sex education curricula name male adolescent sexual desire; girls are taught to recognize and to keep a lid on the sexual desire of boys but not taught to acknowledge or even to recognize their own sexual feelings (Fine 1988; Tolman 1991). The few feminist empirical studies of girls' sexuality suggest that sexual desire is a complicated, important experience for adolescent girls about which little is known. In an ethnographic study, Fine noticed that adolescent girls' sexuality was acknowledged by adults in school, but in terms that denied the sexual subjectivity of girls; this "missing discourse of desire" was, however, not always absent from the ways girls themselves spoke about their sexual experiences (Fine 1988). Rather than being "educated," girls' bodies are suppressed under surveillance and silenced in the schools (see also Lesko 1988). Although Fine ably conveys the existence of girls' discourse of desire, she does not articulate that discourse. Thompson collected 400 girls' narratives about sexuality, romance, contraception and pregnancy (Thompson 1984, 1990) in which girls' desire seems frequently absent or not relevant to the terms of their sexual relationships. The minority of girls who spoke of sexual pleasure voiced more sexual agency than girls whose experiences were devoid of pleasure. Within the context of girls' psychological development, Fine's and Thompson's work underscore the need to understand what girls' experiences of their sexual desire are like.

A psychological analysis of this experience for girls can contribute an understanding of both the possibilities and limits for sexual freedom for women in the current social climate. By identifying how the culture has become anchored in the interior of women's lives—an interior that is birthed through living in the exterior of material conditions and relationships—this approach can keep distinct women's psychological responses to sexual oppression and also the sources of that oppression. This distinction is necessary for avoiding the trap of blaming women for the ways our minds and bodies have become constrained.

METHODOLOGICAL DISCUSSION

Sample and Data Collection

To examine this subject, I interviewed 30 girls who were juniors in an urban and a suburban public high school ($n = 28$) or members of a gay and lesbian youth group ($n = 2$). They were 16.5 years old on average and randomly selected. The girls in the larger study are a heterogeneous group, representing different races and ethnic backgrounds (Black, including Haitian and African American; Latina, including Puerto Rican and Colombian; Euro-American, including Eastern and Western European), religions (Catholic, Jewish, and Protestant), and sexual experiences. With the exception of one Puerto Rican girl, all of the girls from the suburban school were Euro-American; the racial/ethnic diversity in the sample is represented by the urban school. Interviews with school personnel confirmed that the student population of the urban school was almost exclusively poor or working class and the students in the suburban school were middle and upper-middle class. This information is important in that my focus is on how girls' social environments shape their understanding of their sexuality. The fact that girls who live in the urban area experience the visibility of and discourse about violence, danger and the consequences of unprotected sex, and that the suburban girls live in a community that offers a veneer of safety and stability, informs their experiences of sexuality. Awareness of these features of the social contexts in which these girls are developing is essential for listening to and understanding their narratives about sexual experiences.

The data were collected in one-on-one, semi-structured clinical interviews (Brown and Gilligan 1992). This method of interviewing consists of following a structured interview protocol that does not direct specific probes but elicits narratives. The interviewer listens carefully to a girl, taking in her voice, and responding with questions that will enable the girl to clarify her story and know she is being heard. In these interviews, I asked girls direct questions about desire to elicit descriptions and narratives. Most of the young women wove their concerns about danger into the narratives they told.

Analytic Strategy

To analyze these narratives, I used the Listening Guide—an interpretive methodology that joins hermeneutics and feminist standpoint epistemology (Brown et al. 1991). It is a voice-centered, relational method by which a researcher becomes a listener, taking in the voice of a girl, developing an interpretation of her experience. Through multiple readings of the same text, this method makes audible the "polyphonic and complex" nature of voice and experience (Brown and Gilligan 1992, 15). Both speaker and listener are recognized as individuals who bring thoughts and feelings to the text, acknowledging the necessary subjectivity of both participants. Self-consciously embedded in a standpoint acknowledging that patriarchal culture silences and obscures women's experiences, the method is explicitly psychological and feminist in providing the listener with an organized way to respond to the coded or indirect language of girls and women, especially regarding topics such as sexuality that girls and women are not supposed to speak of. This method leaves a trail of evidence for the listener's interpretation, and thus leaves room for other interpretations by other listeners consistent with the epistemological stance that there is multiple meaning in such stories. I present a way to understand the stories these young women chose to tell me, our story as I have heard and understood it. Therefore, in the interpretations that follow I include my responses, those of an adult woman, to these girls' words, providing information about girls' experiences of sexual desire much like countertransference informs psychotherapy.

Adolescent Girls' Experiences of Sexual Desire

The first layer of the complexity of girls' experiences of their sexual desire was revealed initially in determining whether or not they felt sexual feelings, A majority of these girls (two-thirds) said unequivocally that they experienced sexual desire; in them I heard a clear and powerful way of speaking about the experience of feeling desire that was explicitly relational and also embodied. Only three of the girls said they did not experience sexual feelings, describing silent bodies and an absence of or intense confusion about romantic or sexual relationships. The remaining girls evidenced confusion or spoke in confusing ways about their own sexual feelings. Such confusion can be understood as a psychic solution to sexual feelings that arise in a culture that denigrates, suppresses, and heightens the dangers of girls' sexuality and in which contradictory messages about women's sexuality abound.

For the girls who said they experienced sexual desire, I turned my attention to how they said they responded to their sexual feelings. What characterized their responses was a sense of struggle; the question of "doing desire"—that is, what to do when they felt sexual desire—was not straightforward for any of them. While speaking of the power of their embodied feelings, the girls in this sample described the difficulties that their sexual feelings posed, being aware of both the potential for pleasure and the threat of danger that their desire holds for them. The struggle took different shapes for different girls, with some notable patterns emerging. Among the urban girls, the focus was on how to stay safe from bodily harm, in and out of the context of relational or social consequences, whereas among the suburban girls the most pronounced issue was how to maintain a sense of themselves as "good" and "normal" girls (Tolman 1992). In this article, I will offer portraits of three girls. By focusing on three girls in depth, I can balance an approach to "variance" with the kind of case study presentation that enables me to illustrate both similarities and differences in how girls in the larger sample spoke about their sexual feelings. These three girls represent different sexual preferences—one heterosexual, one bisexual, and one lesbian.[1] I have chosen to forefront the difference of sexual preference because it has been for some women a source of empowerment and a route to community; it has also been a source of divisiveness among feminists. Through this approach, I can illustrate *both* the similarities and differences in their experiences of sexual desire, which are nested in their individual experiences as well as their social contexts. Although there are many other demarcations that differentiate these girls—social class, race, religion, sexual experience—and this is not the most pervasive difference in this sample,[2] sexual preference calls attention to the kinds of relationships in which girls are experiencing or exploring their sexual desire and which take meaning from gender arrangements and from both the presence and absence of institutionalization (Fine 1988; Friend 1993). Because any woman whose sexuality is not directly circumscribed by heterosexual, monogamous marriage is rendered deviant in our society, all adolescent girls bear suspicion regarding their sexuality, which sexual preference highlights. In addition, questions of identity are heightened at adolescence.

Rochelle Doing Desire

Rochelle is a tall, larger, African American girl who is heterosexual. Her small, sweet voice and shy smile are a startling contrast to her large body, clothed in white spandex the day of our interview. She lives in an urban area where violence is embedded in the fabric of everyday life. She speaks about her sexual experience with a detailed knowledge of how her sexuality is shaped, silenced, denigrated, and possible in relationships with young men. As a sophomore, she thought she "had to get a boyfriend" and became "eager" for a sexual relationship. As she describes her first experience of sexual intercourse, she describes a traditional framing of male-female relationships:

> I felt as though I had to conform to everything he said that, you know, things that a girl and a guy were supposed to do, so like, when the sex came, like, I did it without thinking, like, I wish I would have waited... we started kissing and all that stuff and it just happened. And when I got, went home, I

> was like, I was shocked, I was like, why did I do that? I wish I wouldn't a did it.

Did you want to do it?

> Not really. Not really. I just did it because, maybe because he wanted it, and I was always like tryin' to please him and like, he was real mean, mean to me, now that I think about it, I was like kind of stupid, cause like I did everything for him and he just treated me like I was nothing and I just thought I had just to stay with him because I needed a boyfriend so bad to make my life complete but like now it's different.

Rochelle's own sexual desire is absent in her story of defloration—in fact, she seems to be missing altogether. In a virtual caricature of dominant cultural conventions of femininity, Rochelle connects her disappearance at the moment of sex—"it just happened"—to her attempts to fulfill the cultural guidelines for how to "make [her] life complete." She has sex because "he wanted it," a response that holds no place for whether or not she feels desire. In reflecting on this arrangement, Rochelle now feels she was "stupid...to do everything for him" and in her current relationship, things are "different." As she explains: "I don't take as much as I did with the first guy, cause like, if he's doin' stuff that I don't like, I tell him, I'll go, I don't like this and I think you shouldn't do it and we compromise, you know. I don't think I can just let him treat me bad and stuff."

During the interview, I begin to notice that desire is not a main plot line in Rochelle's stories about her sexual experiences, especially in her intimate relationships. When I ask her about her experiences of sexual pleasure and sexual desire, she voices contradictions. On one hand, as the interview unfolds, she is more and more clear that she does not enjoy sex: "I don't like sex" quickly becomes "I hate sex...I don't really have pleasure." On the other hand, she explains that

> there are certain times when I really really really enjoy it, but then, that's like, not a majority of the times, it's only sometimes, once in a while...if I was to have sex once a month, then I would enjoy it...if I like go a long period of time without

havin' it then, it's really good to me, cause it's like, I haven't had something for a long time and I miss it. It's like, say I don't eat cake a lot, but say, like every two months, I had some cake, then it would be real good to me, so that's like the same thing.

Rochelle conveys a careful knowledge of her body's hunger, her need for tension as an aspect of her sexual pleasure, but her voiced dislike of sex suggests that she does not feel she has much say over when and how she engages in sexual activity.

In describing her experiences with sexuality, I am overwhelmed at how frequently Rochelle says that she "was scared." She is keenly aware of the many consequences that feeling and responding to her sexual desire could have. She is scared of being talked about and getting an undeserved reputation: "I was always scared that if I did that (had sexual intercourse) I would be portrayed as, you know, something bad." Even having sex within the confines of a relationship, which has been described by some girls as a safe haven for their sexuality (Rubin 1990; Tolman 1992), makes her vulnerable; she "could've had a bad reputation, but luckily he wasn't like that"; he did not choose to tell other boys (who then tell girls) about their sexual activity. Thinking she had a sexually transmitted disease was scary. Because she had been faithful to her boyfriend, having such a disease would mean having to know that her boyfriend cheated on her and would also make her vulnerable to false accusations of promiscuity from him. Her concern about the kind of woman she may be taken for is embedded in her fear of using contraception: "When you get birth control pills, people automatically think you're having sex every night and that's not true." Being thought of as sexually insatiable or out of control is a fear that many girls voice (Tolman 1992); this may be intensified for African American girls, who are creating a sexual identity in a dominant cultural context that stereotypes Black women as alternately asexual and hypersexual (Spillers 1984).

Rochelle's history provides other sources of fear. After her boyfriend "flattened [her] face," when she realized she no longer wanted to be with

him and broke off the relationship, she learned that her own desire may lead to male violence. Rochelle confided to me that she has had an abortion, suffering such intense sadness, guilt, and anxiety in the wake of it that, were she to become pregnant again, she would have the baby. For Rochelle, the risk of getting pregnant puts her education at risk, because she will have to sacrifice going to college. This goal is tied to security for her; she wants to "have something of my own before I get a husband, you know, so if he ever tries leavin' me, I have my own money." Given this wall of fears, I am not surprised when Rochelle describes a time when simply feeling desire made her "so scared that I started to cry." Feeling her constant and pervasive fear, I began to find it hard to imagine how she can feel any other feelings, including sexual ones.

I was thus caught off guard when I asked Rochelle directly if she has felt desire and she told me that she does experience sexual desire; however, she explained "most of the time, I'm by myself when I do." She launched, in breathless tones, into a story about an experience of her own sexual desire just the previous night:

Last night, I had this crank call.... At first I thought it was my boyfriend, cause he likes to play around, you know. But I was sitting there talking, you know, and thinking of him and then I found out it's not him, it was so crazy weird, so I hang the phone up and he called back, he called back and called back. And then I couldn't sleep, I just had this feeling that, I wanted to have sex so so bad. It was like three o'clock in the morning. And I didn't sleep the rest of the night. And like, I called my boyfriend and I was tellin' him, and he was like, what do you want me to do, Rochelle, I'm sleeping! [Laughs.] I was like, okay, okay, well I'll talk to you later, bye. And then, like, I don't know, I just wanted to, and like, I kept tossin' and turnin'. And I'm trying to think who it was, who was callin' me, cause like, it's always the same guy who always crank calls me, he says he knows me. It's kinda scary.... I can't sleep, I'm like, I just think about it, like, oh I wanna have sex so bad, you know, it's like a fever, drugs, something like that. Like last night, I don't know, I think if I woulda had the car and stuff, I probably woulda left the house. And went over to his house, you know. But I couldn't, cause I was babysitting.

When I told her that it sounds a little frightening but it sounds like there's something exciting about it, she smiled and leaned forward, exclaiming, "Yeah! It's like sorta arousing." I was struck by the intensity of her sexual feelings and also by the fact that she is alone and essentially assured of remaining alone due to the late hour and her responsibilities. By being alone, not subject to observation or physical, social, emotional, or material vulnerability, Rochelle experienced the turbulent feelings that are awakened by this call in her body. Rochelle's desire has not been obliterated by her fear; desire and fear both reverberate through her psyche. But she is not completely alone in this experience of desire, for her feelings occur in response to another person, whom she at first suspects is her boyfriend speaking from a safe distance, conveying the relational contours of her sexual desire. Her wish to bring her desire into her relationship, voiced in her response of calling her boyfriend, is in conflict with her fear of what might happen if she did pursue her wish—getting pregnant and having a baby, a consequence that Rochelle is desperate to avoid.

I am struck by her awareness of both the pleasure and danger in this experience and how she works the contradiction without dissociating from her own strong feelings. There is a brilliance and also a sadness in the logic her body and psyche have played out in the face of her experiences with sexuality and relationships. The psychological solution to the dilemma that desire means for her, of feeling sexual desire only when she cannot respond as she says she would like to, arises from her focus on these conflicts as personal experiences, which she suffers and solves privately. By identifying and solving the dilemma in this way, Rochelle is diminished, as is the possibility of her developing a critique of these conflicts as not just personal problems but as social inequities that emerge in her personal relationships and on her body. Without this perspective, Rochelle is less likely to become empowered through her own desire to identify that the ways in which she must

curtail herself and be curtailed by others are socially constructed, suspect, and in need of change.

Megan Doing Desire

Megan, a small, freckled, perky Euro-American, is dressed in baggy sweats, comfortable, unassuming, and counterpointed by her lively engagement in our interview.[3] She identifies herself as "being bisexual" and belongs to a gay youth group; she lives in a city in which wealth and housing projects coexist. Megan speaks of knowing she is feeling sexual desire for boys because she has "kind of just this feeling, you know? Just this feeling inside my body." She explains: "My vagina starts to kinda like act up and it kinda like quivers and stuff, and like I'll get like tingles and and, you can just feel your hormones (laughing) doing something weird, and you just, you get happy and you just get, you know, restimulated kind of and it's just, and Oh! Oh!" and "Your nerves feel good." Megan speaks about her sexual desire in two distinct ways, one for boys and one for girls. In our interview, she speaks most frequently about her sexual feelings in relation to boys. The power of her own desire and her doubt about her ability to control herself frighten her: "It scares me when I'm involved in a sexual situation and I just wanna go further and further and cause it just, and it scares me that, well, I have control, but if I even just let myself not have control, you know?...I'd have sex and I can't do that." Megan knows that girls who lose control over their desire like that can be called "sluts" and ostracized.

When asked to speak about an experience of sexual desire, Megan chooses to describe the safety of a heterosexual, monogamous relationship. She tells me how she feels when a boyfriend was "feeling me up"; not only is she aware of and articulate about his bodily reactions and her own, she narrates the relational synergy between her own desire and his:

> *I just wanted to go on, you know? Like I could feel his penis, you know, 'cause we'd kinda lied down you know, and, you just really get so into it and intense and, you just wanna, well you just kinda keep wanting to go on or something, but it just feels*

good.... His penis being on my leg made, you know, it hit a nerve or something, it did something because it just made me start to get more horny or whatever, you know, it just made me want to do more things and stuff. I don't know how, I can't, it's hard for me to describe exactly how I felt, you know like, (intake of breath)... when he gets more excited then he starts to do more things and you can kind of feel his pleasure and then you start to get more excited.

With this young man, Megan knows her feelings of sexual desire to be "intense," to have a momentum of their own, and to be pleasurable. Using the concrete information of his erection, she describes the relational contours of her own embodied sexual desire, a desire that she is clear is her own and located in her body but that also arises in response to his excitement.

Although able to speak clearly in describing a specific experience she has had with her desire, I hear confusion seep into her voice when she notices that her feelings contradict or challenge societal messages about girls and sexuality:

It's so confusing, 'cause you have to like say no, you have to be the one to say no, but why should you be the one to, cause I mean maybe you're enjoying it and you shouldn't have to say no or anything. But if you don't, maybe the guy'll just keep going and going, and you can't do that because then you would be a slut. There's so [much] like, you know, stuff that you have to deal with and I don't know, just I keep losing my thought.

Although she knows the logic offered by society—that she must "say no" to keep him from "going and going," which will make her "a slut"—Megan identifies what is missing from that logic, that "maybe you're"—she, the girl—"the one who is enjoying it." The fact that she may be experiencing sexual desire makes the scripted response—to silence his body—dizzying. Because she does feel her own desire and can identify the potential of her own pleasure, Megan asks the next logical question, the question that can lead to outrage, critique, and empowerment: "Why should you have to be the one to [say no]?" But Megan also gives voice to why sustaining the question is difficult; she knows that if she does not

conform, if she does not "say no"—both to him and to herself—then she may be called a slut, which could lead to denigration and isolation. Megan is caught in the contradiction between the reality of her sexual feelings in her body and the absence of her sexual feelings in the cultural script for adolescent girls' sexuality. Her confusion is an understandable response to this untenable and unfair choice: a connection with herself, her body, and sexual pleasure or a connection with the social world.

Megan is an avid reader of the dominant culture. Not only has she observed the ways that messages about girls' sexuality leave out or condemn her embodied feelings for boys, she is also keenly aware of the persuasiveness of cultural norms and images that demand heterosexuality:

Every teen magazine you look at is like, guy this, how to get a date, guys, guys, guys, guys, guys. So you're constantly faced with I have to have a boyfriend, I have to have a boyfriend, you know, even if you don't have a boyfriend, just [have] a fling, you know, you just want to kiss a guy or something. I've had that mentality for so long.

In this description of compulsory heterosexuality (Rich 1983), Megan captures the pressure she feels to have a boyfriend and how she experiences the insistence of this demand, which is ironically in conflict with the mandate to say no when with a boy. She is aware of how her psyche has been shaped into a "mentality" requiring any sexual or relational interests to be heterosexual, which does not corroborate how she feels. Compulsory heterosexuality comes between Megan and her feelings, making her vulnerable to a dissociation of her "feelings" under this pressure.

Although she calls herself bisexual, Megan does not describe her sexual feelings for girls very much in this interview. In fact, she becomes so confused that at one point she says she is not sure if her feelings for girls are sexual:

I mean, I'll see a girl I really really like, you know, because I think she's so beautiful, and I might, I don't know. I'm so confused.... But there's, you know, that same mentality as me liking a guy if he's really cute, I'm like, oh my God, you know, he's so cute. If I see a woman that I like, a girl, it's just like wow, she's so pretty, you know. See I can picture like hugging a girl; I just can't picture the sex, or anything, so, there's something being blocked.

Megan links her confusion with her awareness of the absence of images of lesbian sexuality in the spoken or imagistic lexicon of the culture, counterpointing the persuasiveness of heterosexual imagery all around her. Megan suggests that another reason that she might feel "confused" about her feelings for girls is a lack of sexual experience. Megan knows she is feeling sexual desire when she can identify feelings in her own body—when her "vagina acts up"—and these feelings occur for her in the context of a sexual relationship, when she can feel the other person's desire. Because she has never been in a situation with a girl that would allow this embodied sexual response, she posits a connection between her lack of sexual experience with girls and her confusion.

Yet she has been in a situation where she was "close to" a girl and narrates how she does not let her body speak:

There was this one girl that I had kinda liked from school, and it was really weird 'cause she's really popular and everything. And we were sitting next to each other during the movie and, kind of her leg was on my leg and I was like, wow, you know, and that was, I think that's like the first time that I've ever felt like sexual pleasure for a girl. But it's so impossible, I think I just like block it out, I mean, it could never happen. . . . I just can't know what I'm feeling. . . . I probably first mentally just say no, don't feel it, you know, maybe. But I never start to feel, I don't know. It's so confusing. 'Cause finally it's all right for me to like a girl, you know? Before it was like, you know, the two times that I really, that it was just really obvious that I liked them a lot, I had to keep saying no no no no, you know, I just would not let myself. I just hated myself for it, and this year now that I'm talking about it, now I can start to think about it.

Megan both narrates and interprets her dissociation from her embodied sexual feelings and de-

scribes the disciplinary stance of her mind over her body in how she "mentally" silences her body by saying "no," preempting her embodied response. Without her body's feelings, her embodied knowledge, Megan feels confused. If she runs interference with her own sexual feelings by silencing her body, making it impossible for her to feel her desire for girls, then she can avoid the problems she knows will inevitably arise if she feels sexual feelings she "can't know"—compulsory heterosexuality and homophobia combine to render this knowledge problematic for her. Fearing rejection, Megan keeps herself from feelings that could lead to disappointment, embarrassment or frustration, leaving her safe in some ways, yet also psychologically vulnerable.

Echoing dominant cultural constructions of sexual desire, Megan links her desire for girls with feelings of fear: "I've had crushes on some girls . . . you can picture yourself kissing a guy but then if you like a girl a lot and then you picture yourself kissing her, it's just like, I can't, you know, oh my God, no (laughs), you know it's like scary . . . it's society . . . you never would think of, you know, it's natural to kiss a girl." Megan's fear about her desire for girls is different from the fears associated with her desire for boys; whereas being too sexual with boys brings the stigma of being called a "slut," Megan fears "society" and being thought of as "unnatural" when it comes to her feelings for girls. Given what she knows about the heterosexual culture in which she is immersed— the pressure she feels to be interested in "guys" and also given what she knows about homophobia—there is an inherent logic in Megan's confused response to her feelings for girls.

Melissa Doing Desire

Melissa, dressed in a flowing gypsy skirt, white skin pale against the lively colors she wears, is clear about her sexual desire for girls, referring to herself as "lesbian"; she is also a member of a gay/lesbian youth group. In speaking of her desire, Melissa names not only powerful feelings of "being excited" and "wanting," but also more contained feelings; she has "like little crushes on like millions of people and I mean, it's enough for me." Living in a world defined as heterosexual, Melissa finds that "little crushes" have to suffice, given a lack of opportunity for sexual exploration or relationship: "I don't know very many people my age that are even bisexual or lesbians...so I pretty much stick to that, like, being hugely infatuated with straight people. Which can get a little touchy at times...realistically, I can't like get too ambitious, because that would just not be realistic."

At the forefront of how Melissa describes her desire is her awareness that her sexual feelings make her vulnerable to harm. Whereas the heterosexual girls in this study link their vulnerability to the outcomes of responding to their desire—pregnancy, disease, or getting a bad reputation—Melissa is aware that even the existence of her sexual desire for girls can lead to anger or violence if others know of it: "Well I'm really lucky that like nothing bad has happened or no one's gotten mad at me so far, that, by telling people about them, hasn't gotten me into more trouble than, it has, I mean, little things but not like, anything really awful. I think about that and I think it, sometimes, I mean, it could be more dangerous." In response to this threat of violence, Melissa attempts to restrain her own desire: "Whenever I start, I feel like I can't help looking at someone for more than a few seconds, and I keep, and I feel like I have to make myself not, stare at them or something." Another strategy is to express her desire covertly by being physically affectionate with other girls, a behavior that is common and acceptable; by keeping her sexuality secret, she can "hang all over [girls] and stuff and they wouldn't even think that I meant anything by it." I am not surprised that Melissa associates feeling sexual desire with frustration; she explains that she "find(s) it safer to just think about the person than what I wanna do, because if I think about that too much and I can't do it, then that'll just frustrate me," leading her to try to intervene in her feelings by "just think[ing] about the person" rather than about the more sexual things she "want(s) to do." In this way, Melissa

may jeopardize her ability to know her sexual desire and, in focusing on containing what society has named improper feelings, minimize or exorcise her empowerment to expose that construction as problematic and unjust.

My questions about girls' sexual desire connect deeply with Melissa's own questions about herself; she is in her first intimate relationship, and this interview proves an opportunity to explore and clarify painful twinges of doubt that she had begun to have about it. This relationship began on the initiative of the other girl, with whom she had been very close, rather than out of any sexual feelings on Melissa's part. In fact, Melissa was surprised when her friend had expressed a sexual interest, because she had not "been thinking that" about this close friend. After a history of having to hold back her sexual desire, of feeling "frustrated" and being "hugely infatuated with straight people," rather than having the chance to explore her sexuality, Melissa's response to this potential relationship was that she "should take advantage of this situation." As the interview progresses, Melissa begins to question whether she is sexually attracted to this girl or "it's just sort of like I just wanted something like this for so long that I'm just taking advantage of the situation."

When I ask Melissa questions about the role of her body in her experience of sexual desire, her confusion at first intensifies:

> Is that [your body] part of what feels like it might be missing?

> *(eight-second pause) It's not well, sometimes, I mean I don't know how, what I feel all the time. It's hard like, because I mean I'm so confused about this. And it's hard like when it's actually happening to be like, ok, now how do I feel right now? How do I feel right now? How am I gonna feel about this?...I don't know, 'cause I don't know what to expect, and I haven't been with anyone else so I don't know what's supposed to happen. So, I mean I'm pretty confused.*

The way she speaks about monitoring her body suggests that she is searching for bodily feelings, making me wonder what, if anything, she felt. I discern what she does not say directly; that her body was silent in these sexual experiences. Her hunger for a relationship is palpable: "I really wanted someone really badly, I think, I was getting really sick of being by myself.... I would be like God, I really need someone." The desperation in her voice, and the sexual frustration she describes, suggest that her "want" and "need" are distinctly sexual as well as relational.

One reason that Melissa seems to be confused is that she felt a strong desire to be "mothered," her own mother having died last year. In trying to distinguish her different desires in this interview, Melissa began to distinguish erotic feelings from another kind of wanting she also experienced: she said that "it's more of like but I kind of feel like it's really more of like a maternal thing, that I really want her to take care of me and I just wanna touch someone and I just really like the feeling of just how I mean I like, when I'm with her and touching her and stuff. A lot, but it's not necessarily a sexual thing at this point." In contrast to her feelings for her girlfriend, Melissa describes feeling sexually attracted to another girl. In so doing, Melissa clarifies what is missing in these first sexual adventures, enabling her to know what had bothered her about her relationship with her girlfriend:

> I don't really think I'm getting that much pleasure, from her, it's just, I mean it's almost like I'm getting experience, and I'm sort of having fun, it's not even that exciting, and that's why I think I don't really like her...because my friend asked me this the other day, well, I mean does it get, I mean when you're with her does it get really, I don't remember the word she used, but just really, like what was the word she used? But I guess she meant just like, exciting [laughing]. But it doesn't, to me. It's weird, because I can't really say that, I mean I can't think of like a time when I was really excited and it was like really, sexual pleasure, for me, because I don't think it's really like that. I mean not that I think that this isn't good because, I don't know, I mean, I like it, but I mean I think I have to, sort of realize that I'm not that much attracted to her, personally.

Wanting both a relationship and sexual pleasure, a chance to explore closeness and her sexual curiosity, and discovering that this relationship leaves out her sexual desire, Melissa laments her silent body: "I sort of expect or hope or whatever that there would be some kind of more excited feeling just from feeling sexually stimulated or whatever. I would hope that there would be more of a feeling than I've gotten so far." Knowing consciously what she "knows" about the absence of her sexual feelings in this relationship has left her with a relational conflict of large proportions for her: "I'm not that attracted to her and I don't know if I should tell her that. Or if I should just kind of pretend I am and try to...anyway." I ask her how she would go about doing that—pretending that she is. She replies, "I don't think I could pretend it for too long." Not being able to "pretend" to have feelings that she knows she wants as part of an intimate relationship, Melissa faces a dilemma of desire that may leave her feeling isolated and lonely or even fraudulent.

ADOLESCENT GIRLS' SEXUAL DESIRE AND THE POSSIBILITIES OF EMPOWERMENT

All of the girls in this study who said they felt sexual desire expressed conflict when describing their responses to their sexual feelings—conflict between their embodied sexual feelings and their perceptions of how those feelings are, in one way or another, anathema or problematic within the social and relational contexts of their lives. Their experiences of sexual desire are strong and pleasurable, yet they speak very often not of the power of desire but of how their desire may get them into trouble. These girls are beginning to voice the internalized oppression of their women's bodies; they knew and spoke about, in explicit or more indirect ways, the pressure they felt to silence their desire, to dissociate from those bodies in which they inescapably live. Larger societal forces of social control in the form of compulsory heterosexuality (Rich 1983), the policing of girls' bodies through school codes (Lesko 1988), and media images play a clear part in forcing this silence and dissociation. Specific relational dynamics, such as concern about a reputation that can easily be besmirched by other girls and by boys, fear of male violence in intimate relationships, and fear of violent repercussion of violating norms of heterosexuality are also audible in these girls' voices.

To be able to know their sexual feelings, to listen when their bodies speak about themselves and about their relationships, might enable these and other girls to identify and know more clearly the sources of oppression that press on their full personhood and their capacity for knowledge, joy, and connection. Living in the margins of a heterosexual society, the bisexual and lesbian girls voice an awareness of these forces as formative of the experiences of their bodies and relationships; the heterosexual girls are less clear and less critical about the ways that dominant constructions of their sexuality impinge on their embodied and relational worlds. Even when they are aware that societal ambivalence and fears are being played out on their minds and bodies, they do not speak of a need for collective action, or even the possibility of engaging in such activities. More often, they speak of the danger of speaking about desire at all. By dousing desire with fear and confusion, or simple, "uncomplicated" denial, silence, and dissociation, the girls in this study make individual psychological moves whereby they distance or disconnect themselves from discomfort and danger. Although disciplining their bodies and curbing their desire is a very logical and understandable way to stay physically, socially, and emotionally safe, it also heightens the chance that girls and women may lose track of the fact that an inequitable social system, and not a necessary situation, renders women's sexual desire a source of danger, rather than one of pleasure and power in their lives. In "not knowing" desire, girls and women are at risk for not knowing that there is nothing wrong with having sexual feelings and responding to them in ways that bring joy and agency.

Virtually every girl in the larger study told me that no woman had ever talked to her about sexual desire and pleasure "like this"—in depth, listening

to her speak about her own experiences, responding when she asked questions about how to masturbate, how to have cunnilingus, what sex is like after marriage. In the words of Rubin: "The ethos of privacy and silence about our personal sexual experience makes it easy to rationalize the refusal to speak [to adolescents]" (1990, 83; Segal 1993). Thompson (1990) found that daughters of women who had talked with them about pleasure and desire told narratives about first intercourse that were informed by pleasure and agency. The recurrent strategy the girls in my study describe of keeping their desire under wraps as a way to protect themselves also keeps girls out of authentic relationships with other girls and women. It is within these relationships that the empowerment of women can develop and be nurtured through shared experiences of both oppression and power, in which collectively articulated critiques are carved out and voiced. Such knowledge of how a patriarchal society systematically keeps girls and women from their own desire can instigate demand and agency for social change. By not talking about sexual desire with each other or with women, a source for empowerment is lost. There is a symbiotic interplay between desire and empowerment: to be empowered to desire one needs a critical perspective, and that critical perspective will be extended and sustained through knowing and experiencing the possibilities of desire and healthy embodied living. Each of these girls illustrates the phenomenon observed in the larger study—the difficulty for girls in having or sustaining a critical perspective on the culture's silencing of their sexual desire. They are denied full access to the power of their own desire and to structural supports for that access.

Common threads of fear and joy, pleasure and danger, weave through the narratives about sexual desire in this study, exemplified by the three portraits. Girls have the right to be informed that gaining pleasure and a strong sense of self and power through their bodies does not make them bad or unworthy. The experiences of these and other adolescent girls illustrate why girls deserve to be educated about their sexual desire.

Thompson concludes that "to take possession of sexuality in the wake of the anti-erotic sexist socialization that remains the majority experience, most teenage girls need an erotic education" (1990, 406). Girls need to be educated about the duality of their sexuality, to have safe contexts in which they can explore both danger and desire (Fine 1988) and to consider why their desire is so dangerous and how they can become active participants in their own redemption. Girls can be empowered to know and act on their own desire, a different educational direction than the simplistic strategies for avoiding boys' desire that they are offered. The "just say no" curriculum obscures the larger social inequities being played out on girls' bodies in heterosexual relationships and is not relevant for girls who feel sexual feelings for girls. Even adults who are willing or able to acknowledge that girls experience sexual feelings worry that knowing about their own sexual desire will place girls in danger (Segal 1993). But keeping girls in the dark about their power to choose based on their own feelings fails to keep them any safer from these dangers. Girls who trust their minds and bodies may experience a stronger sense of self, entitlement, and empowerment that could enhance their ability to make safe decisions. One approach to educating girls is for women to speak to them about the vicissitudes of sexual desire— which means that women must let themselves speak and know their own sexual feelings, as well

as the pleasures and dangers associated with women's sexuality and the solutions that we have wrought to the dilemma of desire: how to balance the realities of pleasure and danger in women's sexuality.

Asking these girls to speak about sexual desire, and listening and responding to their answers and also to their questions, proved to be an effective way to interrupt the standard "dire consequences" discourse adults usually employ when speaking at all to girls about their sexuality. Knowing and speaking about the ways in which their sexuality continues to be unfairly constrained may interrupt the appearance of social equity that many adolescent girls (especially white, middle-class young women) naively and trustingly believe, thus leading them to reject feminism as unnecessary and mean-spirited and not relevant to their lives. As we know from the consciousness-raising activities that characterized the initial years of second-wave feminism, listening to the words of other girls and women can make it possible for girls to know and voice their experiences, their justified confusion and fears, their curiosities. Through such relationships, we help ourselves and each other to live in our different female bodies with an awareness of danger, but also with a desire to feel the power of the erotic, to fine-tune our bodies and our psyches to what Audre Lorde has called the "yes within ourselves" (Lorde 1984, 54).

NOTES

1. The bisexual girl and the lesbian girl were members of a gay/lesbian youth group and identify themselves using these categories. As is typical for members of privileged groups for whom membership is a given, the girls who feel sexual desire for boys and not for girls (about which they were asked explicitly) do not use the term "heterosexual" to describe themselves. Although I am aware of the debate surrounding the use of these categories and labels to delimit women's (and men's) experience, because my interpretive practice is informed by the ways society makes meaning of girls' sexuality, the categories that float in the culture as ways of describing the girls are relevant to my analysis. In addi-

tion, the bisexual and lesbian girls in this study are deeply aware of compulsory heterosexuality and its impact on their lives,

2. Of the 30 girls in this sample, 27 speak of a desire for boys and not for girls. This pattern was ascertained by who appeared in their desire narratives and also by their response to direct questions about sexual feelings for girls, designed explicitly to interrupt the hegemony of heterosexuality. Two of the 30 girls described sexual desire for both boys and girls and one girl described sexual desire for girls and not for boys.

3. Parts of this analysis appear in Tolman (1994).

REFERENCES

Brown, L. 1991. Telling a girl's life: Self authorization as a form of resistance. In *Women, girls and psychotherapy: Reframing resistance,* edited by C. Gilligan, A. Rogers, and D. Tolman. New York: Haworth.

Brown, L., E. Debold, M. Tappan, and C. Gilligan. 1991. Reading narratives of conflict for self and moral voice: A relational method. In *Handbook of moral behavior and development: Theory, research, and application,* edited by W. Kurtines and J. Gewirtz. Hillsdale, NJ: Lawrence Erlbaum.

Brown, L., and C. Gilligan. 1992. *Meeting at the crossroads: Women's psychology and girls' development.* Cambridge, MA: Harvard University Press.

Fine, Michelle. 1988. Sexuality, schooling and adolescent females: The missing discourse of desire. *Harvard Educational Review* 58:29–53.

Friend, Richard. 1993. Choices, not closets. In *Beyond silenced voices,* edited by M. Fine and L. Weis. New York: State University of New York Press.

Gilligan, Carol. 1989. Teaching Shakespeare's sister. In *Making connections: The relational world of adolescent girls at Emma Willard School,* edited by C. Gilligan, N. Lyons, and T. Hamner. Cambridge, MA: Harvard University Press.

———. 1990. Joining the resistance: Psychology, politics. girls and women. *Michigan Quarterly Review* 29:501–36.

Lees, Susan. 1986. *Losing out: Sexuality and adolescent girls.* London: Hutchinson.

Lesko, Nancy. 1988. The curriculum of the body: Lessons from a Catholic high school. In *Becoming feminine: The politics of popular culture,* edited by L. Roman. Philadelphia: Falmer.

Lorde, Audre. 1984. The uses of the erotic as power. In *Sister outsider: Essays and speeches.* Freedom, CA: Crossing Press.

Miller, Jean Baker. 1976. *Towards a new psychology of woman.* Boston: Beacon Press.

Rick Adrienne. 1983. Compulsory heterosexuality and lesbian existence. In *Powers of desire: The politics of sexuality,* edited by A. Snitow, C. Stansell, and S. Thompson. New York: Monthly Review Press.

Rubin. Lillian. 1990. *Erotic wars: What happened to the sexual revolution?* New York: HarperCollins.

Segal, Lynne. 1993. Introduction. In *Sex exposed: Sexuality and the pornography debate,* edited by L. Segal and M. McIntosh. New Brunswick, NJ: Rutgers University Press.

Spillers, Hortense. 1984. Interstices: A small drama of words. In *Pleasure and danger: Exploring female sexuality,* edited by C. Vance. Boston: Routledge and Kegan Paul.

Thompson, Sharon. 1984. Search for tomorrow: On feminism and the reconstruction of teen romance. In *Pleasure and danger: Exploring female sexuality,* edited by C. Vance. Boston: Routledge and Kegan Paul.

———. 1990. Putting a big thing in a little hole: Teenage girls' accounts of sexual initiation. *Journal of Sex Research* 27:341–61.

Tolman, Deborah L. 1991. Adolescent girls, women and sexuality: Discerning dilemmas of desire. *Women, girls and psychotherapy: Reframing resistance,* edited by C. Gilligan, A. Rogers, and D. Tolman. New York: Haworth.

———. 1992. Voicing the body: A psychological study of adolescent girls' sexual desire. Unpublished dissertation, Harvard University.

———. 1994. Daring to desire: Culture and the bodies of adolescent girls. In *Sexual cultures: Adolescents, communities and the construction of identity,* edited by J. Irvine. Philadelphia: Temple University Press.

Tolman, Deborah, and Elizabeth Debold. 1993. Conflicts of body and image: Female adolescents, desire, and the no-body. In *Feminist treatment and therapy of eating disorders,* edited by M. Katzman, P. Fallon, and S. Wooley. New York: Guilford.

21

Anita Hill, Sexual Harassment, and Gender Politics in the Black Community

ROBERT STAPLES

One can only marvel at the circumstances that in 1991 brought together a Black man and a Black woman, on national television, to debate charges that the Black man had made inappropriate and offensive sexual remarks to the Black woman. For three days a television audience composed primarily of Euro-Americans sat mesmerized by the sexual candor of the two protagonists, Clarence Thomas and Anita Hill. After all, the Thomas hearings, ostensibly to evaluate Thomas's moral suitability as a Supreme Court nominee, were excellent theater that combined the combustible elements of politics, sex, and race. During the hearings, the nation pretended that the most important aspect of a Supreme Court nominee's qualifications was his dating style and consumption of pornography. Little attention focused on Thomas's ability to do the work of the Court, to render decisions about affirmative action, abortion, and workers' rights—decisions that could result in the fulfillment or waste of millions of American lives. And, during the hearings, the nation suddenly pretended to care about a Black woman's sexual sensibilities, after ignoring vicious and blatant transgressions against her body for 400 years.

HISTORICAL BACKGROUND

The stereotype of the Black woman is that she is the most sensual of all female creatures. One Black writer even described her as "potentially, if not already, the most sexual animal on this planet."[1] Although his description was meant as a compliment, the traditional White view of Black sexuality is rife with negative connotations. The lusty sexuality that many Whites impute to Blacks represents to Whites the most abnormal, vulgar and base instincts of mankind. The image of the Black woman as innately sexual is a combination of fact and myth. That image has been used as a justification of racist practices because it suggests that she has unrestrained sexual urges that "civilized" people do not possess.

Predictably, the slave woman was subject to the carnal desires of the slavemaster and his overseers. She was used and abused, sexually, by many White males on the plantation. Though there may have been some slave women who voluntarily submitted to the slavemaster's sexual advances, there is sufficient historical evidence to show that many Black women, because of their captive status, were compelled to enter into various sexual associations with White males. As one observer noted, the American slaveholder's sexual domination never lost its openly terroristic character.[2]

Slave women were deprived of any protection against the sexual assaults of White males. Under slavery, Blacks were not permitted to be witnesses against Whites in a court of law. There were no legal provisions that could save the Black woman from surrendering her body. For example, the North Carolina Supreme Court ruled in the nineteenth century that no White male could be convicted for fornication with a slave woman. The North Carolina Constitutional Convention of 1835 declared that any White man might go to the house of a free Black, mistreat and abuse him, and commit any outrage upon his family. If a White person did not witness the act, no legal remedies were available.[3]

If a Black man defended a Black woman against sexual assault from a White man, the consequence for the Black man was often death. This does not mean that Black men did not try to defend Black women. After emancipation, when the marriages of Black women were legally recognized, Black men began to demand that Black women be treated with respect and courtesy, that White men cease their seduction and rape of Black womanhood. In 1874 one Black congressman declared: "We want more protection from the Whites invading our homes and destroying the virtue of our woman than they from us."[4]

The sexual exploitation of Black women was not always accompanied by violence. White men were able to use the economic deprivation of Black women to their sexual advantage. The sexual exploitation of Black women who worked as domestic servants is legendary. Hernton reports that even today, throughout the entire South, White men sexually use Black women in the course of the women's employment or in the course of their seeking employment.[5]

One such example of the White man's economic advantage serving sexual ends is reported by John Howard Griffin. He quoted the following revelations of a White employer:[6]

He told me how all of the White men in the region crave colored girls. He said he hired a lot of them both for house work and in his business. [He said], "And I guarantee you, I've had it in every one of them before they get on the payroll."

"Surely some refuse," I suggested cautiously.

"Not if they want to eat—or feed their kids," he snorted. "If they don't put out, they don't get the job."

From a review of the conditions under which Black women lived, it is easy to understand why there failed to emerge in the Black culture the rigid

sexual regulations so prevalent in the dominant American society. As the violation of her body became routine, Black women could not value that which was not available to her—virginity.

Some writers point out that Black women have been sexually used by men of both races. It has been noted that, after emancipation, many Black men had a sexual life of a casual nature. Many of them wandered from town to town, seeking employment. Frequently, as a result of telling hard-luck stories of their life on the road, they were taken in by lonely women engaged in domestic service. Once the men's sexual hunger was satisfied, they took to the road again.[7]

Only middle-class Black women had any measure of protection against the unwelcome sexual advances of White men. Middle-class Black males preferred that their wives stay at home; therefore, middle-class Black women did not often encounter White men.[8] This middle-class element in the Black population was very conscious of its unique position in relation to the masses of Black folk. Contrary to their lower-class brethren, they placed an exaggerated emphasis upon moral conduct and developed a puritanical restraint in contrast to the free sexual behavior of the larger Black population.

Considering the different history of Blacks and the different conditions under which they live, White sexual standards may not be applicable to Black females. Although Blacks are influenced by the majority culture's moral code, that code does not necessarily guide their behavior, especially in the lower class. According to Ladner, Blacks in the lower economic classes do not regard premarital sex, for example, as an immoral act but rather as a human function that is engaged in because it is natural.[9]

The Black experience has produced a sexual style that is unique. Talking plays an important role. In talking to a Black woman, a Black man must be able to use such words as *cool, baby, what's happening,* and *right on* properly. Proper use shows that the man is "with it" and worth her attention. Such words have a special meaning in the

Black community, and their use is labeled "heavy talking." A man should use a different rap for lower-class women than for middle-class women. Since a woman may be either attracted or repelled by the man's rap, it is important that the male use words appropriate to the context.[10]

Most Black women expect men to try and seduce them. Whether they agree to have sexual relations does not depend solely on a man's rap, however. Most Black women want to feel that they are not just casual sexual partners and that the man really cares for them. The rapper has to convey a feeling of sincerity or he fails to complete the seductive process. Because, although most Black women enjoy the physical aspects of sex, for many it represents an emotional bond. It signifies human relatedness.

THE THOMAS HEARINGS IN THE CONTEXT OF BLACKS' ATTITUDES ABOUT SEX

Given the liberality of Black sexual attitudes, why was Anita Hill charging Clarence Thomas with what was, in terms of Black culture, a relatively mild form of sexual harassment? This situation can only be understood in its political context. Had Clarence Thomas been a Jesse Jackson or Thurgood Marshall (warts and all)—someone who had paid some dues in the Black community—it is highly improbable that she would have come forth with sexual harassment charges, even if sexual harassment had transpired. Until Hill's emergence Thomas's confirmation seemed a done deal. She was the Black community's last chance to prevent a Black man representing racist interests from sitting on the highest court in the land. Her actions were most likely based on who Clarence Thomas was and why he was nominated to the U.S. Supreme Court. One columnist wrote, "President Bush, who has done nothing for African-Americans but use them to scare white voters, pushed Thomas in the Black community's face. There, he said, fight about that for a while."[11] Another equally observant columnist noted, "the obscenity is nominating a nothing of a right wing

Judge, with very little experience, to take the place of a jurist of the stature of Thurgood Marshall. The fact that Thomas is Black, staunchly supported by former segregationists Strom Thurmond [as well as Jesse Helms and David Duke], is Bush's big racial joke."[12] The political strategy was that, by making the conservative a Black man, there were too many Democrats in an all-White Senate who could not afford to oppose any Black nominee, though he be to the right of Genghis Khan.

In effect, Clarence Thomas became the racist nominee by proxy. He had earned the support of Thurmond, Helms, and Duke not only by his words and deeds against civil rights laws and affirmative action regulations, but by his willingness to validate the right-wing Republican agenda across the board. He was a threat to the rights of women, the elderly, and workers. First and foremost, however, Bush intended to use Thomas as a racial symbol. If, as a Supreme Court justice, Thomas supported an anti-civil rights ruling, the ruling would have a legitimacy that one supported by an all-White court would not. As a justice of the Supreme Court, Thomas's elite position would cast him in a leadership role in the Black community.

Although some Black organizations (such as the Urban League) remained neutral in regard to Thomas's nomination and a few (such as the Southern Christian Leadership Conference) endorsed him, most Black organizations viewed Thomas as a racist in blackface, and on that basis they opposed him. Among the Black leaders on record, the most prominent who supported Thomas and who were not known as Black conservatives were writer Maya Angelou and the president of Lincoln University, Niara Sudarkasa. Most progressive groups, representing 70 percent of the American population, opposed him. Up to the time of Anita Hill's charges, the polls showed that a larger percentage of Whites than Blacks supported Thomas's nomination.[13]

Enter Anita Hill, whom Jesse Jackson ranks along with Rosa Parks for her contribution to the Black struggle.[14] Had Thomas not been a racist by proxy, would certain events have occurred? Would Hill's elderly parents and members of her family have accompanied her to the judiciary hearings to deny a Black man his seat on the Supreme Court? Would Hill herself have testified against a Black man to an all-White male panel? Knowing Black women's reluctance to testify against Black men in divorce court and child support cases, I think not. Would White feminists have taken on Thomas if they knew doing so would pit them against Black organizations? Despite Thomas's support among Blacks at the grass roots level, he had no visible support among Black leaders except the two Black women mentioned earlier, and Angelou and Sudarkasa had to be embarrassed by the sexual allegations.

The hearings were based on the sexual harassment charges, but a great deal more was at stake. Under the circumstances, old alliances meant nothing. The former segregationists and current users of racial buzzwords (such as *quotas, welfare,* and *crime*) found themselves supporting a Black man with a White wife. Anita Hill's most visible supporters were middle-class White women, who identified with her issue—if not with her. Most non-Southern White Democratic males sided with Hill and White Republican males overwhelmingly supported Thomas. Since people claimed it was impossible to tell who was telling the truth, they sided according to race, gender, or political preference and interest—at least the Whites did. After Hill came forward, Blacks were almost divided down the middle over Thomas (about 60 percent supported him after the hearings). One person's explanation for the Black support of Thomas reflects the continuing significance of race in American life. He said, "there is a lot of diversity of Blacks with respect to where they fall in terms of identity. A lot also depends on where they are and what's going on in their lives."[15]

Guessing at the veracity of the protagonists is fruitless and beside the point. Still, I am inclined to believe Hill's claims about what Thomas said and did. Besides the polygraph test she passed, she has no discernible motive for not telling the truth. And everything we know about Thomas leads us to believe he is capable of such deeds. Any man who is capable of selling out his race is certainly capable of a crude sexual approach to women, and several women alleged that Thomas had made crude sexual advances to them.[16] So, why did the TV viewers believe him over her? In a racist, sexist society, it is relatively easy for White men with power to discredit and to dismiss a Black woman. All she had on her side was the truth. He had a better television performance, more aggressive Republican interviewers, and the willingness of White male viewers to see the attack on Thomas as an attack on themselves. Ultimately, Thomas won because of his racial views—not on the basis of whether he sexually harassed Anita Hill. The Republican members of the Senate were already committed to voting for him. The key Southern Democrats, who provided the votes necessary, voted for Thomas out of fear of offending White conservatives in their home states, while knowing they stood to lose few Black votes for their decision.[17]

What was so startling was the high percentage of Blacks who supported Thomas, as high as 67 percent in some polls.[18] What is more, his Black support appears to have come from a cross section of Afro-Americans, albeit few polls gave a detailed breakdown of the Black vote. One journalist concluded that "for Blacks, there was a solid show of support for an embattled Black man, even one assailed as an enemy of civil rights, that reinforced the degree to which Blacks have behaved as a unified political force."[19] A Black minister claimed that some of Thomas's Black support was a result of slavery. Reverend Amos Brown said, "you don't go and tell the White man on a member of the family. That's why many Blacks are still sympathetic to him. It clouds the real issue."[20] My own reading of the situation is that many Blacks supported Thomas despite his philosophy, not because of it. I also suspect that most Afro-Americans began to pay attention to Thomas's nomination only after the Hill charges were aired on television. Many of them, at that point, probably did not know what Thomas stood for, why he was nominated, and who his supporters were. Being unaware of what was at stake, their instinctual reaction was to support a Black man besieged by Whites in a nationally televised hearing.

Politically sophisticated Blacks, especially the leadership class, knew why Anita Hill was there and what her role was. Much has been made of the fact that she was a conservative. However, her testimony before the judiciary committee showed she had philosophical differences with Thomas, and one of them was the need for affirmative action. Probably more than most, because she had worked with him, she knew what a danger Thomas was to the Black community. By testifying against Thomas, she has probably ruined her political career. The greatest injury she may suffer is the knowledge that her own people turned against her and became political bedfellows with their worst enemies.

Sexual harassment was ostensibly the issue on which Clarence Thomas was to be questioned. It is an issue of grave importance, but it is so vaguely and subjectively defined that it may be one of the most divisive issues of our time. In part, men and women are divided because of their different sexual socialization and values. The courts have said that the more conservative sexual values of women will determine what constitutes sexual harassment. Consequently, 50 percent of American men say they have been guilty of sexual harassment in the past and 44 percent of American women say they have been subjected to sexual harassment.[21] One must raise the question: If a standard of behavior pits half of each gender group against half the opposite gender group, is the standard valid or practical?

The implications of the courts' definition of sexual harassment are even greater for the Black community than for the White community. The historical sexual liberality of the Black community conflicts with current definitions of sexual harassment. In his study of Black and White cultural styles, Kochman observed that "In Black culture it is customary for Black men to approach Black women in a manner that openly expresses a sexual interest, while in white culture it is equally customary for 'respectable' women to be offended by an approach that presumes sexual interest and availability."[22]

Although Kochman's statement more accurately reflects lower-income, urban, and non-Southern Blacks than other Black groups, it serves to explain Orlando Patterson's claim that "Professor Hill perfectly understood the psycho-cultural context in which judge Thomas allegedly regaled her with his Rabelaisian humor (possibly as a way of affirming their common origins) which is precisely why she never filed a complaint against him."[23]

While she may have understood the cultural context of his courtship style, that does not mean she liked it when it came from a man who was her supervisor and who held absolute authority over her hiring and firing. I suspect she was more bothered by his insistence on a personal relationship she did not desire than some of the sexually oriented conversation. Either way, Thomas's behavior qualified as sexual harassment according to the prevailing definition. Thomas knew that; he told Hill that, if she revealed his behavior, she would ruin his career. Yet Patterson, himself a Black neo-conservative, charges Hill with "lifting a verbal style that carries only minor sanction in one subcultural context and throwing it in the overheated cultural arena of mainstream, neo-Puritan America where it incurs professional extinction."[24] That distinction is probably irrelevant to an upwardly mobile, quasi-religious woman like Anita Hill.

THE EFFECTS OF THE THOMAS HEARINGS ON THE BLACK COMMUNITY

What are the consequences of the Thomas hearings for the Black community? Poussaint says the hearings will reinforce negative sexual stereotypes of Black men and that the hearings "will increase [Black men's] level of tension and vulnerability around charges of this type and make them tip-toe carefully because they may feel that they will be more likely targets."[25] Certainly, the White-dominated media has highlighted Black males accused of sexual harassment, rape, and violence against women. Although most Black males are not in a position to sexually harass women, they may need to adjust to changing norms of male-female interaction.

The controversy over Clarence Thomas revealed widening splits in the Afro-American community and Euro-American political strategies for the twenty-first century. The splits are along gender and class lines. Gender lines are divisive because some Black men feel that Black women are given preference over them, that White men like to put Black women between themselves and Black men. Many Blacks accused Anita Hill of acting as a tool for White men to ruin the life of a Black man at the peak of his career. That many Black leaders did not share that view is reflected in a statement by Representative Craig Washington: "it is not Black women who have lynched Black men. It is White racism that has been tolerated for so long by many of Judge Thomas's supporters. It is a problem that will not be addressed by attacking and demeaning Black women."[26] Thomas's claim that he was the victim of racism was the real irony. Most of the racists in America were his supporters, and the White supporters of civil rights were his opponents.

The Thomas hearings may represent the worst of all worlds for Black Americans. Anita Hill's attempt to prevent Thomas's confirmation to the U.S. Supreme Court failed, and he is likely to be the sole Black Supreme Court justice for two generations. His first year on the bench confirmed the worst fears about his commitment to a reactionary interpretation of the Constitution. Meanwhile, Anita Hill has become a feminist icon and travels throughout the country giving speeches on sexual harassment for $10,000 each.[27] Although there is a need for a reduction in sexual violence against Black women, the history of American justice is that White males can use their power and privilege to escape punishment for sexual crimes against

women while Black males pay the full price. The acquittal of William Kennedy Smith, White, and the conviction of Mike Tyson, Black, on rape charges is one example. When rape was a capital offense in the United States, 89 percent of those executed for that crime were Black males; almost all their alleged victims were White.[28] Because sexual harassment regulations conflict with Black dating styles, we may once more see a repetition of this travesty of justice, this time with the imposition of Eurocentric values on Black behavior.

However, the penalty for alleged sexual harassment is, in most cases, a suspension or loss of employment. Most Black males do not have jobs to lose. Those who are employed are often in the type of job where there is little interaction with women. Moreover, anecdotal evidence suggests that it is White males who sexually harass women in blue-collar occupations that have been traditionally dominated by men. Nevertheless, a disproportionate number of the highly publicized sexual harassment cases involved Black males. One Black male executive committed suicide when confronted with sexual harassment charges by a White female employee, an accusation that other Black executives claimed was the most dangerous a Black male executive can face.[29] When the alleged victim is a White female, the harsh penalties meted out to the accused Black male reflect the fact that, for a Black man, expressing sexual interest in a White woman is taboo.

The worst consequence of Anita Hill's spotlight on sexual harassment is its potential for increasing tension and conflict between Black men and Black women. Already inculcated in the public mind is the image of Black men as criminals, something that can be seen in the reaction of White women to every strange Black male they encounter. In recent years, the highly publicized cases of *two* Black males, Clarence Thomas and Mike Tyson, have caused even Black women to think of *all* Black men as potential date rapists and sexual harassers. Many Black women, particularly those in the acculturated middle class, refuse to go indoors alone with them. In a community with a sex ratio of four eligible Black women to every one "desirable" Black male, where only one-third of all adult Black females are married and living with their spouse, the current trend toward distrust may create the worst crisis for the Black family since slavery. History may declare Anita Hill the Rosa Parks of her era. Or, she may have sowed the seeds of an irreparable rift in the Afro-American world. Only time will tell.

NOTES

1. Calvin Hernton, *Sex and Racism in America.* Garden City, N.Y.: Doubleday, 1965, p. 136.
2. Angela Davis, "Reflections on the Black Woman's Role in the Community of Slaves." *The Black Scholar 3,* December 1971, p. 8.
3. Quoted in Louis Wirth and Herbert Guldhammer, "The Hybrid and the Problems of Miscegenation," in Otto Klineberg, *Characteristics of the American Negro.* New York: Harper & Row, 1944, p. 263.
4. Quoted in Joseph Washington, Jr., *Marriage in Black and White.* Boston: Beacon Press, 1970, p. 66.
5. Hernton, *op cit.,* p. 128.
6. John Howard Griffin, *Black Like Me.* New York: Signet, 1963, p. 100.
7. E. Franklin Frazier, *The Negro Family in the United States,* Chicago: University of Chicago Press, p. 214.
8. E. F. Frazier, *The Black Bourgeois.* New York: Collier, 1957.
9. Joyce Ladner, *Tomorrow's Tomorrow,* Garden City, N.Y.: Doubleday, 1971, pp. 51–52.
10. Thomas Kochman, *Black and White Styles in Conflict.* Chicago: University of Chicago Press, 1981.
11. Bill Mandel, "Thomas Stars in America's Nightmare." *San Francisco Examiner* October 14, 1991, p. A-3.
12. Rob Morse, "The Thomas Clown Affair." *San Francisco Examiner* October 15, 1991, p. A-3.
13. "How the Poll was Taken." *The New York Times* October 15, 1991, p. A-3.
14. Teresa Moore, "Jesse Jackson Gives Hill a Spot in History." *San Francisco Chronicle* October 14, 1991, p. A-2.
15. Dr. Robert T. Carter, quoted in Leno Williams, "Blacks Say the Blood Spilled in the Thomas Case Stains All." *The New York Times* October 14, 1991, p. A-1.
16. "A Moment of Truth." *Newsweek* October 2, 1991, p. 323.
17. "Playing White Male Politics" *Newsweek* October 28, l991, p. 27.
18. "New Polls Show Most Americans Favoring Thomas." *San Francisco Examiner* October 14, 1991, p. A-9.
19. Peter Applebome, "Despite Talk of Sexual Harassment, Thomas Hearings Turned on Race Issue." *The New York Times* October 19, 1991, p. A-7.
20. Reverend Amos Brown, quoted in Gregory Lewis, "Strong Feelings among Blacks in Bay Area." *San Francisco Examiner* October 15, 1991, p. A-12.
21. Elizabeth Kolbert, "Sexual Harassment at Work is Pervasive, Survey Suggests." *The New York Times* October 11, 1991, p. A-1.
22. Thomas Kochman, *Black and White Styles in Conflict.* Chicago: University of Chicago Press, 1981, p. 75.
23. Orlando Patterson, "Race, Gender and Liberal Fallacies." *The New York Times* October 20, 1991, p. A-15.
24. *Ibid.*
25. Alvin Poussaint, quoted in Williams, "Blacks Say Blood...Stains All."
26. Representative Craig Washington, quoted in "Black Caucus Decries Thomas Racism Defense." *San Francisco Chronicle* October 16, 1991, p. A-9.
27. David Brock, *The Real Anita Hill.* New York: Free Press, 1993.
28. William J. Bowers, *Executions in America.* Lexington, Mass.: Lexington Books, 1974.
29. Jonathan Kaufman, "The Pressures on a Black Executive." *The Boston Globe* February 8, 1983, pp. 1, 16.

22

It Takes More Than Two

The Prostitute, the Soldier, the State,
and the Entrepreneur

CYNTHIA ENLOE

Since U.S. occupation troops in Japan are unalterably determined to fraternize, the military authorities began helping them out last week by issuing a phrase book. Sample utility phrases: "You're very pretty"... "How about a date?"... "Where will I meet you?" And since the sweet sorrow of parting always comes, the book lists no less than 14 ways to say goodbye.

Time, July 15, 1946

On a recent visit to London, I persuaded a friend to play hooky from work to go with me to Britain's famous Imperial War Museum. Actually, I was quite embarrassed. In all my trips to London, I had never visited the Imperial War Museum. But now, in the wake of the Gulf War, the time seemed ripe. Maybe the museum would help put this most recent military conflict in perspective, mark its continuities with other wars, and clarify its special human, doctrinal, and technological features. I was in for a disappointment.

Only selective British experiences of the "great" wars were deemed worthy of display. Malaya, Aden, Kenya, the Falklands—these British twentieth-century war zones didn't rate display cases. In fact, Asia, Africa, and the West Indies didn't seem much on the curators' minds at all. There were two formal portraits of turbaned Indian soldiers who had won military honors for their deeds, but there were no displays to make visible to today's visitors how much the British military had relied on men and women from its colonies to fight both world wars. I made a vow

on my next trip to take the train south of London to the Gurkha Museum.

The only civilians who received much attention in the Imperial War Museum were British. Most celebrated were the "plucky" cockney Londoners who coped with the German blitz by singing in the Underground. Women were allocated one glass case showing posters calling on housewives to practice domestic frugality for the cause. There was no evidence, however, of the political furor set off when white British women began to date—and have children with—African-American GIs.

Our disappointment with the museum's portrayal of Britain's wars served to make us trade hunches about what a realistic curatorial approach might be. What would we put on display besides frontline trenches (which at least showed the rats), cockney blitz-coping lyrics, and unannotated portraits of Sikh heroes?

Brothels. In my war museum there would be a reconstruction of a military brothel. It would show rooms for officers and rooms for rank and file soldiers. It would display separate doors for

193

white soldiers and black soldiers. A manikin of the owner of the business (it might be a disco rather than a formal brothel) would be sitting watchfully in the corner—it could be a man or a woman, a local citizen or a foreigner. The women serving the soldiers might be White European, Berber, Namibian, or Puerto Rican; they might be Korean, Filipina, Japanese, Vietnamese, African-American, or Indian. Depending on the era and locale, they could be dressed in sarongs, saris, or miniskirts topped with T-shirts memorializing resort beaches, soft drinks, and aircraft carriers.

In this realistic war museum, visitors would be invited to press a button to hear the voices of the women chart the routes by which they came to work in this brothel and describe the children, siblings, and parents they were trying to support with their earnings. Several of the women might compare the sexual behavior and outlook of these foreign men with those of the local men they had been involved with. Some of the women probably would add their own analyses of how the British, U.S., French, or United Nations troops had come to be in their country.

Museum goers could step over to a neighboring tape recorder to hear the voices of soldiers who patronized brothels and discos while on duty abroad. The men might describe how they imagined these women were different from or similar to the women from their own countries. The more brazen might flaunt their sexual prowess. They might compare their strength, chivalry, or earning power with that of the local men. Some of the soldiers, however, would describe their feelings of loneliness, their uncertainty of what it means to be a man when you're a soldier, their anxieties about living up to the sexual performance expectations of their officers and buddies.

War—and militarized peace—are occasions when sexual relations take on particular meanings. A museum curator—or a journalist, novelist, or political commentator—who edits out sexuality, who leaves it on the cutting-room floor, deliv-

ers to the audience a skewed and ultimately unhelpful account of just what kinds of myths, anxieties, inequalities, and state policies are required to fight a war or to sustain a militarized form of peace.

A letter from a former CIA analyst, now an academic, suggests one reason why prostitution is so invisible, not only in military museums, but also in "serious" official discussions of security. He noted that in a recent book I had surmised from a Rand Corporation report that Soviet commanders had banned prostitution from their bases in Afghanistan during the counterinsurgency of the 1980s. He warned me not to jump to conclusions. While working as a CIA analyst in the 1970s, he had conducted a classified study of morale and discipline among Soviet forces. During the course of the study, he had interviewed an émigré who had been a conscript on a remote Soviet air force base in Russia's Far North. In reply to the analyst's inquiry about the presence of women on the base, the former conscript recalled that there had been approximately one hundred. What were their functions? *Prostituki!* The U.S. analyst found this pertinent and included the information in his report. But when the official CIA version came out, this was the only information excised by his superiors from the original draft. The analyst, looking back, speculated: "Since the U.S. military represses its bases' dependency on sexual access to local women, the organizational incentive is to avoid mentioning the Soviet problems for fear of drawing attention to the issue in the U.S. The tendency," he went on to explain, "to use information about the USSR as a means of discussing U.S. problems was something I commonly encountered in the CIA."[1]

It is for this reason that feminist ethnographies and oral histories are so vital. They help us to make sense of militaries' dependence on—yet denial of—particular presumptions about masculinity to sustain soldiers' morale and discipline. Without sexualized rest and recreation, would the

U.S. military command be able to send young men off on long, often tedious sea voyages and ground maneuvers? Without myths of Asian or Latina women's compliant sexuality, would many American men be able to sustain their own identities, their visions of themselves as manly enough to act as soldiers?

Women who have come to work as prostitutes around U.S. bases tell us that a militarized masculinity is constructed and reconstructed in smoky bars and sparsely furnished rented rooms. If we confine our curiosity only to the boot camp and the battlefield—the focus of most investigations into the formations of militarized masculinity— we will be unable to explain just how masculinity is created and sustained in the peculiar ways still imagined by officials to be necessary to sustain a modern military organization.

We will also miss just how much governmental authority is being expended to insure that a peculiar definition of masculinity is sustained. Military prostitution differs from other forms of industrialized prostitution in that there are explicit steps taken by state institutions to protect the male customers without undermining their perceptions of themselves as sexualized men.

"Close to 250,000 men a month paid three dollars for three minutes of the only intimacy most were going to find in Honolulu."[2] These figures come from records kept in Hawaii during 1941 and 1944. Historians have these precise figures because Honolulu brothel managers, most of whom were White women, had to submit reports to Hawaii's military governor. American soldiers' sexual encounters with local prostitutes were not left to chance or to the market; they were the object of official policy consideration among the military, the police, and the governor's staff. Two hundred and fifty prostitutes paid $1.00 per year to be registered merely as "entertainers" with the Honolulu Police Department because the federal government had passed the May Act in 1941, making prostitution illegal, to assuage the fears of many American civilians that mobilizing for war

would corrupt the country's sexual mores.[3] Hawaii's military governor disagreed. He had police and military officers on his side. They saw a tightly regulated prostitution industry as necessary to bolster male soldiers' morale, to prevent sexually transmitted diseases, and to reassure the Hawaiian White upper class that wartime would not jeopardize their moral order. The navy and the army set up prophylaxis distribution centers along Honolulu's Hotel Street, the center of the city's burgeoning prostitution industry. The two departments collaborated with the local police to try to ensure that licensed prostitutes kept their side of the bargain: in return for the license, women servicing soldiers and sailors up and down Hotel Street had to promise to have regular medical examinations, not to buy property in Hawaii, not to own an automobile, not to go out after 10:30 at night, and not to marry members of the armed forces. The objective was to keep prostitutes quite literally in their place.

The effort was only partially successful. Women working in the most successful brothels, White women, many of whom came by ship from San Francisco to work as prostitutes, made enough money to violate the official rules and buy homes outside Honolulu. They kept $2 of the $3 from each customer. Out of their earnings they paid $100 per month to the brothel manager for room and board, plus extra for laundry and $13 for each required monthly venereal disease test.

Before the war, most Hotel Street brothels had two doors, one for White male customers and one for men of color, most of whom were Asian men who worked on the island's pineapple and sugar plantations. Brothel managers believed this segregation prevented violent outbursts by White men who objected to the women they were paying for servicing men of any other race. As the wartime influx of White soldiers and sailors tilted the brothels' business ever more toward a White clientele, most managers decided that any risk of offending White male customers was bad business;

they did away with the second door and turned away men of color altogether.

Opening time for the typical Honolulu brothel during the war years was 9 A.M. It operated on an efficient assembly-line principle. From prostitutes and soldiers recalling the arrangement, we learn that most of the brothels used what was called a 'bull-ring' setup consisting of three rooms. "In one room a man undressed, in a second the prostitute engaged her customer, in a third a man who had finished put his clothes back on."[4] Prostitutes learned to tailor their services to the sexual sophistication of their military clients. They offered oral sex to the more nervous and inexperienced men. A senior military police officer in the middle of the war speculated before an audience of local citizen reformers that those sailors who performed oral sex with the Honolulu prostitutes were those men most likely to engage in homosexual behavior once they were back on board ship. The U.S. military's policymakers tried to think of everything.

Today British and Belize officials work hard together to develop a complex policy to ensure a steady but safe supply of military prostitutes for the British troops stationed in that small ex-colony perched on the edge of Latin America.[5] A new nine-hundred-man batallion arrives every six months. British soldiers have special brothels designated for their patronage, although they slip out of the carefully woven policy net to meet local women in bars and discos in Belize City. Most of the women who work in the officially approved brothels are Latinas, rather than Afro-Belize women; many have traveled across the border from war-torn Guatemala to earn money as prostitutes.

The government-to-government agreement requires that every brothel worker, with the cooperation of the owners, have a photo identification card and undergo weekly medical examinations by a Belizean doctor. Prostitutes are required to use condoms with their military customers, although it is not clear how many women may be paid extra by their customers to break the condom rule. If a soldier-patron does show symptoms of a sexually transmitted disease or tests positive for HIV, it is assumed that the prostitute is to blame. The infected soldier gives his British superiors the name of the prostitute who he believes infected him. On the basis of the soldier's word as well as on test results, on a first "offense" the woman is reprimanded by the brothel owner; on a second offense she is fined; on a third she is fired.

British-born soldiers and their Nepali Gurkha comrades, both in Belize under a Belize-British defense pact, have rather different racial/sexual preferences. Whereas the former are likely to frequent both Latina and Afro-Belize women, the Gurkhas reportedly prefer Latina women, which means that the Gurkhas are more likely to stick to the government-approved prostitutes. The fact that any Gurkha troops go to prostitutes at all, however, contradicts the long-standing British portrayal of Nepali militarized masculinity: though White British men's masculinity is presumed by their officers to require a diet of local sex while overseas, Nepali men's masculinity is constructed as more disciplined, faithful when home and celibate while on assignment abroad.[6] With the end of the Cold War and the relaxation of political tensions between Belize and Guatemala, the future of the government-to-government prostitution agreement has become uncertain. But in early 1992, Britain's Chief of Defence Staff, Field Marshal Sir Richard Vincent, made it known publicly that the Conservative government of John Major was hoping that the British troop rotation in Belize could be continued. Though no longer needed to defend Belize, the British army, according to the field marshal, now finds Belize's climate and topography especially attractive for jungle warfare training.[7] Do the field marshal and his superiors back in London perhaps also find the Belize government's willingness to cooperate in the control of local women's sexuality a military attraction?

The United States fashioned a rather different policy to regulate soldiers' relationships with prostitutes around major U.S. bases such as Clark and Subic Bay in the Philippines. Like the British, the Americans supported compulsory medical examinations of women working as prostitutes. Similarly, women without the license issued with these examinations were prevented from working by the local—in this case Filipino—municipal authorities. U.S. soldiers who contracted sexually transmitted diseases (STDs) were not required to report the woman whom they believe gave them the disease. Nonetheless, it was the practice of the Angeles City and Olongapo health authorities to pass on to U.S. base officials the names of sex workers who had contracted STDs. The base commanders then ordered that the photographs of infected Filipinas be pinned upside down on the public notice board as a warning to the American men.[8]

Apparently believing that "stable" relationships with fewer local women would reduce the chances that their personnel would become infected, base commanders allowed Filipinas hired out by bar owners to stay with their military boyfriends on the base. U.S. officials occasionally sent out a "contact" card to a club owner containing the name of a Filipina employee whom the Americans suspected of having infected a particular sailor or air force man. However, they refused to contribute to the treatment of prostitutes with sexually transmitted diseases or AIDS and turned down requests that they subsidize Pap smears for early cancer detection for the estimated one hundred thousand women working in the entertainment businesses around Clark and Subic.

The closing of both Clark Air Force Base and Subic Naval Base in 1992 forced many Filipinas in precarious states of health into the ranks of the country's unemployed. Their few options included migrating to Okinawa or Guam, or even to Germany, to continue working as prostitutes for U.S. military men. They may also have been vulnerable to recruiters procuring Filipina women for Japan's entertainment industry, an industry that is increasingly dependent on young women from abroad.[9] Olongapo City's businessman mayor, with his own entertainment investments now in jeopardy, has been in the forefront of promoters urging that

Subic Bay's enormous facilities be converted into private enterprises, although the Filipino military is also eager to take over at least part of the operations for its own purposes. Military base conversion is always an intensely gendered process. Even if women working the entertainment sector are not at the conversion negotiation table, they will be on many of the negotiators' minds. For instance, the above-mentioned mayor, among others, has urged not only that privatized ship maintenance be developed at Subic Bay, but also that tourism development be high on the new investment list.[10] In the coming years, the politics of prostitution in Olongapo City may take on a civilian look, but many of the tourists attracted may be slightly older American men trying to relive their earlier militarized sexual adventures with Filipina women.

There is no evidence thus far that being compelled by the forces of nature and nationalism to shut down two of their most prized overseas bases has caused U.S. military planners to rethink their prostitution policies. Shifting some of the Philippines operations to Guam or Singapore or back home to the United States does not in itself guarantee new official presumptions about the kinds of sexual relations required to sustain U.S. military power in the post-Cold War world. The governments of Singapore and the United States signed a basing agreement in Tokyo in mid-1992. But, despite popular misgivings about the implications of allowing U.S. Navy personnel to use the small island nation for repairs and training, the basing agreement itself was kept secret. Thus, Singapore citizens, as well as U.S. citizens, are left with little information about what policing formulas, public health formulas, and commercial zoning formulas have been devised by the two governments to shape the sexual relations between American and Singapore men and the women of Singapore.[11]

The women who have been generous enough to tell their stories of prostitution have revealed that sexuality is as central to the complex web of relationships between civil and military cultures as are more talked-about security doctrines and economic quid pro quo. Korean and Filipino women interviewed by Sandra Sturdevant and Brenda Stoltzfus for their oral history collection *Let the Good Times Roll* also remind us of how hard it is sometimes to map the boundaries between sexual relations and economics.[12] They found that the local and foreign men who own the brothels, bars, and discos catering to soldiers are motivated by profit. These men weigh the market value of a woman's virginity, her "cherry," as well as her age. They constantly reassess their male clients' demands. Thus, by the early 1990s, bar owners and procurers concluded that AIDS-conscious U.S. soldiers were competing to have sex with younger and younger Filipinas, and so the proprietors sought to supply them, driving down the value of the sexual services supplied by "older" women—women in their early twenties.[13]

Over the decades, U.S. Navy veterans stayed in the Philippines and set up bars and discos, both because they liked living outside the United States (often with Filipina wives) and because they could make a comfortable livelihood from sexualized entertainment. Australian men immigrated to launch their own businesses in the base towns and eventually made up a large proportion of the owners of the military-dependent entertainment industry.[14] Local military personnel, especially officers, also used their status and authority in the rural areas to take part in the industry. Some men in the Philippines military have been known to supplement their salaries by acting as procurers of young rural women for the tourist and military prostitution industries.[15] Similarly, among the investors and managers of Thailand's large prostitution industry are Thai military officers.[16] Militarized, masculinized sexual desire, by itself, isn't sufficient to sustain a full-fledged prostitution industry. It requires (depends on) rural poverty, male entrepreneurship, urban commercialized demand, police protection, and overlapping governmental economic interest to ensure its success.

Yet military prostitution is not simply an economic institution. The women who told their stories to Sturdevant and Stoltzfus were less concerned with parsing analytical categories—what is "economic," what is "social," and what is "political"—than with giving us an authentic account of the pressures, hopes, fears, and shortages they had to juggle every day in order to ensure their physical safety, hold onto some self-respect, and make ends meet for themselves and their children.

The stories that prostitutes tell also underscore something that is overlooked repeatedly in discussions of the impact of military bases on local communities: local women working in military brothels and discos mediate between two sets of men, the foreign soldiers and the local men—some of whom are themselves soldiers, but many of whom are civilians. Outside observers rarely talk about these two sets of men in the same breath. But the women who confided in Stoltzfus and Sturdevant knew that they had to be considered simultaneously. The Korean and Filipina women detailed how their relationships with local male lovers and husbands had created the conditions that initially made them vulnerable to the appeals of the labor-needy disco owners. Unfaithfulness, violent tempers, misuse of already low earnings, neglectful fathering—any combination of these behaviors by their local lovers and husbands might have launched these women into military prostitution. Children, too, have to be talked about. Most of the women servicing foreign soldiers sexually have children, some fathered by local men and others fathered by the foreign soldiers. Prostitution and men's ideas about fathering: the two are intimately connected in these women's lives.

In deeply militarized countries such as the Philippines, South Korea, Honduras, and Afghanistan, a woman working in prostitution may have to cope with local as well as foreign soldiers who need her services to shore up their masculinity. Because it is politically less awkward to concentrate on foreign soldiers' exploitation of local women, local soldiers' militarized and sexualized masculinity is frequently swept under the analytical rug, as if it were nonexistent or harmless. And in fact the local soldiery may have more respect for local women, may have easier access to noncommercialized sex, or may have too little money to spend to become major customers of local prostitutes. But none of those circumstances should be accepted as fact without a close look.

For instance, Anne-Marie Cass, an Australian researcher who spent many months in the late 1980s both with the Philippine government's troops and with insurgent forces, found that Filipino male soldiers were prone to sexualizing their power. Cass watched as many of them flaunted their sexualized masculinity in front of their female soldier trainees, women expected from respectable families to be virgins. She also reported that many Filipino soldiers "expect to and receive rides on civilian transport, and drinks and the services of prostitutes in discos and bars without payment."[17]

This is not, of course, to argue that local men are the root of the commercialized and militarized sex that has become so rife, especially in countries allied to the United States. Without local governments willing to pay the price for the lucrative R and R business, without the U.S. military's strategies for keeping male soldiers content, without local and foreign entrepreneurs willing to make their profits off the sexuality of poor women—without each of these conditions, even an abusive, economically irresponsible husband would not have driven his wife into work as an Olongapo bar girl. Nonetheless, local men must be inserted into the political equation; the women who tell their stories make this clear. In fact, we need to widen our lens considerably if we are to fully understand militarized prostitution. Here is a list—probably an incomplete list—of the men we need to be curious about, men whose actions may contribute to the construction and maintenance of prostitution around any government's military base:

- husbands and lovers
- bar and brothel owners, local and foreign
- local public health officials
- local government zoning board members
- local police officials
- local mayors
- national finance ministry officials
- national defense officials
- male soldiers in the national forces
- local civilian male prostitution customers
- local male soldier-customers
- foreign male soldier-customers
- foreign male soldiers' buddies
- foreign base commanders
- foreign military medical officers
- foreign national defense planners
- foreign national legislators

Among these men there may be diverse forms of masculinity. Women in Okinawa, Korea, and the Philippines described to Sturdevant and Stoltzfus how they had to learn what would make American men feel manly during sex; it was not always what they had learned would make their Korean, Japanese, or Filipino sexual partners feel manly.

Sexual practice is one of the sites of masculinity's—and femininity's—daily construction. That construction is international. It has been so for generations. Tourists and explorers, missionaries, colonial officials and health authorities, novelists, development technocrats, businessmen, and soldiers have long been the internationalizers of sexualized masculinity. Today the U.S. military's "R and R" policy and the industry it has spawned function only if thousands of poor women are willing and able to learn those sexual acts that U.S. military men rely on to bolster their sense of masculinity. Thus, bar owners, military commanders, and local finance ministry bureaucrats depend on local women to be alert to the historically evolving differences between masculinities.

Korean women have been among the current historical investigators of militarized prostitution. Korean women petitioners, together with a small, supportive group of Japanese feminists and Japanese historians, recently pressed the Japanese government to admit that the Japanese military had a deliberate policy of conscripting Korean, Thai, and Burmese women into prostitution during World War II.[18] In the past, Japanese officials insisted that any Asian women pressed into servicing Japanese soldiers sexually during the war were organized and controlled by civilian businessmen. The military itself was institutionally immune. Senior officers had simply accepted the prostituted women as part of the wartime landscape. This defense is strikingly similar to that employed by U.S. officials when asked about the Pentagon's current prostitution policy. Their Japanese counterparts, however, have had to give up their long-time defense in the face of convincing bureaucratic evidence uncovered by Yoshiaki Yoshimi, a professor of history at Chuo University. In the Self-Defense Agency's library he found a document entitled "Regarding the Recruitment of Women for Military Brothels" dating from the late 1930s, when the Japanese army was moving southward into China. It ordered the military to build "facilities for sexual comfort." The official rationale was that brothels would stop Japanese soldiers from raping Chinese and other women along the route of the army's invasion. Eventually, an estimated 100,000 to 200,000 Asian women were forcibly conscripted to work as *Karayuki-san,* "comfort women," in these military brothels.[19]

Although the uncovering of the document evoked a formal apology from Prime Minister Kiichi Miyazawa, the issue is not resolved. Kim Hak Sun, one of the survivors of the "comfort women" program, and other elderly Korean women are calling on their government and the Japanese government to reach a settlement that will include monetary compensation for the hardships they suffered.[20]

Furthermore, the internationalizing dynamics which have shaped military prostitution in the past grind on. Thus, the uncovering of 1930s and 1940s Japanese policy on prostitution led to a spate of articles in the U.S. media at a time when many Americans were in search of evidence that they were morally superior to, albeit economically lagging behind, Japan. Thus the story was set in a Pearl Harbor context by many U.S. readers, even if not intentionally by its authors. It could have been quite a different story. The research by Yoshiaki Yoshimi, Nakahara Michiko, and other Japanese historians about their country's military's prostitution policies could have been written—and read—so as to draw attention to U.S., British, French, and other militaries' past and present prostitution policies.

This possibility was what inspired Rita Nakashima Brock to write to the *New York Times* in the wake of the discovery of the Tokyo document. A researcher studying the sex industries in Southeast Asia, she is also an Asian-American woman who spent her childhood on U.S. military bases in the United States, Germany, and Okinawa. She recalls that, as a girl, "I faced the assumption that any woman who looked Asian was sexually available to soldiers. I was often called 'geisha-girl' or 'Suzy Wong' (soldiers usually couldn't tell Japanese from Chinese). Every base I ever lived on...had a thriving red-light district near it." When she was older, Brock began to wonder about official military policies that led to the prostitution she had witnessed as a child. "A former Navy chaplain who served in Japan during the post–World War II occupation told me that when he protested the American base commander's efforts to set up prostitution centers using Japanese women, he was reassigned stateside."[21]

Thanh-Dam Truong, a Vietnamese feminist who has investigated the political economy of Thailand's prostitution industry, also reminds us to view sexuality historically. Thai women working in prostitution, she discovered, had to learn new sexual skills in the 1980s that they hadn't needed in the 1960s because by the 1980s their male customers, now mainly local and foreign civilians, had acquired new tastes, new insecurities, and new grounds for competing with other men.[22] Similarly, around the U.S. Navy base at Subic Bay in the late 1980s, bar owners, still dependent on military customers, introduced "foxy boxing." These entrepreneurs believed that having women wrestle and box each other on stage would make the American sailors in the audience more eager for sex with the Filipina employees. Women, in turn, learned that they would be paid for their performance only if at the end of a bout they could show bruises or had drawn blood.[23] At about the same time, women in the bars were instructed by their employers to learn how to pick up coins with their vaginas. This, too, was designed as a new way to arouse the American customers.[24]

Each group of men involved in militarized sexuality is connected to other groups by the women working in the base town bars. But they also may be connected to each other quite directly. At least some Filipino male soldiers are adopting what they see as an American form of militarized masculinity. The men most prone to adopting such attitudes are those in the Scout Rangers, the elite fighting force of the Philippine Constabulary. They act as though Rambo epitomizes the attributes that make for an effective combat soldier: "a soldier in khaki or camouflage, sunglasses or headbands, open shirt, bare head, and well armed, lounging in a roofless jeep traveling down a Davao City street, gun held casually, barrel waving in the air."[25] One consequence of this form of borrowed masculinized intimidation is that local prostitutes servicing Filipino soldiers perform sexual acts that they otherwise would refuse to perform.

A woman who comes to work in a foreign military brothel or disco finds that she must negotiate among all of these male actors. She has direct contact, however, with only some of them. She never hears what advice the foreign base commander passes on to his troops regarding the alleged unhealthiness or deviousness of local women. She never hears what financial arrangements local and foreign medical officials devise

to guarantee the well-being of her soldier-customers. She rarely learns what a soldier who wants to marry her and support her children is told by his military chaplain or superior officer. She is not invited into the conference room when U.S., British, or French legislators decide it is politically wise not to hold hearings on their government's military prostitution policy. The Latina woman working as a prostitute in Belize or the Filipina woman working in the Philippines or Okinawa makes her assessments using only what information she has.

Much of that information comes from the women with whom she works. The women who told their stories to Sturdevant and Stoltzfus did not romanticize the sistership between women working in the bars. The environment is not designed to encourage solidarity. Women *have* engaged in collective actions—for instance, bar workers in Olongapo protested against being forced to engage in boxing matches for the entertainment of male customers. But, despite growing efforts by local feminists to provide spaces for such solidarity, collective action remains the exception. Most women rely on a small circle of friends to accumulate the information necessary to walk the minefield laid by the intricate relationships between the various groups of men who define the military prostitution industry. The women teach each other how to fake orgasms, how to persuade men to use a condom, how to avoid deductions from their pay, how to meet soldier-customers outside their employers' supervision, and how to remain appealing to paying customers when they are older and their valued status as a "cherry girl" is long past.

Women are telling their prostitution stories at a time when the end of the Cold War and the frailty of an industrialized economy are combining to pressure governments in North America and Europe to "downsize" their military establishments. The U.S. Department of Defense has announced the closing of military bases at home and abroad. One of the apparent lessons of the Gulf

War in the eyes of many American strategists is that the United States now has the administrative capacity to deploy large numbers of troops overseas rapidly without maintaining a costly and often politically risky base in the region. Simultaneously, Mount Pinatubo spewed its deadly ash so thickly over Clark Air Force Base that even this facility, which until 1991 the Bush administration had deemed vital to American national security, was classified as uneconomical. The Philippine Senate, for its part, rejected Corazón Aquino's requests that the Subic Bay Navy Base agreement be renewed.

Base closings have their own sexual consequences. U.S. military and civilian men and their Filipina lovers had to discuss the possibility of marriage, perhaps each with quite different fears and expectations. There were reports of a number of quick marriages.[26] In March 1992 Pat Ford, National Public Radio's reporter in the Philippines, described the departure of the last U.S. ship from Subic Bay. Filipina women from Olongapo's bars cried and hugged their sailor boyfriends and customers at the gates of the base.[27] What sexual expectations would the American men take home with them? Perhaps the Filipinas' tears and hugs prompted many men to imagine that they had experienced not commercialized sex but rather relationships of genuine affection. What were women shedding tears for? Perhaps for the loss of some temporary emotional support. Or maybe for the loss of their livelihoods. How many women who have lost their jobs around Subic Bay will seek out the employment agencies that, for a fee, will send them to Kuwait to work as maids?[28] Despite the efforts of the Filipino anti-base campaign, the government had no operative base conversion plan ready to launch that would put women's health and autonomy high on its list of objectives.[29]

It might be tempting to listen to Asian women's stories as if they were tales of a bygone era. That would, I think, be a mistake. Large bases still exist in South Korea and Guam. Over forty thousand American military personnel were stationed in Japan (including Okinawa) at the end of 1991; even more will be redeployed from Clark and Subic Bay. In early 1992, the U.S. government made agreements with officials in Australia, Singapore, and Malaysia to use facilities in their countries for repairs, communications, and training. Even with some cutbacks, the number of American men going through those bases on long tours and on shorter-term maneuvers will be in the thousands. Governments in Seoul, Tokyo, and Manila have made no moves to cancel the R and R agreements they have with Washington, agreements that spell out the conditions for permitting and controlling the sort of prostitution deemed most useful for the U.S. military. The no-prostitution formula adopted to fight the Gulf War—a no-prostitution formula not initiated by Washington policymakers, but rather imposed on the United States by a Saudi regime nervous about its own Islamic legitimacy—has not been adopted anywhere else. What discussions have U.S. military planners had with their counterparts in Singapore, Canberra, and Kuala Lumpur about morale, commerce, health, and masculinity?

Listening to women who work as prostitutes is as important as ever. For political analysts, listening to them can provide information necessary for creating a more realistic picture of how fathering, child-rearing, man-to-man borrowing, poverty, private enterprise, and sexual practice play vital roles in the construction of militarized femininity and masculinity. For non-feminist anti-base campaigners, listening to these women will shake the conventional confidence that has come from relying only on economic approaches to base conversion. Marriage, parenting, male violence, and self-respect will all have to be accepted as serious political agenda items if the women now living on wages from prostitution are to become actors, and not mere symbols, in movements to transform foreign military bases into productive civilian institutions. Listening is political.

NOTES

An earlier version of this chapter appeared as an introductory essay in Saundra Sturdevant and Brenda Stoltzfus, *Let the Good Times Roll: The Sale of Women's Sexual Labor around U.S. Military Bases in the Philippines, Okinawa and the Southern Part of Korea* (New York: New Press, 1992). This is a wonderful collection of oral histories by Filipina and Korean women working as prostitutes around U.S. bases in the Philippines, South Korea, and Guam.

1. Letter from a former CIA analyst and Defense Department consultant, August 20, 1991.
2. Beth Bailey and David Farber, *The First Strange Place: The Alchemy of Race and Sex in World War II Hawaii* (New York: Free Press, 1992), 95.
3. Ibid., 102–3. The material that follows is based on Bailey and Farber, 95–107.
4. Ibid., 102–3.
5. The information on Belize is contained in a manuscript by Stephanie C. Kane, "Prostitution and the Military: Planning AIDS Intervention in Belize" (Department of American Studies and African-American Studies, State University of New York at Buffalo, 1991); information on the Gurkhas is form correspondence from Stephanie Kane, December 11, 1991.
6. Tamang, "Nepali Women as Military Wives."
7. "Troops Want to Stay in Belize," *Carib News* (New York:), March 17, 1992.
8. The information on Subic Bay and Clark bases is derived from Anne-Marie Cass, "Sex and the Military: Gender and Violence in the Philippines" (Ph.D. diss., Department of Sociology and Anthropology, University of Queensland, Brisbane, Australia, 1992), 206–209; and Saundra Sturdevant and Brenda Stoltzfus, *Let the Good Times Roll: The Sale of Women's Sexual Labor around U.S. Military Bases in the Philippines, Okinawa and the Southern Part of Korea* (New York: New Press, 1992).
9. For descriptions and analyses of the lives of Filipino women and men who have migrated to Japan, including many women who went there for exploitative work in the entertainment industry catering to male customers—see Randolf S. David, "Filipino Workers in Japan: Vulnerability and Survival," *Kasarinlan: A Philippine Quarterly of Third World Studies* (Quezon City: University of the Philippines) 6, no. 3 (1991): 9–23; Rey Ventura, *Underground in Japan,* London, Jonathan Cape, 1992.
10. Rigoberto Tiglao, "Open for Offers" *Far Eastern Economic Review,* October 15, 1992, 62–63.

11. I am grateful to Suzaina Abdul Kadii, of the University of Wisconsin political science graduate program, for her analysis of the U.S.–Singaporean basing agreement process: conversation with the author, Madison, Wisconsin, October 29, 1992.
12. Sturdevant and Stoltzfus, *Let the Good Times Roll.*
13. Cass, "Sex and the Military," 210.
14. Ibid., 205.
15. Ibid., 215.
16. The most complete account of the Thai military's role in Thailand's prostitution industry is Thanh-Dam Truong, *Sex, Money and Morality: Prostitution and Tourism in Southeast Asia* (London: Zed Press, 1990). I am also indebted to Alison Cohn for sharing her as yet unpublished research in Thailand with me at Clark University, Worcester, MA, February–April, 1992. For an investigation of Indonesia's prostitution business, a system which is not organized around either foreign tourists or foreign soldiers but is deeply affected by Indonesia's militarized national politics, see Saraswati Sunindyo's forthcoming Ph.D. dissertation (Department of Sociology, University of Wisconsin, Madison). Saraswati Sunindyo has also written a collection of poetry, entitled *Yakin* (typescript, 1992), which describes some of her own responses to conducting research in a coastal town's government-owned hotel, which was shared by a number of Indonesian women working as prostitutes servicing Indonesian military officers, civil servants, businessmen, farmers, and schoolboys.
17. Cass, "Sex and the Military."
18. Nakahara Michiko, "Forgotten Victims: Asian and Women Workers on the Thai-Burma Railway," *AMPO: Japan-Asia Quarterly* 23, no. 2 (1991): 21–25; Yoshiaki Yoshimi, "Japan Battles Its Memories" (Editorial), *New York Times,* March 11, 1992; Sanger, "Japan Admits"; David E. Sanger, "History Scholar in Japan Exposes a Brutal Chapter," *New York Times,* January 27, 1992.
19. Sanger, "History Scholar."
20. Ibid. See also: George Hicks, "Ghosts Gathering: Comfort Women Issue Haunts Tokyo as Pressure Mounts", *Far Eastern Economic Review,* February 18, 1993, 32–37.
21. Rita Nakashima Brock, "Japanese Didn't Invent Military Sex Industry" (Letter to the Editor), *New York Times,* February 23, 1992.
22. Truong, "Sex, Money and Morality."
23. Cass, "Sex and the Military," 210.

24. Sturdevant and Stoltzfus, *Let the Good Times Roll.* In a slide and tape show produced by Sturdevant and Stoltzfus, Filipinas describe being ashamed at having to perform demeaning acts. "Pussy Cat III," 726 Gilman St., Berkeley, CA 94710.

25. Anne-Marie Cass, "Sexuality, Gender and Violence in the Militarized Society of the Philippines" (Paper presented at the annual conference of the Australian Sociological Association, Brisbane, December 12–16, 1990), 6.

26. Donald Goertzen, "Withdrawal Trauma," *Far Eastern Economic Review,* January 30, 1992, 10.

27. Pat Ford, "Weekend Edition," National Public Radio, March 21, 1992.

28. I am grateful to Lauran Schultz for bringing to my attention the *Philippine Journal of Public Administration* 34, no. 4 (October 1990), a special issue devoted to articles on the current conditions of Filipina women, including women as migrants. See, in particular, Bievenda M. Amarles, "Female Migrant Labor: Domestic Helpers in Singapore," 365–389; Prosperina Domingo Tapales, "Women, Migration and the Mail-Order Bride Phenomenon: Focus on Australia," 311–322.

29. American Friends Service Committee Peace Education Division and the Alliance for Philippine Concerns, *Swords into Plowshares: Economic Conversion and the U.S. Bases in the Philippines* (Philadelphia, PA: American Friends Service Committee, 1991). See also Sheila Coronel, "With Hope and Tears, U.S. Closes Philippine Base," *New York Times,* November 25, 1992; P. N. Abinales, "Searching for the Philippine Eden—the Post-Bases Era," *Kasarinlan: A Philippine Quarterly of Third World Studies* 7, no. 4 (1992): 8–12.

23

Lesbian "Sex"[1]

MARILYN FRYE

The reasons the word "sex" is in quotation marks in my title are two: one is that the term "sex" is an inappropriate term for what lesbians do, and the other is that whatever it is that lesbians do that (for lack of a better word) might be called "sex" we apparently do damned little of it. For a great many lesbians, the gap between the high hopes we had some time ago for lesbian sex and the way things have worked out has turned the phrase "lesbian sex" into something of a bitter joke. I don't want to exaggerate: many lesbians are having gratifying erotic lives. But there is much grumbling among us about "lesbian bed death," especially in long-term relationships.[2] I want to explore the meanings of the relative dearth of what (for lack of a better word) we call lesbian "sex."...

Recent discussions of lesbian "sex" frequently cite the findings of a study on couples by Blumstein and Schwartz,[3] which is perceived by most of those who discuss it as having been done well, with a good sample of couples—lesbian, male homosexual, heterosexual non-married and heterosexual married couples. These people apparently found that lesbian couples "have sex" far less frequently than any other type of couple, that lesbians couples are less "sexual" as couples and as individuals than anyone else. In their sample, only about one third of lesbians in relationships of two years or longer "had sex" once a week or more; 47% of lesbians in long term relationships "had sex" once a month or less, while among heterosexual married couples only 15% had sex once a month or less. And they report that lesbians seem to be more limited in the range of their "sexual" techniques than are other couples.

When this sort of information first came into my circle of lesbian friends, we tended to see it as conforming to what we know from our own experience. We were not surprised to hear that we "had" less "sex" than anyone else or that in our long-term relationships we "had sex" a great deal less frequently than other sorts of couples....

But it was brought to our attention during our ruminations on this that what 85% of long-term heterosexual married couples do more than once a month takes on the average 8 minutes to do.[4]

Although in my experience lesbians discuss their "sex" lives with each other relatively little (a point to which I will return), I know from my own experience and from the reports of a few other lesbians in long-term relationships, that what we do that, on average, we do considerably less frequently, takes on the average, considerably more than 8 minutes to do. Maybe about 30 minutes at the least. Sometimes maybe about an hour. And it is not uncommon that among these relatively uncommon occurrences, an entire afternoon or evening is given over to activities organized around doing it. The suspicion arises that what 85% of heterosexual married couples are doing more than once a month and what 47% of lesbians couples are doing less than once a month is not the same thing....

I remember that one of my first delicious tastes of old gay lesbian culture occurred in a bar where I was chatting with some other lesbians I was just getting acquainted with. One was talking about being busted out of the Marines for being gay. She had been put under suspicion somehow, and was sent off to the base psychiatrist to be questioned, her perverted tendencies to be assessed. He wanted to convince her she had only been engaged in a little youthful experimentation and wasn't really gay. To this end, he questioned her about the extent of her experience. What he asked was, "How many times have you had sex with a woman?" At this, we all laughed and giggled: what an ignorant fool he was! What does he think he means by "times"? What will we count? What's to *count*?

Another of my friends years later, discussing the same conundrum, said that she thought maybe every time you got up to go to the bathroom, that marked a "time." The joke about "how many times" is still good for a chuckle from time to time in my life with my lover. I have no memory of any such topic providing any such merriment in my years of sexual encounters and relationships with men. It would have been very rare indeed that we would not have known how to answer the question "How many times did you do it?"

If what heterosexual married couples do that the individuals report under the rubric "sex" or "have sex" is something that in most instances can easily be individuated into countable instances, this is more evidence that it is not what long-term lesbian couples do . . . or, for that matter, what short-term lesbian couples do.[5]

What violence did the lesbians do their experience by answering the same question the heterosexuals answered, as though it had the same meaning for them? How did the lesbians figure out how to answer the questions "How frequently?" or "How many times?" My guess is, for starters, that different individuals figured it out differently, to some degree. Some might have counted a two or three-cycle evening as one "time" they "had sex"; some might have counted that as two or three "times." Some may have counted as "times" only the times both partners had orgasms; some may

have counted as "times" occasions on which at least one had in orgasm; some may not have orgasms or have them rarely and may not have figured orgasms into the calculations; perhaps they counted as a "time" every episode in which both touched the other's vulva more than fleetingly and not for something like a health examination. For some, to count every reciprocal touch of the vulva would have made them count as "having sex" more than most people with work to do would dream of having time for; how do we suppose those individuals counted "times"? Is there any good reason why they should not count all those as "times"? Does it depend on how fulfilling it was? (Was anybody else counting by occasions of fulfillment?)

We have no idea how individual lesbians individuated their so-called "sexual acts" or encounters; we have no idea what it means when they said they did it less than once a month. But this raises questions for how the heterosexuals individuated and counted *their* sexual acts or encounters. . . . I think that if the heterosexual woman counted "times" according to the standard meaning of "have sex" in English, they counted not according to their own experience of orgasm or even arousal, but according to their partners' orgasms and ejaculations. . . .

So, do lesbian couples really "have sex" any less frequently than heterosexual couples? My own view is that lesbian couples "have sex" a great deal less frequently than heterosexual couples: I think, in fact, we don't "have sex" at all. By the criteria that I'm betting most of the heterosexual people used in reporting the frequency with which they have sex, lesbians don't have sex. . . . (I'm willing to draw the conclusion that heterosexual women don't have sex either, that what they report is the frequency with which their partners had sex.)

It has been said before by feminists that the concept of "having sex" is a phallic concept; that it pertains to heterosexual intercourse, in fact, primarily to heterosex*ist* intercourse, that is, male-dominant-female-subordinate-copulation-whose-

completion-and-purpose-is-the-male's-ejaculation.
... For some of us, myself included, the move
from heterosexual relating to lesbian relating was
occasioned or speeded up or brought to closure
by our recognition that what we had done under
the heading "having sex" had indeed been male-
dominant-female-subordinate-copulation-whose-
completion-and-purpose-is-the-male's-ejaculation,
and it was not worthy of doing. Yet now, years
later, we are willing to answer questionnaires that
ask us how frequently we "have sex," and are dissatisfied with ourselves and with our relationships because we don't "have sex" enough. We
are so dissatisfied that we keep a small army of
therapists in business trying to help us "have sex"
more.

We quit having sex years ago, and for excellent and compelling reasons. What exactly is our
complaint now?

In all these years I've been doing and writing
feminist theory, I have not until very recently
written, much less published, a word about sex. I
did not write, though it was suggested to me that I
do so, anything in the SM debates; I left entirely
unanswered an invitation to be the keynote
speaker at a feminist conference about women's
sexuality (which by all reports turned out to be an
excellent conference). I was quite unable to think
of anything but vague truisms to say, and very
few of those. Feminist theory is grounded in experience; I have always written feminist political
and philosophical analysis from the bottom up,
starting with my own encounters and adventures,
frustrations, pain, anger, etc.... When I put to
myself the task of theorizing about sex and sexuality, it was as though I had no experience, as
though there was no ground on which and from
which to generate theory. But, if I understand the
terminology rightly, I have in fact been what they
call "sexually active" for about a quarter of a
century.... Surely I have experience. But I seem
not to have experiential knowledge of the sort I
need.

Reflecting on all that history, I realize that in
many of its passages this experience has been a

muddle. Acting, being acted on, choosing, desir-
ing, pleasure and displeasure all akimbo—not
coherently determining each other. Even in its
greatest intensity it has for the most part been
somehow rather opaque to me, not fully in my
grasp. My "experience" has in general the character more of a buzzing blooming confusion than
of experience. And it has occurred in the midst of
almost total silence on the part of others about
their experience. The experience of others has for
the most part also been opaque to me; they do not
discuss or describe it in detail at all....

I once perused a large and extensively illustrated book on sexual activity by and for homosexual men. It was astounding to me for one thing
in particular, namely, that its pages constituted a
huge lexicon of specific vocabulary: words for
acts and activities, their sub-acts, preludes and
denouements, their stylistic variation, their se-
quences. Gay male sex, I realized then, is articulate. It is articulate to a degree that, in my world,
lesbian "sex" does not remotely approach. Lesbian "sex" as I have known it most of the time I
have known it is utterly inarticulate. Most of my
lifetime, most of my experience in the realms
commonly designated as "sexual" has been pre-
linguistic, noncognitive. I have, in effect, no linguistic community, no language, and therefore in
one important sense, no knowledge....

Meanings should arise from our bodily self-
knowledge, bodily play, tactile communication,
the ebb and flow of intense excitement, arousal,
tension, release, comfort, discomfort, pain and
pleasure (and I make no distinctions here among
bodily, emotional, intellectual, aesthetic). But
such meanings are more completely muted, less
coalesced into discrete elements of a coherent pattern of meanings (of an experience) than any other
dimensions of our lives. In fact, there are for many
of us virtually no meanings in this realm because
nothing of it is crystallized in a linguistic matrix.[9]

What we have for generic words to cover this
terrain are the words "sex," "sexual" and "sexuality." In our efforts to liberate ourselves from the
stifling woman-hating denial that women even

have bodily awareness, arousal, excitement, orgasms and so on, many of us actively took these
words for ourselves, and claimed that we do "do
sex" and we are sexual and we have sexuality.
This has been particularly important to lesbians
because the very fact of "sex" being a phallocentric term has made it especially difficult to get
across the idea that lesbians are not, for lack of a
penis between us [as Alix Dobkin put it in a song
lyric], making do with feeble and partial and pathetic half-satisfactions.... But it seems to me that
the attempt to encode our lustiness and lustful-
ness, our passion and our vigorous carnality in the
words "sex," "sexual" and "sexuality" has back-
fired. Instead of losing their phallocentricity, these
words have imported the phallocentric meanings
into and onto experience which is not in any way
phallocentric. A web of meanings which maps
emotional intensity, excitement, arousal, bodily
play, orgasm, passion and relational adventure
back onto a semantic center in male-dominant-
female-subordinate-copulation has been so utterly
inadequate as to leave us speechless, meaningless,
and ironically, according to the Blumstein and
Schwartz report, "not as sexual" as couples or as
individuals as any other group.

Our lives, the character of our embodiment,
cannot be mapped back on to that semantic center.
When we try to synthesize and articulate it by the
rules of that mapping, we end up trying to mold
our loving and passionate carnal intercourse into
explosive 8-minute events. But that is the timing
and the ontology of an alienated and patriarchal
penis, not of the lesbian body. When the only
things that count as "doing it" are those passages
of our interactions which most closely approximate a paradigm that arose from the meanings of
the rising and falling penis, no wonder we discover ourselves to "do it" rather less often than do

pairs with one or more penises present. Interpreting our desires and determining our acts by the
rules of that semantic map, we have tended to discount, discontinue, never try, or never even imagine acts, activities, practices, rituals, forms of play,
ways of touching, looking, talking, which might
be woven into a fabric of our erotic experience....

My positive recommendation is this: Instead
of starting with a point (a point in the life of a
body unlike our own) and trying to make meanings along vectors from that point, we would do
better to start with a wide field of our passions and
bodily pleasures and make meanings that weave a
web across it. I suggest that we begin the creation
of a vocabulary that can encode and expand our
meanings by adopting a very wide and general
concept of "doing it." Let it be an open, generous,
commodious concept encompassing all the acts
and activities by which we generate with each
other pleasures and thrills, tenderness and ecstasy,
passages of passionate carnality of whatever dura-
tion or profundity. Everything from vanilla to lico-
rice, from puce to tangerine, from velvet to ice,
from cuddles to cunts, from chortles to tears.
Starting from there, we can let our experiences
generate a finer-tuned descriptive vocabulary that
maps and expresses the differences and distinctions among the things we do, the kinds of pleasures we get, the stages and styles of our acts and
activities, the parts of our bodies centrally engaged
in the different kinds of "doing it," and so on. Our
vocabulary will arise among us as we explain and
explore and define our pleasures and our preferences across this field, teaching each other what
the possibilities are and how to make them real.

The vocabulary will arise among us, of
course, only if we talk with each other about what
we're doing and why, and what it feels like. Language is social. So is "doing it."...

NOTES

1. This essay was first published in *Sinister Wisdom,*
vol. 35 (Summer/Fall 1988). It was first presented as a
paper at the meeting of the Society for Women in Philosophy, Midwestern Division, November 13–15, 1987.

It was occasioned by Claudia Card's paper "What Lesbians Do," which was published under the title "Intimacy and Responsibility: What Lesbians Do," as the
Institute for Legal Studies, University of Wisconsin-

Madison Law School Working Papers Series 2, No. 10. Carolyn Shafer has contributed a lot to my thinking here, and I am indebted also to conversations with Sue Emmert and Terry Grant. For more writing by lesbians on sex, see *An Intimate Wilderness: Lesbian Writers on Sexuality,* edited by Judith Barrington (Portland, OR: Eighth Mountain Press, 1991).

2. When I speak of "we" and "our communities," I actually don't know exactly who that is. I know only that such issues are being discussed in my own circles and in communities other than mine as well (as witness, e.g., discussion in the pages of the *Lesbian Connection*). If what I say here resonates for you, so be it. If not, at least you can know it resonates for some range of lesbians and some of them probably are your friends or acquaintances.

3. Philip Blumstein and Pepper Schwartz, *American Couples* (NY: William Morrow and Company, 1983).

4. Dotty Calabrese gave this information in her workshop on long-term lesbian relationships at the Michigan Womyn's Music Festival, 1987. (Thanks to Terry Grant for this reference.)

5. In their questionnaire, Blumstein and Schwartz use the term "have sexual relations." In the text of their book, they use "have sex."

6. It was brought to my attention by Carolyn Shafer. See pp. 156–7 of my book *The Politics of Reality* (Freedom, CA: The Crossing Press, 1983).

7. *Websters' First New Intergalactic Wickedary of the English Language* (Boston: Beacon Press, 1987).

8. I use the word 'encoding' as it is used in the novel *Native Tongue,* by Suzette Haden Elgin (NY: Daw Books, Inc., 1984). She envisages women identifying concepts, feelings, types of situations, etc., for which there are no words in English (or any other language), and giving them intuitively appropriate names in a women-made language called Laadan.

9. Carolyn Shafer has speculated that one significant reason why lesbian SM occasioned so much excitement, both positive and negative, is that lesbians have been starved for language—for specific, detailed, literal, particular, bodily talk with clear non-metaphorical references to parts of our bodies and the ways they can be stimulated, to acts, postures, types of touch. Books about SM like *Coming to Power* (Boston: Alyson Publications, 1982) feed that need, and call forth more words in response.

24

Miguel
Sexual Life History
of a Gay Mexican American

JOSEPH CARRIER

The following brief sexual life history of an acculturated gay Mexican-American male, born in an east Los Angeles barrio in 1948, illustrates some important cultural and behavioral differences that exist between the Anglo and the Latino gay worlds. Gay liberation in the United States has essentially been a middle-class Anglo phenomenon, a social movement organized and run by middle-class Anglo-American males. Gay neighborhoods and establishments in large American cities are thus predominantly populated by Anglo males. Ethnic minority gay males who move in the mainstream Anglo gay world are generally highly acculturated Latino, Black, and Oriental males....

Miguel's sexual life history must...be viewed as an example of only one of the many paths that males of Mexican origin might follow in the development of individual patterns of homosexual behavior. In Miguel's case, it is the pattern of one first-generation U.S.-born Mexican American. It is of interest to note that the largest Latino population is composed of Mexican immigrants and first- and second-generation U.S.-born Mexican Americans. They make up close to two-thirds of the Latino population in the United States. In California, they make up over 85 percent of the total. Recent estimates by Robert Burciaga-Valdez indicate that "35 percent of the Mexican-origin population in California are immigrants and another 42 percent are first generation U.S.-born."[1]...

The available data on sexual behavior indicate that significant differences exist between the homosexual behaviors of Mexican males in Mexico and middle-class Anglo males in California.[2] A major difference also exists in the way in which homosexuality is conceptualized in the United States and in Mexico.

A large majority of Mexican males involved in homosexual behavior appear to have strong preferences for playing either the anal insertive or the anal receptive sexual role, but not both; and, although they may engage in fellatio, anal intercourse provides the ultimate sexual satisfaction. A sizable minority play both sexual roles but may still have a preference for playing one sexual role over the other in anal intercourse. The foreignness of males in Mexico playing both sexual roles, however, is illustrated by the fact that in the Mexican "gay world" they are called "internationals."

Homosexual role playing appears to be the result of the sharp dichotomization of gender roles in Mexico. This dichotomization leads to a widely held belief that feminine males basically prefer to play the female role rather than the male. The link between male effeminacy and homosexuality is the additional belief that as a result of this role preference feminine males are sexually interested only in masculine males with whom they play the passive sexual role.

Although the motivations of males participating in homosexual encounters are without question diverse and complex, the fact remains that in Mexico cultural pressure is brought to bear on feminine males to play the receptive role in anal intercourse, and a kind of de facto cultural approval is given (i.e., no particular stigma is attached) to masculine males who want to play the active insertor role in anal intercourse.

One effect of homosexual role playing in Mexican society is that only the feminine male is labeled a "homosexual." By societal standards, the masculine self-image of Mexican males is not threatened by their homosexual behavior as long as they play the anal insertive role and also have a reputation for having sexual relations with women.

Recent data on the attitudes and sexual behaviors of Mexican males in California who emigrated at the age of puberty or older indicate that as a result of their sexual socialization in Mexico the majority continue to hold the same beliefs about homosexuality as they did before emigrating.[3] Those immigrant males previously involved in homosexual behaviors in Mexico continue to prefer either the anal insertive or the receptive sexual role and to follow cruising patterns similar to those found in their home states in Mexico.

Compared to Mexican males, Anglo males are generally believed not to have as strongly developed preferences for playing one sexual role over the other and not necessarily to look on anal intercourse as the preferred or ultimate sexual technique in homosexual encounters. The prevailing findings in the research literature are that it appears to be unusual for middle-class Anglo males to adhere to a particular sexual role and that fellatio is the most frequently practiced sexual technique....

Another major difference is that in mainstream Anglo culture in the United States the harsh judgment is often made that *all* males involved in homosexual behavior, no matter how infrequent, are "homosexual." Thus, even males with only a few homosexual encounters, regardless of sexual role played, may be given this stigmatizing label. The major effect of this is that "straight" Anglo males in general appear to be far more concerned about being approached by homosexual males than do "straight" Mexican males. "Queer bashing" for example, is an Anglo phenomenon that occurs only rarely in Mexico....

Sexual life histories of our Mexican-American respondents suggest that, although there are some variations in attitudes toward homosexuality held by persons living in traditional Mexican-American barrios, in general they parallel the belief systems held by the *mestizo* Mexican population in Mexico.[4] Machismo still provides an important guideline for masculine behavior. Little boys are taught to be "tough," not "soft and feminine like," by their older brothers, cousins, and neighbors. And they are made aware of the fact that males not considered tough or masculine run the risk of being labeled "puto" or "joto" (i.e., feminine and homosexual). As one respondent put it, "During junior and senior high school years male classmates could be vicious about kidding anyone not tough...it was not uncommon for them to show their prowess with the challenge: 'I'll show you how tough you are, I'll punk you...if you don't cool it, *me voy a chapetear* [i.e., make a woman of you].'" *Puto* and *joto* are commonly used expletives between young males in their barrios and may "be often used to call friends assholes or to harass someone known or suspected to be gay...it is used relentlessly for any male with feminine traits."[5] As long as a male lives in his barrio, all-male socialization tends to continue, as is the case in Mexico, even after marriage.

MIGUEL'S SEXUAL LIFE HISTORY

The following sexual life history of Miguel is based on participant observation and interviews conducted by the author over a period of sixteen years, from 1969 to 1985. At the time of our first formal interview, Miguel had just celebrated his twenty-first birthday. Our last formal interview took place a few weeks before he died at the age of thirty-seven. Miguel was my first research subject when I embarked on what has turned out to be a lifelong study of Mexican and Mexican-American male sexual behavior. He was, however, much more than an object of study. He was a close and dear friend who shared his family and friends as well as the most intimate details of his life. He helped me understand the joys and the sorrows of being a gay Mexican American. Miguel did not die as a result of AIDS. He died from a long bout with an equally dread disease that afflicts gay people, alcoholism.

Miguel's Family Background

Miguel was a first-generation *mestizo* Mexican American. His father was born in northern Mexico, his mother in east Los Angeles of Mexican parentage; all his grandparents were born in Mexico. He was the second of five children. He had one older sister and three younger brothers. Along with many aunts, uncles, and cousins, they grew up together in a Mexican-American barrio referred to as "East Los."

Miguel's father spoke to his children only in Spanish; his mother spoke mostly in English but at times in a mixture of English and Spanish. The father wanted his family run according to Mexican traditions. He was a quiet man, who never had much to say to his children. When he did, he usually spoke to them through their mother: "Why don't you tell Miguel not to do that," or, "I don't think he should go there."

Miguel recalled that while growing up he and his brothers and sister were afraid of their authoritarian father. The mother disciplined with words, the father with a strap. He recalled that the relationship between his mother and his father was relatively good. He and his siblings, however, were closer to their mother than to their father. She is remembered as being "more sympathetic with American ways, more reasonable"—a bridge to the Anglo world. The father always wanted them to behave like good Mexican children. And, although they had rather limited financial resources, the children were sent to private Catholic schools that were run mainly by Anglo nuns.

The Barrio

Miguel's barrio, "East Los" is located in an unincorporated area of Los Angeles County, a short distance from the center of downtown Los Angeles. It is populated mainly by low- and moderate-income immigrant Mexican and Mexican-American families who generally live in small houses on narrow and sometimes irregularly shaped lots. As is the custom in Mexico, the barrio contains a central *mercado* (market), many churches, small grocery stores, restaurants, night clubs, and cantina-style bars. The population density is high.

There are no "gay bars" in the barrio, but as noted above males searching for sexual encounters with other males often find partners in some of the "straight" restaurants, nightclubs, and cantina-style bars. Just a short distance outside the barrio, there are two neighborhood-type gay bars; one attracts mainly Anglo males, the other Latino males.

Miguel's Childhood

Miguel remembered his childhood as a very happy time. He and his older sister were very close and played a lot with cousins from both sides of the family who lived nearby. Because of large age differences—the oldest of his brothers was four years younger—he did not feel as close to his brothers. Compared to his male cousins, he remembered himself as a child being more quiet and somewhat aloof. From his early teens onward, he considered himself to be a loner. On looking back, he believed that this personality trait could be related to his being quiet and aloof as a child.

Miguel also recalled that his mother was very religious and that he was active in the Catholic church from a very early age. He said that outside the family the person that influenced his childhood the most was a German Dominican nun. From the third grade up to his first year in high school he spent most Saturday mornings helping her with her chores at the private Catholic school he attended.

Prepubertal Sexual Experiences

Miguel's first remembered sexual experiences were between the ages of four and five. They were with a male cousin one year older and his sister and consisted of games that included touching each other's bodies and sex organs. He remembered feeling that "we shouldn't get caught doing it" which gave their games an aura of secrecy and shame.

The three-way sexual games with his cousin and sister continued once or twice a month for about six years and were played in the nude when possible. Their games were never discovered by either set of parents or other family members. They ceased when Miguel's sister reached puberty at thirteen and no longer wanted to play sexual games with them. The three nevertheless continued to be close friends.

Adolescence

Miguel's first ejaculation occurred in bed a couple of years later at the age of thirteen while lying next to a younger brother who was seven at the time. They had been sleeping together for two years but had not been involved in any sexual games. Miguel said that he did not think his brother was aware of what had happened because they were wearing pajamas. They continued to sleep together, and several years later they occasionally engaged in mutual masturbation.

Miguel's major sexual target at that time, however, was his male cousin. They got together at least once a month for mutual masturbation. When his cousin moved to a different neighborhood, they exchanged letters and used a coded sentence to denote desire for sex: "Do you want your flowers watered?" Their meetings together were almost always for sexual relations and continued for the next ten years.

As their sexual relationship progressed, Miguel began to realize that his desire for sex was much stronger than his cousin's. He wanted to do much more than just mutual masturbation. During his last year of high school, he finally got his cousin to try something new, anal intercourse. His cousin agreed to play the receptive role. Miguel, however, always managed, as he put it, "to avoid being used anally." He was able "to get away with it" he said, "because my cousin enjoyed being

fucked and because I was happy to go down on him and he would go down on me." Miguel's sexual relationship with his cousin continued even after the cousin married at age twenty. His cousin would arrange meetings when his wife and child were away. Their sexual relationship ended only because Miguel found "other guys" he liked "having sex with better."

Miguel's reason for not wanting "to be used anally" was clearly revealed in a conversation about his first "one-night stand with a stranger" when he was seventeen: "He wanted to fuck me! I resisted. ... I wouldn't let him. I thought it would break my manhood. It's too passive and unmanly." Miguel had grown up knowing that there was one thing he "didn't want to be, a *puto* or *joto*... one of those female-like guys that take it up the ass."

When asked whether he remembered feeling guilty after having a homosexual encounter, Miguel replied that he had "no feelings of remorse." He said that he had loved to look at the male nude from as far back as he could remember and had never had any problems about his choice of male sexual partners. Although religious, he did not believe that his sexual practices were sinful. ...

Young Adulthood

... To establish independence from his family just prior to graduating from high school, he moved into a small house his parents had purchased next door. But within a few months, in response to his religious calling and with the encouragement of his family, he moved to northern California and became a brother in a Catholic monastery. The monastic life, however, did not suit Miguel. He left after six months because he felt he was "missing too much on the outside." He returned to his barrio and moved back into the little house next door to his parents. His mother was very unhappy over his leaving the monastery. His father said little but was also not pleased.

Miguel's coming home turned out to be a major milestone in his life: he came out to himself and accepted that his homosexual feelings were more important than his heterosexual. He said he "had no guilt feelings over giving up the church," that he had been "celibate while living at the monastery." But he realized on returning home that he had never really felt sexually attracted to women. He was a loner in high school and "made no attempt to put up a front by taking out girls." As a part-time janitor's helper in a girls-only school, he remembered that he was "around girls a lot...used to notice boys at the school's gate waiting to see girls...and there I was right there with them and had no feelings about them." He rationalized his disinterest in women at the time on the grounds that since he worked after school he had no time anyway.

Miguel, at age eighteen, decided to explore the outside Anglo World for male sexual partners. Still concerned about maintaining a masculine appearance to outsiders, he nevertheless accepted that he was sexually attracted to men, not women. He intended to keep his sexual relationship going with his cousin, but he wanted to enlarge his homosexual world.

Shortly after returning from the monastery, he decided to spend a weekend in Ensenada, Mexico, with one of his few high school friends, an Anglo named Fred. Miguel had always been physically attracted to Fred, so even if nothing happened he felt "it would be a fun weekend." But, on the last night of their trip, Miguel said, "I lucked out. We were both drunk when we got back to the motel...we took a piss at the same time...Fred saw me looking down at his cock and started getting a hard on. I followed him back into the bedroom and pushed him onto his back on the bed and went down on him. I jacked off while sucking him. He pretended to be asleep. We never talked about it...it was a one time thing."

Miguel also soon discovered that he could get picked up while walking or waiting for the bus along the streets of nearby downtown Los Angeles. His first experience was with a forty-year-old man who asked him if he "wanted to screw a woman." The second was with a thirty-year-old man who approached him at a bus stop and asked "what [he] was up to." Miguel said he "screwed both of them" at their apartments. He

was delighted to find that he could easily maintain his preferred sexual practice, insertive anal intercourse.

After being home only two months, he realized that he was living too close to his family to carry out his new life-style. His mother made comments, and his brothers started harassing him about the "weird friends" he sometimes brought back to his little house. His sister, having difficulty with her father over her independent ways, left the house to live with some friends in another neighborhood. Miguel decided that it was also time for him to move, but into the Anglo world. He got a job with a large downtown department store as a messenger, bought an old car, and moved into an apartment with some newly found friends.

First "Gay" Year Homosexual Encounters

Miguel's sexual life opened up about halfway through his eighteenth year, in part as a result of having his own automobile. Driving along Sunset Boulevard one day in November 1966 near downtown Los Angeles he picked up a twenty-two-year-old effeminate Anglo male hitchhiker named Edward. They went to Edward's apartment, where for the first time Miguel had sex with an uninhibited gay-identified male. Miguel said, "We did everything...'69,' I screwed him, got screwed." On recalling the event just three years after it had occurred, he got very excited and said that it changed forever the way he felt about his body and what he could do sexually.

Miguel and Edward continued their sexual relationship for the next three months. During those months, he also had sex with Edward's twenty-two-year-old gay roommate Charlie, but he only "screwed him." As time passed, playing the anal receptive role with Edward left him feeling guilty afterward and somewhat depressed. Miguel also French kissed Edward, but he did not really enjoy it either; it made him feel "kind of stupid, silly, to tongue kiss another guy." He had French kissed girls first—something he had learned from his barrio friends during his early teens—so it was a more acceptable feeling.

A couple of months later, Miguel decided he had to change the way he cruised. He had been arrested by an undercover police officer while cruising along Hollywood Boulevard. It was his first contact with the law as a result of his homosexual behavior, and he was extremely fearful about being sent to jail and having his parents find out the reason for his arrest. Luckily, a female judge dropped the charges to disturbing the peace, and he was fined only fifty dollars. Miguel decided to stop picking up hitchhikers.

Since he was still too young to get into gay bars legally, Miguel decided it would be safer to spend most of his cruising time looking for sexual partners in a predominantly gay teenager's coffeehouse called Geno's, which Edward and Charlie had taken him to near Hollywood. The people Miguel met at Geno's further opened up the Los Angeles Anglo gay world for him. . . .

Miguel further expanded his sexual repertoire during this year of intense homosexual activity. The two partners he was most involved with, George and Tim, introduced him to the pleasures of "rimming" (anal-oral contact). Miguel said that he had always been fascinated by the anus during sexual intercourse and knew that rimming existed. "They call it *beso negro* in Spanish" he said. But it seemed to him to be a disgusting practice, so he had not previously tried it with his cousin. When George first did it to him, Miguel noted that he was willing to let it happen because he was intoxicated not only with alcohol but also with George's looks, his first real blond, blue-eyed "paddy." George did it to him from the "69" position, so Miguel reciprocated by rimming him. Rimming also turned out to be a regular part of his sexual experiences with Tim, another blond, blue-eyed "paddy," and continued to be an important part of his sexual repertoire for the rest of his life with those males that especially "turned him on."

The Next Eleven Years

During the following eleven years, Miguel participated almost exclusively in the Anglo gay world. On reaching twenty-one, he phased out Geno's and turned to drinking and cruising in the gay bars of Hollywood and downtown Los Angeles. He also started having sex in bathhouses and in Griffith Park, a wilderness park adjacent to Hollywood. He said that he found the majority of his sexual partners in bars. Most of the rest he found in bathhouses and the park, a few occasionally while walking along Hollywood Boulevard. Looking back on these years, he estimated that he had on the average at least one or two different sexual partners weekly and that a large majority of them (80–90 percent) were one-night stands.

Most of his sexual partners were Anglo males, whom he loved to dominate as the anal insertor. He usually allowed them to take the lead in the kind of sex carried out, but he preferred to end up "screwing them in the ass." And he liked sleeping curled around them, his "cock against their ass." He was anal receptive only occasionally—with someone with whom he really felt a strong sexual attraction. Even then, being receptive usually left him feeling "grouchy and depressed."

Miguel became a part of the Anglo gay world, but he never lost the feeling drummed into him since early childhood by his male friends and relatives in the barrio that playing the female role in anal intercourse caused a "breaking of manhood . . . was too passive, unmanly." Every time he went to visit his parents in the barrio, he was reminded of it by graffiti on walls that had gang names marked out with asterisks and *putos* written nearby by rival gang members, indicating that the marked-out gang members "took it up the ass."

Miguel did not have male lovers. Instead, he occasionally had what he described as "short-time regulars: guys I can do things with like going to the beach and making trips. We have sex . . . no lovey dovey stuff . . . I don't like kissing and all those mushy things." But he did like to cuddle after sex, so when possible he liked spending nights with his regulars and his one-night stands.

Miguel had only two long-lasting intimate relationships with gay men. Both were with relatively wealthy Anglo gay men about ten years older and were established through sexual contact. He moved in and out of both of their lives during these eleven years. Miguel lived with one of them on and off for several years but always carefully noted to outsiders that he paid his share of expenses and that they no longer had sex and were thus just close friends. He lived with the other, "a Hollywood type" with a luxurious apartment, only on occasional weekends and also always wanted outsiders to know that it was not an exploitative relationship. He often credited himself with providing younger sex partners for the older man. One of the things he shared with both men was a love for travel. Through them he was able to travel places he would not have otherwise been able to afford. These travels helped motivate him to become a flight attendant when he as in his mid-twenties.

Miguel had some homosexual encounters with Mexican males during this period, most taking place in Mexico. He made his first trio south of the border a few months after his twenty-first birthday. He visited me in Guadalajara, where I was living at the time, and then took off on his own to visit Mexico City and Acapulco. He spoke Spanish well but was shy being around Mexicans and felt somewhat embarrassed about his Mexican-American accent. One of the friendship circles I was studying at the time was made up of very young (fifteen to eighteen) effeminate gay males who preferred to play only the receptive role in anal intercourse. On finding Miguel in my apartment, they immediately befriended him, complemented him on how well he spoke Spanish, and took him sight-seeing. When they returned to my apartment, they played their version of "spin the bottle" in which the winner had the option of having sex with Miguel. By the time he left Guadalajara, he had had sex with all but one member of the friendship circle.

On his way back to Los Angeles, Miguel stopped off in Guadalajara and told me about the many homosexual encounters he had had in Acapulco and Mexico City. He was surprised by how easy it was for him to find Mexican sexual partners, the more so since he was sightseeing most of the time and not cruising. In Acapulco, he was also surprised to find American and European men coming on to him for sex.

Miguel returned to Mexico several times, but he told me that finding sexual partners was never his motive for traveling there; rather it was for the pleasure of being in the country of his origin. He usually took his parents or some of his family members with him. His major sexual interest during this time was still with "paddy."

Family Relationships

For his emotional needs, Miguel maintained close contact with his family and friends in the barrio throughout his life. He visited his parents weekly when living in Los Angeles and participated in most family celebrations. After becoming a flight attendant, he took them on many vacations not only to Mexico but also to other parts of the world served by his airline.

Miguel believed that his mother knew that he was gay, but they never talked openly about it. The only exception was when she was mad; then she would say things like, "I know about your friends." He further believed that his father did not know. He said, "He'd be broken by news about it." Only the oldest of his three younger brothers knew for sure; the other two probably suspected, he thought, since he had never married.

Miguel's relation with his sister was especially close. They had their secret past together, and she knew he was gay because he had told her shortly after returning from the monastery. Also, she had discovered a few months after he had come out to her that she was a lesbian and had divorced her husband. She and Miguel, along with an understanding female cousin, spent a lot of time together. Whenever the Anglo world was too much for him, he would turn to his sister and cousin for support and understanding.

Miguel's sister confirmed that their mother knew he was gay. She told me that on divorcing her husband and returning home she had confided in her mother that she had had a sexual affair with another woman and was a lesbian. Her mother responded to the news with anger and disappointment. She was perplexed as to what she had done wrong that made her two oldest children homosexual. She knew with certainty, however, that their father must never be told. So far as I know, he never has been....

Heterosexual Relationships

One result of Miguel's becoming a flight attendant was a series of close relationships with some female coworkers. When first interviewed at age twenty-one, he said that he had never felt sexually attracted to women and so had never developed any close heterosexual relationships. He tried to change his feelings as he grew older, however, because he feared loneliness in old age and believed that one hedge against it would be the companionship of a wife and children. Age heightened his fear of rejection. "Age is a disturbing thing," he said. "I feel I'm not good looking.... Getting older isn't helping me.... The older I get, the less people are bound to approach me."

In his early twenties, Miguel started "taking some girls out from work" and would go "as far as French kissing, fondling their breasts, and getting an erection," but he never tried to have sexual intercourse with them. When asked how he thought his girlfriends felt when he did not try to take them to bed, he replied that it made him "all the more desirable in their eyes."

Miguel's first major heterosexual affair was with an Anglo flight attendant named Susan. They worked the same flights to Hawaii and the Far East for almost a year. During turn-around time, they spent many days together at the same hotel, enjoyed each other's company, became very close friends, and then lovers. According to Miguel, Susan really believed that they would eventually get married. He said that he had also hoped that they would get married and have children, but he was uneasy about his ability to maintain a marriage and cope with his homosexual desires at the same time. Their relationship was

terminated close to a year after it started, but prior to marriage, when Susan discovered that he was having a sexual relationship with another (male) flight attendant as well as with her.

Miguel's second major heterosexual affair, which started a few months after he broke up with Susan and got on a different route, was with a Mexican-American flight attendant named Lupita. He and Lupita did not work the same flights but were on the same route, so they were able to be together often during turn-around time. Once again, Miguel hoped that he would eventually feel comfortable enough with Lupita and she with him to get married and have children. While their relationship was relatively good, it was never as close as the one he had had with Susan. Miguel attributed this to the fact that Lupita was probably suspicious from the beginning that he was also having sexual relations with men as well as with her. Although they talked openly about homosexuality and about male flight attendants known to be gay, something he never did with Susan, he still did not have the courage to tell her about his bisexuality and thus directly find out whether she would consider marriage knowing about this aspect of his life. Fearing rejection once again, Miguel terminated the relationship after he and Lupita had been going together about six months and got himself transferred to another route.

Following his breakup with Lupita, Miguel became preoccupied with the notion that he was losing his reputation as a macho heterosexual flight attendant, a reputation that he had carefully built to counter the belief held by many in the industry that most male flight attendants are gay. He was very disturbed by this probable change in his image but felt powerless to do anything to prevent it from happening. He was convinced that Susan and Lupita were spreading rumors among his colleagues in the airline that he was gay.

With the realization that his interest in men was so strong that he would never be able to give up having homosexual relations and would never be able to find a woman interested in marrying a bisexual man, Miguel decided that he must accept the fact that he would never get married and never have a family. He also decided that, while he would continue to present himself as macho and straight, he had to accept the fact that behind his back people at work would continue their gossip that he was gay.

Miguel's Drinking Problem

It was about this point in time that Miguel's excessive consumption of alcohol began to interfere with his work. Though his dilemmas at the time about aging, loneliness, marriage, and self-image probably contributed to his drinking problem, they were not the only factors since he had been drinking excessively for several years and had been previously arrested for drunk driving. . . .

Additionally, Miguel's gay life-style and access to alcohol as a flight attendant reinforced a compulsive drinking pattern that probably started when he worked as a salesman for a liquor distributor in Los Angeles, his job for a couple of years prior to joining the airline. . . .

Miguel's Final Years

On turning thirty, Miguel changed his gay life-style. He was beginning to have to deal with the fact that he was an alcoholic. He also began to feel acutely the effects of the ageist Anglo gay world, which penalizes its members for growing old. He found it more and more difficult to find "paddy" sex partners in gay bars and elsewhere. This in turn led to longer drinking bouts in bars. When he was put on medical disability by the airline for stress-related alcoholism, he decided to move back to his barrio.

During his final seven years, Miguel reestablished to himself and to others his Mexican-American identity. He grew a mustache, bought a motorcycle, and got a couple of tatoos. He lived in a rented house on the edge of his old barrio and continued his close relationship with his family. He did not give up all his Anglo friends, but he spent most of his time socializing with a small circle of gay Mexican-American friends at his house and at local Latino gay bars.

Miguel fought for a monetary settlement with the airline over his stress-related medical leave for alcoholism. He maintained that he could no longer effectively work as a flight attendant because the stress of flying would not allow him to recover from his alcoholism. He also declined to accept lower-paying jobs offered by the airline. He did accept medical services in the form of psychotherapy.

After close to a year on medical leave, the airline refused to make a monetary settlement, terminated the medical leave, and offered to reinstate Miguel as a flight attendant. Miguel accepted the offer. He was not happy to be back at his old job, but he was not able to face the alternative prospect of having to find a new job and the possibility of having to train himself for another profession.

Throughout what were his final years, Miguel had a rich and varied sex life. He told me that he had no difficulty in finding interested neighborhood boys as sexual partners; in fact, many came knocking on his door as the word got out about the availability of "sex and pot." But he had to be discreet and not let the barrio know about the sexual nature of their visits to his house.

Miguel shared his house and rent—and also sexual partners—with a relatively younger Mexican-American gay friend. He also established ongoing sexual relationships with several teenage boys in the barrio, two of them brothers. Though Miguel still enjoyed fellatio, he always ended up his sexual sessions playing the anal insertive role.

In addition, Miguel cruised the local Latino gay bars for sexual partners. Two of his best "Chicano" gay friends worked at one of them, and he would often stay there until closing time, when they would return to his house with selected "tricks" for a party. From time to time, he would return to the Anglo gay world in search of "paddy" sexual partners, but with little success.

Miguel tried to deal with his drinking problem through psychological counseling and Alcoholics Anonymous, but neither worked for him.

He also tried to use marijuana as a substitute for alcohol, but that did not work either. Nothing seemed to help. He continued to drink as heavily at home as he did in gay bars.

Miguel developed pancreatitis and was warned that he must severely limit his consumption of alcohol or face a life-threatening coma. For about a year after the diagnosis, he went on and off the "antabuse" drug as a means of controlling his consumption of alcohol. He then stopped using it and slipped back into uncontrolled drinking. After a week of sustained heavy drinking, he became comatose and was hospitalized for about one week. His physician told him on leaving the hospital that his next coma might be his last one.

Miguel went back on the antabuse drug program, but on recovering his health once again discontinued it and resumed his old drinking practices. I remember going into his favorite Latino gay bar late one evening during this period and being told by his bartender friend that he had started drinking again and had just left. Six months later, on a Sunday morning, he died in a coma after a weekend of unabated heavy drinking.

CONCLUSION

Miguel's brief life had a tragic ending that is not unique to Mexican-American gay men. Alcoholism is an endemic disease in the gay world, one facilitated by the oppression of society at large, by gay cruising patterns that utilize drinking establishments as primary locations for meeting potential sexual partners, and by gay social events and

parties that often include extensive alcohol consumption by participants as part of socialization.

Gay Mexican-American men may in addition have to deal with a cultural drinking pattern that leads many Mexicans and Mexican Americans to alcoholism.[6] Miguel often complained about finding his father and sometimes his mother inebriated. Although he never blamed his parents for his alcoholism, Miguel knew that his pattern of drinking was affected by their behavior.

Miguel's sex life was obviously influenced by both Mexican and Anglo cultural patterns of sexual behavior. He believed that he had had the best of both worlds and reflected happily many times about his good luck in having had access to both of them. Although he had enjoyed the Anglo gay world while he was in it, he felt fortunate about being able also to be sexually excited by men of Mexican origin.

During his final year, Miguel occasionally talked about the possibility of dying young. He looked at the possibility fatalistically. He had lived a good life by his reckoning and was happy about having moved back to his barrio and maintaining close relationships with his family and old friends.

Not too long before he died, Miguel told me about one of his many flying dreams. He said he had looked down and saw a line of people filing past a young man in a coffin. He was upset over the possibility that people would look down at him when he was dead and feel pity. He did not want that to happen and told his family that, should he die as a result of his disease, they should make sure that his coffin was closed at the rosary and the funeral. His family respected his wishes.

NOTES

1. Robert Burciaga-Valdez, "A Framework for Policy Development for the Latino Population: Testimony before the California Hispanic Legislative Conference," Paper no. 7207 (Santa Monica, Calif.: Rand Corp., 1986), p. 1.

2. For *mestizo* Mexican behavior patterns, see Joseph M. Carrier, "Cultural Factors Affecting Urban Mexican Male Homosexual Behavior," *Archives of Sexual Behavior* 3 (1976): 103–24, and "Mexican Male Bisexuality," in *Bisexualities: Theory and Research,* ed. F. Klein

and T. Wolf (New York: Haworth, 1985). For Anglo patterns, see Alan P. Bell and Martin S. Weinberg, *Homosexualities: A Study of Diversity among Men and Women* (New York: Simon and Schuster, 1978).

3. See Raul Magana and Joseph M. Carrier, "Mexican and Mexican American Male Sexual Behavior and Spread of AIDS in California," *Journal of Sex Research* (in press).

4. The majority population in Mexico is *mestizo,* i.e., people of mixed Spanish and American Indian ancestry.

5. The quote is from a Mexican-American interviewer.

6. See Gilbert, ed., *Alcohol Consumption among Mexicans and Mexican Americans.*

25

Sexuality and Sexual Politics

Conflicts and Contradictions for Contemporary Women in the Middle East

EVELYNE ACCAD

Sexuality seems to have a revolutionary potential so strong that many political women and men are afraid of it. They prefer, therefore, to dismiss its importance by arguing that it is not as central as other factors, such as economic and political determinations which are easily recognizable as the major factors that produce revolution—class inequalities, hunger, poverty, lack of job opportunities. In this essay, I would like to argue that sexuality is much more central to social and political problems in the Middle East than previously thought, and that unless a sexual revolution is incorporated into political revolution, there will be no real transformation of social relations.

By sexual revolution, I mean one which starts at the level of personal life, with a transformation of attitudes toward one's mate, family, sexuality, and society; specifically, a transformation of the traditional rapports of domination and subordination which permeate interpersonal, particularly sexual, relationships (such as power struggles, jealousy, possession). Change is fundamental at the level of sexual and familial intimacy. We need to develop an exchange of love, tenderness, equal sharing, and recognition among people. This would create a more secure and solid basis for change in other spheres of life—political, economic, social, religious, and national as they are often characterized by similar rapports of domination. By political revolution, I mean one primarily motivated by nationalism. I would argue that if all of the various

political parties who are trying to dominate a small piece of territory in Lebanon were to unite and believe in their country as an entity not to be possessed and used, but to be loved and respected, much of the internal violence, destruction, and conflicts would begin to cease, and we could work more positively toward resolution. Nationalism—belief in and love of one's country—in this context seems a necessity.

In the Middle East, nationalism and feminism have never mixed very well. Women have been used in national liberation struggles—Algeria, Iran, Palestine, to name a few—only to be sent back to their kitchens after "independence" was gained. To those who believe that it is utopian to think that the two can ever blend, I would like to suggest first, that it has never been tried, since sexuality has never been conceptualized as being at the center of the problems in the Middle East. Second, if an analysis of sexuality and sexual relations were truly incorporated into the revolutionary struggle in Lebanon, nationalism could be transformed into a more viable revolutionary strategy.

In most discussions of third world feminism, sexuality and the privatized oppression of women by men are relegated to secondary issues. When sexuality and/or male domination is raised as a significant factor, conflicts arise over the validity of Marxism versus feminism, economic equality versus sexual equality, national revolution versus women's rights—as if these concepts must be opposed, as if the life of one means the death of the other. For instance, at the "Common Differences: Third World Women and Feminist Perspectives" conference (University of Illinois at Urbana-Champaign, April 1983), a major conflict arose between those women who believed sexuality and male domination to be central, and those who believed class and imperialism to be central. Mostly Marxist women, speaking in the name of all third world women, claimed that economic issues—such as food and shelter—were far more important than sex. They accused U.S. lesbians at the conference of overemphasizing sex, particularly lesbianism. As I listened, I felt that their arguments were very "paternalistic," and somewhat irrelevant: first, because sex is one of the basic needs—like food and sleep—in any culture; second, because no mention was made of the spiritual and/or psychological needs for love, affection, and tenderness, intimately connected with sexuality, which are felt by people in all cultures. To claim that some women live without these needs because of more pressing economic factors seems not only very unfair but an exercise which only some intellectuals can afford. And third, from my research and analysis, I believe that sexuality and sex-role socialization are intimately connected to the national conflicts and on-going war in Lebanon.

In the past five years, I have conducted extensive research throughout the Middle East, interviewing women in rural and urban areas about their sexuality, relations with men (husbands, brothers, sons), relations with other women, and the social conditions of their lives. I also attended a conference, "What Feminism for the Maghreb" (Tunisia, 1985), which addressed issues of feminism, nationalism, and, peripherally, sexuality, and taught a course on the role of Arab women at Beirut University College in 1985, living the war in Lebanon that year (as well as previous years). My research, teaching, discussing, and own thinking about these issues have helped me to clarify my perspectives on the role of feminism in nationalist struggles, and the centrality of sexuality to

the social and political relations of whole groups of people. In this essay I would like to suggest the importance of sexuality and sexual relations to third world women's lives, and the centrality of sexuality and male domination to the political and national struggles occurring in the Middle East.

First of all, contrary to the perspectives of many intellectuals and political women and men involved in the U.S. and/or the Middle East, my interviews with rural and urban women indicate that sexuality is of utmost concern to women. In fact it is often women from the neediest levels of society who are the most outspoken on the subject of sex, love, and their relationships to their husbands and family, and who, contrary to what some intellectuals have expressed, see the need for change in these areas of their lives. Perhaps it is because they have not interpreted and analyzed their needs from within the framework of patriarchal ways of thinking (i.e., Marxism, nationalism, capitalism) that they can be so outspoken. For example, in Oran, Algeria (1984), I interviewed a group of maids at the hotel where I was staying. The majority of them lived in polygamous relationships and had to wear the veil when going out. Most of them expressed anger toward both customs—polygamy and the veil—and wished for different conditions for their daughters. Similarly, in 1978, I visited hospitals in the United Arab Emirates, and conducted interviews with women living in different oases and remote places. They too expressed to me their anger about the conditions of their lives—having to produce children every year under the threat of repudiation, or having to accept their husbands' taking younger wives if they did not, and having to wear the *burqa* (a mask-type leatherlike face cover which left purplish-blue marks from sweating).

Secondly, it seems clear to me that given the way in which political intellectuals have dealt with sexuality, at least at the conferences that I have attended, the issues are far more central than anyone is willing to admit. At the conference "What Feminism for the Maghreb" (1985) at the Club Taher in Tunisia, and at the "Common Dif-

ferences" conference in Illinois, the topic of sexuality, with all of its ramifications, divided women
and created enormous amounts of tension. In Tunisia, women who chose to speak out on sexuality
were ostracized by the majority of other feminist
intellectuals. The most open and frank woman on
the subject decided to leave the country because
she felt misunderstood and rejected even by the
feminist movement. Some women asked me to
shut off the cassette recorder when they talked
about sexuality, and some burst into tears when
talking about intimate experiences in their lives. I
wondered as I listened and talked with women
why there was so much pain in remembering past
events in their lives connected with sexuality, yet
so much resistance and denial around a political
analysis of sexuality. Similarly at the conference
in Illinois, women viciously attacked one another
over the issues of sexuality and their place in the
lives of third world women.

One of the participants at the conference in
Tunisia provided some analysis of the centrality of
sexuality, and yet its denial on the part of political
women. Unfortunately, because of her analysis
and her willingness to speak in such an environment, she felt she had to leave her country. When I
wrote her, asking if I could mention her by name,
or if she preferred to remain anonymous, she replied, "Please get me out of anonymity which
weighs on me, and is slowly killing me. But what
name should I use? Ilham Bint Milad—my father's? Bousseu—my mother's? Ben Ghadifa—
my husband's? or just my surname which is not
enough? How does one solve this problem?" At
the conference, Ilham began her speech with a
discussion of why she had decided to lift the veil
of silence over her condition, to get rid of autocensorship (a word which acquired great significance
when I lived in Tunisia, witnessing its way of killing creativity and freedom in several women I became close to), so that she would no longer be her
own enemy.

She felt that the silence of Tunisian feminists
had fallen over three spheres: (1) the feminine
body, (2) women's personal relationships, and

(3) sexual identity. Silence, she suggested, reigns
over the subject of periods, virginity, masturbation, sexual pleasure in general, abortion, birth,
and the feminine body as a whole. She recited poetry she had written about her period in French
and in Arabic—noticing how it was harder to talk
about it in Arabic. The following excerpts from
her speech give a sense of her analysis:

> *The myth of virginity is such an idiocy. The ritual
> takes place in pain. It is like a green bubble to be
> burst. And it is for this bubble, this hollowness,
> this emptiness, that women are taught repulsion,
> shame, disgust toward their bodies, and the fear of
> sexuality....*
>
> *The first sexual pleasure known by the child is
> masturbation.... In certain families, it is called
> "to do evil." We live in a situation where the body
> is morally neglected. In such a context, how can
> one learn to love one's body? How can one learn
> to read one's desires, and even more to let them
> rise in oneself? How can sexual pleasure, con-
> demned for so long, exercise itself freely just be-
> cause it has become approved by an institution on
> the basis of having a partner?... The child learns
> to associate pleasure with culpability. The body,
> instead of being an object of pleasure, becomes an
> enemy which hurts.... How can a body which
> never learns to love or to speak, develop in a har-
> monious sexual relationship?...*
>
> *Silence prevails, not only on the topic of the
> feminine body but also, more generally, on every-
> thing that touches upon intimate relations, which
> are constantly shifting between dream and reality,
> between love and hate.... Why do my tears fall
> when my neighbor is beaten up? Why do I feel per-
> sonally humiliated? The pain she experiences in
> her life affects me for many reasons. The life of
> such a woman is like a magnifying glass, which re-
> flects back to me an exaggerated image of my own
> condition. Obtaining the respect of others is a con-
> stant struggle for women. The enslavement of
> other women sets limits to my own blossoming....
> But above all, her life reminds me of another
> woman's suffering, to which I was for a long time
> a spectator—that of my mother....*

Ilham also raised the problem of women turning
on each other when one or another brought up is-

sues of sexuality. I found this particularly relevant
because I have faced similar responses from feminist intellectuals. Fear and autocensorship are two
key factors preventing women from wanting to explore these issues. The subject of sexuality is too
close to home and to one's personal life. At this
conference, when the topic was raised, women
gossiped openly about each other, about individual sexualities and sexual practices, thereby widening the malaise and tensions. As Ilham herself
suggested:

> Women's hatred expresses itself in many ways....
> Feminism and gossiping appear as a contradic-
> tion. Unfortunately, it is not so. I was a target of
> gossip by feminists, the preceding year, after my
> communication on "Femininity and Fecundity."
> They accused me of being a prostitute, a divorcee,
> a lesbian, a robber of husbands, and a scandal be-
> cause I refused maternity! I would like to empha-
> size how all these accusations are related to
> sexuality.
>
> While the purpose of gossiping is to alleviate
> what is bothersome, to make oneself feel more se-
> cure, it also expresses anxiety over marginality, and
> tries to disarm one's sense of culpability.... Apart
> from trying to repress the other, because one is not
> able to free oneself, gossip has two consequences:
> (1) It prevents the woman who pronounced it from
> fulfilling her own desires, therefore of knowing her-
> self deeply, (2) it destroys the woman who uttered
> it, especially when one adds to it bad conscience,
> and the feeling—more or less diffused—of having
> made a dangerous concession to society, and to the
> mother....
>
> Gossiping and hostility between women upsets
> the followers of unconditional feminine love. But
> their protests do not go as far as defending or even
> pronouncing the word homosexuality. This would
> entail too much subversion. It is a point of no re-
> turn, a path which society cannot forgive. At the
> personal level, it is too risky to return to the love
> affair with the mother. Homosexuality is also con-
> demned by society because it shakes its founda-
> tions. Not only is it not productive—in terms of
> procreation, therefore threatening the survival of
> society—but it also shakes the foundation of capi-
> talism where production is very much valued.

> Above all, it affirms the right to pure pleasure, a
> suspicious concept, because anarchist by essence.
> ... Isn't the Third World characterized by a dan-
> gerous confusion between individuality and indi-
> vidualism, through a most repressive structure of
> duty?...
>
> One more issue I would like to address is jeal-
> ousy in the context of love. The woman who arouses
> one's jealousy is one we feel is stealing something
> from us, as our mother stole from us, our in-depth
> being, our body. The more a person lives under re-
> pression, with no satisfaction, the greater his or her
> jealousy will be. In this context, love and pleasure
> are necessarily threatened if shared. When some-
> one gives to another, she feels she has necessarily
> lost something of her own. Jealousy also increases
> when the person we envy also stirs our love and
> admiration.... Jealousy is the expression of a lack
> of confidence in oneself.... One can understand
> why intellectuals have kept silent in this domain:
> analysis and reasoning are hardly protections
> against jealousy....

The topic of women's personal relations was
charged with meaning. It brought to the surface
much of the uneasiness I had felt in my relationships with some of the women at the conference.
Because I had raised issues connecting sexuality
to war, I had been the target of gossip by some of
the women of the group, as if to make what I had
to say less important and even suspect. I was accused of being CIA, engaging in orgies, and
stealing boyfriends. Ilham's speech made me feel
less isolated, and explained to me some of the
problems we face as women who are committed
to nationalism as well as to feminism and sexual
freedom.

Ilham's speech is worthy of notice for a variety of reasons. It is important to note that there
was no discussion of the issues she raised at the
conference. Rather than take up her points, the
talk centered on issues of language and Arab nationalism. Sexuality was hardly touched upon, despite the fact that the focus of the conference was
to be "What Feminism for the Maghreb?" Only
one other woman used a frank and personal approach, and when she gave testimony about what

had led her to feminism, it was done with extreme uneasiness. Part of the malaise came from the split between the women themselves, their search for identity and the simultaneous realization of the political, economic, and social tensions created by the crisis the Arab world is undergoing.

Another method of silencing the discussion of sexuality and its relationship to political and social conflicts is through unquestioning adherence to dogmatic political systems of thinking. Many nationalist and leftist women at both conferences felt that women should rally behind already existing leftist movements and ideologies. Yet in these movements, traditional morality often filters through the dogmas, setting new barriers between women's sense of obligation and their search for truth and freedom. Yolla Polity-Charara (1980) provides an incisive analysis of this problem as exemplified in Lebanese politics. According to her, many Lebanese women joined political parties thinking that the condition of women would change. In 1975, during the activities organized for International Women's Year, the Democratic party invited the delegates of the political parties in Lebanon to a meeting aimed at weighing the possibilities for organizing a joint action. Women from the Phalangist party, the National Bloc, the Progressive Socialist party, the Ba'ath party, and the Communist party, as well as others from smaller groups, found themselves suspicious and indeed rivals because "how could it be possible with so many ideological differences and antagonisms, representing the whole range of political forces of Lebanon, not to be divergent on the details of women's demands" (p. 141)?

According to Polity-Charara, the party and ideological loyalties made women loath to complain about their fate to other unknown women, and even more so to rivals. The militants among them, when conscious of the discrimination women faced, when they were not themselves token women in the party, preferred to wash their dirty laundry within the family; they refused to publicly question the men of their party, to admit that their men were not the most advanced, the most egali-

tarian, and the most revolutionary. Thus, in such a context, loyalty and siding with a group become more important than discussing the issues with frankness and openness in order to find solutions to the problems.

It is obvious from all of my experiences in the Middle East, as well as in the United States, that sexuality stirs in people reactions that go much deeper than mere intellectual exercises. It brings out gut-feeling reactions that go far beyond conscious levels of explanation. It is also evident that sexuality often works together with what may appear as more tangible factors—political, economic, social, and religious choices. It is part of the psychological, physical, and spiritual aspects of human existence. As such, it seems quite obvious that if sexuality is not incorporated into the main feminist and political agenda, the struggles for freedom will remain on a very superficial level. A problem cannot be solved without going to its roots.

If women do not begin to see the necessity of dealing with issues of sexuality, more women will feel isolated, rejected, and misunderstood, even within a group leading the same struggle. More will feel pushed to leave for other places, or simply drop out of political struggle, in the hope of finding better acceptance and tolerance. Under the cover of progressive dogmas, some Western and Eastern feminists will continue to speak in the name of third world women, triggering in all women a retreat into a "national identity" or selfless and sexless socialist system, neither of which speaks to women's experience and struggles in their own lives. What happened at the "Common Differences" conference is an illustration of such reaction. In the name of leftist ideology, some feminists argued that for third world women, development, food, and shelter take precedence over issues of sexuality. This resulted in such violent arguments that many women felt caught and pressured into "taking sides," which led some to leave the conference altogether. These reactions are struggles for power and a repetition of male patterns of behavior. Many of the debates involve some women who speak on behalf of another group through an already existing dogma, rather than working toward an analysis which would incorporate the pain and suffering women are subjected to in all parts of our lives.

The importance of incorporating a discourse on sexuality when formulating a revolutionary feminist theory became even more evident as I started analyzing and writing about the Lebanese war. I have grown convinced that the war itself is closely connected with the way people perceive and act out their sense of love and power, as well as their sense of relationship to their partners, to the family, and to the general society. Usually the argument has been made that wars create such conditions of despair, and that within such a context women's issues are unimportant. Many argue that if the "right" side in a war were to win, then women's problems would automatically be solved. I would like to argue the reverse. I would suggest that if sexuality and women's issues were dealt with from the beginning, wars might be avoided, and revolutionary struggles and movements for liberation would become more effective. Justice cannot be won in the midst of injustice. Each of the levels is connected to the others.

The whole range of oppression women suffer in the Middle East, including forced marriage, virginity, and the codes of honor, claustration, the veil, polygamy, repudiation, beating, lack of freedom, and the denial of the possibility to achieve their aims and desires of life, etc.—practices that I ran away from in Lebanon at the age of twenty-two—are closely connected to the *internal* war in Lebanon (I am not referring to the Israeli and Syrian occupations, or the foreign interferences). There are at least eighteen—with many subdivisions—political parties fighting each other in Lebanon. Each of these parties has different interests; each tries to dominate a small piece of territory and impose its vision of Lebanon onto that territory; and each tries to dominate the others largely through the control of women.

One of the codes of Arab tribes is *sharaf* (honor), which also means the preservation of girls' virginity, to ensure that the women are kept exclusively for the men of their tribe. Women's lives are regulated not by national laws but by community ones. All legal questions related to individual status are legislated by denominational laws. Each creed has a different legislation according to its religion. For example, there is no civil marriage in Lebanon. Marriage, divorce, separation, custody of children, and inheritance are resolved according to one's confession—religious denomination. Each of the group's laws, rites, practices, and psychological and sexual pressures aims at keeping their women exclusively for the men of their community.

Arab society in general, and Lebanese in particular, has always had pride in the *za'im* (leader, chief, hero). The *za'im* is the macho man par excellence. Not only does he embody all the usual masculine values of conquest, domination, competition, fighting, boasting, etc., but also that of *shatara* (cleverness). *Shatara* means to succeed and get what one wants, even through lying and perfidy. *Za'im* and *shatara* are concepts much valued in tribal society. The Lebanese war has transformed the *za'im* into the *askari* (man with the gun, militiaman).

The *askari* has technical military training, and his goal is "self-preservation" of his group. In addition to his military and his economic-social functions, he has played and continues to play a role that is most violently destructive of his country, and therefore of his sexuality as well. He uses weapons of war to destroy and seize control of one region or of another group. He participates in looting to benefit his clientele and to extend the range of his influence. Given the extension of his influence, he builds a system of wealth distribution and gains more power. Material gains are obtained through his gun and other weapons of war. It is a "primitive" system, and a vicious destructive cycle, rather than a self-preserving one. The more men desire omnipotence and the control of others, the more weapons are used. The means of conquest are given a value in proportion to their success. The gun, the machine gun, the cannon—

all of the masculine sexual symbols which are extensions of the phallus—are put forward and used to conquer and destroy.

The meaning and importance given to a military weapon and to the sexual weapon are equal. Man uses his penis in the same way he uses his gun: to conquer, control, and possess. The whole macho society must be unveiled and condemned because in the present system one tries to obtain material goods and territory, not in order to enjoy them, not out of need, but only to enlarge one's domain and authority. Similarly, sexual relations are not built on pleasure, tenderness, or love, but on reproduction, the preservation of girls' virginity (so-called "honor" of the family), the confinement and control of women for the increase in male prestige, and the overestimation of the penis.

Lebanese society, which is currently composed of these groups, values such individuals because people believe that they will save the society and guarantee its survival. Yet, in reality, they are leading the society more and more toward death and destruction. The Lebanese people are blinded by their immediate needs, and by values they have been taught to take pride in. The whole system must be rethought and changed.

If the attitude of the people does not undergo a profound transformation—a radical change in the way they perceive power and love—there can be no solution to the inextricable dilemma Lebanon is going through. Outside powers may continue to play with and on Lebanon, trying to impose their views and interests. If the Lebanese people were to successfully unite and believe in their country; if they would strive not to possess a small part of it, but could develop a love for it outside material interests; if nationalism could unite all the various factions fighting each other under a common aim and belief, it could move toward a real solution. In this respect, nationalism (although often mixed with sexism) may appear to be the more urgent need. But I would argue that if nationalism remains at a sexist stage, and does not move beyond ownership and possession as final goals, the cycle of hell will repeat itself and the violence will start all over again. In Lebanon, then, both nationalism and feminism are necessary: nationalism in order to save Lebanon, and feminism in order to change the values upon which social relationships are created and formed. Only with the two combined will salvation become more lasting. And thus the work must begin at the most personal levels: with a change in attitudes and behavior toward one's mates, one's family, one's sexuality, one's society. From such a personal beginning, at least some of the internal conflicts might work toward resolution. With a stronger nationhood based in real love, rather than domination, the strength might radiate and push out outside influences.

The analysis I have given is clearly not restricted to Lebanon, but involves most geographical areas afflicted with war. The ideas about sexuality, its centrality to the social relations among and between women and men, and its relationship to war and national interests, probably make sense to different degrees everywhere. What makes the situation in Lebanon unique is that these questions take on huge proportions and are more obvious than elsewhere. Lebanon is a Mediterranean country, highly dominated by Islamo-Arab influences. As such, it carries the codes of honor and women's oppression, as well as masculine-macho values, to their farthest limits. The tragedy of this situation holds its own answer.

In conclusion, I would like to stress that the conflicts and contradictions which contemporary Middle Eastern women face in their society, in their families, and even within feminist and political groups working for social change, have their roots in sexuality and sexual politics. Sexuality is at the core of most debates and choices of human existence. It is urgent to acknowledge this fact, and to start dealing with it openly, frankly, and probably painfully. It also must be incorporated into any analysis, theory, and/or practice of revolution. If the conflicts and tensions surrounding our sexual and emotional lives are not incorporated into our struggle for freedom, we are not likely to see tangible and lasting results.

I hope that my observations, analysis, and deductions will help women all over the world realize that their common struggle is far more important and binding than the differences that might lead some of them to want to disengage from the feminist movement. I also hope that sexuality—the right to sexual pleasure, the emo-

tional relationship between two persons, as well as the problems connected with it: virginity, genital mutilation, etc., in the East, rape, pornography, etc., in the West—will grow to be recognized as an important element, as serious and as essential as food, shelter, jobs, and development in the struggles for revolutionary change.

REFERENCES

Abunasr, Junlinda. 1980. *The Development of the Three to Six Year-Old Lebanese Children and Their Environment.* Beirut: I.W.S.A.W.

Accad, Evelyne. 1978. *Veil of Shame: Role of Women in the Contemporary Fiction of North Africa and the Arab World.* Sherbrooke, Quebec: Naaman.

———. 1986. *Contemporary Arab Women Writers and Poets.* Beirut: Institute for Women's Studies in the Arab World.

———. 1988. *Coquelicot du Massacre.* [Novel on the war in Lebanon with a cassette of songs.] Paris: L'Harmattan.

———. 1989. *L'Excisée: The Mutilated Woman.* Washington: Three Continents Press.

———. 1989. *Women Unmask War Unveils Men: Sexuality, War and Literature in the Middle East.* New York: NYUP.

Adnan, Etel. 1982. *Sitt Marie Rose.* Sausalito, Calif.: Post-Apollo Press.

Ajami, Fouad. 1987. "The Silence in Arab Culture." *The New Republic* 6.

Al-Shaykh, Hanan. 1986. *The Story of Zahra.* London/New York: Readers International.

Antonius, Soraya. 1983. "Fighting on Two Fronts: Conversations with Palestinian Women." In Miranda Davies, ed., *Third World, Second Sex.* London: Zed Press.

Aibid, Marie Therese. 1980. *Ma Guerre, Pourquoi Faire?* Beirut: An-Nahar.

Awwad, Tawfiq Yusuf. 1976. *Death in Beirut.* London: Heineman.

Badinter, Elisabeth. 1986. *Lun est l'autre: Des Relations Entre Hommes et Femmes.* Paris: Odile Jacob.

Barakat, Halim. 1977. *Lebanon in Strife.* Austin: University of Texas Press.

———. 1983. *Days of Dust.* Washington: Three Continents Press.

Barry, Kathleen. 1984. *Female Sexual Slavery.* New York/London: New York University Press.

Boukhedenna, Sakinna. 1987. *Journal "Nationalité: Immigré(e)."* Paris: L'Harmattan.

Brownmiller, Susan. 1976. *Against Our Will: Men, Women, and Rape.* New York: Bantam.

Chedid, Andrée. 1976. *Cérémonial de la Violence.* Paris: Flammarion.

———. 1985. *La Maison sans Racines.* Paris: Flammarion.

———. 1987. *The Sixth Day.* London: Serpent's Tail.

Connell, Bob. 1985. "Masculinity, Violence and War." In Paul Patton and Ross Poole, eds., *War/Masculinity.* Sydney: Intervention.

Cooke, Miriam. 1987. *Women Write War: The Centering of the Beirut Decentrists.* Oxford: Center for Lebanese Studies.

———. 1988. *War's Other Voices: Women Writers on the Lebanese Civil War, 1975–1982.* Cambridge: Cambridge University Press.

Corm, Georges. 1986. *Géopolitique du Conflit Libanais.* Paris: La Decouverte.

Davies, Miranda, ed. 1983. *Third World—Second Sex: Women's Struggles and National Liberation, Third World Women Speak Out.* London: Zed Press.

Davis, Angela. 1983. *Women, Race and Class.* New York: Vintage Books.

Dworkin, Andrea. 1980. *Marx and Gandhi Were Liberals: Feminism and the "Radical" Left.* Palo Alto, Calif.: Frog in the Well.

———. 1980. *Pornography: Men Possessing Women.* New York: Perigee Books.

el Saadawi, Nawal. 1980. *The Hidden Face of Eve.* Boston: Beacon Press.

———. 1983. *Woman at Point Zero.* London: Zed Press.

———. 1984. *Douze Femmes dans Kanater.* Paris: Des Femmes.

Enloe, Cynthia. 1983. *Does Khaki Become You?: The Militarisation of Women's Lives.* London: Pluto Press.

Erlich, Michel. 1986. *La Femme Blessée: Essai sur Les Mutilations Sexuelles Féminines* Paris: L'Harmattan.

Farrar, Adam. 1985. "War: Machining Male Desire." In *War/Masculinity.* Sydney: Intervention.

"Femmes et Violences." 1981. *Alternatives Non Violentes,* no. 40, Printemps.

Gadant, Monique, ed. 1986. *Women of the Mediterranean.* London: Zed Press.

Gebeyli, Claire. 1985. *Dialogue Avec le Feu* (Carnets du Liban). Caen: Le Pave.

———. 1975. *Mémorial d'exil.* Paris: St-Germain-des-Prés.

———. 1982. *La Mise à Jour.* Paris: St-Germain-des-Prés.

Ghousoub, Maï. "Feminism—or the Eternal Masculine—in the Arab World." *New Left Review,* no. 161.

Jabbra, N. W. 1980. "Sex Roles and Language in Lebanon." *Ethnology 19,* no. 4:459–74.

Joseph, Suad. 1978. "Women and the Neighborhood Street in Borj Hammoud, Lebanon." In Lois Beck and Nikki Reddie, eds., *Women in the Muslim World.* London: Harvard.

"Jouir." 1983. *Les Cahiers du Grif,* no. 26 (dir., ed. Francoise Collin). Trimestriel-Mars.

Khair-Badawi. 1986. *Le Désir Amputé* (vécu sexuel des femmes libanaises). Paris L'Harmattan.

Khaled, Leila. 1973. *Mon Peuple Vivra* (L'autobiographie d'une révolutionaire rédigée par George Hajjar). Paris: Gailimard.

Khayat-Bennaï El, Ghita. 1985. *Le Monde Arabe au Féminin.* Paris: L'Harmattan.

Laborit, Henri. 1970. *L'agressivité Detournée.* Paris: U.G.E.

Lapierre, Jean-William, and Anne-Marie de Vilaine. 1981. "Femmes: Une Oppression Millénaire." *Alternatives Non-Violentes: Femmes et Violences,* no. 40, Printemps.

Lemsine, Aïcha. 1983. *Ordalie des Viox: Les Femmes Arabes Parlent.* Paris: Encre.

"Liban, Remises en Cause." 1982. *Peuples Méditerranéens,* no. 20. Paris, Juillet–Sept. (Direct. de Publ. Paul Vieille.)

"L'Indépendance Amoureuse." 1985. *Les Cahiers du Grif,* no. 32 (dir., ed. Francoise Collin). Editions Tierce, Hiver.

Macciocchi, Maria-Antonietta. 1974–75. *Eléments Pour une Analyse du Fascisme.* Paris VIII: Vincennes, Tome 1, no. 1026.

———. 1978. *Les Femmes et Leurs Maîtres.* Paris: Bourgeois.

Makarem, May. 1988. "Avec la Non-Violence Laure Moghaïzel, L'autre Visage du Liban." *L'Orient-Le Jour* (Beirut), 16 March.

Makhlouf, Issa. 1988. *Beyrouth au la Fascination de la Mort.* Paris: La Passion.

Mernissi, Fatima. 1983. *Sexe, Idéologie, Islam.* Paris: Tierce.

Mikdadi, Lina. 1983. *Surviving the Siege of Beirut: A Personal Account.* London: Onyx.

Mokhtar, Khaoula. 1983. "Se Libérer à Beyrouth." *Peuples Méditerranéens,* nos. 22–23, Paris, Janv.–Juin.

Moraga, Cherríe. 1983. *Loving in the War Years.* Boston: South End Press.

Patton, Paul, and Ross Poole, eds. 1985. *War/Masculinity.* Sydney: Intervention.

Peristiany, J. G. 1976. *Mediterranean Family Structures.* Cambridge: University Press. (Three articles on Lebanon.)

Peters, Emrys. 1978. "The Status of Women in Four Middle East Communities." In Lois Beck and Nikki Keddie, eds., *Women in the Muslim World.* London: Harvard.

Pierce, Judith. 1983. "Outside the Tribe." *The Middle East* (London, September).

Polity-Charara, Yolla. 1980. "Women in Politics in Lebanon." In *Femme et Politique.* Paris: L'Harmattan.

———. 1983. "Women and Politics in Lebanon." In Miranda Davies, ed., *Third World—Second Sex.* London: Zed Press.

Reardon, Betty A. 1985. *Sexism and the War System.* New York/London: Teachers College Press, Columbia University.

Reich, Wilhelm. 1981. *L'irruption de la Morale Sexuelle.* Paris: Payot (first published in German in 1932).

Samman, Ghada. 1975. *Bayrut 75* (novel). Beirut: Ghada Samman.

Saoudi, Fathia. 1986. *L'oubli Rebelle* (Beyrouth 82). Paris: L'Harmattan.

Sayegh, Rosemary. 1979. *Palestinians, from Peasants to Revolutionaries: A People's History.* London: Zed Press.

Scarry, Elaine. 1985. *The Body in Pain: The Making and Unmaking of the World.* New York: Oxford University Press.

Souriau, Christiane, ed. 1980. *Femmes et Politique autour de la Méditerranée.* Paris: L'Harmattan.

Stephen, Wafa. 1984. "Women and War in Lebanon." *Al-Raïda,* no. 30. Beirut: I.W.S.A.W.

Tabbara, Lina Mikdadi. 1979. *Survival in Beirut: A Diary of Civil War.* London: Onyx Press.

Timerman, Jacobo. 1982. *The Longest War.* New York: Vintage.

Turni. Nadia. 1979. *Liban, Vingt Poèmes Pour un Amour.* Beirut: Zakka.

———. 1982. *Archives Sentimentales d'une Guerre au Liban.* Paris: Pauvert.

———. 1984. *La Terre Arrêtée.* Paris: Belfond.

Vial-Mannessier, Thérèse. 1981. "Fascisme et Mystification Misogyne." *Alternatives Non-Violentes: Femmes et Violences,* no. 40, Printemps.

Vilaine, Anne-Marie de. 1981. "La Maternité Detournée." *Alternatives Non-Violentes: Femmes et Violences,* no. 40, Printemps.

Waring, Marilyn. 1985. *Women, Politics and Power.* Foreword by Robin Morgan. Wellington, London: Unwin.

Woolf, Virginia. 1966. *Three Guineas.* London/New York/San Diego: Harvest/HBJ.

PART FOUR

Identities

Chapter 8   Defining the Self through Difference

Our sense of who we are as women and men is not likely to remain the same over the span of our lives, but how are our identities formed and contested? How do our gendered identities change as they feed into our identities as members of religious groups, nations, or social movements? There is nothing automatic about identities. Identities are fluid rather than primordial, socially constructed rather than inherited, and they shift with changing social contexts. As the world grows more complex and interconnected, our identities, or self-definitions, respond to diverse, and sometimes competing, pulls and tugs.

Identities are both intensely private and vociferously public. Racial-ethnic, religious, national, and sexual identities are at the core of contemporary social movements and political conflicts. Intertwined with these emergent and contested identities are strong ideas—stated or implicit—of what it is to be feminine or masculine. The articles in Part Four rely on strong, first-person narratives as a vehicle to reflect how gender interacts with the creation and contestation of multifaceted identities. Together, the authors suggest some of the ways in which identities are actively shaped and defined in contradistinction to other identities. In this view, identities involve a process of simultaneously defining and erasing difference.

Feminist identity does not fall from the sky but emerges through struggle. In the first article, Slavenka Drakulic challenges some of the assumptions about Eastern European women and feminism made by a U.S. feminist. Drakulic suggests that feminist identities are cultivated through struggle, autonomy, and processes that include discussion and reflection, and she gives voice to all those who have fought against the imposition of identity by outsiders.

The two following articles, by Michael Kimmel and Gloria Anzaldúa, respectively, examine racial-ethnic identities. Kimmel explores some of the connections among Jewish cultural traits, counterhegemonic masculinities, and oppositional identities of resistance.

Anzaldúa urges us to consider identities based on ambiguity, rather than fixed certainty. By rejecting dualism and celebrating the new consciousness that emerges from mixing heritages and identities, Anzaldua challenges simple models of identity construction based on exclusionary principles.

As many commentators have pointed out elsewhere, there is no clear-cut correlation between behavior and identity. This point is probably best illustrated by the examples of homosexually active people who do not identify as gays or lesbians and heterosexually active individuals who align themselves with gay and lesbian groups. The last article in the section considers some of the ways in which sexuality interacts with feminist identity. Anastasia Higginbotham, a young feminist, narrates how feminism has prompted dramatic changes in the way she perceives her sexuality, and she discusses some of the implications of adopting bisexual identity. In all these articles, gender emerges as both constitutive and responsive to racial-ethnic, national, sexual, and feminist identities.

26

A Letter from the United States
The Critical Theory Approach

SLAVENKA DRAKULIC

"Dear Slavenka," her letter began; a two-page, single-spaced letter written on a computer. (By the way, I don't remember receiving a handwritten letter from the United States in the last couple of years.) *"I am writing to you about the interview I did with you in New York, in April, right after the Socialist Scholars' Conference (in a luncheonette near Gloria Steinem's apartment, if you remember)..."*

I remember—indeed I do. We were sitting on red plastic chairs, leaning over a plastic table, holding plastic cups with insipid American coffee, and B asked me about the position of women in Eastern Europe after the "velvet revolution." I also remember a kind of geographical map appearing in my mind: Poland, Czechoslovakia, East Germany, Hungary, Bulgaria, Romania, Yugoslavia too—we are talking about perhaps 70 million women there, living in different regions and cultures, speaking different languages, yet all reduced to a common denominator, the system they were living under.

It was after I spoke at the plenary session at that conference that B approached me. The big midtown auditorium at CUNY was almost filled. I was to give a paper on the same subject: women in Eastern Europe. But before I started my speech, I took out one sanitary napkin and one Tampax and, holding them high in the air, I showed them to the audience. "I have just come from Bulgaria," I said, "and believe me, women there don't have either napkins or Tampaxes—they never had them, in fact. Nor do women in Poland, or Czechoslova-

kia, much less in the Soviet Union or Romania. This I hold as one of the proofs of why communism failed, because in the seventy years of its existence it couldn't fulfil the basic needs of half the population."

The audience were startled at first; they hadn't expected this, not at a scholarly conference where one could expect theories, analyses, conclusions—words, words, words. Then, people started applauding. For me, the sight of a sanitary napkin and a Tampax was a necessary precondition for understanding what we are talking about: not the generally known fact that women wait in long lines for food or that they don't have washing machines—one could read about this in *Time* or *Newsweek*—but that besides all the hardship of living in Eastern Europe, if they can't find gauze or absorbent cotton, they have to wash bloody cloth pads every month, again and again, as their mothers and grandmothers and great-grandmothers did hundreds of years ago. For them, communism has changed nothing in that respect.

But I wasn't sure that my audience grasped this fact, after all: first, because they were mostly men and, by some caprice of Mother Nature, men usually don't have to wash bloody cloth pads every month; second, because they were leftists. I know them, the American men (and women) of the left. Talking to them always makes me feel like the worst kind of dissident, a right-wing freak (or a Republican, at best), even if I consider myself an honest social democrat. For every mild criticism of life in the system I have been living under for

233

the last forty years they look at me suspiciously, as if I were a CIA agent (while my folks, communists back home, never had any doubts about it—perhaps this is the key difference between Eastern and Western comrades?) But one can hardly blame them. It is not the knowledge about communism that they lack—I am quite sure they know all about it—it's the experience of living under such conditions. So, while I am speaking from "within" the system itself, they are explaining it to me from without. I do not want to claim that you have to be a hen to lay an egg, only that a certain disagreement between these two starting positions is normal. But they don't go for that; they need to be right. They see reality in schemes, in broad historical outlines, the same as their brothers in the East do. I love to hear their great speeches or read their long analyses after brief visits to our poor countries, where they meet with the best minds the establishment can offer (probably speaking English!) I love the way they get surprised or angry when the food is too greasy, there is no hot water in their hotel, they can't buy Alka Seltzer or aspirin, or their plane is late. But best of all I love the innocence of their questions. Sitting in that luncheonette on Seventy-fifth Street with B, I resented the questions she asked me, the way she asked them, as if she didn't understand that menstrual pads and Tampax are both a metaphor for the system and the reality of women living in Eastern Europe. Or as if she herself were not a woman—slim, tall, smart-looking and, surprisingly, dressed with style. Feeling the slick plastic cup in my hand, it came to my mind that her questions are like that—cold, artificial, slippery, not touching my reality.

"I am sorry to have taken so long to get in touch with you. I was in Berlin for a while this summer," the letter continued. *"I am doing a bigger project now on women and Eastern Europe—trying to put together an anthology on this topic. There is already a publisher who has expressed interest. I hope it will be more than a description of events, but some kind of analysis about women and democracy, the public sphere, civil society,*

modernization, etc. A kind of Critical Theory approach..."

I picked up this letter from my mailbox on my way to the office (together with an American Express bill, which I didn't want to open right away because I knew it would upset me). "She spent several weeks in Berlin," I thought, reading it in the streetcar, "and here she is, making an anthology!" How easy, how incredibly easy it is for her; she even has an editor. Women in Eastern Europe hardly existed as a topic, especially for leftists. And now, what is wanted is no less than a Critical Theory approach! I admit this letter upset me much more than the American Express bill would have. Following her instructions, I am to write *"some article specifically on women in Yugoslavia, dealing with the kinds of interventions women have made in the public discourse, eg, about abortion, women's control over women's bodies, what sorts of influence women have had in the public discourse on these topics, and what sorts of influence the non-feminist media have had on women's issues now."*

Reading all this, I couldn't help laughing out loud. A few people turned their heads in surprise, but I didn't stop laughing. Women's influence in the public discourse? For God's sake, what does she mean? There is hardly any public discourse, except the one about politics. Women don't have any influence, they barely even have a voice. All media are non-feminist, there are no feminist media. All that we could talk about is the absence of influence, of voice, of debate, of a feminist movement. *"Do the women in Yugoslavia argue for an 'essentialism,' i.e., that women are different from men or is it a matter of choice?"* I read in her letter, with utter amazement. With each of her words, the United States receded further and further, almost disappearing from my horizon. Argue what? Argue where? Somehow, in spite of her good intentions, I felt trapped by this letter, the views she expressed in it, like a white mouse in an experimental laboratory. Sitting in her office at the university, with a shelf full of books on Marxism, feminism, or Critical Theory within reach, B asks me about discussion on *"essentialism" in Yugoslavia.* I can imagine her, in her worn-out jeans and fashionable T-shirt, with her trimmed black hair, looking younger than she is (aerobics, macrobiotics), sitting at her computer and typing this letter, these very words that—when I read them in a streetcar in Zagreb ten days later—sound so absurd that I laugh even more, as if I were reading some very good news. *"No, dear B, we don't discuss this matter,"* I will answer in my letter. *"It is not a matter of choice, it is simply not a matter at all, see? And I cannot answer your questions, because they are all wrong."*

But if she doesn't understand us, who will? What is the way to show her what our life—the life of women and feminists—looks like? Maybe instead of answers, I could offer her something else. Suppose that my mind is an album of myriads of pictures, photos, images, paintings, snapshots, collages. And suppose I could show her some of them...

It is the autumn of 1978 and eight of us are sitting in Rada's room on Victims of Fascism Square in Zagreb. It is a little chilly because a balcony door is open, but it has to be that way. Rada hates smoking and yet we all smoke in the excitement—even Rada herself. This is because we have just come back from Beograd, from the first international feminist conference, "Comrade Woman," where we met the well-known Western European feminists Alice Schwarzer, Christine Delphy, and Dacia Maraini for the first time. We thought they were too radical when they told us that they were harassed by men on our streets. We don't even notice it, we said. Or when they talked about wearing high-heeled shoes as a sign of women's subordination. We didn't see it quite like that; we wore such shoes and even loved them. I remember how we gossiped about their greasy hair, no bra, no make-up. But all that didn't stop us from deciding to form our own group, the first feminist group in Yugoslavia. We didn't know how to organize; it even seemed impossible. First we talked. Then we published some articles—nothing big, of course. In a matter

of days we were attacked by the official women's organization, Women's Conference, by politicians, university professors, famous columnists—for importing foreign ideology.

So we discover that a feminist is not only a man-eater here, she is an enemy of the state. Some of us received threatening letters. Some got divorced, accused of neglecting their families. A maniac broke into my friend's apartment (convinced that he could understand her!); a writer wrote a porno story about two of us, feminists. Women themselves accused us of being elitist. A man wanted to chain me in the main square; someone spat on my door every night, for years ... On the other hand, more and more women were joining in, attending our monthly meetings, participating in discussions, forming their own groups—a hundred, perhaps, at the beginning. But it was lonely being one of a few feminists twelve years ago. Sitting in Rada's room and making plans, it's good that we didn't know it then.

Twelve years later, when I was in Warsaw in 1990, Jola took me to another similar room. In fact, it looked like a replica of Rada's, even if this one was not in an ambassador's apartment, with original paintings, antiques, and Ming vases all around. It was in a skyscraper somewhere on the outskirts of town, but the atmosphere was the same: nine young women and their expectations. I ask them why they joined the group. One—a teacher, tall, married, no children—answers jokingly: "Because my husband always interrupts when I talk. It's hard to recognize discrimination when you live with it." They don't know how to organize yet, but they do know that feminism is about prejudices, about woman's self. Three of them had already participated in organizing the first demonstration against the anti-abortion law proposed in the Polish Parliament in May 1989. One came for the first time this very evening. When you think about feminism in Poland, you can count the women on your fingers: Ana, Malgorzata, Stanka, Barbara, Renata, people in this room. "You might laugh at us, but we *are* the Polish Feminist Union," says Jola. "It's hard. Women don't take the initiative here; they wait for some-body to solve their problems—that's very typical for Polish women."

That evening, in her apartment, still in War-saw, Ana takes down a book from her shelf—a rather thick, ordinary paperback. It looks old, be-cause it's worn out and somehow shabby. But it's not ordinary. I can tell by the way she handles it so carefully, like something unique. "This is the book I told you about," she says, holding out the *Anthology of Feminist Texts,* a collection of early American feminist essays, "the only feminist book translated into the Polish language," the only such book to turn to when you are sick and tired of reading about man-eater/man-killer femi-nists from the West, I think, looking at it, imagin-ing how many women have read this one copy. "Sometimes I feel like I live on Jupiter, among Jupiterians, and then one day, quite by chance, I discover that I belong to another species. And I discover it in this book. Isn't that wonderful?"

She reminds me of Klara. In Klara's bedroom in Budapest there is a small shelf with about twenty such books. She has collected more be-cause she is an English translator, and she travels to London from time to time. "I read these books when I'm tired and depressed from my everyday life, from the struggle to survive and keep my head above water in spite of everything. Then I just close the door—leaving my job, two kids, the high prices, outside, no men—and read Kate Mil-lett, Betty Friedan, Susan Brownmiller. It's like reading science fiction, an escape from reality. It's so difficult to be a woman here."

I see that when I visit the novelist Erzsébet. She is a thin, quiet woman, and even though she has written four novels, she doesn't sound self-assured at all. We talk. Her husband—a journalist and novelist, too—sits there, drinking vodka and pretending he is not interested in a discussion about women in Hungary. "I'm lucky," she says. "I didn't have to work." When I ask her what she thinks of feminism, she pauses. "I don't under-stand what these women want," she responds, glancing shyly at her husband. At this point, he just can't stand it anymore. "You want to know

who, in my opinion, was the first feminist?" he asks me, as if his argument is so strong that it will persuade me forever against feminism, his face al-ready red from vodka and barely concealed anger. "I'll tell you who she was—Sappho from Les-bos." I see Erzsébet blushing, nervously playing with her glass. But she doesn't utter a word.

In a dark, smoky writer's club in Sofia, Kris-tina sits opposite me. She looks disappointed. Her words are bitter as she tells me about a question-naire she sent out some time ago. "I wrote a hun-dred letters, asking women if they think we need a feminist organization in Bulgaria. Everyone answered, yes, we do. But I also asked them whether they were prepared to join such an orga-nization, and imagine, only ten out of a hundred women answered positively." I tell her about the eight of us in Zagreb, about Jola and her group in Warsaw, about Enikö and her group of thirty stu-dents in Szeged—the first feminist group in Hun-gary. They were seven at the beginning. "Ten women out of a hundred?" I say. "But I think you're doing splendidly." "You think so?" she says, cheering up a bit. "Then maybe it's worth trying."

"Dear B," I will write in my letter to the United States, *"we live surrounded by newly opened porno shops, porno magazines, peep-shows, stripteases, unemployment, and galloping poverty. In the press they call Budapest 'the city of love, the Bangkok of Eastern Europe.' Romanian women are prostituting themselves for a single dollar in towns on the Romanian-Yugoslav border. In the midst of all this, our anti-choice nationalist governments are threatening our right to abortion and telling us to multiply, to give birth to more Poles, Hungarians, Czechs, Croats, Slovaks. We are unprepared, confused, without organization or movement yet. Perhaps we are even afraid to call ourselves feminists. Many women here see the movement as a 'world without men,' a world of lesbians, that they don't understand and cannot accept. And we definitely don't have answers for you. A Critcal Theory approach? Maybe in ten years. In the meantime, why don't you try asking us something else?"*

27

Judaism, Masculinity and Feminism

MICHAEL S. KIMMEL

In the late 1960s, I organized and participated in several large demonstrations against the war in Vietnam. Early on—it must have been 1967 or so—over 10,000 of us were marching down Fifth Avenue in New York urging the withdrawal of all U.S. troops. As we approached one corner, I noticed a small but vocal group of counter-demonstrators, waving American flags and shouting patriotic slogans. "Go back to Russia!" one yelled. Never being particularly shy, I tried to engage him. "It's my duty as an American to oppose policies I disagree with. This is patriotism!" I answered. "Drop dead, you commie Jew fag!" was his reply.

Although I tried not to show it, I was shaken by his accusation, perplexed and disturbed by the glib association of communism, Judaism, and homosexuality. "Only one out of three," I can say to myself now, "is not especially perceptive." But yet something disturbing remains about that linking of political, religious, and sexual orientations. What links them, I think, is a popular perception that each is not quite a man, that each is less than a man. And while recent developments may belie this simplistic formulation, there is, I believe, a kernel of truth to the epithet, a small piece I want to claim, not as vicious smear, but proudly. I believe that my Judaism did directly contribute to my activism against that terrible war, just as it currently provides the foundation for my participation in the struggle against sexism.

What I want to explore here are some of the ways in which my Jewishness has contributed to becoming an anti-sexist man, working to make this world a safe environment for women (and men) to fully express their humanness. Let me be clear that I speak from a cultural heritage of Eastern European Jewry, transmuted by three generations of life in the United States. I speak of the culture of Judaism's effect on me as an American Jew, not from either doctrinal considerations—we all know the theological contradictions of a biblical reverence for women, and prayers that thank God for not being born one—nor from an analysis of the politics of nation states. My perspective says nothing of Middle-Eastern machismo; I speak of Jewish culture in the diaspora, not of Israeli politics.

The historical experience of Jews has three elements that I believe have contributed to this participation in feminist politics. First, historically, the Jew is an *outsider.* Wherever the Jew has gone, he or she has been outside the seat of power, excluded from privilege. The Jew is the symbolic "other," not unlike the symbolic "otherness" of women, gays, racial and ethnic minorities, the elderly and the physically challenged. To be marginalized allows one to see the center more clearly than those who are in it, and presents grounds for alliances among marginal groups.

But the American Jew, the former immigrant, is "other" in another way, one common to many ethnic immigrants to the United States. Jewish culture is, after all, seen as an ethnic culture, which allows it to be more oppressive and emotionally rich than the bland norm. Like other ethnic subgroups, Jews have been characterized as emotional, nurturing, caring. Jewish men hug and kiss, cry and laugh. A little too much. A little too loudly. Like ethnics.

Historically, the Jewish man has been seen as less than masculine, often as a direct outgrowth of this emotional "respond-ability." The historical consequences of centuries of laws against Jews, of anti-Semitic oppression, are a cultural identity and even a self-perception as "less than men," who are too weak, too fragile, too frightened to care for our own. The cruel irony of ethnic oppression is that our rich heritage is stolen from us, and then we are blamed for having no rich heritage. In this, again, the Jew shares this self-perception with other oppressed groups who, rendered virtually helpless by an infantilizing oppression, are further victimized by the accusation that they are, in fact, infants and require the beneficence of the oppressor. One example of this cultural self-hatred can be found in the comments of Freud's colleague and friend Weininger (a Jew) who argued that "the Jew is saturated with femininity. The most feminine Aryan is more masculine than the most manly Jew. The Jew lacks the good breeding that is based upon respect for one's own individuality as well as the individuality of others."

But, again, Jews are also "less than men" for a specific reason as well. The traditional emphasis on literacy in Jewish culture contributes in a very special way. In my family, at least, to be learned, literate, a rabbi, was the highest aspiration one could possibly have. In a culture characterized by love of learning, literacy may be a mark of dignity. But currently in the United States literacy is a cultural liability. Americans contrast egghead intellectuals, divorced from the real world, with men of action—instinctual, passionate, fierce, and masculine. Senator Albert Beveridge of Indiana counseled in his 1906 volume *Young Man and the World* (a turn of the century version of *Real Men Don't Eat Quiche*) to "avoid books, in fact, avoid all artificial learning, for the forefathers put America on the right path by learning from completely, natural experience." Family, church and synagogue, and schoolroom were cast as the enervating domains of women, sapping masculine vigor.

Now, don't get me wrong. The Jewish emphasis on literacy, on mind over body, does not ex-

empt Jewish men from sexist behavior. Far from it. While many Jewish men avoid the Scylla of a boisterous and physically harassing misogyny, we can often dash ourselves against the Charybdis of a male intellectual intimidation of others. "Men with the properly sanctioned educational credentials in our society," writes Harry Brod, "are trained to impose our opinions on others, whether asked for or not, with an air of supreme self-confidence and aggressive self-assurance." It's as if the world were only waiting for our word. In fact, Brod notes, "many of us have developed mannerisms that function to intimidate those customarily denied access to higher educational institutions, especially women."[1] And yet, despite this, the Jewish emphasis on literacy has branded us, in the eyes of the world, less than "real" men.

Finally, the historical experience of Jews centers around, hinges upon our sense of morality, our ethical imperatives. The preservation of a moral code, the commandment to live ethically, is the primary responsibility of each Jew, male or female. Here, let me relate another personal story. Like many other Jews, I grew up with the words "Never Again" ringing in my ears, branded indelibly in my consciousness. For me they implied a certain moral responsibility to bear witness, to remember—to place my body visibly on the side of justice. This moral responsibility inspired my participation in the anti-war movement, and my active resistance of the draft *as a Jew.* I remember family dinners in front of the CBS Evening News, watching Walter Cronkite recite the daily tragedy of the war in Vietnam. "Never again," I said to myself, crying myself to sleep after watching napalm fall on Vietnamese villagers. Isn't this the brutal terror we have sworn ourselves to preventing when we utter those two words? When I allowed myself to feel the pain of those people, there was no longer a choice; there was, instead, a moral imperative to speak out, to attempt to end that war as quickly as possible.

In the past few years, I've become aware of another war. I met and spoke with women who had been raped, raped by their lovers, husbands, and fathers, women who had been beaten by those husbands and lovers. Some were even Jewish women. All those same words—Never Again—flashed across my mind like a neon meteor lighting up the darkened consciousness. Hearing that pain and that anger prompted the same moral imperative. We Jews say "Never Again" to the systematic horror of the Holocaust, to the cruel war against the Vietnamese, to Central American death squads. And we must say it against this war waged against women in our society, against rape and battery.

So in a sense, I see my Judaism as reminding me every day of that moral responsibility, the *special* ethical imperative that my life, as a Jew, gives to me. Our history indicates how we have been excluded from power, but also, as men, we have been privileged by another power. Our Judaism impels us to stand against any power that is illegitimately constituted because we know only too well the consequences of that power. Our ethical vision demands equality and justice, and its achievement is our historical mission.

NOTE

[1]Harry Brod, "Justice and a Male Feminist" in *The Jewish Newspaper* (Los Angeles) June 6, 1985, p. 6.

28

La Conciencia de la Mestiza

Towards a New Consciousness

GLORIA ANZALDÚA

*Por la mujer de mi raza
hablará el espíritu.*[1]

Jose Vasconcelos, Mexican philosopher, envisaged *una raza mestiza, una mezcla de razas afines, una raza de color—la primera raza síntesis del globo.* He called it a cosmic race, *la raza cósmica,* a fifth race embracing the four major races of the world.[2] Opposite to the theory of the pure Aryan, and to the policy of racial purity that white America practices, his theory is one of inclusivity. At the confluence of two or more genetic streams, with chromosomes constantly "crossing over," this mixture of races, rather than resulting in an inferior being, provides hybrid progeny, a mutable, more malleable species with a rich gene pool. From this racial, ideological, cultural and biological cross-pollinization, an "alien" consciousness is presently in the making—a new *mestiza* consciousness, *una conciencia de mujer.* It is a consciousness of the Borderlands.

UNA LUCHA DE FRONTERAS/
A STRUGGLE OF BORDERS

Because I, a *mestiza,*
continually walk out of one culture
and into another,
because I am in all cultures at the same time,
*alma entre dos mundos, tres, cuatro,
me zumba la cabeza con lo contradictorio.
Estoy norteada por todas las voces que me hablan
simultáneamente.*

The ambivalence from the clash of voices results in mental and emotional states of perplexity. Internal strife results in insecurity and indecisiveness. The *mestiza's* dual or multiple personality is plagued by psychic restlessness.

In a constant state of mental nepantilism, an Aztec word meaning torn between ways, *la mestiza* is a product of the transfer of the cultural and spiritual values of one group to another. Being tricultural, monolingual, bilingual or multilingual, speaking a patois, and in a state of perpetual transition, the *mestiza* faces the dilemma of the mixed breed: which collectivity does the daughter of a darkskinned mother listen to?

El choque de un alma atrapado entre el mundo del espíritu y el mundo de la técnica a veces la deja entullada. Cradled in one culture, sandwiched between two cultures, straddling all three cultures and their value systems, *la mestiza* undergoes a struggle of flesh, a struggle of borders, an inner war. Like all people, we perceive the version of reality that our culture communicates. Like others having or living in more than one culture, we get multiple, often opposing messages. The coming together of two self-consistent but habitually incompatible frames of reference[3] causes *un choque,* a cultural collision.

Within us and within *la cultura chicana,* commonly held beliefs of the white culture attack commonly held beliefs of the Mexican culture, and both attack commonly held beliefs of the indigenous culture. Subconsciously, we see an attack on ourselves and our beliefs as a threat and we attempt to block with a counterstance.

But it is not enough to stand on the opposite river bank, shouting questions, challenging patriarchical, white conventions. A counterstance locks one into a duel of oppressor and oppressed; locked in mortal combat, like the cop and the criminal, both are reduced to a common denominator of violence. The counterstance refutes the dominant culture's views and beliefs, and, for this, it is proudly defiant. All reaction is limited by, and dependent on, what it is reacting against. Because the counterstance stems from a problem with authority—outer as well as inner—it's a step towards liberation from cultural domination. But it is not a way of life. At some point, on our way to a new consciousness, we will have to leave the opposite bank, the split between the two mortal combatants somehow healed so that we are on both shores at once and, at once, see through serpent and eagle eyes. Or perhaps we will decide to disengage from the dominant culture, write it off altogether as a lost cause, and cross the border into a wholly new and separate territory. Or we might go another route. The possibilities are numerous once we decide to act and not react.

A TOLERANCE FOR AMBIGUITY

These numerous possibilities leave *la mestiza* floundering in uncharted seas. In perceiving conflicting information and points of view, she is subjected to a swamping of her psychological borders. She has discovered that she can't hold concepts or ideas in rigid boundaries. The borders and walls that are supposed to keep the undesirable ideas out are entrenched habits and patterns of behavior; these habits and patterns are the enemy within. Rigidity means death. Only by remaining flexible is she able to stretch the psyche horizontally and vertically. *La mestiza* constantly has to shift out of habitual formations; from convergent thinking, analytical reasoning that tends to use rationality to move toward a single goal (a Western mode), to divergent thinking,[4] characterized by movement away from set patterns and goals and toward a more whole perspective, one that includes rather than excludes.

The new *mestiza* copes by developing a tolerance for contradictions, a tolerance for ambiguity. She learns to be an Indian in Mexican culture, to be Mexican from an Anglo point of view. She learns to juggle cultures. She has a plural personality, she operates in a pluralistic mode—nothing is thrust out, the good, the bad and the ugly, nothing rejected, nothing abandoned. Not only does she sustain contradictions, she turns the ambivalence into something else.

She can be jarred out of ambivalence by an intense, and often painful, emotional event which inverts or resolves the ambivalence. I'm not sure exactly how. The work takes place underground—subconsciously. It is work that the soul performs. That focal point or fulcrum, that juncture where the *mestiza* stands, is where phenomena tend to collide. It is where the possibility of uniting all that is separate occurs. This assembly is not one where severed or separated pieces merely come together. Nor is it a balancing of opposing powers. In attempting to work out a synthesis, the self has added a third element which is greater than the sum of its severed parts. That third element is a new consciousness—a *mestiza* consciousness—and though it is a source of intense pain, its energy comes from a continual creative motion that keeps breaking down the unitary aspect of each new paradigm.

En unas pocas centurias, the future will belong to the *mestiza.* Because the future depends on the breaking down of paradigms, it depends on the straddling of two or more cultures. By creating a new mythos—that is, a change in the way we perceive reality, the way we see ourselves and the ways we behave—*la mestiza* creates a new consciousness.

The work of *mestiza* consciousness is to break down the subject-object duality that keeps her a prisoner and to show in the flesh and through the images in her work how duality is transcended. The answer to the problem between the white race and the colored, between males and females, lies in healing the split that originates in the very foundation of our lives, our culture, our languages, our thoughts. A massive uprooting of dualistic thinking in the individual and collective consciousness is the beginning of a long struggle, but one that could, in our best hopes, bring us to the end of rape, of violence, of war.

LA ENCRUCIJADA/THE CROSSROADS

A chicken is being sacrificed
 at a crossroads, a simple mound of earth
a mud shrine for *Eshu,*
 Yoruba god of indeterminacy,
who blesses her choice of path.
 She begins her journey.

Su cuerpo es una bocacalle. La mestiza has gone from being the sacrificial goat to becoming the officiating priestess at the crossroads.

As a *mestiza* I have no country, my homeland cast me out; yet all countries are mine because I am every woman's sister or potential lover. (As a lesbian I have no race, my own people disclaim me; but I am all races because there is the queer of me in all races.) I am cultureless because, as a feminist, I challenge the collective cultural/religious male-derived beliefs of Indo-Hispanics and Anglos; yet I am cultured because I am participating in the creation of yet another culture, a new story to explain the world and our participation in it, a new value system with images and symbols that connect us to each other and to the planet. *Soy un amasamiento,* I am an act of kneading, of uniting and joining that not only has produced both a creature of darkness and a creature of light, but also a creature that questions the definitions of light and dark and gives them new meanings.

We are the people who leap in the dark, we are the people on the knees of the gods. In our flesh, (r)evolution works out the clash of cultures. It makes us crazy constantly, but if the center holds, we've made some kind of evolutionary step forward. *Nuestra alma el trabajo,* the opus, the great alchemical work; spiritual *mestizaje,* a "morphogenesis,"* an inevitable unfolding. We have become the quickening serpent movement.

Indigenous like corn, like corn, the *mestiza* is a product of crossbreeding, designed for preservation under a variety of conditions. Like an ear of corn—a female seed-bearing organ—the *mestiza* is tenacious, tightly wrapped in the husks of her culture. Like kernels she clings to the cob; with thick stalks and strong brace roots, she holds tight to the earth—she will survive the crossroads.

Lavando y remojando el maíz en agua de cal, despojando el pellejo. Moliendo, mixteando, amasando, haciendo tortillas de masa.** She steeps the corn in lime, it swells, softens. With stone roller on *metate,* she grinds the corn, then grinds again. She kneads and moulds the dough, pats the round balls into *tortillas.*

We are the porous rock in the stone *metate*
squatting on the ground.
We are the rolling pin, *el maíz y agua,*
la masa harina. Somos el amasijo.
Somos lo molido en el metate.
We are the *comal* sizzling hot,
the hot *tortilla,* the hungry mouth.
We are the coarse rock.
We are the grinding motion,
the mixed potion, *somos el molcajete.*
We are the pestle, the *comino, ajo, pimienta,*
We are the *chile colorado,*
the green shoot that cracks the rock.
We will abide.

---

*To borrow chemist Ilya Prigogine's theory of "dissipative structures." Prigogine discovered that substances interact not in predictable ways as it was taught in science, but in different and fluctuating ways to produce new and more complex structures, a kind of birth he called "morphogenesis," which created unpredictable innovations.[5]

***Tortillas de masa harina:* corn tortillas are of two types, the smooth uniform ones made in a tortilla press and usually bought at a tortilla factory or supermarket, and *gorditas,* made by mixing *masa* with lard or shortening or butter (my mother sometimes puts in bits of bacon or *chicharrones*).

EL CAMINO DE LA MESTIZA/
THE *MESTIZA* WAY

> *Caught between the sudden contraction, the breath sucked in and the endless space, the brown woman stands still, looks at the sky. She decides to go down, digging her way along the roots of trees. Sifting through the bones, she shakes them to see if there is any marrow in them. Then, touching the dirt to her forehead, to her tongue, she takes a few bones, leaves the rest in their burial place.*
>
> *She goes through her backpack, keeps her journal and address book, throws away the muni-bart metromaps. The coins are heavy and they go next, then the greenbacks flutter through the air. She keeps her knife, can opener and eyebrow pencil. She puts bones, pieces of bark,* hierbas, *eagle feather, snakeskin, tape recorder, the rattle and drum in her pack and she sets out to become the* complete *tolteca.*

Her first step is to take inventory. *Despojando, desgranando, quitando paja.* Just what did she inherit from her ancestors? This weight on her back—which is the baggage from the Indian mother, which the baggage from the Spanish father, which the baggage from the Anglo?

Pero es difícil differentiating between *lo heredado, lo adquirido, lo impuesto.* She puts history through a sieve, winnows out the lies, looks at the forces that we as a race, as women, have been a part of. *Luego bota lo que no vale, los desmientos, los desencuentos, el embrutecimiento. Aguarda el juicio, hondo y enraízado, de la gente antigua.* This step is a conscious rupture with all oppressive traditions of all cultures and religions. She communicates that rupture, documents the struggle. She reinterprets history and, using new symbols, she shapes new myths. She adopts new perspectives toward the darkskinned, women and queers. She strengthens her tolerance (and intolerance) for ambiguity. She is willing to share, to make herself vulnerable to foreign ways of seeing and thinking. She surrenders all notions of safety, of the familiar. Deconstruct, construct. She becomes a *nahual,* able to transform herself into a tree, a coyote, into another person. She learns to transform the small "I" into the total Self. *Se hace*

moldeadora de su alma. Según la concepción que tiene de sí misma, así será.

QUE NO SE NOS OLVIDE LOS HOMBRES

> "Tú no sirves pa' nada—
> you're good for nothing.
> *Eres pura vieja.*"

"You're nothing but a woman" means you are defective. Its opposite is to be *un macho.* The modern meaning of the word "machismo," as well as the concept, is actually an Anglo invention. For men like my father, being "macho" meant being strong enough to protect and support my mother and us, yet being able to show love. Today's macho has doubts about his ability to feed and protect his family. His "machismo" is an adaptation to oppression and poverty and low self-esteem. It is the result of hierarchical male dominance. The Anglo, feeling inadequate and inferior and powerless, displaces or transfers these feeling to the Chicano by shaming him. In the Gringo world, the Chicano suffers from excessive humility and self-effacement, shame of self and self-deprecation. Around Latinos he suffers from a sense of language inadequacy and its accompanying discomfort; with Native Americans he suffers from a racial amnesia which ignores our common blood, and from guilt because the Spanish part of him took their land and oppressed them. He has an excessive compensatory hubris when around Mexicans from the other side. It overlays a deep sense of racial shame.

The loss of a sense of dignity and respect in the macho breeds a false machismo which leads him to put down women and even to brutalize them. Coexisting with his sexist behavior is a love for the mother which takes precedence over that of all others. Devoted son, macho pig. To wash down the shame of his acts, of his very being, and to handle the brute in the mirror, he takes to the bottle, the snort, the needle and the fist.

Though we "understand" the root causes of male hatred and fear, and the subsequent wounding of women, we do not excuse, we do not condone and we will not longer put up with it. From the men of our race, we demand the admission/acknowledgement/disclosure/testimony that they wound us, violate us, are afraid of us and of our power. We need them to say they will begin to eliminate their hurtful put-down ways. But more than the words, we demand acts. We say to them: we will develop equal power with you and those who have shamed us.

It is imperative that *mestizas* support each other in changing the sexist elements in the Mexican-Indian culture. As long as woman is put down, the Indian and the Black in all of us is put down. The struggle of the *mestiza* is above all a feminist one. As long as *los hombres* think they have to *chingar mujeres* and each other to be men, as long as men are taught that they are superior and therefore culturally favored over *la mujer,* as long as to be a *vieja* is a thing of derision, there can be no real healing of our psyches. We're halfway there—we have such love of the Mother, the good mother. The first step is to unlearn the *puta/virgen* dichotomy and to see *Coatlapopeuh—Coatlicue* in the Mother, *Guadalupe.*

Tenderness, a sign of vulnerability, is so feared that it is showered on women with verbal abuse and blows. Men, even more than women, are fettered to gender roles. Women at least have had the guts to break out of bondage. Only gay men have had the courage to expose themselves to the woman inside them and to challenge the current masculinity. I've encountered a few scattered and isolated gentle straight men, the beginnings of a new breed, but they are confused, and entangled with sexist behaviors that they have not been able to eradicate. We need a new masculinity and the new man needs a movement.

Lumping the males who deviate from the general norm with man, the oppressor, is a gross injustice. *Asombra pensar que nos hemos quedado en ese pozo oscuro donde el mundo encierra a las lesbianas. Asombra pensar que hemos, como feministas y lesbianas, cerrado nuestros corazónes a los*

hombres, a nuestros hermanos los jotos, desheredados y marginales como nosotros. Being the supreme crossers of cultures, homosexuals have strong bonds with the queer white, Black, Asian, Native American, Latino and with the queer in Italy, Australia and the rest of the planet. We come from all colors, all classes, all races, all time periods. Our role is to link people with each other—the Blacks with Jews with Indians with Asians with whites with extraterrestrials. It is to transfer ideas and information from one culture to another. Colored homosexuals have more knowledge of other cultures; have always been at the forefront (although sometimes in the closet) of all liberation struggles in this country; have suffered more injustices and have survived them despite all odds. Chicanos need to acknowledge the political and artistic contributions of their queer. People, listen to what your *jotería* is saying.

The *mestizo* and the queer exist at this time and point on the evolutionary continuum for a purpose. We are a blending that proves that all blood is intricately woven together, and that we are spawned out of similar souls.

SOMOS UNA GENTA

> *Hay tantísimas fronteras*
> que dividen a la gente,
> pero por cada frontera
> existe también un puente.

> —Gina Valdés[6]

Divided Loyalties

Many women and men of color do not want to have any dealings with white people. It takes too much time and energy to explain to the downwardly mobile, white middle-class women that it's okay for us to want to own "possessions," never having had any nice furniture on our dirt floors or "luxuries" like washing machines. Many feel that whites should help their own people rid themselves of race hatred and fear first. I, for one, choose to use some of my energy to serve as mediator. I think we need to allow whites to be our allies. Through our literature, art, *corridos* and folktales we must share our history with them so when they set up committees to help Big Mountain Navajos or the Chicano farmworkers or *los Nicaragüenses* they won't turn people away because of their racial fears and ignorances. They will come to see that they are not helping us but following our lead.

Individually, but also as a racial entity, we need to voice our needs. We need to say to white society: we need you to accept the fact that Chicanos are different, to acknowledge your rejection and negation of us. We need you to own the fact that you looked upon us as less than human, that you stole our lands, our personhood, our self-respect. We need you to make public restitution: to say that, to compensate for your own sense of defectiveness, you strive for power over us, you erase our history and our experience because it makes you feel guilty—you'd rather forget your brutish acts. To say you've split yourself from minority groups, that you disown us, that your dual consciousness splits off parts of yourself, transferring the "negative" parts onto us. (Where there is persecution of minorities, there is shadow projection. Where there is violence and war, there is repression of shadow.) To say that you are afraid of us, that to put distance between us, you wear the mask of contempt. Admit that Mexico is your double, that she exists in the shadow of this country, that we are irrevocably tied to her. Gringo, accept the doppelganger in your psyche. By taking back your collective shadow the intracultural split will heal. And finally, tell us what you need from us.

BY YOUR TRUE FACES
WE WILL KNOW YOU

I am visible—see, this Indian face—yet I am invisible. I both blind them with my beak nose and am their blind spot. But I exist, we exist. They'd like to think I have melted in the pot. But I haven't, we haven't.

The dominant white culture is killing us slowly with its ignorance. By taking away our self-determination, it has made us weak and empty. As a people we have resisted and we have taken expedient positions, but we have never been allowed to develop unencumbered—we have never been allowed to be fully ourselves. The whites in power want us people of color to barricade ourselves behind our separate tribal walls so they can pick us off one at a time with their hidden weapons; so they can whitewash and distort history. Ignorance splits people, creates prejudices. A misinformed people is a subjugated people.

Before the Chicano and the undocumented worker and the Mexican from the other side can come together, before the Chicano can have unity with Native Americans and other groups, we need to know the history of their struggle and they need to know ours. Our mothers, our sisters and brothers, the guys who hang out on street corners, the children in the playgrounds, each of us must know our Indian lineage, our afro-*mestisaje*, our history of resistance.

To the immigrant *mexicano* and the recent arrivals we must teach our history. The 80 million *mexicanos* and the Latinos from Central and South America must know of our struggles. Each one of us must know basic facts about Nicaragua, Chile and the rest of Latin America. The Latinoist movement (Chicanos, Puerto Ricans, Cubans and other Spanish-speaking people working together to combat racial discrimination in the market place) is good but it is not enough. Other than a common culture we will have nothing to hold us together. We need to meet on a broader communal ground.

The struggle is inner: Chicano, *indio,* American Indian, *mojado, mexicano,* immigrant Latino, Anglo in power, working class Anglo, Black, Asian—our psyches resemble the bordertowns and are populated by the same people. The struggle has always been inner, and is played out in the outer terrains. Awareness of our situation must come before inner changes, which in turn come before changes in society. Nothing happens in the "real" world unless it first happens in the images in our heads.

EL DÍA DE LA CHICANA

> I will not be shamed again
> Nor will I shame myself.

I am possessed by a vision: that we Chicanas and Chicanos have taken back or uncovered our true faces, our dignity and self-respect. It's a validation vision.

Seeing the Chicana anew in light of her history. I seek an exoneration, a seeing through the fictions of white supremacy, a seeing of ourselves in our true guises and not as the false racial personality that has been given to us and that we have given to ourselves. I seek our woman's face, our true features, the positive and the negative seen clearly, free of the tainted biases of male dominance. I seek new images of identity, new beliefs about ourselves, our humanity and worth no longer in question.

Estamos viviendo en la noche de la Raza, un tiempo cuando el trabajo se hace a lo quieto, en el oscuro. El día cuando aceptamos tal y como somos y para en donde vamos y porque—ese día será el día de la Raza. Yo tengo el conpromiso de expresar mi visión, mi sensibilidad, mi percepción de la re-validación de la gente mexicana, su mérito, estimación, honra, aprecio y validez.

On December 2nd when my sun goes into my first house, I celebrate *el día de la Chicana y el Chicano.* On that day I clean my altars, light my *Coatlalopeuh* candle, burn sage and copal, take *el baño para espantar basura,* sweep my house. On that day I bare my soul, make myself vulnerable to friends and family by expressing my feelings. On that day I affirm who we are.

On that day I look inside our conflicts and our basic introverted racial temperament. I identify our needs, voice them. I acknowledge that the self and the race have been wounded. I recognize the need to take care of our personhood, of our racial self.

On that day I gather the splintered and disowned parts of *la gente mexicana* and hold them in my arms. *Todas las partes de nosotros valen.*

On that day I say, "Yes, all you people wound us when you reject us. Rejection strips us of self-worth; our vulnerability exposes us to shame. It is our innate identity you find wanting. We are ashamed that we need your good opinion, that we need your acceptance. We can no longer camouflage our needs, can no longer let defenses and fences sprout around us. We can no longer withdraw. To rage and look upon you with contempt is to rage and be contemptuous of ourselves. We can no longer blame you, nor disown the white parts, the male parts, the pathological parts, the queer parts, the vulnerable parts. Here we are weaponless with open arms, with only our magic. Let's try it our way, the *mestiza* way, the Chicana way, the woman way.

On that day, I search for our essential dignity as a people, a people with a sense of purpose—to belong and contribute to something greater than our *pueblo.* On that day I seek to recover and reshape my spiritual identity. *¡Anímate! Raza, a celebrar el día de la Chicana.*

EL RETORNO

> *All movements are accomplished in six stages, and the seventh brings return.*
> —I Ching[7]

> *Tanto tiempo sin verte casa mía, mi cuna, mi hondo nido de la huerta.*
> —"Soledad"[8]

I stand at the river, watch the curving, twisting serpent, a serpent nailed to the fence where the mouth of the Rio Grande empties into the Gulf.

I have come back. *Tanto dolor me costó el alejamiento.* I shade my eyes and look up. The bone beak of a hawk slowly circling over me, checking me out as potential carrion. In its wake a little bird flickering its wings, swimming sporadically like a fish. In the distance the expressway and the slough of traffic like an irritated sow. The sudden pull in my gut, *la tierra, los aguac-*

eros. My land, *el viento soplando la arena, el lagartijo debajo de un nopalito. Me acuerdo como era antes. Una región desértica de vasta llanuras, costeras de baja altura, de escasa lluvia, de chaparrales formados por mesquites y huizaches.* If I look real hard I can almost see the Spanish fathers who were called "the cavalry of Christ" enter this valley riding their burros, see the clash of cultures commence.

Tierra Natal

This is home, the small towns in the Valley, *los pueblitos* with chicken pens and goats picketed to mesquite shrubs. *En las colonias* on the other side of the tracks, junk cars line the front yards of hot pink and lavender-trimmed houses—Chicano architecture we call it, self-consciously. I have missed the TV shows where hosts speak in half and half, and where awards are given in the category of Tex-Mex music. I have missed the Mexican cemeteries blooming with artificial flowers, the fields of aloe vera and red pepper, rows of sugar cane, of corn hanging on the stalks, the cloud of *polvareda* in the dirt roads behind a speeding truck, *el sabor de tamales de rez y venado.* I have missed *la yegua colorada* gnawing the wooden gate of her stall, the smell of horse flesh from Carito's corrals. *He hecho menos las noches calientes sin aire, noches de linternas y lechuzas* making holes in the night.

I still feel the old despair when I look at the unpainted, dilapidated, scrap lumber houses consisting mostly of corrugated aluminum. Some of the poorest people in the U.S. live in the Lower Rio Grande Valley, an arid and semi-arid land of irrigated farming, intense sunlight and heat, citrus groves next to chaparral and cactus. I walk through the elementary school I attended so long ago, that remained segregated until recently. I remember how the white teachers used to punish us for being Mexican.

How I love this tragic valley of South Texas, as Ricardo Sánchez calls it; this borderland between the Nueces and the Rio Grande. This land

has survived possession and ill-use by five countries: Spain, Mexico, the Republic of Texas, the Confederacy, and the U.S. again. It has survived Anglo-Mexican blood feuds, lynchings, burnings, rapes, pillage.

Today I see the Valley still struggling to survive. Whether it does or not, it will never be as I remember it. The borderlands depression that was set off by the 1982 peso devaluation in Mexico resulted in the closure of hundreds of Valley businesses. Many people lost their homes, cars, land. Prior to 1982, U.S. store owners thrived on retail sales to Mexicans who came across the borders for groceries and clothes and appliances. While goods on the U.S. side have become 10, 100, 1000 times more expensive for Mexican buyers, goods on the Mexican side have become 10, 100, 1000 times cheaper for Americans. Because the Valley is heavily dependent on agriculture and Mexican retail trade, it has the highest unemployment rates along the entire border region; it is the Valley that has been hardest hit.*

"It's been a bad year for corn," my brother, Nune, says. As he talks, I remember my father scanning the sky for a rain that would end the drought, looking up into the sky, day after day, while the corn withered on its stalk. My father has been dead for 29 years, having worked himself to death. The life span of a Mexican farm laborer is 56—he lived to be 38. It shocks me that I am older than he. I, too, search the sky for rain. Like the ancients, I worship the rain god and the maize goddess, but unlike my father I have recovered their names. Now for rain (irrigation) one offers not a sacrifice of blood, but of money.

"Farming is in a bad way," my brother says. "Two to three thousand small and big farmers

---

*Out of the twenty-two border counties in the four border states, Hidalgo County (named for Father Hidalgo who was shot in 1810 after instigating Mexico's revolt against Spanish rule under the banner of *la Virgen de Guadalupe*) is the most poverty-stricken county in the nation as well as the largest home base (along with Imperial in California) for migrant farmworkers. It was here that I was born and raised. I am amazed that both it and I have survived.

went bankrupt in this country last year. Six years ago the price of corn was $8.00 per hundred pounds," he goes on. "This year it is $3.90 per hundred pounds." And, I think to myself, after taking inflation into account, not planting anything puts you ahead.

I walk out to the back yard, stare at *los rosales de mamá.* She wants me to help her prune the rose bushes, dig out the carpet grass that is choking them. *Mamagrande Ramona también tenía rosales.* Here every Mexican grows flowers. If they don't have a piece of dirt, they use car tires, jars, cans, shoe boxes. Roses are the Mexican's favorite flower. I think, how symbolic—thorns and all.

Yes, the Chicano and Chicana have always taken care of growing things and the land. Again I see the four of us kids getting off the school bus, changing into our work clothes, walking into the field with Papí and Mamí, all six of us bending to

the ground. Below our feet, under the earth lie the watermelon seeds. We cover them with paper plates, putting *terremotes* on top of the plates to keep them from being blown away by the wind. The paper plates keep the freeze away. Next day or the next, we remove the plates, bare the tiny green shoots to the elements. They survive and grow, give fruit hundreds of times the size of the seed. We water them and hoe them. We harvest them. The vines dry, rot, are plowed under. Growth, death, decay, birth. The soil prepared again and again, impregnated, worked on. A constant changing of forms, *renacimientos de la tierra madre.*

This land was Mexican once
was Indian always
and is.
And will be again.

NOTES

1. This is my own "take-off" on Jose Vasconcelos' idea. Jose Vasconcelos, *La Raza Cósmica: Missión de la Raza Ibero-Americana* (México: Aguilar S.A. de Ediciones, 1961).
2. Vasconcelos.
3. Arthur Koestler termed this "bisociation." Albert Rothenberg, *The Creative Process in Art, Science, and Other Fields* (Chicago, IL: University of Chicago Press, 1979), 12.
4. In part, I derive my definitions for "convergent" and "divergent" thinking from Rothenberg, 12–13.
5. Harold Gilliam, "Searching for a New World View," *This World* (January, 1981), 23.
6. Gina Valdés, *Puentes y Fronteras: Coplas Chicanas* (Los Angeles, CA: Castle Lithograph, 1982), 2.
7. Richard Wilhelm, *The I Ching or Book of Changes,* trans. Cary F. Baynes, (Princeton. NJ: Princeton University Press, 1950), 98.
8. *"Soledad"* is sung by the group Haciendo Punto en Otro Son.

29

Chicks Goin' at It

ANASTASIA HIGGINBOTHAM

Aside from the occasional dream of being chased by a man throwing hot dogs at me, I consider myself a fairly well-adjusted feminist. Yes, I sometimes imagine myself alone, late at night, surrounded by candles; the scent of incense fills the air as I scribble on little slips of paper, "Howard Stern—AWAY," while a small doll, cut off at the waist and doused in gasoline, awaits its grim fate.... Still, for all intents and purposes, I think I coexist quite reasonably with the phallo-explosive media and institutions that surround me. Oh, there was that time I talked all through Thanksgiving dinner about why I consider the clitoris to be the jewel of human anatomy and the source of my strength and magic as a woman and feminist. But everyone was telling stories and I just wanted to participate.

I know now that I've overcome the angry stage. When the evening news made me cry and fraternity boys made me vomit. When I thought men who hate women were cowering assholes with too much testosterone and too little brain power. When I thought the fight to bring patriarchy to a screeching, jubilant halt was the only fight worth my time or anyone else's.

But, oh, I've changed from that bitter girl of seventeen. I'm now a bitter woman of twenty-three. I don't watch the news, and I'm convinced that men who hate women are indeed cowering assholes with an exorbitant amount of testosterone and very little brain power, if any. I know that the fight to end patriarchy, to devour it, to deplete and dismember it in favor of a system that does not achieve cosmic orgasm through the oppression of others is a just and valiant fight. And I will continue to pursue this glorious end as long as my soul wanders the earth. Fraternity boys still make me vomit. But now I imagine vomiting on them rather than because of them. I've become a gastric avenger of sorts.

I wasn't always a feminist. In fact, I used to think feminists were sexually undesirable and perpetually angry. (Boy, was I wrong. Feminists are perpetually desirable, and I am sexually angry.) Prior to my feminist epiphany, I felt I was nothing more than big hair with a fellatio fetish, the worst part about this being that I thought I was pretty cool. In the time that has passed since then, I have grown from girl to woman, but more dramatically, I have been transformed from masochist to feminist.

The big hair, accompanied by moderately big breasts and a dancer's ass, all bundled into a squeezy purple dress, attracted all sorts of attention—all sorts dangerous. For one thing, I could have brought my high school to its knees on charges of sexual misconduct. My most serious encounter nearly led to an affair with a teacher who, despite the inappropriateness of his forty-seven-year-old affections for a fifteen-year-old girl, won me over somehow. Being near him made my stomach churn, my throat ache, my eyes blur. Though I wish it had been a temporary virus, I realize now it was probably terror, and at the time it seemed quite romantic. Another of my faculty suitors had a nasty habit of pressing his bulging manhood against my back as I sat in his class furiously taking notes to prove I was smart. They were charmers, all right.

It's appalling to me now, but at the time it felt normal and hardly bothered me. In fact, I thrived on making them all hard and then laughing in their faces at the obvious fact that they could never have me. I thought I was god's gift to men because I could play glam, sweetheart and harlot all in one shot. I had my pick, and like your typical fallen angel-to-be, I chose poorly.

I lost my virginity, or rather, rid myself of its intolerable presence. Virginity implied immaturity, stupidity and a dearth of passion—as such, I wanted no part of it. To me, virginity represented all the qualities of "girliness," none of which merited any respect at all from anyone, anywhere.

Furthermore, coming from a long line of passionate women, I felt drawn to the pleasures of flesh. But more than sexual contact, I wanted the hard edges that come from having a lot of sex with many lovers. My role models were the prostitutes in old Westerns who played poker with mean cowboys (and won). They swore in low, husky voices, were cynical but funny, carried guns in their garter belts and never needed men. I wanted to be scarred by love the way these women were. For what it's worth, I was successful in achieving my goal.

I began having vaginal intercourse—I'd already done everything else—with one of the men who, in middle school, had thrown my brother over a wall to prove his seventh-grade masculinity. Though he was never violent with me, I had yet to recognize a separation between sex/iness, violence and the romantic intrigue of scars. For example, I recall an incident in which my friends and I discussed going to see *The Accused*. They shared my sexually curious desire to see "the gang rape," as I said to them with a mischievous grin, "I heard they show it."

I left the movie theater the following weekend in tears, completely traumatized (scarred, in fact). I spent the next two days in exactly the same condition, crying for that woman, crying for myself and convinced that I would inevitably find myself pinned to a table by hovering, raping, evil men. My fear of rape and of men culminated in frequent nightmares about incest, murder and, of course, more rape.

The problem was not that I suffered an abusive childhood or bad luck, because I didn't. It

was also not that I was weak or ill-prepared for life as a young adult in a world full of "adult" bookstores. It was simply that I was born a girl in a society that devalues women and girls. Bam. That easy. And because I lacked the words to describe my demons, I had no power to address them.

I know all kinds of words now. Words like revolution, equality, dignity, reproductive freedom. I've mistressed phrases like subvert the patriarchy, run with the wolves, and take back the night. Words of empowerment. The one word all phallocrats most fear (and well they should), I wear like a badge of honor, my pride, my work, my glowing, spiked tiara. That word is "feminist."

I became a feminist through other forms of activism—race education (my own) and gay rights. One shining moment of radicalization occurred in my Speech 105 class. I'd given a speech on gay, lesbian and bisexual rights—you know the ones I'm talking about. The right to not be beaten up, the right to not be thrown out of the house/church/military, the right to not die from a disease the ruling class chooses to ignore, that is, until they're the ones to get it, blah, blah, blah. Unreasonable demand after unreasonable demand.

So, I've just finished my tribute to queers everywhere, when a student raises his hand to ask me (the only question I received at all), "When you say 'homosexuals,' do you mean guys? Or chicks goin' at it, too?" Chicks goin' at it. Obviously, my rhetoric had sung its way into his tender, eager-to-be-enlightened heart. My calling into the world of gay activism.

Then there was the time I bought these hunky purple hiking boots, a look I'd admired from atop my three-and-a-half-inch heels for some time. I enhanced my purchase by wearing them with dresses, the nonclinging kind, and the most alarming thing happened. I began to walk differently. I no longer wobbled. I took bigger steps, surer steps, harder steps. A friend of mine wears boots anytime she waits tables to combat wobbliness in the face of the inevitable harassment endured by women in the service industry. It's clear to me now that every feminist, indeed every woman, needs a good, solid pair of boots. It's not just a symbolic assault on the patriarchy, it's a fashion statement. Like short hair.

I know because I cut the hell out of my long, curly hair. My mother loved it; my boyfriend hated it. (Duh.) He said it made him feel like he was making love to a boy. I found this particularly amusing since he had very long, very female hair, which provided just the touch I needed to reach orgasm with him. I suddenly realized why he was so upset. I apologized for not having warned him and told him I hoped that he would never cut his own hair. "I know exactly what you mean," I said.

So now we have the boots, the hair, the lesbian fantasy (more on this later), and, in my effort to dive headlong into the stereotypical/archetypal image of a feminist, I offer what was my next, triumphant step toward full-blown feminist liberation. Susan B. Anthony did it. Mary Ann Shadd Cary did it. Ida B. Wells did it, and so did Margaret Sanger. Heck, all the kids were doin' it. On the campus of Vanderbilt University, a place that quite resembles an old southern plantation crawling with J. Crew models and debutantes, I started a feminist newspaper with two womenfriends. The initiation, my rebirth—feminist at last.

We took on woman haters, Limbaugh lovers, date rapers, and the ever-popular, oh-so-predictable brothers (and sisters) of backlash. We lost sleep, I lost a three-year dean's list streak, we nearly went insane, and it was still some of the best fun I ever had in my life. Every heartbeat, every bit of energy, our very souls, we spent for that paper and for each other.

In my prefeminist incarnation, I was incapable of this kind of close relationship with women. Vanity, competition and superficial alliances more accurately describe my friendships with women then. But imagine my surprise as I took this intimacy even one step further when I ended up in bed with a dear friend and coeditor.

We only slept—that day. But we wrapped our bodies around one another and stayed that way, from early one Saturday afternoon to late in the evening. Some of the time I slept, some of the time I contemplated the curve of her hip, some of the time I imagined how we looked, lying there, me with this warm grin crawling across my face. We only slept. Anything more would have been redundant, excessive. I'd been introduced to a feeling I never knew existed. That moment of revelation satisfied me more than any sex ever could.

It also came as a shock to me, for about a minute. Then I put it into my own historical context. I had wondered whether or not I might be lesbian ever since the time the sound of k.d. lang's voice over my headphones made me blush. Plus, I consistently fantasized about women in order to get through sex with men. For, contrary to the much-publicized, rather unfortunate words of Naomi Wolf, the male body is neither home nor shelter to me. It's more like a really itchy blanket with some holes in it. And while I, too, have seen the word "love" trigger an erection, I have also seen the word "rape" inspire much of the same.

And though I know that my rejection of men is not what led me to the arms of women, my experiences with them certainly provided me with the impetus to go looking for something (and someone) else. Sleeping with men required more compromise and more effort than I was willing to make. Sleeping with women felt like just another extension of my sexuality and identity. It is also something I aspired to as a die-hard advocate for women. That's what troubled me.

My bedroom, as you might well expect, was full of politics. Ever since the moment I inherited the fiery skull of knowledge, my head and my bed swarmed with the power dynamics of sex: Who leads, who follows, when is it rape, when is it just bad sex and why do I so desperately hate it these days? But women, I thought, sex with women must be different.

It tormented me for months. I had these massive crushes on my best friend and my boss, and suddenly I was in angst over whether or not to tattoo a pink triangle on my forehead. But I worried (and still do occasionally) that I was taking on lesbianism out of loyalty to a cause, fearful that my capacity to sleep with the bad guys was bad for PR. Was I trying too hard to sleep with my politics? After all, with all my issues there was hardly room for anyone else in the bed. Why not take advantage? Or, worse yet, was I a wanna-be? A baby dyke? A lesbian chic groupie, flashing in the pan, wanting my fifteen minutes of fame on the cover of *Newsweek*? Or was I truly falling more in love with women, with spirited feminists and with my own womanhood than I had ever been with anyone?

Um . . . yes.

I figure you can fantasize about sleeping with women only so much before it stops being a fantasy and starts becoming a reality. And while I still have a bed full of feminist ideologies—combined with the world of women-loving women—I find they practically serve as erotica. "Tell me again in your sexiest voice how pathetic the Senate Judiciary Committee is while I light some candles and slip into my sleeveless 'Patriarchy Bites!' T-shirt." Rrowll.

Now, instead of arguing over the well-known fact (known by delinquent assholes) that "some women *like* hard-core S/M porn, eh, eh, whine, whine," I can argue over who knows more lines from *Thelma and Louise.* "You said you and me wuz gonna git outta town and for once jus' really let our hair down. Well, darlin', look out, 'cause my hair is comin' down."

So I'll tell you the truth: I still don't know if all of this makes me a lesbian. I'm definitely bisexual. And I only recently claimed that label for myself without fear of it implying indecisiveness, internalized all-out-lesbian homophobia or the perception that I'm just plain easy. I've known both straight and gay people who shunned it (the word, the deed and the person) for each of the biphobic reasons I just expressed. In the wake of this paranoia, on my part and theirs, I've allowed myself to conclude a few things.

I'm a Libra for goddess' sake. You better believe I'm indecisive! It's the only thing I know for sure at all! I can't even determine whether I'm right-handed or left-handed, just in case my left hand one day decides to assert itself. I'd feel terrible having given up on it before it was ready to come out—if you know what I mean. Needless to

say, I only assumed I was straight all those years because nothing led me to believe otherwise. Hallelujah, I believe otherwise!

As far as fearing status as a true-blue lesbian, I'll tell ya, I came out two or three times in front of large audiences before it was even relevant to my personal life. In the heat of many a debate, we needed a lesbian, I took the bulldyke by the horns and BAM: instant lesbian. Short hair, raging feminist, swearing in front of faculty? As if they didn't already think it.

My campus environment proved just slightly less than fascist when it came to gay rights. I mean, it's not as if we had drag queens and biker dykes screamin' across the delicately manicured lawn. (If only we had! The mere thought makes my heart leap.) The atmosphere was more than hostile to even the most meager queer on campus. How can I say this without offending anyone? Do the words Bible-bangin' freaks all carryin' plastic fetuses in their backpacks mean anything to you? The only lesbians we had were these badass, underappreciated grad students and a philosophy professor. I think all the other lesbians transferred.

Besides, my alliance with lesbians, as a women-loving woman and feminist, has always been core to my political activism and identity. Feminists are routinely "accused" of being lesbians or manhaters (as if the two are synonymous). Straight feminists often scramble to defy this stereotype by proclaiming their unfailing love for men and their affinity for bikini waxes. Some subtly distance themselves from lesbians by wearing buttons that claim "straight but not narrow." This is bullshit to me. If being called a lesbian is an insult to me, then I am an insult to lesbians. Any feminist who fears being called lesbian, or who fears association with a movement demanding civil rights for gays, lesbians and bisexuals, is not worthy of being called feminist.

The only other reason that could prevent me from embracing my bisexual identity is the implication to others that I might be easy. Ain't no might about it. I am easy. But, as long as I'm safe, what the hell?

My favorite term (other than plain old "queer") is "bisexual lesbian." It just works for me. I don't expect a man to understand me; I don't applaud him if he does. My heart and my mind belong with other women-loving women.

So here I am. I have birthed of myself a wild and unruly feminist. I feast as often as possible with my womensisters under new and full moons. I am seriously in love with Susan B. Anthony, and I have the dearest little crush on Gloria Steinem (especially during her big hair stage—probably some kind of narcissistic throwback to my past). I don't think I could be prouder of the cause that fuels my existence. I certainly didn't expect this much support, encouragement and spiritual nourishment outside of the womb, but what a lovely surprise!

I offer my feminist flamboyance as a personal attack on the patriarchy. And to further hack at the roots of patriarchal power, I would like to co-opt a statement made by Sarah Grimké in 1838. (If there had been a Miss Feminist America Pageant in 1838, this answer to world peace would surely have taken the crown.) She wrote: "All I ask our brethren is, that they will take their feet from off our necks and permit us to stand upright on that ground which God designed us to occupy."[1] I'd like to reiterate (without the "God" part—whole other story), since apparently SOMEBODY wasn't in class that day. Give it up, would you? I'm so over it.

1. Gerda Lerner, *The Creation of Feminist Consciousness: From the Middle Ages to Eighteen-seventy* (New York: Oxford University Press, 1993), p. 162.

PART FIVE

Families

Chapter 9   Constructing Motherhood and Fatherhood

Chapter 10   Work and Families

Family life is shrouded in myth. No matter how much families change, they are idealized as natural or biological units based on the timeless functions of love, motherhood, and childbearing. Family evokes warmth, caring, and unconditional love in a refuge set apart from the public world. In this image, family and society are separate. Relations *inside* the family are idealized as nurturant, and those *outside* the family are seen as competitive. This ideal assumes a gendered division of labor: a husband/father associated with the public world and a wife/mother defined as the heart of the family. Although this image bears little resemblance to present family situations, it is still recognizable in our cultural ideals.

In the past two decades, feminist thought has been in the forefront of efforts to demythologize the family. Feminist thinkers have demonstrated that family forms are socially and historically constructed, not monolithic universals that exist for all times and all peoples, and that the arrangements governing family life are not the inevitable result of unambiguous differences between women and men. Feminist thinkers have drawn attention to disparities in family life, to the contradictions within families between love and power and between family images on the one hand and lived family experiences on the other. They have directed attention to the close connection between families and other structures and institutions in society.

Early feminist critiques of the family characterized it as the primary site of women's oppression and argued in support of women's increased participation in the labor force as a means of attaining greater autonomy. But this analysis did not apply well to women of color or working-class women generally, because it falsely universalized the experiences of White middle-class women who had the option of staying home to raise their children. More recently, feminist thought has begun to create a more complex understanding of the relationship between family and work by examining differences among women and taking men's experiences into account.

Questioning motherhood has been a central theme in recent feminist studies. Chapter 9 explores both symbolic meanings and concrete realities of motherhood. It uncovers experiences that are not simply gendered but shaped by other lines of difference as well. In her study of mother love and infant death on Alto de Cruzo, Nancy Scheper-Hughes discovers an ambiguous form of mothering that is far removed from the essentialized and mythical portrait. Instead, the local context produces differences that seem impossible and even unthinkable. Next, Patricia Hill Collins takes race and class into account in rethinking motherhood. Distinctive sociohistorical realities engender more generalized and collective mothering relationships for Black women. The article by Denise Segura compares conceptions of motherhood among Chicanas and recent Mexican immigrants. She probes the underlying social conditions that allow for different ways of viewing motherhood and employment among these Latinas. Finally, we move to fatherhood as Ralph LaRossa confronts the idea that fathering in the United States has undergone dramatic changes.

Chapter 10 takes up questions about work and family, giving us new insights into women's and men's experiences in public and private spheres. First, in a study of women and men in southern Spain, David Gilmore exposes the false dichotomy of public and private power. We cannot assume that men's public activities automatically give them freedom and power, nor that women's domestic activities render them powerless. Looking carefully at what goes on within and between households reveals a female infrastructure of control that challenges conventional wisdom about gender and power.

By now it is a truism that families throughout the world have been affected by the movement of women into the work force. But on closer look, women's new work patterns are part of a much larger upheaval in the relationship between work and family. The next two articles address the shaping power of larger economic forces on women's family roles. The impact of shifting economies on women and their families varies considerably by class. Patricia Fernández Kelly's comparison of industrial housework among Mexican American and Cuban women shows how the class context gives rise to different work and family patterns. While Cuban women's employment enhances their families' middle-class status, Mexican American women must rely on their work for survival. Next, Nazli Kibria discovers wide-ranging class differentiation in how Bangladeshi women workers view and experience their income and their bargaining power. Finally, research by Elizabeth Higginbotham and Lynn Weber raises intriguing questions about the role of the family in the upward mobility of Black and White professional women.

30

(M)Other Love

Culture, Scarcity, and Maternal Thinking

NANCY SCHEPER-HUGHES

*Maternal practices begin in love, a love which for most women is
as intense, confusing, ambivalent, poignantly sweet as any they will
experience.*

Sara Ruddick (1980:344)

... The subject of my study is love and death on the Alto do Cruzeiro, specifically *mother* love and *child* death. It is about the meanings and effects of deprivation, loss, and abandonment on the ability to love, nurture, trust, and have and keep faith in the broadest senses of these terms. It treats the individual and the personal as well as the collective and cultural dimensions of maternal practices in an environment hostile to the survival and well-being of mothers and infants. I argue that a high expectancy of child death is a powerful shaper of maternal thinking and practice as evidenced, in particular, in delayed attachment to infants sometimes thought of as temporary household "visitors." This detachment can be mortal at times, contributing to the severe neglect of certain infants and to a "failure" to mourn the death of very young babies. I am *not* arguing that mother love, as we understand it, is deficient or absent in this threatened little human community but rather that its life history, its course, is different, shaped by overwhelming economic and cultural constraints. And so I trace the gradual unfolding of maternal love and attentive, "holding" care once the risk of loss (through chaotic and unpredictable early death) seems to have passed. This discussion is embedded in an examination of the cultural construction of emotions, and it attempts to overcome the distinctions between "natural" and "socialized" affects, between "deep" private feelings and "superficial" public sentiments, between conscious and unconscious emotional expressions. In its attempts to show how emotion is shaped by political and economic context as well as by culture, this discussion can be understood as a "political economy" of the emotions....

Mother love is anything *other* than natural and instead represents a matrix of images, meanings, sentiments, and practices that are everywhere socially and culturally produced. In place of a poetics of motherhood, I refer to the pragmatics of motherhood, for, to paraphrase Marx, these shantytown women create their own culture, but they do not create it just as they please or under circumstances chosen by themselves....

What I discovered while working as a medic in the Alto do Cruzeiro during the 1960s was that while it was possible, and hardly difficult, to rescue infants and toddlers from premature death from diarrhea and dehydration by using a simple sugar, salt, and water solution (even bottled Coca-Cola worked fine in a pinch), it was more difficult to enlist mothers themselves in the rescue of a child they perceived as ill-fated for life or as better off dead. More difficult still was to coax some desperate young mothers to take back into the bosom of the family a baby they had already come to think of as a little winged angel, a fragile bird, or a household guest or visitor more than as a permanent family member. And so Alto babies "successfully" rescued and treated in the hospital rehydration clinic or in the creche and returned home were sometimes dead before I had the chance to make a follow-up house call. Eventually I learned to inquire warily before intervening: "Dona Maria, do you think we should try to save this child?" or, even more boldly, "Dona Auxiliadora, is this a child worth keeping?" And if the answer was no, as it sometimes was, I learned to keep my distance.

Later, I learned that the high expectancy of death and the ability to face death with stoicism and equanimity produced patterns of nurturing that differentiated those infants thought of as "thrivers" and as "keepers" from those thought of as born "already wanting to die." The survivors and keepers were nurtured, while the stigmatized or "doomed" infants were allowed to die *à míngua,* "of neglect." Mothers sometimes stepped back and allowed nature to take its course. This pattern I first (and rather unfortunately) labeled "ethnoeugenic selective neglect." Today I simply call it "mortal neglect." Both are unhappy terms, and it is little wonder that some critics have been offended by what they saw as a lapse in cultural relativism or as a failure of solidarity with my female "subjects." An earlier notion of "benign neglect" perhaps comes closer to the women's own perceptions of their actions. Nevertheless, translated to the North American context, "benign neglect" conjures up images of unkempt and unsupervised, yet otherwise happy and carefree, older street urchins riding subway trains on hot summer nights in New York City. The mortally neglected infants and babies I am referring to here are often (although not always) prettily kept: washed, such hair as they have combed, and their emaciated little bodies dusted with sweet-smelling talcum powders. When they die, they usually do so with candles propped up in tiny waxen hands to light their way to the afterlife. At least some of these little "angels" have been freely "offered up" to Jesus and His Mother, although "returned" to whence they came is closer to the popular idiom....

LORDES AND ZEZINHO: THE AMBIGUITIES OF MOTHER LOVE

In 1966 I was called on for a second time to help Lordes, my young neighbor, deliver a child, this one a fair and robust little tyke with a lusty cry. But while Lordes showed great interest in the newborn, she ignored Zé, who spent his days miserably curled up in a fetal position and lying on a piece of urine-soaked cardboard beneath his mother's hammock. The days passed and with Lordes's limited energy and attention given over to the newborn, Zezinho's days seemed numbered. I finally decided to intervene. In taking Zé away from Lordes and bringing him to the relative safety of the creche, I repeated the words that Alto women often used when deciding to rescue a *criança condenada* (condemned child) from a relative or neighbor. "Give me that child," I said, "for he'll never escape death in your house!" Lordes did not protest, but the creche mothers laughed at my efforts on behalf of such a hopeless case. Zezinho himself resisted the rescue with a perversity matching my own. He refused to eat, and he wailed pitifully whenever anyone approached him. The creche mothers advised to leave Zezinho alone. They said that they had seen many babies like this one, and "if a baby *wants* to die, it *will* die." There was no sense in frustrating him so, for here was a child who was completely "lifeless," without any "fight" at all. His eyes were already sinking to the back of his head, a sign that he had already begun his journey into the next life. It was very wrong, the creche mothers warned, to fight with death.

Their philosophy was alien to me, and I continued to do battle with the boy, who finally succumbed: he began to eat, although he never did more than pick at his food with lack of interest. Indeed, it did seem that Zé had no *gosto,* no "taste" for life. As he gained a few kilos, Zé's huge head finally had something to balance on. His wispy, light hair began to grow in, and his funny, wizened, old man face grew younger once his first two teeth (long imprisoned in shrunken gums) erupted. Gradually, too, Zezinho developed an odd and ambivalent attachment to his surrogate mother, who, when frustrated, was known to angrily force-feed him. Then the power struggle was on in earnest; once when Zé spit his *mingau* in my face, I turned him over and swatted him soundly on his skinny, leathery backside. He wouldn't even give the satisfaction of crying. Throughout all, Zé's legs remained weak and bowed, and long before he could stand upright, he would drag them behind him in a funny sort of hand crawl. Once he became accustomed to it, Zé liked being held, and he would wrap his spindly arms tightly around my neck and his legs around my waist. He reminded one of a frightened Brazilian spider monkey. His anger at being loosed from that uncomfortable, stranglehold position was formidable. Zé even learned to smile, although it more resembled a pained grimace. Withal, I was proud of my "success" and of proving the creche mothers wrong. Zé *would* live after all!

There were many other little ones in the creche like Zezinho, but none had arrived quite so wasted as he, and none ever engaged me in quite the same way. But as the time approached to return Zé to his mother, my first doubts began to surface. Could it be true, as the creche mothers hinted, that Zé would never be "quite right," that he would always live in the shadows "looking" for death, a death I had tricked once but would be unable to forestall forever? Such "fatalistic" sentiments were not limited to the creche mothers by any means. A visiting pediatrician from the American Midwest took a dim view of the creche. At first I could not understand his negative reactions. What could be wrong? Each of the thirty-some creche babies wore hand-laundered cotton diapers with the monogram UPAC stitched onto each. There were handmade canvas cot-cribs and even a playpen donated by the German sisters of the local convent. In the midst of the tour of the facilities, the doctor turned away and wearily rested his head on his elbow against the wall. "What do you think you are doing?" he asked.

I had to shake myself out of my own accommodation to see what the American pediatrician was noting: that the diapers, so white from having been beaten against stones and bleached by the sun to sterilize them, were covering fleshless little bottoms. The high point of the day was the weighing-in ritual, and we would cheer when a ten-month-old would weigh in at a fraction over his "normal" six or seven kilos: *Gordinho* [fatty]!" or "*Guloso* [greedy]," we would say in mocking jest but also in encouragement. The "toddlers" in their playpens sat on their mats passively, without crying but also without playing. They moved themselves away from the brightly colored plastic toys, unfamiliar objects altogether. The creche had something of the grotesque about it, for it was a child care center, a place where healthy, active babies should have been howling and laughing and fighting among themselves. From the visiting doctor's clinical perspective, virtually all the creche babies were seriously physically and "developmentally delayed" and likely to remain so, carrying their early damage into what could only become highly compromised adult lives.

What *was* I doing, indeed? Could Zé ever be "right" again? Could he develop normally after the traumas he had been through? Worse, perhaps, were the traumas yet to come, as I would soon be returning him to Lordes in her miserable lean-to on the trash-littered Vultures' Path. Would he have been better off dead after all that I had put him through? And what of Lordes? Was this fair to her? She barely had enough to sustain herself and her newborn. But Lordes did agree to take Zezinho back, and she seemed more interested in him now that he looked a bit more human than spider monkey. Meanwhile, my own interest in the child began to wane. I was beginning to "let go." By this time I was becoming better socialized to Alto life. Never again would I put so much effort where the odds were so poor.

When I returned to Bom Jesus and the Alto in 1982 among the women who formed my original research sample was Lordes, no longer living in her lean-to but still in desperate straits and still fighting to put together some semblance of a life for her five living children, the oldest of whom was Zé, now a young man of seventeen. Zé struck me as a slight, quiet, reserved young man with an ironic, inward-turning smile and a droll sense of humor. He had long, thin, yet obviously strong, arms; I could see that they had always served him well, compensating for legs still somewhat bowed. Much was made of my reunion with Lordes and Zé, and the story was told again and again of how I had whisked Zé away from Lordes when he was all but given up for dead and had force-fed him like a fiesta turkey. Zé laughed the hardest of all at these "survivor tales" and at his own near-miss with death at the hands of an "indifferent" mother who often forgot to feed and bathe him. Zé and his mother obviously enjoyed a close and affectionate relationship, and while we spoke, Zé draped his arm protectively around his little mother's shoulders. There was no bitterness or resentment, and when I asked Zé alone and in private who had been his best friend in life, the one person he could always count on for support, he took a long drag on his cigarette and replied without a trace of irony, "Mãezinha [my little mother], of course! "For her part, Lordes gave "homage" to her son as her *filho eleito,* her "elect," or favorite, son, her "arms and legs," she called him, more important to her than the shadowy, older man with whom she was then living and more beloved than any other of her living children. . . .

OUR LADY OF SORROWS

Mother, behold your Son; Son, behold your Mother.
John 19:25

. . . On my next return to Bom Jesus in 1987 I was told the news immediately: "Go find Lordes—she has suffered a terrible tragedy. She is mad with grief." I found Lordes at home disconsolate,

plunged into a profound mourning. With tears coursing freely down her suddenly, prematurely aged cheeks, Lordes explained that her favorite son, "her arms and legs," had been brutally murdered on the night of the feast of São Pedro by his lover's ex-husband. Zé had been fooled; he never knew that his girlfriend had a husband. Lordes struck her breast in grief.

"If only my Zé were alive today, my life would not be one of suffering and misery. Not one of my other children turned out like him. On the day he died he left my house filled with enough groceries for a month. It was as if he knew he would be leaving me. I couldn't eat for weeks after the murder, and it pained me to look at all the food he had left me: yams, manioc, pimientos, beans. . . . These other wretched children of mine, they only know how to drive me crazy by asking for things. As soon as Zé was old enough to work, he said to me, 'Little Mama, now you are free. You will never have to worry again. You won't have to depend on some worthless bum to feed and protect you. I will see that you always have enough to eat and a bed to sleep on. I will be your protector.' And he was! He was like a mother to me! He never forgot me, even after he found a woman of his own. How many mothers can say that about their son?". . .

MOTHER LOVE AND CHILD DEATH

Love is always ambivalent and dangerous. Why should we think that it is any less so between a mother and her children? And yet it has been the fate of mothers throughout history to appear in strange and distorted forms. Mothers are sometimes portrayed as larger than life, as all-powerful, and sometimes as all-destructive. Or mothers are represented as powerless, helplessly dependent, and angelic. Historians, anthropologists, philosophers, and the "public" at large are influenced by old cultural myths and stereotypes about childhood innocence and maternal affection as well as their opposites. The "terrible" power attributed to mothers is based on the perception that the infant cannot survive for very long without considerable nurturing love and care, and normally that has been the responsibility of mothers. The infant's life is a vulnerable thing and depends to a great extent on the mother's good will. Sara Ruddick has captured the contradictions well in noting that mothers, while so totally in control of the lives and well-being of their infants and small babies, are themselves under the dominion and control of others, usually of men. Simultaneously powerful and powerless, it is no wonder that artists, scholars, and psychoanalysts can never seem to agree whether "mother" was the primary *agent* or the primary *victim* of various domestic tragedies. And so myths of a savagely protective "maternal instinct" compete at various times and places with the myth of the equally powerful, devouring, "infanticidal" mother.

Whenever we try to pierce the meanings of lives very different from our own, we face two interpretive risks. On the one hand, we may be tempted to attribute our own ways of thinking and feeling to "other" mothers. Any suggestion of radically different existential premises (such as those, for example, that guide selective neglect in Northeast Brazil) is rejected out of hand as impossible, unthinkable. To describe some poor women as aiding and abetting the deaths of certain of their infants can only be seen as "victim blaming." But the alternative is to cast women as passive "victims" of their fate, as powerless, without will, agency, or subjectivity. Part of the difficulty lies in the confusion between *causality* and *blame*. There must be a way to look dispassionately at the problem of child survival and conclude that a child died from mortal neglect, even at her or his mother's own hands, without also blaming the mother—that is, without holding her personally and morally accountable.

Related to this is the persistent idea that mothers, *all* mothers, *must* feel grief, a "depth of sorrow," in reaction to infant death. Women who do not show an "appropriate" grief are judged by psychoanalytic fiat to be "repressing" their "natural" maternal sentiments, to be covering them over with a culturally prescribed but *superficial* stoicism, or they may be seen as emotionally ravaged, "numbed" by grief, and traumatized by shock. But it was indifference, not numbing or shock, that I often observed. The traumatized individual does not shrug her shoulders and say cheerily, "It's better the baby should die than either you or me" and quickly become pregnant because little babies are interchangeable and easily replaced.

One may experience discomfort in the face of profound human differences, some of which challenge our cultural notions of the "normal" and the "ethical." But to attribute "sameness" across vast social, economic, and cultural divides is a serious error for the anthropologist, who must begin, although cautiously, from a respectful assumption of difference. Here we want to direct our gaze to the ways of seeing, thinking, and feeling that represent these women's experience of being-in-the-world and, as faithful Catholics, their being-beyond-this-world. This means avoiding the temptation of all "essentializing" and "universalizing" discourses, whether they originate in the biomedical and psychological sciences or in philosophical or cultural feminism.

On the other hand, there is the danger of over-distancing ourselves from those we are trying to understand so as to suggest that there is no common ground at all. This is found in some deconstructionist and postmodernist theories of gender politics where the categories of "woman" and "mother" are rigorously problematized and deconstructed out of existence. Less radically, one can see the "overproduction of difference" in the writings of those modern social historians who have suggested that mother love is an invention of the "modern" world and that until very recently in human history women scarcely knew how to love their children. The language of these historians can be extreme and off-putting. . . .

So perhaps there is a middle ground between the two rather extreme approaches to mother love—the sentimentalized maternal "poetics" and the mindlessly automatic "maternal bonding" theorists, on the one hand, and the "absence of love" theorists, on the other. Between these is the reality of maternal thinking and practice grounded in specific historical and cultural realities and bounded by different economic and demographic constraints. Maternal practices always begin as a response to "the historical reality of a biological child in a particular social world."

Seen in the context of a particular social world and historical reality, the story of Lordes and Zé conveys the ambiguities of mothering on the Alto do Cruzeiro where mortal selective neglect and intense maternal attachment coexist. Alto mothers, like Lordes, do sometimes turn away from certain ill-fated babies and abandon them to an early death in which their own neglect sometimes plays a final and definitive part. But maternal indifference does not always lead to death, and should an infant or a toddler show, like Zé, that he has a hidden "talent" for life, his mother may greet the "doomed" child's surprising turnabout with grateful joy and deep and lasting affection. And these same "neglectful" mothers can exclaim, like Lordes, that they live only for their grown children, some of whom only survived in spite of them. In so doing, these women are neither hypocritical nor self-delusional. . . .

HOLDING ON AND LETTING GO—
THE PRAGMATICS OF MOTHERING

. . . Sara Ruddick has suggested that although some economic and social conditions, such as extreme poverty or social isolation, can erode maternal affection, they do not kill that love. Her understanding of mother love carried resonances of Winnicott as she referred to the metaphysical attitude of "holding"—holding *on,* holding *up,* holding *close,* holding *dear.* Maternal thinking, she suggested, begins with a stance of protectiveness, "an attitude governed, above all, by the priority of keeping over acquiring, of conserving the fragile, of maintaining whatever is at hand and necessary to the child's life" (1980:350). . . .

But what of mothering in an environment like the Alto where the risks to child health and safety

are legion, so many, in fact, that mothers must necessarily concede to a certain "humility," even "passivity," toward a world that is in so many respects beyond their control? Among the mothers of the Alto maternal thinking and practice are often guided by another, quite opposite metaphysical stance, one that can be called, in light of the women's own choice of metaphors, "letting go." If holding has the double connotations of loving, maternal care (to have and to hold), on the one hand, and of retentive, restraining holding on or holding back, on the other, letting go also has a double valence. In its most negative sense, letting go can be thought of as letting loose destructive maternal power, as in child-battering and other forms of physical abuse. But malicious child abuse is extremely rare on the Alto do Cruzeiro, where babies and young children are often idealized as "innocents" who should not be physically disciplined or restrained. But letting go in the form of abandonment is not uncommon on the Alto, and the occasional neonate is found from time to time where he or she was let go in a backyard rubbish heap. And the abandonment of newborns by their overwrought mothers is so common in the maternity wing of the local hospital that a copybook is kept hanging on a cord just outside the nursery in which the data on abandonments and informal adoptions are recorded. There is no stigma in leaving an infant behind, although the birth mother is required by the nursing staff to remain in the hospital until a prospective adoptive parent can be found. The mother rarely has to wait more than a few days. Once an adoptive parent or couple appears—and there is no regulation of the process save for the few instances in which the nurse on duty takes a personal dislike to a potential adoptive parent—the birth mother need only sign her name (or affix her mark) after a statement declaring that she has freely given up her infant son or daughter born on such a date and time at the hospital. The adoptive parent is free to register the infant as her own birth child at the *cartório civil,* and most do so. In 1986 twelve newborns, eight males and four females, were left behind in the nursery by their mothers. In 1987 ten newborns, seven girls and three boys, were abandoned. Although all the birth mothers were poor, some of them wretchedly so, and only six could sign their own names, as many of them were older (thirty and older) as younger mothers (sixteen to twenty-nine), and almost an equal number were living with a spouse or lover as those who reported themselves to be "single," "separated," or "abandoned."

But here I want to reflect on another meaning of letting go. Among the women of the Alto to let go also implies a metaphysical stance of calm and reasonable resignation to events that cannot easily be changed or overcome. This is expressed in the women's frequent exhorting of each other, especially in times of great difficulty, to "let it go," "let it pass," "let it be": *Deixe, menina—deixe isso, deixe as coisas como são para ver como ficam.* In other words, "Leave it be, girl; leave things alone, and see how they turn out for themselves."... It is present each time Alto mothers say that their infants are "like birds," nervous and flighty creatures that are here today and gone tomorrow. A perfectly good mother can in good faith and with a clear conscience let go of an infant who "wants" to escape life, just as one may set free into the heavens a miserable wild bird that was beating its wings against its cage.

"What does it mean, *really,*" I asked Doralice, an older woman of the Alto who often intervenes in poor households to rescue young and vulnerable mothers and their threatened infants, "to say that infants are like birds?"

"It means that...well, there is another expression you should know first. It is that all of us, our lives, are like burning candles. At any moment we can suddenly 'go out without warning [*a qualquer momento apaga*].' But for the infant this is even more so. The grownup, the adult, is very attached to life. One doesn't want to leave it with ease or without a struggle. But infants are not so connected, and their light can be extinguished very easily. As far as they are concerned, *tanto faz,* alive or dead, it makes no real difference to them. There is not that strong *vontade* to live that marks the big person. And so we say that 'infants are like little birds,' here one moment, flying off the next. That is how we like to think about their deaths, too. We like to imagine our dead infants as little winged angels flying off to heaven to gather noisily around the thrones of Jesus and Mary, bringing pleasure to them and hope for us on earth."

And so a good part of learning how to mother on the Alto includes knowing when to let go of a child who shows that he wants to die. The other part is knowing just when it is safe to let oneself go enough to love a child, to trust him or her to be willing to enter the *luta* that is this life on earth....

NOTES

1. Ruddick, Sarah. 1980. "Maternal Thinking." *Feminist Studies* 6:342–364.

31

The Meaning of Motherhood in Black Culture
and Black Mother–Daughter Relationships

PATRICIA HILL COLLINS

"What did your mother teach you about men?" is a question I often ask students in my courses on African-American women. "Go to school first and get a good education—don't get too serious too young," "Make sure you look around and that you can take care of yourself before you settle down," and "Don't trust them, want more for yourself than just a man," are typical responses from Black women. My students share stories of how their mothers encouraged them to cultivate satisfying relationships with Black men while anticipating disappointments, to desire marriage while planning viable alternatives, to become mothers only when fully prepared to do so. But, above all, they stress their mothers' insistence on being self-reliant and resourceful.

These daughters, of various ages and from diverse social class backgrounds, family structures and geographic regions, had somehow received strikingly similar messages about Black womanhood. Even though their mothers employed diverse teaching strategies, these Black daughters had all been exposed to common themes about the meaning of womanhood in Black culture.[1]

This essay explores the relationship between the meaning of motherhood in African-American culture and Black mother–daughter relationships by addressing three primary questions. First, how have competing perspectives about motherhood intersected to produce a distinctly Afrocentric ideology of motherhood? Second, what are the enduring themes that characterize this Afrocentric ideology of motherhood? Finally, what effect might this

Afrocentric ideology of motherhood have on Black mother–daughter relationships?

COMPETING PERSPECTIVES
ON MOTHERHOOD

The Dominant Perspective: Eurocentric Views of White Motherhood

The cult of true womanhood, with its emphasis on motherhood as woman's highest calling, has long held a special place in the gender symbolism of White Americans. From this perspective, women's activities should be confined to the care of children, the nurturing of a husband, and the maintenance of the household. By managing this separate domestic sphere, women gain social influence through their roles as mothers, transmitters of culture, and parents for the next generations.[2]

While substantial numbers of White women have benefited from the protections of White patriarchy provided by the dominant ideology, White women themselves have recently challenged its tenets. On one pole lies a cluster of women, the traditionalists, who aim to retain the centrality of motherhood in women's lives. For traditionalists, differentiating between the experience of motherhood, which for them has been quite satisfying, and motherhood as an institution central in reproducing gender inequality, has proved difficult. The other pole is occupied by women who advocate dismantling motherhood as an institution. They suggest that compulsory motherhood be outlawed and that the experience of motherhood can only be satisfying if women can also choose not to be mothers. Arrayed between these dichotomous positions are women who argue for an expanded, but not necessarily different, role for women—women can be mothers as long as they are not *just* mothers.[3]

Three themes implicit in White perspectives on motherhood are particularly problematic for Black women and others outside of this debate. First, the assumption that mothering occurs within the confines of a private, nuclear family household where the mother has almost total responsibility for child-rearing is less applicable to Black families. While the ideal of the cult of true womanhood has been held up to Black women for emulation, racial oppression has denied Black families sufficient resources to support private, nuclear family households. Second, strict sex-role segregation, with separate male and female spheres of influence within the family, has been less commonly found in African-American families than in White middle-class ones. Finally, the assumption that motherhood and economic dependency on men are linked and that to be a "good" mother one must stay at home, making motherhood a full-time "occupation," is similarly uncharacteristic of African-American families.[4]

Even though selected groups of White women are challenging the cult of true womanhood and its accompanying definition of motherhood, the dominant ideology remains powerful. As long as these approaches remain prominent in scholarly and popular discourse, Eurocentric views of White motherhood will continue to affect Black women's lives.

Eurocentric Views of Black Motherhood

Eurocentric perspectives on Black motherhood revolve around two interdependent images that together define Black women's roles in White and in African-American families. The first image is that of the Mammy, the faithful, devoted domestic servant. Like one of the family, Mammy conscientiously "mothers" her White children, caring for them and loving them as if they were her own.

Mammy is the ideal Black mother for she recognizes her place. She is paid next to nothing and yet cheerfully accepts her inferior status. But when she enters her own home, this same Mammy is transformed into the second image, the too-strong matriarch who raises weak sons and "unnaturally superior" daughters.[5] When she protests, she is labeled aggressive and unfeminine, yet if she remains silent, she is rendered invisible.

The task of debunking Mammy by analyzing Black women's roles as exploited domestic workers and challenging the matriarchy thesis by demonstrating that Black women do not wield disproportionate power in African-American families has long preoccupied African-American scholars.[6] But an equally telling critique concerns uncovering the functions of these images and their role in explaining Black women's subordination in systems of race, class, and gentler oppression. As Mae King points out, White definitions of Black motherhood foster the dominant group's exploitation of Black women by blaming Black women for their characteristic reactions to their own subordination.[7] For example, while the stay-at-home mother has been held up to all women as the ideal, African-American women have been compelled to work outside the home, typically in a very narrow range of occupations. Even though Black women were forced to become domestic servants and be strong figures in Black households, labeling them Mammys and matriarchs denigrates Black women. Without a countervailing Afrocentric ideology of motherhood, White perspectives on both White and African-American motherhood place Black women in a no-win situation. Adhering to these standards brings the danger of the lowered self-esteem of internalized oppression, one that, if passed on from mother to daughter, provides a powerful mechanism for controlling African-American communities.

African Perspectives on Motherhood

One concept that has been constant throughout the history of African societies is the centrality of motherhood in religions, philosophies, and social institutions. As Barbara Christian points out, "There is no doubt that motherhood is for most African people symbolic of creativity and continuity."[8]

Cross-cultural research on motherhood in African societies appears to support Christian's claim.[9] West African sociologist Christine Oppong suggests that the Western notion of equating household with family be abandoned because it obscures women's family roles in African cultures.[10] While the archetypal White, middle-class nuclear family conceptualizes family life as being divided into two oppositional spheres—the "male" sphere of economic providing and the "female" sphere of affective nurturing—this type of rigid sex role segregation was not part of the West African tradition. Mothering was not a privatized nurturing "occupation" reserved for biological mothers, and the economic support of children was not the exclusive responsibility of men. Instead, for African women, emotional care for children and providing for their physical survival were interwoven as interdependent, complementary dimensions of motherhood.

In spite of variations among societies, a strong case has been made that West African women occupy influential roles in African family networks.[11] First, since they are not dependent on males for economic support and provide much of their own and their children's economic support, women are structurally central to families.[12] Second, the image of the mother is one that is culturally elaborated and valued across diverse West African societies. Continuing the lineage is essential in West African philosophies, and motherhood is similarly valued.[13] Finally, while the biological mother-child bond is valued, child care was a collective responsibility, a situation fostering cooperative, age-stratified, woman-centered "mothering" networks.

Recent research by Africanists suggests that much more of this African heritage was retained among African-Americans than had previously been thought. The retention of West African culture as a culture of resistance offered enslaved Africans and exploited African-Americans alternative ideologies to those advanced by dominant groups. Central to these reinterpretations of African-American institutions and culture is a reconceptualization of Black family life and the role of women in Black family networks.[14] West African perspectives may have been combined with the changing political and economic situations framing African-American communities to produce certain enduring themes characterizing an Afrocentric ideology of motherhood.

ENDURING THEMES OF AN AFROCENTRIC IDEALOGY OF MOTHERHOOD

An Afrocentric ideology of motherhood must reconcile the competing worldviews of these three conflicting perspectives of motherhood. An ongoing tension exists between efforts to mold the institution of Black motherhood for the benefit of the dominant group and efforts by Black women to define and value their own experiences with motherhood. This tension leads to a continuum of responses. For those women who either aspire to the cult of true womanhood without having the resources to support such a lifestyle, or who believe the stereotypical analyses of themselves as dominating matriarchs, motherhood can be oppressive. But the experience of motherhood can provide Black women with a base of self-actualization, status in the Black community, and a reason for social activism. These alleged contradictions can exist side by side in African-American communities, families, and even within individual women.

Embedded in these changing relationships are four enduring themes that I contend characterize an Afrocentric ideology of motherhood. Just as the issues facing enslaved African mothers were quite different from those currently facing poor Black women in inner cities, for any given historical moment the actual institutional forms that these themes take depend on the severity of oppression and Black women's resources for resistance.

Bloodmothers, Othermothers, and Women-Centered Networks

In African-American communities, the boundaries distinguishing biological mothers of children from other women who care for children are often fluid and changing. Biological mothers or bloodmothers are expected to care for their children. But African and African-American communities have also recognized that vesting one person with full responsibility for mothering a child may not be wise or possible. As a result, "othermothers," women who assist bloodmothers by sharing mothering responsibilities, traditionally have been central to the institution of Black motherhood.[15]

The centrality of women in African-American extended families is well known.[16] Organized, resilient, women-centered networks of bloodmothers and othermothers are key to this centrality. Grandmothers, sisters, aunts, or cousins acted as othermothers by taking on childcare responsibilities for each other's children. When needed, temporary child care arrangements turned into long-term care or informal adoption.[17]

In African-American communities, these women-centered networks of community-based childcare often extend beyond the boundaries of biologically related extended families to support "fictive kin."[18] Civil rights activist Ella Baker describes how informal adoption by othermothers functioned in the Southern, rural community of her childhood:

> My aunt who had thirteen children of her own raised three more. She had become a midwife, and a child was born who was covered with sores. Nobody was particularly wanting the child, so she took the child and raised him...and another mother decided she didn't want to be bothered with two children. So my aunt took one and raised him...they were part of the family.[19]

Even when relationships were not between kin or fictive kin, African-American community norms were such that neighbors cared for each other's children. In the following passage, Sara Brooks, a Southern domestic worker, describes the importance of the community-based childcare that a neighbor offered her daughter. In doing so, she also shows how the African-American cultural value placed on cooperative childcare found institutional support in the adverse conditions under which so many Black women mothered:

> She kept Vivian and she didn't charge me nothin either. You see, people used to look after each other, but now it's not that way. I reckon it's because we all was poor, and I guess they put theirself in the place of the person that they was helpin.[20]

Othermothers were key not only in supporting children but also in supporting bloodmothers who, for whatever reason, were ill-prepared or had little desire to care for their children. Given the pressures from the larger political economy, the emphasis placed on community-based childcare and the respect given to othermothers who assume the responsibilities of childcare have served a critical function in African-American communities. Children orphaned by sale or death of their parents under slavery, children conceived through rape, children of young mothers, children born into extreme poverty, or children who for other reasons have been rejected by their bloodmothers have all been supported by othermothers who, like Ella Baker's aunt, took in additional children, even when they had enough of their own.

Providing as Part of Mothering

The work done by African-American women in providing the economic resources essential to Black family well-being affects motherhood in a contradictory fashion. On the one hand, African-American women have long integrated their activities as economic providers into their mothering relationships. In contrast to the cult of true womanhood, in which work is defined as being in opposition to and incompatible with motherhood, work for Black women has been an important and valued dimension of Afrocentric definitions of Black motherhood. On the other hand, African-

American women's experiences as mothers under oppression were such that the type and purpose of work Black women were forced to do had a great impact on the type of mothering relationships bloodmothers and othermothers had with Black children.

While slavery both disrupted West African family patterns and exposed enslaved Africans to the gender ideologies and practices of slaveowners, it simultaneously made it impossible, had they wanted to do so, for enslaved Africans to implement slaveowner's ideologies. Thus, the separate spheres of providing as a male domain and affective nurturing as a female domain did not develop within African-American families.[21] Providing for Black children's physical survival and attending to their affective, emotional needs continued as interdependent dimensions of an Afrocentric ideology of motherhood. However, by changing the conditions under which Black women worked and the purpose of the work itself, slavery introduced the problem of how best to continue traditional Afrocentric values under oppressive conditions. Institutions of community-based childcare, informal adoption, greater reliance on othermothers, all emerge as adaptations to the exigencies of combining exploitative work with nurturing children.

In spite of the change in political status brought on by emancipation, the majority of African-American women remained exploited agricultural workers. However, their placement in Southern political economics allowed them to combine childcare with field labor. Sara Brooks describes how strong the links between providing and caring for others were for her:

> When I was about nine I was nursin my sister Sally—I'm about seven or eight years older than Sally. And when I would put her to sleep, instead of me goin somewhere and sit down and play, I'd get my little old hoe and get out there and work right in the field around the house.[22]

Black women's shift from Southern agriculture to domestic work in Southern and Northern towns and cities represented a change in the type of work done, but not in the meaning of work to women and their families. Whether they wanted to or not, the majority of African-American women had to work and could not afford the luxury of motherhood as a noneconomically productive, female "occupation."

Community Othermothers and Social Activism

Black women's experiences as othermothers have provided a foundation for Black women's social activism. Black women's feelings of responsibility for nurturing the children in their own extended family networks have stimulated a more generalized ethic of care where Black women feel accountable to all the Black community's children.

This notion of Black women as community othermothers for all Black children traditionally allowed Black women to treat biologically unrelated children as if they were members of their own families. For example, sociologist Karen Fields describes how her grandmother, Mamie Garvin Fields, draws on her power as a community othermother when dealing with unfamiliar children.

> She will say to a child on the street who looks up to no good, picking out a name at random, "Aren't you Miz Pinckney's boy?" in that same reproving tone. If the reply is, "No, ma'am, my mother is Miz Gadsden," whatever threat there was dissipates.[23]

The use of family language in referring to members of the Black community also illustrates this dimension of Black motherhood. For example, Mamie Garvin Fields describes how she became active in surveying the poor housing conditions of Black people in Charleston.

> I was one of the volunteers they got to make a survey of the places where we were paying extortious rents for indescribable property. I said "we," although it wasn't Bob and me. We had our own home, and so did many of the Federated Women. Yet we still fell like it really was "we" living in those terrible places, and it was up to us to do something about them.[24]

To take another example, while describing her increasingly successful efforts to teach a boy who had given other teachers problems, my daughter's kindergarten teacher stated, "You know how it can be—the majority of children in the learning disabled classes are *our children*. I know he didn't belong there, so I volunteered to take him." In these statements, both women invoke the language of family to describe the ties that bind them as Black women to their responsibilities to other members of the Black community as family.

Sociologist Cheryl Gilkes suggests that community othermother relationships are sometimes behind Black women's decisions to become community activists.[25] Gilkes notes that many of the Black women community activists in her study became involved in community organizing in response to the needs of their own children and of those in their communities. The following comment is typical of how many of the Black women in Gilkes' study relate to Black children: "There were a lot of summer programs springing up for kids, but they were exclusive . . . and I found that most of *our kids* (emphasis mine) were excluded."[26] For many women, what began as the daily expression of their obligations as community othermothers, as was the case for the kindergarten teacher, developed into full-fledged roles as community leaders.

Motherhood as a Symbol of Power

Motherhood, whether bloodmother, othermother, or community othermother, can be invoked by Black women as a symbol of power. A substantial portion of Black women's status in African-American communities stems not only from their roles as mothers in their own families but from their contributions as community othermothers to Black community development as well.

The specific contributions Black women make in nurturing Black community development form the basis of community-based power. Community othermothers work on behalf of the Black community by trying, in the words of late nine-

teenth century Black feminists, to "uplift the race," so that vulnerable members of the community would be able to attain the self-reliance and independence so desperately needed for Black community development under oppressive conditions. This is the type of power many African-Americans have in mind when they describe the "strong, Black women" they see around them in traditional African-American communities.

When older Black women invoke this community othermother status, its results can be quite striking. Karen Fields recounts an incident described to her by her grandmother illustrating how women can exert power as community othermothers:

> One night . . . as Grandmother sat crocheting alone at about two in the morning, a young man walked into the living room carrying the portable TV from upstairs. She said, "Who are you looking for this time of night?" As Grandmother [described] the incident to me over the phone, I could hear a tone of voice that I know well. It said, "Nice boys don't do that." So I imagine the burglar heard his own mother or grandmother at that moment. He joined in the familial game just created: "Well, he told me that I could borrow it." "Who told you?" "John." "Um um, no John lives here. You got the wrong house."[27]

After this dialogue, the teenager turned around, went back upstairs and returned the television.

In local Black communities, specific Black women are widely recognized as powerful figures, primarily because of their contributions to the community's well-being through their roles as community othermothers. Sociologist Charles Johnson describes the behavior of an elderly Black woman at a church service in rural Alabama of the 1930s. Even though she was not on the program, the woman stood up to speak. The master of ceremonies rang for her to sit down but she refused to do so claiming, "I am the mother of this church, and I will say what I please." The master of ceremonies later explained to the congregation—"Brothers, I know you all honor Sister Moore. Course our time is short but she has acted as a mother to me . . . Any time old folks get up I give way to them."[28]

IMPLICATIONS FOR BLACK MOTHER–DAUGHTER RELATIONSHIPS

In her discussion of the sex-role socialization of Black girls, Pamela Reid identifies two complementary approaches in understanding Black mother-daughter relationships.[29] The first, psychoanalytic theory, examines the role of parents in the establishment of personality and social behavior. This theory argues that the development of feminine behavior results from the girls' identification with adult female role models. This approach emphasizes how an Afrocentric ideology of motherhood is actualized through Black mothers' activities as role models.

The second approach, social learning theory, suggests that the rewards and punishments attached to girls' childhood experiences are central in shaping women's sex-role behavior. The kinds of behaviors that Black mothers reward and punish in their daughters are seen as key in the socialization process. This approach examines specific experiences that Black girls have while growing up that encourage them to absorb an Afrocentric ideology of motherhood.

African-American Mothers as Role Models

Feminist psychoanalytic theorists suggest that the sex-role socialization process is different for boys and girls. While boys learn maleness by rejecting femaleness via separating themselves from their mothers, girls establish feminine identities by embracing the femaleness of their mothers. Girls identify with their mothers, a sense of connection that is incorporated into the female personality. However, this mother-identification is problematic because, under patriarchy, men are more highly valued than women. Thus, while daughters identify with their mothers, they also reject them, since in patriarchal families, identifying with adult women as mothers means identifying with persons deemed inferior.[30]

While Black girls learn by identifying with their mothers, the specific female role with which Black girls identify may be quite different than that modeled by middle-class White mothers. The presence of working mothers, extended family othermothers, and powerful community othermothers offers a range of role models that challenge the tenets of the cult of true womanhood.

Moreover, since Black mothers have a distinctive relationship to White patriarchy, they may be less likely to socialize their daughters into their proscribed role as subordinates. Rather, a key part of Black girls' socialization involves incorporating the critical posture that allows Black women to cope with contradictions. For example, Black girls have long had to learn how to do domestic work while rejecting definitions of themselves as Mammies. At the same time they've had to take on strong roles in Black extended families without internalizing images of themselves as matriarchs.

In raising their daughters, Black mothers face a troubling dilemma. To ensure their daughters' physical survival, they must teach their daughters to fit into systems of oppression. For example, as a young girl in Mississippi, Black activist Ann Moody questioned why she was paid so little for the domestic work she began at age nine, why Black women domestics were sexually harassed by their White male employers, and why Whites had so much more than Blacks. But her mother refused to answer her questions and actually became angry whenever Ann Moody stepped out of her "place."[31] Black daughters are raised to expect to work, to strive for an education so that they can support themselves, and to anticipate carrying heavy responsibilities in their families and communities because these skills are essential for their own survival as well as for the survival of those for whom they will eventually be responsible.[32] And yet mothers know that if daughters fit too well into the limited opportunities offered Black women, they become willing participants in their own subordination. Mothers may have ensured their daughters' physical survival at the high cost of their emotional destruction.

On the other hand, Black daughters who offer serious challenges to oppressive situations may not physically survive. When Ann Moody became involved in civil rights activities, her mother first begged her not to participate and then told her not to come home because she feared the Whites in Moody's hometown would kill her. In spite of the dangers, many Black mothers routinely encourage their daughters to develop skills to confront oppressive conditions. Thus, learning that they will work, that education is a vehicle for advancement, can also be seen as ways of preparing Black girls to resist oppression through a variety of mothering roles. The issue is to build emotional strength, but not at the cost of physical survival.

This delicate balance between conformity and resistance is described by historian Elsa Barkley Brown as the "need to socialize me one way and at the same time to give me all the tools I needed to be something else."[33] Black daughters must learn how to survive in interlocking structures of race, class, and gender oppression while rejecting and transcending those very same structures. To develop these skills in their daughters, mothers demonstrate varying combinations of behaviors devoted to ensuring their daughters' survival—such as providing them with basic necessities and ensuring their protection in dangerous environments to helping their daughters go farther than mothers themselves were allowed to go.

The presence of othermothers in Black extended families and the modeling symbolized by community othermothers offer powerful support for the task of teaching girls to resist White perceptions of Black womanhood while appearing to conform to them. In contrast to the isolation of middle-class White mother/daughter dyads, Black women-centered extended family networks foster an early identification with a much wider range of models of Black womanhood, which can lead to a greater sense of empowerment in young Black girls.

Social Learning Theory and Black Mothering Behavior

Understanding this goal of balancing the needs of ensuring their daughters' physical survival with the vision of encouraging them to transcend the boundaries confronting them sheds some light on some of the apparent contradictions in Black mother-daughter relationships. Black mothers are often described as strong disciplinarians and overly protective parents; yet these same women manage to raise daughters who are self-reliant and assertive.[34] Professor Gloria Wade-Gayles offers an explanation for this apparent contradiction by suggesting that Black mothers "do not socialize their daughters to be passive or irrational. Quite the contrary, they socialize their daughters to be independent, strong and self-confident. Black mothers are suffocatingly protective and domineering precisely because they are determined to mold their daughters into whole and self-actualizing persons in a society that devalues Black women."[35]

Black mothers emphasize protection either by trying to shield their daughters as long as possible from the penalties attached to their race, class, and gender or by teaching them how to protect themselves in such situations. Black women's autobiographies and fiction can be read as texts revealing the multiple strategies Black mothers employ in preparing their daughters for the demands of being Black women in oppressive conditions. For example, in discussing the mother-daughter relationship in Paule Marshall's *Brown Girl, Brownstones*, Rosalie Troester catalogues some of these strategies and the impact they may have on relationships themselves:

Black mothers, particularly those with strong ties to their community, sometimes build high banks around their young daughters, isolating them from the dangers of the larger world until they are old and strong enough to function as autonomous women. Often these dikes are religious, but sometimes they are built with education, family, or the restrictions of a close-knit and homogeneous community...this isolation causes the currents between Black mothers and daughters to run deep and the relationship to be fraught with an emotional intensity often missing from the lives of women with more freedom.[36]

Black women's efforts to provide for their children also may affect the emotional intensity of Black mother–daughter relationships. As Gloria Wade-Gayles points out, "Mothers in Black women's fiction are strong and devoted... but ...they are rarely affectionate."[37] For far too many Black mothers, the demands of providing for children are so demanding that affection often must wait until the basic needs of physical survival are satisfied.

Black daughters raised by mothers grappling with hostile environments have to confront their feelings about the difference between the idealized versions of maternal love extant in popular culture and the strict, assertive mothers so central to their lives.[38] For daughters, growing up means developing a better understanding that offering physical care and protection is an act of maternal love. Ann Moody describes her growing awareness of the personal cost her mother paid as a single mother of three children employed as a domestic worker. Watching her mother sleep after the birth of another child, Moody remembers:

> *For a long time I stood there looking at her. I didn't want to wake her up. I wanted to enjoy and preserve that calm, peaceful look on her face, I wanted to think she would always be that happy...Adline and Junior were too young to feel the things I felt and know the things I knew about Mama. They couldn't remember when she and Daddy separated. They had never heard her cry at night as I had or worked and helped as I had done when we were starving.*[39]

Renita Weems's account of coming to grips with maternal desertion provides another example of a daughters efforts to understand her mother's behavior. In the following passage, Weems struggles with the difference between the stereotypical image of the super strong Black mother and her own alcoholic mother, who decided to leave her children:

> *My mother loved us. I must believe that. She worked all day in a department store bakery to buy shoes and school tablets, came home to curse out neighbors who wrongly accused her children of any impropriety (which in an apartment complex usually meant stealing), and kept her house cleaner than most sober women.*[40]

Weems concludes that her mother loved her because she provided for her to the best of her ability.

Othermothers often play central roles in defusing the emotional intensity of relationships between bloodmothers and their daughters and in helping daughters understand the Afrocentric ideology of motherhood. Weems describes the women teachers, neighbors, friends, and othermothers that she turned to for help in negotiating a difficult mother/daughter relationship. These women, she notes, "did not have the onus of providing for me, and so had the luxury of talking to me."[41]

June Jordan offers one of the most eloquent analyses of a daughter's realization of the high personal cost Black women have paid as bloodmothers and othermothers in working to provide an economic and emotional foundation for Black children. In the following passage, Jordan captures the feelings that my Black women students struggled to put into words:

> *As a child I noticed the sadness of my mother as she sat alone in the kitchen at night...Her woman's work never won permanent victories of any kind. It never enlarged the universe of her imagination or her power to influence what happened beyond the front door of our house. Her woman's work never tickled her to laugh or shout or dance. But she did raise me to respect her way of offering love and to believe that hard work is often the irreducible factor for survival, not something to avoid. Her woman's work produced a reliable home base where I could pursue the privileges of books and music. Her woman's work invented the potential for a completely different kind of work for us, the next generation of Black women: huge, rewarding hard work demanded by the huge, new ambitions that her perfect confidence in us engendered.*[42]

Jordan's words not only capture the essence of the Afrocentric ideology of motherhood so central to the well-being of countless numbers of Black women. They simultaneously point the way into the future, one where Black women face the challenge of continuing the mothering traditions painstakingly nurtured by prior generations of African-American women.

NOTES

1. The definition of culture used in this essay is taken from Leith Mullings, "Anthropological Perspectives on the Afro-American Family," *American Journal of Social Psychiatry* 6 (1986): 11–16. According to Mullings, culture is composed of "the symbols and values that create the ideological frame of reference through which people attempt to deal with the circumstances in which they find themselves" (13).

2. For analyses of the relationship of the cult of true womanhood to Black women, see Leith Mullings, "Uneven Development: Class, Race and Gender in the United States Before 1900," in *Women's Work, Development and the Division of Labor by Gender,* ed. Eleanor Leacock and Helen Safa (South Hadley, MA: Bergin & Garvey, 1986), pp. 41–57; Bonnie Thornton Dill, "Our Mothers' Grief: Racial Ethnic Women and the Maintenance of Families," Research Paper 4, Center for Research on Women (Memphis, TN: Memphis State University, 1986); and Hazel Carby, *Reconstructing Womanhood: The Emergence of the Afro-American Woman Novelist* (New York: Oxford University Press, 1987), esp. chapter 2.

3. Contrast, for example, the traditionalist analysis of Selma Fraiberg, *Every Child's Birthright: In Defense of Mothering* (New York: Basic Books, 1977) to that of Jeffner Allen, "Motherhood: The Annihilation Of Women," in *Mothering, Essays in Feminist Theory,* ed. Joyce Trebilcot (Totawa, NJ: Rowan & Allanheld, 1983). See also Adrienne Rich. *Of Woman Born: Motherhood as Experience and Institution* (New York: Norton, 1976). For an overview of how traditionalists and feminists have shaped the public policy debate on abortion, see Kristin Luker, *Abortion and the Politics of Motherhood* (Berkeley, CA: University of California, 1984).

4. Mullings, "Uneven Development"; Dill. "Our Mother's Grief"; and Carby, *Reconstructing Womanhood.* Feminist scholarship is also challenging Western notions of the family. See Barrie Thorne and Marilyn Yalom, eds., *Rethinking the Family* (New York: Longman, 1982).

5. Since Black women are no longer heavily concentrated in private domestic service, the Mammy image may be fading. In contrast, the matriarch image, popularized in Daniel Patrick Moynihan's, *The Negro Family: The Case for National Action* (Washington, D.C.: U.S. Government Printing Office, 1965), is reemerging in public debates about the feminization of poverty and the urban underclass. See Maxine Baca Zinn, "Minority Families in Crisis: The Public Discussion," Research Paper 6, Center for Research on Women (Memphis, TN: Memphis State University, 1987).

6. For an alternative analysis of the Mammy image, see Judith Rollins, *Between Women: Domestics and Their Employers* (Philadelphia: Temple University, 1985). Classic responses to the matriarchy thesis include Robert Hill, *The Strengths of Black Families* (New York: Urban League, 1972); Andrew Billingsley, *Black Families in White America* (Englewood Cliffs, NJ: Prentice-Hall, 1968); and Joyce Ladner, *Tomorrow's Tomorrow,* (Garden City, NY: Doubleday, 1971). For a recent analysis, see Linda Burnham, "Has Poverty Been Feminized in Black America?" *Black Scholar* 16 (1985): 15–24.

7. Mae King, "The Politics of Sexual Stereotypes," *Black Scholar* 4 (1973):12–23.

8. Barbara Christian, "An Angle of Seeing: Motherhood in Buchi Emecheta's *Joys of Motherhood* and Alice Walker's *Meridian,"* in *Black Feminist Criticism,* ed. Barbara Christian (New York: Pergamon, 1985), p. 214.

9. See Christine Oppong, ed., *Female and Male in West Africa* (London: Allen & Unwin, 1983); Niara Sudarkesa, "Female Employment and Family Organization in West Africa," in *The Black Woman Cross-Culturally,* ed. Filomina Chiamo Steady (Cambridge, MA: Schenkman, 1981), pp. 49-64; and Nancy Tanner, "Matrifocality in Indonesia and Africa and Among Black Americans," in *Woman, Culture, and Society,* ed. Michelle Rosaldo and Louise Lamphere (Stanford, CA: Stanford University Press, 1974), pp. 129–56.

10. Christine Oppong, "Family Structure and Women's Reproductive and Productive Roles: Some Conceptual and Methodological Issues," in *Women's Roles and Population Trends in the Third World,* ed. Richard Anker, Myra Buvinic, and Nadia Youssef (London: Croom Heim, 1982), pp. 133–50.

11. The key distinction here is that, unlike the matriarchy thesis, women play central roles in families and this centrality is seen as legitimate. In spite of this centrality, it is important not to idealize African women's family roles. For an analysis by a Black African feminist, see Awa Thiam, *Black Sisters, Speak Out: Feminism and Oppression in Black Africa* (London: Pluto, 1978).

12. Sudarkasa, "Female Employment."

13. John Mbiti, *African Religions and Philosophies* (New York: Anchor, 1969).

14. Niara Sudarkasa, "Interpreting the African Heritage in Afro-American Family Organization," in *Black Families,* ed. Harriette Pipes McAdoo (Beverly Hills, CA: Sage, 1981), pp. 37–53; and Deborah Gray White, *Ar'n't I a Woman? Female Slaves in the Plantation South* (New York: W. W. Norton, 1985).

15. The terms used in this section appear in Rosalie Riegle Troester's "Turbulence and Tenderness: Mothers, Daughters, and "Othermothers" in Paule Marshall's *Brown Girl, Brownstones," SAGE: A Scholarly Journal on Black Women* 1 (Fall 1984):13–16. [Reprinted in this collection.]

16. See Tanner, "Matrifocality"; see also Carrie Allen McCray, "The Black Woman and Family Roles," in *The Black Woman,* ed. LaFrances Rogers-Rose (Beverly Hills, CA: Sage, 1980), pp. 67–78; Elmer Martin and Joanne Mitchell Marlin, *The Black Extended Family* (Chicago: University of Chicago Press, 1978); Joyce Aschenbrenner, *Lifelines, Black Families in Chicago* (Prospect Heights, IL: Waveland, 1975); and Carol B. Stack, *All Our Kin* (New York: Harper & Row, 1974).

17. Martin and Martin, *The Black Extended Family*; Stack, *All Our Kin*; and Virginia Young, "Family and Childhood in a Southern Negro Community," *American Anthropologist* 72 (1970):269–88.

18. Stack, *All Our Kin.*

19. Ellen Cantarow, *Moving the Mountain: Women Working for Social Change* (Old Westbury, NY: Feminist Press, 1980), p. 59.

20. Thordis Simonsen, ed., *You May Plow Here, The Narrative of Sara Brooks* (New York: Touchstone, 1986), p. 181.

21. White, *Ar'n't I a Woman?*; Dill, "Our Mothers' Grief"; Mullings, "Uneven Development."

22. Simonsen, *You May Plow Here*, p. 86.

23. Mamie Garvin Fields and Karen Fields, *Lemon Swamp and Other Places, A Carolina Memoir* (New York: Free Press, 1983), p. xvii.

24. Ibid, p. 195.

25. Cheryl Gilkes, "'Holding Back the Ocean with a Broom,' Black Women and Community Work," in *The Black Woman,* ed. Rogers-Rose, 1980, pp. 217–31, and "Going Up for the Oppressed: The Career Mobility of Black Women Community Workers," *Journal of Social Issues* 39 (1983):115–39.

26. Gilkes, " 'Holding Back the Ocean.'" p. 219.

27. Fields and Fields, *Lemon Swamp,* p. xvi.

28. Charles Johnson, *Shadow of the Plantation* (Chicago: University of Chicago Press, 1934, 1979), p. 173.

29. Pamela Reid, "Socialization of Black Female Children," in *Women: A Developmental Perspective,* ed. Phyllis Berman and Estelle Ramey (Washington, DC: National Institutes of Health, 1983).

30. For works in the feminist psychoanalytic tradition, see Nancy Chodorow, "Family Structure and Feminine Personality," in *Woman, Culture, and Society,* ed. Rosaldo and Lamphere, 1974; Nancy Chodorow, *The Reproduction of Mothering* (Berkeley, CA: University of California, 1978); and Jane Flax, "The Conflict Between Nurturance and Autonomy in Mother-Daughter Relationships and Within Feminism," *Feminist Studies* 4 (1978):171–89.

31. Ann Moody, *Coming of Age in Mississippi* (New York: Dell, 1968).

32. Ladner, *Tomorrow's Tomorrow;* Gloria Joseph, "Black Mothers and Daughters: Their Roles and Functions in American Society," in *Common Differences*, ed. Gloria Joseph and Jill Lewis (Garden City, NY: Anchor, 1981), pp. 75–126; Lena Wright Myers, *Black Women, Do They Cope Better?* (Englewood Cliffs, NJ: Prentice-Hall, 1980).

33. Elsa Barkley Brown, "Hearing Our Mothers' Lives," paper presented at fifteenth anniversary of African-American and African Studies at Emory College, Atlanta, 1986. This essay appeared in the Black Women's Studies issue of *SAGE: A Scholarly Journal on Black Women*, vol. 6, no. 1:4–11.

34. Joseph, "Black Mothers and Daughters"; Myers, 1980.

35. Gloria Wade-Gayles, "The Truths of Our Mothers' Lives: Mother-Daughter Relationships in Black Women's Fiction," *SAGE: A Scholarly Journal on Black Women* 1 (Fall 1984):12.

36. Troester, "Turbulence and Tenderness," p. 13.

37. Wade-Gayles, "The Truths," p. 10.

38. Joseph, "Black Mothers and Daughters."

39. Moody, *Coming of Age*, p. 57.

40. Renita Weems, "'Hush. Mama's Gotta Go Bye Bye': A Personal Narrative," *SAGE: A Scholarly Journal on Black Women* 1 (Fall 1984):26.

41. Ibid, p. 27.

42. June Jordan, *On Call, Political Essays* (Boston: South End Press, 1985), p. 145.

32

Working at Motherhood

Chicana and Mexican Immigrant Mothers and Employment[1]

DENISE A. SEGURA

In North American society, women are expected to bear and assume primary responsibility for raising their children. This socially constructed form of motherhood encourages women to stay at home during their children's early or formative years, and asserts activities that take married mothers out of the home (for instance, paid employment) are less important or "secondary" to their domestic duties.[2] Motherhood as a social construction rests on the ideological position that women's biological abilities to bear and suckle children are "natural," and therefore fundamental to women's "fulfillment." This position, however, fails to appreciate that motherhood is a culturally formed structure whose meanings can vary and are subject to change.

Despite the ideological impetus to mother at home, over half of all women with children work for wages.[3] The growing incongruence between social ideology and individual behaviors has prompted some researchers to suggest that traditional gender role expectations are changing (for example, greater acceptance of women working outside the home).[4] The profuse literature on the "ambivalence" and "guilt" employed mothers often feel when they work outside the home, however, reminds us that changes in expectations are neither absolute nor uncontested.

Some analysts argue that the ambivalence felt by many employed mothers stems from their discomfort in deviating from a socially constructed "idealized mother," who stays home to care for her family.[5] This image of motherhood, popularized in the media, schoolbooks, and public policy, implies that the family and the economy constitute two separate spheres, private and public. Dubois and Ruiz argue, however, that the notion of a private-public dichotomy largely rests on the experiences of White, leisured women, and lacks immediate relevance to less privileged women (for instance, immigrant women, women of color), who have historically been important economic actors both inside and outside the home.[6] The view that the relationship between motherhood and employment varies by class, race, and/or culture raises several important questions. Do the ideology of motherhood and the "ambivalence" of employed mothers depicted within American sociology and feminist scholarship pertain to women of Mexican descent in the United States? Among these women, what is the relation between the ideological constructions of motherhood and employment? Is motherhood mutually exclusive from employment among Mexican-heritage women from different social locations?

In this chapter I explore these questions using qualitative data gathered from thirty women of Mexican descent in the United States—both native-born Chicanas (including two Mexico-born women raised since preschool years in the U.S.) and resident immigrant Mexicanas.[7] I illustrate that notions of motherhood for Chicanas and Mexicanas are embedded in different ideological constructs operating within two systems of patriarchy. Contrary to the expectations of acculturation models, I find that Mexicanas frame motherhood in ways that foster a more consistent labor market presence than do Chicanas. I argue that this distinction—typically bypassed in the sociological literature on motherhood, women and work, or Chicano Studies—is rooted in their dissimilar social locations—that is, the "social spaces" they engage within the social structure created by the intersection of class, race, gender, and culture.[8]

I propose that Mexicanas, raised in a world where economic and household work often merged, do not dichotomize social life into public and private spheres, but appear to view employment as one workable domain of motherhood. Hence, the more recent the time of emigration, the less ambivalence Mexicanas express regarding employment. Chicanas, on the other hand, raised in a society that celebrates the expressive functions of the family and obscures its productive economic functions, express higher adherence to the ideology of stay-at-home motherhood, and correspondingly more ambivalence toward full-time employment—even when they work.

These differences between Mexicanas and Chicanas challenge current research on Mexican-origin women that treats them as a single analytic category (for instance, "Hispanic") as well as research on contemporary views of motherhood that fails to appreciate diversity among women. My examination of the intersection of motherhood and employment among Mexican immigrant women also reinforces emerging research focusing on women's own economic and social motivations to emigrate to the U.S. (rather than the behest of husbands and/or fathers).[9]

My analysis begins with a brief review of relevant research on the relationship between motherhood and employment. Then I explore this relationship in greater detail, using in-depth interview data. I conclude by discussing the need to recast current conceptualizations of the dilemma between motherhood and employment to reflect women's different social locations.

THEORETICAL CONCERNS

The theoretical concerns that inform this research on Chicana/Mexicana employment integrate feminist analyses of the hegemonic power of patriarchy over work and motherhood with a critique of rational choice models and other models that overemphasize modernity and acculturation. In much of the literature on women and work, familial roles tend to be portrayed as important constraints on both women's labor market entry and mobility. Differences among women related to immigrant status, however, challenge this view.

Within rational choice models, motherhood represents a prominent social force behind women's job decisions. Becker and Polachek, for example, argue that women's "preference" to mother is maximized in jobs that exact fewer penalties for interrupted employment, such as part-time, seasonal, or clerical work.[10] According to this view, women's pursuit of their rational self-interest reinforces their occupational segregation within low-paying jobs (for example, clerical work) and underrepresentation in higher-paying, male-dominated jobs that typically require significant employer investments (for example, specialized training). Employers may be reluctant to "invest" in or train women workers who, they perceive, may leave a job at any time for familial reasons.[11] This perspective views motherhood as a major impediment to employment and mobility. But it fails to consider that the organization of production has developed in ways that make motherhood an impediment. Many feminist scholars view this particular development as consistent with the hegemonic power of patriarchy.

Distinct from rational choice models, feminist scholarship directs attention away from individual preferences to consider how patriarchy (male domination/female subordination) shapes the organization of production resulting in the economic, political, and social subordination of women to men.[12] While many economists fail to consider the power of ideological constructs such as "family" and "motherhood" in shaping behavior among women, employers, and the organization of production itself, many feminist scholars focus on these power dynamics.

Within feminist analyses, motherhood as an ideology obscures and legitimizes women's social subordination because it conceals particular interests within the rubric of a universal prerogative (reproduction). The social construction of motherhood serves the interest of capital by providing essential childbearing, child care, and housework at a minimal cost to the state, and sustains women as a potential reservoir of labor power, or a "reserve army of labor."[13] The strength of the ideology of motherhood is such that women continue to try to reconcile the "competing urgencies"[14] of motherhood and employment despite the lack of supportive structures at work or within the family....

Research on women of Mexican descent and employment indicates their labor force participation is lower than that of other women when they have young children[15] Moreover, Chicanas and Mexicanas are occupationally segregated in the lowest-paying of female-dominated jobs.[16] Explanations for their unique employment situation range from analyses of labor market structures and employer discriminations[17] to deficient individual characteristics (for instance, education, job skills)[18] and cultural differences.[19]

Analyses of Chicana/Mexicana employment that utilize a cultural framework typically explain the women's lower labor force participation, higher fertility, lower levels of education, and higher levels of unemployment as part of an ethnic or cultural tradition.[20] That is, as this line of argument goes, Chicano/Mexican culture emphasizes a strong allegiance to an idealized form of motherhood and a patriarchal ideology that frowns upon working wives and mothers and does not encourage girls to pursue higher education or employment options. These attitudes are supposed to vary by generation, with immigrant women (from Mexico) holding the most conservative attitudes.[21]

There are two major flaws in the research on Chicana/Mexicana employment, however. First, inconsistency in distinguishing between native-born and resident immigrant women characterizes much of this literature. Second, overreliance on linear acculturation persists. Both procedures imply either that Chicanas and Mexicanas are very similar, or that they lie on a sort of "cultural continuum," with Mexican immigrants at one end holding more conservative behaviors and attitudes grounded in traditional (often rural) Mexican culture, and U.S.-born Chicanos holding an amalgamation of cultural traditions from Mexico and the United States.[22] In terms of motherhood and employment, therefore, Mexicanas should have more "traditional" ideas about motherhood than U.S.-born Chicanas. Since the traditional ideology of motherhood typically refers to women staying home to "mother" children rather than going outside the home to work, Mexicanas theoretically should not be as willing to work as Chicanas or North American women in general—unless there is severe economic need. This formulation, while logical, reflects an underlying emphasis on modernity—or the view that "traditional" Mexican culture lags behind North American culture in developing behaviors and attitudes conducive to participating fully in modern society.[23] Inasmuch as conventional North American views of motherhood typically idealize labor market exit to care for children, embracing this prototype may be more conducive to maintaining patriarchal privilege (female economic subordination to men) than facilitating economic progress generally. In this sense, conceptualizations of motherhood that affirm its economic character may be better accommodating to women's market participation in the U.S.

The following section discusses the distinct views of motherhood articulated by Chicanas and Mexicanas and their impact on employment attitudes and behaviors. In contrast to the notion that exposure to North American values enhances women's incentives to work, proportionately more Chicanas than Mexicanas express ambivalence toward paid employment when they have children at home. I analyze these differences among a selected sample of clerical, service, and operative workers.

METHOD AND SAMPLE

This paper is based on in-depth interviews with thirty Mexican origin women—thirteen Chicanas and seventeen Mexicanas—who had participated in the 1978 to 79 or 1980 to 81 cohorts of an adult education and employment training program in the greater San Francisco Bay Area.[24] All thirty respondents had been involved in a conjugal relationship (either legal marriage or informal cohabitation with a male partner) at some point in their lives before I interviewed them in 1985, and had at least one child under eighteen years of age. At the time of their interviews, six Chicanas and fourteen Mexicanas were married; seven Chicanas and three Mexicanas were single parents.

On the average, the married Chicanas have 1.2 children at home; the Mexicanas report 3.5 children. Both Chicana and Mexicana single mothers average 1.6 children. The children of the Chicanas tend to be preschool or in elementary school. The children of the Mexicanas exhibit a greater age range (from infant to late adolescence), reflecting their earlier marriages and slightly older average age.

With respect to other relevant characteristics, all but two Mexicanas and Chicanas had either a high school diploma or its equivalent (GED). The average age was 27.4 years for the Chicanas; and thirty-three for the Mexicanas.[25] Upon leaving the employment training program, all the women secured employment. At the time of their interviews about half of the Chicanas (n = 7) and three-fourths of the Mexicanas were employed (n = 12). Only two out of the seven (twenty-eight percent) employed Chicanas worked full-time (thirty-five or more hours per week) whereas nine out of the twelve (seventy-five percent) employed Mexicanas worked full-time. Most of the Chicanas found clerical or service jobs (for example, teacher assistants); most of the Mexicanas labored in operative jobs or in the service sector (for example, hotel maids), with a small minority employed as clerical workers.

I gathered in-depth life and work histories from the women to ascertain:

1. What factors motivated them to enter, exit, and stay employed in their specific occupations;
2. whether familial roles or ideology influenced their employment consistency; and
3. whether other barriers limited their job attachment and mobility.

My examination of the relationship between motherhood and employment forms part of a larger study of labor market stratification and occupational mobility among Chicana and Mexican immigrant women.[29]

MOTHERHOOD AND EMPLOYMENT

Nearly all of the respondents, both Chicana and Mexicana, employed and nonemployed, speak of motherhood as their most important social role. They differ sharply in their employment behaviors and views regarding the relationship between motherhood and market work. Women fall into four major groups. The first group consists of five *Involuntary Nonemployed Mothers* who are not employed but care full-time for their children. All of these women want to be employed at least part time. They either cannot secure the job they want and/or they feel pressured to be at home mothering full-time.

The second group consists of six *Voluntary Nonemployed Mothers* who are not employed but remain out of the labor force by *choice*. They feel committed to staying at home to care for preschool and/or elementary school age children.

The third category, *Ambivalent Employed Mothers,* includes eleven employed women. They have either preschool or elementary school age children. Women in this group believe that employment interferes with motherhood, and feel "guilty" when they work outside the home. Despite these feelings, they are employed at least part-time.

The fourth group, *Nonambivalent Employed Mothers* includes eight employed women. What distinguishes these women from the previous group is their view that employment and motherhood seem compatible social dynamics irrespective of the age of their children. All eight women are Mexicanas. Some of these women believe employment could be problematic, however, *if* a family member could not care for their children or be at home for the children when they arrived from school.

Chicanas tend to fall in the second and third categories, whereas Mexicanas predominate in the first and fourth groups. Three reasons emerged as critical in explaining this difference:

1. the economic situations of their families;
2. labor market structure (four-fifths of the non-employed Mexicanas were involuntarily unemployed); and
3. women's conceptualizations of motherhood, in particular, their expressed *need* to mother.

Age of the women and number of children did not fall into any discernible pattern, therefore I did not engage them in depth within my analysis.

First, I consider the situation of the *Voluntary Nonemployed Mothers*, including three married Chicanas, one single-parent Mexicana and one single-parent Chicana. All but one woman exited the labor market involuntarily (for reasons such as layoffs or disability). All five women remain out of the labor force by choice. Among them, the expressed need to mother appears strong—overriding all other concerns. They view motherhood as mutually exclusive from employment. Lydia, a married Chicana with a small toddler, articulates this perspective:

> Right now, since we've had the baby, I feel, well he [her husband] feels the same way, that I want to spend this time with her and watch her grow up. See, because when I was small my grandmother raised me so I felt this loss [her emphasis] when my grandmother died. And I've never gotten that real love, *that mother love from my mother.* We have a friendship, but we don't have that "motherly love." I want my daughter to know that I'm here, especially at her age, it's very important for them to know that when they cry that mama's there. Even if it's not a painful cry, it's still impor-

> tant for them to know that mommy's there. She's my number one—she's all my attention...so working-wise, it's up to [her husband] right now.

Susana, a Chicana single parent with a five-year-old child said:

> I'm the type of person that has always wanted to have a family. I think it was more like I didn't have a family-type home when I was growing up. I didn't have a mother and a father and the kids all together in the same household all happy. I didn't have that. And that's what I want more than anything! I want to be different from my mother, who has worked hard and is successful in her job. I don't want to be successful in the same way.

Lydia, Susana, and the other voluntarily unemployed Chicanas adamantly assert that motherhood requires staying home with their children. Susana said: "A good mother is there for her children all the time when they are little and when they come home from school." All the Chicanas in this category believe that motherhood means staying home with children—even if it means going on welfare (AFDC). This finding is similar to other accounts of working-class women.[26]...

This group of Chicanas seems to be pursuing the social construction of motherhood that is idealized within their ethnic community, their churches, and society at large.[27] Among Chicanos and Mexicanos the image of *la madre* as self-sacrificing and holy is a powerful standard against which women often compare themselves.[28] The Chicana informants also seem to accept the notion that women's primary duty is to provide for the emotional welfare of the children, and that economic activities which take them outside the home are secondary. Women's desire to enact the socially constructed motherhood ideal was further strengthened by their conviction that many of their current problems (for instance, low levels of education, feelings of inadequacy, single parenthood) are related to growing up in families that did not conform to the stay-at-home mother/father-as-provider configuration....

Only one married Mexicana, Belen, articulated views similar to those of the Chicanas. Belen left the labor market in 1979 to give birth and care for her newborn child. It is important to note that she has a gainfully employed husband who does not believe mothers should work outside the home. Belen, who has two children and was expecting a third when I interviewed her, said:

> I wanted to work or go back to school after having my first son, but my husband didn't want me to. He said, "no one can take care of your child the way you can." He did not want me to work. And I did not feel right having someone else care for my son. So I decided to wait until my children were older.

Belen's words underscore an important dynamic that impacted on both Mexicana and Chicana conceptualizations of motherhood: spousal employment and private patriarchy. Specifically, husbands working in full-time, year-round jobs with earnings greater than those of their wives, tended to pressure women to mother full-time. Women who succumb to this pressure become economically dependent on their husbands and reaffirm male authority in the organization of the family. These particular women tend to consider motherhood and employment in similar ways. This suggests that the form the social construction of motherhood takes involves women's economic relationship to men as well as length of time in the U.S.

Four Mexicanas and one Chicana were involuntarily nonemployed. They had been laid off from their jobs or were on temporary disability leave. Three women (two Mexicanas/one Chicana) were seeking employment; the other two were in the last stages of pregnancy but intended to look for a job as soon as possible after their child's birth. All five women reported feeling "good" about being home with their children, but wanted to rejoin the labor force as soon as possible. Ideologically these women view motherhood and employment as reconcilable social dynamics. As Isabel, an unemployed production worker, married with eight children, said:

> I believe that women always work more. We who are mothers work to maintain the family by work-

ing outside, but also inside the house caring for the children.

Isabel voiced a sentiment held by all of the informants—that women work hard at motherhood. Since emigrating to the U.S. about a decade ago, Isabel had been employed nearly continuously, with only short leaves for childbearing. Isabel and nearly all of the Mexicanas described growing up in environments where women, men, and children were important economic actors. In this regard they are similar to the *Nonambivalent Employed Mothers*—all of whom are also Mexicanas. They tended not to dichotomize social life in the same way as the *Voluntary Nonemployed Chicanas* and *Ambivalent Employed* informants.

Although all of the Chicanas believe that staying home best fulfills their mother roles, slightly fewer than half actually stay out of the labor market to care for their young children. The rest of the Chicanas are employed and struggling to reconcile motherhood with employment. I refer to these women as *Ambivalent Employed Mothers*. They express guilt about working and assert they *would not work* if they did not have to for economic reasons. Seven of these women are Chicanas; four are Mexicanas.

To try and alleviate their guilt and help meet their families' economic goals, most of the Chicanas work in part-time jobs. This option permits them to be home when their children arrive from school. Despite this, they feel guilty and unhappy about working. As Jenny, a married Chicana with two children, ages two and four, who is employed part-time, said:

> Sure, I feel guilty. I should [her emphasis] be with them [her children] while they're little. He [her husband] really feels that I should be with my kids all the time. And it's true....

The Mexicana mothers who are employed express their ambivalence somewhat differently from the Chicanas. One Mexicana works full-time; the other three are employed part-time. Angela, a Mexicana married with one child and employed full-time as a seamstress, told me with glistening eyes:

*Always I have had to work. I had to leave my son
with the baby-sitter since he was six months old. It
was difficult. Each baby-sitter has their own way
of caring for children which isn't like yours. I
know the baby-sitter wouldn't give him the food I
left. He always had on dirty diapers and was starv-
ing when I would pick him up. But there wasn't
any other recourse. I had to work. I would just
clean him and feed him when I got home.*

Angela's "guilt" stemmed from her inability to
find good, affordable child care. Unlike most of
the Mexicanas, who had extensive family networks, Angela and her husband had few relatives
to rely on in the U.S. Unlike the Chicana informants, Angela did not want to exit the labor market to care for her child. Her desire is reinforced
by economic need; her husband is irregularly employed.[29] For the other three Mexicanas in this
group guilt as an employed mother appears to
have developed with stable spousal employment.
That is, the idea of feeling guilty about full-time
employment emerged *after* husbands became
employed in secure, well-paying jobs and "reminded" them of the importance of stay-at-home,
full-time motherhood. . . .

Women seem particularly troubled when they
have to work on weekends. This robs them of precious family time. As Elena, a Chicana single parent with two children, ages nine and three, who
works part-time as a hotel maid, said:

*Yes, I work on weekends. And my kids, you know
how kids are—they don't like it. And it's hard. But
I hope to find a job soon where the schedule is
fixed and I won't have to work on weekends—because that time should be for my kids.*

There is a clear sense among the women I interviewed that a boundary between *time for the
family* and *market time* should exist. During times
when this boundary folds, women experience both
internal conflict (within the woman herself) and
external conflict (among family members). They
regard jobs that overlap on family time with disfa-
vor and unhappiness. When economic reasons
compel women to work during what they view a
family time, they usually try to find as quickly as

possible a different job that allows them to better
meet their mother roles.

Interestingly, the Chicanas appear less flexible
in reconciling the boundaries of family time and
market time than the Mexicanas. That is, Chicanas
overwhelmingly "choose" part-time employment
to limit the amount of spillover time from employment on motherhood and family activities. Mexicans, on the other hand, overwhelmingly work full
time (n = 9) and attempt to do both familial caretaking and market work as completely as possible,

This leads us to consider the fourth category I
call *Nonambivalent Employed Mothers*. This category consists of Mexicana immigrants, both married and single-parent (six and two women,
respectively). Mexicanas in this group do not describe motherhood as a *need* requiring a separate
sphere for optimal realization. Rather, they refer to
motherhood as one function of womanhood compatible with employment insofar as employment
allows them to provide for their family's economic
subsistence or betterment. As Pilar, a married
Mexicana with four children, employed full-time
as a line supervisor in a factory, said: "I work to
help my children. That's what a mother should
do." This group of Mexicanas does not express
guilt over leaving their children in the care of others so much as *regret* over the limited amount of
time they could spend with them. As Norma, a
Mexicana full-time clerical worker, who is married
with two children ages three and five, said:

*I don't feel guilty for leaving my children because
if I didn't work they might not have the things they
have now. . . . Perhaps if I had to stay at home I
would feel guilty and frustrated. I'm not the type
that can stay home twenty-four hours a day. I don't
think that would help my children any because I
would feel pressured at being cooped up [encer-
rada] at home. And that way I wouldn't have the
same desire to play with my daughters. But now,
with the time we have together, we do things that
we want to, like run in the park, because there's so
little time.*

All of the Mexicanas in this group articulate views
similar to Norma's. Their greater comfort with the

demands of market and family work emanates from their social locations. All of the Mexicanas come from poor or working-class families, where motherhood embraced both economic and affective features. Their activities were not viewed as equal to those of men, however, and ideologically women saw themselves as *helping* the family rather than *providing* for it.

Few Mexicanas reported that their mothers were wage-laborers (n = 3), but rather, described a range of economic activities they remembered women doing "for the family."[30] Mexicanas from rural villages (n = 7) recounted how their mothers had worked on the land and made assorted products or food to sell in local marketplaces. Mexicanas from urban areas (n = 5) also discussed how their mothers had been economically active. Whether rural or urban, Mexicanas averred that their mothers had taught them to "help" the family as soon as possible. As Norma said:

> My mother said: "it's one thing for a woman to lie around the house but it's a different thing for the work that needs to be done. As the saying goes, work is never done; the work does you in [el trabajo acaba con uno; uno nunca acaba con el trabajo]. . . .

Although the Mexicanas had been raised in worlds where women were important economic actors, this did not signify gender equality. On the contrary, male privilege, or patriarchy, characterizes the organization of the family, the economy, and the polity in both rural and urban Mexican society.[31] In the present study, Mexicanas indicated that men wielded greater authority in the family, the community and the state than women. Mexicanas also tended to uphold male privilege in the family by viewing both domestic work and women's employment as "less important" than the work done by men. As Adela, a married Mexicana with four children, said: "Men are much stronger and do much more difficult work than women." Mexicanas also tended to defer to husbands as the "head" of the family—a position they told me was both "natural" and "holy."[32]

WORKING AT MOTHERHOOD

The differences presented here between the Chicanas and Mexicanas regarding motherhood and employment stem from their distinct social locations. Raised in rural or working-class families in Mexico, the Mexicanas described childhoods where they and their mothers actively contributed to the economic subsistence of their families by planting crops, harvesting, selling homemade goods, and cleaning houses. Their situations resonate with what some researchers term a family economy, where all family members work at productive tasks differentiated mainly by age and sex.[33] In this type of structure, there is less distinction between economic life and domestic life. Motherhood in this context is both economic and expressive, embracing both employment as well as childrearing.

The family economy the Mexicanas experienced differs from the family organization that characterizes most of the Chicanas' childhoods. The Chicanas come from a world that idealizes a male wage earner as the main economic "provider," with women primarily as consumers, and only secondarily as economic actors.[34] Women in this context are mothers first, wage earners second. Families that challenge this structure are often discredited, or perceived as dysfunctional and the source of many social problems.[35] The ambivalence Chicanas recurrently voice stems from their belief in what Kanter calls "the myth of separate worlds."[36] They seek to realize the popular notion or stereotype that family is a separate structure—a haven in a heartless world. Their attachment to this ideal is underscored by a harsh critique of their own employed mothers and themselves *when* they work full-time. Motherhood framed within this context appears irreconcilable with employment.

There are other facets to the differences between Chicanas and Mexicanas. The Mexicanas, as immigrant women, came to the United States with a vision of improving the life chances of their families and themselves. This finding intersects with research on "selective immigration." That is, that Mexican immigrants tend to possess higher levels of education than the national average in Mexico, and a wide range of behavioral characteristics (for instance, high achievement orientation) conducive to success in the U.S.[37]

The Mexicanas emigrated hoping to work—hence their high attachment to employment, even in physically demanding, often demeaning jobs. Mexican and Chicano husbands support their wives' desires to work *so long as* this employment does not challenge the patriarchal structure of the family. In other words, so long as the Mexicanas: (1) articulate high attachment to motherhood *and* family caretaker roles, (2) frame their employment in terms of family economic goals, and (3) do not ask men to do equal amounts of housework or childcare, they encounter little resistance from husbands or other male family members.

When Mexican and Chicano husbands secure good jobs, however, they begin pressuring wives to quit working or to work only part-time. In this way, Mexican and Chicano men actively pursue continuity of their superordinate position within the family. This suggests that the way motherhood is conceptualized in both the Mexican and Chicano communities, particularly with respect to employment, is wedded to male privilege, or patriarchy. Ironically then, Mexicanas' sense of employment's continuity with motherhood enhances their job attachment but does not challenge a patriarchal family structure or ethos.

Similarly, Chicanas' preference for an idealized form of motherhood does not challenge male privilege in their community. Their desire to stay at home to mother exercised a particularly strong influence on the employment behavior of single-parent Chicanas and women with husbands employed in relatively good jobs. This preference reflects an adherence both to an idealized, middle-class life-style that glorifies women's domestic roles, as well as to maintenance of a patriarchal family order. Chicanas feel they should stay at home to try and provide their children with the mothering they believe children should have—mothering that many or them had not experienced.

Chicanas also feel compelled by husbands and the larger community to maintain the status of men as "good providers." Men earning wages adequate to provide for their families' needs usually urged their wives to leave the labor market. While the concept of the good provider continues to be highly valued in our society, it also serves as a rationale that upholds male privilege ideologically and materially, and reinforces the myth of separate spheres that emanates from the organization of the family and the economy.

CONCLUSION

By illustrating how Chicanas and Mexicanas differ in their conceptualizations and organization of the motherhood and employment nexus, this study demonstrates how motherhood is a culturally formed structure with various meanings and subtexts. The vitality of these differences among a group who share a common historical origin and many cultural attributes underscores the need for frameworks that analyze diversity among all groups of women. Most essential to such an undertaking is a critique of the privileging of the "separate spheres" concept in analyses of women and work.

The present study provides additional coherence to recent contentions that the private-public dichotomy lacks immediate relevance to less privileged women (for instance, Chicana and Mexican immigrant women). In the process of illustrating how Chicanas and Mexicanas organized the interplay between motherhood and employment, it became clear that a more useful way of understanding this intersection might be to problematize motherhood itself. Considering motherhood from the vantage point of women's diverse social locations revealed considerable heterogeneity in how one might speak of it. For example, motherhood has an economic component for both groups of women, but it is most strongly expressed by Mexicana immigrants. The flavor of the expressive, however, flows easily across both groups of women, and for the Mexicanas embraces the eco-

Chapter 9: Constructing Motherhood and Fatherhood   **285**

nomic. What this suggests is that the dichotomy of the separate spheres lacks relevance to Chicanas and Mexicanas, and other women whose social origins make economic work necessary for survival.

This leads us to consider the relative place and function of the ideology of motherhood prevalent in our society. Motherhood constructed to privilege the woman who stays at home serves a myriad of functions. It pushes women to dichotomize their lives rather than develop a sense of fluidity across roles, responsibilities, and preferences. Idealized, stay-at-home motherhood eludes most American women with children. As an ideology, however, it tells them what "should be," rendering them failures *as women* when they enter the labor market. Hence the feelings of ambivalence that characterized employed mothers' lives for the most part—except those who had not yet internalized these standards. The present research provided examples of such women, along with the understanding that other women from different social locations may demonstrate distinct ways of organizing the motherhood-employment nexus as well.

Feminist analyses of women and work emphasize the role of patriarchy to maintain male privilege and domination economically and ideologically. It is important to recognize that male privilege is not experienced equally by all men, and that patriarchy itself can be expressed in dif-

ferent ways. The present study found that notions of motherhood among Mexicanas and Chicanas are embedded in different ideological constructs operating within two systems of patriarchy. For Mexicanas, patriarchy takes the form of a corporate family model, with all members contributing to the common good. For Chicanas, the patriarchal structure centers more closely around a public-private dichotomy that idealizes men as economic providers, and women primarily as caretakers-consumers.

The finding that women from more "traditional" backgrounds (such as rural Mexico) are likely to approach full-time employment with less ambivalence than more "American" women (such as the Chicanas) rebuts linear acculturation models that assume a negative relationship between ideologies (such as motherhood) constructed within "traditional" Mexican society, and employment. It also complements findings on the negative relationship between greater length of time in the U.S. and high aspirations among Mexicans.[38] This suggests that employment problems (for example, underemployment, unemployment) are related less to "traditional" cultural configurations than to labor market structure and employment policies. Understanding the intersections between employment policy, social ideology, and private need is a necessary step toward expanding possibilities for women in our society.

NOTES

1. This article is a revised version of "Ambivalence or Continuity?: Motherhood and Employment among Chicanas and Mexican Immigrant Women," *AZTLAN, International Journal of Chicano Studies Research* (1992). I would like to thank Maxine Baca Zinn, Evelyn Nakano Glenn, Arlie Hochschild, Beatriz Pesquera, and Vicki Ruiz for their constructive feedback and criticism of earlier drafts of this paper. A special thanks goes to Jon Cruz for his assistance in titling this paper. Any remaining errors or inconsistencies are my own responsibility. This research was supported in part by a

1986–87 University of California President's Postdoctoral Fellowship.

2. Betsy Wearing, *The Ideology of Motherhood, A Study of Sydney Suburban Mothers* (Sydney: George Allen and Unwin, 1994); Barbara J. Berg, *The Crisis of the Working Mother, Resolving the Conflict Between Family and Work* (New York: Summit Books, 1986). Nancy Folbre "The Pauperization of Motherhood: Patriarchy and Public Policy in the United States," *Review of Radical Political Economics* 16 (1994). The view that mothers should not work outside the home typically pertains to married

women. Current state welfare policies (e.g., Aid to Families with Dependent Children [AFDC], workfare) indicate that single, unmarried mothers belong in the labor force, not at home caring for their children full-time. See Naomi Gerstel and Harriet Engel Gross, "Introduction," in N. Gerstel and H. E Gross, eds., *Families and Work* (Philadelphia: Temple University Press, 1987), pp. 1–12; Deborah K. Zinn and Rosemary C. Sarri, Turning Back the Clock on Public Welfare," in *Signs: Journal of Women in Culture and Society* 10 (1984), pp. 355–370; Nancy Folbre "The Pauperization of Motherhood; Nancy A. Naples, "A Socialist Feminist Analysis of the Family Support Act of 1988," AFFILIA 6 (1991), pp. 23–38.

3. Allyson Sherman Grossman, "More than Half of All Children Have Working Mothers," Special Labor Force Reports—Summaries, *Monthly Labor Review* (February, 1982), pp. 41–43; Howard Hayghe, "Working Mothers Reach Record Number in 1984," *Monthly Labor Review* 107 (December, 1984), pp. 31–34; U.S. Bureau of the Census "Fertility of American Women: June 1990," *Current Population Report*, Series P-20, No. 454, (Washington D.C.: United States Government Printing Office, 1991). In June 1990, over half (53.1 percent) of women between the ages of 18–44 who had had a child in the last year were in the labor force. This proportion varied by race: 54.9 percent of White women, 46.9 percent of Black women, and 44.4 percent of Latinas were in the labor force. See U.S. Bureau of the Census (1991), p. 5.

4. Simon and Landis report that a 1986 Gallup Poll indicates that support for married women to work outside the home is considerably greater than 1938 levels: 76 percent of women and 78 percent of men approve (1989: 270). Comparable 1938 levels are 25 percent and 19 percent, respectively of women and men. The 1985 Roper Poll finds the American public adhering to the view that a husband's career supersedes that of his wife: 72 percent of women and 62 percent of men agree that a wife should quit her job and relocate if her husband is offered a good job in another city (1989: 272). In the reverse situation, 20 percent of women and 22 percent of men believe a husband should quit his job and relocate with his wife (1989: 272). Simon and Landis conclude: "The Women's Movement has not radicalized the American woman: she is still prepared to put marriage and children ahead of her career and to allow her husband's status to determine the family's position in society" (1989: 269). Rita J. Simon and Jean M. Landis, "Women's and Men's Attitudes About a Woman's Place

and Role," *Public Opinion Quarterly* (1989), 53: 265–276.

5. Arlie Hochschild with Anne Machung, *The Second Shift, Working Parents and the Revolution at Home* (New York: Viking Penguin Books, 1989); Kathleen Gerson, *Hard Choices* (Berkeley, California: University of California Press, 1985); Barbara J. Berg, *The Crisis of the Working Mother, Resolving the Conflict Between Family and Work* (New York: Summit Books, 1996). The concept of "separate spheres" is approached in a variety of ways and often critiqued. See Michele Barrett, *Women's Oppression Today, Problems in Marxist Feminist Analysis* (London, Verso Press, 1980); Nona Glazer "Servants to capital: Unpaid domestic labor and paid work," *Review of Radical Economics 16* (1984), pp. 61–87. Zaretsky contends that distinct family and market spheres arose with the development of industrial capitalism: "men and women came to see the family as separate from the economy, and personal life as a separate sphere of life divorced from the larger economy." See Eli Zaretsky, *Capitalism, The Family and Personal Life* (New York: Harper Colophon Books, 1976), p. 78. This stance is substantially different from that of early radical feminist approaches including Firestone, who argued that the separation antedates history. See Shulamith Firestone, *The Dialectic of Sex* (New York: Bantam Books, 1970). Other scholars assert that the relations of production and reproduction are intertwined and virtually inseparable. See Heidi Hartmann, "Capitalism, Patriarchy and Job Segregation by Sex," in Martha Blaxall and Barbara Reagan, eds., *Women and the Work Place* (Chicago, Illinois: University of Chicago Press, 1976), pp. 137–169.

6. Hood argues that the "ideal" of stay-at-home motherhood and male provider has historically been an unrealistic standard for families outside the middle and upper classes. She points out that early surveys of urban workers indicate between 40% and 50% of all families supplemented their income with the earnings of wives and children. See Jane C. Hood, "The Provider Role: Its Meaning and Measurement," *Journal of Marriage and the Family* 49 (May, 1986), pp. 349–359.

7. It should be noted that native-born status is not an essential requirement for the ethnic label, "Chicana/o." There are numerous identifiers used by people of Mexican descent, including: Chicana/o, Mexican, Mexican-American, Mexicana/o, Latina/o, and Hispanic. Often people of Mexican descent use two or three of the above labels, depending on the social situation (e.g., "Mexican-American" in the family or "Chicana/o" at school).

See John A. Garcia, "Yo Soy Mexicano . . .: Self-identity and Sociodemographic Correlates," *Social Science Quarterly 62* (March, 1981), pp. 88–98; Susan E. Keefe and Amado M. Padilla, *Chicano Ethnicity* (Albuquerque, NM: University of New Mexico Press, 1987). My designation of study informants as either "Chicana" or "Mexicana" represents an analytic separation that facilitates demonstrating the heterogeneity among this group.

8. Patricia Zavella, "Reflections on Diversity among Chicanos," *Frontiers* 2 (1991), p. 75.

9. See Rosalia Solorzano-Torres, "Female Mexican Immigrants in San Diego County," in V. L Ruiz and S. Tiano, eds., *Women on the U.S.-Mexico Border: Responses to Change* (Boston: Allen and Unwin, 1987), pp. 41–59; Reynaldo Baca and Bryan Dexter, "Mexican Women, Migration and Sex Roles," *Migration Today 13* (1985), pp. 14–18; Sylvia Guendelman and Auristela Perez-Itriago, "Double Lives: The Changing Role of Women in Seasonal Migration," *Women's Studies* 13 (1987), pp. 249–271.

10. Gary S. Becker, "Human Capital, Effort, and the Sexual Division of Labor," *Journal of Labor Economics* 3 (1985 Supplement), pp. S33–S58; Gary S. Becker, *A Treatise on the Family* (Cambridge, MA: Harvard University Press, 1981); Solomon W. Polachek, "Occupational Self-Selection: A Human Capital Approach to Sex Differences in Occupational Structure," *Review of Economics and Statistics* 63 (1981), pp. 60–69; S. Polachek "Occupational Segregation Among Women: Theory, Evidence, and a Prognosis" in C. B. Lloyd, E. S. Andrews and C. L. Gilroy, eds., *Women in the Labor Market* (New York: Columbia University Press, 1981), pp. 137–157; S. Polachek, "Discontinuous Labor Force Participation and Its Effect on Women's Market Earnings," in C. Lloyd, ed., *Sex Discrimination and the Division of Labor* (New York: Columbia University Press, 1975), pp. 90–122. Becker's classic treatise, *Human Capital*, uses the following example borrowed from G. Stigler, "The Economics of Information," *Journal of Political Economy* (June 1961): "Women spend less time in the labor force than men and, therefore, have less incentive to invest in market skills; tourists spend little time in any one area and have less incentive than residents of the area to invest in knowledge of specific consumption activities." See Gary S. Becker, *Human Capital* (Chicago: University of Chicago Press, 1975), p. 74.

11. Some institutional economists argue that "statistical discrimination" is one critical labor market dynamic that often impedes women and minorities. See Kenneth Arrow, "Economic Dimensions of Occupational Segregation: Comment I," *Signs: Journal of Women in Culture and Society* 1 (1987), pp. 233–237; Edmund Phelps, "The Statistical Theory of Racism and Sexism," in A. H. Amsden, ed., *The Economics of Women and Work* (New York: St. Martin's Press, 1980), pp. 206–210. This perspective suggests that prospective employers often lack detailed information about individual applicants and therefore utilize statistical averages and normative views of the relevant group(s) to which the applicant belongs in their hiring decisions (e.g., college-educated men tend to be successful and committed employees; all women are potential mothers; or women tend to exit the labor force for childbearing).

Bielby and Baron pose an important critique to the underlying rationale of statistical discrimination. They argue that utilizing perceptions of group differences between the sexes is "neither as rational nor as efficient as the economists believe." That is, utilizing stereotypical notions of "men's work" and "women's work" is often costly to employers and therefore irrational. This suggests that sex segregation is imbedded in organizational policies which reflect and reinforce "belief systems that are also rather inert." See William T. Bielby and James N. Baron, "Undoing Discrimination: Job Integration and Comparable Worth," in C. Bose and G. Spitze, eds., *Ingredients for Women's Employment Policy* (New York: State University of New York Press, 1987), p. 216, pp. 221–222.

12. Annette Kuhn, "Structure of Patriarchy and Capital in the Family," in A. Kuhn and Annemarie Wolfe, eds., *Feminism and Materialism: Women and Modes of Production* (London: Routledge and Kegan Paul, 1978); Heidi Hartmann, "Capitalism, Patriarchy, and Job Segregation by Sex," in Martha Blaxall and Barbara Reagan, eds., *Women and the Work Place* (Chicago, Illinois: University of Chicago Press, 1976), pp. 137–169; H. Hartmann, "The Family as the Locus of Gender, Class, and Political Struggle: The Example of Housework," *Signs: Journal of Women in Culture and Society* 6 (1981), pp. 366–394; Michele Barrett, *Women's Oppression Today, Problems in Marxist Feminist Analysis* (London: Verso Press, 1980).

13. Lourdes Beneria and Martha Roldan, *The Crossroads of Class and Gender, Industrial Homework, Subcontracting, and Household Dynamics in Mexico City* (Chicago: The University of Chicago Press, 1987); L. Beneria and Gita Sen, "Accumulation, Reproduction, and Women's Role in Economic Development: Boserup

Revisited," in E. Leacock and H. I. Safa, eds., *Women's Work: Development and Division of Labor by Gender* (Massachusetts: Bergin and Garvey Publishers, 1986), pp. 141–157; Dorothy Smith, "Women's Inequality and the Family," in N. Gerstel and H. E. Gross, eds., *Families and Work* (Philadelphia: Temple University Press, 1987), pp. 23–54.

14. This phrase was coined by Arlie R. Hochschild and quoted in Lillian B. Rubin, *Intimate Strangers, Men and Women Together* (New York: Harper and Row, 1983).

15. Howard Hayghe, "Working Mothers Reach Record Number in 1984," *Monthly Labor Review* 107 (December, 1984), pp. 31–34; U.S. Bureau of the Census, "Fertility of American Women: June 1990" in Current Population Report, Series P-20, No. 454 (Washington D.C.: United States Government Printing Office, 1991); U.S. Bureau of Census Report, "Fertility of American Women: June 1986" in Current Population Report, Series P-20, No. 421 (Washington D.C.: United States Printing Press). In June 1986 (the year closest to the year I interviewed the respondents where I found relevant data), 49.8 percent of all women with newborn children were in the labor force. Women demonstrated differences in this behavior: 49.7 percent of white women, 51.1 percent of Black women, and 40.6 percent of Latinas with newborn children were in the labor force. See U.S. Bureau of the Census "Fertility of American Women: June 1986" (1987), p. 5.

16. Bonnie Thornton Dill, Lynn Weber Cannon, and Reeve Vanneman, "Pay Equity: An Issue of Race, Ethnicity, and Sex" (Washington D.C.: National Commission on Pay Equity, February, 1987); Julianne Malveaux and Phyllis Wallace, "Minority Women in the Workplace," in K. S. Koziara, M. Moskow, and L. Dewey Tanner, eds., *Women and Work: Industrial Relations Research Association Research Volume* (Washington D.C.: Bureau of National Affairs, 1987), pp. 265–298; Vicki L. Ruiz, "'And Miles to go. . . .': Mexican Women and Work, 1930–1985" in L. Schlissel, V. L. Ruiz, and J. Monk, eds., *Western Women, Their Land, Their Lives* (Albuquerque: University of New Mexico Press, 1988), pp. 117–136.

17. Mario Barrera, *Race and Class in the Southwest: A Theory of Racial Inequality* (Notre Dame, IN: University of Notre Dame Press, 1979); Tomas Almaguer, "Class, Race, and Chicano Oppression," in *Socialist Revolution* 5 (1975), pp. 71–99; Denise Segura, "Labor Market Stratification: The Chicana Experience," *Berkeley Journal of Sociology*, 29 (1984), pp. 57–91.

18. Maria Tienda and P. Guhleman, "The Occupational Position of Employed Hispanic Women," in G. J. Borjas and M. Tienda, eds., *Hispanics in the U.S. Economy* (New York: Academic Press, 1985), pp. 243–273.

19. Edgar J. Kranau, Vicki Green, and Gloria Valencia-Weber, "Acculturation and the Hispanic Woman: Attitudes Towards Women, Sex-Role Attribution, Sex-Role Behavior, and Demographics," *Hispanic Journal of Behavioral Sciences* 4 (1982), pp. 21–40; Alfredo Mirande and Evangelina Enriquez, *La Chicana, The Mexican American Woman* (Chicago: The University of Chicago Press, 1979).

20. Kranau, Green, and Valencia-Weber, "Acculturation and the Hispanic Woman," pp. 21–40; Alfredo Mirande, *The Chicano Experience: An Alternative Perspective* (Notre Dame: University of Notre Dame Press, 1985).

21. Vilma Ortiz and Rosemary Santana Cooney, "Sex-Role Attitudes and Labor Force Participation among Young Hispanic Females and Non-Hispanic White Females." *Social Science Quarterly 65* (June, 1984), pp. 392–400.

22. Susan E. Keefe and Amado M. Padilla, *Chicano Ethnicity* (Albuquerque. NM: University of New Mexico Press, 1987); Richard H. Mendoza, "Acculturation and Sociocultural Variability," in J. L. Martinez Jr. and R. H. Mendoza, eds., *Chicano Psychology*, Second Edition (New York: Academic Press, 1984), pp. 61–75.

23. Maxine Baca Zinn, "Mexican-American Women in the Social Sciences," *Signs: Journal of Women in Culture and Society* 8 (1982), pp. 259–272; M. Baca Zinn, "Employment and Education of Mexican-American Women: The Interplay of Modernity and Ethnicity in Eight Families," *Harvard Educational Review* 50 (February 1980), pp. 47–62; M. Baca Zinn, "Chicano Family Research: Conceptual Distortions and Alternative Directions," *Journal of Ethnic Studies* 7 (1979) pp. 59–71.

24. For additional information on the methods and sample selection, I refer the reader to Denise A. Segura, "Chicanas and Mexican Immigrant Women in the Labor Market: A Study of Occupational Mobility and Stratification," unpublished Ph.D. dissertation. Department of Sociology, University of California, Berkeley (1986).

25. The ages of the Chicanas range from 23 to 42 years. The Mexicanas reported ages from 24 to 45. The age profile indicates that most of the women were in peak childbearing years.

26. For example, see Betsy Wearing, *The Ideology of Motherhood, A Study of Sydney Suburban Mothers* (Sydney: George Allen and Unwin, 1984).

27. Manuel Ramirez III and Alfredo Castaneda, *Cultural Democracy, Bicognitive Development, and Education* (New York: Academic Press, 1974); Robert F. Peck and Rogelio Diaz-Guerrero, "Two Core-Culture Patterns and the Diffusion of Values Across Their Borders," *International Journal of Psychology* 2 (1967), pp. 272–282; Javier I. Escobar and E. T. Randolph, "The Hispanic and Social Networks," in R. M. Becerra, M. Karno, and J. I. Escobar, eds., *Mental Health and Hispanic Americans: Clinical Perspectives* (New York: Grune and Stratton, 1982).

28. Alfredo Mirande and Evangelina Enriquez, *La Chicana, The Mexican American Woman* (Chicago: The University of Chicago Press 1979); Margarita Melville, "Introduction" and "Matrascence," in M. B. Melville, ed., *Twice a Minority: Mexican American Women* (St. Louis: The C. V. Mosby Co., 1980), pp. 1–16; Gloria Anzaldua, *Borderlands, La Frontera: The New Mestiza* (San Francisco: Spinsters/Aunt Lute Book Co., 1987); Linda C. Fox, "Obedience and Rebellion: Re-Vision of Chicana Myths of Motherhood," *Women's Studies Quarterly* (Winter, 1993), pp. 20–22.

29. For a full discussion of the interplay between economic goals and economic status of the respondents and their employment decisions, I refer the reader to Denise Segura, "The Interplay of Familism and Patriarchy on Employment among Chicana and Mexican Immigrant Women," in the *Renato Rosaldo Lecture Series Monograph* 5 (Tucson, AZ: The University of Arizona, Center for Mexican American Studies, 1989), pp. 35–53.

30. Two of the Mexicanas reported that their mothers had died while they were toddlers and therefore were unable to discuss their economic roles.

31. Patricia M. Fernandez Kelly, "Mexican Border Industrialization, Female Labor-Force Participation and Migration," in J. Nash and M. P. Fernandez Kelly, eds., *Women, Men, and the International Division of Labor* (Albany: State University of New York Press, 1983), pp. 205–223; Sylvia Guendelman and Auristela Perez-Itriago, "Double Lives: The Changing Role of Women in Seasonal Migration," *Women's Studies* 13 (1987), pp. 249–271; Reynaldo Baca and Dexter Bryan, "Mexican Women, Migration and Sex Roles," *Migration Today* 13 (1985), pp. 14–18.

32. Research indicates religious involvement plays an important role in gender beliefs. See Ross K. Baker, Laurily K. Epstein, and Rodney O. Forth, "Matters of Life and Death: Social, Political, Religious Correlates of Attitudes on Abortion," *American Politics Quarterly* 9 (1981), pp. 89–102; Charles E. Peek and Sharon Brown, "Sex Prejudice among White Protestants: Like or Unlike Ethnic Prejudice?" *Social Forces* 59 (1980), pp. 169–185. Of particular interest for the present study is that involvement in fundamentalist Christian churches is positively related to adherence to traditional gender role ideology. See Clyde Wilcox and Elizabeth Adell Cook, "Evangelical Women and Feminism: Some Additional Evidence," *Women and Politics* 9 (1989), pp. 27–49; Clyde Wilcox, "Religious Attitudes and Anti-Feminism: An Analysis of the Ohio Moral Majority," *Women and Politics* 48 (1987), pp. 1041–1051. Half of the Mexicanas (and all but two Chicanas) adhered to the Roman Catholic religion; half belonged to various fundamentalist Christian churches (e.g., Assembly of God). Two Chicanas belonged to other Protestant denominations. I noticed that the women who belonged to the Assembly of God tended to both work full-time in the labor market and voice the strongest convictions of male authority in the family. During their interviews many of the women brought out the Bible and showed me the biblical passages that authorized husbands to "rule" the family. Catholic women also voiced traditional beliefs regarding family structure but did not invoke God.

33. Frances Rothstein, "Women and Men in the Family Economy: An Analysis of the Relations Between the Sexes in Three Peasant Communities," *Anthropological Quarterly* 56 (1983), pp. 10–23; Ruth Schwartz Cowan, "Women's Work, Housework, and History: The Historical Roots of Inequality in Work-Force Participation," in N. Gerstel and H. E. Gross, eds., *Families and Work* (Philadelphia: Temple University, 1987), pp. 164–177; Louise A. Tilly and Joan W. Scott, *Women, Work, and Family* (New York: Holt, Rinehart, and Winston, 1978).

34. Jessie Bernard, "The Rise and Fall of the Good Provider Role," *American Psychologist* 36 (1981), pp. 1–12; J. Bernard, *The Future of Motherhood* (New York: Penguin Books, 1974); Jane C. Hood, "The Provider Role: Its Meaning and Measurement," *Journal of Marriage and the Family* 48 (May, 1986), pp. 349–359.

35. Lorraine O. Walker and Mary Ann Best, "Well-Being or Mothers with Infant Children: A Preliminary Comparison of Employed Women and Homemakers," *Women and Health* 17 (1991), pp. 71–88; William J. Doherty and Richard H. Needle. "Psychological Adjustment and Substance Use Among Adolescents Before and After a Parental Divorce," *Child Development*

62 (1991), pp. 328–337; Eugene E. Clark and William Ramsey, "The Importance of Family and Network of Other Relationships in Children's Success in School," *International Journal of Sociology of the Family* 20 (1990), pp. 237–254.

36. Rosabeth Moss Kanter, *Men and Women of the Corporation* (New York: Basic Books, 1977).

37. John M. Chavez and Raymond Buriel, "Reinforcing Children's Effort: A Comparison of Immigrant, Native-Born Mexican American and Euro-American Mothers," *Hispanic Journal of Behavioral Sciences* 8 (1986), pp. 127–142; Raymond Buriel, "Integration with Traditional Mexican-American Culture and Sociocultural Adjustment," in J. L. Martinez, Jr. and R. H. Mendoza, eds., *Chicano Psychology*, Second Edition (New York: Academic Press, 1984), pp. 95–130; Lee R. Chavez, "Households, Migration and Labor Market Participation: The Adaptation of Mexicans to Life in the United States," *Urban Anthropology* 14 (1985), pp. 301–346.

38. Raymond Buriel, "Integration with Traditional Mexican-American Culture and Sociocultural Adjustment," in J. L. Martinez, Jr. and R. H. Mendoza, eds., *Chicano Psychology*, Second Edition (New York: Academic Press, 1984), pp. 95–130. In their analysis of differences in educational goals among Mexican-Americans, Buriel and his associates found that: "third generation Mexican Americans felt less capable of fulfilling their educational objectives." See Raymond Buriel, Silverio Caldaza, and Richard Vasquez, "The Relationship of Traditional Mexican American Culture to Adjustment and Delinquency among Three Generations of Mexican American Adolescents," *Hispanic Journal of Behavioral Sciences* 4 (1982), p. 50. Similar findings were reported by Nielsen and Fernandez: "we find that students whose families have been in the U.S. longer have *lower* [their emphasis] aspirations than recent immigrants." See Francois Nielsen and Roberto M. Fernandez, *Hispanic Students in American High Schools: Background Characteristic and Achievement* (Washington D.C.: United States Government Printing Office, 1981), p. 76.

In their analysis of Hispanic employment, Bean and his associates reported an unexpected finding—that English-proficient Mexican women exhibit a greater "constraining influence of fertility" on their employment vis-à-vis Spanish-speaking women. They speculate that more acculturated Mexican women may have "a greater desire for children of higher quality," and, therefore "be more likely to devote time to the informal socialization and education of young children." They wonder "why this should hold true for English-speaking but not Spanish-speaking women." See Frank D. Bean, C. Gray Swicegood, and Allan G. King, "Role Incompatibility and the Relationship Between Fertility and Labor Supply Among Hispanic Women," in G. J. Borjas and M. Tienda, eds., *Hispanics in the U.S. Economy* (New York: Academic Press, 1985), p. 241.

33

Fatherhood and Social Change

RALPH LaROSSA

The consensus of opinion in American society is that something has happened to American fathers. Long considered minor players in the affairs of their children, today's fathers often are depicted as major parental figures, people who are expected to—people who presumably want to—*be there* when their kids need them. "Unlike their own fathers or grandfathers," many are prone to say.

But, despite all the attention that the so-called "new fathers" have been receiving lately, only a few scholars have systematically conceptualized the changing father hypothesis, and no one to date has marshalled the historical evidence needed to adequately test the hypothesis (Demos, 1982; Hanson & Bozett, 1985; Hanson & Bozett, 1987; Lamb, 1987; Lewis, 1986; Lewis & O'Brien, 1987; McKee & O'Brien, 1982; Pleck, 1987; Rotundo, 1985).

Given that there is not much evidence to support the hypothesis, (a) how do we account for the fact that many, if not most, adults in America believe that fatherhood has changed, and (b) what are the consequences—for men, for women, for families—resulting from the apparent disparity between beliefs and actuality? The purpose of this article is to answer these two questions.

THE ASYNCHRONY BETWEEN THE CULTURE AND CONDUCT OF FATHERHOOD

The institution of fatherhood includes two related but still distinct elements. There is the *culture of fatherhood* (specifically the shared norms, values, and beliefs surrounding men's parenting), and

there is the *conduct of fatherhood* (what fathers do, their paternal behaviors). The distinction between culture and conduct is worth noting because although it is often assumed that the culture and conduct of a society are in sync, the fact is that many times the two are not synchronized at all. Some people make a habit of deliberately operating outside the rules, and others do wrong because they do not know any better (e.g., my 4-year-old son). And in a rapidly changing society like ours, countervailing forces can result in changes in culture but not in conduct, and vice-versa.

The distinction between culture and conduct is especially relevant when trying to assess whether fatherhood has changed because the available evidence on the history of fatherhood suggests that the *culture of fatherhood has changed more rapidly than the conduct.* For example, E. Anthony Rotundo (1985) argues that since 1970 a new style of American fatherhood has emerged, namely "Androgynous Fatherhood." In the androgynous scheme,

> *A good father is an active participant in the details of day-to-day child care. He involves himself in a more expressive and intimate way with his children, and he plays a larger part in the socialization process that his male forebears had long since abandoned to their wives. (p. 17)*

Rotundo (1985) is describing not what fathers lately have been doing but what some people would *like* fathers to *begin* doing. Later on he says that the new style is primarily a middle-class phenomenon and that "even within the upper-middle class ... there are probably far more men who still practice the traditional style of fathering than the new style." He also surmises that "there are more *women* who *advocate* 'Androgynous Fatherhood' than there are *men* who *practice* it" (p. 20). Similarly, Joseph Pleck (1987) writes about the history of fatherhood in the United States and contends that there have been three phases through which modern fatherhood has passed. From the early 19th to mid-20th centuries there was the father as distant breadwinner. Then, from 1940 to 1965 there was the father as sex role model. Finally, since around 1966 there has emerged the father as nurturer. Pleck's "new[est] father," like Rotundo's "androgynous father" is an involved father. He is also, however, more imagined than real. As Pleck acknowledges from the beginning, his analysis is a history of the "dominant *images* [italics added] of fatherhood" (p. 84).

Rotundo and Pleck are clear about the fact that they are focusing on the culture of fatherhood, and they are careful about drawing inferences about the conduct of fatherhood from their data. Others, however, have not been as careful. John Mogey, for example, back in 1957, appears to have mistaken cultural for behavioral changes when, in talking about the emerging role of men in the family, he asserts that the "newer" father's "behavior is best described as participation, the reintegration of fathers into the conspicuous consumption as well as the child rearing styles of family life" (Mogey, as cited in Lewis, 1986, p. 6). Ten years later, Margaret Mead (1967), too, extolled the arrival of the new father:

> We are evolving a new style of fatherhood, in which young fathers share very fully with mothers in the care of babies and little children. In this respect American men differ very much from their own grandfathers and are coming to resemble much more closely men in primitive societies. (p. 36)

And recently there appeared in my Sunday newspaper the comment that "[Modern men] know more about the importance of parenting. They're aware of the role and of how they are doing it. Fifty years ago, fathers didn't think much about what kind of job they were doing" (Harte, 1987, p. 4G).

Neither Mogey nor Mead nor the newspaper presented any evidence to support their views. One can only guess that they were reporting what they assumed—perhaps hoped—was true generally (i.e., true not only for small "pockets" of fathers here and there), for, as was mentioned before, no one to date has carried out the kind of historical study needed to test the changing father hypothesis. If, however, the professional and lay public took seriously the thesis that fathers have changed and if others writing for professional and popular publications have echoed a similar theme, then one can easily understand how the notion that today's fathers are "new" could become implanted in people's minds. Indeed, there is a good chance that this is exactly what has happened. That is to say, Rotundo (1985) and Pleck (1987) probably are correct: there has been a shift in the culture of fatherhood—the way fathers and mothers think and feel about men as parents. But what separates a lot of fathers and mothers from Rotundo and Pleck is that, on some level of consciousness, the fathers and mothers also believe (incorrectly) that there has been a proportionate shift in the conduct of fatherhood.

I say on "some" level of consciousness because, on "another" level of consciousness, today's fathers and mothers *do* know that the conduct of fatherhood has not kept pace with the culture. And I include the word "proportionate" because, while some researchers have argued that there have been changes in paternal behavior since the turn of the century, no scholar has argued that these changes have occurred at the same rate as the ideological shifts that apparently have taken place. These two points are crucial to understanding the consequences of the asynchrony between culture and conduct, and they will soon be discussed in more detail. But first another question: If the behavior of fathers did not alter the ideology of fatherhood, then what did?

The answer is that the culture of fatherhood changed primarily in response to the shifts in the conduct of motherhood. In the wake of declines in the birth rate and increases in the percentage of mothers in the labor force, the culture of motherhood changed, such that it is now more socially acceptable for women to combine motherhood with employment outside the home (Margolis, 1984). The more it became apparent that today's mothers were less involved with their children, on a day-to-day basis, than were their own mothers or grandmothers, the more important it became to ask the question: Who's minding the kids? Not appreciating the extent to which substitute parents (day-care centers, etc.) have picked up the slack for mothers, many people (scholars as well as the lay public) assumed that fathers must be doing a whole lot more than before and changed their beliefs to conform to this assumption. In other words, mother–child interaction was erroneously used as a "template" to measure father–child interaction (Day & Mackey, 1986).

Generally speaking, culture follows conduct rather than vice-versa (Stokes & Hewitt, 1976). Thus, the fact that the culture of fatherhood has changed more rapidly than the conduct of fatherhood would seem to represent an exception to the rule. However, it may not be an exception at all. What may be happening is that culture *is* following conduct, but not in a way we normally think it does. Given the importance that American society places on mothers as parents, it is conceivable that the conduct of motherhood has had a "cross-fertilizing" effect on the culture of fatherhood. There is also the possibility that the conduct of fatherhood is affecting the culture of fatherhood, but as a stabilizer rather than a destabilizer. As noted, research suggests that androgynous fatherhood as an ideal has failed to become widespread. One reason for this may be that the conduct of fatherhood is arresting whatever "modernizing" effect the conduct of motherhood is having. Put differently, the conduct of fatherhood and the conduct of motherhood may, on a societal level, be exerting contradictory influences on the culture of fatherhood.

THE CONDUCT OF FATHERHOOD VERSUS THE CONDUCT OF MOTHERHOOD

Contending that the conduct of fatherhood has changed very little over the course of the 20th century flies in the face of what many of us see every day: dads pushing strollers, changing diapers, playing in the park with their kids. Also, what about the men who publicly proclaim that they have made a conscientious effort to be more involved with their children than their own fathers were with them?

What cannot be forgotten is that appearances and proclamations (both to others and ourselves) can be deceiving; everything hinges on how we conceptualize and measure parental conduct. Michael Lamb (1987) notes that scholars generally have been ambiguous about what they mean by parental "involvement," with the result that it is difficult to compare one study with the next, and he maintains that if we ever hope to determine whether or not fathers have changed, we must arrive at a definition that is both conceptually clear and comprehensive. The definition which he thinks should be used is one that separates parental involvement into three components: engagement, accessibility, and responsibility. *Engagement* is time spent in one-on-one interaction with a child (whether feeding, helping with homework, or playing catch in the backyard). *Accessibility* is a less intense degree of interaction and is the kind of involvement whereby the parent is doing one thing (cooking, watching television) but is ready or available to do another (respond to the child, if the need arises). *Responsibility* has to do with who is accountable for the child's welfare and care. Responsibility includes things like making sure that the child has clothes to wear and keeping track of when the child has to go to the pediatrician.

Reviewing studies that allow comparisons to be made between contemporary fathers' involvement with children and contemporary mothers' involvement with children, Lamb (1987) estimates that in two-parent families in which mothers are unemployed, fathers spend about one fifth to one quarter as much time as mothers do in an engagement status and about a third as much time as mothers do just being accessible to their children. In two-parent families with employed mothers, fathers spend about 33% as much time as mothers do in an engagement status and 65% as much time being accessible. As far as responsibility is concerned, mothers appear to carry over 90% of the load, regardless of whether they are employed or not. Lamb also notes that observational and survey data indicate that the behavioral styles of fathers and mothers differ. Mother–child interaction is dominated by caretaking whereas father–child interaction is dominated by play.

> *Mothers actually play with their children more than fathers do but, as a proportion of the total amount of child–parent interaction, play is a much more prominent component of father–child interaction, whereas caretaking is more salient with mothers. (p. 10)*

In looking for trends, Lamb relies on one of the few studies which allows historical comparisons to be made—a 1975 national survey that was repeated in 1981 (Juster, 1985). No data apparently were collected on parents' accessibility or responsibility levels, but between 1975 and 1981, among men and women aged 18 to 44, there was a 26% increase in fathers' engagement levels and a 7% increase in mothers'. Despite these shifts, paternal engagement was only about one third that of mothers, increasing from 29% in 1975 to 34% in 1981 (Lamb, 1987).

While there is nothing intrinsically wrong with talking about percentage changes, one should be careful about relying on them and them alone. If, for example, one examines the tables from which Lamb drew his conclusions (Juster, 1985), one finds that the number of hours per week that the fathers spent in child care was 2.29 hours in 1975, compared to 2.88 hours in 1981, which is an increase of about 35 minutes per week or 5 minutes per day. The mothers in the sample, on the other hand, spent 7.96 hours per week in child care in 1975, compared to 8.54 hours per week in

child care in 1981, which also is an increase of about 35 minutes per week or 5 minutes per day. Thus, in absolute terms, fathers and mothers increased their child care by the same amount.

Bear in mind also that we are still talking about only one component of parental involvement, namely engagement. The two national surveys provide little, if any, information about changes in the accessibility and responsibility levels of fathers and mothers. Perhaps I am being overly cautious, but I cannot help but feel that until we gather historical data which would allow us to compare all three components of fatherhood, we should temper our excitement about surveys which suggest changes in the conduct of fatherhood over time. (For a tightly reasoned alternative viewpoint, see Pleck, 1985.)

Comparisons over time are difficult to make not only because so few scholars have chosen to study the history of fatherhood, but also because the studies carried out over the years to measure family trends provide scant information about fatherhood, per se. For instance, during a recent visit to the Library of Congress, I examined the Robert and Helen Lynd archival collection which I had hoped would include copies of the interview schedules from their two Middletown studies. It had occurred to me that if I could review the raw data from the studies, then I could perhaps plot paternal involvement trends from 1924 to 1935 to 1978, the times of the first, second, and third data collections in the Middletown series (Lynd & Lynd, 1929, 1937; Caplow, Bahr, Chadwick, Hill, & Williamson, 1982). Unfortunately, only four sample interviews from the earlier studies were in the archives The rest apparently were destroyed. It is a shame that the Middletown data were not saved because the most recent book in the series presents a table which shows an increase in the weekly hours that fathers spent with their children between 1924 and 1987 (Caplow et al., 1982). There is no indication whether this represents an increase in engagement or accessibility or both. Had I been able to look at the interviews themselves, however, I might have been able to discern subtle variations.

What about the dads who are seen interacting with their kids in public (see Mackey & Day, 1979)? A thoughtful answer to this question also must address how we conceptualize and measure paternal involvement. Does the paternal engagement level of fathers in public square with the paternal engagement level of fathers in private, or are we getting an inflated view of fatherhood from public displays? If we took the time to scrutinize the behavior of fathers and mothers in public would we find that, upon closer examination, the division of child care is still fairly traditional. When a family with small children goes out to eat, for example, who in the family—mom or dad—is more accessible to the children; that is to say, whose dinner is more likely to be interrupted by the constant demands to "put ketchup on my hamburger, pour my soda, cut my meat"? And how can one look at a family in public and measure who is responsible for the children? How do we know, for instance, who decides whether the kids need clothes; indeed, how do we know who is familiar with the kids' sizes, color preferences, and tolerance levels for trying on clothes? The same applies to studies of paternal involvement in laboratory settings (see Parke, 1981). What can a study of father–child interaction in, say, a hospital nursery tell us about father–child interaction in general? The fact that fathers are making their presence known in maternity wards certainly is not sufficient to suggest that the overall conduct of fathers has changed in any significant way. Finally, the fact that fathers can be seen in public with their children may not be as important as the question, How much time do fathers spend *alone* with their children? One recent study found that mothers of young children spent an average of 44.45 hours per week in total child-interaction time (which goes beyond engagement), while fathers spent an average of 29.48 hours per week, a 1.5 to 1 difference. If one looked, however, at time spent alone with children, one discovered that 19.56 hours of mothers' child-interaction time, compared with 5.48 hours of fathers' child-interaction, was solo time, a 3.6 to 1 difference. Moreover, while fathers' total interaction time was

positively affected by the number of hours their wives worked, fathers' solo time was not affected at all (Barnett & Baruch, 1987).

As for the public proclamations, almost all the books and articles which tout the arrival of "new" fatherhood are written not by a cross-section of the population but by upper-middle class professionals. Kort and Friedland's (1986) edited book, for instance, has 57 men writing about their pregnancy, birth, and child-rearing experiences. But who are these men? For the most part, they are novelists, educators, sculptors, real estate investors, radio commentators, newspaper editors, publishers, physicians, performers, psychologists, social workers, and attorneys. Not exactly a representative sample. As Rotundo (1985) notes, androgynous fatherhood as an ideal has caught the attention of the upper-middle class more than any other group, but that even in this group, words seem to speak louder than actions.

While the perception of fathers in public and the Kort and Friedland (1986) book may not accurately represent what fathers in general are *doing*, they can most certainly have an effect of what people *think* fathers are doing and should be doing. Which brings us back to the question, What are the consequences that have resulted from the apparent disparity between beliefs and actuality?

THE CONSEQUENCES OF ASYNCHRONOUS SOCIAL CHANGE

Thirty years ago, E. E. LeMasters (1957) made the point that parenthood (and not marriage, as many believe) is the real "romantic complex" in our society, and that even middle-class couples, who do more than most to plan for children, are caught unprepared for the responsibilities of parenthood. Later on, he and John DeFrain (1983) traced America's tendency to romanticize parenthood to a number of popular folk beliefs or myths, some of which are: raising children is always fun, children are forever sweet and cute, children will invariably turn out well if they have "good" parents, and having children will never disrupt but in fact will always improve marital communication and adjustment. Needless to say, anyone who is a parent probably remembers only too vividly the point at which these folk beliefs began to crumble in her/his mind.

The idea that fathers have radically changed —that they now are intimately involved in raising their children—qualifies also as a folk belief, and it too is having an impact on our lives and that of our children. On the positive side, people are saying that at least we have made a start. Sure, men are not as involved with their children as some of us would like them to be, but, so the argument goes, the fact that we are talking about change represents a step in the right direction. (Folk beliefs, in other words, are not necessarily negative. The myth that children are always fun, for example, does have the positive effect of making children more valued than they would be if we believed the opposite: that they are always a nuisance.) But what about the negative side of the myth of the changing father? Is there a negative side? My objective is to focus here on this question because up to now scholars and the media have tended to overlook the often unintentional but still very real negative consequences that have accompanied asynchronous change in the social institution of fatherhood.

I am not saying that professionals have been oblivious to the potentially negative consequences of "androgynization" on men's lives, for one could point to several articles and chapters which have addressed this issue (e.g., Benokraitis, 1985; Berger, 1979; Lamb, Pleck, & Levine, 1987; Lutwin & Siperstein, 1985; Pleck, 1979; Scanzoni, 1979). Rather, the point being made is that scholars and the media, for the most part, have overlooked the difficulties associated with a *specific* social change, namely the asynchronous change in the social institution of fatherhood.

The Technically Present But Functionally Absent Father

The distinction between engagement and accessibility outlined by Lamb (1987) is similar to the distinction between *primary time* and *secondary time* in our study of the transition to parenthood (LaRossa & LaRossa, 1981). The social organization of a family with children, especially young children, parallels the social organization of a hospital in that both are *continuous coverage social systems* (Zerubavel, 1979). Both are set up to provide direct care to someone (be it children or patients) on a round-the-clock or continuous basis. And both the family and the hospital, in order to give caregivers a break every now and then, will operate according to some formal or informal schedule such that some person or persons will be "primarily" involved with the children or patients (on duty) while others will be "secondarily" involved (on call or accessible).

Like Lamb, we also found that the fathers' levels of engagement, accessibility, and responsibility were only a fraction of the mothers', and that fathers tended to spend a greater part of their care giving time playing with their children. Moreover, we found that the kinds of play that fathers were likely to be involved in were the kinds of activities that could be carried out at a secondary (semi-involved) level of attention, which is to say that it was not unusual for fathers to be primarily involved in watching television or doing household chores while only secondarily playing with their children.

When asked why they wanted to be with their children, the fathers often would answer along the lines that a father has to "put in some time with his kids" (LaRossa, 1983, p. 585). Like prisoners who "do time" in prison many fathers see themselves as "doing time" with their children. If, on some level of consciousness, fathers have internalized the idea that they should be more involved with their children, but on another level of consciousness they do not find the idea all that attractive, one would expect the emergence of a hybrid style: the technically present but functionally absent father (cf. Feldman & Feldman, 1975, cited in Pleck, 1983).

The technically present but functionally absent father manifests himself in a variety of ways. One father in our study prided himself on the fact that he and his wife cared for their new baby on an alternating basis, with him "covering" the mornings and his wife "covering" the afternoons. "We could change roles in a night," he said; "it wouldn't affect us." But when this father was asked to describe a typical morning spent alone with his infant son, he gave the distinct impression that he saw fatherhood as a *job* and that while he was "there" in body, he was someplace else in spirit.

> *I have the baby to be in charge of, [which has] really been no problem for me at all. But that's because we worked out a schedule where he sleeps a pretty good amount of that time.... I generally sort of have to be with him in the sense of paying attention to his crying or dirty diapers or something like that for any where between 30 to 45 minutes, sometimes an hour, depending. But usually I can have two hours of my own to count on each morning to do my own work, so it's no problem. That's just the breaks that go with it.*

Another example: Recently, there appeared an advertisement for one of those minitelevisions, the kind you can carry around in your pocket. Besides promoting the television as an electronic marvel, the man who was doing the selling also lauded how his mini-TV had changed his life: "Now when I go to my son's track meets, I can keep up with other ball games" (Kaplan, 1987, p. 32a). The question is: Is this father going to the track meets to see his son race, or is he going simply to get "credit" from his son for being in the stands? One more example: A newspaper story about a father jogging around Golden State Park in San Francisco who is so immersed in his running that he fails to notice his 3-year-old daughter—whom he apparently had brought with him—crying "Daddy, Daddy" along the side of the running track. When he finally notices her, he stops only long enough to tell his daughter that it is not his job to watch her, but her job to watch for him (Gustatis, 1982).

What will be the impact of the mixed messages that these children—and perhaps countless others—are getting from their fathers? Research capable of measuring and assessing the complex-

ity of these encounters is needed to adequately answer this question (Pleck, 1983).

Marital Conflict in Childbearing and Child-Rearing Families

Because our study was longitudinal, we were able to trace changes over time; and we found that from the third, to the sixth, to the ninth month postpartum, couples became more traditional, with fathers doing proportionately less child care (LaRossa & LaRossa, 1981). It was this traditionalization process that provided us with a close-up view of what happens when the bubble bursts; that is, what happens when the romanticized vision of dad's involvement starts to break down.

One father, first interviewed around the third month after his daughter's birth, wanted to communicate that he was not going to be an absentee father like some of his friends were:

> *I've got a good friend of mine, he's the ultimate male chauvinist pig. He will not change a diaper.... [But] I share in changing the diapers, and rocking the baby, and in doing those kinds of things.... I love babies.*

During the sixth month interview, however, it was revealed that he indeed had become very much the absentee father. In fact, almost every evening since the first interview he had left the house after dinner to play basketball, or participate in an amateur theater group, or sing in the local choir.

Since what he was doing contradicted what he said he would do, he was asked by his wife to "account" for his behavior. *Accounts* are demanded of social actors whose behavior is thought to be out of line. By submitting an account, which in common parlance generally takes the form of an excuse or justification, and having it honored or accepted by the offended party, a person who stands accused can manage to create or salvage a favorable impression (Scott & Lyman, 1968). Because the wife did not honor the accounts that her husband offered, the father was put in the position of either admitting he was wrong (i.e., apologizing) or coming up with more accounts. He chose the latter, and in due course offered no fewer than 20 different explanations for his conduct, to include "I help out more than most husbands do" and "I'm not good at taking care of the baby." At one dramatic point during the second interview, the husband and wife got into a verbal argument over how much of the husband's contribution to child care was "fact" and how much was "fancy." (He, with his head: "I *know* I was [around a lot]." She, with her heart: "[To me] it just doesn't *feel* like he was.")

This couple illustrates what may be happening in many homes as a result of the asynchrony between the culture and conduct of fatherhood. In the past, when (as best we can tell) both the culture and conduct of fatherhood were more or less traditional, fathers may not have been asked to account for their low paternal involvement. If the culture said that fathers should not be involved with their children and if fathers were not involved with their children, then fathers were perceived as doing what they should be doing. No need for an explanation. Today, however, the culture and conduct of fatherhood appear to be out of sync. The culture has moved toward (not to) androgyny much more rapidly than the conduct. On some level of consciousness, fathers and mothers believe that the behavior of fathers will measure up to the myth. Usually, this is early in the parental game, before or just after the birth of the first child. In time, however, reality sets in, and on another level of consciousness it becomes apparent that mom is doing more than planned because dad is doing less than planned. The wife challenges the legitimacy of the (more unequal than she had foreseen) division of child care, demanding an explanation from her husband, which may or may not be offered, and if offered may or may not be honored, and so on.

In short, one would expect more conflict in marriage today centered around the legitimacy of the division of child care than, say, 40 years ago because of the shift in the culture of fatherhood that has occurred during this time. Some may say, "Great, with more conflict there will be needed change." And their point is valid. But what must be kept in mind is that conflict also can escalate and destroy. Given that at least one recent study has reported that the most likely conflict to lead a couple to blows is conflict over children (Straus, Gelles, & Steinmetz, 1980), family researchers and practitioners would be well advised to pay attention to the possibility that violence during the transition to parenthood may be one negative consequence of asynchronous social change.

Fathers and Guilt

Several years ago, Garry Trudeau (1985), who writes *Doonesbury,* captured to a tee the asynchrony between the culture and conduct of fatherhood when he depicted a journalist-father sitting at his home computer and working on an autobiographical column on "The New Fatherhood" for the Sunday section of the newspaper. "My editor feels there's a lot of interest in the current, more involved generation of fathers," the journalist tells his wife who has just come in the room. "He asked me to keep an account of my experiences." Trudeau's punch line is that when Super Dad is asked by his wife to watch his son because she has to go to a meeting, he says no because if he did, he would not meet his deadline. In the next day's *Doonesbury,* Trudeau fired another volley at the new breed of fathers. Now the son is standing behind his computer-bound father and ostensibly is asking for his father's attention. But again Super Dad is too busy pecking away at his fatherhood diary to even look up: "Not now, son. Daddy's busy" (March 24 & 25).

Trudeau's cartoons, copies of which sit on my wall in both my office and my den, are a reminder to me not to be so caught up in writing about what it means to be a father (thus contributing to the culture of fatherhood) that I fail to *be* a father. The fact, however, that I took the time to cut the cartoons out of the newspaper (and make not one but two copies) and the fact that Trudeau, who is himself a father, penned the cartoons in the first place is indicative of a feeling that many men today experience, namely ambivalence over their performance as fathers.

To feel "ambivalent" about something is to feel alternately good and bad about it. The plethora of autobiographical books and articles written by fathers in the past few years conveys the impression that men do feel and, perhaps most importantly, should feel good about their performance as fathers. A lot of men do seem to be proud of their performance, what with all the references to "new" fatherhood and the like. At the same time, however, men are being almost constantly told—and can see for themselves, if they look close enough—that their behavior does not square with the ideal, which means that they are being reminded on a regular basis that they are *failing* as fathers. Failing not when compared with their own fathers or grandfathers perhaps, but failing when compared with the image of fatherhood which has become part of our culture and which they, on some level of consciousness, believe in.

This is not to suggest that in the past men were totally at ease with their performance as fathers, that they had no doubts about whether they were acting "correctly." For one thing, such an assertion would belie the fact that role playing is, to a large degree, improvisational, that in everyday life (vs. the theater) scripts almost always are ill defined and open to a variety of interpretations (Blumer, 1969). Perhaps more importantly, asserting that men in the past were totally at ease with their performance as fathers would ignore the fact that, contrary to what many think, some of our fathers and grandfathers were ambivalent about the kind of job they were doing. In a study just begun on the history of fatherhood in America, I have come across several cases of men in the early 1900s expressing concern over the quality of their paternal involvement. In 1925, for example, one father wrote to a psychologist to ask whether he was *too involved* with his 2-year-old son. Apparently, he had taught the boy both the alphabet and how to count, and he now wondered whether he had forced his son to learn too much too soon (LaRossa, 1988).

So, what *is* the difference between then and now? I would say it is a difference in degree not kind. I would hypothesize that, given the asynchrony between the culture and conduct of fatherhood, the number of fathers who feel ambivalent and, to a certain extent, guilty about their performance as fathers has increased over the past three generations. I would also hypothesize that, given it is the middle class which has been primarily responsible for the changes in the culture of fatherhood, it is the middle-class fathers who are likely to feel the most ambivalent and suffer from the most guilt.

There is a certain amount of irony in the proposition that middle-class men are the ones who are the most likely to experience ambivalence and guilt, in that middle-class men are also the ones who seem to be trying the hardest to act according to the emerging ideal. As noted, the testimonials from the so-called androgynous fathers almost invariably are written by middle-class professionals. But it is precisely because these middle-class professionals are trying to conform to the higher standards that one would expect that they would experience the most ambivalence and guilt. Like athletes training for the Olympics, androgynous-striving fathers often are consumed with how they are doing as fathers and how they can do better. For example:

> *Should I play golf today, or should I spend more time playing with Scott and Julie? Should I stay late in the office to catch up or should I leave early to go home and have dinner with the children? There is an endless supply of these dilemmas each day.* (Belsky, 1986, p. 64)

Some may argue that the parental anxiety that men are beginning to experience is all for the better, that they now may start feeling bad enough about their performance to really change. This argument does have merit. Yes, one positive outcome of asynchronous social change is that ultimately men may become not only more involved with their children but also more sensitive to what it is like to be a mother. After all, for a long time women have worried about *their* performance as parents. It should not be forgotten, however, that the guilt which many women experience as mothers (and which has been the subject of numerous novels, plays, and films) has not always been healthy for mothers—or families. In sum, when it comes to parenthood, today it would appear that both men and women can be victims as well as benefactors of society's ideals.

CONCLUSION

Fatherhood is different today than it was in prior times but, for the most part, the changes that have occurred are centered in the culture rather than in the conduct of fatherhood. Whatever changes have taken place in the behavior of fathers, on the basis of what we know now, seem to be minimal at best. Also, the behavioral changes have largely occurred within a single group—the middle class.

The consequences of the asynchrony between the (comparatively speaking) "modern" culture of fatherhood and the "less modern" or "traditional" conduct of fatherhood are (a) the emergence of the technically present but functionally absent father, (b) an increase in marital conflict in childbearing and child-rearing families, and (c) a greater number of fathers, especially in the middle class, who feel ambivalent and guilty about their performance as fathers.

A number of recommendations seem to be in order. First, more people need to be made aware of the fact that the division of child care in America has not significantly changed, that—despite the beliefs that fathers are a lot more involved with their children—mothers remain, far and away, the primary child caregivers. The reason for publicizing this fact is that if our beliefs represent what we want (i.e., more involved fathers) and we mistakenly assume that what we want is what we have, our complacency will only serve to perpetuate the culture-conduct disjunction. Thus, scholars and representatives of the media must commit themselves to presenting a balanced picture of "new fatherhood."

Second, and in line with the above, men must be held responsible for their actions. In our study of the transition to parenthood, we found that the language that couples use to account for men's lack of involvement in infant care does not simply reflect the division of infant care, it constructs that division of infant care. In other words, the accounts employed by new parents to excuse and justify men's paternal role distance serves as a social lubricant in the traditionalization process (LaRossa & LaRossa, 1981). Thus, when men say things like "I'm not good at taking care of the baby" or "I can't be with Junior now, I have to go to the office, go to the store, go to sleep, mow the lawn, pay the bills, and so forth" the question must be raised, are these reasons genuine (i.e., involving insurmountable role conflicts) or are they nothing more than rationalizations used by men to do one thing (not be with their children) but believe another ("I like to be with my children")? If they are rationalizations, then they should not be honored. Not honoring rationalizations "de-legitimates" actions and, in the process, puts the burden of responsibility for the actions squarely on the person who is carrying out the actions. Only when men are forced to seriously examine their commitment to fatherhood (vs. their commitment to their jobs and avocations) can we hope to bring about the kinds of changes that will be required to alter the division of child care in this country (LaRossa, 1983).

What kinds of changes are we talking about? Technically present but functionally absent fathers are products of the society in which we live. So also, the traditionalization process during the transition to parenthood and the conflict and guilt it apparently engenders cannot be divorced from the socio-historical reality surrounding us and of which we are a part. All of which means that if we hope to alter the way men relate to their children, we cannot be satisfied with individualistic solutions which see "the problem" as a private, therapeutic matter best solved through consciousness raising groups and the like. Rather, we must approach it as a public issue and be prepared to alter the institutional fabric of American society (cf. Mills, 1959). For example, the man-as-breadwinner model of fatherhood, a model which emerged in the 19th and early 20th centuries and which portrays fathers primarily as breadwinners whose wages make family consumption and security possible, remains dominant today (Pleck, 1987). This model creates structural barriers to men's involvement with their children, in that it legitimates inflexible and highly demanding job schedules which, in turn, increase the conflict between market work and family work (Pleck, 1985). More flex-time jobs would help to relieve this conflict. So would greater tolerance, on the part of employers, of extended paternity leaves (Levine, 1976). I am not suggesting that the only reason that men are not as involved with their children is that their jobs keep them from getting involved. The fact that many women also contend with inflexible and highly demanding job schedules and still are relatively involved with their children would counter

such an assertion. Rather, the point is that the level of achievement in market work expected of men in America generally is higher than the level of achievement in market work expected of women and that this socio-historical reality must be entered into any equation which attempts to explain why fathers are not more involved.

When we will begin to see significant changes in the conduct of fatherhood is hard to say. The past generally provides the data to help predict the future. But, as the historian John Demos (1982) once noted, "Fatherhood has a very long history, but virtually no historians" (p. 425). Hence, our ability to make informed predictions about the future of fatherhood is severely limited. Hopefully, as more empirical research—historical and otherwise—on fatherhood is carried out, we will be in a better position to not only see what is coming but to deal with what is at hand.

REFERENCES

Barnett, R. C., & Baruch, G. K. (1987). Determinants of fathers' participation in family work. *Journal of Marriage and the Family, 49,* 29–40.

Belsky, M. R. (1986). Scott's and Julie's Daddy. In C. Kort & R. Friedland (Eds.), *The father's book: Shared experiences* (pp. 63–65). Boston: G. K. Hall.

Benokraitis, N. (1985). Fathers in the dual-earner family. In S. M. H. Hanson & F. W. Bozett (Eds.), *Dimensions of fatherhood* (pp. 243–268). Beverly Hills, CA: Sage Publications.

Berger, M. (1979). Men's new family roles—Some implications for therapists. *Family Coordinator, 28,* 638–646.

Blumer, H. (1969). *Symbolic interactionism: Perspective and method.* Englewood Cliffs, NJ: Prentice Hall.

Caplow, T. with Bahr, H. M., Chadwick, B. A., Hill, R., & Williamson, M. H. (1982). *Middletown families: Fifty years of change and continuity.* Minneapolis: University of Minnesota Press.

Day, R. D., & Mackey, W. C. (1986). The role image of the American father: An examination of a media myth. *Journal of Comparative Family Studies, 17,* 371–388.

Demos, J. (1982). The changing faces of fatherhood: A new exploration in American family history. In S. H. Cath, A. R. Gurwitt, & J. M. Ross (Eds.), *Father and child: Developmental and clinical perspectives* (pp. 425–445). Boston: Little, Brown.

Gustatis, R. (1982, August 15). Children sit idle while parents pursue leisure. *Atlanta Journal and Constitution,* pp. 1D, 4D.

Hanson, S. M. H., & Bozett, F. W. (1985). *Dimensions of fatherhood.* Beverly Hills, CA: Sage Publications.

Hanson, S. M. H., & Bozett, F. W. (1987). Fatherhood: A review and resources. *Family Relations, 36,* 333–340.

Harte, S. (1987, June 21). Fathers and sons. Narrowing the generation gap: Atlanta dads reflect a more personal style of parenting. *Atlanta Journal and Constitution,* pp. 4G, 6G.

Juster, F. T. (1985). A note on recent changes in time use. In F. T. Juster & F. P. Stafford (Eds.), *Time,* goods, and well-being (pp. 313–332). Ann Arbor, MI: Institute for Social Research.

Kaplan, D. (1987, Early Summer). The great $39.00 2" TV catch. *DAK Industries Inc.,* p. 32A.

Kort, C., & Friedland, R. (Eds.), (1986). *The father's book: Shared experiences.* Boston: G. K. Hall.

Lamb, M. E. (1987). Introduction: The emergent American father. In M. E. Lamb (Ed.), *The father's role: Cross-cultural perspectives* (pp. 3–25). Hillsdale, NJ: Lawrence Erlbaum.

Lamb, M. E., Pleck, J. H., & Levine, J. A. (1987). Effects of increased paternal involvement on fathers and mothers. In C. Lewis & M. O'Brien (Eds.), *Reassessing fatherhood: New observations on fathers and the modern family* (pp. 109–125). Beverly Hills, CA: Sage Publications.

LaRossa, R. (1983). The transition to parenthood and the social reality of time. *Journal of Marriage and the Family, 45,* 579–589.

LaRossa, R. (1988, November). *Toward a social history of fatherhood in America.* Paper presented at the Theory Construction and Research Methodology Workshop, Annual Meeting of National Council of Family Relations, Philadelphia, PA.

LaRossa, R., & LaRossa, M. M. (1981). *Transition to parenthood: How infants change families.* Beverly Hills, CA: Sage Publications.

LeMasters, E. E. (1957). Parenthood as crisis. *Marriage and Family Living, 19,* 352–355.

LeMasters, E. E., & DeFrain, J. (1983). *Parents in contemporary America: A sympathetic view* (4th ed.). Homewood, IL: Dorsey.

Levine, J. A. (1976). *Who will raise the children?* New York: Bantam.

Lewis, C. (1986). *Becoming a father.* Milton Keynes, England: Open University Press.

Lewis, C., & O'Brien, M. (1987). *Reassessing fatherhood: New observations on fathers and the modern family.* Beverly Hills, CA: Sage Publications.

Lutwin, D. R., & Siperstein, G. N. (1985). Househusband fathers. In S. M. H. Hanson & F. W. Bozett (Eds.), *Dimensions of fatherhood* (pp. 269–287). Beverly Hills, CA: Sage Publications.

Lynd, R. S., & Lynd, H. M. (1929). *Middletown: A study in American culture.* New York: Harcourt & Brace.

Lynd, R. S., & Lynd, H. M. (1937). *Middletown in transition: A study in cultural conflicts.* New York: Harcourt & Brace.

Mackey, W. C., & Day, R. D. (1979). Some indicators of fathering behaviors in the United States: A crosscultural examination of adult male-child interaction. *Journal of Marriage and the Family, 41,* 287–297.

Margolis, M. L. (1984). *Mothers and such: Views of American women and why they changed.* Berkeley: University of California Press.

McKee, L., & O'Brien, M. (Eds.), (1982). *The father figure.* London: Tavistock.

Mead, M. (1967). Margaret Mead answers: How do middle-class American men compare with men in other cultures you have studied? *Redbook, 129,* 36.

Mills, C. W. (1959). *The sociological imagination.* London: Oxford University Press.

Parke, R. D. (1981). *Fathers.* Cambridge, MA: Harvard University Press.

Pleck, J. H. (1979). Men's family work: Three perspectives and some data. *Family Coordinator, 28,* 481–488.

Pleck, J. H. (1983). Husbands' paid work and family roles: Current research issues. In H. Z. Lopata & J. H. Pleck (Eds.), *Research in the interweave of social roles, Vol. 3, Families and jobs* (pp. 251–333). Greenwich, CT: JAI Press.

Pleck, J. H. (1985). *Working wives/Working husbands.* Beverly Hills, CA: Sage Publications.

Pleck, J. H. (1987). American fathering in historical perspective. In M. S. Kimmel (Ed.), *Changing men: New directions in research on men and masculinity* (pp. 83–97). Beverly Hills, CA: Sage Publications.

Rotundo, E. A. (1985). American fatherhood: A historical perspective. *American Behavioral Scientist, 29,* 7–25.

Scanzoni, J. (1979). Strategies for changing male family roles: Research and practice implications. *Family Coordinator, 28,* 435–442.

Scott, M. B., & Lyman, S. M. (1968). Accounts. *American Sociological Review, 33,* 46–62.

Stokes, R., & Hewitt, J. P. (1976). Aligning actions. *American Sociological Review, 41,* 838–849.

Straus, M., Gelles, R. J., & Steinmetz, S. K. (1980). *Behind closed doors: Violence in the American family.* New York: Anchor/Doubleday.

Trudeau, G. B. (1985, March 24 & March 25). *Doonesbury.* United Press Syndicate.

Zerubavel, E. (1979). *Patterns of time in hospital life: A sociological perspective.* Chicago: University of Chicago Press.

34

Men and Women in Southern Spain
"Domestic Power" Revisited[1]

DAVID D. GILMORE

Anthropologists have begun to challenge standard assumptions about gender in southern Europe. Initiated by feminists compensating for male bias in data collection, recent studies[2] have revitalized Mediterranean ethnography by transcending sexual stereotypes of woman as reticent, passive, and submissive, and man as active, powerful, and assertive. Disavowing the alleged "invisibility" of peasant women and providing new insight into women's daily routines both in and out of doors, these studies take us far beyond the crude sex-based oppositions such as honor/shame, kinship/friendship, and public/private, with their often hidden androcentric biases.

The argument is that if we look at what goes on within and among households rather than public policy-making, women are neither so recessive nor so powerless as male anthropologists and their informants have stated. My topic here is the question of "domestic power" and who has it. Data are taken from two rural communities in western Andalusia (Seville Province). "Fuenmayor" and "El Castillo"[3] are located some ten miles apart on either side of the national highway linking the provincial capitals of Seville and Cordoba. No comparison is intended here; the two examples are treated as a single case study.

RURAL TOWNS

Fuenmayor is an agricultural town of about 8,000 people in the alluvial Guadalquivir River Basin. Its economy is based on dry cultivation of Mediterranean staple crops such as olives, wheat, and sunflowers. El Castillo is about half the size of its neighbor, with about 4,000 people. The two towns represent matched "twins" sharing similar market

adaptations, history, and mutual participation in a generally shared ritual cycle. As in the larger town, the Castilleros are almost all involved in rainfall agriculture. The smaller community has somewhat more land under garden irrigation and so has a slightly higher per capita income.

El Castillo also has a vestigial cottage industry of esparto-grass manufacturing, producing tiny quantities of sandals, mats, and bridles, but this is hardly thriving today with the competition of mass-produced goods. In contrast, Fuenmayor has one of the few liquor mills in the *comarca* (ecological zone), producing small amounts of bottled anisette and cheap brandy. Sometimes this contrasting specialization gives rise to jokes about drunks versus cobblers, but otherwise the two towns enjoy friendly relations and their people mingle freely, intermarrying without comment.

Both towns are class-stratified, with relatively minor differences in wealth being the source of much discussion and concern. The main difference is that El Castillo does not have a significant resident gentry (*señoritos*) because its municipal territory is more subdivided. In addition, El Castillo has no aristocratic absentee landowners as does Fuenmayor, whose municipal territory includes a huge latifundium[4] owned by a Madrid-based duke. So, while the people of Fuenmayor recognize three resident social classes—the gentry, the peasants (*mayetes*), and the landless laborers (*jornaleros*)—the Castilleros proudly say they are more egalitarian, with only peasants and farm workers present. "We are more together," they say, glossing over the fact that there are a few wealthy peasant families who hire labor.

Today, both communities are Left-leaning, with strong Communist and Socialist representa-

303

tion, although in keeping with the generally more sophisticated quality of Fuenmayor's political life, most of the current regional leaders come from Fuenmayor. In most other respects, also, the two towns are similar, especially in their lingering observation of traditional sex and gender distinctions. In what follows I discuss primarily the men and women of the working classes: smallholding peasants and rural proletarians. The gentry of Fuenmayor and the relatively few rich farmers of El Castillo form an important contrast that I will address later.

The rigid sexual segregation typical of Andalusian agrotowns prevailed in these two towns until the 1970s, which represents our ethnographic present. As throughout the region, men are expected to remain outside the home, either at work, or, when unemployed or after hours, at the neighborhood tavern. Men who linger at home are morally suspect; their manhood is questionable. Community gossip is relentless on this score. Men who avoid the male camaraderie of the bars at night are often likened to "motherhens," and "brooding cows." Very concerned about their manly image, most men avoid spending too much time indoors.

In El Castillo, there is one exception to this. Some men have organized an "eating club," which meets alternately in each club member's home. The man in question prepares a feast with his wife's help and invites all the others to the festivities. This, however, is somewhat of an anomaly, and even the Castilleros say openly that this is daring and "modern."

Men and women in both towns say that men "belong" in the streets, women in the home. A good woman is "mistress of her house": chaste, housebound, secluded, a careful housekeeper and a devoted mother. A good man, conversely, although he is a concerned husband and father and a good provider, is not expected to be deeply involved in domestic activities. As we have seen, any retreat away from the hurly-burly and the often exhausting male rivalries of the extra-domestic world is, for a self-respecting man, a cultural solecism as damaging to reputation as a woman's immodesty.

Thus, while women are "forced" to avoid the public places, one may say equally that men are "forced" to give up the tranquility and comfort of the home for the greater part of the day.

Depending upon individual personality, this spatial "gender schema" can be said to be equally repressive for both sexes. One is tempted to add that the association of "public" with freedom and power, and of "private" with deprivation and oppression, is an ethnocentric imposition upon a much richer reality.

CONJUGAL DECISION MAKING

Prenuptial Example

In Andalusia, the engagement is usually a long, drawn-out process often involving years. Consequently, such decisions often presage future directions and set the stage for marital relations to come. The following incident involves fiances (*novios*) from El Castillo. It involves the most important decision a couple can make: when to marry.

Eulogio, a man of about 30, and Carmen, 28, had been engaged for four years—a relatively long period, but not unusual by any means. Carmen decided it was time to marry: she had compiled her *ajuar* or trousseau; her parents had finally rebuilt and furnished an upstairs apartment in the parental home for the newlyweds. Besides, she was impatient for the big day. However, Eulogio resisted setting a date, and the wedding was becoming a bone of contention. A trucker with a growing business transporting comestibles to and from Seville, he felt he needed more time to amass capital before marriage. As he put it to friends, a man wants to gain financial independence before, not after, marriage—a common sentiment finding wide approval among his friends and confidants. So a basic disagreement erupted, setting the stage for a battle of wills, directly observed by Eulogio's male friends.

The unfolding of their rather stormy nuptial story is revealing for two reasons: first, because of the personal characteristics of the fiances, and second, because of the fact that within Eulogio's circle of bachelor friends, he was considered an exemplary "strong man," whose relations with his fiancee were watched closely for evidence of the hoped-for male domestic prerogative. That is, Eulogio was considered somewhat of a test case in the sense of masculine "right," a model for other as-yet unmarried men in his circle. Whether or not he would prevail over a woman was therefore regarded among his fellows as an augury. As elsewhere in Spain, El Castillo men pay lip service to an ideology of patriarchal privilege—at least in their bachelor days.

Eulogio was a gregarious man, tall and athletic, a successful risk-taker in business, stentorian in conversation, somewhat boastful, generous, "correct" in his dealings with men. Up to that point, too, he had appeared dominant in courtship (he appeared to be in charge, at least in public). In his teens, he had been a leader of his *pandilla,* or youthful clique, had achieved noncommissioned officer's rank in the army, and was considered to have leadership qualities. Independence and self-assurance were his hallmarks, consciously cultivated and acknowledged among both men and women in El Castillo. Contrariwise, Carmen was a small, demure, physically unimpressive women, who gave no indication, at least among men, of any outstanding qualities of character.

When Eulogio told his friends that his wedding would be postponed for another year because, as he put it, *he dicho* ("I have spoken"), there was general agreement that Carmen would simply have to wait. Yet within a month, Eulogio astonished his friends by sheepishly confiding that the wedding date had been set, that Carmen had gotten her way on an early marriage and that there was "no remedy." What had caused this dramatic turnaround? One day I sat in a bar with a number of mutual friends who were discussing the fiasco.

The men earnestly debated Eulogio's demise. One bachelor, Geraldo, expressed shock over his friend's craven capitulation. How was it possible, he asked, that a big strong man like Eulogio could relent so easily, put up so weak a struggle, and be so dominated by a small and apparently demure woman? "Who rules," Geraldo asked plaintively, "the man or the woman?"

The verb used here is *mandar,* "to command or dictate," a commonly heard term in discussions of politics. This concept of *manda,* or rule, has historically played an important role in masculine self-image in Andalusia, especially among rural farm workers. For these men to maintain their honor they must rule themselves, be their own master; hence they are manly. To be "ruled," by which is meant to be controlled by or dependent upon others, is to be dominated, with almost a ring of emasculation about it. One who is ruled is *manso,* "tame," the same term used in the farm context for a steer, a castrated bull (Marvin 1984:65). The "rule" concept finds symbolic expression in all walks of life, political, sexual, and interpersonal. Hence its use is effectively important in contexts in which male self-image is involved. Geraldo's question therefore had resonance beyond the call to colors in the battle of the sexes. It brought a reflective response from another, older man.

This man, Carlos, himself married, had the advantage of personal experience in such matters and also knew the fiances better than the rest. As such men often do in Andalusian bars, Carlos gave a little speech, beginning with the standard pontifical prelude: "look man, what happens is the following" (*lo que paza e' lo ziguiente*). Listening attentively, the others found his subsequent comments both amusing and profoundly true.

Carlos spoke candidly about the balance of power between the sexes. He allowed that the man rules in Spain, except, he added ironically, "when he doesn't." This latter occurs in most matters that are important to the woman. The reason for this is that the man is preoccupied by other matters and cannot give his full attention to details to which his wife, or fiancee, devotes all her energies. The final say in such matters, according to Carlos, is held not by the man or the woman, but by the support they can muster from interested kin. In this sense, the woman will prevail in domestic matters because she has the unfailing support of her mother, whose role in life is to protect her daughter and to advance her interests, while the man stands alone. The women, then, in tandem, can almost always "wear the man down." Carlos thus introduced two important principles: the inherent power of women in conjugal matters as a result of the divided attention and solitariness of men; and more telling, the considerable role played by the infamous *bête noire* of Andalusian husbands, the mother-in-law (*suegra*), in terrorizing her son-in-law. The invocation of the mother-in-law drew sighs of recognition and self-pity from most men present.

Carlos added that personality is of course very important here. For the man to prevail against wife and *suegra* he must be unusually "strong," meaning stubborn. However, even if he is strong and his wife is "submissive" (*floja*), his *suegra* is always strong, and the alliance of women is too potent to resist without an intolerable exhaustion of male energies. Equally important is the fact that the husband is rarely at home, leaving the field open to usurpation by wife and *suegra,* who are deeply invested in matters of the home. In any case, it is clear that "power" in this case, at least from the male perspective, was wielded by a woman, or perhaps more accurately, women in domestic alliance, since the ability to prevail in an important decision was "unexpected," unequivocal, and independent of "right" as men see it. Although my informants would be surprised to hear the word power used in this seemingly trivial context, they would nevertheless agree that important decisions affecting a man's life are often beyond his control and in the hands of manipulative or scheming women.

As Carlos was finishing his peroration about the power of the *novia* allied with the dreadful mother-in-law, one of the most popular local poets and comedians, a man known to everyone by his nickname "Juanito el Chocho," walked into the bar. Overhearing our conversation, the poet joined in by performing a credible pantomime of his "pugilistic" *suegra,* replete with right hooks and uppercuts. These comical convulsions culminated in a crescendo of obscene gestures indicating "she has me by the ass." Finally, before wandering off to the bar to reward his own performance with a drink, he sang a *copla* from one of his own epics, entitled "La Vida del Hombre" ("Man's Life")—a

typical way of concluding such discussions by invoking the summary power of wit. After catching the lyrics, the other men joined in:

Yo pelé con mi novia	I had a fight with my novia
Y mi suegra se enteró.	And my mother-in-law (to be) found out.
Me pegó con una caña	She jumped on top of me with a club
Y encima me la cascó!	And gave me a thorough drubbing!

Again, the term *encima* has emotional resonance. Literally "above," or "on top of," it is used to express social hierarchy and domination, as in the commonly heard expression *los ricos nos están encima,* "the rich are on top of us." To be "encima" also has obvious sexual connotations.

While these men clearly felt abused by the outcome of Eulogio's premarital squabble, I am unfortunately unable to provide his antagonists' view. For reasons of discretion, I was unable to interview Carmen or her mother alone. Despite recent arguments to the contrary, it is still inadvisable for a male fieldworker to approach unchaperoned women in places like Andalusia, because men take umbrage at such things.

Yet I did get some casual female input. The few women I was able to query regarded Carmen's victory as "only natural" because, as they said, technical matters involving marriage are a "woman's business" (*cosa de mujeres*). For a man to interfere in such matters was to them as unseemly as his attempting to dictate a silverware pattern or an upholstery color. So here is an area where male "right" seems to contrast with female "prerogative" or sexual "seemliness," and the former may indeed be contested, since the prerogatives of sex role seem ambiguous.

CONJUGAL DECISIONS

Once a couple marries, the newlyweds are faced with three immediate problems, the solutions of which will have permanent impact upon their future: first, where to set up residence; second, how to administer domestic finances and how to allocate previous savings in order to set up an immediately comfortable home; and, finally, when to have children and how many to have. Naturally there are other questions that arise, depending upon idiosyncrasies, but these three represent the major, initial, seminal or "organic" decisions that all newlyweds must make at the outset of establishing an independent household.

Postmarital residence in Fuenmayor shows a very strong neolocal, but "matrivicinal" tendency; that is, newlyweds tend to choose a new home that is near that of the wife's family. By "near" is normally meant within five minutes' walking distance. Minuscule degrees of distance are a major issue among engaged couples. I have heard both men and women state seriously that a house two blocks away was *lejos,* or "distant." People describe a house on the other side of town (about ten minutes' walking time) as *muy lejos,* or very far away. In addition, when the newlyweds must remain in one of the parental homes because of financial constraints (neolocality is preferred), there is a marked uxorilocal [residence with the parents of the bride] tendency. In Fuenmayor, 71 percent of households show a matrilateral extension. This same matrilateral tendency is equally well marked in El Castillo, where 79 percent of the extended multigenerational families were living with the wife's parents in the 1970s.

As a result, many Andalusian towns display a female-oriented residence pattern and sororal neighborhoods [neighborhoods in which sisters live close together], as is true of some Greek, Portuguese, and southern Italian peasants. These data challenge conventional wisdom about patriarchal, patrilocal peasantries. As Davis reports for the town of Pisticci in southern Italy, this residential preference tends to create a permanent female infrastructure, or matri-core; that is, neighborhoods are dominated by women's ties because women remain co-residential more often and longer than men and because they reside in close association with childhood neighbors, kinswoman, and parents after marriage. According to village perceptions of spatial-social distance, it is the husband who is most often the "stranger" in his home or neighborhood, residing "very far" from his parents, who

may be located more than two blocks away, and from his agnates.[5] In a statement that may serve for Andalusia, Davis writes: "The neighborhood is a community of women: women bring their husbands to live there; women have their close kin there; daughters will continue to live there when parents are dead." As Davis astutely notes, this matri-core is a woman's "chief source of power," since it provides her access to allies and to sources of information and gossip, and establishes a continual basis of kinship support.

Equally true in western Andalusia, this quasi-matrilocality raises two epistemological questions in considering domestic power: first, to what degree is this matrilocal-matrivicinal pattern consonant with the assumed male domestic prerogatives; and second, what is the effect of such a residence pattern on conjugal decision making? Although there is the usual amount of individual variation, certain patterns emerge.

When I first became aware of the matrilocal tendency, I queried men about it, since it seemed at variance with the androcentric emphasis. Most men said that they quietly acquiesced to the wife's request to "live near mamma," for a number of reasons, any one of which may have been paramount in any particular case. As in Seville City, some men said they wanted to evade the continuing supervision of their fathers, although this seems less pressing in these rural towns. The most common response was that residence was an issue that meant a great deal to women and less to men, as men are by nature more "independent" of parental ties. The wife, men allow, especially a new bride, needs the support of her mother in establishing a new home; so why break up this proven domestic team?

Basically the men felt that any attempt on their part to "come between" wife and mother-in-law by insisting on virilocal residence [residence with the parents of the groom] would backfire, leading to a passive-aggressive campaign by both to undermine his comfort and his peace of mind for the rest of his life, and that therefore the battle for dominance was just not worth the penalty.

To be sure, part of the answer reflects selfishness rather than mere passivity, since men want their homes to be run well and efficiently. Andalusians believe that since women are in charge of domestic operations they must be allowed full control; otherwise the man's life will suffer from disorganization. As one man put it: wife and mother are a "clique" that works well only when there is physical proximity. In a sense, therefore, the mother-in-law is regarded as a necessary nuisance, a kind of existential penance. The most common response to questions about the uxorial dominance in residence choice was therefore a resigned acceptance of proven practice with the frequently heard conversational suffix: *no hay remedio* (there is no remedy for it). This is a rhetorical device that one encounters in many male pronouncements concerning wives, mothers-in-law, and women's capacity to get their own way in general. Although this may reflect, in part, the usual male indifference to "feminine" preoccupations, it also seems to indicate a degree of moral surrender, as the issues concerned were indeed of great importance to men and were often, as they knew, the sources of dissatisfaction later. In this sense, we may characterize male abstention from such domestic matters as de facto, although ambivalent, recognition of uncontested female authority in domestic decision making.

The most important consequence of the husband's ambiguous acquiescence is that the *suegra* maintains a high profile in the man's life, often intruding into domestic arrangements and sometimes asserting the balance of power in marital quarrels or disagreements. The powerful image of this invasive female scourge is found also among urbanites in western Andalusia, testifying to a regional stereotype deeply rooted in male consciousness. On the surface, the Andalusian's fearful attitude about his mother-in-law seems ubiquitous rather than area-specific, aside from the possibly anomalous intensification of affinal ties as a result of matrivicinal residence. Most bilateral societies, including our own, have their own folklore about the horrors of this stock villain in the domestic comedy. Yet, because of the associated structural preponderance of the domestic matri-core, the Andalusian husband often finds himself outmatched by the weight this fierce harridan throws in supporting her daughter, and his laments often evoke a revealing sense of masculine alienation before a female dyad elevated to domestic sovereignty.

Naturally the *suegra*'s power is enhanced by simple residential propinquity, but even more psychologically salient is the fact that she and her daughter enjoy a moral symbiosis that the husband cannot match. Although he may have many friends, his male friendships are founded as much on competition as cooperation, and he cannot plead for help in domestic skirmishes without endangering his reputation as a "strong man." His own mother of course may intercede, but no man wants to have his mother fight his battles. So for various reasons, he acquiesces, maintaining a respectable facade of indifference before his peers. In addition the husband knows all too well that "trouble" (*jaleo*) with the *suegra* leads to marital discord, unless the wife is "strong" and prefers to mollify her husband while alienating her own mother. However, this is said to be rare.

With their vibrant oral traditions, Andalusians are consummate artists of the human condition. Because of the powerful proscription on fighting and violence in their culture, they prefer to express their sorrows and troubles in song and art rather than in outbursts. Accordingly, the alliance of wife and *suegra*, with the latter assuming mythopoetic status as a masculine nemesis, has achieved a kind of apotheosis in verse and poetry. In both Fuenmayor and El Castillo, the men sing *coplas* during Carnival to great acclaim and applause, reflecting common male concerns. What is most interesting about these verses is the formidable physical power ascribed to the *suegra* in metaphors and tropes of specifically virile animal and military imagery, a tradition rendering "marital" as "martial," in which the male appears victimized and indecisive. This may reflect, as Driessen perceptively suggests, deep-seated insecurity or cognitive dissonance about the power of women, which the "cover" of male indifference or self-abstention is meant to assuage. During the Fuenmayor Carnival of 1970, one famous poet sang the following *copla,* receiving accolades from the cheering men:

All mothers-in-law in the world
Are pretty much the same.
I fight with mine, too,
So listen how it goes.
She kicks me out of her house
Forty times a day.
Good, bad, indifferent,
They all belong in the cavalry.[6]

Another poet describes his *suegra* as a *bicho fiero* ("fierce beast") which he hopes someday to *desbravacer* ("tame" or, more colorfully, "geld") as though she were a wild animal.[7] One man told me that his *suegra* was a "dragon" who expelled him from "her house" (which was his house, as well) whenever he disagreed with her. Other men described their *suegra* as a "brave bull," a "tom-cat," an "armor-plated lizard," and other such scaly or vicious animals.

With all their hyperbole, these pseudo-jocular laments are revealing because of the intimations of sex-role reversal and power inversion with their unconscious implications of sublimated male gender-identity insecurities. Also revealing is the sense of powerlessness expressed as an evanescent integration into the domestic setting as a result of the man's tenuous connection to the home, which is, after all, haunted—sometimes owned outright—by his *suegra*. Even if the man lives neolocally, the *suegra*'s intrusion into his home is so all-encompassing that the man feels menaced in his own house. As we have seen, this domestic weakness is partly attributable to a masculine abdication of domestic responsibilities in exchange for a full larder and efficient housekeeping, but belying the ready acceptance of this domestic "service" is the continual eulogizing over lost powers.

Faced with this powerful matri-core, the working-class husband often finds some of the most basic decisions in his life taken over unilaterally by affines. For example, many men complain plaintively that although they hate to emigrate to work outside of Andalusia, they are literally forced to go when faced with the *fait accompli* of a decision made by wife and *suegra*. One man in El Castillo, a peasant farmer, echoed a commonly heard complaint when he confided that

he went to work in Madrid after his wife decided they needed a new refrigerator—a prestige item that many women buy for competitive "show" rather than real need (since women shop daily, the refrigerator often stands empty in the kitchen). Most men are committed to providing as well as possible for their families, but often decisions about consumption needs and therefore about employment, are made by the joint demands of kinswoman, with the *suegra* again figuring demonically in this process. Another popular carnival *copla* puts it this way:

Working, working,
Working night and day,
Because when I'm unemployed
And not earning any money,
No one can control my
Wife and mother-in-law.[8]

Later in this song the *suegra* and wife are scolded for their voracious appetite for consumer goods, which forces the poor man to emigrate to Germany as "the only way to pay back what I owe in Spain." Again, the point to be made is that a worker or poor peasant, who has very little input into purchasing decisions, senses a helplessness before the power of the matri-core. The wife, in alliance with her mother, may make the most important life decision, and the man may feel a passive victim.

Occasionally, a man may express the opinion that his wife cares more about her mother than her husband, a complaint that may convey a hidden sense of both injustice and affective exclusion. For example, there was one man in Fuenmayor, Adolfo, whose wife kept forgetting his lunch (the main meal of the day). Her excuse was that her mother was old and needed her constant attention. One day I went home with Adolfo directly from the bar where we had been enjoying a pre-prandial beer. He had invited me home for the midday meal, after which I was to interview him. But when we arrived, Adolfo was chagrined to find that no lunch had been prepared and there was nothing in the family larder but a small sausage. A note taped on the wall announced that his wife had gone to visit her ill mother. Although embarrassed and disappointed, Adolfo took it all in stride, confiding to me that "that's how women are." A man is a fifth wheel in his own house, he noted, adding peevishly that at least he had the consolation of knowing that the "old dragon" would not be bossing him around that day, since she was sick. It is clear that many lower-class men feel marginalized in their own homes.

In addition to her dominance in economic planning (with her mother's active support), the non-elite Andalusian wife usually acts as the un-official administrator of domestic finances. This is especially true among the rural proletarians in both Fuenmayor and El Castillo, where the hus-band may surrender his entire day-wage to his wife each night. In return he expects the house to be run properly, and will himself be given a small "allowance" for his expenses at the bar and for his nightly card game. Many laborers refer to their wives in a semi-ironic vein as the *ama* ("boss") or *jefa* ("chief") of the house—words reserved in the wider public context for such au-thority figures as employers and political leaders. One man in Fuenmayor spoke of his wife seri-ously as the "generalissima" of household fi-nances (using the feminized form of Generalis-simo Franco's[9] title), adding that he did not care what she did with the money he earned so long as he was returned enough to buy refreshments at the neighborhood tavern.

I remember one worker getting up from an exciting card game to run home to wheedle his wife for more money. His fellows remarked that his wife was a "peseta pincher," but they agreed that her supervision of his gambling was probably a good thing, as he tended to bet poorly at cards. Most men present admitted that their own wives held the family purse strings and that this was unavoidable, since they (the men) were rarely at home. They said that a man works (or "sacri-fices") to give money to his wife and his family and that a man who withheld his wages from his wife was "mean" and a reprobate: he was depriv-ing his children. Again, male acquiescence here may be seen as morally ambivalent. Men evade onerous responsibilities by giving the wife final

authority, but there is a lingering self-doubt about it; as usual, this tension finds expression in self-deprecating humor.

DOMESTIC POWER AND CLASS

This tendency to let the wife and her mother run the family's finances correlates with class status. Among the wealthier peasants, most husbands re-tain rights over the domestic economy and play a more active part in allocating resources for the family. Among the gentry in Fuenmayor, most husbands take a more active role in finances and may even control the family purse strings through bank accounts and investments that the wife rarely knows about. Or, in some landowning families, a husband may simply provide his wife with a monthly allowance, while she does little more than distribute this to various domestic employees with instructions on purchases.

In the working classes, however, where sur-plus cash is a rarity and where the domestic econ-omy is often managed on a credit or deficit basis because of the vagaries of agrarian employment, the wife "rules" the household economy and the husband accepts this. Although he may realize that it further diminishes his "power" in the do-mestic sphere, he is often willing to trade this power for the peace of mind that comes from be-ing shielded from petty fiscal annoyances. Again, working-class male remoteness here is a trade-off in which the man sacrifices control for a modicum of comfort. Conversely, in the propertied classes, comfort is assured through the practice of hiring servants; in addition, or perhaps because of this, the rich tend to live either patrilocally or patrivici-nally after marriage: the *suegra* is not "needed."

POWER AND SEXUALITY

Finally, there is the "power" exercised by wives through their ability to withhold sex, which is the same in all classes. Generally it is assumed among men in Andalusia that women are highly sexed, although it is the man who awakens and directs this amorphous source of female sexual energy.

Yet there is also a general understanding that in marital relations, it is the woman who "uses" the strategy of withholding sex as a means of controlling or persuading.

Some men naturally are "flojo" sexually (weak or impotent), and their wives may be frustrated by this lamentable failing. But according to informants—both male and female—a husband never withholds sex purposefully in order to manipulate his wife. "He could not do that if he were a man," one man asserted firmly, adding that this is an exclusively feminine weapon that would be humiliating for a man.

Withholding sex is also a weapon that carries more than just psychological weight. I was once talking to a couple of newlyweds, who quite spontaneously asked me and my wife (a medical doctor, as they knew) about the best way to conceive a child. They had heard rumors that the impregnation of the wife could be assured and the sex of the child could be determined by "positions."

Although we could not advise them on this issue, the conversation soon turned to more concrete subjects, such as the importance of having a first child exactly nine months after the wedding. Husband and wife agreed that this is necessary to quell gossip about the man's potency. If a first child is delayed, they added, people assume that the husband has sexual problems and they gossip about his manhood. They also implied that since this is so, some brides are able to "lead the groom about by the nose" by threatening to withhold sex. The man has to placate her so that she quickly becomes pregnant. This is another example of female "power" wielded without respect to "right."

CONCLUSIONS

If power is defined as personal autonomy and the ability to impose one's will regardless of the source of this ability, then one must conclude, along with Rogers that men have less of this ability than their wives—at least in the lower classes of these Andalusian communities. Although the lower-class men claim that this imbalance is by design and that it "frees" them to concentrate on more important matters, I am inclined to regard this as Rogers seems to do, as farcical face-saving, rather than an inverse "power" to evade work.

Beyond the domestic realm, real power is a scarce commodity denied to most men. Most Andalusian workers have little or no political power; nor do they exercise power in relations with their peers, all of whom start from the same point of equivalency in basically egalitarian relationships. They may have influence with their cronies, but few men can be said to have power, whatever its provenance—except perhaps over their sons, but even this is equivocal (Murphy 1983). Since working-class men have virtually no alternative sources of power over their peers in communities like Fuenmayor and El Castillo, one may conclude that they are relatively powerless compared to women, whose domestic power is real and unqualified.

One very important point should be made about relations of dominance and subordination in the context of class-stratified marginal communities like those in rural Andalusia. This is that any approach to the dimension of power that uses only gender as a criterion is probably epistemologically invalid. Where power is concerned, there are men and men, and there are women and women. As Davis has pointed out, what matters is not only sex, but also relative access to resources. One may not speak of a category "men" opposed to another category "women," because this is an oversimplification that, in Herzfeld's phrase, "sacrifices *complementarity* to *opposition*" and conflates theoretically subtle symbols. Europeanist ethnography shows us the pervasiveness of social class and its power to determine, not sex of course, but the principles of group formation. Gender is one additional or parallel dimension of the social organization of production, not an arbitrary symbolic schema imposed independent of structural and historical context. Almost everywhere we look, "Alpha males"[10] dominate women *because* they dominate men and so one must speak more generally of multidimensional *human* rather than unidimensional gender hierarchies.

NOTES

1. Research for this study was made possible by grants from the National Institute of Mental Health, the National Science Foundation, the Wenner-Gren Foundation, the National Endowment for the Humanities, the Council for the International Exchange of Scholars, and the H. F. Guggenheim Foundation.

2. See, for example, Giovannini (1985); Uhl (1985); Dubisch (1986). I also follow Dubisch (1986:16); and Salamone and Stanton (1986:97) in use of the term "domestic power."

3. Names of both towns are pseudonyms.

4. A latifundium is a landed estate on which workers in a state of partial servitude practice labor-intensive agriculture.

5. Agnates are kin related through the male line.

6. From a poem by Marcelin Lora.

7. From a poem by Juanillo "El Gato."

8. From a poem by Juanillo "El Gato."

9. Generalissimo Franco ran Spain with an iron hand from 1936 until his death in 1975.

10. "Alpha male" is a term developed in studies of non-human primates. It refers to the dominant male of a local primate group.

REFERENCES

Bem, Sandra. 1983. "Gender Schema Theory and Its Implications for Child Development." *Signs,* 8: 598–616.

Brandes, Stanley H. 1980. *Metaphors of Masculinity.* Philadelphia: University of Philadelphia Press.

Brøgger, Jan. 1990. *Pre-Bureaucratic Europeans.* Oslo: Norwegian University Press.

Carrasco, Pedro. 1963. "The Locality Referent in Residence Terms." *American Anthropologist,* 65: 133–134.

Casselberry, Samuel F. and Nancy Valavanes. 1976. "Matrilocal Greek Peasants and Reconsideration of Residence Terminology." *American Ethnologist,* 3:215–226.

Davis, John. 1973. *Land and Family in Pisticci.* London: Athlone Press.

Driessen, Henk. 1983. "Male Sociability and Rituals of Masculinity in Rural Andalusia." *Anthropological Quarterly,* 56:125–133.

Dubisch, Jill, ed. 1986. *Gender and Power in Rural Greece.* Princeton: Princeton University Press.

Giovannini, Maureen J. 1985. "The Dialectics of Women's Factory Work in a Sicilian Town." *Anthropology,* 9:45–64.

Gregory, James R. 1984. "The Myth of the Male Ethnographer and the Woman's World." *American Anthropologist,* 86:316–327.

Herzfeld, Michael. 1986. "Within and Without: The Category of 'Female' in the Ethnography of Modern Greece," in Jill Dubisch, ed., *Gender and Power in Rural Greece.* Princeton: Princeton University Press.

Murphy, Michael. 1983. "Emotional Confrontations between Sevillano Fathers and Sons: Cultural Foundations and Social Consequences." *American Ethnologist,* 10:650–664.

Pina-Cabral, João de. 1986. *Sons of Adam, Daughters of Eve: The Peasant Worldview of the Alto Minho.* Oxford: Clarendon Press.

Press, Irwin. 1979. *The City as Context: Urbanism and Behavioral Constraints in Seville.* Urbana: University of Illinois Press.

Rogers, Susan C. 1975. "Female Forms of Power and the Myth of Male Dominance: A Model of Female/Male Interaction in Peasant Society." *American Ethnologist.* 2:727–756.

Salamone, S. D., and J. B. Stanton. 1986. "Introducing the Nikokyra: Ideality and Reality in Social Process," in Jill Dubisch, ed., *Gender and Power in Rural Greece.* Princeton: Princeton University Press.

Uhl, Sarah C. 1985. "Special Friends; The Organization of Intersex Friendship in Escalona (Andalusia) Spain." *Anthropology,* 9:129–152.

35

Delicate Transactions

Gender, Home, and Employment among Hispanic Women

M. PATRICIA FERNÁNDEZ KELLY

The days have vanished when scholars could comfortably speak about the roles of men and women as if they were immutable biological or temperamental traits. More than a decade of feminist thought and research in the social sciences has brought about a complex understanding of gender as a process reflecting political, economic, and ideological transactions, a fluid phenomenon changing in uneasy harmony with productive arrangements. The theoretical focus of this essay is on the way class, ethnicity, and gender interact.

I compare two groups of Hispanic women involved in apparel manufacturing: One includes native- and foreign-born Mexicans in Southern California; another, Cuban exiles in Southern Florida.[1] All the women have worked in factories at different stages in their lives, and they have also been involved in industrial work in the home. In a broad sense, women's incorporation into the work force is part and parcel of economic strategies that have allowed manufacturing firms to compete in domestic and international markets. From a more restricted perspective, it is also the result of personal negotiations between men and women in households and workplaces. Combining these perspectives, it is possible to compare the two groups of women to see the influence of economic resources and immigration histories on conceptions and institutions of gender. Despite sharing important characteristics, the two groups represent distinct economic classes and social situations. I use the cases to examine how economic and social factors can reinforce or undermine patriarchal values and affect women's attitudes toward and relationships with men.

A complex conceptualization of gender has emerged over the past two decades from the dialogue between Marxist and feminist scholars. In this dialogue, theorists have focused on the relationship between productive and reproductive spheres to uncover the varied content of gender relations under differing conditions of production and in different periods.[2] Here "gender" refers to meshed economic, political, and ideological relations. Under capitalism gender designates fundamental economic processes that determine the allocation of labor into remunerated and nonremunerated spheres of production. Gender also circumscribes the alternatives of individuals of different sexes in the area of paid employment. Women's specific socioeconomic experience is grounded in the contradiction that results from the wage labor/unpaid domestic labor split.

In addition, gender is political as it contributes to differential distributions of power and access to vital resources on the basis of sexual difference. The political asymmetry between men and women is played out both within and outside of the domestic realm. In both cases it involves conflict, negotiation, and ambivalent resolutions which are, in turn, affected by economic and ideological factors.

Finally, gender implicates the shaping of consciousness and the elaboration of collective discourses which alternatively explain, legitimate, or question the position of men and women as members of families and as workers. While all societies assign roles to individuals on the basis of perceived sexual characteristics, these roles vary significantly and change over time. Gender is part of a broader ideological process in constant flux. Moreover, adherence to patriarchal mores may have varying outcomes depending on their economic and political context.

This interplay of economic, political, and ideological aspects of gender is particularly evident in studying the relationship between women's paid employment and household responsibilities. Women's work—whether factory work, industrial homework, or unpaid domestic work—always involves negotiations of gendered boundaries, such as the line between wage labor and domestic responsibilities, and the arrangements that tie household organization and family ideals. Industrial homework, for example, both contradicts and complies with the ideological split between "work" and "family" as this sets standards for male-female differentiation; women who do homework work for wages but do not leave their homes and families.

Employers rely on homework to lower the wage bill, evade government regulations, and maintain competitiveness in the market;[3] none of these goals seem consistent with women's attempts to raise their economic status. Yet homework has been used by women to reconcile the responsibilities of domestic care with the need to earn a wage. Furthermore, women use and interpret homework as a strategy for bridging employment and family goals in a variety of ways. Women move between factory work, homework, and unpaid domestic labor on different trajectories, depending on both household organization and class-based resources.

Some conceptual clarification is needed for this analysis. It is necessary to distinguish "family" and "household." "Family" is an ideological notion that includes marriage and fidelity, men's roles as providers and women's roles as caretakers of children, and the expectation that nuclear families will reside in the same home. Rayna Rapp

notes the prevalence of a family ideal shared by working- and middle-class people in the United States.[4] While "family" designates the way things should be, "household" refers to the manner in which men, women, and children actually join each other as part of domestic units. Households represent mechanisms for the pooling of time, labor, and other resources in a shared space. As households adjust to the pressures of the surrounding environment, they frequently stand in sharp, even painful, contrast to ideals regarding the family.

Class accounts largely for the extent to which notions about the family can be upheld or not. The conditions necessary for the maintenance of long-term stable unions where men act as providers and women as caretakers of children have been available among the middle and upper classes but absent among the poor. Nuclear households are destabilized by high levels of unemployment and underemployment or by public policy making it more advantageous for women with children to accept welfare payments than to remain dependent upon an irregularly employed man. The poor often live in highly flexible households where adherence to the norms of the patriarchial family are unattainable.

Class differences in the relation between household patterns and family ideals are apparent in women's changing strategies of factory work, homework, and unpaid labor. Homework, for example, can maintain family objectives or help compensate for their unattainability. In describing two contrasting ways women link household organization, paid employment, and gender and family ideals, my study creates a model for class and ethnic specific analyses of gender negotiations.

THE HISPANIC COMMUNITIES IN MIAMI AND LOS ANGELES

Although there are many studies comparing minorities and whites in the U.S., there have been few attempts to look at variations of experience within ethnic groups. This is true for Hispanics in general and for Hispanic women in particular; yet contrasts abound. For example, Mexicans comprise more than half of all Hispanics between eighteen and sixty-four years of age living in the U.S. Of these, approximately 70% were born in this country. Average levels of educational attainment are quite low with less than 50% having graduated from high school. In contrast, Cubans represent about 7% of the Hispanic population. They are mostly foreign-born; 58% of Cubans have 12 or more years of formal schooling.[5]

Both in Southern California and in Southern Florida most direct production workers in the garment industry are Hispanic. In Los Angeles most apparel firm operatives are Mexican women, in Miami, Cuban women.[6] The labor force participation rates of Mexican and Cuban women dispel the widespread notion that work outside the home is a rare experience for Hispanic women.[7] Yet the Los Angeles and Miami communities differ in a number of important respects. One can begin with contrasts in the garment industry in each area.

The two sites differ in the timing of the industry, its evolution, maturity, and restructuring. In Los Angeles, garment production emerged in the latter part of the nineteenth-century and expanded in the 1920s, stimulated in part by the arrival of runaway shops evading unionization drives in New York. The Great Depression sent the Los Angeles garment industry into a period of turmoil, but soon fresh opportunities for the production of inexpensive women's sportswear developed, as the rise of cinema established new guidelines for fashion. During the 1970s and 1980s the industry reorganized in response to foreign imports; small manufacturing shops have proliferated, as has home production. In contrast, the apparel industry in Miami has had a shorter and more uniform history. Most of the industry grew up since the 1960s, when retired manufacturers from New York saw the advantage of opening new businesses and hiring exiles from the Cuban Revolution.

The expansion of the Los Angeles clothing industry resulted from capitalists' ability to rely on continuing waves of Mexican immigrants, many of whom were undocumented. Mexican migration over the last century ensured a steady supply of workers for the apparel industry; from the very beginning, Mexican women were employed in nearly all positions in the industry.[8] By contrast, the expansion of garment production in Miami was due to an unprecedented influx of exiles ejected by a unique political event. Cubans working in the Florida apparel industry arrived in the United States as refugees under a protected and relatively privileged status. Exile was filled with uncertainty and the possibility of dislocation but not, as in the case of undocumented Mexican aliens, with the probability of harassment, detention, and deportation.

Mexican and Cuban workers differ strikingly in social class. For more than a century, the majority of Mexican immigrants have had a markedly proletarian background. Until the 1970s, the majority had rural roots, although in more recent times there has been a growing number of urban immigrants.[9] In sharp contrast, Cuban waves of migration have included a larger proportion of professionals, mid-level service providers, and various types of entrepreneurs ranging from those with previous experience in large companies to those qualified to start small family enterprises. Entrepreneurial experience among Cubans and reliance on their own ethnic networks accounts, to a large extent, for Cuban success in business formation and appropriation in Miami.[10] Thus, while Mexican migration has been characterized by relative homogeneity regarding class background, Cuban exile resulted in the transposition of an almost intact class structure containing investors and professionals as well as unskilled, semiskilled, and skilled workers.

In addition to disparate class compositions, the two groups differ in the degree of their homogeneity by place of birth. Besides the sizable undocumented contingent mentioned earlier, the Los Angeles garment industry also employs U.S.-born citizens of Mexican heritage. First-hand reports and anecdotal evidence indicate that the fragmentation between "Chicana" and "Mexicana" workers causes an unresolved tension and animosity within the labor force. Cubans, on the other hand, were a highly cohesive population until the early 1980s, when the arrival of the so-called "Marielitos" resulted in a potentially disruptive polarization of the community.

Perhaps the most important difference between Mexicans in Los Angeles and Cubans in Florida is related to their distinctive labor market insertion patterns. Historically, Mexicans have arrived in the U.S. labor market in a highly individuated and dispersed manner. As a result, they have been extremely dependent on labor market supply and demand forces entirely beyond their control. Their working-class background and stigma attached to their frequent undocumented status has accentuated even further their vulnerability vis-à-vis employers. By contrast, Cubans have been able to consolidate an economic enclave formed by immigrant businesses, which hire workers of a common cultural and national background. The economic enclave partly operates as a buffer zone separating and often shielding members of the same ethnic group from the market forces at work in the larger society. The existence of an economic enclave does not preclude exploitation on the basis of class; indeed, it is predicated upon the existence of a highly diversified immigrant class structure. However, commonalities of culture, national background, and language between immigrant employers and workers can become a mechanism for collective improvement of income levels and standards of living. As a result, differences in labor market insertion patterns among Mexicans and Cubans have led to varying social profiles and a dissimilar potential for socioeconomic attainment.

THE WOMEN GARMENT WORKERS

These differences between the two Hispanic communities have led to important differences between the two groups of women who work in the garment industry. For Mexican women in Southern California, employment in garment production is the consequence of long-term economic need. Wives and daughters choose to work outside the home in order to meet the survival requirements of their families in the absence of satisfactory earnings by men. Some female heads of household join the labor force after losing male support through illness, death, and, more often, desertion. In many of these instances, women opt for industrial homework in order to reconcile child care and the need for wage employment. They are particularly vulnerable members of an economically marginal ethnic group.

By contrast, Cuban women who arrived in Southern Florida during the 1960s saw jobs in garment assembly as an opportunity to recover or attain middle-class status. The consolidation of an economic enclave in Miami, which accounts for much of the prosperity of Cubans, was largely dependent upon the incorporation of women into the labor force. While they toiled in factories, men entered business or were self-employed. Their vulnerability was tempered by shared goals of upward mobility in a foreign country.

Despite their different nationalities, migratory histories, and class backgrounds, Mexicans and Cubans share many perceptions and expectations. In both cases, patriarchal norms of reciprocity are favored; marriage, motherhood, and devotion to family are high priorities among women, while men are expected to hold authority, to be good providers, and to be loyal to their wives and children. However, the divergent economic and political conditions surrounding Mexicans in Southern California and Cubans in Southern Florida have had a differing impact upon each group's ability to uphold these values. Mexican women are often thrust into financial "autonomy" as a result of men's inability to fulfill their socially assigned role. Among Cubans, by contrast, men have been economically more successful. Indeed, ideological notions of patriarchal responsibility have served to maintain group cohesion; that offers women an advantage in getting and keeping jobs within the ethnic enclave.

Cuban and Mexican women both face barriers stemming from their subordination in the family and their status as low-skilled workers in highly competitive industries. Nevertheless, their varying class backgrounds and modes of incorporation into local labor markets entail distinctive political and socioeconomic effects. How women view their identities as women is especially affected. Among Mexican garment workers disillusion about the economic viability of men becomes a desire for individual emancipation, mobility, and financial independence as women. However, these ideals and ambitions for advancement are most often frustrated by poverty and the stigmas attached to ethnic and gender status.

Cuban women, on the other hand, tend to see no contradiction between personal fulfillment and a strong commitment to patriarchal standards. Their incorporation and subsequent withdrawal from the labor force are both influenced by their acceptance of hierarchical patterns of authority and the sexual division of labor. As in the case of Mexicans in Southern California, Cuban women's involvement in industrial homework is an option bridging domestic and income-generating needs. However, it differs in that homework among them was brought about by relative prosperity and expanding rather than diminishing options. Women's garment work at home does not contradict patriarchal ideals of women's place at the same time as it allows women to contribute to the economic success that confirms gender stratification.

The stories of particular women show the contrasts in how women in each of these two groups negotiate the links among household, gender, and employment arrangements. Some of the conditions surrounding Mexican home workers in Southern California are illustrated by the experience of Amelia Ruíz.[11] She was born into a family of six children in El Cerrito, Los Angeles County. Her mother, a descendant of Native American Indians, married at a young age the son of Mexican immigrants. Among Amelia's memories are the fragmentary stories of her paternal grandparents working in the fields and, occasionally, in canneries. Her father, however was not a stoop laborer but a trained upholsterer. Her mother was always a homemaker. Amelia grew up with a distinct sense of the contradictions that plague the relationships between men and women:

> All the while I was a child, I had this feeling that my parents weren't happy. My mother was smart but she could never make much of herself. Her parents taught her that the fate of woman is to be a wife and mother; they advised her to find a good man and marry him. And that she did. My father was reliable and I think he was faithful but he was also distant; he lived in his own world. He would come home and expect to be served hand and foot. My mother would wait on him but she was always angry about it. I never took marriage for granted.

After getting her high school diploma, Amelia found odd jobs in all the predictable places: as a counter clerk in a dress shop, as a cashier in a fast-food establishment, and as a waitress in two restaurants. When she was 20, she met Miguel—Mike as he was known outside the barrio. He was a consummate survivor, having worked in the construction field, as a truck driver, and even as an English as a Second Language instructor. Despite her misgivings about marriage, Amelia was struck by Mike's penchant for adventure:

> He was different from the men in my family. He loved fun and was said to have had many women. He was a challenge. We were married when I was 21 and he 25. For a while I kept my job but when I became pregnant, Miguel didn't want me to work any more. Two more children followed and then, little by little, Miguel became abusive. He wanted to have total authority over me and the children. He said a man should know how to take care of a family and get respect, but it was hard to take him seriously when he kept changing jobs and when the money he brought home was barely enough to keep ends together.

After the birth of her second child, Amelia started work at Shirley's, a women's wear factory in the area. Miguel was opposed to the idea. For Amelia, work outside the home was an evident need prompted by financial stress. At first, it was also a means to escape growing disenchantment,

I saw myself turning into my mother and I started thinking that to be free of men was best for women. Maybe if Miguel had had a better job, maybe if he had kept the one he had, things would have been different, but he didn't....We started drifting apart.

Tension at home mounted over the following months. Amelia had worked at Shirley's for almost a year when, one late afternoon after collecting the three children from her parents' house, she returned to an empty home. She knew, as soon as she stepped inside, that something was amiss. In muted shock, she confirmed the obvious: Miguel had left, taking with him all personal possessions; even the wedding picture in the living room had been removed. No explanations had been left behind. Amelia was then 28 years of age, alone, and the mother of three small children.

As a result of these changes, employment became even more desirable, but the difficulty of reconciling home responsibilities with wage work persisted. Amelia was well regarded at Shirley's, and her condition struck a sympathetic chord among the other factory women. In a casual conversation, her supervisor described how other women were leasing industrial sewing machines from the local Singer distributor and were doing piecework at home. By combining factory work and home assembly, she could earn more money without further neglecting the children. Mr. Driscoll, Shirley's owner and general manager, made regular use of home workers, most of whom were former employees. That had allowed him to retain a stable core of about 20 factory seamstresses and to depend on approximately 10 home workers during peak seasons.

Between 1979, the year of her desertion, and 1985, when I met her, Amelia had struggled hard, working most of the time and making some progress. Her combined earnings before taxes fluctuated between $950 and $1,150 a month. Almost half of her income went to rent for the two-bedroom apartment which she shared with the children. She was in debt and used to working at least 12 hours a day. On the other hand, she had

bought a double-needle sewing machine and was thinking of leasing another one to share additional sewing with a neighbor. She had high hopes:

Maybe some day I'll have my own business; I'll be a liberated woman...I won't have to take orders from a man. Maybe Miguel did me a favor when he left after all....

With understandable variations, Amelia's life history is shared by many garment workers in Southern California. Three aspects are salient in this experience. First, marriage and a stable family life are perceived as desirable goals which are, nonetheless, fraught with ambivalent feelings and burdensome responsibilities.

Second, tensions between men and women result from contradictions between the intent to fulfill gender definitions and the absence of the economic base necessary for their implementation. The very definition of manhood includes the right to hold authority and power over wives and children, as well as the responsibility of providing adequately for them. The difficulties in implementing those goals in the Mexican communities I studied are felt equally by men and women but expressed differently by each. Bent on restoring their power, men attempt to control women in abusive ways. Women often resist their husbands' arbitrary or unrealistic impositions. Both reactions are eminently political phenomena.

Third, personal conflict regarding the proper behavior of men and women may be tempered by negotiation. It can also result in the breach of established agreements, as in the case of separation or divorce. Both paths are related to the construction of alternative discourses and the redefinition of gender roles. Women may seek personal emancipation, driven partly by economic need and partly by dissatisfaction with men's performance as providers. In general, individuals talk about economic and political conflict as a personal matter occurring in their own homes. Broader contextual factors are less commonly discussed.

The absence of economic underpinnings for the implementation of patriarchal standards may bring about more equitable exchanges between men and women, and may stimulate women's search for individual well-being and personal autonomy as women. However, in the case at hand, such ideals remain elusive. Mexican garment workers, especially those who are heads of households, face great disadvantages in the labor market. They are targeted for jobs that offer the lowest wages paid to industrial workers in the United States; they also have among the lowest unionization rates in the country. Ironically, the breakdown of patriarchal norms in the household draws from labor market segmentation that reproduces patriarchal (and ethnic) stratification.

Experiences like the ones related are also found among Cuban and Central American women in Miami. However, a larger proportion have had a different trajectory. Elvira Gómez's life in the U.S. is a case in point. She was 34 when she arrived in Miami with her four children, ages three to twelve. The year was 1961.

Leaving Havana was the most painful thing that ever happened to us. We loved our country. We would have never left willingly. Cuba was not like Mexico: we didn't have immigrants in large numbers. But Castro betrayed us and we had to join the exodus. We became exiles. My husband left Cuba three months before I did and there were moments when I doubted I would ever see him again. Then, after we got together, we realized we would have to forge ahead without looking back.

We lost everything. Even my mother's china had to be left behind. We arrived in this country as they say, "covering our nakedness with our bare hands" (una mano delante y otra detrás). My husband had had a good position in a bank. To think that he would have to take any old job in Miami was more than I could take; a man of his stature having to beg for a job in a hotel or in a factory? It wasn't right!

Elvira had worked briefly before her marriage as a secretary. As a middle-class wife and mother, she was used to hiring at least one maid. Coming to the United States changed all that:

Something had to be done to keep the family together. So I looked around and finally found a job in a shirt factory in Hialeah. Manolo (her hus-

band) joined a childhood friend and got a loan to start an export-import business. All the time they were building the firm, I was sewing. There were times when we wouldn't have been able to pay the bills without the money I brought in.

Elvira's experience was shared by thousands of women in Miami. Among the first waves of Cuban refugees there were many who worked tirelessly to raise the standards of living of their families to the same levels or higher than those they had been familiar with in their country of origin. The consolidation of an ethnic enclave allowed many Cuban men to become entrepreneurs. While their wives found unskilled and semi-skilled jobs, they became businessmen. Eventually, they purchased homes, put their children through school, and achieved comfort. At that point, many Cuban men pressed their wives to stop working outside of the home; they had only allowed them to have a job, in the first place, out of economic necessity. In the words of a prominent manufacturer in the area:

You have to understand that Cuban workers were willing to do anything to survive. When they became prosperous, the women saw the advantage of staying at home and still earn additional income. Because they had the skill, owners couldn't take them for granted. Eventually, owners couldn't get operators anymore. The most skilled would tell a manager "my husband doesn't let me work out of the home." This was a worker's initiative based on the values of the culture. I would put ads in the paper and forty people would call and everyone would say "I only do homework." That's how we got this problem of the labor shortages. The industry was dying; we wouldn't have survived without the arrival of the Haitians and the Central Americans.

This discussion partly shows that decisions made at the level of the household can remove workers, actively sought and preferred by employers, from the marketplace. This, in turn, can threaten certain types of production. In those cases, loyalty to familial values can mitigate against the interests of capitalist firms. Interviews with Cuban women involved in homework confirm the general accuracy of this interpretation. After leaving factory employment, many put their experience to good use by becoming subcontractors and employing neighbors or friends. They also transformed so-called "Florida rooms" (the covered porches in their houses) into sewing shops. It was in one of them that Elvira Gómez was first interviewed. In her case, working outside the home was justified only as a way to maintain the integrity of her family and as a means to support her husband's early incursions into the business world:

> For many long years I worked in the factory but when things got better financially, Manolo asked me to quit the job. He felt bad that I couldn't be at home all the time with the children. But it had to be done. There's no reason for women not to earn a living when it's necessary; they should have as many opportunities and responsibilities as men. But I also tell my daughters that the strength of a family rests on the intelligence and work of women. It is foolish to give up your place as a mother and a wife only to go take orders from men who aren't even part of your family. What's so liberated about that? It is better to see your husband succeed and to know you have supported one another.

Perhaps the most important point here is the unambiguous acceptance of patriarchal mores as a legitimate guideline for the behavior of men and women. Exile did not eliminate these values; rather, it extended them in telling ways. The high labor force participation rates of Cuban women in the United States have been mentioned before. Yet, it should be remembered that, prior to their migration, only a small number of Cuban women had worked outside the home for any length of time. It was the need to maintain the integrity of their families and to achieve class-related ambitions that precipitated their entrance into the labor force of a foreign country.

In descriptions of their experience in exile, Cuban women often make clear that part of the motivation in their search for jobs was the preservation of known definitions of manhood and womanhood. Whereas Mexican women worked as a response to what they saw as a failure of patriarchal arrangements, Cuban women worked in the name of dedication to their husbands and children, and in order to preserve the status and authority of the former. Husbands gave them "permission" to work outside the home, and only as a result of necessity and temporary economic strife. In the same vein, it was a ritual yielding to masculine privilege that led women to abandon factory employment. Conversely, men "felt bad" that their wives had to work for a wage and welcomed the opportunity to remove them from the marketplace when economic conditions improved.

As with Mexicans in Southern California, Cuban women in Miami earned low wages in low- and semi-skilled jobs. They too worked in environments devoid of the benefits derived from unionization. Nevertheless, the outcome of their experience as well as the perceptions are markedly different. Many Cuban women interpret their subordination at home as part of a viable option ensuring economic and emotional benefits. They are bewildered by feminist goals of equality and fulfillment in the job market. Yet, the same women have had among the highest rates of participation in the U.S. labor force.

CONCLUSIONS

For Mexican women in Southern California, proletarianization is related to a high number of female-headed households, as well as households where the earnings provided by women are indispensable for maintaining standards of modest subsistence. In contrast, Cuban women's employment in Southern Florida was a strategy for raising standards of living in a new environment. These contrasts in the relationship between households and the labor market occurred despite shared values regarding the family among Mexicans and Cubans. Both groups partake of similar mores regarding the roles of men and women; nevertheless, their actual experience has differed significantly. Contrasting features of class, educational background, and immigration history have created divergent gender and family dilemmas for each group.

This analysis underscores the impact of class on gender. Definitions of manhood and womanhood are implicated in the very process of class formation. At the same time, the norms of reciprocity sanctioned by patriarchal ideologies can operate as a form of social adhesive consolidating class membership. For poor men and women, the issue is not only the presence of the sexual division of labor and the persistence of patriarchal ideologies but the difficulties of upholding either.

Thus, too, the meaning of women's participation in the labor force remains plagued by paradox. For Mexican women in Southern California, paid employment responds to and increases women's desires for greater personal autonomy and financial independence. Ideally, this should have a favorable impact upon women's capacity to negotiate an equitable position within their homes and in the labor market. Yet these women's search for paid employment is most often the consequence of severe economic need; it expresses vulnerability not strength within homes and in the marketplace. Indeed, in some cases, women's entry into the labor force signals the collapse of reciprocal exchanges between men and women. Women deserted by their husbands are generally too economically marginal to translate their goals of gender equality and autonomy into socially powerful arrangements. Conversely, Cuban women in Southern Florida have more economic power, but this only strengthens their allegiance to patriarchal standards. The conjugal "partnership for survival" Elvira Gómez describes is not predicated on the existence of a just social world, but rather an ideological universe entailing differentiated and stratified benefits and obligations for men and women.

NOTES

A different version of this essay appears in Women, Work, and Politics, *Louise Tilly and Patricia Guerin, eds. (New York: Russell Sage Foundation, 1990).*

1. This essay is based on findings from the "Collaborative Study of Hispanic Women in Garment and Electronics Industries" supported by the Ford Foundation under grant number 870 1149. Initial funding for the same project was also provided by the Tinker Foundation. The author gratefully acknowledges the continued encouragement of Dr. William Díaz from the Ford Foundation.

2. Joan W. Scott, "Gender: A Useful Category of Historical Analysis," *The American Historical Review,* 91, 5 (1986): 1053–75; Felicity Edholm, "Conceptualizing Women," *Critique of Anthropology,* 3, 9/10: 101–30. For a relevant analysis of class, see Michael Buroway, *The Politics of Production* (London: New Left Books, 1985).

3. M. Patricia Fernández Kelly and Anna M. García, "Informalization at the Core: Hispanic Women, Homework and the Advanced Capitalist State," in *The Informal Economy: Comparative Studies in Advanced and Third World Societies,* eds. Alejandro Portes, Manuel Castels, and Lauren Benton (Baltimore: Johns Hopkins University Press, 1989).

4. Rayna Rapp, "Family and Class in Contemporary America: Notes Toward an Understanding of Ideology," in *Rethinking the Family,* eds. Barrie Thorne and Marilyn Yalom (New York: Longman, 1982). See also Eli Zaretsky, *Capitalism, The Family and Personal Life* (New York: Harper and Row, 1976).

5. Frank D. Bean and Marta Tienda, *The Hispanic Population of the United States* (New York: Russell Sage Foundation, 1987). There are almost twenty million Hispanics in the United States, that is, 14.6% of the total population.

6. Approximately 75% and 67% of operatives in Los Angeles and Miami apparel firms are Mexican and Cuban women, respectively.

7. Note 54.2% of native-born and 47.5% of foreign-born Mexican women were employed outside the home in 1980. The equivalent figure for the mostly foreign-born Cuban women was almost 65%. Non-Hispanic white women's labor force participation in 1980 was assessed at 57.9% (U.S. Census of Population, 1980).

8. Peter S. Taylor, "Mexican Women in Los Angeles Industry in 1928," *Aztlán: International Journal of Chicano Studies Research,* 11, 1 (Spring, 1980): 99–129.

9. Alejandro Portes and Robert L. Bach, *Latin journey: Cuban and Mexican Immigrants in the United States* (Berkeley: University of California Press, 1985), 67.

10. Alejandro Portes, "The Social Origins of the Cuban Enclave Economy of Miami," *Pacific Sociological Review,* Special Issue on the Ethnic Economy. 30, 4 (October, 1987): 340–372. See also Lisandro Perez,

"Immigrant Economic Adjustment and Family Organization: The Cuban Success Story Reexamined," *International Migration Review,* 20 (1986): 4–20.

11. The following descriptions are chosen from a sample of 25 Mexican and 10 Cuban women garment workers interviewed in Los Angeles and Miami Counties. The names of people interviewed, and some identifying characteristics, have been changed.

36

Culture, Social Class, and Income Control in the Lives of Women Garment Workers in Bangladesh

NAZLI KIBRIA

My father and mother can't feed me, my brothers can't feed me, my uncles can't feed me. So that is why I am working in garments, to stand on my own feet. Since I am taking care of my own expenses, I have no obligation to give money to my family. (Unmarried garment worker, late teens)

It's natural that I give my wages to my husband. It is the custom (niyom) *of our society to cater to the wishes of the husband. For a woman, heaven is at her husband's feet. In this world, a woman without a husband is no better off than a beggar on the street. (Married garment worker, late thirties)*

The recent emergence of export-oriented garment production factories in Bangladesh, the first modern industry in the country to employ primarily women, has been accompanied by vigorous debate among scholars and policymakers about its effects on women (Bangladesh Unnayan Parishad 1990; Chaudhuri and Majumdar 1991; United Nations Industrial Development Organization 1991). In this article I explore this issue through an in-depth analysis of how Bangladeshi women garment workers view and experience their income. Of particular interest is the ability of the women workers to exercise authority over their wages, because income control has been identified as a

critical variable in the relationship of women's wagework to family power (Blumberg 1984, 1991).

Analyses of gender and wage control in developing societies emphasize the role of traditional social and cultural patterns in determining the ability of women to control their income (Fapohunda 1988; Hoodfar 1988; Papanek and Schwede 1988; Wolf 1992). The experience of Bangladeshi women workers, however, suggests the need to move away from an analysis of income control that relies heavily on *tradition* as an explanation.

Despite the fact that cultural traditions in Bangladesh are not favorable to the economic autonomy of women, the relationship of women workers to their wages is varied, ranging from complete control over its expenditure to virtually none. Underlying this diversity are differences in the socioeconomic background of the women workers, which shape the relevance and meaning of cultural traditions, particularly those surrounding family life, for women.

SOCIAL CLASS AND THE RELATIONSHIP OF CULTURAL TRADITION TO INCOME CONTROL

Women's access to wage income has the potential to generate egalitarian shifts in gender relations at the household level by providing women the bargaining chips with which to assert power in

AUTHOR'S NOTE: I would like to thank M. Anisul Islam and Ashrafe Khandekar for their research assistance, and Susan Eckstein, Hanna Papanek, and Diane Wolf for their helpful comments on earlier drafts.

household decision-making processes; however, this potential for positive change is not always realized (Sen 1990). One of the crucial intervening factors is the ability of women to exercise control over their income. As Blumberg (1984, 1991) notes in her work on gender stratification, it is women's *control* over key economic resources rather than mere economic ownership or participation that is critical to women's family power. When women exercise control over the expenditure of their income, they can more effectively use it as a bargaining chip with the implicit threat of withdrawing their wages from the household economy.

Studies on the ability of Third World women to control their wages emphasize the importance of traditional social patterns (Fapohunda 1988; Hoodfar 1988; Papanek and Schwede 1988; Wolf 1992). That is, established cultural beliefs and expectations about women furnish a normative template, one that guides the relationship of employed women to their income. Across societies, the ability of women to control their wages varies by the degree of social and economic autonomy that they have traditionally enjoyed.

Clearly, societies in which women have traditionally engaged in valued productive activities and maintained control over the fruits of their labor are social settings in which the potential ability of women to control their wages is high. For example, sub-Saharan African societies, in which women and men have traditionally maintained separate economic activities and resources, are a context in which women are likely to govern their own wages (Fapohunda 1988; Kandiyoti 1988). Women are also more likely to control their income within kinship systems that have traditionally accorded power and authority to women in their relations with men. The Javanese kinship system, favorable to women because of bilateral inheritance, descent, and flexible rules of residence, is one in which women are able to resist the authority of men over their wages (Wolf 1991). In stark contrast, the Chinese kinship system, with its patriarchal rules of descent, inherit-

ance, and residence, is one that expects women to defer to male authority, an expectation that women factory workers fulfill by turning over their wages to the male household head (Gallin 1990; Greenhalgh 1988; Kung 1983; Salaff 1981).

The emphasis on cultural tradition that marks the analysis of gender and wage control in developing societies has fostered a perspective that is inattentive to differentiation among women and its consequences for income control processes. Cultural traditions regarding the autonomy of women vary in meaning and relevance for women, depending on such factors as age and stage in the family life cycle. A major source of differentiation among women, one that is important to consider when evaluating the impact of tradition on income control, is social class.

By determining access to social and economic resources, social class can shape the ability of women and their families to fulfill the dictates of cultural tradition. Economic necessity, for example, often triggers the movement of women into the labor force, despite traditional cultural prohibitions against women's employment (Geschwender 1992). When families are unable to meet traditional gender expectations, women may deal with their income in ways that are a departure from traditional patterns. In the context of a patriarchal family system that assumes the social and economic protection of women by men, the inability of male kin to offer such protection may shift the dynamics of power within the family (Fernandez Kelly 1990). Under such circumstances, women may refuse to relinquish control of their wages to men. In short, social class can affect income control patterns by either affirming or challenging the traditional dynamics of relations between women and men.

Social class will also influence income control patterns by shaping the symbolic meanings that are attached to women's income earning. Scholars concerned with the familial consequences of women's wagework have argued that how income is viewed by the woman and her family may be far more important to understanding family power dynamics than the material value of the money per se (Hochschild and Machung 1989; Hood 1983; Pyke 1994). As suggested by the following discussion, the impact of a woman's income on her family power depends on the symbolic meanings and interpretations that are attached to the income by the woman and her family members:

> *A woman married to a man who views her employment as a threat rather than as a gift for which he should reciprocate will derive less power from her employment. Similarly, a nonemployed woman married to a man who values his wife's domestic work as a gift will derive more power from her role. Conversely, the extent to which a woman views her own paid and unpaid labor as a gift or burden will also affect her marital power. (Pyke 1994, 75)*

Studies suggest that understandings of women's employment are shaped by the socioeconomic status of those involved. For example, in her research on marital power, Pyke (1994) found that among working-class men, the absence of a sense of control in the workplace resulted in a need to assert one's authority at home. The woman's wagework was then viewed unfavorably, as something for which she was expected to compensate to her husband. Such situations, in which the employment of the woman is burdensome due to status insecurities, may detract from the ability of women to control their wages. This is suggested by Safilios-Rothschild (1988), who observes that in patriarchal societies, men may be less inclined to directly assert their authority and demand control of the income of women when their economic superiority and headship over women is firmly established and not under question. In short, social class, through its impact on perceptions of male dominance and authority, affects the symbolic meaning of women's income, and thus potentially the patterns of control that surround women's wages.

In the analyses that follow, I explore the impact of variations in socioeconomic status on women's income-related experiences. Contrary to the widespread image of Bangladeshi women as a monolithic mass, one whose behavior is guided in uniform ways by cultural tradition, women garment workers relate to the traditional family system in diverse ways. The diversity of women's experiences reflects recent economic and social shifts in Bangladesh, which have increased socioeconomic differentiation among women.

CHALLENGES TO TRADITION AND THE RISE OF THE GARMENT INDUSTRY

The basic features of the traditional normative family system in Bangladesh concur with those noted by Kandiyoti (1988) in her description of "classic patriarchy." The system's rules of residence, inheritance, and lineage work to limit the social and economic autonomy of women. Although the status and power of women improve with age, women remain dependent on men throughout the life cycle. At a young age, girls are married and go to live in their husband's home. The custom of village exogamy, or marrying outside the home village, only heightens the isolation of the new bride, who finds herself in a position of subordination to not only the men but also the older women (mother-in-law and sisters-in-law) in the joint family household.[1] Marriage is traditionally accompanied by gifts from the groom's family to the bride, and sometimes to the bride's family. There is also an agreement of a bride price (*mahre*) that is typically deferred with the understanding that it can be claimed by the wife in the event of divorce. Besides this, women enter into marriage with no independent economic assets of their own. As specified by Islamic law, daughters have the right to inherit the equivalent of half the son's share of the father's property; however, the customary practice is for women to waive their land rights to their brothers in exchange for the promise of future economic protection in the event of divorce, abandonment, or other calamity.

The subordination of women in the traditional Bangladeshi family system as I have described is powerfully supported by the institution of *purdah*, or female seclusion. *Purdah* functions as a system of social control that emphasizes the separation of women from men and the seclusion of women from the world outside the home. Whereas the outward symbol of *purdah* is the veil, in Bangladesh, *purdah* operates through a more generalized system in which women are confined to the household compound (*ghare*), away from the outside (*baire*) world of men. The seclusion of women is supported by a powerful ideological apparatus whereby women are socialized into modesty and submission, and family honor (*izzat*) rests on the ability of the family to seclude its women. As Feldman and McCarthy (1983) have observed, it is a system that simultaneously ensures women's participation in agricultural production as well as the inability of women to control the fruits of production. Within the confines of the household compound, women are involved in the processing of crops (e.g., winnowing, husking) as well as the maintenance of household gardens and livestock (Chen 1983). Men, on the other hand, specialize in those economic activities carried out in public spaces, such as the marketplace, thus facilitating their control over economic resources.

As this brief description suggests, the traditional context in Bangladesh is clearly not favorable to women's control over their income, but in Bangladesh, as elsewhere, cultural traditions are not experienced and interpreted by people in uniform ways. Contemporary social and economic shifts in Bangladesh have in fact heightened the diversity of women's understanding of and relationship to the traditional normative family system. The expansion of the state sector following national independence in 1971 has resulted in the expansion of an urban, salaried middle class whose family life is shaped by nonagrarian economic concerns and exposure to Western ideas (Siddiqui et al. 1990). The more widespread challenge to the traditional organization of family life, however, has come from the growing landlessness and impoverishment of rural Bangladesh, trends that have been sharply evident since the 1970s.[2] Under the pressures of extreme poverty, the traditional family system is becoming increasingly dis-

tant from the immediate realities of life for many in rural Bangladesh. For women, it is a system that is increasingly unreliable, one on which they cannot depend for survival.

One of the effects of landlessness has been the disintegration of the joint family household, an economic unit previously held together by shared land interests. Observers of rural Bangladesh have also noted how, under the pressures of extreme poverty, traditional familial and village-based mutual-aid networks have declined in value, and subsistence has become a largely individual matter (Cain, Khanan, and Nahar 1979; Feldman 1992). For women, the erosion of traditional sources of mutual aid, including the ability to rely on the natal family in the event of calamity, has been especially devastating because of a rise in the number of women who find themselves without men's economic support. Conditions of widespread impoverishment and the concurrent inability of men to economically support their families are reflected in the growing incidence of divorce and abandonment by men of their wives and children. As a result, there has been a steady rise in the number of female-headed households in the country.[3]

A central assumption of the traditional family system—the economic and social protection of women by men in exchange for deference to male authority—has been challenged by the widespread poverty of rural Bangladesh. In light of these conditions, growing numbers of women in contemporary Bangladesh have been compelled to go outside the bounds of the traditional family system to ensure their livelihood. The 1970s witnessed the movement of growing numbers of rural women into wagework (e.g., road construction), despite both the traditional prohibitions against women's presence in public spaces and extremely limited employment opportunities for women (Hossain, Jahan, and Sobhan 1990, 34).

Since the mid-1980s, the garment industry has been an important source of urban employment for women. The Bangladesh Garment Manufacturers and Exporters Association (BGMEA 1992) reports more than 1,000 garment manufacturing units in the country in 1992, compared to just 47 in 1983. In fact, by 1992, Bangladesh had become the eighth largest exporter of garments to the United States and the tenth largest to the EEC (European Economic Community). Two factors favored the entry of Bangladesh into the global clothing market at this time. First, the rising costs of production and the imposition of export quotas on major garment-supplying countries, such as Taiwan and South Korea, spurred the movement of garment production to quota-free countries such as Bangladesh that had cheap labor. Second, government policy in Bangladesh, as reflected in the New Industrial Policy (NIP) of 1982, sought to create a favorable investment climate for export-oriented industries by such measures as the creation of export processing zones and the extension of tax benefits and tariff protection to investors (Hossain, Jahan, and Sobhan 1990, 37).

The BGMEA (1992) reports that of the 500,000 workers employed by the industry, more than 78 percent were women who had no previous work experience in the organized industrial sector. The high numbers of women in the industry reflect both the preference of employers for women workers and the growing need for income generation among women. How much control do these women workers retain over their wages? It is clear that the traditional Bangladeshi family system, centered on the deference and dependence of women on men, is a setting in which women are likely to defer to men in the control of their wages. How does this normative system operate to affect income control, particularly in light of structural challenges to traditional family life in Bangladesh?

STUDY METHODS

The analyses that follow draw on materials from a study of the Bangladesh garment industry conducted in 1992. As part of this study, I interviewed garment factory workers, as well as managers and owners. On two occasions, I also observed recruitment interviews for workers at a small-sized factory. I conducted my research in five different export garment production facilities. In two of the factories, managers allowed me to approach workers randomly and ask for interviews; in others, the management selected interviewees. Whereas the majority of the interviews were conducted at the production site, a few were done at the homes of interviewees.

I conducted 46 interviews with workers in their native language, Bengali. The analysis here focuses on the 34 female sewing machine operators in the sample who had similar salary levels and who faced potential demands for control of their income from male kin.[4] The semistructured interviews, which lasted an average of an hour to an hour and a half, were tape-recorded and later transcribed. Whereas the interviews covered a range of issues surrounding socioeconomic status, work, and family, a series of questions focused on what women did with their income and how they felt about it.

The majority of the women workers had not been employed prior to their work in the garment industry, a finding that concurs with that noted by other studies of the industry (Bangladesh Unnayan Parishad 1990; Chaudhuri and Majumdar 1991). In other ways, the sample was a diverse group. The median age of workers ranged from early to late 20s. Of the 41 women, 26 lived in households that were conventionally structured, headed by husbands or male family elders. Eight of the interviewees were young, unmarried women who were living in the city without family elders, either in a dormitory (*mess*) or in an apartment shared with other young women workers.

Reflecting the general paucity of employment opportunities for women in Bangladesh, the female sewing machine operators came from socioeconomically diverse backgrounds. This is suggested by the range of education levels among the women. A total of 12 women had been to school for one to five years, 13 for six to ten years, and 1 had attended a year of college. Based on the women's years of schooling as well as other factors that have been identified as important in

determining social class in contemporary Bangladesh (e.g., family income, occupation, involvement in formal versus informal sector, land ownership), I analyzed the socioeconomic background
of the women (Siddiqui et al. 1990). Sixteen of
the women were from urban working-class backgrounds, as suggested by the relatively low levels
of income, schooling (six years or less), and involvement in manual jobs in the informal sector
(e.g., rickshaw puller) of family members. Ten of
the women were distinguished from others in the
sample by their relative economic prosperity, as
indicated by their levels of education and household income. On average, these women had completed 7 to 10 years of schooling, and they had at
least one family member in a low-level salaried
government job—all indicators of lower-middle-
class status. Eight of the interviewees were from
poor rural backgrounds. These were women who
had arrived in the city from the villages with the
specific intent of working in the garment factories.
Their families were from the impoverished, landless sectors of rural Bangladesh. In what follows, I
explore the relationship of these variations in socioeconomic background to the income control
experiences of the women.

Urban Working-Class Women: Handing over Wages

The women from urban working-class backgrounds lived with what may be described as
male-dominant budgets—financial arrangements
in which a male family member exercised substantial or complete control over the woman's income. Many of these women initially indicated
that they placed their money into a common
household fund. Further questioning revealed,
however, that most had little say over the uses of
the common fund, revealed by the fact that they
were unable to provide any specific accounting of
the areas of income expenditure. The dominant
pattern was to hand over their entire pay to the
male household heads who maintained complete
control over household expenditures. In many
cases the household head, after receiving the

woman's pay, would then give her a small allowance from it for supplemental housekeeping and/
or personal expenses. I encountered only three
cases among male-dominant budgets in which
women were in charge of basic housekeeping expenses. The absence of women's control over
even housekeeping budgets may be explained by
the responsibility traditionally held by men in
Bangladesh for purchasing food for the household, because of cultural prohibitions against
women appearing in public places such as the
market. Reinforcing this tradition of male responsibility for grocery shopping was the women's
long working hours at the factory; many women
said that they simply did not have the time or
energy to undertake the time-consuming task of
shopping for food.

Not surprisingly, the imprint of traditional
Bangladeshi familial principles emerged in the
sharpest and most predictable fashion in the interviews with women in male-dominant budgets.
These women, both married and unmarried, legitimated their surrender of pay to the male household heads with reference to ideological elements
of the traditional Bangladeshi family system. The
first of these was a view of the family as a unit
with common interests and a single, unified identity. Women spoke of how the distinction between
their own wages and that of other household
members was an artificial one, because all of
these were collective rather than individual resources. The reality of conflicting intrahousehold
interests was also minimized as women spoke of
the male household head as the *benevolent dicta-
tor,* whose authority over financial matters was
justified by the fact that he acted in ways that protected the interests of all household members.
These views emerged in the words of Rokeya, an
unmarried 18-year-old woman who had been
working as a sewing machine operator for almost
two years. She lived in her brother's household
and dutifully handed over her wages to him every
month:

> *I give all my pay to my brother. I can't imagine act-
> ing in another way. After all, my brother is not
> spending the money on his own pleasure, on luxu-*

ries for himself. When he spends the money it's for my own good, for the good of our family.

Further bolstering the legitimacy of the financial authority of the male household head were traditional beliefs regarding the *natural* place of men and women. Because financial matters were in the realm of the *baire* rather than the *ghare,* they fell under the purview of men's responsibility and expertise. A number of the women garment workers remarked that men were naturally more clever at outside worldly matters, in contrast to women who were smart in household matters.

The traditional family system entered into the construction of the male-dominant budgets not only by furnishing ideological justifications for women's relinquishment of income control but also by providing the basis for the expectation that conformity to traditional norms, specifically, acts of deference to male authority, would ensure the fulfillment of male familial economic responsibilities. In other words, women's surrender of their income solidified the gender contract that was a central dynamic of the traditional family system, that of women's submission to male authority in exchange for the economic and social protection of men.

Of central importance to understanding the significance and value that the women placed on the traditional gender contract is their socioeconomic status. As members of the urban working class, these women had entered into garment work in a context of financial scarcity and insecurity. Despite the added household income generated by their garment factory work, their families had trouble making ends meet and had little or no surplus income. In fact, the urban working-class women, both married and unmarried, had entered into garment factory work because of the inability of men in the family to adequately meet basic household costs, a situation that also provided the justification for women breaking the norms of *purdah* to enter the workplace. They thus saw themselves as living on the edge of poverty, a situation that strengthened their resolve to solidify the contract that ensured men's participation in the household economy.

Further highlighting women's fears about men's economic participation were the financial struggles of fellow women workers who had become heads of household in the absence of men. The impoverished women heads of households, struggling to support themselves and their children, were symbolic warnings of the dire consequences of men's withdrawal from familial economic responsibilities. This view was shared by the women heads of households themselves, who saw their poverty to be a result of the failure of the family system to deliver on its promise of protection to women.

The significance of these economic fears to the income control behavior of the women in male-dominant budgets was vividly illustrated by the situation of Ameena, a married woman in her mid-20s with two children. Ameena said that a year ago, she had fought with her husband when he discovered that to generate savings she had been withholding about 20 percent of her pay from him. Ameena eventually acceded to her husband's demands that she turn over all her pay to him. She saw this as an act that preserved the implicit gender contract of the marriage:

> *After that time I stopped keeping money for myself; every time I get paid I come home and give all the money to my husband. I see some of the marriages of women in the garment factory be ruined over money; they don't give all the money when he asks for it, the husband leaves her, and then she and her children will be struggling to find rice to eat. After all, women have only one dream in life, to remain with their husband forever.*

If the fear of men's withdrawal from their familial economic responsibilities caused women to hand over their wages, it also, somewhat ironically, encouraged women to covertly withhold a portion of their pay from the male household heads. Women were extremely aware of the potential for breakdown of the traditional gender contract. Six of the 16 women in the male-dominant budgets said that they secretly withheld a portion of their pay, despite the possibility of physical violence and other retribution from family members. One of the most common means of withholding money was not to inform family members of special holiday and overtime bonus pay received at work. The withheld money was typically accumulated and then used by women to purchase gold jewelry—a common method of saving in Bangladesh. The women saw such savings as protective insurance that could enable them to survive if faced with such calamity as the departure of the male family breadwinner, an increasingly common occurrence. The income control behavior of women in male-dominant budgets, while driven by the promises of the traditional gender contract, was also being affected by the contract's growing unreliability.

To summarize, women garment workers from urban working-class backgrounds did not exercise much control over their income; however, women's acceptance of male financial authority was not a simple reflection of patriarchal cultural tradition. Rather, the male-dominant budgets were the outcome of the complex interaction of cultural tradition and economic circumstance. Economic conditions affected the symbolic meanings that were attached to the women's income earning. Used to meet basic household subsistence costs, the women's pay symbolized the inadequacy of men's breadwinning capacities. Women worked, however, to mute the potential challenge of this situation to men's authority in the family. The handing over of wages to men was a gesture that diverted attention from men's economic inadequacies. Women also affirmed the economic primacy and, thus, the authority of men by the ways in which they spoke of their pay. For example, they spoke of their pay as a supplement rather than a replacement for male wages.

Such efforts to affirm male authority were not simply a reflection of women's socialization into patriarchal cultural tradition. They reflected a concern for maintaining male participation in the household economy. Whereas the men's income was not enough to support the household completely, it was essential to keep the household from sinking into extreme poverty. Given these circumstances, it is not surprising that entry into wage-

work had not apparently increased the women's family power in significant ways. Whereas many of the women felt that employment had enhanced their sense of self-worth, they did not associate wagework with a strengthened ability to exercise authority in family decision making.

Lower-Middle-Class Women: Keeping Wages with Permission

In stark contrast to the budgetary arrangements described above, the women workers from lower-middle-class backgrounds said that they did not pool their money with other household members; they maintained control of 90 percent or more of their own income. Although the women paid heed to the financial advice of knowledgeable elders, they alone made decisions about how to spend their pay, and they also spent the money themselves, *with their own hands (nijer hate)*.

The financial autonomy of the women reflects, I suggest, the symbolic meanings attached to their wagework, meanings that were deeply colored by the meaning of lower-middle-class status in Bangladesh. Unlike the previous case, the entry of these women into the outside world of the garment industry could not be justified by basic economic scarcity. Instead, the women spoke of how their wagework was legitimated by the fact that they were working to achieve economic mobility into the secure upper sectors of the middle class for their families. The unmarried women in this group, for example, spoke of how garment factory work enabled them to save money for marriage expenses. Not only would these savings spare their families from incurring wedding and dowry costs on their behalf, but they could also facilitate marriage into a prosperous family, a situation that held potential economic and social benefits both for themselves and for their families. They could also use their earnings to purchase luxury goods such as televisions and VCRs for the household, items that promoted a middle-class identity.

Among married women, the notion that their wagework was of benefit to the family was even more strongly invoked; they argued that they were being good wives and mothers by working. One woman told me that she was saving her wages to pay the bribe that was necessary for her husband to get a salaried government job, an important marker of middle-class status in Bangladesh. Simmi, a 22-year-old married woman with two children, felt that she was fulfilling the dictates of good motherhood by working. Whereas the household was financially able to get by on the income of her husband, who was a shopkeeper, she felt compelled to work for some extra money. Her husband had initially opposed her employment arguing that the factories were filled with uncouth lower-class persons who generated an unsuitable environment for women. Simmi persisted in her request, however, arguing that her income would give them the extra means necessary to ensure a middle-class future for their children. In keeping with this goal, Simmi indicated that she placed a large share of her monthly income into a savings account that was earmarked for the private schools and tutoring that were necessary to ensure the educational success of her children. She spent the remainder of her income on milk (an expensive item in Bangladesh) for the children, household goods, and personal expenses. These items had become indispensable to her, and she could not imagine not working.

Despite the fact that these women spoke of their wagework as an activity aimed toward the collective welfare of their households, they maintained virtually complete control of their wages. The lower-middle-class women spoke of their wage control as an expression of the ability of men to fulfill their provider obligations. Some told of how, according to Islamic principles, men were expected to provide for the upkeep of their families, regardless of the women's resources. It was a matter of honor and pride for men to not take money from women in the family. Nasreen, a single woman who lived in the household of her older brother, said that no one touched her pay because, after all, it was the family's responsibility to look after her, a young woman, rather than the

other way around; her brother would feel shameful to take her money.

The status-related meanings surrounding men's insistence that women keep their wages are revealed by the comments of a married woman. Her words also show how the belief that the woman's wages went only toward incidental expenses, publicly affirmed by all involved, was not always entirely accurate:

> My husband likes that my income is for luxuries, for the little things that catch my fancy. Although sometimes I pay for household things, during difficult months. He tells me, it is his job to provide for food, clothing, rent and other necessities. Why should he take my money like the lower-class men?

Whereas the income control of these women was a sharp contrast to the patterns noted among working-class women, in both cases, budgetary arrangements were legitimated by traditional family ideology, albeit different elements of it. These differing interpretations of tradition highlight the malleability of family ideologies and the critical role of social class in structuring interpretations of tradition. For the working-class women, male authority was affirmed by women's relinquishment of wages to men, but for the lower-middle-class women, male authority was affirmed by men's refusal to touch their wages. Indeed, allowing one's wife or daughter to retain her wages for incidental luxury expenses was perhaps especially important for the lower-middle-class men, given their insecurity about their place in the middle class. That is, the ability of the men to adequately provide for their families was an important marker of middle-class status, a way of affirming distance from the lower socioeconomic strata.

Given the ways in which women's income control symbolically affirmed rather than challenged male authority, it is not surprising that the wage earning of the lower-middle-class women had only modest effects on their family power. The women did not associate their entry into wagework with a notably enhanced ability to assert their power in family decision-making processes. At the same time, almost all of the women felt that greater respect was accorded them because of their status as income earners.

Rural Poor Women: Controlling Wages

Women garment workers who controlled their income included eight young unmarried women who were living in the city without family elders. Like that of the lower-middle-class women, the income control of these women is counterintuitive when viewed against the backdrop of cultural tradition. In the traditional Bangladeshi family system, before marriage, women are under the authority of fathers, brothers, and other male kin who control all aspects, including economic aspects, of their lives; however, contrary to the dictates of tradition, none of these young women remitted all or even a portion of their wages to family members. Underlying this pattern of financial independence were conditions of poverty, which had challenged the set of expectations traditionally guiding relations between daughters and kin.

The women in this group were from impoverished and typically landless rural families. It was the inability of the families to economically provide for daughters that allowed the young women to enter into garment work in the city unaccompanied by family members. In Bangladeshi tradition, the honor of the family is tied to its ability to protect the sexual purity of its women. Young unmarried women who do not conform to *purdah* norms and whose activities are not subject to familial supervision are automatically sexually suspect and a threat to family honor. It is not surprising, then, that for these women, entering into garment factory work and relocating to the city were both events that were typically accompanied by a period of opposition to these moves from parents and other family elders because of the implications for family honor. The ability of families to persist in their opposition was weakened by their poverty and subsequent inability to adequately provide for basic subsistence needs as well as the ever-rising costs of providing a dowry to daugh-

ters.[5] This was suggested by the words of two young women who had initially encountered family opposition to their plans to work in the garment industry:

> *Rehana: At first, my mother and uncle [chacha] said no, if you work in garments and live alone in Dhaka city you will lose your innocence; you will mix with men and all kinds of low people, and you will learn undesirable things from them. But then I said, how long can I eat your rice? Now there's not enough for two meals a day, and I'm just another mouth to feed. They had no reply to what I said.*

> *Sayeeda: In my home in the village there were five of us [brothers and sisters] and my father couldn't support us. When I heard about garments work from some people in the village I asked my father about it and he said that if it was necessary I would eat just one meal a day but still I couldn't work in garments. That was how much he opposed it. But later I persuaded him to change his mind. I asked him to think about my future because if I worked in garments I would be self-sufficient and I could save some money for my married life.*

Within the traditional family system, girls could expect natal families to ensure their upkeep and eventual marriage. But poverty had eroded the ability of these families to fulfill obligations to daughters. This familial failure enabled the young women to take the unconventional step of working and living in the city alone and also maintain virtually no financial ties with their families. As I have mentioned, young single women did not remit money to parents or other family members in the home village. Their wages instead went toward personal living expenditures and, occasionally, consumer items (e.g., clothes, cosmetics, and small pieces of gold jewelry). The only regular flow of resources from daughters to their families occurred on such occasions as Eid (a Muslim religious holiday), when the young women traveled back to their home villages, armed with gifts of clothes, food, and other items.

The failure to remit wages, a sharp contrast to the behavior of working daughters in many societies (Fernandez Kelly 1982; Greenhalgh 1988;

Harevan 1982; Ong 1987; Tilly and Scott 1978), reflected the inability of families to provide for their daughters and the subsequent breakdown of obligation in daughter-parent relations. One young woman, when questioned about how her parents felt about the fact that she did not send money home, replied that they did not expect her to do so. On the contrary, they felt shameful about the fact that they could not provide for her, and so they did not want to accept her money. Another woman refused to cave in to her elder brother's demands for her wages. She resented that he and other family members had been unable to take care of her. It was clear that the circumstances under which the young women had entered into garment work had shaped the symbolic meanings of the work. Rather than daughterly obligation, the work was associated with familial inefficacy and perhaps even shame.

The financial autonomy of these young women was the outcome of a process in which economic circumstances, specifically, conditions of poverty, had worked to challenge the traditional dynamics of family life. To put it simply, the traditional family system had little meaning for these young women, certainly far less than it did for the other groups of women that I have described. Unlike the other women in the study, these young women expressed ideals and conceptions of family life that were far removed from traditional ones. They spoke with great satisfaction about their greater freedom of movement (in contrast to their village sisters) and their ability to exercise control over such important life events as marriage. Whereas it was clear that garment factory work, combined with an independent living situation, damaged the sexual reputation and thus marriage opportunities of young women, the benefits of such work, including the ability to make one's own marriage choices, far outweighed the disadvantages. Perhaps most significantly, these women spoke of how, after marriage, they expected to continue to move around freely and to make their own decisions about such issues as employment and the expenditure of their income:

If you work in garments you can better yourself. What's the use of sitting at home? If I lived in the village I would be married by now, but I'm glad that my life is different. Because I'm self-sufficient I can go where I want and marry whom I want. Even after I'm married, I will continue to live my life in my own way.

Both the working-class and lower-middle-class women related to their income within a social context in which the traditional family system was meaningful and attractive, at least in certain aspects. But this was not the case for the young women from poor rural families. These young women felt that they were economically better off at present than they were when they lived with their families in the home village. Unencumbered by economic dependents, they experienced their financial situation as adequate, one that enabled them to meet basic living as well as occasional discretionary expenses. They did not place much meaning or significance on what is perhaps the fundamental attraction of the patriarchal family system for the women—the promise of men's economic support. Also relevant were the combined effects of the young age (mid- to late teens) and the living situation of the women. Unlike the other women in the sample, they had moved out of the parental home during early to mid-adolescence, thus avoiding the critical gender socialization processes of this phase of the life cycle. This, combined with the absence of family guardians who could monitor their activities in the city, was potent ground for change. It was the combined effect of these conditions, rather than income control per se, that made wage employment an extremely powerful force of change for these women.

CONCLUSION

Research on Third World women is often marked by an inattention to the sources of differentiation in their lives. This is particularly the case with studies of Bangladeshi women, who are often portrayed as a monolithic group whose behavior is uniformly guided by cultural traditions such as that of *purdah.*[6] My analyses reveal Bangladeshi women garment workers to be a diverse group, one that experiences employment in varied ways.

The diversity of the women's experiences highlights the difficulty of assuming a simple relationship between cultural tradition and women's income control, particularly in societies that are in the throes of rapid economic and social transformation. In Bangladesh, one of the effects of such transformation has been to heighten socioeconomic differentiation among women. It is not surprising that women workers deal with the issue of male control over their income differently, in ways that reflect the particular socioeconomic realities of their lives. These socioeconomic realities place them in varied relationships to the traditional family system. For example, the financial autonomy of the young, unmarried women garment workers living without family in the city reflects the failure of the traditional family system to deliver on its promise of economic and social protection; however, as illustrated by the situation of the women in male-headed, working-class and lower-middle-class households, the traditional family system remains economically attractive to some women, despite increasing uncertainty about it (cf. Kandiyoti 1988). The varied ways in which women relate to the traditional family system highlight the fact that family life is in a process of rapid change in Bangladesh.

There were, however, important differences in income control patterns even among those women who valued the maintenance of the traditional family system. Lower-middle-class women retained control over their wages, whereas working-class women relinquished control to men. These divergent patterns stemmed from differences in socioeconomic status, which colored the ways in which men viewed the implications of women's income earning for their own authority in the family. Working-class men associated women's wagework with their own economic impotence; seizing control of women's income was a gesture that affirmed their economic headship. In contrast, lower-middle-class men affirmed their economic authority by allowing women to control

their wages. By not touching the women's pay, they affirmed an understanding of women's income as peripheral and inessential to the household economy. Ironically, whereas quite different in substance, both sets of behaviors served to affirm rather than challenge male authority in the family. Efforts to maintain male dominance in the family can result, then, in quite different patterns of income control. The relationship of social class to women's income control may be explored in more detail by studies that look at the effects of household economic mobility, or how the ability of women to control income shifts along with changes in socioeconomic status.

Income control is not a guarantee of greater family power for women, as highlighted by the experiences of the lower-middle-class women. More significant than income control per se is the extent to which the broader social context that surrounds women's income earning offers opportunities and options for women. The importance of the broader context is also suggested by Blumberg (1991) when she asserts that the relationship between women's income control and family power is one that is mediated by a variety of complex factors such as the extent of gender inequality at the macrosocietal level and the gender role ideology of family members. For the young unmarried *unaccompanied* women workers, the larger social context surrounding their work accounts for the seemingly dramatic changes in their lives. It is not simply their income earning but a combination of circumstances, including the independent living situation of the young women and the economic inefficacy of their families, that creates the conditions for both their financial and social autonomy. Unlike the other women in the sample, these women responded to the growing uncertainty of the traditional family system with a new and more egalitarian vision of family life. Further research may illuminate the specific conditions that generate changes in attitudes and ideals for these women. It is possible, for example, that the workplace subcultures in which the young women are involved play an important role in the construction of egalitarian family ideals.

Given the controversy that has surrounded the participation of women in the garment industry of Bangladesh, it is worth noting that the overwhelming majority of the women garment workers spoke of their employment in positive terms, as an activity that had enhanced their sense of self-esteem and worth in the household. Because of the paucity of other job opportunities, they valued the presence of the garment factories in the country. At the same time, for those who are concerned with the improvement of women's status in Bangladesh, the women's experiences do not legitimate an overly optimistic view of the consequences of the industry for women. With respect to family power, the benefits of garment factory work for women in Bangladesh seem to be uneven at best. The most significant and powerful challenge to patriarchal family relations stems not from women's involvement in the industrial sector but from the ongoing macrostructural shifts that have questioned the core dynamics of traditional family relations.

NOTES

1. The term *joint family household* refers to a household in which the sons of the family continue to live under one roof, with their parents, after marriage.
2. Feldman (1992, 220) reports that in 1978, 80 percent of the rural population was found to be landless or functionally landless, owning less than one acre of land. For other statistics on this issue, see Hossain, Jahan, and Sobhan (1990, 32).
3. In 1982, 16.5 percent of all households were estimated to be female headed, based on a sample survey by Bangladesh Bureau of Statistics (Islam 1991).
4. Besides the operators, the sample included two quality inspectors, women who inspected garments for errors after they had been produced. It also included three "helpers" or assistants to sewing machine operators. To control for levels of income, the analysis here is confined to operators because of their similar salary levels. Because control over wages was not a problematic issue for these women, I have also not included the seven women who were heads of their households. The female heads of households tended to have only distant relations with fathers, brothers, and other male kin who could potentially challenge their authority.
5. Whereas marriage was traditionally accompanied by a flow of gifts from the groom's family to the bride, the past three decades have witnessed a steady inflation in the economic demands made by the groom of the bride's family, a situation that both signifies and reinforces the low economic value of women (Lindenbaum 1981).
6. For a review and critique of the monolithic depiction of Bangladeshi women in academic literature, see Kabeer (1991) and White (1992).

REFERENCES

Bangladesh Garment Manufacturers and Exporters Association (BGMEA). 1992. The garment industry: A look ahead at Europe of 1992. Bangladesh Garment Manufacturers and Exporters Association, Dhaka, Bangladesh. Mimeographed.

Bangladesh Unnayan Parishad (BUP). 1990. A study on female garment workers in Bangladesh: A draft report. Bangladesh Unnayan Parishad, Dhaka, Bangladesh.

Blumberg, R. L. 1984. A general theory of gender stratification. In *Sociological theory,* edited by R. Collins. San Francisco: Jossey-Bass.

———. 1991. Income under female versus male control: Hypotheses from a theory of gender stratification and data from the Third World. In *Gender, family and economy: The triple overlap,* edited by R. L. Blumberg. Newbury Park CA: Sage.

Cain, M., S. R. Khanan and S. Nahar. 1979. Class, patriarchy, and women's work in Bangladesh. *Population and Development Review* 5:408–16.

Chaudhuri, S., and P. P. Majumdar. 1991. The conditions of garment workers in Bangladesh: An appraisal. Bangladesh Institute of Development Studies, Dhaka, Bangladesh.

Chen, Martha. 1983. *A quiet revolution: Women in transition in rural Bangladesh.* Cambridge, MA: Schenkman.

Fapohunda, E. R. 1988. The nonpooling household: A challenge to theory. In *A home divided: Women and income in the Third World,* edited by D. Dwyer and J. Bruce. Stanford, CA: Stanford University Press.

Feldman, S. 1992. Crisis, Islam and gender in Bangladesh: The social construction of a female labor force. In *Unequal burden: Economic crises, persistent poverty and women's work,* edited by L. Beneria and S. Feldman. Boulder, CO: Westview.

Feldman, S., and F. E. McCarthy. 1983. Purdah and changing patterns of social control among rural women in Bangladesh. *Journal of Marriage and the Family* 4:949–59.

Fernandez Kelly, Maria Patricia. 1982. *For we are sold, I and my people: Women and industry in Mexico's frontier.* Albany, NY: SUNY Press.

———. 1990. Delicate transactions: Gender, home, and employment among Hispanic women. In *Uncertain terms: Negotiating gender in American culture,* edited by P. Ginsburg and A. L. Tsing. Boston: Beacon.

Gallin, R. 1990. Women and the export industry in Taiwan: The muting of class consciousness. In *Women, work and global restructuring,* edited by K. Ward. Ithaca, NY: ILR.

Geschwender, James A. 1992. Ethgender, women's waged labor, and economic mobility. *Social Problems* 39:1–16.

Greenhalgh, S. 1988. Intergenerational contacts: Familial roots of sexual stratification in Taiwan. In *A home divided: Women and income in the Third World,* edited by D. Dwyer and J. Bruce. Stanford, CA: Stanford University Press.

Harevan, Tamara. 1982. *Family time and industrial time.* New York: Cambridge University Press.

Hochschild, A., and A. Machung. 1989. *The second shift.* New York: Viking.

Hood, Jane. 1983. *Becoming a two-job family.* New York: Praeger.

Hoodfar, H. 1988. Household budgeting and financial management in a lower-income Cairo neighborhood. In *A home divided: Women and income in the Third World,* edited by D. Dwyer and J. Bruce. Stanford, CA: Stanford University Press.

Hossain, H., R. Jahan, and S. Sobhan. 1990. *No better option? Industrial women workers in Bangladesh.* Dhaka, Bangladesh: University Press Limited.

Islam, Mahmuda. 1991. *Women heads of household in Bangladesh: Strategies for survival.* Dhaka, Bangladesh: Flair Print.

Kabeer, Naila. 1991. Cultural dopes or rational fools? Women and labour supply in the Bangladesh garment industry. *European Journal of Development Research* 3:133–60.

Kandiyoti, Deniz. 1988. Bargaining with patriarchy. *Gender & Society* 2:274–90.

Kung, Lydia. 1983. *Factory women in Taiwan.* Ann Arbor: University of Michigan Press.

Lindenbaum, Shirley. 1981. Implications for women of changing marriage transactions in Bangladesh. *Studies in Family Planning* 1:394–401.

Ong, Aihwa. 1987. *Spirits of resistance and capitalist discipline: Factory women in Malaysia.* Albany, NY: SUNY Press.

Papanek, H., and L. Schwede. 1988. Women are good with money: Earning and managing in an Indonesian city. In *A home divided: Women and income in the Third World,* edited by D. Dwyer and J. Bruce. Stanford, CA: Stanford University Press.

Pyke, Karen D. 1994. Women's employment as gift or burden? Marital power across marriage, divorce and remarriage. *Gender & Society* 8:73–91.

Safilios-Rothschild, C. 1988. The impact of agrarian reform on men's and women's incomes in rural Honduras. In *A home divided: Women and income in the Third World,* edited by D. Dwyer and J. Bruce. Stanford, CA: Stanford University Press.

Salaff, Janet. 1981. *Working daughters of Hong Kong.* New York: Cambridge University Press.

Sen, A. K. 1990. Gender and cooperative conflicts. In *Persistent inequalities: Women and world development,* edited by I. Tinker. New York: Oxford University Press.

Siddiqui, K., S. Qadir, S. Alamgir, and S. Huq. 1990. *Social formation in Dhaka city.* Dhaka, Bangladesh: University Press Limited.

Tilly, L. and J. Scott. 1978. *Women, work and family.* New York: Holt, Rinehart and Winston.

United Nations Industrial Development Organization (UNIDO). 1991. Bangladesh's textile and clothing industry: A working paper. United Nations Industrial Development Organization, Dhaka, Bangladesh.

White, Sarah. 1992. *Arguing with the crocodile: Gender and class in Bangladesh.* London: Zed Books.

Wolf, D. L. 1991. Female autonomy, the family and industrialization in Java. In *Gender, family and economy: The triple overlap,* edited by R. L. Blumberg. Newbury Park CA: Sage.

———. 1992. *Factory daughters: Gender, household dynamics and rural industrialization in Java.* Berkeley: University of California Press.

37

Moving Up with Kin and Community

Upward Social Mobility for
Black and White Women

ELIZABETH HIGGINBOTHAM
LYNN WEBER

…When women and people of color experience upward mobility in America, they scale steep structural as well as psychological barriers. The long process of moving from a working-class family of origin to the professional-managerial class is full of twists and turns: choices made with varying degrees of information and varying options; critical junctures faced with support and encouragement or disinterest, rejection, or active discouragement; and interpersonal relationships in which basic understandings are continuously negotiated and renegotiated. It is a fascinating process that profoundly shapes the lives of those who experience it, as well as the lives of those around them. Social mobility is also a process engulfed in myth. One need only pick up any newspaper or turn on the television to see that the myth of upward mobility remains firmly entrenched in American culture: With hard work, talent, determination, and some luck, just about anyone can "make it."…

The image of the isolated and detached experience of mobility that we have inherited from past scholarship is problematic for anyone seeking to understand the process for women or people of color. Twenty years of scholarship in the study of both race and gender has taught us the importance of interpersonal attachments to the lives of women

and a commitment to racial uplift among people of color….

…Lacking wealth, the greatest gift a Black family has been able to give to its children has been the motivation and skills to succeed in school. Aspirations for college attendance and professional positions are stressed as *family* goals, and the entire family may make sacrifices and provide support…. Black women have long seen the activist potential of education and have sought it as a cornerstone of community development—a means of uplifting the race. When women of color or White women are put at the center of the analysis of upward mobility, it is clear that different questions will be raised about social mobility and different descriptions of the process will ensue….

Research Design

These data are from a study of full-time employed middle-class women in the Memphis metropolitan area. This research is designed to explore the processes of upward social mobility for Black and White women by examining differences between women professionals, managers, and administrators who are from working- and middle-class backgrounds—that is, upwardly mobile and middle-class stable women. In this way, we isolate subjective processes shared among women who have been upwardly mobile from those common to women who have reproduced their family's

AUTHORS' NOTE: The research reported here was supported by National Institute for Mental Health Grant MH38769.

professional-managerial class standing. Likewise, we identify common experiences in the attainment process that are shared by women of the same race, be they upwardly mobile or stable middle class. Finally, we specify some ways in which the attainment process is unique for each race-class group....

...We rely on a model of social class basically derived from the work of Poulantzas (1974), Braverman (1974), Ehrenreich and Ehrenreich (1979), and elaborated in Vanneman and Cannon (1987). These works explicate a basic distinction between social class and social status. Classes represent bounded categories of the population, groups set in a relation of opposition to one another by their roles in the capitalist system. The middle class, or professional-managerial class, is set off from the working class by the power and control it exerts over workers in three realms: economic (power through ownership), political (power through direct supervisory authority), and ideological (power to plan and organize work; Poulantzas 1974; Vanneman and Cannon 1987).

In contrast, education, prestige, and income represent social statuses—hierarchically structured relative rankings along a ladder of economic success and social prestige. Positions along these dimensions are not established by social relations of dominance and subordination but, rather, as rankings on scales representing resources and desirability. In some respects, they represent both the justification for power differentials vested in classes and the rewards for the role that the middle class plays in controlling labor.

Our interest is in the process of upward social class mobility, moving from a working-class family of origin to a middle-class destination—from a position of working-class subordination to a position of control over the working class. Lacking inherited wealth or other resources, those working-class people who attain middle-class standing do so primarily by obtaining a college education and entering a professional, managerial, or administrative occupation. Thus we examine carefully the process of educational at-

tainment not as evidence of middle-class standing but as a necessary part of the mobility process for most working-class people.

Likewise, occupation alone does not define the middle class, but professional, managerial, and administrative occupations capture many of the supervisory and ideologically based positions whose function is to control workers' lives. Consequently, we defined subjects as *middle class* by virtue of their employment in either a professional, managerial, or administrative occupation.... Classification of subjects as either professional or managerial-administrative was made on the basis of the designation of occupations in the U.S. Bureau of the Census's (1983) "Detailed Population Characteristics: Tennessee." Managerial occupations were defined as those in the census categories of managers and administrators; professionals were defined as those occupations in the professional category, excluding technicians, whom Braverman (1974) contends are working class.

Upwardly mobile women were defined as those women raised in families where neither parent was employed as a professional, manager, or administrator. Typical occupations for working-class fathers were postal clerk, craftsman, semiskilled manufacturing worker, janitor, and laborer. Some working-class mothers had clerical and sales positions, but many of the Black mothers also worked as private household workers. *Middle-class stable* women were defined as those women raised in families where *either* parent was employed as a professional, manager, or administrator. Typical occupations of middle-class parents were social worker, teacher, and school administrator as well as high-status professionals such as attorneys, physicians, and dentists....

Family Expectations for Educational Attainment

Four questions assess the expectations and support among family members for the educational attainment of the subjects. First, "Do you recall your father or mother stressing that you attain an education?" Yes was the response of 190 of the 200 women. Each of the women in this study had obtained a college degree, and many have graduate degrees. It is clear that for Black and White women, education was an important concern in their families....

The comments of Laura Lee, a 39-year-old Black woman who was raised middle class, were typical:

> Going to school, that was never a discussable issue. Just like you were born to live and die, you were going to go to school. You were going to prepare yourself to do something.

It should be noted, however, that only 86 percent of the White working-class women answered yes, compared to 98 percent of all other groups. Although this difference is small, it foreshadows a pattern where White women raised in working-class families received the least support and encouragement for educational and career attainment.

"When you were growing up, how far did your father expect you to go in school?" While most fathers expected college attendance from their daughters, differences also exist by class of origin. Only 70 percent of the working-class fathers, both Black and White, expected their daughters to attend college. In contrast, 94 percent of the Black middle-class and 88 percent of the White middle-class women's fathers had college expectations for their daughters.

When asked the same question about mother's expectations, 88 percent to 92 percent of each group's mothers expected their daughters to get a college education, except the White working-class women, for whom only 66 percent of mothers held such expectations. In short, only among the White working-class women did a fairly substantial proportion (about one-third) of both mothers and fathers expect less than a college education from their daughters. About 30 percent of Black working-class fathers held lower expectations for their daughters, but not the mothers; virtually all middle-class parents expected a college education for their daughters.

Sara Marx is a White, 33-year-old director of counseling raised in a rural working-class family. She is among those whose parents did not expect a college education for her. She was vague about the roots of attending college:

> It seems like we had a guest speaker who talked to us. Maybe before our exams somebody talked to us. I really can't put my finger on anything. I don't know where the information came from exactly.

"Who provided emotional support for you to make the transition from high school to college?" While 86 percent of the Black middle-class women indicated that family provided that support, 70 percent of the White middle class, 64 percent of the Black working class, and only 56 percent of the White working class received emotional support from family.

"Who paid your college tuition and fees?" Beyond emotional support, financial support is critical to college attendance. There are clear class differences in financial support for college. Roughly 90 percent of the middle-class respondents and only 56 percent and 62 percent of the Black and White working-class women, respectively, were financially supported by their families. These data also suggest that working-class parents were less able to give emotional or financial support for college than they were to hold out the expectation that their daughters should attend.

Family Expectations for Occupation or Career

When asked, "Do you recall your father or mother stressing that you should have an occupation to succeed in life?" racial differences appear. Ninety-four percent of all Black respondents said yes. In the words of Julie Bird, a Black woman raised-middle-class junior high school teacher:

> My father would always say, "You see how good I'm doing? Each generation should do more than the generation before." He expects me to accomplish more than he has.

Ann Right, a 36-year-old Black attorney whose father was a janitor, said:

> They wanted me to have a better life than they had. For all of us. And that's why they emphasized education and emphasized working relationships and how you get along with people and that kind of thing.

Ruby James, a Black teacher from a working-class family, said:

> They expected me to have a good-paying job and to have a family and be married. Go to work every day. Buy a home. That's about it. Be happy.

In contrast, only 70 percent of the White middle-class and 56 percent of the White working-class women indicated that their parents stressed that an occupation was needed for success. Nina Pentel, a 26-year-old white medical social worker, expressed a common response: "They said 'You're going to get married but get a degree, you never know what's going to happen to you.' They were pretty laid back about goals."

When the question focuses on a career rather than an occupation, the family encouragement is lower and differences were not significant, but similar patterns emerged. We asked respondents, "Who, if anyone, encouraged you to think about a career?" Among Black respondents, 60 percent of the middle-class and 56 percent of the working-class women answered that family encouraged them. Only 40 percent of the White working-class women indicated that their family encouraged them in their thinking about a career, while 52 percent of the White middle-class women did so. . . .

When working-class White women seek to be mobile through their own attainments, they face conflicts. Their parents encourage educational attainment, but when young women develop professional career goals, these same parents sometimes become ambivalent. This was the case with Elizabeth Marlow, who is currently a public interest attorney—a position her parents never intended her to hold. She described her parents' traditional expectations and their reluctance to support her career goals fully.

> My parents assumed that I would go college and meet some nice man and finish, but not necessarily work after. I would be a good mother for my children. I don't think that they ever thought I would go to law school. Their attitude about my interest in law school was, "You can do it if you want to, but we don't think it is a particularly practical thing for a woman to do."

Elizabeth is married and has three children, but she is not the traditional housewife of her parents' dreams. She received more support outside the family for her chosen lifestyle.

Although Black families are indeed more likely than white families to encourage their daughters to prepare for careers, like White families, they frequently steer them toward highly visible traditionally female occupations, such as teacher, nurse, and social worker. Thus many mobile Black women are directed toward the same gender-segregated occupations as White women. . . .

Marriage

Although working-class families may encourage daughters to marry, they recognize the need for working-class women to contribute to family income or to support themselves economically. To achieve these aims, many working-class girls are encouraged to pursue an education as preparation for work in gender-segregated occupations. Work in these fields presumably allows women to keep marriage, family, and child rearing as life goals while contributing to the family income and to have "something to fall back on" if the marriage does not work out. This interplay among marriage, education, financial need, and class mobility is complex (Joslin 1979).

We asked, "Do you recall your mother or father emphasizing that marriage should be your primary life goal?" While the majority of all respondents did not get the message that marriage was the *primary life* goal, Black and White women's parents clearly saw this differently. Virtually no Black parents stressed marriage as the primary life goal (6 percent of the working class and 4 percent of the middle class), but significantly more White parents did (22 percent of the working class and 18 percent of the middle class).

Some White women said their families expressed active opposition to marriage, such as Clare Baron, a raised-working-class nursing supervisor, who said, "My mother always said, 'Don't get married and don't have children!'"

More common responses recognized the fragility of marriage and the need to support oneself. For example, Alice Page, a 31-year-old White raised-middle-class librarian, put it this way:

> *I feel like I am really part of a generation that for the first time is thinking, "I don't want to have to depend on somebody to take care of me because what if they say they are going to take care of me and then they are not there? They die, or they leave me or whatever." I feel very much that I've got to be able to support myself and I don't know that single women in other eras have had to deal with that to the same degree.*

While White working-class women are often raised to prepare for work roles so that they can contribute to family income and, if necessary, support themselves, Black women face a different reality. Unlike White women, Black women are typically socialized to view marriage separately from economic security, because it is not expected that marriage will ever remove them from the labor market. As a result, Black families socialize all their children—girls and boys—for self-sufficiency (Clark 1986; Higginbotham and Cannon 1988)....

...Fairly substantial numbers of each group had never married by the time of the interview, ranging from 20 percent of the White working-class to 34 percent of the Black working-class and White middle-class respondents. Some of the women were pleased with their singlehood, like Alice Page, who said:

> *I am single by choice. That is how I see myself. I have purposely avoided getting into any kind of romantic situation with men. I have enjoyed going out but never wanted to get serious. If anyone wants to get serious, I quit going out with him.*

Other women expressed disappointment and some shock that they were not yet married. When asked about her feeling about being single, Sally Ford, a 32-year-old white manager, said:

> *That's what I always wanted to do: to be married and have children. To me, that is the ideal. I want a happy, good marriage with children. I do not like being single at all. It is very, very lonesome. I don't see any advantages to being single. None!*

Subjective Sense of Debt to Kin and Friends

McAdoo (1978) reports that upwardly mobile Black Americans receive more requests to share resources from their working-class kin than do middle-class Black Americans. Many mobile Black Americans feel a "social debt" because their families aided them in the mobility process and provided emotional support. When we asked the White women in the study the following question: "Generally, do you feel you owe a lot for the help given to you by your family and relatives?" many were perplexed and asked what the question meant. In contrast, both the working- and middle-class Black women tended to respond immediately that they felt a sense of obligation to family and friends in return for the support they had received. Black women, from both the working class and the middle class, expressed the strongest sense of debt to family, with 86 percent and 74 percent, respectively, so indicating. White working-class women were least likely to feel that they owed family (46 percent), while 68 percent of white middle-class women so indicated. In short, upwardly mobile Black women were almost twice as likely as upwardly mobile White women to express a sense of debt to family.

Linda Brown, an upwardly mobile Black woman, gave a typical response, "Yes, they are there when you need them." Similar were the words of Jean Marsh, "Yes, because they have been supportive. They're dependable. If I need them I can depend upon them."

One of the most significant ways in which Black working-class families aided their daughters and left them with a sense of debt related to care for their children. Dawn March expressed it thus:

> They have been there more so during my adult years than a lot of other families that I know about. My mother kept all of my children until they were old enough to go to day care. And she not only kept them, she'd give them a bath for me during the daytime and feed them before I got home from work. Very, very supportive people. So, I really would say I owe them for that.

Carole Washington, an upwardly mobile Black woman occupational therapist, also felt she owed her family. She reported:

> I know the struggle that my parents have had to get me where I am. I know the energy they no longer have to put into the rest of the family even though they want to put it there and they're willing. I feel it is my responsibility to give back some of that energy they have given to me. It's self-directed, not required.

White working-class women, in contrast, were unlikely to feel a sense of debt and expressed their feelings in similar ways. Irma Cox, part owner of a computer business, said, "I am appreciative of the values my parents instilled in me. But I for the most part feel like I have done it on my own." Carey Mink, a 35-year-old psychiatric social worker, said, "No, they pointed me in a direction and they were supportive, but I've done a lot of the work myself." Debra Beck, a judge, responded, "No, I feel that I've gotten most places on my own."...

Commitment to Community

The mainstream "model of community stresses the rights of individuals to make decisions in their own self interest, regardless of the impact on the larger society" (Collins 1990, 52). This model may explain relations to community of origin for mobile white males but cannot be generalized to other racial and gender groups. In the context of well-recognized structures of racial oppression, America's racial-ethnic communities develop collective sur-

vival strategies that contrast with the individualism of the dominant culture but ensure the community's survival (Collins 1990; McAdoo 1978; Stack 1974; Valentine 1978). McAdoo (1978) argues that Black people have *only* been able to advance in education and attain higher status and higher paying jobs with the support of the wider Black community, teachers in segregated schools, extended family networks, and Black mentors already in those positions. This widespread community involvement enables mobile people of color to confront and challenge racist obstacles in credentialing institutions, and it distinguishes the mobility process in racial-ethnic communities from mobility in the dominant culture. For example, Lou Nelson, now a librarian, described the support she felt in her southern segregated inner-city school. She said:

> There was a closeness between people and that had a lot to do with neighborhood schools. I went to Tubman High School with people that lived in the Tubman area. I think that there was a bond, a bond between parents, the PTA...I think that it was just that everybody felt that everybody knew everybody. And that was special.

Family and community involvement and support in the mobility process means that many Black professionals and managers continue to feel linked to their communities of origin. Lillian King, a high-ranking city official who was raised working class, discussed her current commitment to the Black community. She said:

> Because I have more opportunities, I've got an obligation to give more back and to set a positive example for Black people and especially for Black women. I think we've got to do a tremendous job in building self-esteem and giving people the desire to achieve.

Judith Moore is a 34-year-old single parent employed as a health investigator. She has been able to maintain her connection with her community, and that is a source of pride.

> I'm proud that I still have a sense of who I am in terms of Black people. That's very important to

me. No matter how much education or professional status I get, I do not want to lose touch with where I've come from. I think that you need to look back and that kind of pushes you forward. I think the degree and other things can make you lose sight of that, especially us Black folks, but I'm glad that I haven't and I try to teach that [commitment] to my son.

For some Black women, their mobility has enabled them to give to an even broader community. This is the case with Sammi Lewis, a raised-working-class woman who is a director of a social service agency. She said, "I owe a responsibility to the entire community, and not to any particular group."...

Crossing the Color Line

Mobility for people of color is complex because in addition to crossing class lines, mobility often means crossing racial and cultural ones as well. Since the 1960s, people of color have increasingly attended either integrated or predominantly White schools. Only mobile White ethnics have a comparable experience of simultaneously crossing class and cultural barriers, yet even this experience is qualitatively different from that of Black and other people of color. White ethnicity can be practically invisible to White middle-class school peers and co-workers, but people of color are more visible and are subjected to harsher treatment. Our research indicates that no matter when people of color first encounter integrated or predominantly White settings, it is always a shock. The experience of racial exclusion cannot prepare people of color to deal with the racism in daily face-to-face encounters with White people.

For example, Lynn Johnson was in the first cohort of Black students at Regional College, a small private college in Memphis. The self-confidence and stamina Lynn developed in her supportive segregated high school helped her withstand the racism she faced as the first female and the first Black to graduate in economics at Regional College. Lynn described her treatment:

I would come into class and Dr. Simpson (the Economics professor) would alphabetically call the roll. When he came to my name, he would just jump over it. He would not ask me any questions, he would not do anything. I stayed in that class. I struggled through. When it was my turn, I'd start talking. He would say, "Johnson, I wasn't talking to you" [because he never said Miss Johnson]. I'd say, "That's all right, Dr. Simpson, it was my turn. I figured you just overlooked me. I'm just the littlest person in here. Wasn't that the right answer?" He would say, "Yes, that was the right answer." I drove him mad, I really did. He finally got used to me and started to help me.

In southern cities, where previous interaction between Black and White people followed a rigid code, adjustments were necessary on both sides. It was clear to Lynn Johnson and others that college faculty and students had to adapt to her small Black cohort at Regional College.

Wendy Jones attended a formerly predominantly White state university that had just merged with a formerly predominantly Black college. This new institution meant many adjustments for faculty and students. As a working-class person majoring in engineering, she had a rough transition. She recalled:

I had never gone to school with White kids. I'd always gone to all Black schools all my life and the Black kids there [at the university] were snooty. Only one friend from high school went there and she flunked out. The courses were harder and all my teachers were men and White. Most of the kids were White. I was in classes where I'd be the only Black and woman. There were no similarities to grasp for. I had to adjust to being in that situation. In about a year I was comfortable where I could walk up to people in my class and have conversations.

For some Black people, their first significant interaction with White people did not come until graduate school. Janice Freeman described her experiences:

I went to a Black high school, a Black college and then worked for a Black man who was a former teacher. Everything was comfortable until I had to go to State University for graduate school. I felt very insecure. I was thrown into an environment that was very different—during the 1960s and 1970s there was so much unrest anyway—so it was extremely difficult for me.

It was not in graduate school but on her first job as a social worker that Janice had to learn to work *with* White people. She said, "After I realized that I could hang in school, working at the social work agency allowed me to learn how to work *with* White people. I had never done that before and now I do it better than anybody."

Learning to live in a White world was an additional hurdle for all Black women in this age cohort. Previous generations of Black people were more likely to be educated in segregated colleges and to work within the confines of the established Black community. They taught in segregated schools, provided dental and medical care to the Black communities, and provided social services and other comforts to members of their own communities. They also lived in the Black community and worshiped on Sunday with many of the people they saw in different settings. As the comments of our respondents reveal, both Black and White people had to adjust to integrated settings, but it was more stressful for the newcomers.

SUMMARY AND CONCLUSIONS

Our major aim in this research was to reopen the study of the subjective experience of upward social mobility and to begin to incorporate race and gender into our vision of the process. In this exploratory work, we hope to raise issues and questions that will cast a new light on taken-for-granted assumptions about the process and the people who engage in it. The experiences of these women have certainly painted a different picture from the one we were left some twenty years ago. First and foremost, these women are not detached, isolated, or driven solely by career goals. Relationships with family of origin, partners, children, friends, and the wider community loom large in

the way they envision and accomplish mobility and the way they sustain themselves as professional and managerial women.

Several of out findings suggest ways that race and gender shape the mobility process for baby boom Black and White women. Education was stressed as important in virtually all of the families of these women; however, they differed in how it was viewed and how much was desired. The upwardly mobile women, both Black and White, shared some obstacles to attainment. More mobile women had parents who never expected them to achieve a college education. They also received less emotional and financial support for college attendance from their families than the women in middle-class families received. Black women also faced the unique problem of crossing racial barriers simultaneously with class barriers.

There were fairly dramatic race differences in the messages that the Black and White women received from family about what their lives should be like as adults. Black women clearly received the message that they needed an occupation to succeed in life and that marriage was a secondary concern. Many Black women also expressed a sense that their mobility was connected to an entire racial uplift process, not merely an individual journey.

White upwardly mobile women received less clear messages. Only one-half of these women said that their parents stressed the need for an occupation to succeed, and 20 percent said that marriage was stressed as the primary life goal. The most common message seemed to suggest that an occupation was necessary, because marriage could not be counted on to provide economic survival. Having a career, on the other hand, could even be seen as detrimental to adult happiness.

Upward mobility is a process that requires sustained effort and emotional and cognitive, as well as financial, support. The legacy of the image of mobility that was built on the White male experience focuses on credentialing institutions, especially the schools, as the primary place where talent is recognized and support is given to ensure that the talented among the working class are mobile. Family and friends are virtually invisible in this portrayal of the mobility process.

Although there is a good deal of variation in the roles that family and friends play for these women, they are certainly not invisible in the process. Especially among many of the Black women, there is a sense that they owe a great debt to their families for the help they have received. Black upwardly mobile women were also much more likely to feel that they give more than they receive from kin. Once they have achieved professional managerial employment, the sense of debt combines with their greater access to resources to put them in the position of being asked to give and of giving more to both family and friends. Carrington (1980) identifies some potential mental health hazards of such a sense of debt in upwardly mobile Black women's lives.

White upwardly mobile women are less likely to feel indebted to kin and to feel that they have accomplished alone. Yet even among this group, connections to spouses and children played significant roles in defining how women were mobile, their goals, and their sense of satisfaction with their life in the middle class.

These data are suggestive of a mobility process that is motivated by a desire for personal, but also collective, gain and that is shaped by interpersonal commitments to family, partners and children, community, and the race. Social mobility involves competition, but also cooperation, community support, and personal obligations. Further research is needed to explore fully this new image of mobility and to examine the relevance of these issues for White male mobility as well.

NOTE

1. This and all the names used in this article are pseudonyms.

REFERENCES

Braverman, Harry. 1974. *Labor and monopoly capital.* New York: Monthly Review Press.

Carrington, Christine. 1980. Depression in Black women: A theoretical appraisal. In *The Black woman*, edited by La Frances Rodgers Rose. Beverly Hills, CA: Sage.

Clark, Reginald. 1986. *Family life and school achievement.* Chicago: University of Chicago Press.

Collins, Patricia Hill. 1990. *Black feminist thought: Knowledge, consciousness, and the politics of empowerment.* Boston: Routledge.

Ehrenreich, Barbara, and John Ehrenreich. 1979. The professional-managerial class. In *Between labor and capital*, edited by Pat Walker. Boston: South End Press.

Higginbotham, Elizabeth, and Lynn Weber Cannon. 1988. *Rethinking mobility: Towards a race and gender inclusive theory.* Research Paper no. 8.

Center for Research on Women, Memphis State University.

Joslin, Daphne. 1979. Working-class daughters, middle-class wives: Social identity and self-esteem among women upwardly mobile through marriage. Ph.D. diss., New York University, New York.

McAdoo, Harriette Pipes. 1978. Factors related to stability in upwardly mobile Black families. *Journal of Marriage and the Family* 40:761–76.

Poulantzas, Nicos. 1974. *Classes in contemporary capitalism.* London: New Left Books.

U.S. Bureau of the Census. 1983. Detailed population characteristics: Tennessee. Census of the Population, 1980. Washington, DC: GPO.

Vanneman, Reeve, and Lynn Weber Cannon. 1987. *The American perception of class.* Philadelphia: Temple University Press.

PART SIX

Public Institutions
Work and Education

Chapter 11   Constructing Gender in Workplaces

Chapter 12   Negotiating Gender in Schools

How much does gender influence one's status in the public institutions of work and education? Does the feminization of paid labor around the world place women on a more equal footing with men? Do schools mitigate against the social inequalities experienced by women and men of different groups? The readings in this part discuss gender relations in the public arenas of workplaces and schools.

Today's average worker in the global economy may be either a man or a woman, of any age, race, class, sexual orientation, or nationality. The average worker in the global economy may labor virtually unseen inside the home or may work in a public workplace, as a mechanic, teacher, secretary, or assembler. Whatever the average worker does for a living, he or she is very likely to work at a job assigned on the basis of gender.

Everywhere, gender differentiation organizes workplaces. Women's jobs and men's jobs are structured with different characteristics and different rewards. In every society, we find a familiar pattern: women earn less than men, even when they work in similar occupations and have the same level of education. But exactly *how* does work become gendered? How does occupational segregation take hold? Can gender boundaries be dismantled? Such questions are addressed in the first two readings of Chapter 11. Peter Nardi takes us into the social worlds of magicians, at both structural and interpersonal levels, to show how magic became and remains dominated by male performers. By probing the work environment of male secretaries, Rosemary Pringle reveals how their secretarial jobs become redefined as men's work.

Workplaces are racialized as well as gendered. Racism and sexism interact so that women and men of different races, national origins and immigrant groups become clustered in certain kinds or work. Job opportunities are shaped by *who* people are—by their being women or men, educated or uneducated, of a certain race, sexual orientation, and residents of specific geopolitical settings—rather than by their skills and talents. These hierarchies also define what constitute acceptable behavior on the job. In their study of restaurant workers, Patti A. Giuffre and Christine L. Williams discover that even the definition of sexual harassment depends on *who* the perpetrator is and *who* the victim is. Double standards of race and class mask a good deal of sexual discrimination in workplaces.

As the global economy presses forward, relying on established patterns of race and gender subordination to structure local workplaces, women and men throughout the world are affected differently. The same changes making women the main facilitators of the economic transformations have eroded many men's ability to be breadwinners. This would appear to benefit women by expanding their opportunities, but most women around the world continue to earn low wage levels and face limited opportunities for advancement.

The last three readings in Chapter 11 consider some of the complex matters related to race, gender, and economic transformations in the United States. Karen Hossfeld's study illustrates how divisions of race and gender can also be used by workers themselves to resist coercive measures of control in the workplace. Teresa Amott explains how economic earthquakes have reconfigured work for women and men in different races and classes. Esther Ngan-Ling Chow describes how the combined effects of gender, race, and class place Asian American women at the bottom of the job hierarchy.

Among public institutions, education looms as one of the most gendered. From elementary school through higher education, gender differences prevail. Schools shortchange girls in myriad ways, from achievement scores, to curriculum design, to student–teacher interactions. Schools also sift and sort by economic background and race. So while schooling may serve as a primary avenue of social mobility, schools also reproduce social inequalities.

Schools also structure different opportunities for achieving manhood and womanhood. Not all students possess the resources required to achieve the culture's idealized forms of masculinity and femininity. Far from a simple gender divide, we find a range of genders. Masculinities are not merely different, but they operate in relation to each other. And different forms of femininity are also power relations in their own right. Chapter 12 moves us beyond common stereotypes of the "opposite sex," as they analyze multiple forms of masculinity and femininity. R. W. Connell examines the place of schooling in the lives of two groups of Australian young men who are distanced in different ways from the dominant models of masculinity. Wendy Luttrell unravels race and class relations in the school and workplace struggles of two groups of women whose aspirations and images of womanhood are profoundly different. Both articles point us in the direction of a more complex and dynamic understanding of gender's multiple meanings and how these come into being and are sustained in the schools.

38

The Social World of Magicians
Gender and Conjuring[1]

PETER M. NARDI

Gender role differences are visible in almost every facet of entertainment magic (conjuring) in Western cultures, whether it be performance, participation in magical associations, or audience behavior. Specifically, the number of women magicians is relatively small, both historically and today. When they do participate in magic, women are either assisting male magicians or performing the more psychic and occult forms, such as mind reading, seances, and fortune-telling. Why women's roles in magic have been so limited and why so few women actively perform magic is the focus of this article.

Consider the stereotypical magical image of "sawing the woman in half." The powerful male with his sharp instrument penetrates and mutilates the woman ("I always feel a twinge of pain whenever I watch a magician's assistant climb into her coffin-like box.... Once again, woman is being put on display as the victim of a male-dominated torture fantasy"; Marshall, 1984, p. 41). And only he can restore her to her original wholeness. One need not, however, resort to simplistic Freudianism to make sense out of these images. The reasons may have more to do with (1) the socio-cultural and historical tradition of performing, (2) the social organization of the magic profession, (3) the socialization of gender roles in conversation and play in Western society, (4) the nature of magic, and (5) the relationship of power and control between a performer and an audience. Each of these will be discussed as possible explanations for the dearth of women magicians.

Adelaide Hermann (1981, p. 5), one of the few famous women conjurers, wrote,

> *Magic is a graceful art, and, as those of my own sex are the real exponents of grace, I have often wondered why more young girls do not turn their attention to the study and practice of magic, as it develops every one of the attributes necessary to social success—grace, dexterity, agility, ease of movement, perfection of manner, and self-confidence.*

Although the promise of grace and social success may attract some women to the practice of magic, there are a number of social-structural reasons for the limited appeal that magic has to women in general.

HISTORICAL PERSPECTIVE

The virtual absence of women in conjuring circles prior to the mid-19th century can be traced to several cultural sources. Foremost is the association of women with witchcraft. For a woman even to attempt a magical performance would have been tantamount to a public declaration of witchcraft. The earliest extant book on magic, *Discoverie of Witchcraft* (Scot, 1584/1972), emphasized the link that existed in the public's mind in the 16th century between conjuring tricks and witchcraft. Scot's purpose was to debunk the existence of actual witchcraft and to demonstrate its dependency on ordinary sleight-of-hand magic tricks. Scot argued that anything unexplainable or out of the ordinary was not necessarily due to the intervention of the Devil and his forces. He demonstrated that what witches were accused of doing in cooperation with satanic forces could also be performed by popular entertainers using explainable means.

The almost universal association in Western societies of women with witchcraft and sorcery has been substantiated by many historians (Demos, 1982; Macfarlane, 1970; Russell, 1980; Thomas, 1970). Russell (1980) argues that sexist religious assumptions led to the belief in the preponderance of women as witches. Women had little influence and legal power during the 15th, 16th, and 17th centuries. They were often socially isolated, financially destitute, and viewed by religious tradition as responsible for carnality (Russell, 1980). In short, the position of women in the social structure was subservient; they were vulnerable to charges of being mysterious and performing evil deeds. In the *Malleus Maleficarum* of 1486, according to Russell (1972), women were described as susceptible to demonic temptation because of their "manifold weaknesses." Coupled with this misogynist view was an exaggerated respect for women's magical powers. The *Malleus Maleficarum* described women as carnal and impressionable, as liars and deceivers unable to conceal, and as having weak memories. At the same time, there existed a belief that they had power to perform dark and mysterious deeds.

Within such a context, any woman engaging in ordinary conjuring tricks or juggling (as it was called until the 18th century) would have been viewed as dangerous. Christopher (1973) tells the story of a girl who, after publicly performing a torn-and-restored handkerchief trick in Cologne in the 15th century, was subsequently tried for witchcraft. While similar fates and diabolical labels often awaited male performers, women were more at risk and culturally less acceptable as public performers. Magical entertainment typically was offered by performers traveling from fair to fair, street corner to street corner, and tavern to tavern (Clarke, 1928, 1983), and it was unlikely that respectable women would perform in such public places.

For that matter, women rarely performed in the theater in England until the Restoration, and even then men continued to portray witches, magicians, and comic old women (Brockett, 1968; Bullough, 1974). Although women occasionally performed on the stage in Italy, France, and Spain, they were not always greeted warmly: "When two French companies appeared in London, the first in 1629 and the second a few years later, their actresses were hissed and pelted with rotten apples" (Macgowan & Melnitz, 1955). Since women were essentially forbidden participation in public performances, conjuring and juggling were occupations primarily limited to male performers. Few documents before the 16th century refer to conjurers, but those that do, describe only males as jugglers in the British courts (Clarke, 1928/1983). Even in fiction, many of the noted magicians were men such as Merlin, Faustus, Friar Bacon, and Prospero (Traister, 1984).

Occasional reference is made to women performers—usually before or after the witch craze of the 14th–17th centuries. Clarke (1928/1983, p. 24) notes that "it is clear that long before the Christian era there was a class of public performers, of both sexes, who specialized in juggling, fire-eating, sword-swallowing, and ventriloquism." Women were shown juggling in 10th century illuminations, and the *Domesday Book* mentions Adelina, "a Joculatrix who is described as being a landowner in Hamsphire" (Clarke, 1928/1983, p. 13). But historical accounts, both the original sources and secondary ones, make few references to women magicians. Like priests, conjurers and other public performers were almost always male (see Butler, 1948). In short, as Apte (1985, p. 72) notes, "Historical and analytical studies of the development of court jesters, clowns, buffoons, and fools...show that women rarely, if ever, played such roles."

Perhaps the earliest recorded evidence of a woman performer, according to Clarke (1928/1983) is a French conjurer, Mlle. Regnault. The wife of a showman during the late 17th century, she presented a cups-and-balls routine. Christopher (1973) writes about Mrs. Brenon, the wife of an 18th-century Irish conjurer, as the first woman to perform magic professionally in North America. In both cases, however, the conjurer followed in the path of her performing husband rather than originating the magic act herself.

Around the 19th century, the style and popularity of conjuring began to change from street-corner and parlor sleights-of-hand to larger effects performed on stages (see Pecor, 1977). The new style of magic required assistants to participate in the performance and to help manipulate the equipment. Usually these assistants were the wife, daughter, or son of the magician. These assistants, almost always a (more powerless) woman or child, were the ones the magic was performed on by a (more powerful) male magician.

Furthermore, as playbills and posters from the 19th century illustrate, magicians were typically referred to as "professors of scientific experiments." They performed illusions that were essentially newly discovered scientific principles, staying just one step ahead of the general public's knowledge of them. The roles of professor and scientist in the 19th century also had a predominantly male image, thereby making it even more difficult for a woman to take on the magician's persona.

As magic shows developed into more elaborate productions and became part of a music hall or vaudeville tradition in the late 19th century, women were often given their own spot in them. Interestingly, it typically was as a medium or a mentalist performing a "second-sight" routine. For example, Barnado Eagle, a mid-19th century performer, was assisted by his daughter, known as the "Clairvoyant Lady" and "Fore-Sighted Lady." After her father died in 1873, she performed alone as Madame Gilliland Card until about 1886 (Clarke, 1928/1983). Women often entered this career by taking over when a husband or father, whom they assisted, died.

A content analysis by the author of 19th-century posters and playbills on file at the Harvard University performing arts library supports the idea that early women magicians were typically performing a mentalism routine or assisting in their husband's or father's shows.[2] Ten out of 87 playbills included a reference to women performers. In 7 cases, these references were to a second-sight mentalism routine or to some equivalent supernatural powers. One example is an 1899 playbill for Mme. Konorah, who was described as a "modern witch." Another is an 1843 London poster for the "Mysterious Lady" asking "what would the people of Salem in the days of witchcraft have said or done to a woman whose wonderful faculties would have enabled her to name articles that she saw not?" Other noted women performers of the day, such as Madame Bosco, Miss Anderson, and Miss Heller, all performed second-sight routines in their husband's or father's shows.

It was not until Adelaide Hermann carried on the show of her famous husband (Alexander) for almost 30 years after his death in 1896 that a woman performer finally achieved a fame that lasted many years beyond the influence of a husband or father. Hermann became one of the most renowned performers in Europe and North and South America, and the most famous woman magician in the world. Yet the historical accounts of her work are sketchy. The much-quoted histories of magic by Christopher (1962), Clarke (1928/1983), Dawes (1979), and Lamb (1976) barely mention her shows and give only fleeting acknowledgment to the performances of such other noted women conjurers and spiritualists as Nella Davenport, the Fox Sisters, Anna Eva Fay, Aimee Desiree ("Mystia"), Annie Vernone ("The Only Female Professor of Modern Magic in the World"), Madame Cora de Lamond, Talma, Ionia, Okita, Vonetta, and Dell O'Dell. Despite the notoriety of these performers and of some contemporary magicians, the woman magician remains overlooked in many historical accounts and is the exception in this strongly male-dominated entertainment field. Why this is so today in a society that no longer supports beliefs in witchcraft and no longer refuses women access to the entertainment fields is the focus of the following sections.

THE SOCIAL ORGANIZATION OF MAGIC

Magic is one of the few fields in the world of entertainment that remains strongly male dominated. Comedy, acting, singing, and dancing are occupations more open to females than is performing magic. According to the U.S. Bureau of the Census (1984), 42.5% of writers, artists, entertainers, and athletes are female. Females are 28% of musicians, 46.7% of authors, and 47.4% of artists. Over 30% of a sample of actors and 12% of a sample of comics were female (Fisher & Fisher, 1981). Yet according to the International Brotherhood of Magicians (personal communication), approximately 5% of their membership are female magicians. Only among comics is the proportion of female entertainers close to the proportion that characterizes the field of magic. Interestingly, stand-up comedy is an entertainment field that also demands an aggressive, powerful role, involving one-upping people. The relationship of humor and gender (see Apte, 1985, and Canter, 1976), and how these in turn relate to magic, is discussed below.

In a survey of 169 magician members of the leading U.S. magic club (the Magic Castle in Hollywood), only 7% of the respondents were women, and not all of them were performing solo shows (Nardi, 1983). A magic-shop owner interviewed by the author reported that about 1 out of every 20 people entering the store to buy magic was female. Stebbins's (1984) study of 56 magicians included only 2 women. Furthermore, a review of a list of performers in 1987 at the Magic Castle reveals that about 3% were female. In short, magic is dominated by male performers; women, when present, are almost exclusively used as assistants.

The organization of the world of magic resembles a male social club. Like any secret society, magic clubs work to preserve their identity, in this case their male identity, by controlling access to it. One of the oldest magic associations in the world, London's Magic Circle, remains closed to women, a decision upheld by the British courts. It is an association, described in its brochures, "for gentlemen, 18 years of age and older." Although American magic organizations are open to both men and women, access is often through personal references, auditions, and contacts. When the gatekeepers of the profession, the images in the literature, and the role models are predominantly male, access is difficult for women to attain. Although magic clubs are open to women, the message conveyed by the brochures, books, magazines, and magic kits is that this is really an activity for males. The magic world is dominated by male leaders, masculine imagery (such as swords, top hats, and wands), positive male role models (such as Houdini, Blackstone, and Henning), and male-oriented language (such as the International Brotherhood of Magicians). With this generally masculine image and with so few female role models, it is not likely that many women will consider the field of magic for a hobby or a career.

IMPLICATIONS OF SEX ROLE SOCIALIZATION FOR LEARNING MAGIC

Most magicians enter the field through years of amateur play and apprenticeships. Hanging out at magic stores, many boys begin to learn the field and gain entry into the school arena of magic. The social organization of leisure and amateurism (see Stebbins, 1979) in this case tends to benefit men and to discourage the participation of women.

Magic is usually a hobby for the people engaged in it, rather than their career (Nardi, 1983). Most professional magicians began practicing magic at some early point in their lives as a hobby. Gender differences in the ways that children and adults organize leisure time and play help explain the greater concentration of males in the field of magic. Fine (1983) estimates that only 5–10% of the participants in fantasy role-playing games are female. Lever (1978) found that boys' play activities are more competitively structured, more complex, and involve face-to-face confrontation. Girls emphasize more cooperation, less interaction and interdependence, and play in smaller groups with less structure and fewer rules. Performing magic is more male in this regard. It is a structured activity, involves face-to-face interaction of a competitive nature, and requires a dominant leader.

Differences in conversational styles between males and females similarly give males an advantage in magic. Maltz and Borker (1982, p. 200) state that "American men and women come from different sociolinguistic subcultures." Boys posture and counterposture, using speech to assert their dominance even when others have the floor and to attract and maintain an audience. In other words, boys perform while speaking. Girls, on the other hand, use speech to create relationships of closeness and equality, to share secrets, and to establish intimacy. In adulthood, female conversations emphasize harmony and interaction maintenance. Males perform narratives, argue aggressively with jokes and put-downs, and make challenging statements (Maltz & Borker, 1982). Furthermore, Stebbins found that men are more likely to deceive women by putting them on than women are likely to deceive men or even each other (Stebbins, 1975). Apte (1985) found that very few ethnographic accounts of women playing practical jokes or pranks in everyday interactions exist. He argues that cultural norms of propriety preclude women from engaging in totally uninhibited ways, especially in ways that involve belittling others. Women's humor rarely involves competition or enhancing one's own status through putting down others.

An analysis of a magic performance indicates the congruence with male styles of humor, conversation, and interaction. Magic involves challenges, jokes, and narratives. A magician needs to be able to perform and take control. Secrets cannot be shared (except among selective others) and equality is not the goal in the interaction.

In sum, the ways in which sex role socialization shapes play, leisure time, and interaction styles may be an important factor in the selection of hobbies and careers, especially magic. In general, socialization patterns for males are more congruent with the ways that magic is performed and structured.

MAGICAL ACTS BY MALE AND FEMALE PERFORMERS

The process of performing a magic trick involves a kind of deceit that involves power, control, and one-up-man(*sic*)ship. Magic is an aggressive, competitive form involving challenges and winning at the expense of others. Parlee (1985) made similar arguments in her discussion of why so few women play poker. The illusion created is not simply putting on makeup or altering one's character, as in a play or other type of performance (as would an actress or clown). It is creating an illusion that involves putting something over someone, to establish who is in control, and to make the other (the audience) appear fooled.

Males in our culture are more likely to be encouraged to demonstrate power, control, and competitive manipulation of others. Magic is an activity that ideally exploits these characteristics and gives them a more benign, socially approved context. We tend to socialize males in roles and characteristics that lend themselves to expression in magic performances.

Social approval from audiences and its correlates (frequent bookings, career mobility, etc.) may not be generated as readily for women magicians. For magic to work, the audience must believe a rational explanation exists, yet find it impossible to offer one, even an incorrect one (Nardi, 1984). Some people in audiences believe women engage in real magic—seances, palm readings, and witchcraft—and that there is no rational explanation. What they experience, then, is "real" magic and not entertainment. Women are capable of making things appear through the "magic of childbirth" and of seeing what someone is thinking by means of "women's intuition." The rapport between performer and audience and the style of the performance as perceived by the audience may be subtly affected by the gender of the interacting parties.

Furthermore, most magic performances make use of instruments of some form, such as swords, wands, and boxes. Using the traditional dichotomy of expressive vs. instrumental, the nature of magic can be defined as instrumental. Men play the instrumental roles in magic, creating and controlling with tools of the trade and following rational rules to create the effect. Power appears to emanate from the performer. However, the roles women have traditionally performed in magic, such as psychics, mediums, and palm readers, reflect an expressive nature in which power is transmitted through the mediator. They touch hands, communicate with the dead, read minds, and share secrets. Cooperation and intimacy are essential for the interaction to be successful.

Mediums and psychics become the conduit of power rather than the source of power. Gyspy fortune-tellers, often using admitted confidence tricks, play a nurturing, listening role, almost therapeutic (Okely, 1983). They transmit, interpret, and mediate. They themselves do not create, alter, or make objects disappear. Power is not in them, it is through them. These remain relatively safer cultural roles for women to enact and for others to interact with. McLaughlin (1980, p. 43) concluded that "Fortune-telling is a skill in character analysis rather than an exhibition of extrasensory powers."

THE AUDIENCE'S VIEW OF MAGIC: POWER, CONTROL, AND STATUS

All interactions involve a performer and an audience. Magicians normally select women as participants and as assistants in their acts. The woman is sawed in half or placed in the box through which swords are pushed. Canter (1976, p. 166) makes the argument that "in humor, the sex of the target of ridicule is an important determinant of the humor response, and . . . it is still funnier to see a woman than a man disparaged."

Observations of magic performances by the author also show a difference in responses according to gender. Although most people respond similarly to a trick, men more often than women state they know one also or publicly attempt to figure out how it was done. What role gender plays in defining audience behavior is a subject in need of more systematic analysis.

Audience composition and location for different magic events usually are gender typed. Fortune-tellers tend to meet privately with their customers rather than perform in theaters or halls. Furthermore, their audience is mostly female (McLaughlin, 1980). Motivation for attending is also a factor in the interrelationship between performer and audience. The customers of psychics and fortune-tellers generally seek advice while audiences for traditional magic performances want to be entertained. In other words, what goes on in the performance is partly a function of who the audience is and why they are there. Silverman (1982, p. 395) found in her work on impression management and urban gypsies that "different performances are enacted for various non-Gypsy audiences. . . . Language, appearance, demeanor, and props are manipulated so that the audience receives selective information."

In general, both male and female audience members of magic performances, in order to be entertained, must allow themselves to be tricked, to be one-upped. They must relinquish control to the performer. This also may be related to gender differences in the performer. Perhaps audiences are not likely to do this with someone of perceived lower status. Women, blacks, and other minorities (with the exception of Asians whose image fits with a magical and mysterious one) rarely perform magic, and each is perceived to be of lower status in our society. To be one-upped or tricked by those less powerful or to have control coopted by them may make it difficult for audiences and the gatekeepers in the field to support minority performers of magic. While this is probably not a conscious process, the structure of social interactions in everyday life verifies that such dynamics are at work (see LaFrance & Mayo, 1978).

CONCLUSION

No single explanation can account for the relative invisibility of women in magic; there is likely to be a complex interaction of sociological and social-psychological processes. There are, of course, some women magicians. Conversations with a few of them confirm many of the factors discussed in this article. Interest seems a major variable. Those women who did enter the profession or became hobbyists did so because they were attracted to the magic itself. They found it fun, intriguing, and fascinating. Women who are not magicians typically say they never thought of it as an option, not because they perceived obstacles and discrimination ahead, but because they were just not interested enough to pursue it. Their responses underline the importance of the lack of female magician role models and of gender differences in socialization and play.

Why study gender and magic? One answer lies in the usefulness of magic as a metaphor for illustrating the properties of everyday interactions. By looking at women's roles that involve both power and assistance, such as those in a magic performance, an understanding of women's and men's roles in contemporary society is enhanced. Goffman (1974, p. 564) argues that realms other than the ordinary can be "a subject matter of interest in their own right [and can] provide natural experiments in which a property of ordinary activity is displayed or contrasted in a clarified or clarifying way." The social world of magic and its allocation of roles according to gender clarify similar relationships in everyday life. The metaphor of magic, as opposed to the more dramaturgical model often used in symbolic interactionist studies, suggests looking beyond the mask, and focusing on the various levels of interaction and reality ongoing in a magic performance and in everyday life. The attribution of power and control to the male persona and the indifference enacted toward the female assistants by the audience illustrate the multiple levels of reality occurring in everyday interactions (see Berger & Luckmann, 1966; Schutz, 1970).

In the world of magic and often in the "real" world as well, the social structure either allocates powerless roles to women or assumes they have some secret manipulative power hidden from men's worlds. This duality of images that women have been assigned—a dualism that can be traced back to the Bible's depiction of Eve and to the *Malleus Maleficarum* with its picture of women as both powerful and weak—reinforces a type of oppression that becomes difficult to eliminate. The world of conjuring clearly describes this stage version of a mundane world made up of women's roles as assistants and victims yet holding some secret power and control. This perception of women as having some secret magic but not being legitimate participants in the exercise of power is concisely summarized by Mauss (1955, p. 28) in his study of religious magic:

> *[Women are] everywhere recognized as being more prone to magic than men. . . . They are said to be the font of mysterious activities, the sources of magical power. . . . The magical attributes of women derive primarily from their social position and consequently are more talked about than real. In fact, there are fewer female practitioners of magic than public opinion would have us believe. The curious result is that on the whole, it is the men who perform the magic while women are accused of it.*

NOTES

1. An earlier version of this paper was presented at the American Sociological Association meetings in Washington, DC, August 1985. Comments were generously provided by Ruth Borker, Gary Alan Fine, Glenn Goodwin, Meredith Gould, Danny Maltz, Myriam Ruthchild, Susan Seymour, Molly Squire, and Robert Stebbins.

2. This content analysis does not represent a random sample of all possible playbills in the Harvard collection. Several boxes were made available to the author. These contained a variety of posters illustrating several types of performing arts, such as music hall performances, magic shows, and other vaudeville acts. Eighty-seven focused on magic and were analyzed for references to female performers. It should also be noted that these posters are not a random selection of all possible 19th-century playbills dealing with magic. The majority of them referred to acts in the Northeastern United States and in England. However, based on what is portrayed in Christopher (1973), the Harvard posters appear typical of 19th-century magic act playbills.

REFERENCES

Apte, M. *Humor and laughter.* Ithaca, NY: Cornell University Press, 1985.

Berger, P., & Luckmann, T. *The social construction of reality.* Garden City. NY: Doubleday Anchor, 1966.

Brockett, O. *History of the theatre.* Boston: Allyn and Bacon, 1968.

Bullough, V. Transvestites in the middle ages. *American Journal of Sociology,* 1974, *79*(6), 1381–1394.

Butler, E. *The myth of the magus.* New York: Macmillan, 1948.

Canter, J. What is funny to whom? The role or gender. *Journal of Communication,* 1976, *26*(3) 164–172.

Christopher, M. *Panorama of magic.* New York: Dover, 1962.

Christopher, M. *The illustrated history of magic.* New York: Crowell, 1973.

Clarke, S. *The annals of conjuring.* New York: Magico, 1928/1983.

Dawes, E. *The great illusionists.* Secaucus. NJ: Chartwell, 1979.

Demos, J. *Entertaining satan.* New York: Oxford University Press, 1982.

Fine, G. *Shared fantasy.* Chicago: University of Chicago Press, 1983.

Fisher, S., & Fisher, R. *Pretend the world is funny and forever: A psychological analysis of comedians, clowns, and actors.* Hillsdale, NJ: Lawrence Erlbaum Associates, 1981.

Goffman, E. *Frame analysis.* New York: Harper & Row, 1974.

Hermann, A. Popularity of magic. *New York Dramatic Mirror, 67,* p. 5, 1912.

LaFrance, M., & Mayo, R. *Moving bodies: Nonverbal communication in social relationships.* Monterey, CA: Brooks/Cole, 1978.

Lamb, G. *Victorian magic.* London: Routledge and Kegan Paul, 1976.

Lever, J. Sex differences in the games children play. *American Sociological Review,* 1978, *43,* 471–483.

Macfarlane, A. *Witchcraft in Tudor and Stuart England.* London: Routledge and Kegan Paul, 1970.

Macgowan, K., & Melnitz, W. *The living stage: A history of the world theater.* Englewood Cliffs, NJ: Prentice-Hall, 1955.

Maltz, D., & Borker, R. A cultural approach to male-female miscommunication. In John Gumperz (Ed.), *Language and social identity.* Cambridge: Cambridge University Press, 1982.

Marshall, F. *Those beautiful dames.* Chicago: Magic Inc., 1984.

Mauss, M. *A general theory of magic.* New York: Norton, 1930.

McLaughlin, J. *Gypsy lifestyle.* Lexington, MA: D. C. Heath/Lexington Books, 1980.

Nardi, P. M. *Amateurs and professionals: The case of magicians.* Unpublished paper, Pitzer College, 1983.

Nardi, P. M. Toward a social psychology of entertainment magic (conjuring). *Symbolic Interaction,* 1984, *7*(1), 25–42.

Okely, J. *The traveller gypsies.* Cambridge: Cambridge University Press, 1983.

Parlee, M. Deal me in: Why women should play poker. *Ms. Magazine,* pp. 14–15, January 1985.

Pecor, C. *The magician on the American stage: 1752–1874.* Washington, DC: Emerson and West, 1977.

Russell, J. *Witchcraft in the middle ages.* Ithaca, NY: Cornell University Press, 1972.

Russell, J. *A history of witchcraft.* London: Thames and Hudson, 1980.

Schutz, A. *On phenomenology and social relations.* Chicago: University of Chicago Press, 1970.

Scot, R. *The discoverie of witchcraft.* New York: Dover, 1584/1972.

Silverman, C. Everyday drama: Impression management of urban Gypsies. *Urban Anthropology,* 1982, *11*(3–4), 395.

Stebbins, R. Putting people on. *Sociology and Social Research,* 1975, *59,* 189–200.

Stebbins, R. *Amateurs: On the margins between work and leisure.* Beverly Hills: Sage Publications, 1979.

Stebbins, R. *The magician: Career, culture, and social psychology in a variety art.* Toronto: Clarke Irwin, 1984.

Thomas, K. The relevance of social anthropology to the historical study of English witchcraft. In M. Douglas (Ed.), *Witchcraft: Confessions and accusations.* London: Tavistock, 1970.

Traister, B. *Heavenly necromancers: The magician in English Renaissance drama.* Columbia: University of Missouri Press, 1984.

U.S. Bureau of the Census. Washington: U.S. Government Printing Office, 1984.

39

Male Secretaries

ROSEMARY PRINGLE

Two years ago I was appointed to a promotions committee at a provincial university. Complicated travel arrangements had to be made each time for the 12 or so out-of-town members, and there were difficulties finding dates that were mutually compatible. Extensive documentation had to be collected and circulated, interviews arranged, referees contacted. At each meeting Pat, the secretary, not only took minutes but frequently left the room to make telephone calls and send faxes. Pat's role was clearly to do the bidding of the chair. Pat did all this cheerfully and was warmly thanked by members of the committee at the end for taking care of them. The work was secretarial in the broadest sense, including organizing lunches and daily travel arrangements, and helping to clear the cups away after morning tea. But Pat was a man. And nobody thought it at all odd that he should be doing this work. It was, after all, a high-level, confidential committee chaired by the Vice-Chancellor. Pat was a besuited, slightly swarthy man in his late forties, not in any way effeminate. He was doing work that was clearly defined as appropriate to a man, and he was formally classified, not as a secretary but as an administrative officer.

Pat is not unique. Every large organization has dozens of men like him, performing a similar range of tasks to those done by female secretaries, often under the direction of a "boss" and often, as in Pat's case, including a range of semipersonal services. Rather than being called secretaries, they are generally classified as clerical, administrative, or even managerial workers. At the same time, male secretaries are thought to be few and far between. The media have found novelty value in

such role reversals, and have posed the question of whether, in response to feminist demands for equality in the workplace, men will return to secretarial work, perhaps serving women bosses. It is important, therefore, to consider the relationship between the minority who are labeled "male secretaries" and the much larger group who are doing broadly secretarial work.

This chapter derives from a larger study, *Secretaries Talk* (Pringle, 1988), based on historical and statistical data, census returns, representations of secretaries in the media and in student text books, and interviews with both secretarial and nonsecretarial workers in a range of workplaces, large and small, government and nongovernment. While the material on which I draw is mostly Australian, similar processes have taken place throughout the Western industrialized world (Benet, 1972; Crompton & Jones, 1984; Davies, 1982; Kanter, 1977). Some variation can be expected at the level of the region, the firm, and the individual. It will be argued that while there are key discourses that structure secretaries' working lives, these discourses are not imposed in a deterministic way. Rather, they exist as frameworks of meaning within which individuals negotiate their relationships: There is room for different outcomes and for shifts in emphasis. Though male secretaries were sought, there are only 7 in the sample of 149 secretaries interviewed for *Secretaries Talk,* and most of these were found only after I eventually stopped asking for "male secretaries" and substituted job profiles (Pringle, 1988, p. 271). Once I began to realize how the categorization was limiting the data, it became relatively easy to locate men doing broadly similar work. Had I started doing this earlier, I might well have included a higher proportion of men. This is indicative of the extent to which occupational groupings, which at first seem self-evident, are shaped by the categories that are used to organize them. The emphasis on gender polarity can mask a great deal of common ground between men's and women's work. It was thus not only the changing labor process of secretarial work that needed to be studied but also shifts in its definition and meaning.

FEMINIST APPROACHES

Feminist scholars have provided a clear outline of the processes whereby secretarial work, which until the third quarter of the nineteenth century was done almost entirely by men, came in the twentieth century to be perceived as quintessentially women's work. Once an apprenticeship for management, or a way of learning the business before taking it over, secretarial work changed dramatically as the result of both new office technology and the growth of a more complex corporate economy. Middle management expanded, opening up new opportunities to men who might once have been clerks and simultaneously creating new low-status keyboard and stenographic positions that were filled by women. Secretarial work became mechanized and deskilled, and no longer served as a gateway to power. The sexual division of labor was redefined to include a sharp differentiation between secretarial jobs on the one hand and administrative and managerial jobs on the other. Work has continued to be organized around gender polarities, with clear-cut distinctions between men's and women's work. As argued in *Gender at Work,* gender is not only about difference but also about power: the domination of men and the subordination of women. This power relation is maintained by the creation of distinctions between male and female spheres (Game & Pringle, 1983, p. 16). Not only are jobs defined according to a clear gender dichotomy, but the gendering of jobs has been important to the construction of gender

identity. Gender is not constructed in the family and then taken out to work but is continually reconstituted in a number of arenas, including work. Men need to experience their work as empowering. Performing secretarial work, as it conveyed ancillary service functions carried out by women, was increasingly seen as a threat to masculine power and identity.

One of the limitations of such an analysis is that it assumes that both occupational and gender categories are empirically given. It will be argued here that neither occupational titles nor gender labels merely describe a pregiven reality, but exist in discourses that actively constitute that reality. Discourse is precisely this—the ways of understanding, interpreting, and responding to a "reality," which it is impossible to know in any other way. This is not to imply that reality does not exist—in this case, substantial differences in the tasks performed by men and women. But occupations do not emerge straightforwardly from an observation of the labor process. These occupational divisions could equally well have been described in a number of other ways and need not have assumed a gender polarity. In any case, secretaries are not sitting at their desks waiting to be counted. Their numbers vary enormously, depending on which meaning is being produced: In Australia it could range between 25,000 and a half million, depending on whether one wanted to differentiate between executive assistants and routine filing clerks. It is notable, too, that secretarial work is still routinely described in terms of individual boss/secretary relationships, even though such relationships are now largely restricted to senior management (Pringle, 1988, pp. 174–194).

If we cannot take occupations as given in reality, neither can we take gender as given. Kessler and McKenna (1978, pp. 102–103) point out that by assuming in advance the centrality of gender categories, we inevitably reproduce such categories. The possibility of describing social relations in any other way is then systematically excluded, and gender is presented as fixed and given. Most questions posed about gender assume a sharp dichotomy, that is, that everyone fits one and only one category, and that one's gender is invariant. On the contrary, they suggest, it is "our seeing two genders" that leads to the "discovery" of biological, psychological, and social differences. They argue for a more open approach, suggesting that if gender is a social construction, it might be treated as more fluid. Judith Butler has made the case against essentialism even more strongly, arguing that gender coherence is a regulatory fiction (1990, pp. 329–339). She rejects the assumption that individuals have a deep psychic investment in gender identity, socially constructed or otherwise, and insists that this is imposed purely through discourse.

While Butler's anti-essentialist position is extreme, it does open up new ways of thinking about gender and occupations. It calls into question the deep connections between gender and occupational identities and suggests that it may be possible to resituate the issues. The subject of male secretaries is a particularly promising area to investigate this approach, for it poses the contradiction between men's horror of being labeled "male secretaries," while they are willing to do the same or very similar work as long as they are not so labeled. Why does a simple change of label make it acceptable? On the one hand gender seems so rigid that secretarial work presents a threat to a man's core gender identity. On the other, it may be relatively straightforward to resituate the subject in a different occupational discourse, recasting the "reality" in a different frame. The question that needs to be raised is not, why there are so few male secretaries; but rather, why the title "secretary" is reserved almost exclusively for women, and how it affects the negotiation of workplace identities and power relations.

WHAT IS A SECRETARY?

It is impossible to answer the question "what is a secretary?" by describing what a secretary *does*. If it were so, the many thousands of Pats in existence would surely be included. There are actually a range of discourses, statistical and cultural, in which meanings are produced about what a secretary *is* (Pringle, 1988). We come to know secretaries and to identify them as a group through the ways in which they are represented. This is true of all groups, but in most cases the emphasis is on the actual work and the social relations surrounding it. A plumber, or for that matter a stenographer or typist, does not have a particularly strong cultural presence. By contrast, the secretary is constructed in popular culture in a way that plays down the importance of what she does, in favor of discussion of what she is. Secretary is one of the few employment categories for which there has never been a clear job description. Secretaries do a wide variety of things, and there is not even one task, such as typing, that we can confidently say they all perform. This ambiguity about what constitutes a secretary's work makes it easily available for cultural redefinition. Secretaries are part of folklore and popular culture and are represented in stereotypical ways in advertising and the media, even in pornography.

In the twentieth century secretaries have come to be defined first as exclusively women, and second in familial and sexual terms. If, as the psychoanalysts suggest, woman is perceived as lacking what it takes to be a man, so secretaries were assumed to lack the qualities that make a successful boss. The equating of secretary with woman or wife, and boss with man, has been important in establishing the normative versions of what a secretary is. So powerful are these norms that female bosses and male secretaries are perceived as out of step, and the relationship may be difficult to read in traditional boss/secretary terms—it may simply be perceived as two people working together (Pringle, 1988, pp. 82–83).

The question "what is a secretary" may be answered with reference to three discourses, which have coexisted at times peacefully and at others in open competition with one another. The first of these, the "office wife," emerged early this century and had its origins in the debate about whether (middle-class) women should work outside the home. It may be found in serious journals, teaching manuals, and the practices of a good many secretarial studies teachers, as well as the more traditional bosses and secretaries. It signified that women's primary place was in the home, that her other tasks would be redefined in relation to this and restricted to support roles. The two main requirements of the office wife were that she be deferential and that she be ladylike. The office wife is portrayed as the extension of her boss: loyal, trustworthy, and devoted. Though the discourse has been modernized, debate about changes in secretarial work is frequently cast in terms of how far office marriages are changing. Are they being transformed into more compassionate and egalitarian relations, where the wife might have other interests or refuse to do certain aspects of the housework?

By the 1950s the prim, spinsterish figure with the bun had been challenged by alternative images, appearing regularly in tabloid cartoons, of the blonde "dolly bird" figure, with large breasts, long legs, and short skirts. Where the office wife had been a workhorse, putting order into the office, the dolly was presented as a source of chaos and diversion. The office wife is subservient, passive, and reserved; but the dolly is cheeky and loud and is represented as having an active sexuality and a degree of sexual power over the boss. What the two had in common was their definition in gendered and familial terms. Secretaries could be wives, mothers, mistresses, dragons, or spinster aunts.

A third set of meanings has struggled to emerge, which resists the familial and sexual definitions, treats secretaries as having serious careers, emphasizes skill and experience, and plays down the special relationship between boss and secretary in favor of viewing both as part of a management team. Although this "equal opportunity" discourse gathered strength by the 1970s, and proclaimed that gender should not be important in the construction of occupational categories, the earlier meanings live on and need to be addressed seriously in the discussion of work.

The inclusion of a sexual dynamic in the boss/secretary relationship has largely excluded men from being defined as secretaries. It would be tantamount to declaring both boss and secretary to be gay. Male secretaries are often assumed to be gay. This is both a conventional way of interpreting a male sexuality that is perceived as lacking power and a statement about the place of sexuality in people's perceptions of the boss/secretary relation. Alternately, male secretaries may be incorporated in familial terms as sons and brothers. (Sons who are currently performing filial duties but will, in the course of time, move on to establish their autonomous place in the world.) In the fantasies of women managers, male secretaries may at times appear as toy boys and playthings—but significantly *never* in the powerful subject positions of husbands or fathers. I shall return to these questions, drawing on interview data, in the final section.

SHIFTING DEFINITIONS OF SECRETARIES

The history of men and women in secretarial work must take account of not only technological and organizational change, but also shifting frameworks of meaning. Far from being a fixed, identifiable group, secretaries are a fluid and shifting category; and sociologists, economists, journalists, managers, clerks, keyboard operators, personal assistants, and so on, may have quite different notions of who should be included. The changing definitions of secretaries are amplified by the decisions of the statisticians as to how to count and classify them. Official statistics are no more neutral a discourse than any other; they too produce specific meanings for *secretary*. This section looks at the ongoing presence of men in secretarial work since the late nineteenth century, and the ways in which that presence has been discursively disguised, particularly by statisticians who have interpreted the occupational structure in ways that emphasized sexual polarities.

Even though in the nineteenth century secretaries were men, it is now assumed that secretaries have been women since time immemorial. Secretarial work is now seen as so traditionally women's work that it is hard to remember how recently this work has become feminized. Although in the United States women began to move into secretarial work during the Civil War period, it was not until about 1930 that a clear majority of secretaries were women, and not until the 1950s that male secretaries began to seem strange or unusual (Benet, 1972; Davies, 1982). In the space of a very few decades, the secretarial workforce underwent a sex change. This feminization occurred in conjunction with a major shift in the meaning and status of *secretary.*

The shift is signified by the three definitions offered by the *Oxford English Dictionary* (1979), which will be discussed in turn. The first of these definitions invokes the older meaning, which lives on in titles like Secretary of State or Press Secretary.

> One who is entrusted with private or secret matters; one whose office is to write for another, especially one who is employed to conduct correspondence, to keep records and (usually) to transact other business for another person or for a society, corporation or public body.

It usually appears in capitals and still signifies largely male preserves. While the British Foreign Secretary and the American Defense Secretary are there to serve a monarch and a president, respectively, they exercise enormous power. Men who are Secretaries in this earlier sense are often impatient or uncomfortable about comparing themselves with "small s" secretaries. Had anyone used the word *secretary* to refer to Pat, they would have implicitly added, "in the old sense," more akin to a company or union secretary than to somebody who served a boss.

The second Oxford definition indicates a transition of meaning:

> Private secretary—a secretary employed by a minister of state or other high official for the personal correspondence connected with his official positions. Also applied to a secretary in the employ of

> a particular person (as distinguished from the secretary to a society, etc).

As assistants to senior managers, private secretaries still act as officers of the company or organization, but their continuity with secretaries in the earlier sense goes largely unacknowledged and they are, for counting purposes, usually included with typists and stenographers.

The third definition more accurately conveys what most contemporary secretaries do and is indicative of the shift to "women's work":

> A person employed to help deal with correspondence, typing, filing and similar routine work.

HISTORICAL TRANSITIONS

The changes signified by the dictionary definitions did not take place overnight but happened gradually over half a century. They are linked to major changes in the occupational structure and the development of new tiers of clerical work, made possible by new technologies. This section attempts a broad periodization from the 1890s, when the first two definitions still held sway, to the developments since World War II, when the third definition became the most widely used one.

1890–1920

Of all the components of what is now called secretarial work, telephoning was the first to be designated as feminine (Kingston, 1975, p. 93). Typing was initially considered to require not only manual dexterity but also some practical knowledge of the material being processed (Fitzsimmons, 1980, p. 24). It was therefore perceived as appropriate work for men. As typewriters came into general use, in the first decade of the twentieth century, and the demand for operators increased, typing became accepted as a woman's subject. Shorthand retained a masculine image, but had, before World War I, become paired with typing by employers to create the feminine job classification of "shorthand-typiste." The first two national censuses in

Australia replaced "secretary" with "officer in a public company," a small group which remained predominantly male. Typists and stenographers were included in the general categories of "office caretaker, keeper, attendant" and "clerk, cashier, accountant undefined." The proportion of women in the latter category rose to 35% by 1921 and, when this is checked against the job advertisements for the period, it is reasonable to assume that many of them were typists, stenographers, and private secretaries.

1920–1945

Though men continued to engage in secretarial work in the inter-war period, their proportion steadily declined. The feminine "typiste" came to be used in the job advertisements of the 1920s to distinguish "women's work." The statisticians caught up with this terminology and, in the 1933 census created the gendered category "typiste, office machinist," from which men were absent by definition. Until World War II advertisements for typists (without the "e") still routinely appeared in the classifieds, which indicates that a number of men were employed as typist/clerks. The majority of secretaries, as distinct from stenographers, were also still men. But for the male secretaries, unlike most of the women, stenographic work was the start rather than the end of a career. The key way that young men without a tertiary education could get promotion in the public service, for example, was by going to night school and studying either shorthand or accountancy. Shorthand was taken as a kind of alternative evidence of intellectual ability. Even in the 1980s there were senior male public servants and company managers who had started their careers as stenographic and secretarial workers (Byrne, 1982, p. 10).

Late 1940s–Present

In the late 1940s the term *secretary* began to be used more loosely in the classifieds to describe what had previously been understood in more precise terms as stenographers and typists. The statisticians were obviously concerned that company secretaries might get confused with humbler typing varieties. "Secretary" disappeared entirely as a census category. Rather than making any effort to distinguish private secretaries as a professional group, they collapsed them into the category of "typists and shorthand writers." From a masculinist viewpoint it was convenient to do this because they then did not have to identify or acknowledge levels of skill. "Women's work" could be seen as an undifferentiated category of unskilled labor.

In the 1947 census men were again counted among typists and stenographers, but their numbers were small: 245 out of 71,000. Although officially gender-neutral, the "typist, stenographer" category was treated, by the statisticians, as a feminine one. The coders were actually allowed to take gender into account in deciding how to categorize people. Men who did shorthand or typing (and there were still a large number of them in the public service) were thus recoded as clerks. If "shorthand typist" was a category reserved for women, so too was "receptionist." So that there could be no mistake about this, the 1976 and 1981 censuses actually labeled the group "receptionist, female." A man, by definition, could not be a receptionist and would have to be placed in some other category.

As a result of these processes, men in secretarial work became literally invisible as "secretaries" and were treated as part of a clerical and administrative workforce with a separate career path. Male secretaries gained novelty value. Newspapers have loved to "discover" the occasional "brave" man who is attending secretarial college. In Australia, they have been discovering him every few months since at least 1968! (*Sun-Herald,* November 10, 1968). In 1973, when employers faced the prospect of equal pay, we were told that Caulfield Institute had just enrolled their first male in a secretarial postgraduate course (*Australian,* March 4, 1973); that Stella Cornelius (furrier and arbiter of women's fashion) had a male personal assistant (*Sydney Morning Herald,* March 14,

1973); and that such men were earning nearly twice as much as the women and saw their jobs as stepping-stones to more important careers (*Sydney Morning Herald,* February 7, 1973). After equal pay for work of equal value became official policy in 1975, the popular press threatened that "the first male secretaries are sharpening their pencils to lead the men's lib march down the corridors of power" and that they were "edging out boardroom blondes." One of their number allegedly commented: "Female secretaries are two a penny. Men beat them for efficiency and stability.... We don't fall pregnant and don't come and go" (*Sun-Herald,* January 9, 1977). A year later it was "Take a letter MR Jones" (*Sun-Herald,* March 5, 1977). In 1982 a policeman was chosen as Queensland's Secretary of the Year: As the *Herald* put it, "Sergeant Greg takes on the girls and cops it sweet." He had started 20 years earlier as a foot patrolman and gone on to become assistant to the police commissioner. With admirable secretarial tact, he commented: "The police in Queensland have received a lot of unwarranted criticism lately and I hope my award can do a little bit to help our cause" (*Sydney Morning Herald,* April 22, 1982).

The strong associations of "secretary" with femininity and sexuality have a number of implications for men doing broadly secretarial work. Currently, men are rarely called secretaries. They are generally described as assistants of some kind, or as computer operators, clerks, or trainees. As late as 1970 a textbook for secretarial students noted that:

> In industries where secretaries are required to represent their employers, in factories or on construction sites, and in strictly masculine provinces, male secretaries are in great demand...they are frequently employed in the legal field, in purchasing, mining, the oil and rubber industries, public utilities and in the newspaper field. (Solly et al., 1970, pp. 6–7)

Men continued to use stenographic skills in the armed forces, the police, and journalism. The State Rail Authority insisted that its junior recruits learn to type, and in the 1960s still required shorthand as a qualification for its clerks. Court reporting also remained a male preserve, although women had taken over the typing side. In what seems a strange division of labor, the reporters took down the proceedings in shorthand and dictated them directly to typists. Men only dropped out in the 1980s, when the work apparently became less attractive to them after equal pay was implemented (Pringle, 1988, p. 170). While the number of men doing secretarial work has undoubtedly dropped, a number remain who are simply not perceived as secretaries because of their gender. As a result, the extent to which secretarial work has been feminized has been overemphasised.

"MALE SECRETARIES"

While the majority of men in secretarial work are not called secretaries, a few are quite self-consciously given that label, and it is necessary to ask why they have been singled out in this way, rather than incorporated into an "assistant" category. According to my research, men labeled as secretaries are often thought, by those with whom they work, to have some "problem" with their masculinity. Said one manager:

> I had a male secretary once. He was a clerk who came from the Air Force and I discovered one day, quite by accident, that he wrote shorthand and he typed.... I didn't have a secretary at the time and he was one of those guys who was quite happy to fill a secretarial role.... He was an effeminate sort of person and he appeared to enjoy the subservient role. He was one of those people who always wanted to help you.

The boss's assumption appeared to be: What "real" man would want to be subservient, let alone helpful! Male secretaries may also be sensitive to assumptions made about their sexuality, as another interviewee insists:

> An old retired bloke comes in regularly to relive the old days.... The other morning he came in. He stopped and he looked at me and I was typing. And

I was aware that he was looking at me...and he said, what's your name, Miss? And I looked at him and said, it's Jacqueline, actually! He didn't get it. He just sort of grunted and walked off.

I don't object to having overtones of femininity. I mean, everyone's got their yin and their yang. But the implication in a male-dominated society, and particularly in the last bastion of male domination...is that femininity is associated with homosexuality, which is taboo...which conjures up all sorts of nasty images. So that's what I cope with every day.

Any "feminized" occupation is presumed to draw homosexual men: Fashion, hairdressing, entertainment, and more recently nursing are cases in point. A firm connection is made between gender and sexual preference, and the stronger the sex-typing of the job, the stronger the resulting stereotype. The popular press reinforces such connections, for example, by seeking out gay secretaries. The Sydney *Sun-Herald,* for example, in an article titled "Sex Changes in the Typing Pool" (July 1982), described the unhappy experience of Ashley, before he joined the safety of the public service: "'It was disastrous,' he said. 'The boss tried to chase me around the desk. I left after only three-and-a-half weeks.'" The passage probably says more about the fear expressed by the interviewer, of what happens to men in an occupation that is not only subordinate and feminized, but perceived in such strongly sexual terms. The sexuality of the boss is not problematical here—he is represented as sexually dominant and willing to take sexual liberties with the secretary, regardless of either gender or sexual preference.

Ashley *was* actually gay (I interviewed him 4 years later) but he is in the minority. In my research it was easier to find gay nurses than gay secretaries; and even in nursing, gays are a minority. Gay secretaries were largely a newspaper fiction of the 1970s and 1980s. There is no reason to believe that gay men are congregated in secretarial work. A gay lawyer, with a high proportion of gay clients, told me he had advertised widely for a male secretary and had not been able to find anyone suitably qualified. He thought the legal profession was probably too staid for such people. A spokesman for the Gay Business Association in Sydney suggested that gay men may perceive secretaries as "dowdy," and the work as involving long hours of drudgery. He suggested that they were more likely to be working as receptionists or switchboard operators than as secretaries. Secretarial work does not necessarily represent femininity for gay men. In some cases it may represent the opposite. The only other gay secretary I interviewed grew up in a country town and wanted to be a court or Hansard reporter, he explained, to reconcile his sexuality with "something masculine." When he did not get the necessary speeds, he joined the State Rail Authority, which had also retained a masculine image, and it was only when he became dissatisfied with the promotional prospects there that he became willing to consider more stereotypically secretarial positions in the private sector.

The media discourse about gay male secretaries now seems a little dated, particularly since the emergence of "gay machismo." Since the mid-1980s more women have moved into senior executive positions (particularly in the public service) and often find themselves dealing with male subordinates. These women often joked to me about the "male secretary" as a subject of titillation, a possible object of desire or a status symbol (a toy boy or a handbag). Given the notorious difficulties that women bosses often report with female secretaries (Pringle, 1998, pp. 57–83), a male personal assistant has both practical and erotic appeal. To reverse the master/slave relationship is to represent the woman as both powerful and stylish. It is to imply that she is cared for by a man, who both finds her sexually attractive and admires and respects her, offering the same kind of loyalty that men have in the past extracted from their female secretaries. It is also to exploit the traditionally higher status of the manservant or butler over the female domestic (the status of male secretaries might be lower than that of men in many other occupations, but they are likely to earn more than their female counterparts). The numbers of female boss/male secretary pairs are not vast, but their appearance in the discourse of women managers is indicative of a shift in the way male secretaries are being regarded. It is notable that they continue to be sexually defined, though in new ways. Perhaps because of this sexualization, most men doing secretarial work still express discomfort at the prospect of being labeled "male secretaries."

MALE BOSSES

Some male managers said they "could not imagine" having a man as a secretary, and it is quite possible that male applicants face discrimination. One of my subjects recalled that when he was living in London two other men he knew were "temping" for solicitors and found it very difficult to get work "until they had tried them once. And it took 3 or 4 months for these guys to get established. It is a very staid industry." To many male bosses the relationship with a "secretary" is of an intimate nature and is more appropriately with a woman. Yet managers are constantly in the position of supervising those below them in the chain of command. Why should it be so different in principle when the person concerned is a "secretary"? As soon as the person concerned is renamed an "assistant" of some kind, the problem appears to go away. A professor spoke warmly of his "technical officer," who, "to my delight writes letters almost in the words I would have used." He relies on him for "higher level secretarial tasks" and sees a future for a lot more men in these positions.

Bosses may deal with the sexualization issue by denying that their male secretaries are secretaries or by treating them differently. One senior manager commented:

A male secretary... would not be called my secretary but my assistant.... I think I would get a male secretary to do additional work because he was male.... Simply because other males here that are helping me, the marketing manager, the accountant, the product manager... are doing work of a particular level.... I would imagine this guy taking on more and more responsibility and then one day I would say, "Why don't we get a typist?"

Once appointed, male secretaries appear to receive very favorable treatment and the "discrimination" works to their advantage. In a rather similar way male doctors, embarrassed by the sexual connotations of the doctor/nurse relationship, often treat male nurses as junior doctors, explain more processes to them, and facilitate their speedier progress through the system (Game & Pringle, 1983, pp. 110–111). Since it is "unimaginable" that men might be secretaries, they tend to be paid more and to move quickly up the career ladder.

Male secretaries earn about 20% more than their female counterparts, a figure that directly parallels the differential for full-time workers overall (Pringle, 1988, p. 171). The self-confidence and assertiveness of the two male secretaries discussed below thus has a solid financial basis. The higher rate cannot be explained in terms of the different occupation distributions of men and women, and can only signify that the men are receiving more favorable treatment and moving into personal assistant positions.

FAMILY GAMES

Where male secretaries are not defined sexually, they may be integrated, in family terms, as brothers or sons. Tim, for example, works in the family law firm. He tells close friends that he is a secretary but otherwise describes himself as a legal clerk. He picked up typing while working in a bank and works from Dictaphone. He does not take shorthand. His brother and sister, both solicitors, say he is the best secretary they have had because he wants to know exactly what each piece of work is about. He behaves as though he were one of the legal staff and, like many other male secretaries, is treating it as a stepping-stone. He is currently taking an accountancy course.

Phillip Warton works for a family-based pharmaceutical company, where he is treated by both husband and wife as the son. While this has its frustrations, particularly with the wife, it also gives him a stronger power base than that usually available to sisters or daughters. Phillip agreed to talk to me after a woman friend of his saw my advertisement for "male secretaries" and volunteered him. He had not identified himself as a secretary until that time because his description says he is a "marketing assistant." Now in his early 20s he had started work in a bank and had taken it upon himself to learn to type when he found he kept making mistakes on bank cheques and international drafts.

> I went to tech for 6 months and learned to type.... There was two other guys there but it was very sexist actually in that the woman who was teaching me to type came to me and said that I didn't have to bother too much about spacing and those aspects of typing because I wouldn't be using that in my role. And I said, but if I was going to be a secretary I would. She said, "But you're not—what are you doing it for?" She automatically presumed I was not going to be a secretary.... I didn't have to do typing tests on spacing and setting out letters and what have you. I just went strictly on speed typing.

He earns 30% to 40% more than he was getting in the bank. Despite his lack of a science or pharmacy degree, he is being groomed for a long-term position in the company. But he does not see a future in it, and it is unlikely that he will stay. Phillip has taken the job to get marketing experience and plans to do a marketing diploma. How does he describe his current job?

> Basically it is to look after the managing director. I run after him, and organize him, keep his desk tidy, make sure he goes to appointments.... Get things done that he should do and doesn't get time for.

But he is always introduced as "my assistant," my offsider, Phillip who runs around after me... never as secretary. Phillip claims a degree of power in relation to his boss:

> I think he feels, not threatened by me, but I feel I have the ability to tell him what to do. I tell him what to do and he does it. I'll go in there and I'll say, "Your desk is utterly disgusting. How can you

find anything?" And I'll come back into his office and there will be piles on the floor for me to take away to file. His wife thinks it's wonderful that he's got me to run around after him.... But in regard to a power play he's still M.D., and he knows he still is...and knows that it's just a game.... Sometimes I feel like that and other times I feel he's a bit wimpy, because someone who's only been in the company for 3 months has the ability to say something to him.

It was unusual to hear female secretaries talk like this in an interview situation, regardless of what they might have felt privately.

Though he replaced a woman who did a lot of typing, Phillip rarely uses his typing skills at work. He says:

> ...The only time I'll type is if I need it and there's no one to do it. I've heard it said that the girl that is doing the typing now has had to do more because I'm there.... Mind you, typing was a stipulation of the job...but he [the boss] didn't even ask me if I could type...he just assumed I didn't.
>
> And I said to him, "You didn't ask me about typing." He said, "Do you type?" I said, "Of course I do, I did a tech course." "Oh, really? That's an added advantage, isn't it?" I thought, oh, well, he must have taken me on on the basis of my other attributes.

This "girl" appears a few minutes later as the boss's wife and a director of the company. Her relationship with Phillip is complex. He asserts his ascendancy over her, too, as the typist who lacks many of his skills, but at the same time he regards her as the power behind the throne.

> So you give typing to her?
> Yes but it doesn't work that way because she...is not the typist. She is a director and she will take time out.

As the interview continues, her authority increases rapidly. She controls the office, keeps everything under surveillance, and basically manages things. If there is conflict between her and her husband, she gets her way. She intervenes on every level. She insists on a high standard of dress and routinely comments on Phillip's ties, clothes, hairstyle, and so on. At first this is presented in terms of mother-son intimacy. The two of them talk about PLU—people like us. You are either PLU or you are not. But before long, he switches again and says that if he were going to resign, it would be because of her. He finds it "frustrating" that she constantly goes behind his back to the boss:

> If I do something that she disagrees with . . . she won't tell me, she'll go to Douglas. And then he will ask me, "Why did you do that?" . . . Everything that goes on, she is always overseeing. If I resign from the job, it will be basically because of her. I find her a very frustrating woman to deal with. Because I cannot find my footing with her. She is not direct. She is behind my back.

Perhaps it is not accidental that Phillip's own mother had been a secretary and in all likelihood intervened in similar ways in his relationship with his father.

Phillip's role is considerably more high profile than that of the "girl" he replaced. He does no routine typing, and as a result the boss's wife, herself a director and actively engaged in managing the company, takes on additional typing work. A conflict ensues in which she is constantly putting him in his place, showing that ultimately it is she rather than he who will have her way with Douglas, the patriarch. He can be the favored son only by conforming to her whims, and he has made the judgment that his future will be better served by moving on.

GENDER AND POWER

Clearly, gender does alter the boss-secretary relationship. Raoul, unlike Phillip, is actually defined as a secretary and is thus placed at a cultural disadvantage, subject to ridicule. Yet he is able to develop strategies of asserting masculine power. His boss, Geraldine Milner, is a senior manager with a large merchant bank, for which she has worked for the past 15 years. Her main responsibilities are with advisory services and public relations. She is 41 and single. Beyond that she revealed virtually nothing about her private life.

Though very aware of the problems of being a woman in a male-dominated industry, she does not attach any significance to having a male secretary. I asked her what she thought about the common view that it would be hard for men to be in those sorts of support positions:

> Rubbish! What a load! Have they ever tried it? I mean, this is it! It's crazy! I've always had men working for me and I haven't noticed any difference. . . . I've never really expected my secretaries to get my cups of coffee or cups of tea or anything like that . . . if that's what they term support. . . . I suppose some men expect their secretaries to go out and buy their wives' birthday presents and all that sort of nonsense. . . . I would never consider asking them to do anything other than what was required in a professional capacity.

Her secretary, Raoul Wicks, is 26 and single. He was dressed in a crumpled suit, which barely fulfilled the formal dress requirements, and he appeared to thumb his nose at the style associated with merchant banks. Having dropped out of a Bachelor of Business degree halfway through, he has had a rather checkered career as an actor and odd-jobs person. He is in this position rather accidentally, having originally contacted the bank about another clerical job.

Geraldine stressed there was no difference between what Raoul did and what previous female secretaries had done:

> I want someone who can do the basic school lectures for us. Someone who can handle the phones and preferably who knows the industry, at least enough to answer a lot of the basic queries. I don't really have sufficient typing and normal things like that to warrant a full-time secretary.
>
> Raoul's here because he studied and wants to work in the industry, so it's a very good training position for someone in the long term. Another former secretary has now gone into a broker's office and is doing extremely well.

Raoul, on the other hand, is not happy about being called a secretary, and goes out of his way to explain why the term is inappropriate. He says that when the job was first discussed, the term *secretary* was never mentioned. They just said:

I would need to do a little bit of typing.... It looked like an attractive job. There's a certain amount of prestige in working for this organization.... At that point in time I couldn't type but I rapidly learned.... I went and did one of those bloody student receptionist center courses...

He stressed the ways in which his job is different from that of a secretary—and went on to give what is a very typical job description:

My job involves doing all the administration in the department.... I answer all the mail...and discern where it should go and who should answer it. If I can answer it, I answer it. I handle all the bookings for schools for our educational talks...for community organizations...and for companies.... I also take lectures for school and community groups. I handle all the merchandising for the department. I sell all the sweatshirts. I am in charge of the accounts.... I do the banking.... I also take phone inquiries.

"Lecturing" to school and community groups is beyond the duties of most secretaries, but it is the only task that stands out. There had been some concern to find him an alternative title, befitting his status as a male, but Geraldine would have none of this. Where his strategy of power was to emphasize his difference from secretaries, hers was to assert his similarity with his female predecessors. The connections between discourse and power are very obvious here, in the two quite different interpretations of "secretary" that are put forward as the terms of the relationship are negotiated.

On this occasion Geraldine won. As Raoul describes it:

The personnel officer rang me.... She was updating the telephone directory...and she said to me. "Oh, Raoul, what are we going to call you? You're not really a "secretary," are you...you do more than that...how about we call you "Information Officer"? I said that's fine, that sounds good. And she said, "I'll talk to Geraldine and get back to you.".... No more was said...and when the telephone list came out, there I was, a secretary and that was that.... I didn't say anything to Geraldine about it. I didn't feel I could.

He goes to some lengths to enlist sympathy for his "predicament":

If one wants to belong to a club, particularly a men's club, there are certain do's and don'ts. There are certain mores, and it therefore doesn't augur well to be a secretary. Maybe 30 years ago...if you had been a private secretary...that may have been different.... Now if you're doing a woman's job, the implication is that you are somehow feminine. And femininity has no place in a men's club.

He claims to get teased by young girls in the office who imply he is not a proper man. And yet what comes across is the power that this man is able to exercise. Typically, when I interviewed both members of a boss/secretary pair, the male boss was loquacious and open, while the female secretary was more guarded. On this occasion, the female boss restricts her range of comments, while the male secretary talks freely, explicitly. and quite personally about her. I did not meet a single female secretary who talked in quite this way about a boss, male or female. On this occasion gender clearly overrides formal position in determining what can be said. Thus he comments:

I think she's perceived as a hard arse. But I think she's had to be a hard arse to get where she's got to. I also think she's perceived as pretty neurotic and I do know that she has a nickname around here.

She gets bad-mouthed a lot behind her back. I have to be careful, as there may be times when I agree with what people are saying. I have found myself slip on a couple of occasions and say, yes, you're right...or enforce their prejudices rather than just taking a neutral stance.

Yes, she's perceived as being hard and tough, particularly with women. She's tougher on women than she is on men.... So I think...you know, jobs for the boys doesn't necessarily operate with jobs for the girls.

He talks at length about the way in which Geraldine exercises power over him. As he talks it becomes clear that the flow of power between them fluctuates very much more than is the case with female secretaries and either male or female bosses. He thinks she has "very definite limits and very definite boundaries that cannot be overstepped," but seems to delight in playing games with them. On one occasion Geraldine asserts her authority because Raoul has forgotten to leave her a message. His comeback is, first, that only a woman would be concerned with such "trivia," dismissing the possibility that it may have been important to make every effort to return the call. Second, he implies it is because he is a man that she has to bother asserting herself in this way at all:

> I think she expects that she doesn't have to exert any authority with women. I mean, someone who has authority doesn't feel the need to display it.... With women I don't think she feels the need to display it. But with men she does have a need to display it.

Raoul continues in this vein, ostensibly describing her power and his subordination, but actually imposing his own power in the situation and reducing hers through stereotyping her—first as a dragon and then as a typical neurotic woman.

> The male bosses I have had are more even. They're less prone to ups and downs. With my boss at the moment...I leave her alone for at least a good hour. I've learned that now. Leave her alone till half past 10 and probably it'll be okay. But as soon as she walks in the door, the first thing I have to do is sum her up...and see what kind of mood she's in.

It is hardly unusual for secretaries to discern their bosses' moods, and adjust their behavior accordingly. But he turns this into a kind of reverse power base. He concedes that men's moods fluctuate too:

> ...but I don't think it's as visible.... That's kind of more dangerous because they're actually prone to exploding on you without any warning, whereas with Geraldine, I've got a pretty fair idea in advance.

He claims the power to read her accurately, literally placing her via a detailed description of her

clothes. None of the women interviewed said anything like this of her boss:

> I can tell a lot from the way she's dressed.... There was one dress that has a very high collar...it's quite rigid...and it's pleated all the way down.... I know that she's in a very no-nonsense mood when I see that dress.... Like today we've got work to do.... She has a little crimson suit and that's another no-nonsense outfit. But it says...I'm more available today. I'm more open. I will probably be meeting executives or important VIPs.... There is another dress that has a split up the center, and that has its own connotations. And that's usually when she's far more relaxed. The perfume she wears tells me how she feels that day, too. So I try to sum those things up.

While Geraldine denies that the gender of her secretary makes any difference, Raoul thinks she is very aware of his maleness. Unlike female secretaries, he is quite happy to talk about sexual fantasies and interactions, assuming that he has control.

> I can imagine having an affair with Geraldine. But I can't imagine having an affair with Geraldine and working here, because I just think it would just alter the relationship entirely, and it would become untenable for her and for me.

He thinks in the first few weeks in the job there was a kind of sexual attraction going on. Whether the attraction was mutual or his fantasy we do not know, but he curtailed it. As if to have the last word he says:

> I've never told her when I'm pissed off, never. I think that would be to take advantage of the relationship between the sexes, so I don't. Because I couldn't do it with a man. I couldn't go to a man and say, "Look, what you have just done really annoys me," or "The way you've spoken to me really annoys me."

In other words, he believes he could take advantage of male power but claims he does not. The implication is that she depends on his gallantry and cooperation. Remembering his unease at being called secretary, he has had to turn the situation around in fantasy, and to some extent in practice, to make it acceptable to his masculine ego. Geraldine's counter-strategy is to deny that his masculinity has any relevance to the situation and to try to ensure that it brings him no extra privileges. It is clear that, on this occasion at least, gender does matter.

SUMMARY

The normative boss/secretary relationship involves a male boss and a female secretary. When the gender of either is changed, the relationship is quite considerably transformed. Despite stereotyping of male secretaries as "inadequate" men, they are often able to draw on images of masculine power and competence to negotiate significant power in relation to managers. While one must be cautious about generalizing on the basis of a small number of interviews, the discursive strategies that are available to men in secretarial work are fairly clear.

Men have always maintained a presence, albeit a minority one, in secretarial work; the reason this cannot be seen is because of the sexual and gendered nature of the cultural construction of "secretary." Men can and do type, though they often decline to do so at work, for fear of losing their status or their masculinity. Increasingly, managers have computer terminals on their desks, and the old distinction between clerical and secretarial work is breaking down.

The question is not how to get more men into secretarial work but the terms on which they come in. As with other areas of "traditional" women's work, the danger for women is that men will take over the best-paid, most prestigious jobs; that the division between gendered categories of work will be replaced by a horizontal division in which women are restricted to the bottom rungs. This has already happened to some extent in nursing, where men become charge nurses more quickly and move up the administrative hierarchy. But in nursing the movement of some men into positions of power has been counter-balanced by powerful unions, by strong moves toward professionalization and the upgrading of nursing qualifications. It can be argued that the presence of men has assisted in the upgrading of status and working conditions for everyone. In secretarial work the position is quite different. Outside the public sector, the unions are weak and the movement of men into the area does not signify that secretarial work is being acknowledged as professional or managerial in any genuine sense. The fact that "male secretaries" as well as female ones are so often perceived in sexual terms probably does currently limit their capacity to challenge women for many of the most prestigious jobs. While in the short term it may be to the benefit of the women that the sexual definitions are extended in this way, in the long term it will be necessary to challenge the sexualized meanings of "secretary" to ensure that it does not continue to be used to limit the areas available to women. This involves not only a change of label but also struggles around the discursive frameworks within which meanings are constituted.

REFERENCES

Australian. (1973, March 3).

Benet, M. K. (1972). *Secretary: An inquiry into the female ghetto.* London: Sidgwick & Jackson.

Butler, J. (1990). Gender trouble, feminist theory and psychoanalytic discourse. In L. J. Nicholson (Ed.), *Feminism/postmodernism* (pp. 324–340). New York: Routledge.

Byrne, R. (1982). Occupation—secretary: An historical perspective. A paper presented at the seminar, Secretarial Education: A New Direction. Melbourne: Chisholm Institute of Technology.

Crompton, R., & Jones, G. (1984). *White collar proletariat: Deskilling and gender in clerical work.* London: Macmillan.

Davies. M. (1982). *Woman's place is at the typewriter.* Philadelphia: Temple University Press.

Fitzsimmons, K. (1980). The involvement of women in the commercial sector 1850–1891. *Second women and labor conference papers.* Melbourne: Melbourne University.

Game, A., & Pringle, R. (1983). *Gender at work.* Sydney: Allen & Unwin.

Kanter, R. M. (1977). *Men and women of the corporation.* New York: Basic Books.

Kessler, S., & McKenna, W. (1978). *Gender: An ethnomethodological approach.* London: Verso.

Kingston. B. (1975). *My wife, my daughter and poor Mary Ann.* Melbourne: Nelson.

Oxford English dictionary. (1979). Oxford: Oxford University Press.

Pringle. R. (1988). *Secretaries talk.* London: Verso.

Solly, E., et al. (1970). *The secretary at work* (3rd ed.) Melbourne: McGraw-Hill.

Sun-Herald. (1968, November 10).

Sun-Herald. (1977, January 9).

Sun-Herald. (1977, March 5).

Sydney Morning Herald. (1973, February 7).

Sydney Morning Herald. (1973, March 14).

Sydney Morning Herald. (1982, April 22).

Sydney Sun-Herald. (1982, July).

40

Boundary Lines

Labeling Sexual Harassment in Restaurants

PATTI A. GIUFFRE
CHRISTINE L. WILLIAMS

Sexual harassment occurs when submission to or rejection of sexual advances is a term of employment, is used as a basis for making employment decisions, or if the advances create a hostile or offensive work environment (Konrad and Gutek 1986). Sexual harassment can cover a range of behaviors, from leering to rape (Ellis, Barak, and Pinto 1991; Pryor 1987; Reilly et al. 1992; Schneider 1982). Researchers estimate that as many as 70 percent of employed women have experienced behaviors that may legally constitute sexual harassment (MacKinnon 1979; Powell 1986); however, a far lower percentage of women claim to have experienced sexual harassment. Paludi and Barickman write that "the great majority of women who are abused by behavior that fits legal definitions of sexual harassment—and who are traumatized by the experience—do not label what has happened to them 'sexual harassment'" (1991, 68).

Why do most women fail to label their experiences as sexual harassment? Part of the problem is that many still do not recognize that sexual harassment is an actionable offense. Sexual harassment was first described in 1976 (MacKinnon 1979), but it was not until 1986 that the U.S. Su-

preme Court included sexual harassment in the category of gender discrimination, thereby making it illegal (Paludi and Barickman 1991); consequently, women may not yet identify their experiences as sexual harassment because a substantial degree of awareness about its illegality has yet to be developed.

Many victims of sexual harassment may also be reluctant to come forward with complaints, fearing that they will not be believed, or that their charges will not be taken seriously (Jensen and Gutek 1982). As the Anita Hill-Clarence Thomas hearings demonstrated, women who are victims of sexual harassment often become the accused when they bring charges against their assailant.

There is another issue at stake in explaining the gap between experiencing and labeling behaviors "sexual harassment": many men and women experience some sexual behaviors in the workplace as pleasurable. Research on sexual harassment suggests that men are more likely than women to enjoy sexual interactions at work (Gutek 1985; Konrad and Gutek 1986; Reilly et al. 1992), but even some women experience sexual overtures at work as pleasurable (Pringle 1988). This attitude may be especially strong in organizations that use and exploit the bodies and sexuality of the workers (Cockburn 1991). Workers in many jobs are hired on the basis of their attractiveness and solicitousness—including not only sex industry workers, but also service sector workers such as receptionists, airline attendants,

AUTHORS' NOTE: We would like to thank Margaret Andersen, Dana Britton, Kirsten Dellinger, Ricardo Gonzalez, Elizabeth Grauerholz, Suzanne Harper, Beth Schneider, Tracey Steele, Teresa Sullivan, and an anonymous reviewer for their helpful comments and criticisms.

and servers in trendy restaurants. According to Cockburn (1991), this sexual exploitation is not completely forced: many people find this dimension of their jobs appealing and reinforcing to their own sense of identity and pleasure; consequently, some men and women resist efforts to expunge all sexuality from their places of work.

This is not to claim that all sexual behavior in the workplace is acceptable, even to some people. The point is that it is difficult to label behavior as sexual harassment because it forces people to draw a line between illicit and "legitimate" forms of sexuality at work—a process fraught with ambiguity. Whether a particular interaction is identified as harassment will depend on the intention of the harasser and the interpretation of the interchange by the victim, and both of these perspectives will be highly influenced by workplace culture and the social context of the specific event.

This article examines how one group of employees—restaurant workers—distinguishes between sexual harassment and other forms of sexual interaction in the workplace. We conducted an in-depth interview study of waitpeople and found that complex double standards are often used in labeling behavior as sexual harassment: identical behaviors are labeled sexual harassment in some contexts and not others. Many respondents claimed that they enjoyed sexual interactions involving co-workers of the same race/ethnicity, sexual orientation, and class/status backgrounds. Those who were offended by such interactions nevertheless dismissed them as natural or inevitable parts of restaurant culture.[1] When the same behavior occurred in contexts that upset these hegemonic heterosexual norms—in particular, when the episode involved interactions between gay and heterosexual men, or men and women of different racial/ethnic backgrounds—people seemed willing to apply the label sexual harassment

We argue that identifying behaviors that occur only in counterhegemonic contexts as sexual harassment can potentially obscure and legitimate more insidious forms of domination and exploita-

tion. As Pringle points out, "Men control women through direct use of power, but also through definitions of pleasure—which is less likely to provoke resistance" (1988, 95). Most women, she writes, actively seek out what Rich (1980) termed "compulsory heterosexuality" and find pleasure in it. The fact that men and women may enjoy certain sexual interactions in the workplace does not mean they take place outside of oppressive social relationships, nor does it imply that these routine interactions have no negative consequences for women. We argue that the practice of labeling as "sexual harassment" only those behaviors that challenge the dominant definition of acceptable sexual activity maintains and supports men's institutionalized right of sexual access and power over women.

METHODS

The occupation of waiting tables was selected to study the social definition of sexual harassment because many restaurants have a blatantly sexualized workplace culture (Cobble 1991; Paules 1991). According to a report published in a magazine that caters to restaurant owners, "Restaurants . . . are about as informal a workplace as there is, so much so as to actually encourage—or at the very least tolerate—sexual banter" (Anders 1993, 48). Unremitting sexual banter and innuendo, as well as physical jostling, create an environment of "compulsory jocularity" in many restaurants (Pringle 1988, 93). Sexual attractiveness and flirtation are often institutionalized parts of a waitperson's job description; consequently, individual employees are often forced to draw the line for themselves to distinguish legitimate and illegitimate expressions of sexuality, making this occupation an excellent context for examining how people determine what constitutes sexual harassment. In contrast, many more sexual behaviors may be labeled sexual harassment in less highly sexualized work environments.[2]

Eighteen in-depth interviews were conducted with male and female waitstaff who work in restaurants in Austin, Texas. Respondents were se-

lected from restaurants that employ equal proportions of men and women on their wait staffs. Overall, restaurant work is highly sex segregated:
women make up about 82 percent of all waitpeople
(U.S. Department of Labor 1989), and it is common for restaurants to be staffed only by either
waitresses or waiters, with men predominating in
the higher-priced restaurants (Cobble 1991; Hall
1993; Paules 1991). We decided to focus only on
waitpeople who work in mixed-sex groups for two
reasons. First, focusing on waitpeople working on
integrated staffs enables us to examine sexual harassment between co-workers who occupy the
same position in an organizational hierarchy. Coworker sexual harassment is perhaps the most
common form of sexual harassment (Pryor 1987;
Schneider 1982); yet most case studies of sexual
harassment have examined either unequal hierarchical relationships (e.g., boss-secretary harassment) or harassment in highly skewed gender
groupings (e.g., women who work in nontraditional occupations) (Benson and Thomson 1982;
Carothers and Crull 1984; Gruber and Bjorn
1982). This study is designed to investigate sexual
harassment in unequal hierarchical relationships,
as well as harassment between organizationally
equal co-workers.

Second, equal proportions of men and women
in an occupation implies a high degree of male-
female interaction (Gutek 1985). Waitpeople are in
constant contact with each other, help each other
when the restaurant is busy, and informally socialize during slack periods. In contrast, men and
women have much more limited interactions in
highly sex-segregated restaurants and indeed, in
most work environments. The high degree of
interaction among the wait staff provides ample
opportunity for sexual harassment between men
and women to occur and, concomitantly, less
opportunity for same-sex sexual harassment to
occur.

The sample was generated using "snowball"
techniques and by going to area restaurants and
asking waitpeople to volunteer for the study. The
sample includes eight men and ten women. Four

respondents are Latina/o, two African American,
and twelve White. Four respondents are gay or
lesbian; one is bisexual; thirteen are heterosexual.
(The gay men and lesbians in the sample are all
"out" at their respective restaurants.) Fourteen respondents are single; three are married; one is divorced. Respondents' ages range from 22 to 37.

Interviews lasted approximately one hour,
and they were tape-recorded and transcribed for
this analysis. All interviews were conducted by
the first author, who has over eight years' experience waiting tables. Respondents were asked
about their experiences working in restaurants; relationships with managers, customers, and other
co-workers; and their personal experiences of
sexual harassment. Because interviews were conducted in the fall of 1991, when the issue was
prominent in the media because of the Hill-
Thomas hearings, most respondents had thought a
lot about this topic.

FINDINGS

Respondents agreed that sexual banter is very
common in the restaurant: staff members talk and
joke about sex constantly. With only one exception, respondents described their restaurants as
highly sexualized. This means that 17 of the 18
respondents said that sexual joking, touching, and
fondling were common, everyday occurrences in
their restaurants. For example, when asked if he
and other waitpeople ever joke about sex, one
waiter replied, "about 90 percent of [the jokes]
are about sex." According to a waitress, "at
work ...[we're] used to patting and touching and
hugging." Another waiter said, "I do not go
through a shift without someone ... pinching my
nipples or poking me in the butt or grabbing my
crotch.... It's just what we do at work."

These informal behaviors are tantamount to
"doing heterosexuality," a process analogous to
"doing gender" (West and Zimmerman 1987).[3]
By engaging in these public flirtations and open
discussions of sex, men and women reproduce the
dominant cultural norms of heterosexuality and

lend an air of legitimacy—if not inevitability—to heterosexual relationships. In other words, heterosexuality is normalized and naturalized through its ritualistic public display. Indeed, although most respondents described their workplaces as highly sexualized, several dismissed the constant sexual innuendo and behaviors as "just joking," and nothing to get upset about. Several respondents claimed that this is simply "the way it is in the restaurant business," or "just the way men are."

With only one exception, the men and women interviewed maintained that they enjoyed this aspect of their work. Heterosexuality may be normative, and in these contexts, even compulsory, yet many men and women find pleasure in its expression. Many women—as well as men—actively reproduce hegemonic sexuality and apparently enjoy its ritual expression; however, in a few instances, sexual conduct was labeled as sexual harassment. Seven women and three men said they had experienced sexual harassment in restaurant work. Of these, two women and one man described two different experiences of sexual harassment, and two women described three experiences. Table 1 describes the characteristics of each of the respondents and their experiences of sexual harassment.

We analyzed these 17 accounts of sexual harassment to find out what, if anything, these experiences shared in common. With the exception of two episodes (discussed later), the experiences that were labeled "sexual harassment" were not distinguished by any specific words or behaviors, nor were they distinguished by their degree of severity. Identical behaviors were considered acceptable if they were perpetrated by some people, but considered offensive if perpetrated by others. In other words, sexual behavior in the workplace was interpreted differently depending on the context of the interaction. In general, respondents labeled their experiences sexual harassment only if the offending behavior occurred in one of three social contexts: (1) if perpetrated by someone in a more powerful position, such as a manager; (2) if by someone of a different race/

ethnicity; or (3) if perpetrated by someone of a different sexual orientation.

Our findings do not imply that sexual harassment did not occur outside of these three contexts. Instead, they simply indicate that our respondents *labeled* behavior as "sexual harassment" when it occurred in these particular social contexts. We will discuss each of these contexts and speculate on the reasons why they were singled out by our respondents.

Powerful Position

In the restaurant, managers and owners are the highest in the hierarchy of workers. Generally, they are the only ones who can hire or fire waitpeople. Three of the women and one of the men interviewed said they had been sexually harassed by their restaurants' managers or owners. In addition, several others who did not personally experience harassment said they had witnessed managers or owners sexually harassing other waitpeople. This finding is consistent with other research indicating people are more likely to think that sexual harassment has occurred when the perpetrator is in a more powerful position (e.g., Ellis et al. 1991).

Carla describes being sexually harassed by her manager:

> One evening, [my manager] grabbed my body, not in a private place, just grabbed my body, period. He gave me like a bear hug from behind a total of four times in one night. By the end of the night I was livid. I was trying to avoid him. Then when he'd do it, I'd just ignore the conversation or the joke or whatever and walk away.

She claimed that her co-workers often give each other massages and joke about sex, but she did not label any of their behaviors sexual harassment. In fact, all four individuals who experienced sexual harassment from their managers described very similar types of behavior from their co-workers, which they did not define as sexual harassment. For example, Cathy said that she and the other waitpeople talk and joke about sex constantly: "Everybody stands around and talks about sex a

TABLE 1   Description of Respondents and Their Reported Experiences of Sexual Harassment at Work

PSEUDONYM	AGE	RACE[a]	SO[b]	MS[c]	YEARS IN RESTAURANT[d]	SEXUALIZED ENVIRONMENT[e]	SEXUALLY HARASSED[f]
Kate	23	W	H	S	1	yes	yes (1)
Beth	26	W	H	S	5	yes	yes (1)
Ann	29	W	H	S	1*	yes	yes (2)
Cathy	29	W	H	S	8 mos.*	yes	yes (3)
Carla	22	W	H	M	5 mos.*	yes	yes (3)
Diana	32	L	H	M	6	no	no
Maxine	30	L	H	M	4	yes	no
Laura	27	W	B	S	2*	yes	yes (1)
Brenda	23	W	L	S	3	yes	yes (2)
Lynn	37	B	L	D	5*	yes	no
Jake	22	W	H	S	1	yes	yes (1)
Al	23	W	H	S	3	yes	no
Frank	29	W	H	S	8	yes	yes (1)
John	31	W	H	S	2	yes	no
Trent	23	W	G	S	1*	yes	no
Rick	24	B	H	S	1.5	yes	yes (2)
David	25	L	H	S	5	yes	no
Don	24	L	G	S	1*	yes	no

a. Race: B = Black, L = Latina/o, W = White.

b. SO = sexual orientation: B = bisexual, G = gay, H = heterosexual, L = lesbian.

c. MS = marital status: D = divorced, M = married, S = single.

d. Years in restaurant refers to length of time employed in current restaurant. An asterisk indicates that respondent has worked in other restaurants.

e. Whether or not the respondent claimed sexual banter and touching were common occurrences in their restaurant.

f. Responded yes or no to the question: "Have you ever been sexually harassed in the restaurant?" Number in parentheses refers to number of incidents described in the interview.

lot.... Isn't that weird? You know, it's something about working in restaurants and, yeah, so we'll all sit around and talk about sex." She said that talking with her co-workers about sex does not constitute sexual harassment because it is "only joking." She does, however, view her male manager as a sexual harasser:

> My employer is very sexist. I would call that sexual harassment. Very much of a male chauvinist pig. He kind of started [saying] stuff like, "You can't really wear those shorts because they're not flattering to your figure.... But I like the way you wear those jeans. They look real good. They're tight." It's like, you know [I want to say to him],

> "You're the owner, you're in power. That's evident. You know, you need to find a better way to tell me these things." We've gotten to a point now where we'll joke around now, but it's never ever sexual ever. I won't allow that with him.

Cathy acknowledges that her manager may legitimately dictate her appearance at work, but only if he does so in professional—and not personal—terms. She wants him "to find a better way to tell me these things," implying that he is not completely out-of-line in suggesting that she wear tight pants. He "crosses the line" when he personalizes his directive, by saying to Cathy "*I like* the way you wear those jeans." This is offensive to

Cathy because it is framed as the manager's personal prerogative, not the institutional requirements of the job.

Ann described a similar experience of sexual harassment from a restaurant owner:

> Yeah, there's been a couple of times when a manager has made me feel real uncomfortable and I just removed myself from the situation.... Like if there's something I really want him to hear or something I think is really important there's no touching. Like, "Don't touch me while I'm talking to you." You know, because I take that as very patronizing. I actually blew up at one of the owners once because I was having a rough day and he came up behind me and he was rubbing my back, like up and down my back and saying, you know, "Oh, is Ann having a bad day?" or something like that and I shook him off of me and I said, "You do not need to touch me to talk to me."

Ann distinguishes between legitimate and illegitimate touching: if the issue being discussed is "really important"—that is, involving her job status—she insists there be no touching. In these specific situations, a back rub is interpreted as patronizing and offensive because the manager is using his powerful position for his *personal* sexual enjoyment.

One of the men in the sample, Frank, also experienced sexual harassment from a manager:

> I was in the bathroom and [the manager] came up next to me and my tennis shoes were spray-painted silver so he knew it was me in there and he said something about, "Oh, what do you have in your hand there?" I was on the other side of a wall and he said, "Mind if I hold it for a while?" or something like that, you know. I just pretended like I didn't hear it.

Frank also described various sexual behaviors among the waitstaff, including fondling, "joking about bodily functions," and "making bikinis out of tortillas." He said, "I mean, it's like, what we do at work.... There's no holds barred. I don't find it offensive. I'm used to it by now. I'm guilty of it myself." Evidently, he defines sexual behav-

iors as "sexual harassment" only when perpetrated by someone in a position of power over him.[4]

Two of the women in the sample also described sexual harassment from customers. We place these experiences in the category of "powerful position" because customers do have limited economic power over the waitperson insofar as they control the tip (Crull 1987). Cathy said that male customers often ask her to "sit on my lap" and provide them with other sexual favors. Brenda, a lesbian, described a similar experience of sexual harassment from women customers:

> One time I had this table of lesbians and they were being real vulgar towards me. Real sexual. This woman kind of tripped me as I was walking by and said, "Hurry back." I mean, gay people can tell when other people are gay. I felt harassed.

In these examples of harassment by customers, the line is drawn using a similar logic as in the examples of harassment by managers. These customers acted as though the waitresses were providing table service to satisfy the customers' private desires, instead of working to fulfill their job descriptions. In other words, the customers' demands were couched in personal—and not professional—terms, making the waitresses feel sexually harassed.

It is not difficult to understand why waitpeople singled out sexual behaviors from managers, owners, and customers as sexual harassment. Subjection to sexual advances by someone with economic power comes closest to the quid pro quo form of sexual harassment, wherein employees are given the option to either "put out or get out." Studies have found that this type of sexual harassment is viewed as the most threatening and unambiguous sort (Ellis et al. 1991; Fitzgerald 1990; Gruber and Bjorn 1982).

But even in this context, lines are drawn between legitimate and illegitimate sexual behavior in the workplace. As Cathy's comments make clear, some people accept the employers' prerogative to exploit the workers' sexuality, by dictating appropriate "sexy" dress, for example. Like airline attendants, waitresses are expected to be friendly, helpful, and sexually available to the male customers (Cobble 1991). Because this expectation is embedded in restaurant culture, it becomes difficult for workers to separate sexual harassment from the more or less accepted forms of sexual exploitation that are routine features of their jobs. Consequently, some women are reluctant to label blatantly offensive behaviors as sexual harassment. For example, Maxine, who claims that she has never experienced sexual harassment, said that customers often "talk dirty" to her:

I remember one day, about four or five years ago when I was working as a cocktail waitress, this guy asked me for a "Slow Comfortable Screw" [the name of a drink]. I didn't know what it was. I didn't know if he was making a move or something. I just looked at him. He said, "You know what it is, right?" I said, "I bet the bartender knows!" (laughs).... There's another one, "Sex on the Beach." And there's another one called a "Screaming Orgasm." Do you believe that?

Maxine is subject to a sexualized work environment that she finds offensive; hence her experience could fit the legal definition of sexual harassment. But because sexy drink names are an institutionalized part of restaurant culture, Maxine neither complains about it nor labels it sexual harassment: Once it becomes clear that a "Slow Comfortable Screw" is a legitimate and recognized restaurant demand, she accepts it (albeit reluctantly) as part of her job description. In other words, the fact that the offensive behavior is institutionalized seems to make it beyond reproach in her eyes. This finding is consistent with others' findings that those who work in highly sexualized environments may be less likely to label offensive behavior "sexual harassment" (Gutek 1985; Konrad and Gutek 1986).

Only in specific contexts do workers appear to define offensive words and acts of a sexual nature as sexual harassment—even when initiated by someone in a more powerful position. The interviews suggest that workers use this label to describe their experiences only when their bosses or their customers couch their requests for sexual at-

tentions in explicitly personal terms. This way of defining sexual harassment may obscure and legitimize more institutionalized—and hence more insidious—forms of sexual exploitation at work.

Race/Ethnicity

The restaurants in our sample, like most restaurants in the United States, have racially segregated staffs (Howe 1977). In the restaurants where our respondents are employed, men of color are concentrated in two positions: the kitchen cooks and bus personnel (formerly called busboys). Five of the White women in the sample reported experiencing sexual harassment from Latino men who worked in these positions. For example, when asked if she had ever experienced sexual harassment, Beth said:

Yes, but it was not with the people...it was not, you know, the people that I work with in the front of the house. It was with the kitchen. There are boundaries or lines that I draw with the people I work with. In the kitchen, the lines are quite different. Plus, it's a Mexican staff. It's a very different attitude. They tend to want to touch you more and, at times, I can put up with a little bit of it but...because I will give them a hard time too but I won't touch them. I won't touch their butt or anything like that.

[Interviewer: So sometimes they cross the line?]

It's only happened to me a couple of times. One guy, like, patted me on the butt and I went off. I lost my shit. I went off on him. I said, "No. Bad. Wrong. I can't speak Spanish to you but, you know, this is it." I told the kitchen manager who is a guy and he's not...the head kitchen manager is not Hispanic.... I've had to do that over the years only a couple of times with those guys.

Beth reported that the waitpeople joke about sex and touch each other constantly, but she does not consider their behavior sexual harassment. Like many of the other men and women in the sample, Beth said she feels comfortable engaging in this sexual banter and play with the other waitpeople (who were predominantly White), but not with the Mexican men in the kitchen.

Part of the reason for singling out the behaviors of the cooks as sexual harassment may involve status differences between waitpeople and cooks. Studies have suggested that people may label behaviors as sexual harassment when they are perpetrated by people in lower status organizational positions (Grauerholz 1989; McKinney 1990); however, it is difficult to generalize about the relative status of cooks and waitpeople because of the varied and often complex organizational hierarchies of restaurants (Paules 1991, 107–10). If the cook is a chef, as in higher-priced restaurants, he or she may actually have more status than waitpeople, and indeed may have the formal power to hire and fire the waitstaff. In the restaurants where our respondents worked, the kitchen cooks did not wield this sort of formal control, but they could exert some informal power over the waitstaff by slowing down food orders or making the orders look and/or taste bad. Because bad food can decrease the waitperson's tip, the cooks can thereby control the waitperson's income; hence servers are forced to negotiate and to some extent placate the wishes and desires of cooks to perform their jobs. The willingness of several respondents to label the cooks' behavior as sexual harassment may reflect their perception that the cooks' informal demands had become unreasonable. In such cases, subjection to the offensive behaviors is a term of employment, which is quid pro quo sexual harassment. As mentioned previously, this type of sexual harassment is the most likely to be so labeled and identified.

Because each recounted case of sexual harassment occurring between individuals of different occupational statuses involved a minority man sexually harassing a White woman, the racial context seems equally important. For example, Ann also said that she and the other waiters and waitresses joke about sex and touch each other "on the butt" all the time, and when asked if she had ever experienced sexual harassment, she said,

I had some problems at [a previous restaurant] but it was a communication problem. A lot of the guys in the kitchen did not speak English. They would see the waiters hugging on us, kissing us and

pinching our rears and stuff. They would try to do it and I couldn't tell them, "No. You don't understand this. It's like we do it because we have a mutual understanding but I'm not comfortable with you doing it." So that was really hard and a lot of times what I'd have to do is just sucker punch them in the chest and just use a lot of cuss words and they knew that I was serious. And there again, I felt real weird about that because they're just doing what they see go on everyday.

Kate, Carla, and Brenda described very similar racial double standards. Kate complained about a Mexican busser who constantly touched her:

This is not somebody that I talk to on a friendly basis. We don't sit there and laugh and joke and stuff. So, when he touches me, all I know is he is just touching me and there is no context about it. With other people, if they said something or they touched me, it would be funny or. . . we have a relationship. This person and I and all the other people do not. So that is sexual harassment.

And according to Brenda:

The kitchen can be kind of sexist. They really make me angry. They're not as bad as they used to be because they got warned. They're mostly Mexican, not even Mexican-American. Most of them, they're just starting to learn English.

[Interviewer: What do they do to you?]

Well, I speak Spanish, so I know. They're not as sexual to me because I think they know I don't like it. Some of the other girls will come through and they will touch them like here [points to the lower part of her waist]. . . . I've had some pretty bad arguments with the kitchen.

[Interviewer: Would you call that sexual harassment?]

Yes. I think some of the girls just don't know better to say something. I think it happens a lot with the kitchen guys. Like sometimes, they will take a relleno in their hands like it's a penis. Sick!

Each of these women identified the sexual advances of the minority men in their restaurants as sexual harassment, but not the identical behaviors of their white male co-workers; moreover, they all recognize that they draw boundary lines differently for Anglo men and Mexican men: each of them willingly participates in "doing heterosexuality" only in racially homogamous contexts. These women called the behavior of the Mexican cooks "sexual harassment" in part because they did not "have a relationship" with these men, nor was it conceivable to them that they *could* have a relationship with them, given cultural and language barriers—and, probably, racist attitudes as well. The white men, on the other hand, can "hug, kiss, and pinch rears" of the white women because they have a "mutual understanding"—implying reciprocity and the possibility of intimacy.

The importance of this perception of relationship potential in the assessment of sexual harassment is especially clear in the cases of the two married women in the sample, Diana and Maxine. Both of these women said that they had never experienced sexual harassment. Diana, who works in a family-owned and -operated restaurant, claimed that her restaurant is not a sexualized work environment. Although people occasionally make double entendre jokes relating to sex, according to Diana, "there's no contact whatsoever like someone pinching your butt or something." She said that she has never experienced sexual harassment:

> Everybody here knows I'm married so they're not going to get fresh with me because they know that it's not going to go anywhere, you know so... and vice versa. You know, we know the guys' wives. They come in here to eat. It's respect all the way. I don't think they could handle it if they saw us going around hugging them. You know what I mean? It's not right.

Similarly, Maxine, who is Colombian, said she avoids the problem of sexual harassment in her workplace because she is married:

> The cooks don't offend me because they know I speak Spanish and they know how to talk with me because I set my boundaries and they know that.... I just don't joke with them more than I should. They all know that I'm married, first of

> all, so that's a no-no for all of them. My brother used to be a manager in that restaurant so he probably took care of everything. I never had any problems anyway in any other jobs because, like I said, I set my boundaries. I don't let them get too close to me.

> [Interviewer: You mean physically?]

> Not physically only. Just talking. If they want to talk about, "Do you go dancing? Where do you go dancing?" Like I just change the subject because it's none of their business and I don't really care to talk about that with them... not because I consider them to be on the lower levels than me or something but just because if you start talking with them that way then you are just giving them hope or something. I think that's true for most of the guys here, not just talking about the cooks.... I do get offended and they know that so sometimes they apologize.

Both Maxine and Diana said that they are protected from sexual harassment because they are married. In effect, they use their marital status to negotiate their interactions with their co-workers and to ward off unwanted sexual advances. Furthermore, because they do not view their co-workers as potential relationship "interests," they conscientiously refuse to participate in any sexual banter in the restaurant.

The fact that both women speak Spanish fluently may mean that they can communicate their boundaries unambiguously to those who only speak Spanish (unlike the female respondents in the sample who only speak English). For these two women, sexual harassment from co-workers is not an issue. Diana, who is Latina, talks about "respect all around" in her restaurant; Maxine claims the cooks (who are Mexican) aren't the ones who offend her. Their comments seem to reflect more mutual respect and humanity toward their Latino co-workers than the comments of the white waitresses. On the other hand, at least from Maxine's vantage point, racial harassment is a bigger problem in her workplace than is sexual harassment. When asked if she ever felt excluded from any groups at work, she said:

Yeah, sometimes. How can I explain this? Sometimes, I mean, I don't know if they do it on purpose or they don't but they joke around you about being Spanish.... Sometimes it hurts. Like they say, "What are you doing here? Why don't you go back home?"

Racial harassment—like sexual harassment—is a means used by a dominant group to maintain its dominance over a subordinated group. Maxine feels that, because she is married, she is protected from sexual harassment (although, as we have seen, she is subject to a sexualized workplace that is offensive to her); however, she does experience racial harassment where she works, and she feels vulnerable to this because she is one of very few nonWhites working at her restaurant.

One of the waiters in the sample claimed that he had experienced sexual harassment from female co-workers, and race may have also been a factor in this situation. When Rick (who is African American) was asked if he had ever been sexually harassed, he recounted his experiences with some White waitresses:

Yes. There are a couple of girls there, waitpeople, who will pinch my rear.

[Interviewer: Do you find it offensive?]

No (laughs) because I'm male.... But it is a form of sexual harassment.

[Interviewer: Do you ever tell them to stop?]

If I'm really busy, if I'm in the weeds, and they want to touch me, I'll get mad. I'll tell them to stop. There's a certain time and place for everything.

Rick is reluctant about labeling this interaction "sexual harassment" because "it doesn't bother me unless I'm, like, busy or something like that." In those cases where he is busy, he feels that his female co-workers are subverting his work by pinching him. Because of the race difference, he may experience their behaviors as an expression of racial dominance, which probably influences his willingness to label the behavior as sexual harassment.

In sum, the interviews suggest that the perception and labeling of interactions as "sexual harassment" may be influenced by the racial context of the interaction. If the victim perceives the harasser as expressing a potentially reciprocal relationship interest they may be less likely to label their experience sexual harassment. In cases where the harasser and victim have a different race/ethnicity and class background, the possibility of a relationship may be precluded because of racism, making these cases more likely to be labeled "sexual harassment."

This finding suggests that the practices associated with "doing heterosexuality" are profoundly racist. The White women in the sample showed a great reluctance to label unwanted sexual behavior sexual harassment when it was perpetrated by a potential (or real) relationship interest—that is, a White male co-worker. In contrast, minority men are socially constructed as potential harassers of White women: any expression of sexual interest may be more readily perceived as nonreciprocal and unwanted. The assumption of racial homogamy in heterosexual relationships thus may protect White men from charges of sexual harassment of White women. This would help to explain why so many White women in the sample labeled behaviors perpetrated by Mexican men as sexual harassment, but not the identical behaviors perpetrated by White men.

Sexual Orientation

There has been very little research on sexual harassment that addresses the sexual orientation of the harasser and victim (exceptions include Reilly et al. 1992; Schneider 1982, 1984). Surveys of sexual harassment typically include questions about marital status but not about sexual orientation (e.g., Fain and Anderton 1987; Gruber and Bjorn 1982; Powell 1986). In this study, sexual orientation was an important part of heterosexual men's perceptions of sexual harassment. Of the four episodes of sexual harassment reported by the men in the study, three involved openly gay men sexually harassing straight men. One case involved a male manager harassing a male waiter (Frank's experience, described earlier). The other two cases involved co-workers. Jake said that he had been sexually harassed by a waiter:

> Someone has come on to me that I didn't want to come on to me.... He was another waiter [male]. It was laughs and jokes the whole way until things got a little too much and it was like, "Hey, this is how it is. Back off. Keep your hands off my ass."... Once it reached the point where I felt kind of threatened and bothered by it.

Rick described being sexually harassed by a gay baker in his restaurant:

> There was a baker that we had who was really, really gay.... He was very straightforward and blunt. He would tell you, in detail, his sexual experiences and tell you that he wanted to do them with you.... I knew he was kidding but he was serious. I mean, if he had a chance he would do these things.

In each of these cases, the men expressed some confusion about the intentions of their harassers—"I knew he was kidding but he was serious." Their inability to read the intentions of the gay men provoked them to label these episodes sexual harassment. Each man did not perceive the sexual interchange as reciprocal, nor did he view the harasser as a potential relationship interest. Interestingly, however, all three of the men who described harassment from gay men claimed that sexual banter and play with other *straight* men did not trouble them. Jake, for example, said that "when men get together, they talk sex," regardless of whether there are women around. He acceded, "people find me offensive, as a matter of fact," because he gets "pretty raunchy" talking and joking about sex. Only when this talk was initiated by a gay man did Jake label it as sexual harassment.

Johnson (1988) argues that talking and joking about sex is a common means of establishing intimacy among heterosexual men and maintaining a masculine identity. Homosexuality is perceived as a direct challenge and threat to the achievement of masculinity and consequently, "the male homo-

sexual is derided by other males because he is not a real man, and in male logic if one is not a real man, one is a woman" (p. 124). In Johnson's view, this dynamic not only sustains masculine identity, it also shores up male dominance over women; thus, for some straight men, talking about sex with other straight men is a form of reasserting masculinity and male dominance, whereas talking about sex with gay men threatens the very basis for their masculine privilege. For this reason they may interpret the sex talk and conduct of gay men as a form of sexual harassment.

In certain restaurants, gay men may in fact intentionally hassle straight men as an explicit strategy to undermine their privileged position in society. For example, Trent (who is openly gay) realizes that heterosexual men are uncomfortable with his sexuality, and he intentionally draws attention to his sexuality in order to bother them:

> [Interviewer: Homosexuality gets on whose nerves?]
>
> The straight people's nerves.... I know also that we consciously push it just because, we know, "Okay. We know this is hard for you to get used to but tough luck. I've had my whole life trying to live in this straight world and if you don't like this, tough shit." I don't mean like we're shitty to them on purpose but it's like, "I've had to worry about being accepted by straight people all my life. The shoe's on the other foot now. If you don't like it, sorry."
>
> [Interviewer: Do you get along well with most of the waitpeople?]
>
> I think I get along with straight women. I get along with gay men. I get along with gay women usually. If there's ever going to be a problem between me and somebody it will be between me and a straight man.

Trent's efforts to "push" his sexuality could easily be experienced as sexual harassment by straight men who have limited experience negotiating unwanted sexual advances. The three men who reported being sexually harassed by gay men seemed genuinely confused about the intentions of their harassers, and threatened by the possibility that they would actually be subjected to and harmed by unwanted sexual advances. But it is important to point out that Trent works in a restaurant owned by lesbians, which empowers him to confront his straight male co-workers. Not all restaurants provide the sort of atmosphere that makes this type of engagement possible; indeed, some restaurants have policies explicitly banning the hiring of gays and lesbians. Clearly, not all gay men would be able to push their sexuality without suffering severe retaliation (e.g., loss of job, physical attacks).

In contrast to the reports of the straight men in this study, none of the women interviewed reported sexual harassment from their gay or lesbian co-workers. Although Maxine was worried when she found out that one of her co-workers was lesbian, she claims that this fact no longer troubles her:

Six months ago I found out that there was a lesbian girl working there. It kind of freaked me out for a while. I was kind of aware of everything that she did towards me. I was conscious if she walked by me and accidently brushed up against me. She's cool. She doesn't bother me. She never touches my butt or anything like that. The gay guys do that to the [straight] guys but they know they're just kidding around. The [straight] guys do that to the [straight] girls, but they don't care. They know that they're not supposed to do that with me. If they do it, I stop and look at them and they apologize and they don't do it anymore. So they stay out of my way because I'm a meanie (laughs).

Some heterosexual women claimed they feel *more* comfortable working with gay men and lesbians. For example, Kate prefers working with gay men rather than heterosexual men or women. She claims that she often jokes about sex with her gay co-workers, yet she does not view them as potential harassers. Instead, she feels that her working conditions are more comfortable and more fun because she works with gay men. Similarly, Cathy prefers working with gay men over straight men because "gay men are a lot like women in that

they're very sensitive to other people's space." Cathy also works with lesbians, and she claims that she has never felt sexually harassed by them.

The gays and lesbians in the study did not report any sexual harassment from their gay and lesbian co-workers. Laura, who is bisexual, said she preferred to work with gays and lesbians instead of heterosexuals because they are "more relaxed" about sex. Brenda said she feels comfortable working around all of her male and female colleagues—regardless of their sexual orientation:

The guys I work with [don't threaten me]. We always run by each other and pat each other on the butt. It's no big deal. Like with my girlfriend [who works at the same restaurant], all the cocktailers and hostesses love us. They don't care that we're gay. We're not a threat. We all kind of flirt but it's not sexual. A lesbian is not going to sexually harass another woman unless they're pretty gross anyway. It has nothing to do with their sexuality; it has to do with the person. You can't generalize and say that gays and lesbians are the best to work with or anything because it depends on the person.

Brenda enjoys flirtatious interactions with both men and women at her restaurant, but distinguishes these behaviors from sexual harassment. Likewise, Lynn, who is a lesbian, enjoys the relaxed sexual atmosphere at her workplace. When asked if she ever joked about sex in her workplace, she said:

Yes! (laughs) All the time! All the time—everybody has something that they want to talk about on sex and it's got to be funny. We have gays. We have lesbians. We have straights. We have people who are real Christian-oriented. But we all jump in there and we all talk about it. It gets real funny at times.... I've patted a few butts...and I've been patted back by men, and by the women, too! (laughs)

Don and Trent, who are both gay, also said that they had never been sexually harassed in their restaurants, even though both described their restaurants as highly sexualized.

In sum, our interviews suggest that sexual orientation is an important factor in understanding each individual's experience of sexual harassment and his or her willingness to label interactions as sexual harassment. In particular, straight men may perceive gay men as potential harassers. Three of our straight male respondents claimed to enjoy the sexual banter that commonly occurs among straight men, and between heterosexual men and women, but singled out the sexual advances of gay men as sexual harassment. Their contacts with gay men may be the only context where they feel vulnerable to unwanted sexual encounters. Their sense of not being in control of the situation may make them more willing to label these episodes sexual harassment.

Our findings about sexual orientation are less suggestive regarding women. None of the women (straight, lesbian, or bisexual) reported sexual harassment from other female co-workers or from gay men. In fact, all but one of the women's reported cases of sexual harassment involved a heterosexual man. One of the two lesbians in the sample (Brenda) did experience sexual harassment from a group of lesbian customers (described earlier), but she claimed that sexual orientation is not key to her defining the situation as harassment. Other studies have shown that lesbian and bisexual women are routinely subjected to sexual harassment in the workplace (Schneider 1982, 1984); however, more research is needed to elaborate the social contexts and the specific definitions of harassment among lesbians.

The Exceptions

Two cases of sexual harassment were related by respondents that do not fit in the categories we have thus far described. These were the only incidents of sexual harassment reported between co-workers of the same race: in both cases, the sexual harasser is a white man, and the victim, a white woman. Laura—who is bisexual—was sexually harassed at a previous restaurant by a cook:

This guy was just constantly badgering me about going out with him. He like grabbed me and took me in the walk-in one time. It was a real big deal. He got fired over it too.... I was in the back doing

something and he said, "I need to talk to you," and I said, "We have nothing to talk about." He like took me and threw me against the wall in the back.... I ran out and told the manager, "Oh my God. He just hit me," and he saw the expression on my face. The manager went back there ... and then he got fired.

This episode of sexual harassment involved violence, unlike the other reported cases. The threat of violence was also present in the other exception, a case described by Carla. When asked if she had ever been sexually harassed, she said,

I experienced two men, in wait jobs, that were vulgar or offensive and one was a cook and I think he was a rapist. He had the kind of attitude where he would rape a woman. I mean, that's the kind of attitude he had. He would say totally, totally inappropriate [sexual] things.

These were the only two recounted episodes of sexual harassment between "equal" co-workers that involved white men and women, and both involved violence or the threat of violence.[5]

Schneider (1982, 1991) found the greatest degree of consensus about labeling behavior sexual harassment when that behavior involves violence. A victim of sexual harassment may be more likely to be believed when there is evidence of assault (a situation that is analogous to acquaintance rape). The assumption of reciprocity among homogamous couples may protect assailants with similar characteristics to their victims (e.g., class background, sexual orientation, race/ethnicity, age)—*unless* there is clear evidence of physical abuse. Defining only those incidents that involve violence as sexual harassment obscures—and perhaps even legitimizes—the more common occurrences that do not involve violence, making it all the more difficult to eradicate sexual harassment from the workplace.

DISCUSSION AND CONCLUSION

We have argued that sexual harassment is hard to identify, and thus difficult to eradicate from the workplace, in part because our hegemonic definition of sexuality defines certain contexts of sexual interaction as legitimate. The interviews with wait-people in Austin, Texas, indicate that how people currently identify sexual harassment singles out only a narrow range of interactions, thus disguising and ignoring a good deal of sexual domination and exploitation that take place at work.

Most of the respondents in this study work in highly sexualized atmospheres where sexual banter and touching frequently occur. There are institutionalized policies and practices in the workplace that encourage—or at the very least tolerate—a continual display and performance of heterosexuality. Many people apparently accept this ritual display as being a normal or natural feature of their work; some even enjoy this behavior. In the in-depth interviews, respondents labeled such experiences as sexual harassment in only three contexts: when perpetrated by someone who took advantage of their powerful position for personal sexual gain; when the perpetrator was of a different race/ethnicity than the victim—typically a minority man harassing a white woman; and when the perpetrator was of a different sexual orientation than the victim—typically a gay man harassing a straight man. In only two cases did respondents label experiences involving co-workers of the same race and sexual orientation as sexual harassment—and both episodes involved violence or the threat of violence.

These findings are based on a very small sample in a unique working environment, and hence it is not clear whether they are generalizable to other work settings. In less sexualized working environments, individuals may be more likely to label all offensive sexual advances as sexual harassment, whereas in more highly sexualized environments (such as topless clubs or striptease bars), fewer sexual advances may be labeled sexual harassment. Our findings do suggest that researchers should pay closer attention to the interaction context of sexual harassment taking into account not only gender but also the race, occupational status, and sexual orientation of the assailant and the victim.

Of course, it should not matter who is perpetrating the sexually harassing behavior: sexual harassment should not be tolerated under any cir-cumstances. But if members of oppressed groups (racial/ethnic minority men and gay men) are selectively charged with sexual harassment, whereas members of the most privileged groups are exonerated and excused (except in cases where institutionalized power or violence are used), then the patriarchal order is left intact. This is very similar to the problem of rape prosecution: minority men are the most likely assailants to be arrested and prosecuted, particularly when they attack white women (LaFree 1989). Straight white men who sexually assault women (in the context of marriage, dating, or even work) may escape prosecution because of hegemonic definitions of "acceptable" or "legitimate" sexual expression. Likewise, as we have witnessed in the current debate on gays in the military, straight men's fears of sexual harassment justify the exclusion of gay men and lesbians, whereas sexual harassment perpetrated by straight men against both straight and lesbian women is tolerated and even endorsed by the military establishment, as in the Tailhook investigation (Britton and Williams, forthcoming). By singling out these contexts for the label "sexual harassment," only marginalized men will be prosecuted, and the existing power structure that guarantees privileged men's sexual access to women will remain intact.

Sexual interactions involving men and women of the same race and sexual orientation have a hegemonic status in our society, making sexual harassment difficult to identify and eradicate. Our interviews suggest that many men and women are active participants in the sexualized culture of the workplace, even though ample evidence indicates that women who work in these environments suffer negative repercussions to their careers because of it (Jaschik and Fretz 1991; Paludi and Barickman 1991; Reilly et al. 1992; Schneider 1982). This is how cultural hegemony works—by getting under our skins and defining what is and is not pleasurable to us, despite our material or emotional interests.

Our findings raise difficult issues about women's complicity with oppressive sexual relationships. Some women obviously experience pleasure and enjoyment from public forms of sexual engagement with men; clearly, many would resist any attempt to eradicate all sexuality from work—an impossible goal at any rate. Yet it is also clear that the sexual "pleasure" many women seek out and enjoy at work is structured by patriarchal, racist, and heterosexist norms. Heterosexual, racially homogamous relationships are privileged in our society: they are institutionalized in organizational policies and job descriptions, embedded in ritualistic workplace practices, and accepted as legitimate, normal, or inevitable elements of workplace culture. This study suggests that only those sexual interactions that violate these policies, practices, and beliefs are resisted and condemned with the label "sexual harassment."

We have argued that this dominant social construction of pleasure protects the most privileged groups in society from charges of sexual harassment and may be used to oppress and exclude the least powerful groups. Currently, people seem to consider the gender, race, status, and sexual orientation of the assailant when deciding to label behaviors as sexual harassment. Unless we acknowledge the complex double standards people use in "drawing the line," then sexual domination and exploitation will undoubtedly remain the normative experience of women in the workforce.

NOTES

1. It could be the case that those who find this behavior extremely offensive are likely to leave restaurant work. In other words, the sample is clearly biased in that it includes only those who are currently employed in a restaurant and presumably feel more comfortable with the level of sexualized behavior than those who have left restaurant work.

2. It is difficult, if not impossible, to specify which occupations are less highly sexualized than waiting tables. Most occupations probably are sexualized in one way or another; however, specific workplaces may be more or less sexualized in terms of institutionalized job descriptions and employee tolerance of sexual banter. For example, Pringle (1988) describes some offices as coolly professional—with minimal sexual joking and play—whereas others are characterized by "compulsory jocularity." Likewise, some restaurants may de-emphasize sexual flirtation between waitpeople and customers, and restrain informal interactions among the staff (one respondent in our sample worked at such a restaurant).

3. We thank Margaret Andersen for drawing our attention to this fruitful analogy.

4. It is also probably significant that this episode of harassment involved a gay man and a heterosexual man. This context of sexual harassment is discussed later in this article.

5. It is true that both cases involved cooks sexually harassing waitresses. We could have placed these cases in the "powerful position" category, but did not because in these particular instances, the cooks did not possess institutionalized power over the waitpeople. In other words, in these particular cases, the cook and waitress had equal organizational status in the restaurant.

REFERENCES

Anders, K. T. 1993. Bad sex: Who's harassing whom in restaurants? *Restaurant Business,* 20 January, pp. 46–54.

Benson, Donna J., and Gregg E. Thomson. 1982. Sexual harassment on a university campus: The confluence of authority relations, sexual interest and gender stratification. *Social Problems* 29:236–51.

Britton, Dana M., and Christine L. Williams. Forthcoming. Don't ask, don't tell, don't pursue: Military policy and the construction of heterosexual masculinity. *Journal of Homosexuality.*

Carothers, Suzanne C., and Peggy Crull. 1984. Contrasting sexual harassment in female- and male-dominated occupations. In *My troubles are going to have trouble with me: Everyday trials and triumphs of women workers,* edited by K. B. Sacks and D. Remy. New Brunswick, NJ: Rutgers University Press.

Cobble, Dorothy Sue. 1991. *Dishing it out: Waitresses and their unions in the twentieth century.* Urbana: University of Illinois Press.

Cockburn. Cynthia. 1991. *In the way of women.* Ithaca, NY: I.L.R. Press.

Crull, Peggy. 1987. Searching for the causes of sexual harassment: An examination of two prototypes. In *Hidden aspects of women's work,* edited by Christine Bose, Roslyn Feldberg, and Natalie Sokoloff. New York: Praeger.

Ellis, Shmuel, Azy Barak, and Adaya Pinto. 1991. Moderating effects of personal cognitions on experienced and perceived sexual harassment of women at the workplace. *Journal of Applied Social Psychology* 21:1320–37,

Fain, Terri C., and Douglas L. Anderton. 1987. Sexual harassment: Organizational context and diffuse status. *Sex Roles* 17:291–311.

Fitzgerald, Louise F. 1990. Sexual harassment: The definition and measurement of a construct. In *Ivory power: Sexual harassment on campus,* edited by Michele M. Paludi. Albany: State University of New York Press.

Grauerholz, Elizabeth. 1989. Sexual harassment of women professors by students: Exploring the dynamics of power, authority, and gender in a university setting. *Sex Roles* 21:789–801.

Gruber, James E., and Lars Bjorn. 1982. Blue-collar blues: The sexual harassment of women auto workers. *Work and Occupations* 9:271–98.

Gutek, B. A. 1985. *Sex and the workplace.* San Francisco: Jossey-Bass.

Hall, Elaine J. 1993. Waitering/waitressing: Engendering the work of table servers. *Gender & Society* 7:329–46.

Howe, Louise Kapp. 1977. *Pink collar workers: Inside the world of women's work.* New York: Avon.

Jaschik, Mollie L., and Bruce R. Fretz. 1991. Women's perceptions and labeling of sexual harassment. *Sex Roles* 25:19–23.

Jensen, Inger W., and Barbara A. Gutek. 1982. Attributions and assignment of responsibility in sexual harassment. *Journal of Social Issues* 38:122–36.

Johnson, Miriam. 1988. *Strong mothers, weak wives.* Berkeley: University of California Press.

Konrad, Alison M., and Barbara A. Gutek. 1996. Impact of work experiences on attitudes toward sexual harassment. *Administrative Science Quarterly* 31:422–38.

LaFree, Gary D. 1989. *Rape and criminal justice: The social construction of sexual assault.* Belmont, CA: Wadsworth.

MacKinnon, Catherine A. 1979. *Sexual harassment of working women: A case of sex discrimination.* New Haven, CT: Yale University Press.

McKinney, Kathleen. 1990. Sexual harassment of university faculty by colleagues and students. *Sex Roles* 23:421–38.

Paludi, Michele, and Richard B. Barickman. 1991. *Academic and workplace sexual harassment.* Albany: State University of New York Press.

Paules, Greta Foff. 1991. *Dishing it out: Power and resistance among waitresses in a New Jersey restaurant.* Philadelphia. Temple University Press.

Powell, Gary N. 1986. Effects of sex role identity and sex on definitions of sexual harassment. *Sex Roles* 14:9–19.

Pringle, Rosemary. 1988. *Secretaries talk: Sexuality, power and work.* London: Verso.

Pryor, John B. 1987. Sexual harassment proclivities in men. *Sex Roles* 17:269–90.

Reilly, Mary Ellen, Bernice Lott, Donna Caldwell, and Luisa DeLuca. 1992. Tolerance for sexual harassment related to self-reported sexual victimization. *Gender & Society* 6:122–38.

Rich, Adrienne, 1980. Compulsory heterosexuality and lesbian existence. *Signs* 5:631–60.

Schneider, Beth E. 1982. Consciousness about sexual harassment among heterosexual and lesbian women workers. *Journal of Social Issues* 38:75–98.

———. 1984. The office affair. Myth and reality for heterosexual and lesbian women workers. *Sociological Perspectives* 27:443–64.

———. 1991. Put up and shut up: Workplace sexual assaults. *Gender & Society* 5:533–48.

U.S. Department of Labor, Bureau of Labor Statistics. 1989, January. *Employment and earnings.* Washington, DC: Government Printing Office.

West, Candace, and Don H. Zimmerman. 1987. Doing gender. *Gender & Society* 1:125–51.

41

"Their Logic against Them"

Contradictions in Sex, Race, and Class in Silicon Valley

KAREN J. HOSSFELD

The bosses here have this type of reasoning like a seesaw. One day it's "you're paid less because women are different than men," or "immigrants need less to get by." The next day it's "you're all just workers here—no special treatment just because you're female or foreigners."

Well, they think they're pretty clever with their doubletalk, and that we're just a bunch of dumb aliens. But it takes two to use a seesaw. What we're gradually figuring out here is how to use their own logic against them.

—*Filipina circuit board assembler in Silicon Valley (emphasis added)*

This chapter examines how contradictory ideologies about sex, race, class, and nationality are used as forms of both labor control and labor resistance in the capitalist workplace today. Specifically, I look at the workplace relationships between Third World immigrant women production workers and their predominantly white male managers in high-tech manufacturing industry in Silicon Valley, California. My findings indicate that in workplaces where managers and workers are divided by sex and race, class struggle can and does take gender- and race-specific forms. Managers encourage women immigrant workers to identify with their gender, racial, and national identities when the managers want to "distract" the workers from their class concerns about working conditions. Similarly, when workers have workplace needs that actually are defined by gender, nationality, or race, managers tend to deny these identities and to stress the workers' generic class position. Immigrant women workers have learned to redeploy their managers' gender and racial tactics to their own advantage, however, in or-der to gain more control over their jobs. As the Filipina worker quoted at the beginning of the chapter so aptly said, they have learned to use managers' "own logic against them.". . .

This chapter draws from a larger study of the articulation of sex, race, class, and nationality in the lives of immigrant women high-tech workers (Hossfeld 1988b). Empirical data draw on more than two hundred interviews conducted between 1982 and 1986 with Silicon Valley workers; their family members, employers, and managers; and labor and community organizers. Extensive in-depth interviews were conducted with eighty-four immigrant women, representing twenty-one Third World nationalities, and with forty-one employers and managers, who represented twenty-three firms. All but five of these management representatives were U.S.-born White males. All of the workers and managers were employed in Santa Clara County, California, firms that engaged in some aspect of semiconductor "chip" manufacturing. I observed production at nineteen of these firms. . . .

SILICON VALLEY

"Silicon Valley" refers to the microelectronics-based high-tech industrial region located just south of San Francisco in Santa Clara County, California.[1]...

Class Structure and the Division of Labor

Close to 200,000 people—one out of every four employees in the San Jose Metropolitan Statistical Area labor force—work in Silicon Valley's microelectronics industry. There are more than 800 manufacturing firms that hire ten or more people each, including 120 "large" firms that each count over 250 employees. An even larger number of small firms hire fewer than ten employees apiece. Approximately half of this high-tech labor force—100,000 employees—works in production-related work: at least half of these workers—an estimated 50,000 to 70,000—are in low-paying, semiskilled operative jobs (Siegel and Borock 1982; *Annual Planning Information* 1983).[2]

The division of labor within the industry is dramatically skewed according to gender and race. Although women account for close to half of the total paid labor force in Santa Clara County both inside and outside the industry, only 18 percent of the managers, 17 percent of the professional employees, and 25 percent of the technicians are female. Conversely, women hold at least 68 percent and by some reports as many as 85 to 90 percent of the valley's high-tech operative jobs. In the companies examined in my study, women made up an average of 90 percent of the assembly and operative workers. Only rarely do they work as production managers or supervisors, the management area that works most closely with the operatives.

Similar disparities exist vis-à-vis minority employment....

Within the microelectronics industry, 12 percent of the managers, 16 percent of the professionals, and 18 percent of the technicians are minorities—although they are concentrated at the lower-paying and less powerful ends of these categories. An estimated 50 to 75 percent of the operative jobs are thought to be held by minorities.[3] My study suggests that the figure may be closer to 80 percent.

Both employers and workers interviewed in this study agreed that the lower the skill and pay level of the job, the higher the percentage of Third World immigrant women who were employed. Thus assembly work, which is the least skilled and lowest-paying production job, tends to be done predominantly by Third World women....

This occupational structure is typical of the industry's division of labor nationwide. The percentage of women of color in operative jobs is fairly standardized throughout various high-tech centers; what varies is *which* minority groups are employed, not the job categories in which they are employed.[4]

Obviously, there is tremendous cultural and historical variation both between and within the diverse national groups that my informants represent. Here I emphasize their commonalities. Their collective experience is based on their jobs, present class status, recent uprooting, and immigration. Many are racial and ethnic minorities for the first time. Finally, they have in common their gender and their membership in family households.

LABOR CONTROL ON THE SHOP FLOOR

Gender and Racial Logic

In Silicon Valley production shops, the ideological battleground is an important arena of class struggle for labor control. Management frequently calls upon ideologies and arrangements concerning sex and race, as well as class, to manipulate worker consciousness and to legitimate the hierarchical division of labor. Management taps both traditional popular stereotypes about the presumed lack of status and limited abilities of women, minorities, and immigrants and the workers' own fears, concerns, and sense of priorities as immigrant women.

But despite management's success in disempowering and devaluing labor, immigrant women workers have co-opted some of these ideologies and have developed others of their own, playing on management's prejudices to the workers' own advantage. In so doing, the workers turn the "logic" of capital against managers, as they do the intertwining logics of patriarchy and racism. The following section examines this sex- and race-based logic and how it affects class structure and struggle. I then focus on women's resistance to this manipulation and their use of gender and racial logics for their own advantage.

From interviews with Silicon Valley managers and employers, it is evident that high-tech firms find immigrant women particularly appealing workers not only because they are "cheap" and considered easily "expendable" but also because management can draw on and further exploit pre-existing patriarchal and racist ideologies and arrangements that have affected these women's consciousness and realities. In their dealings with the women, managers fragment the women's multifaceted identities into falsely separated categories of "worker," "ethnic," and "woman." The effect is to increase and play off the workers' vulnerabilities and splinter their consciousness. But I also found limited examples of the women drawing strength from their multifaceted experiences and developing a unified consciousness with which to confront their oppressions. These instances of how the workers have manipulated management's ideology are important not only in their own right but as models. To date, though, management holds the balance of power in this ideological struggle.

I label management's tactics "gender-specific" and "racial-specific" forms of labor control and struggle, or gender and racial "logic." I use the term *capital logic* to refer to strategies by capitalists to increase profit maximization. Enforcement by employers of a highly stratified class division of labor as a form of labor control is one such strategy. Similarly, I use the terms *gender logic* and *racial logic* to refer to strategies to promote gender and racial hierarchies. Here I am concerned primarily with the ways in which em-

ployers and managers devise and incorporate gender and racial logic in the interests of capital logic. Attempts to legitimate inequality form my main examples.

I focus primarily on managers' "gender-specific" tactics because management uses race-specific (il)logic much less directly in dealing with workers. Management clearly draws on racist assumptions in hiring and dealing with its workforce, but usually it makes an effort to conceal its racism from workers. Management recognizes, to varying degrees, that the appearance of blatant racism against workers is not acceptable, mainly because immigrants have not sufficiently internalized racism to respond to it positively. Off the shop floor, however, the managers' brutal and open racism toward workers was apparent during "private" interviews. Managers' comments demonstrate that racism is a leading factor in capital logic but that management typically disguises racist logic by using the more socially acceptable "immigrant logic." Both American and immigrant workers tend to accept capital's relegation of immigrants to secondary status in the labor market.

Conversely, "gender logic" is much less disguised: management uses it freely and directly to control workers. Patriarchal and sexist ideology is *not* considered inappropriate. Because women workers themselves have already internalized patriarchal ideology, they are more likely to "agree" with or at least accept it than they are racist assumptions. This chapter documents a wide range of sexist assumptions that management employs in order to control and divide workers.

Gender Ideology

A growing number of historical and contemporary studies illustrate the interconnections between patriarchy and capitalism in defining both the daily lives of working women and the nature of work arrangements in general. Sallie Westwood, for example, suggests that on-the-job exploitation of women workers is rooted in part in patriarchal ideology. Westwood states that ideologies "play a vital part in calling forth a sense of self linked to class and gender as well as race. Thus, a patriarchal ideology intervenes on the shop floor culture to make anew the conditions of work under capitalism" (1985:6).

One way in which patriarchal ideology affects workplace culture is through the "gendering" of workers—what Westwood refers to as "the social construction of masculinity and femininity on the shop floor" (page 6). The forms of work culture that managers encourage, and that women workers choose to develop, are those that reaffirm traditional forms of femininity. This occurs in spite of the fact that, or more likely because, the women are engaged in roles that are traditionally defined as nonfeminine: factory work and wage earning. My data suggest that although factory work and wage earning are indeed traditions long held by working-class women, the dominant *ideology* that such tasks are "unfeminine" is equally traditional. For example, I asked one Silicon Valley assembler who worked a double shift to support a large family how she found time and finances to obtain elaborate manicures, makeup, and hair stylings. She said that they were priorities because they "restored [her] sense of femininity." Another production worker said that factory work "makes me feel like I'm not a lady, so I have to try to compensate."

This ideology about what constitutes proper identity and behavior for women is multileveled. First, women workers have a clear sense that wage earning and factory work in general are not considered "feminine." This definition of "feminine" derives from an upper-class reality in which women traditionally did not need (and men often did not allow them) to earn incomes. The reality for a production worker who comes from a long line of factory women does not negate the dominant ideology that influences her to say, "At work I feel stripped of my womanhood. I feel like I'm not a lady anymore. It makes me feel . . . unattractive and unfeminine."

Second, women may feel "unwomanly" at work because they are away from home and fam-

ily, which conflicts with ideologies, albeit changing ones, that they should be home. And third, earning wages at all is considered "unwifely" by some women, by their husbands, or both because it strips men of their identity as "breadwinner."

On the shop floor, managers encourage workers to associate "femininity" with something contradictory to factory work. They also encourage women workers to "compensate" for their perceived loss of femininity. This strategy on the part of management serves to devalue women's productive worth.

Under contemporary U.S. capitalism, ideological legitimation of women's societal roles and of their related secondary position in the division of labor is already strong outside the workplace. Management thus does not need to devote extreme efforts to developing new sexist ideologies within the workplace in order to legitimate the gender division of labor. Instead, managers can call on and reinforce preexisting ideology. Nonetheless, new forms of gender ideology are frequently introduced. These old and new ideologies are disseminated both on an individual basis, from a manager to a worker or workers, and on a collective basis, through company programs, policies, and practices. Specific examples of informal ways in which individual managers encourage gender identification, such as flirting, dating, sexual harassment, and promoting "feminine" behavior, are given below. The most widespread company practice that encourages engenderment, of course, is hiring discrimination and job segregation based on sex.

An example of a company policy that divides workers by gender is found in a regulation one large firm has regarding color-coding of smocks that all employees in the manufacturing division are required to wear. While the men's smocks are color-coded according to occupation, the women's are color-coded by sex, regardless of occupation. This is a classic demonstration of management's encouragement of male workers to identify according to job and class and its discouragement of women from doing the same. Regardless of what women do as workers, the underlying message reads, they are nevertheless primarily women. The same company has other practices and programs that convey the same message. Their company newsletter, for example, includes a column entitled "Ladies' Corner," which runs features on cooking and fashion tips for "the working gal." A manager at this plant says that such "gender tactics," as I call them, are designed to "boost morale by reminding the gals that even though they do unfeminine work, they really are still feminine." But although some women workers may value femininity, in the work world, management identifies feminine traits as legitimation for devaluation.

In some places, management offers "refeminization" perks to help women feel "compensated" for their perceived "defeminization" on the job. A prime example is the now well-documented makeup sessions and beauty pageants for young women workers sponsored by multinational electronics corporations at their Southeast Asian plants (Grossman 1979; Ong 1985). While such events are unusual in Silicon Valley, male managers frequently use flirting and dating as "refeminization" strategies. Flirting and dating in and of themselves certainly cannot be construed as capitalist plots to control workers; however, when they are used as false compensation for and to divert women from poor working conditions and workplace alienation, they in effect serve as a form of labor control. In a society where women are taught that their femininity is more important than other aspects of their lives—such as how they relate to their work—flirting can be divisive. And when undesired, flirting can also develop into a form of sexual harassment, which causes further workplace alienation.

One young Chinese production worker told me that she and a co-worker avoided filing complaints about illegal and unsafe working conditions because they did not want to annoy their White male supervisor, whom they enjoyed having flirt with them. These two women would never join a union, they told me, because the same supervisor told them that all women who join

unions "are a bunch of tough, big-mouthed dykes." Certainly these women have the option of ignoring this man's opinions. But that is not easy, given the one-sided power he has over them not only because he is their supervisor, but because of his age, race, and class.

When women workers stress their "feminine" and female characteristics as being counter to their waged work, a contradictory set of results can occur. On one hand, the women may legitimate their own devaluation as workers, and, in seeking identity and solace in their "femininity," discard any interest in improving their working conditions. On the other hand, if turning to their identities as female, mother, mate, and such allows them to feel self-esteem in one arena of their lives, that self-esteem may transfer to other arenas. The outcome is contingent on the ways in which the women define and experience themselves as female or "feminine." Femininity in white American capitalist culture is traditionally defined as passive and ineffectual, as Susan Brownmiller explores (1984). But there is also a female tradition of resistance.

The women I interviewed rarely pose their womanhood or their self-perceived femininity as attributes meriting higher pay or better treatment. They expect *differential* treatment because they are women, but "differential" inevitably means lower paid in the work world. The women present their self-defined female attributes as creating additional needs that detract from their financial value. Femininity, although its definition varies among individuals and ethnic groups, is generally viewed as something that subtracts from a woman's market value, even though a majority of women consider it personally desirable.

In general, both the women and men I interviewed believe that women have many needs and skills discernible from those of male workers, but they accept the ideology that such specialness renders them less deserving than men of special treatment, wages, promotions, and status. Conversely, both the men and women viewed men's special needs and skills as rendering men more deserving.

Two of the classic perceived sex differentials cited by employers in electronics illustrate this point. First, although Silicon Valley employers consistently repeat the old refrain that women are better able than men to perform work requiring manual skills, strong hand-eye coordination, and extreme patience, they nonetheless find it appropriate to pay workers who have these skills (women) less than workers who supposedly do not have them (men). Second, employers say that higher entry-level jobs, wages, and promotions rightly belong to heads of households, but in practice they give such jobs only to men, regardless of their household situation, and exclude women, regardless of theirs.

When a man expresses special needs that result from his structural position in the family—such as head of household—he is often "compensated," yet when a woman expresses a special need resulting from her traditional structural position in the family-child care or her position as head of household—she is told that such issues are not of concern to the employer or, in the case of child care, that it detracts from her focus on her work and thus devalues her productive contribution. This is a clear illustration of Heidi Hartmann's definition of patriarchy: social relationships between men, which, although hierarchical, such as those between employer and worker, have a material base that benefits men and oppresses women (1976).

Definitions of femininity and masculinity not only affect the workplace but are in turn affected by it. Gender is produced and reproduced in and through the workplace, as well as outside it. Gender identities and relationships are formed on the work floor both by the labor process organized under capitalism and by workers' resistance to that labor process. "Femininity" in its various permutations is not something all-bad and all-disempowering: women find strength, pride, and creativity in some of its forms. . . . I turn now to one of the other tenets of women workers' multitiered consciousness that employers find advantageous: gender logic that poses women's work as "secondary."

THE LOGIC OF "SECONDARY" WORK

Central to gender-specific capital logic is the assumption that women's paid work is both secondary and temporary. More than 70 percent of the employers and 80 percent of the women workers I interviewed stated that a woman's primary jobs are those of wife, mother, and homemaker, even when she works full time in the paid labor force. Because employers view women's primary job as in the home, and they assume that, prototypically, every woman is connected to a man who is bringing in a larger paycheck, they claim that women do not need to earn a full living wage. Employers repeatedly asserted that they believed the low-level jobs were filled only by women because men could not afford to or would not work for such low wages.

Indeed, many of the women would not survive on what they earned unless they pooled resources. For some, especially the nonimmigrants, low wages did mean dependency on men—or at least on family networks and household units. None of the women I interviewed—immigrant or nonimmigrant—lived alone. Yet most of them would be financially better off without their menfolk. For most of the immigrant women, their low wages were the most substantial and steady source of their family's income. *Eighty percent of the immigrant women workers in my study were the largest per annum earners in their households.*

Even when their wages were primary—the main or only family income—the women still considered men to be the major breadwinners. The women considered their waged work as secondary, both in economic value and as a source of identity. Although most agreed that women and men who do exactly the same jobs should be paid the same, they had little expectation that as women they would be eligible for higher-paying "male" jobs. While some of these women—particularly the Asians—believed they could overcome racial and class barriers in the capitalist division of labor, few viewed gender as a division that could be changed. While they may believe that hard work can overcome many obstacles and raise their *families'* socioeconomic class standing, they do not feel that their position in the gender division of labor will change. Many, of course, expect or hope for better jobs for themselves—and others expect or hope to leave the paid labor force altogether—but few wish to enter traditional male jobs or to have jobs that are higher in status or earnings than the men in their families.

The majority of women who are earning more than their male family members view their situation negatively and hope it will change soon. They do not want to earn less than they currently do; rather, they want their menfolk to earn more. This was true of women in all the ethnic groups. . . .

As in the rest of America, in most cases, the men earned more in those households where both the women and men worked regularly. In many of the families, however, the men tended to work less regularly than the women and to have higher unemployment rates. While most of the families vocally blamed very real socioeconomic conditions for the unemployment, such as declines in "male" industrial sector jobs, many women also felt that their husbands took out their resentment on their families. A young Mexicana, who went to a shelter for battered women after her husband repeatedly beat her, described her extreme situation:

> He knows it's not his fault or my fault that he lost his job: they laid off almost his whole shift. But he acts like I keep my job just to spite him, and it's gotten so I'm so scared of him. Sometimes I think he'd rather kill me or have us starve than watch me go to work and bring home pay. He doesn't want to hurt me, but he is so hurt inside because he feels he has failed as a man.

Certainly not all laid-off married men go to the extreme of beating their wives, but the majority of married women workers whose husbands had gone through periods of unemployment said that the men treated other family members significantly worse when they were out of work. When capitalism rejects male workers, they often use patriarchal channels to vent their anxieties. In a world where men are defined by their control over their environment, losing control in one arena, such as that of the work world, may lead them to tighten control in another arena in which they still have power—the family. This classic cycle is not unique to Third World immigrant communities, but as male unemployment increases in these communities, so may the cycle of male violence.

Even some of the women who recognize the importance of their economic role feel that their status and identity as wage earners are less important than those of men. Many of the women feel that men work not only for income but for respect and dignity. They see their own work as less noble. Although some said they derive satisfaction from their ability to hold a job, none of the women considered her job to be a primary part of her identity or a source of self-esteem. These women see themselves as responsible primarily for the welfare of their families: their main identity is as mother, wife, sister, and daughter, not as worker. Their waged work is seen as an extension of caring for their families. It is not a question of *choosing* to work—they do so out of economic necessity.

When I asked whether their husbands' and fathers' waged work could also be viewed as an extension of familial duties, the women indicated that they definitely perceived a difference. Men's paid labor outside the home was seen as integral both to the men's self-definition and to their responsibility vis-à-vis the family; conversely, women's labor force participation was seen as contradictory both to the women's self-image and to their definitions of female responsibility.

Many immigrant women see their wage contribution to the family's economic survival not only as secondary but as *temporary*, even when they have held their jobs for several years. They expect to quit their production jobs after they have saved enough money to go to school, stay home full time, or open a family business. In actuality, however, most of them barely earn enough to live on, let alone to save, and women who think they are signing on for a brief stint may end up staying in the industry for years.

That these workers view their jobs as temporary has important ramifications for both employers and unions, as well as for the workers themselves. When workers believe they are on board a company for a short time, they are more likely to put up with poor working conditions, because they see them as short term. . . .

Employers are thus at an advantage in hiring these women at low wages and with little job security. They can play on the women's *own* consciousness as wives and mothers whose primary identities are defined by home and familial roles. While the division of labor prompts the workers to believe that women's waged work is less valuable than men's, the women workers themselves arrive in Silicon Valley with this ideology already internalized.

A young Filipina woman, who was hired at a walk-in interview at an electronics production facility, experienced a striking example of the contradictions confronting immigrant women workers in the valley. Neither she nor her husband, who was hired the same day, had any previous related work experience or degrees. Yet her husband was offered an entry-level job as a technician, while she was offered an assembly job paying three dollars per hour less. The personnel manager told her husband that he would "find [the technician job] more interesting than assembly work." The woman had said in the interview that she wanted to be considered for a higher-paying job because she had two children to support. The manager refused to consider her for a different job, she said, and told her that "it will work out fine for you, though, because with your husband's job, and you *helping out* [emphasis added] you'll have a nice little family income."

The same manager told me on a separate occasion that the company preferred to hire members of the same families because it meant that workers' relatives would be more supportive about their working and the combined incomes would put less financial strain on individual workers. This concern over workers and their families dissipated, however, when the Filipino couple split up, leaving the wife with only the "helping-

out" pay instead of the "nice little family income." When the woman requested a higher-paying job so she could support her family, the same manager told her that "family concerns were out of place at work" and did not promote her. . . .

RESISTANCE ON THE SHOP FLOOR

There is little incidence in Silicon Valley production shops of *formal* labor militancy among the immigrant women, as evidenced by either union participation or collectively planned mass actions such as strikes. Filling formal grievances is not common in these workers' shop culture. Union activity is very limited, and both workers and managers claim that the incidence of complaints and disturbances on the shop floor is lower than in other industries. Pacing of production to restrict output does occur, and there are occasionally "informal" incidents, such as spontaneous slowdowns and sabotage. But these actions are rare and usually small in scale. Definitions of workplace militancy and resistance vary, of course, according to the observer's cultural background, but by their *own* definitions, the women do not frequently engage in traditional forms of labor militancy.

There is, however, an important, although often subtle, arena in which the women do engage in struggle with management: the ideological battleground. Just as employers and managers harness racist, sexist, and class-based logic to manipulate and control workers, so too workers use this logic against management. In the ideological arena, the women do not merely accept or react to the biased assumptions of managers: they also develop gender-, class-, and race-based logic of their own when it is to their advantage. The goal of these struggles is not simply ideological victory but concrete changes in working conditions. Further, in Silicon Valley, immigrant women workers have found that managers respond more to workers' needs when they are couched in ethnic or gender terms, rather than in class and labor terms. Thus, class struggle on the shop floor is often disguised as arguments about the proper place and appropriate behavior of women, racial minorities, and immigrants.

When asked directly, immigrant women workers typically deny that they engage in any form of workplace resistance or efforts to control their working conditions. This denial reflects not only workers' needs to protect clandestine activities, but also their consciousness about what constitutes resistance and control. In their conversations with friends and co-workers, the women joke about how they outfoxed their managers with female or ethnic "wisdom." Yet most of the women do not view their often elaborate efforts to manipulate their managers' behavior as forms of struggle. Rather, they think of their tactics "just as ways to get by," as several workers phrased it. It is from casual references to these tactics that a portrait of worker logic and resistance emerges....

The vast majority of these women clearly wish to avoid antagonizing management. Thus, rather than engaging in confrontational resistance strategies, they develop less obvious forms than, say, work stoppages, filing grievances, and straightforwardly refusing to perform certain tasks, all of which have frequently been observed in other industrial manufacturing sectors. Because the more "quiet" forms of resistance and struggle for workplace control engaged in by the women in Silicon Valley are often so discrete and the workers are uncomfortable discussing them, it is probable that there are more such acts and they are broader in scope than my examples imply. As a Chinese woman in her forties who has worked as an operative in the valley for six years explained:

> Everybody who does this job does things to get through the day, to make it bearable. There are some women who will tell you they never do anything unproper or sneaky, but you are not to believe them. The ones that look the most demure are always up to something.... There's not anybody here who has never purposefully broken something, slowed down work, told fibs to the supervisor, or some such thing. And there's probably no one but me with my big mouth who would admit it!...

The most frequently mentioned acts of resistance against management and work arrangements were ones that played on the White male managers' consciousness—both false and real—about gender and ethnic culture. Frequently mentioned examples involved workers who turned management's ideologies against them by exploiting their male supervisors' misconceptions about "female problems." A White chip tester testified:

> It's pretty ironic because management seems to have this idea that male supervisors handle female workers better than female supervisors. You know, we're supposed to turn to mush whenever he's around and respect his authority or something. But this one guy we got now lets us walk all over him. He thinks females are flighty and irresponsible because of our hormones—so we make sure to have as many hormone problems as we can. I'd say we each take hormone breaks several times a day. My next plan is to convince him that menstrual blood will turn the solvents bad, so on those days we have to stay in the lunchroom!

A Filipina woman production worker recounted another example:

> The boss told us girls that we're not strong enough to do the heavy work in the men's jobs—and those jobs pay more, too. So, I suddenly realized that gosh, us little weak little things shouldn't be lifting all those heavy boxes of circuit board parts we're supposed to carry back and forth all the time—and I stopped doing it.
>
> The boss no longer uses that "it's too heavy for you girls" line anymore...but I can tell he's working on a new one. That's okay; I got plenty of responses.

A Mexican wafer fabricator, whose unit supervisor was notorious for the "refeminization" perks discussed above, told of how she manipulated the male supervisor's gender logic to disguise what was really an issue of class struggle:

> I was getting really sick from all the chemicals we have to work with, and I was getting a rash from them on my arms. [The manager] kept saying I was exaggerating and gave the usual line about you can't prove what caused the rash. One day we

had to use an especially harsh solvent, and I made up this story about being in my sister's wedding. I told him that the solvents would ruin my manicure, and I'd be a mess for the wedding. Can you believe it? He let me off the work! This guy wouldn't pay attention to my rash, but when my manicure was at stake, he let me go!

Of course, letting this worker avoid chemicals for one day because of a special circumstance is more advantageous to management than allowing her and others to avoid the work permanently because of health risks. Nonetheless, the worker was able to carve out a small piece of bargaining power by playing off her manager's gender logic. The contradiction of these tactics that play up feminine frailty is that they achieve short-term, individual goals at the risk of reinforcing damaging stereotypes about women, including the stereotype that women workers are not as productive as men. From the workers' point of view, however, the women are simply using the prejudices of the powerful to the advantages of the weak.

Another "manicure" story resulted in a more major workplace change at one of the large plants. Two women fabricator operatives, one Portuguese and one Chicana, applied for higher-paying technician jobs whereupon their unit supervisor told them that the jobs were too "rough" for women and that the work would "ruin their nails." The women's response was to pull off their rubber gloves and show him what the solvents and dopants had done to their nails, despite the gloves. (One of the most common chemicals used in chip manufacturing is acetone, the key ingredient in nail polish remover. It also eats right through "protective" rubber gloves.) After additional goading and bargaining, the supervisor provisionally let them transfer to technician work.

Although the above are isolated examples, they represent tactics that workers can use either to challenge or play off sexist ideology that employers use to legitimate women's low position in the segregated division of labor. Certainly there are not enough instances of such behavior to challenge the inequality between worker and boss, but

they do demonstrate to managers that gender logic cannot always be counted on to legitimate inequality between male and female workers. And dissolving divisions between workers is a threat to management hegemony.

RACIAL AND ETHNIC LOGIC

Typically, high-tech firms in Silicon Valley hire production workers from a wide spectrum of national groups. If their lack of a common language (both linguistically and culturally) serves to fragment the labor force, capital benefits. Conversely, management may find it more difficult to control workers with whom it cannot communicate precisely. Several workers said they have feigned a language barrier in order to avoid taking instructions; they have also called forth cultural taboos—both real and feigned—to avoid undesirable situations. One Haitian woman, who took a lot of kidding from her employer about voodoo and black magic, insisted that she could not work the night shift because evil spirits were out then. Because she was a good worker, the employer let her switch to days. When I tried to establish whether she believed the evil spirits were real or imagined, she laughed and said, "Does it matter? The result is the same: I can be home at night with my kids."

Management in several plants believed that racial and national diversity minimized solidarity. According to one supervisor, workers were forbidden from sitting next to people of their own nationality (i.e., language group) in order to "cut down on the chatting." Workers quickly found two ways to reverse this decision, using management's own class, racial, and gender logic. Chinese women workers told the supervisor that if they were not "chaperoned" by other Chinese women, their families would not let them continue to work there. Vietnamese women told him that the younger Vietnamese women would not work hard unless they were under the eyes of the older workers and that a group of newly hired Vietnamese workers would not learn to do the job right unless they had someone who spoke their language to explain it to them. Both of these arguments could also be interpreted as examples of older workers wanting to control younger ones in a generational hierarchy, but this was not the case. Afterwards both the Chinese and the Vietnamese women laughed among themselves at their cleverness. Nor did they forget the support needs of workers from other ethnic groups: they argued with the supervisor that the same customs and needs held true for many of the language groups represented, and the restriction was rescinded.

Another example of a large-scale demonstration of interethnic solidarity on the shop floor involved workers playing off supervisors' stereotypes regarding the superior work of Asians over Mexicans. The incident was precipitated when a young Mexicana, newly assigned to an assembly unit in which a new circuit board was being assembled, fell behind in her quota. The supervisor berated her with racial slurs about Mexicans' "laziness" and "stupidity" and told her to sit next to and "watch the Orientals." As a group, the Asian women she was stationed next to slowed down their production, thereby setting the average quota on the new boards at a slower than usual pace. The women were in fits of laughter after work because the supervisor had assumed that the speed set by the Asians was the fastest possible, since they were the "best" workers.

Hispanic workers also turn management's anti-Mexican prejudices against them, as a Salvadorean woman explained:

> First of all, the bosses think everyone from Latin American is Mexican, and they think all Mexicans are dumb. So, whenever they try to speed up production, or give us something we don't want to do, we just act dumb. It's not as if you act smart and you get a promotion or a bonus anyway.

A Mexicana operative confided, "They [management] assume we don't understand much English, but we understand when we want to."

A Chinese woman, who was under five feet tall and who identified her age by saying she was a "grandmother," laughingly told how she had her White male supervisor "wrapped around [her] finger." She consciously played into his stereotype that Asian women are small, timid, and obedient by frequently smiling at and bowing to him and doing her job carefully. But when she had a special need, to take a day or a few hours off, for example, she would put on her best guileless, ingratiating look and, full of apologies, usually obtained it. She also served as a voice for co-workers whom the supervisor considered more abrasive. On one occasion, when three White women in her unit complained about poor lighting and headaches, the supervisor became irritated and did not respond to their complaint. Later that week the Chinese "grandmother" approached him, saying that she was concerned that poor lighting was limiting the workers' productivity. The lighting was quickly improved. This incident illustrates that managers can and do respond to workers' demands when they result in increased productivity.

Some workers see strategies to improve and control their work processes and environments as contradictory and as "Uncle Tomming." Two friends, both Filipinas, debated this issue. One argued that "acting like a China doll" only reinforced white employers' stereotypes, while the other said that countering the stereotype would not change their situation, so they might as well use the stereotype to their advantage. The same analysis applies to women workers who consciously encourage male managers to view women as different from men in their abilities and characteristics. For women and minority workers, the need for short-term gains and benefits and for long-term equal treatment is a constant contradiction. And for the majority of workers, short-term tactics are unlikely to result in long-term equality.

POTENTIAL FOR ORGANIZING

Obviously, the lesson here for organizing is contradictory. Testimonies such as the ones given in these pages clearly document that immigrant women are not docile, servile people who always follow orders, as many employers interviewed for this study claimed. Orchestrating major actions such as family migration so that they could take control of and better their lives has helped these women develop leadership and survival skills. Because of these qualities, many of the women I interviewed struck me as potentially effective labor and community organizers and rank-and-file leaders. Yet almost none of them were interested in collective organizing, because of time limitations and family constraints and because of their lack of confidence in labor unions, the feminist movement, and community organizations. Many were simply too worn out from trying to make ends meet and caring for their families. And for some, the level of inequality and exploitation on the shop floor did not seem that bad, compared to their past experiences....

Nonetheless, their past torment does not reduce the job insecurity, poor working conditions, pay inequality, and discrimination so many immigrant workers in Silicon Valley experience in their jobs. In fact, as informants' testimonies suggest, in many cases, past hardships have rendered them less likely to organize collectively. At the same time, individual acts of resistance do not succeed on their own in changing the structured inequality of the division of labor. Most of these actions remain at the agitation level and lack the coordination needed to give workers real bargaining power. And, as mentioned, individual strategies that workers have devised can be contradictory. Simultaneous to winning short-run victories, they can also reinforce both gender and racial stereotypes in the long run. Further, because many of these victories are isolated and individual, they can often be divisive. For workers to gain both greater workplace control *and* combat sexism and racism, organized *collective* strategies hold greater possibilities....

My findings indicate that Silicon Valley's immigrant women workers have a great deal to gain from organizing, but also a great deal to contribute. They have their numeric strength, but also a wealth of creativity, insight, and experience that could be a shot in the arm to the stagnating national labor movement. They also have a great deal to teach—and learn from—feminist and ethnic community movements. But until these or new alternative movements learn to speak and listen to these women, the women will continue to struggle on their own, individually and in small groups. In their struggle for better jobs and better lives, one of the most effective tactics they have is their own resourcefulness in manipulating management's "own logic against them."

NOTES

1. For a comprehensive analytical description of the development of Silicon Valley as a region and an industry, see Saxenian 1981.

2. These production jobs include the following U.S. Department of Labor occupational titles: semiconductor processor; semiconductor assembler; electronics assembler; and electronics tester. Entry-level wages for these jobs in Silicon Valley in 1984 were $4.00 to $5.50; wages for workers with one to two years or more experience were $5.50 to $8.00 an hour, with testers sometimes earning up to $9.50.

3. "Minority" is the term used by the California Employment Development Department and the U.S. Department of Labor publications in reference to people of color. The statistics do not distinguish between immigrants and nonimmigrants within racial and ethnic groupings.

4. In North Carolina's Research Triangle, for example, Blacks account for most minority employment, whereas in Albuquerque and Texas, Hispanics provide the bulk of the production labor force. Silicon Valley has perhaps the most racially diverse production force, although Hispanics—both immigrant and nonimmigrant—still account for the majority.

REFERENCES

Annual Planning Information: San Jose Standard Metropolitan Statistical Area, 1983–1984. 1983. Sacramento: California Department of Employment Development.

Brownmiller, Susan. 1984. *Femininity.* New York: Simon and Schuster.

Grossman, Rachel. 1979. "Women's Place in the Integrated Circuit." *Southeast Asia Chronicle 66— Pacific Research* 9:2–17.

———. 1980. "Bitter Wages: Women in East Asia's Semiconductor Plants." *Multinational Monitor* 1 (March):8–11.

Hartmann, Heidi. 1976. "Capitalism, Patriarchy, and Job Segregation by Sex." In *Women in the Workplace,* ed. Martha Blaxall and Barbara Reagan, 137–70. Chicago: University of Chicago Press.

Hossfeld, Karen. 1988a. "Divisions of Labor, Divisions of Lives: Immigrant Women Workers in Silicon Valley." Ph.D. diss., University of California, Santa Cruz.

———. 1988b. "The Triple Shift: Immigrant Women Workers and the Household Division of Labor in Silicon Valley." Paper presented at the annual meetings of the American Sociological Association, Atlanta.

Ong, Aihwa. 1985. "Industrialization and Prostitution in Southeast Asia." *Southeast Asia Chronicle* 96: 2–6.

Saxenian, Annalee. 1981. *Silicon Chips and Spatial Structure: The Industrial Basis of Urbanization in Santa Clara County, California.* Working Paper no. 345. Berkeley: Institute of Urban and Regional Planning, University of California.

Siegel, Lenny, and Herb Borock. 1982. *Background Report on Silicon Valley.* Prepared for the U.S. Commission on Civil Rights. Mountain View, Calif.: Pacific Studies Center.

Westwood, Sallie. 1985. *All Day, Every Day: Factory and Family in the Making of Women's Lives.* Champaign: University of Illinois Press.

42

Shortchanged

Restructuring Women's Work

TERESA AMOTT

... The [economic] crisis has had different effects on men and women. In some ways, and for some women, the economic crisis has not been as severe as it has been for men. In other ways, and for other women, the crisis has been far more severe.

Throughout the crisis women continued to join the labor force, both to support themselves and their families and to find satisfaction in working outside the home. Companies, seeking to bolster their profits, hired women in order to cut labor costs. In fact, hiring women was a central part of the corporate strategy to restore profitability because women were not only cheaper than men, but were also less likely to be organized into unions and more willing to accept temporary work and no benefits. Women were hired rather than men in a variety of industries and occupations, in the United States and abroad. This led to what has been called the "feminization" of the labor force, as women moved into jobs that had previously been held only by men and as jobs that were already predominantly female became even more so.... This "feminization" of the workforce, in which women substitute for men, explains why women's unemployment rates, on average, were lower than men's during the 1980s.

Each of the corporate and government responses to the crisis...had its most damaging effects on a particular group (or groups) of workers. Union-busting, for instance, took its toll *primarily* on the manufacturing jobs that have been dominated by White men (although a weakened labor movement damages the bargaining power of all workers, as we see below). Capital flight also *pri-marily* affected men's manufacturing jobs, although it also affected women in the service sector and women who work in primarily female manufacturing jobs, such as the garment industry.

SEGREGATION AND SEGMENTATION

The way women experience the economic crisis depends on where they are located in the occupational hierarchy. One concept that will help us understand this hierarchy is *occupational segregation,* which can be by gender—most jobs are held by either men *or* women and few are truly integrated. To take one extreme example, in 1990, 82 percent of architects were male; 95 percent of typists were female. Occupational segregation can also be by race-ethnicity, although this is sometimes more difficult to detect—since racial-ethnic workers are a minority, they rarely dominate a job category numerically, although they may be in the majority at a particular workplace or in a geographical region. At the national level, we have to look for evidence of occupational segregation by race-ethnicity by examining whether a particular group is over- or underrepresented relative to its percent of the total workforce. For instance, if African American women make up 5.1 percent of the total workforce, they are underrepresented in an occupation if they hold less than 5.1 percent of the jobs.[1] Law would be such an occupation: African American women made up only 1.8 percent of all lawyers in 1990. In contrast, they are overrepresented in licensed practical nursing, where they hold 16.9 percent of the jobs.

A second concept that will be helpful in our examination of women's situation during the economic crisis is *labor market segmentation,* a term that refers to the division of jobs into categories with distinct working conditions. Economists generally distinguish two such categories, which they call the *primary* and *secondary* sectors. The first includes high-wage jobs that provide good benefits, job security, and opportunities for advancement. The upper level of this sector includes elite jobs that require long years of training and certification and offer autonomy on the job and a chance to advance up the corporate ladder. Access to upper level jobs is by way of family connections, wealth, talent, education, and governmental programs (like the GI bill, which guaranteed higher education to veterans returning from World War II). The lower level includes those manufacturing jobs that offer relatively high wages and job security (as a result of unionization), but do not require advanced training or degrees. The fact that unionized workers are part of this lower level is the result of the capital-labor accord...through which employers offered some unionized workers better pay and working conditions in exchange for labor peace. In both levels of the primary sector, job turnover is relatively low because it is more difficult for employers to replace these workers. Both the upper and lower levels of the primary sector were for many years the preserve of White men, with women (mostly White women) confined to small niches, such as schoolteaching and nursing.

The secondary sector includes low-wage jobs with few fringe benefits and little opportunity for advancement. Here too, there is a predominantly white-collar upper level (which includes sales and clerical workers), where working conditions, pay, and benefits are better than in the blue-collar lower level (private household, laborer, and most service jobs). Turnover is high in both levels of this sector because these workers have relatively few marketable skills and are easily replaced. For decades, the majority of women of all racial-ethnic groups, along with most men of color, were found in the secondary sector. Mobility between

the primary and secondary sectors is limited: no career ladder connects jobs in the secondary sector to jobs in the primary sector.

While most jobs fall into these two sectors...during the economic crisis a third sector began to grow rapidly. This is known as the *informal sector,* or the underground economy. This name is not entirely accurate, however, since these activities do not make up a separate, distinct *economy* but are linked in many ways to the formal, above-ground sectors. Journalist and economist Philip Mattera believes that economic activity can be lined up along a continuum of formality and regulation.[2] At one end there is formal, regulated, and measured activity, where laws are observed, taxes are paid, inspections are frequent, and the participants report their activities to the relevant government entities. At the other end is work "off the books," where regulations are not enforced, participants do not report their activities, and taxes are evaded. Many economic activities exist somewhere in the middle. As the economic crisis deepens, many large corporations, whose own jobs are in the primary sector, have subcontracted some of their work out to underground firms that hire undocumented workers and escape health and safety, minimum wage, and environmental regulations. For example, in El Paso, Texas, only half of all garment industry workers earn adequate wages in union shops.[3] The other half work in sweatshops that contract work from big-name brands, such as Calvin Klein and Jordache, pay the minimum wage, and sometimes fail to pay anything at all. In 1990, the Labor Department fined one contractor for owing $30,000 in back wages and forced him to pay up. Fortunately for the employees, there is some justice in this world: the International Ladies' Garment Workers Union (ILGWU) then won a contract at his shops. According to Mattera,

operating a business off the books—i.e., without any state regulation or union involvement—is the logical conclusion of the restructuring process. It represents the ultimate goal of the profit-maximizing entrepreneur: proverbial free enterprise.... The type of restructuring that has taken place makes it possible for firms that cannot or do not want to go underground to take advantage of un-protected labor nonetheless.[4]

Another reason for the growth in the informal sector is that worsening wages and conditions in the two formal sectors lead people to seek additional work "off the books" to supplement their shrinking incomes and inadequate welfare or social security benefits. Thus the numbers of people suffering what Mattera calls "the nightmarish working conditions of unregulated capitalism" grow rapidly. Women and men of color, particularly immigrants, are those most likely to be found in the informal sector.…

CAPITAL FLIGHT: A FLIGHT TO WOMEN?

…Over the past twenty years, many U.S. corporations shifted manufacturing jobs overseas. The creation of this "global assembly line" became a crucial component of the corporate strategy to cut costs. In their new locations, these companies hired women workers at minimal wages, both in the third world and in such countries as Ireland. Poorly paid as these jobs were, they were attractive to the thousands of women who were moving from impoverished rural villages into the cities in search of a better life for their families.

But in the United States, millions of workers lost their jobs as the result of capital flight or corporate downsizing. When workers lose their jobs because their plants or businesses close down or move, or their positions or shifts are abolished, it is called worker *displacement*. Over 5 million workers were displaced between 1979 and 1983, and another 4 million between 1985 and 1989.[5] In both periods, women were slightly *less* likely to lose their jobs than men of the same racial-ethnic group. Women in secondary sector factory jobs were hit hardest, primarily because they lacked union protection and the education and skills to find better jobs. (In 1989, over 35 percent of the women in manufacturing operative jobs had less than a high school education.)[6]

The overall result was that even though women lost jobs to capital flight and corporate downsizing, they did so at a slower rate than men.

In fact, the share of manufacturing jobs going to women *rose* between 1970 and 1990. Women, in other words, claimed a growing share of a shrinking pie. Sociologist Joan Smith studied this growing tendency to replace male workers with women (as well as a parallel tendency to replace White workers with African Americans and Latinos). In her research on heavy manufacturing industries such as steel and automobiles, Smith found that employers hired men and/or White workers only in those areas of manufacturing where profits were high, jobs were being created, and there was substantial investment in new plant and equipment. In contrast,

in sectors where profits were slipping, the obvious search for less expensive workers led to the use of Black and women workers as a substitute for White workers and for men.… Close to 70 percent of women in these sectors and well over two-fifths of Blacks held their jobs as either substitutes or replacements for Whites or men.[7]

While manufacturing jobs were feminizing, the rapidly expanding service sector was also hiring women in larger and larger numbers—both women entering the labor market for the first time and women displaced from manufacturing. In fact, all the jobs created during the 1980s were in the service sector.…[8]

A large part of this service sector growth took place in what were already predominantly female jobs, such as nurses' aides, child care workers, or hotel chambermaids (jobs that men would not take), as employers took advantage of the availability of a growing pool of women workers who were excluded from male-dominated jobs.[9] Chris Tilly argues that these sectors were able to grow so rapidly during the 1980s precisely *because* they were able to use low-wage, part-time labor.[10] In other words, if no women workers had been available, the jobs would not have been filled by men; instead, service employment would not have grown as rapidly.

The availability of service sector jobs helped hold the average official unemployment rates for women below those for men. However, the overall figure for women masks important differences by race-ethnicity....[11] In addition, the official unemployment rate doesn't tell the whole story. If we construct a measure of underemployment, we get a different sense of the relative hardships faced by women and men. The underemployed are those who are working part-time but would prefer full-time work, those who are so discouraged that they have given up looking for work, and those who want a job but can't work because home responsibilities—such as caring for children or aged parents—or other reasons keep them out of the labor force. If we look at underemployment rather than unemployment, the rankings change: in contrast to the official unemployment rates, the underemployment rates are higher for women than for men....

Even though the entire service sector grew during this period, service workers still risked losing their jobs. According to the Census Bureau's study of displaced workers, nearly half of those who lost their jobs between 1981 and 1983, and nearly two-thirds of those between 1985 and 1989, were in the service sector. As the crisis dragged on, in other words, corporate downsizing hit services as well as manufacturing. The financial sector, where women make up 60 percent of the workforce, was particularly hard hit, as jobs in banking, insurance, and real estate were lost as a result of the savings and loan scandal and other financial troubles.

UNION-BUSTING

...A second corporate strategy to bolster profitability was to attack labor unions. As the assault took its toll, union membership and union representation declined until by 1990 only 14 percent of women and 22 percent of men were represented by a union—compared to 18 percent of women and 28 percent of men only six years earlier. Even though women are less likely to be represented by unions than men, the *drop* in unionization was not as severe for women, largely because they are concentrated in the service sector where there were some organizing victories. In addition, most women do not hold jobs in factories, the area most

vulnerable to union-busting. The drop in unionization was highest among Latinas, who are over-represented in manufacturing, followed closely by African American women. Still, African American women have the highest rate of union representation among women (22 percent) because so many work in the public sector.[12]

The drop in unionized jobs is dangerous for women for several reasons. The most obvious is that unionized women earn an average weekly wage that is 1.3 times that of nonunionized women. The gap is especially large in the service sector, where unionized workers earn 1.8 times as much as nonunionized workers....[13]

The loss of unionized jobs also hurts women in nonunion jobs because of what economists call a "spillover" effect from union to nonunion firms in the area of wages and benefits. While it is difficult to estimate the extent of this spillover, Harvard economists Richard Freeman and James Medoff suggest that it raises wages in blue collar jobs in large nonunion firms (those with lower level primary sector jobs) by anywhere from 10 to 20 percent, and also improves benefits and working conditions.[14] This happens for two reasons: (1) nonunion firms must compete for labor with the union firms and therefore have to meet unionized rates, and (2) some firms will keep wages higher than necessary in order to keep unions out. Thus when union workers lose wages and benefits, these spillover effects diminish, lowering wages and benefits in nonunion jobs as well.

Higher wages are only part of what women achieve when there is a strong labor movement. Unionization has an important spillover effect in the political as well as economic arena. For instance, support from the labor movement is responsible for the passage of most of the major safety net legislation in the United States, including the minimum wage and the Social Security Act. When the labor movement is weakened, important items on labor's agenda—including national health care, national child care, improved enforcement of job safety and health regulations, and broadened unemployment insurance coverage—all become more difficult to achieve, even though they address the needs of *all* workers. Further evidence of the critical role played by the labor movement comes from Europe, where family policies (parental leave, child allowances, and national day care) were all enacted with the backing, and sometimes at the initiative, of the labor movement.

WOMEN AND THE RESTRUCTURING OF WORK

... Another component of restructuring, and one that particularly affects women, is the use of homework. While homework can provide incomes for women who are unable to locate affordable child care or who live in rural areas, far from other employment, it also exposes women to intense exploitation. Both men and women homeworkers typically earn much less than those who do the same work outside the home: according to the federal Office of Technology Assessment, the poverty risk for homeworkers is nearly double that for other workers. In addition, working conditions in the home can be dangerous. In semiconductor manufacturing homework, for instance, workers are exposed to hazardous substances that can also contaminate residential sewage systems.[15]

Many homeworkers are undocumented immigrants who work out of their homes in order to escape detection by the Immigration and Naturalization Service (INS). During the early 1970s, the majority of undocumented immigrants were male, but since then women have begun to arrive in ever larger numbers:

> *Women's migration has traditionally been ignored by researchers.... The INS reported a "dramatic rise" in the number of women apprehended at the U.S.-Mexico border between 1984 and 1986.... Many authors describe a new spirit of "independence" among women choosing to cross the border alone to reunite with family already in the U.S., or to seek employment on their own to support family left behind.[16]*

In the spring of 1990, the Coalition for Immigration and Refugee Rights and Services in San Francisco surveyed over 400 undocumented women in the Bay Area. Nearly half of them reported employment discrimination by employers who abused them sexually, physically, or emotionally, paid them less than their co-workers, or failed to pay them at all. Most of those surveyed worked as domestic servants, in stores, restaurants, and factories.

WOMEN'S RESPONSES TO RESTRUCTURING

As wages fell and employers pushed more and more work into the secondary and informal sectors, women responded with a variety of individual strategies. Some started small businesses. Others sought "nontraditional" jobs in areas formerly dominated by men, hoping to earn a man's wage. And a growing number took on multiple jobs, "moonlighting" in a desperate effort to make a living wage out of two, or even three, different jobs. Each of these individual strategies ... held some promise, but all failed to deliver substantial gains except to the lucky few....

... Self-employment did not solve women's economic problems. The vast majority of these businesses remained small in scale: although they made up nearly 33 percent of all the businesses in the United States, they earned only 14 percent of the receipts. Nearly 40 percent had total receipts of less than $5,000 a year; only 10 percent had any employees.[17] Even the most successful women entrepreneurs faced difficulties finding affordable health insurance and pension coverage, which they had to buy for themselves out of their profits. Despite conservative rhetoric about the glories of entrepreneurship, self-employment has not proved to be a cure-all for women's economic troubles....

As the number of poverty-level jobs has increased, more and more women have been forced to turn to moonlighting to boost their incomes. By 1989, 3.5 times as many women were working two or more jobs as in 1973. In contrast, the number of men moonlighting only rose by a factor of 1.2.[18] And many more women were moonlighting because of economic hardship—to meet regular household expenses or pay off debts—not to save for something special, get experience, or help out a family member or friend. African American women and Latinas were the most likely to report that they were moonlighting to meet *regular* household expenses, while white women were more likely to report saving for the future or other reasons—a difference caused by the lower average income of women of color and the greater likelihood that they were raising children on their own.

But moonlighting is ultimately limited by the number of hours in the day.... As the crisis wears on and more and more women become fully employed, more families turn to children to help out. According to recent estimates, at least 4 million children under the age of 19 are employed legally, while at least 2 million more work "off the books," and the number is growing.[19]

NEW JOBS FOR WOMEN

During the 1980s, the female labor force grew by over 10 million. Most of the new entrants found traditionally female jobs in secondary, sector service and administrative support occupations, since that is where the majority of job growth took place.... However, some women made inroads into traditionally male jobs in the highly paid primary sector, and these gains are likely to be maintained. In addition, graduate degrees show how women are increasingly willing to prepare themselves for male-dominated occupations.... There has been an occupational "trickle down" effect, as white women improved their occupational status by moving into male-dominated professions such as law and medicine, while African American women moved into the *female-dominated* jobs, such as social work and teaching, vacated by white women. There is some evidence that the improvement for white women was related to federal civil rights legislation, particularly the requirement that firms receiving federal contracts comply with affirmative action guidelines.[20]

The movement of women into highly skilled blue-collar work, such as construction and automaking, was sharply limited by the very slow growth in those jobs. Not coincidentally, male resistance to letting women enter these trades stiffened during the 1980s, when layoffs were common and union jobs were under attack. Moreover, all women lost ground in secondary sector manufacturing jobs, such as machine operators and laborers. Latinas were particularly hard hit, losing ground in most manufacturing jobs....

UP THE DOWN ESCALATOR

If the postwar economic boom had continued into the 1970s and 1980s, women's economic status today would be substantially improved. The crisis produced some gains for women, but many of these evaporate on close inspection. The wage gap narrowed, but partly because men's wages fell. The gap between men's and women's rates of unionization and access to fringe benefits fell, but again partly because men's rates fell. More women entered the workforce, but they also worked longer hours than ever before, held multiple jobs, and sought work in the informal economy in order to maintain their standard of living. Finally, women's gains were not evenly distributed: highly educated women moved even further ahead of their less-educated counterparts.

All this took place against a backdrop of rising family responsibilities.... The most serious stress faced by married women ... was associated with the reduced standard of living their families faced as a result of the cutbacks: "Their continued need to reduce what their wages can buy for their families means that the conflicts they feel between work and family life intensify. Earning less makes it feel harder and harder for them to continue to work and take care of their families."[21]

For these women, who depended on manufacturing jobs, it is not surprising that the economic crisis took a heavy toll. What is surprising is that they experienced it most acutely in the home rather than on the job. Work for them was not a career, a satisfying route to self actualization, but a fate they accepted in order to provide for their families. When their earnings fell, it was their work at home—the work of marketing, cooking, cleaning, caring—that became more difficult. An increasing number were the sole support of their households. Others found that their household's standard of living could only be maintained if they took on one—or more—paid jobs in addition to their homemaking. They were caught between shrinking incomes and growing responsibilities....

NOTES

1. Unpublished data, Bureau of Labor Statistics.
2. Philip Mattera, *Off the Books: The Rise of the Underground Economy* (New York: St. Martin's Press, 1985), p. 38.
3. Colatosti, Camille, "A Job Without a Future," *Dollars and Sense* (May 1992), p. 10.
4. Philip Mattera, *Prosperity Lost* (Reading, MA: Addison-Wesley, 1992), pp. 34–35.
5. For instance, between 1985 and 1989 the displacement rate—the number of workers displaced for every 1,000 workers employed—was 6.3 for white women compared to 6.7 for white men; 6.1 for African American women compared to 7.3 for African American men; and 8.3 for Latinas compared to 9.0 for Latinos. See U.S. Department of Labor, Bureau of Labor Statistics, *Displaced Workers, 1985–89*, June 1991, Bulletin 2382, Table 4.
6. U.S. Bureau of the Census, *Statistical Abstract of the United States 1991*, Table 656, p. 400. African American women factory operatives are better educated than whites: only 29 percent lack a high school degree, compared to 36 percent of whites.
7. Joan Smith, "Impact of the Reagan Years: Race, Gender, and the Economic Restructuring," *First Annual Women's Policy Research Conference Proceedings* (Washington, DC: Institute for Women's Policy Research, 1989), p. 20.
8. U.S. Bureau of the Census, *Statistical Abstract of the United States 1991*, Table 658, p. 401. The number of jobs in durable manufacturing fell by 0.8 percent a year between 1980 and 1988 and in nondurable manufacturing (i.e., light manufacturing, such as food processing) fell by 0.2 percent; service jobs grew an average of 2.7 percent. Manufacturing jobs did see some growth in the last half of the 1970s, however, so that over the two decades there was a small amount of overall growth in manufacturing.
9. Because the number of jobs held by women increased more than the number held by men, the percent of service sector jobs held by women increased from 43 percent to 52 percent between 1970 and 1990.
10. Polly Callaghan and Heidi Hartmann, *Contingent Work* (Washington, DC: Economic Policy Institute, 1991), p. 24.
11. For Latinas, on the other hand, women's unemployment was higher than that of men's. While it is difficult to pinpoint the reason for this, it may be because of the relatively rapid growth of Latina participation in the labor force. Although Latinas have lowest labor force participation rate of the three groups of women, their participation rates are growing the most rapidly. It may be that this growth in the Latina workforce outstripped job creation in the secondary sector, which had traditionally hired Latinas while discrimination still barred their way into the primary sector—resulting in high unemployment. See National Council of La Raza, *State of Hispanic America 1991*, p. 26.
12. Paula Ries and Anne J. Stone, eds., *The American Woman 1992–93: A Status Report* (New York, W. W. Norton and Co., 1991), p. 369.
13. U.S. Bureau of Labor Statistics, *Employment and Earnings*, January 1992, Tables 59–60.
14. Richard Freeman and James Medoff, *What Do Unions Do?* (New York: Basic Books, 1981), p. 153.
15. Virginia DuRivage and David Jacobs, "Home-Based Work: Labor's Choices," in *Homework: Historical and Contemporary Perspectives on Paid Labor at Home*, ed. Eileen Boris and Cynthia R. Daniels (Urbana: University of Illinois Press, 1989), p. 259.
16. Chris Hogeland and Karen Rose, *Dreams Lost, Dreams Found: Undocumented Women in the Land of Opportunity* (San Francisco, CA: Refugee Rights and Services, 1990), p. 4.
17. Ries and Stone, *The American Woman*, pp. 347–48.
18. Lawrence Mishel and David M. Frankel, *The State of Working America* (Armonk, NY: M. E. Sharpe, 1991), p. 142.
19. Gina Kolata, "More Children Are Employed, Often Perilously," *New York Times*, 21 June 1992, p. 1.
20. Barbara Bergman, *The Economic Emergence of Women* (New York: Basic Books, 1986), p. 147.
21. Ellen Israel Rosen, *Bitter Choices: Blue Collar Women in and out of Work* (Chicago: University of Chicago Press, 1987), p. 164.

43

Asian American Women at Work

ESTHER NGAN-LING CHOW

Placing Asian American women, a very much ne-glected research population, as a central focus of analysis, this chapter specifically examines how the social context of the work bureaucracy has shaped the labor experience of this group of mi-nority women and has specified their coping strat-egies when they encounter discrimination. . . .

THE STUDY

This study is based on a cross-sectional survey that investigated the effect of major social and psycho-logical factors on occupational outcomes for 161 employed Asian American women.[1] Women who identified themselves as members of one of the four largest Asian American subgroups (Chinese, Filipino, Japanese, and Korean) and who resided in the Washington, D.C., metropolitan area at the time of the study were included in the sample selection.[2] Because over half of the Asian Ameri-can population in the United States was foreign-born, the sample of this study consisted of half for-eign-born and half U.S.-born Asian American women. . . .

LOCAL LABOR CONDITIONS

The first chapter of the immigration history of Asian Americans begins with the arrival of Chi-nese in the United States in the mid-nineteenth century. After many Chinese laborers completed the transcontinental railroad in 1869, a consider-able number remained in California, while some began moving gradually eastward and to other re-gions in search of better economic opportunities.

According to *The Evening Star* (Cohen 1927), Chiang Kai became the first Chinese resident of Washington, D.C., settling on Pennsylvania Ave-nue in 1851. Many more Chinese later arrived to work as laundry personnel, domestic servants, tai-lors, cooks, "coolies" (unskilled laborers), con-struction workers, and merchants. Other Asian groups began to come to the Washington area in the early part of the twentieth century, but Asian American communities grew very slowly prior to World War II. Exclusionary U.S. immigration laws barring first Chinese and later other Asians (the Chinese Exclusion Act of 1882 and the Ex-clusion Act of 1924) discouraged family forma-tion by Asians for more than half a century. The relative absence of female immigrants resulted in a highly skewed sex ratio of Asian men to Asian women, establishment of bachelor communities, stagnant population growth, and limited family lives (Chow 1987; Yung 1986). After 1943, when the repressive immigration laws were repealed, the Chinese community regained its vitality and other Asian American communities eventually de-veloped, concentrating in various localized areas within metropolitan areas (e.g., Chinatown and "Little Saigon") in the 1960s and 1970s.

The Washington, D.C., metropolitan area, though it is not climatically appealing to many Asians, provides job opportunities and security for many Asian American women and their fami-lies because of its proximity to the federal govern-ment and its tourism industries. In the absence of manufacturing and heavy industries, many Asian American women entered typically female and minority jobs, working in hotel and food industries, sales, and other service sectors. Like other immigrant women and women of color, Asian American women in the Washington area participated in the labor market in greater numbers than their White counterparts. With some ethnic variations, their occupational pattern is characterized by a bimodal distribution, with approximately one-fourth in the professional and technical categories and close to two-thirds concentrated in clerical, service, crafts, operative, and nonfarm jobs (U.S. Bureau of the Census 1983, 1988).

Their location in the economic structure is primarily the result of the intersection of class, gender, and race/ethnicity affecting their "place" in the labor market rather than the result of one factor alone. Like other immigrant groups and people of color, Asian men and women, particularly the foreign-born, have provided cheap and exploitable sources of migrant labor to meet the needs of an expanding capitalist economy in the United States (Cheng and Bonacich 1984; Glenn 1986). The decision to immigrate to this country has subjected them, voluntarily or involuntarily, to a segmented labor market composed of two tiers, a primary sector and a secondary one, that basically reflect the class structure. Those who are from middle-class backgrounds, with better education and training, are more likely to enter the primary sector, finding jobs mainly in professional, technical, and administrative categories with relatively high wages, good working conditions, chances of advancement, and relative employment stability. Those who come from class backgrounds that have fewer education and training resources are more likely to have jobs in the semiskilled, unskilled, service, and nonfarm areas of the secondary sector that tend to be low paying, with poor working conditions, little chance of advancement, job instability, and high turnover (Piore 1972)....

Class differences also are a consequence of U.S. immigration policies, which selected certain classes of Asian women to come at different times. Most of the Asian immigrant women of the pre-World War II era were of working-class origin and acquired jobs primarily in the secondary sec-

tor, whereas those of the post-World War II era came from heterogeneous class backgrounds and entered a wide range of occupational fields. Recent immigration policies favoring those with professional skills, high levels of education, and vocational training have allowed more Asian American women to acquire jobs in the primary sector than before....

Furthermore, the patriarchal principle, rooted in both traditional Asian culture and family structure and in the American system, clearly defines gender roles for women in the home as well as in the labor market (Chow and Berheide 1988; Hartmann 1981). The "typically female" jobs in the labor market are extensions of women's domestic roles. Women workers tend to concentrate in "female jobs" (e.g., secretary and file clerk) located in the secondary labor market. When gender is compounded with race and ethnic factors, Asian American women, like other women of color, tend to have "minority female jobs" that are characterized by lower pay, lower rank, more limited job ladders for mobility, and less desirable working conditions than the "typically female" jobs (Segura 1984). In this study, it is clearly evident that Asian women of foreign birth are concentrated in considerable numbers in "minority female jobs" (e.g., waitresses in ethnic restaurants, beauticians, fast food workers, and domestic help). Asian American women who are U.S.-born, highly educated, trained in job skills, and have a good command of English have attained a much higher occupational level than those who are foreign-born, have less education and skill training, and speak little English.

For many Asians, immigration has devastating effects on their labor process and work experience. Encountering status loss, difficulties in searching for or changing jobs, problems of skill transferability, language differences, state licensing requirements (including examinations), unfamiliar work environments, and discrimination affects their job prospects regardless of class and even of gender. The experience of Sau Ling, a Chinese immigrant woman with a high school diploma who worked as a waitress in a Chinese restaurant downtown, typified the kinds of job prospects interviewees found in the Washington, D.C., area.[3] She explained, "Immigrating to the United States seemed to be a dream for me at the beginning. It was my husband who insisted on coming to the U.S.A. and whose decision I do not regret when I think about it now. It is all for the good future of our four kids. We both sweat working in this pit, my husband as a cook and I as a waitress. Day after day, we earn the minimum to get by. When I asked about her chances of getting a better job, she said, "For a Chinese woman like me, it has become a vanishing hope to get out of this place. I am not a Lao Fan (Cantonese for an American). . . .

Veronica, a Filipino doctor working in a local hospital, mentioned difficulties, such as barriers to obtaining licenses for foreign-trained professionals, male dominance, occupational segregation, and professional subordination, that educated Asian women overcome in order to break into jobs in the primary sector:

> I worked as a surgeon for twelve years in my country before I and my children came here to join my husband, who arrived earlier for his import-export business. For the first six years, I could only work as a nursing aide because I had a hell of a time getting a state license. Finally I obtained a medical license to practice community medicine in the District. I don't think that I will have much chance of breaking into the White- and male-dominated medical institution to be a surgeon again.

The employment experiences of these two Asian American women illustrate how sexism, meshed with racism and economic oppression, results in barriers that are quite different from the forms of sexism with which White women contend.

WORK BUREAUCRACY AS AN ORGANIZATION OF INEQUALITY

Almost all (98 percent) of the Asian American women in the survey sample were salaried or wage workers employed in bureaucratic settings that were hierarchically structured into many layers of positions with rank, authority, duties, and privileges clearly specified. Work bureaucracy penetrates social life along many interrelated dimensions, integrating atomized individuals from the private sphere into the public domain of work and linking the macro level of social institutions with the micro level of workers' activities. . . .

The consequences of bureaucratic control are complex and political, with far-reaching effects. A few of the Asian American women interviewed gave vivid descriptions of their organizational experience. One of the logical outcomes is that bureaucratic control tends to intensify the polarized power relationship between the dominant and subordinated groups and among the subordinated groups, attempting to justify the adversarial nature of these power relationships in the name of administration. Control is accomplished through task routinization and depersonalization of relationships within the bureaucracy. Routinization creates fragmentation in the division of labor and cheapens the worth of workers, deskilling them and making them easily replaceable (Braverman 1974; Glenn and Feldberg 1989). The bureaucratic requirement of depersonalization, by imposing rule-governed relationships, produces alienation that isolates workers from one another, threatening group identity and discouraging meaningful social interaction among individuals. One Korean American woman, Kim, who worked as a file clerk in a government agency, was delighted to be interviewed in the middle of her workday so that she could get away from her monotonous, dull, and repetitive filing tasks. She said,

> I began my day early in the morning by putting files, old or new, back into the filing cabinet. It was so boring a job that I was occasionally daydreaming about other things, so that my mind is occupied while my hands are busy. It is an easy job, but very boring. . . . I am not that proud of what I am doing for a living. I guess that I shouldn't complain after all because I get pay, though quite cheap, for do-

ing this kind of lousy job. If I quit, my boss will have no trouble finding someone to replace me.

While Kim did not identify highly with her job, Setsuko, a Japanese clerk-typist in a law firm, achieved dignity by having excellent typing and word-processing skills. However, her competence, while an asset to her supervisor, was a threat to her coworkers in the typing pool, which frequently worked below the output norms regarding time, pace, punctuality, and quality of production. In order to bring the output level up to par, her supervisor imposed a rule forbidding talking about any nonjob-related matters during core office working hours. The supervisor gave Setsuko more typing assignments than others, stationing her in an isolated corner of the office so that she would get more work done and making it more difficult for her to socialize with others.

Moreover, the seemingly obedient and submissive character of Asian American women makes them good candidates for bureaucratic control; their strong task orientation, high achievement motivation, and hard work qualify them as reliable instruments of production. Setsuko was a typical example in her readiness to accept whatever directives she received from her supervisor, even though this involved taking on a disproportionate share of task assignments. Thus, many administrators see Asian American women (as well as men) as ideal candidates for treatment as tokens. Administrators tend to label them a "model minority," a designation many of those so labeled reject or even despise (Cabezas 1986). Tokenism is a powerful and divisive tactic often used by a dominant group to pit individuals or minority groups against each other....

These images were, in many respects, in conflict with the racial/ ethnic backgrounds, cultural expectations, and social practices of these women. A few of the women found it difficult to internalize fully the organizational values of control and to convince others, as well as themselves, of the appropriateness of these values for the organization (Kanter 1977; Laws 1975). For instance, Yang, a Korean woman employed as a social worker, commented, "If I do something well, people will recognize me readily. If I do it poorly, people will think about me as a Korean who is easily to be singled out for bad performance. Then, people don't forgive me that easily.... Sometimes I wonder whether I fit in the office. I was shocked that country of origin can affect me that much."...

Furthermore, the double jeopardy of Asian American women as females and as members of a racial minority adds immense difficulties if they seek to break into the administrative ranks, because sexual and racial stereotypes Whites hold about them generally inhibit the possibility of their presenting a positive image. The women are seen as childlike, possessing little managerial potential (Wright and Delorean 1979), and feminine, possessing weak qualifies of the "second sex" (Acker 1987, Ferguson 1984; Kanter 1977; Martin 1989). Yang, a Korean social worker, perceived that Americans tend to have a low opinion of Korean Americans. A Japanese cafeteria assistant, Mieko, confirmed that observation:

Some people have positive views about Japanese women, but some don't. Although the Americans generally have a high opinion of Japanese, we still do not have an equal footing with the Whites. When it comes to job competition, I was not picked for managerial training sessions, but Clark, a male coworker with less seniority, was selected. I strongly believe that I am a better worker than he is.... This society is not ready for accepting Orientals as a whole in the job market....

In addition, the depersonalization of the organization is an alien element in the cultural experience of many Asian American women, a number of whom come from societies placing high values on collective interest and striving for harmonious interpersonal relations.... As Azucena, a Filipino health administrator, succinctly summed up the situation:

I think that I am an unassimilated kind. After more than ten years of living in the United States, I am still not used to the impersonal, uncaring, and rigid work environment in America and long for the intimate and caring relationships in the workplace which I experienced before I immigrated to this country....

RESISTANCE AND COPING IN THE WORKPLACE

Resistance is an inseparable part of oppression in all forms of power relationships. "Those who resist organizational oppression do so from within the very structure that creates that oppression" (Ferguson 1984:116). Thus, work bureaucracy provides a unique social context in which resistance is manifested in the process of work dynamics. This study presents some interesting results that demonstrate how the Asian American women interacted with supervisors and coworkers when experiencing unfair treatment at work, and reveal how they felt subjectively toward the work dynamics they experienced. Their coping and resistance show struggles against patriarchal rule, racial domination, class exploitation, and cultural barriers.

Dealing with Supervisors

Being brought up in a tradition of deferring to authority, many Asian American women sometimes found themselves in situations that caused difficulties in dealing with supervisors who, in their mind, represented figures with such omnipotent authority that they were not easy to challenge. Given the fact that workers, mostly powerless, depended on the goodwill of the supervisors or bosses, conformity and compliance became important concepts for these women to follow....

One major finding was that women of high occupational status reported having a more difficult time expressing their anger about job problems with their supervisors, especially in demanding a fair share. Those of lower occupational status seemed to have little to lose if they chose to resist and rebel, even when they knew that they could easily be replaced, whereas those of higher occupational status tended to be more concerned with job security and mobility, and were generally afraid of personal repercussions if they were often

at odds with their bosses. Onyoung, a Korean woman working in the housekeeping department of a hotel chain, told me that she occasionally found that other workers took cleaning supplies and equipment home for personal use. When her White female supervisor and male assistant manager investigated the situation, she said, "I learn not to rock the boat, you know. I was not the one who 'squealed' because I knew we were all together on this floor. Many of us depend on this job to support our families. When I am blamed for the things that I do not do and have no part of it, I will yell my guts out to protest. At most I will lose this job. I want my dignity, to be an honorable person, which my parents taught me."

Her case resembles the experience of Black domestic workers (Dill 1988a; Rollins 1985), Chicana private housekeepers (Romero 1988), and Japanese domestic helpers (Glenn 1986), demonstrating how those placed in a low-status occupation can construct personal dignity in managing employer–employee relationships and gain mastery over a situation in which they are socially defined as objects. Fighting back is one of the main keys to survival at work (Dill 1988a).

For professional women, Betty Harragan (1977) and others (Henning and Jardin 1976; Kennedy 1980) advise following Rule No. 1: "absolute deference to the authority invested in your immediate boss." It is important for women workers, especially those aspiring to high positions, to attune carefully to the moods and attitudes of the superior, to present themselves in an approved way, and to shape their image in such a way as to approximate that of their supervisor.... Anger desensitization, tolerance of hostility, and collective shame control are cultural responses to which Asian American women are accustomed in their socialization and responses that are reinforced by their acculturation experience in America. Ichi, a Japanese researcher-scientist, recognized that

People in hiring do not necessarily see Asian women in authority positions, and therefore they do not treat them as seriously as men. When a

problem occurs, I will try to put up with it as much as possible, so that my apparent anger will not bring a bad name to Japanese women [in general]. I will wait until my supervisor is in a good mood; then I will discuss with him and suggest a way in which he could rectify the problem and alter the situation....

Belying their apparently docile and demure appearance, however, some of the Asian American women clearly evidenced inner strength, tenacity, and courage. For these women, resistance was used to undermine organizational tyranny. A firm believer in hard work as a key to success, Bih-Chun, a Chinese computer specialist, described her ways of dealing with her situation:

I work doubly hard at doing my job, to perform at the top of the whole division, and trying to fit into the system in order to overcome the initial problems of being a woman and an Asian American. I got an outstanding achievement award for my exceptional performance. Because of my superiors' dependency on me to do my job as well as theirs, I can be obnoxious sometimes, being critical about how the company works and about how workers are unfairly treated....

Lina, a Filipino executive administrator working in a business firm, presented another view of corporate success, pointing out the naïveté of the "Horatio Alger" myth, which equates hard work with success:

Much of the career advice to women that emphasizes deference to authority, dressing for success, and self-improvement does not always work. To some extent, this career advice is irrelevant to the ways in which the system operates. I see a corporation sometimes promotes incompetence rather than competence, depending on whether one plays the right game or not. My VP is a typical case. I often serve as his scapegoat, being blamed for things that go wrong. For me to keep my job, a lot of energy goes toward covering his mistakes and protecting his incompetence. This is not to deny that my boss does not appreciate my work.... However, the system is such that breaking into it is just like hitting your head against the wall.

Dealing with Coworkers

...Coping strategies used in handling blatant discrimination from coworkers reveal Asian American women's attempts to gain a sense of autonomy, control, and self-worth in situations in which they were socially defined as objects or machines, good only for getting the work done for others. Suffering from unfair treatment helped the women to develop a range of innovative approaches to dealing with oppressive situations. Based on content analysis of the qualitative data, coping strategies used by these women are classified into four main types: confrontational, assertive, affiliative, and indirect/situational adjustment....

The confrontational style, a rather aggressive way of opposing racist, sexist, class-biased circumstances at work, involved head-on protest against those coworkers the women viewed as insensitive and threatening to their survival. The confrontational style was used to fight back in the face of seemingly overwhelming obstacles, to protect one's work rights, and to show unwillingness to compromise oneself when others' wishes were deemed unreasonable. For example, Reiko, a Japanese salesperson in a department store, experienced sexual harassment when a White male customer made sexual remarks and advances toward her. But her White female coworker commented, "Isn't that what a Japanese geisha girl is good for?" Anger was a natural response to this sexually and racially oppressive situation in dealing with her coworker as well as the patron. She recalled angrily,

How others perceive me stereotypically as a geisha girl is beyond me. I asked her [the female coworker] to get off my back. Women tend to be more emotional than men. Once emotion is built up, it might blast off once in a while. White male colleagues are easier to talk to because they handle emotions better than White women. Although I am a U.S.-born Japanese, my ability to speak perfect "American" English has not helped me earn full status as a real American.

Protesting could go as far as quitting one's job rather than putting up with being pushed around.

Quitting was the ultimate form of resistance; the worker walked out of a domination relationship, affirming the importance of her self-respect and of human dignity over job security.

The assertive style was a direct approach by which Asian American women exercised their work rights and independence by negotiating their time, effort, intellect, commitment, and personal involvement with other workers. Perhaps this style represents a combination of the Asian mode of adaptation by tolerance or modesty with the American value placed on internal control. Regardless of ethnicity, nativity, and occupation, about half the women studied chose the assertive coping style, and they were more likely to do so when they dealt with White male workers than with White female ones. The majority reported that they expressed their viewpoints and judgment of the situation, demanded explanations from offensive workers, and focused their efforts on problem solving. In this way, they portrayed themselves as active agents and goal-oriented actors, capable of taking charge of their own lives....

The affiliation style was sometimes used to show the importance of collegial congeniality in approaching problem solving at the workplace. Personal consideration, friendliness, and candidness were mentioned as primary approaches in achieving some kind of parity with coworkers. Asian American women employing this approach tended to emphasize their racial/ethnic and/or gender identification (e.g., consciousness of one's own kind, sisterhood, and "all are fresh from the boat") in order to form an alliance with those in question, to dispel issues of inequity, and to neutralize feelings of injustice....

The last style of coping, indirect/situational adjustment, was basically an indecisive and seemingly passive way of dealing with work problems and with coworkers involved. Instead of tackling the problem directly, some Asian American women chose to take a defensive stand, thereby protecting themselves from the hurt by pushing their tolerance to the limit. Some avoided the problematic situations as much as they possibly could, doing very little about them or hoping that the problems would subside eventually. Some women sought to use the indirect style by writing to or telling the supervisor about an offensive coworker or making an impersonal telephone call to the coworker in question, with the hope that they could discuss the matter and find a solution to the problem. Rizalina, a Filipino program planning assistant, explained, "I was asked to design a system for a project. Janet [white, female] thought that she has the sole privilege to do it. It seems there is a ring of protection around her so that I have difficulty to confront her directly. I went to tell the supervisor about it instead of approaching her. As a rule, I'll try to avoid awkward situations as much is possible."

Their passive resistance sometimes involved not clear-cut coping strategies but indirect strategies of adjusting to situations and personalities as problems occurred. Onyoung, the Korean hotel service worker, while quite aggressive in dealing with the supervisor, in fact protected the interest of her colleagues even though she knew some had transgressed against job norms. Facing interrogation by her supervisors, she narrowly redefined honesty as only applying to herself, but she tried to cover up what other coworkers had blamed her for. "As far as I am concerned, I am an honest person. I didn't do it," she said. But her resistance tended to crystallize around the feeling that her rights were subject to violation, that she was often taken advantage of by others, and that she ought to be prepared to defend herself in order to make her work situation bearable....

Chinese people often say "Silence is golden." Surprisingly, only 6 percent of the Asian American women in the sample said that they elected not to say anything to a problem instigator or to make any statement at all about an incident they perceived to be unfair. Perhaps American acculturation has taught Asian American women to stand up for their rights more readily....

While many scholars (e.g., Dill 1988b; Gilkes 1988; Terrelonge 1989) point out how Black women generally draw their strength from their community, Asian American women, though they have begun to build their diverse communities, gain strength mostly from their families. As revealed in several cases, organizational oppression and resistance seem to hamper their occupational outlook and weaken their work involvement; the family becomes an important resource to sustain them in the work world. Organizational control penetrates family life and increases, directly or indirectly, the dependence of Asian American women on the patriarchy, thus creating a paradox for women in Asian American families. An in-depth study of the interconnectedness between family and work life among Asian American women is needed to gain additional insight into this area.

In essence, women's struggles in the labor market and in the work organization are political in the sense that women have engaged in the kinds of daily activities that are enmeshed in the political and economic processes that challenge the basic power relationships in society. Only when Asian American women and others begin collectively to pressure the dominant groups in society at large to be responsible for these women's oppressed conditions will they be able to initiate structural changes at all levels where they have been denigrated historically. Alternative strategies to redesigning organizations are on the agenda for scholarly research and political action to promote a better quality of work life for all people.

NOTES

Acknowledgments: This article is dedicated to those Asian American women who generously shared their lives with me. The research was supported by the National Institute of Mental Health, Department of Health and Human Services, grant #1-R01 MH31218-01, and by a writing grant from the Pacific Cultural Foundation in Taiwan. The author is solely responsible for this paper's content and form of analysis. Special thanks are given to Elaine Stahl Leo for her editorial help and to Millie DePallo and Michael Zhao for research assistance.

1. This cross-sectional survey is part of a larger multiphase study that empirically examined the effect of specific social and psychological factors on occupational outcomes for Asian American women in the San Francisco and Washington, D.C., metropolitan areas. The San Francisco data set does not include all the information used for the analysis presented in this paper. Detailed information about the study is reported more fully by Esther Chow (1982).

2. The disproportional stratified random sampling design was originally drawn from a comprehensive list of Asian American women compiled from a variety of sources. A checklist was mailed to everyone on this comprehensive list to obtain informed consent, information about the three stratified factors (ethnicity, nativity, and occupation), and other relevant information. A sample based on the results of the returned checklists was randomly selected to include approximately an equal number from each of the subgroups. The final sample included 161 employed Asian American women.

3. To protect the identity of the women being interviewed and the confidentiality of the data provided, I used pseudonyms. The stories provided by the women were accurately presented, but some of the information was recomposed (a technique commonly used in field studies) to assure that distinctive characteristics of certain women could not be clearly identified.

REFERENCES

Acker, Joan. 1987. "Hierarchies, Jobs, and Bodies: A Theory of Gendered Organizations." *Gender and Society* 4: 139–158.

Braverman, Harry. 1974. *Labor and Monopoly Capital.* New York: Monthly Review Press.

Cabezas, Amado. 1986. "The Asian American Today as an Economic Success Model: Some Myths and Realities." Pp. 16–21 in *Break the Silence: A Conference on Anti-Asian Violence,* edited by Bill Ong Hing, Russell Lowe, Ron Wakabayashi, and

Sue Wong. San Francisco: Break the Silence Coalition.

Cheng, Lucie, and Edna Bonacich, eds. 1984. *Labor Immigration Under Capitalism.* Berkeley: University of California Press.

Chow, Esther Ngan-Ling. 1982. *Acculturation of Asian American Professional Women.* Washington, D.C.: National Institute of Mental Health, U.S. Department of Health and Human Services.

———. 1987. "The Development of Feminist Consciousness Among Asian American Women." *Gender and Society* 1(3): 284–299.

Chow, Esther Ngan-Ling, and Catherine White Berheide. 1988. "The Interdependency of Family and Work: A Framework for Family Life Education, Policy, and Practice." *Family Relations* 37:23–28.

Cohen, E. C. 1927. "Chinatown Has Own Spirit of Exclusiveness." *The Evening Star* (Washington, D.C.), August 14.

Davis, Angela. 1981. *Women, Race, and Class.* New York: Random House.

———. 1988a. "'Making Your Job Good Yourself': Domestic Service and the Construction of Personal Dignity." Pp. 33–52 in *Women and the Politics of Empowerment*, edited by Ann Bookman and Sandra Morgen. Philadelphia: Temple University Press.

———. 1988b. "Our Mothers' Grief: Racial Ethnic Women and the Maintenance of Families." *Journal of Family History* 13 (4):415–431.

Edwards, Richard C. 1979. *Contested Terrain.* New York: Basic Books.

Ferguson, Kathy E. 1984. *The Feminist Case Against Bureaucracy.* Philadelphia: Temple University Press.

Gilkes, Cheryl Townsend. 1983. "Going Up for the Oppressed: The Career Mobility of Black Women Community Workers." *Journal of Social Issues* 39 (3):115–139.

———. 1988. "Building in Many Places: Multiple Commitments and Ideologies in Black Women's Community Work." Pp. 53–76 in *Women and the Politics of Empowerment*, edited by Ann Bookman and Sandra Morgen. Philadelphia: Temple University Press.

Glenn, Evelyn Nakano. 1986. *Issei, Nisei, War Bride: Three Generations of Japanese American Women in Domestic Service.* Philadelphia: Temple University Press.

Glenn, Evelyn Nakano, and Roslyn L. Feldberg. 1989. "Clerical Work: The Female Occupation." Pp. 287–311 in *Women: A Feminist Perspective*, edited by Jo Freeman. Fourth edition. Mountain View, Calif.: Mayfield.

Harragan, Betty Lehan. 1977. *Games Mother Never Taught You: Corporate Gamesmanship for Women.* New York: Warner Books.

Hartmann, Heidi. 1981. "The Family as the Locus of Gender, Class and Political Struggle: The Example of Housework." *Signs: Journal of Women in Culture and Society* 6: 366–394.

Henning, Margaret, and Anne Jardin. 1976. *The Managerial Woman.* New York: Pocket Books.

Jones, Jacqueline. 1985. *Labor of Love, Labor of Sorrow: Black Women, Work and the Family from Slavery to the Present.* New York: Basic Books.

Kanter, Rosabeth Moss. 1977. *Men and Women of the Corporation.* New York: Basic Books.

Kennedy, Marilyn Moats. 1980. *Office Politics: Seizing Power, Wielding Clout.* New York: Warner Books.

Ladner, Joyce. 1971. *Tomorrow's Tomorrow: The Black Woman.* Garden City, N.Y.: Doubleday.

Laws, Judith Long. 1975. "The Psychology of Tokenism: An Analysis." *Sex Roles* 1: 51–67.

Martin, Patricia. 1989. "Women's Prospects for Leadership in Social Welfare: A Political Economy Perspective." *Administration in Social Work* 13:117–143.

Piore, Michael J. 1972. "Notes for a Theory of Labor Market Stratification." Working Paper no. 95. Boston: Massachusetts Institute of Technology.

Rollins, Judith. 1985. *Between Women: Domestics and Their Employers.* Philadelphia: Temple University Press.

Romero, Mary. 1988. "Day Work in the Suburbs: The Work Experience of Chicano Private Housekeepers." Pp. 77–92 in *The Worth of Women's Work: A Qualitative Synthesis*, edited by Anne Statham, Eleanor M. Miller, and Hans O. Mauksch. Albany: State University of New York Press.

Terrelonge, Pauline. 1989. "Feminist Consciousness and Black Women." Pp. 556–566 in *Women: A Feminist Perspective*, edited by Jo Freeman. Fourth edition. Mountain View, Calif.: Mayfield.

U.S. Bureau of the Census. 1981. *1980 Census of Population: Supplementary Reports.* Washington, D.C.: U.S. Department of Commerce, Bureau of the Census.

———. 1983. *1980 Census of Population: Detailed Population Characteristics.* Washington, D.C.: U.S. Department of Commerce, Bureau of the Census.

———. 1988. "Asian and Pacific Islander Population in the United States." In *1980 Census of Population.* Washington, D.C.: U.S. Government Printing Office.

Wright, J. Patrick, and John De Lorean. 1979. *On a Clear Day You Can See General Motors.* New York: Avon Books.

Yung, Judy. 1986. *Chinese Women of America: A Pictorial History.* Seattle: University of Washington Press.

44

Disruptions
Improper Masculinities and Schooling

R. W. CONNELL

A couple of decades ago a modest controversy broke out about masculinity and American schooling. The schools, Sexton argued in a widely-read book, were dominated by women and therefore imposed on boys a feminine culture.[1] Red-blooded "boy culture" was marginalized or suppressed, and therefore American males grew to manhood with difficulty in establishing true manliness. This concern was not original with Sexton. As Hantover has shown, the growth of the Boy Scout movement in the United States in the second decade of the century picked up middle-class anxieties about the feminization of boys and offered a kind of masculinizing medicine through Scouting.[2]

This now seems rather comic in the light of the feminist research of the last two decades, which has documented the actual power of men in the education system as in other institutions. The pendulum has swung far in the other direction, with emphasis on the silencing of women's voices in education and in culture more broadly.[3] There can be no honest doubt about the facts of the institutional power of men and the patriarchal character of the public culture.[4]

But this is not to say there are no questions to ask about men. To understand a system of power, one ought to look very closely at its beneficiaries. Indeed, I would argue that one of the cultural supports of men's power is the failure to ask questions about masculinity.

The surge of feminist research on education in the 1970s (epitomized in the remarkable 1975 report of the Australian Schools Commission, *Girls,*

Schools, and Society) found conventional gender stereotypes spread blanket-like through textbooks, career counseling, teacher expectations, and selection processes. This was theorized as the transmission of an oppressive, restrictive "sex role" to girls. It followed that girls would be advantaged by modifying the sex role or even breaking out of it. This led easily to an educational strategy. A program of redress was required, to expand girls' occupational and intellectual horizons, affirm women's worth, and write women into the curriculum.

Almost all this discussion was about girls and their restrictive "sex role." By implication the boys were getting one too. But here the sex-role approach did not translate smoothly into educational reform. Since men are the privileged sex in current gender arrangements, it is not obvious that boys will be advantaged by teachers' efforts to change their "role." On the contrary, boys may resent and resist the attempt.

A puzzled literature on the "male sex role" in the 1970s scratched pretty hard to find ways by which men are disadvantaged or damaged by their sex role.[5] No convincing educational program ever came of it. Teachers grappling with issues of masculinity for boys are now reaching for new concepts.[6] The expectation now is that anyone working on these questions in schools faces a politicized and emotionally charged situation.

This is very much in accord with the development of research since the 1970s. More intensive research techniques, and more sophisticated theories of gender, have brought out two themes in particular. One is the importance of the institutional structure of education and the institutional practices of gender that children encounter in schools. Hansot and Tyack, in an illuminating historical paper, urge us to "think institutionally" about gender and schooling.[7] Thorne shows how situational is the segregation of the sexes in primary schools.[8] Messner shows how the formal structure of organized sport provides a temporary resolution for developmental problems of masculinity.[9] Kessler et al. point to the ways curricula and school organization separate out different kinds of femininity, and different kinds of masculinity, within the same school.[10] They introduce the idea of the "gender regime" of an institution such as a school, the established order of gender relations within it. A remarkable historical study by Heward of a second-echelon private school in England shows how a gender regime intended to produce a particular pattern of masculinity is produced in response to the class and gender strategies of the families who form the school's clientele.[11]

Close-focus historical work, interview research, and ethnography tend to find complexities and contradictions beneath the gender "stereotypes." Thus Walker's 1987 paper on male youth culture in an inner-city school finds several peer groups positioned very differently in relation to the school's cult of competitive sport: some ethnically based peer groups competing through sport, others rejecting it or being marginalized by it.[12] From such research a concern has emerged about the different versions of masculinity to be found in a given cultural context, and the relations of dominance and subordination among them. This gives a new shape to the issue of the formation of masculinity. It is no longer adequate to see this as the absorption of a sex role. It must be seen as an active process of construction, occurring in a field of power relations that are often tense and contradictory, and often involving negotiation of alternative ways of being masculine.

This paper is an attempt to explore how this process works for certain outsiders. It examines the place of schooling in the lives of two groups of

men who are in different ways distanced from the dominant models of masculinity: (a) a group of young unemployed working-class men, recently out of school, growing up in the face of structural unemployment and in the shadow of the prison system; (b) a group of men, mostly some years older and mostly from more affluent backgrounds, who are involved in "green politics," that is, social action on environmental issues.

The first group was contacted mainly through an agency that is responsible for the welfare of unemployed youth and that seeks to place them in training programs. The young men concerned do not consciously reject the hegemonic model of masculinity in their milieu. But where the dominant model of working-class masculinity was built around a wage, a workplace, and the capacity to support a family, these young men *cannot* inhabit such a masculinity; this is ruled out by structural unemployment. They have, in various ways, constructed more fragmented masculinities, some violent and some more passively alienated.[13]

The second group was contacted mainly through organizations in the environmental movement. The men concerned have all been volunteers in "green" campaigns, several of them participating in the famous blockade in the early 1980s that saved the Franklin River from a hydroelectric scheme; some are paid workers in environmental organizations. In the Australian environmental movement there is a strong feminist presence. All these men, accordingly, have had a close encounter with feminism; most, indeed, have been under the necessity of dealing with feminist women on a daily basis. This has put them under strong pressure to adopt a countersexist politics. Several of them have gone on to a conscious attempt at reconstructing masculinity in the light of feminism.[14]

Research on schooling is usually confined to schooling, and thus has difficulty grasping where the school is located in a larger process. This paper is based on life-history interviews with adults that cover family, workplace, sexual relationships, friendships, and politics, in addition to schooling, as settings for the construction of masculinity.

The interviews became the basis of individual case studies, which in turn were grouped for the analysis of collective processes. The interviews were conducted in New South Wales, Australia, in 1985–87; all respondents were English-speaking and mostly of Anglo background.

Rather than following individual narratives, the approach taken in this paper is to identify key moments in the collective process of gender construction, the social dynamic in which masculinities are formed. In such moments the formation of the person, and the history of the educational institution, are simultaneously at issue.

GETTING INTO TROUBLE

Behind Mal Walton's high school is the bush, and at the edge of the bush are the school toilets. This is where Mal and his friends would gather:

> In high school [my friends] were real hoods[†] ["†" indicates an entry in the glossary] too. Like we used to hang down the back... we'd sit down there and smoke cigarettes and talk about women, get dirty books out, going through—what do you call it? I can't think of the word. Just the things you do at high school in the first year.

Mal had been placed in the bottom stream, and was evidently regarded by most of his teachers (though not all) as disruptive. The main reason he was in the bottom stream was that he could not read. He was arrested for theft at fifteen, in the year he left school. He has not had a lasting job in the six years since.

Harry the Eel (so called because of his fanatical devotion to the Parramatta football team "the Eels"), now twenty and about to become a father for the second time, used to practice his school smoking in the same fragrant setting:

> I was in a bit of trouble in the last four years of school. I got busted for—what was it? Second Form it was selling porno books. Third Form it was getting drunk at the school fete, and allegedly holding another bloke down and pouring Scotch down his throat—which we didn't do, he was hassling us for a drink.... They found him drunk and

> they said where did you get it? and he mentioned our names and Biff, straight into it.... Fourth Form, wasn't much happening in fourth form really, busted in the dunnies[†] having a smoke!

Eel started an apprenticeship, but his employer went broke and no one else would take over his training. Since then he has been on the dole, with casual jobs from time to time.

Eel hasn't been arrested, but his friend Jack Harley has. Jack is less of a tactician and fought every authority figure from his parents on. He thinks he was labeled a "troublemaker" at school because of an older cousin. He clashed early and often with teachers: "They bring me down, I'll bring them down." He was expelled from at least one school, disrupting his learning—"I never did any good at school." Eventually he assaulted a teacher. The court "took the teacher's word more than they took mine" and gave him a sentence in a juvenile detention center. Here he learned the techniques of burglary and car theft. About three years later he was doing six months in the big people's prison. At twenty-two he is on the dole, looking for a job to support his one-year-old child and his killer bull terrier.

These three young men come from laboring families, in Mal Walton's case from a very poor family. Their experience of school shows the relationship between the working class and education at its most alienating. What they meet in the school is an authority structure: specifically, the state and its powers of coercion. They are compelled to be at school, and once there—as they see it—they are ordered about arbitrarily by the teachers. The school is a relatively soft part of the state, but behind it stands the "hard" machinery of police, courts, and prisons. Push the school too far, and, like Jack Harley, one triggers an intervention by the enforcers.

Up against an authority structure, acts of resistance or defiance mean "getting into trouble." This is one of Jack Harley's commonest phrases and indicates how his actions are constantly defined in relation to institutional power. Fights with other boys, arguments with teachers, theft, poor learning, conflicts with parents, are all essentially the same. One can try to retreat beyond the routine reach of institutional power, as Mal Walton and his friends did in their idyllic moments in the toilet block on the edge of the bush. Yet even there, one will be "in trouble" when the authorities raid the retreat, as they did to Eel.

At the same time trouble has its attractions, and may be courted. Mal Walton, for instance, was caned a lot when he went to a Catholic primary school. So were his friends. In fact, he recalls, they fell into a competition to see who could get caned most. No one would win: "We just had big red hands." Why this competition? "Nothing to do; or probably proving that I was stronger than him or he was stronger than me." A violent discipline system invites competition in machismo.

More generally, the authority structure of the school becomes the antagonist against which one's masculinity is cut. Jack Harley, in the comment on teachers quoted above, articulated an ethic of revenge that defines a masculine pride common in his milieu. But he lacked the judgment to keep it symbolic. Teachers often put up with verbal aggression as part of their job, but they are hardly likely to stand still when physically attacked. So the courting of trouble calls out an institutional response, which may push an adolescent assertion of masculine pride toward an early-adult criminal career.

"Trouble" is both sexualized and gendered. Getting the "dirty books" out and "talking about women" are as essential a part of the peer group activity as smoking and complaining about teachers. In the mass high school system, sexuality is both omnipresent and illicit. To act or talk sexually becomes a breach of order, a form of "trouble," in itself. But at the same time it is a means of maintaining order—the order of patriarchy—via the subordination of women and the exaltation of one's maleness.

Patrick Vincent, currently on probation for car theft, succinctly explains why he liked being sent to a coeducational high school after being expelled from his boys-only church school: "Excellent, chicks everywhere, good perve."[†] He boasts that within a week all the girls in his class wanted to climb into his bed. The treatment of young women by these young men is often flatly exploitative.

KNOWING WHERE YOU STAND

To other boys, the hoods in the toilet may be objects of fear. Danny Taylor recalls his first year in an urban working-class high school. Despite being big for his age, he hated the physical contest:

> When the First Form[†] joins and all comes together from all different [primary] schools, there's this thing like sorting out who was the best fighter, who is the most toughest and aggressive boy in the form, and all the little mobs* and cliques develop. So it was like this pecking order stuff... and I was really frightened of this.

He did not enjoy high school until Form IV (about age sixteen), when "all the bullies left."

This is not peculiar to urban schools. Stewart Hardy, the son of a laboring family in the dry, flat country in the far west of New South Wales, makes the usual contrast between city and country but paints the same kind of picture:

> In the country... it was easier for us to get along with each other, although there was the usual dividing: the cool guys hang out together, and the cool girls hang out together, and there was the swots[†] and the wimps.... You knew where you stood, which group you belonged to.

Stewart and Danny joined the wimps and the swots, respectively. Both managed to use the education system to win social promotion (though in both cases limited) out of their class of origin.

The process of demarcating masculinities in secondary school has been noticed in ethnographies of working-class schools in Britain and Australia.[15] Willis's vivid picture of the "lads" and the "ear'oles" is justly celebrated. Such demarcation is not confined to working-class schools. A very similar sorting-out has been documented in a ruling-class private school, between the "bloods" (hearty, sporting) and the "Cyrils" (wimpish, academic).[16]

This suggests a typology of masculinities, even a marketplace of masculinities. To "know where you stand," in Stewart Hardy's phrase, seems to mean *choosing* a masculinity, the way one might choose a football team to root for.

It is important to recognize that differing masculinities are being produced in the same school context. But to picture this as a marketplace, a free choice of gender styles, would be misleading. These "choices" are strongly structured by relations of power.

In each of the cases mentioned, the differentiation of masculinities occurs in relation to a school curriculum that organizes knowledge hierarchically and sorts students into an academic hierarchy. By institutionalizing academic failure via competitive grading and streaming, the school forces differentiation on the boys. But masculinity is organized—on the macro scale—around social power. Social power in terms of access to higher education, entry to professions, command of communication, is being delivered by the school system to boys who are academic "successes." The reaction of the "failed" is likely to be a claim to other sources of power, even other definitions of masculinity. Sporting prowess, physical aggression, or sexual conquest may do.

Indeed, the reaction is often so strong that masculinity as such is claimed for the cool guys. Boys who follow an academic path are defined, conversely, as effeminate (the "Cyrils"). When this situation is reached, there is a *contest for hegemony* between rival versions of masculinity. The school, though it has set this contest up, may be highly ambivalent about the outcome. Many school administrations actively seek competitive sporting success as a source of prestige. The first-rate football team, or the school's swimming champions, may attract as much honor and indulgence from the staff as the academic elite.[17]

The differentiation of masculinities, then, is not simply a question of individual difference emerging or individual paths being chosen. It is a

collective process, something that happens at the level of the institution and in the organization of peer group relationships.

Indeed, the relationship of any one boy to the differentiation of masculinities may change over time. Stewart Hardy remembers being terrified on his arrival at high school (and even before, with "horror tales" about high school circulating in his primary class). He and his friends responded by "clinging to each other for security" in a wimpish huddle in Form I. But then:

> Once I started getting used to the place and not so afraid of my own shadow, I felt here was my chance to develop a new identity. Now I can be a coolie, I can be tough. So I started to be a bit more belligerent. I started to get in with the gangs a bit, slag off[†] teachers behind their backs, and tell dirty jokes and stuff like that.

But it didn't last. After a while, as Stewart got older,

> I decided all that stuff was quite boring. It didn't really appeal to me, being a little shit any more, it didn't really suit my personality.

This was not just a matter of Stewart's "personality." His parents and his teachers put on more pressure for academic performance as the School Certificate (Form IV) approached. Indeed, his parents obliged him to stay on at school to Form VI, long after the "gangs" had left.

OVER THE HUMP

The labor market in modern capitalist economies is segmented and stratified in a number of dimensions. Perhaps the most powerful division in it is not any longer the blue-collar/white-collar divide, but the distinction between (a) a broad market for more or less unskilled general labor—whether manual or clerical—and (b) a set of credentialed labor markets for specific trades, semiprofessions, and professions. The public education system, as the main supplier of credentials (certificates, diplomas, degrees), is deeply implicated in this division. When Stewart Hardy's working-class parents ignored his protests and made him stay on in high school, they were pursuing a family strategy to get him over the hump between these two labor markets and into the world of credentialed labor.

For Stewart it was a rocky path. He resented the pressure, slacked off at school, got involved with a girlfriend, and did "miserably" at the Higher School Certificate (HSC). Soon after that, he ditched the girlfriend and got religion. But after he had been a while in the work force, his parents' pressure bore fruit, and he took himself to a technical college to have a second try at the HSC. This time he did so well that he qualified for university. He is now (aged twenty-four) doing a part-time arts degree and, at the same time, a computer training program organized by his employer, a big bank. He does not see computing as a career, but as a fallback: "If things get tight I can always go back to being a programmer, because there are always jobs for that." He may get into a career through his degree.

Stewart has got the message about qualifications, with a vengeance:

All the time I wasted before, I could have been at university getting a degree. Seven years out of school and I have absolutely no qualification at all. All I did was bum around and take whatever jobs came up.

The contrast with Mal Walton, Jack Harley, and Patrick Vincent is stark. They are glad of "whatever jobs come up" and expect to be at the mercy of such economic chances as far as they can see into the future. To them it isn't "time wasted," it is life.

Through the mechanism of educational credentials, Stewart Hardy has bought into a different construction of masculinity, in which the notion of a long-term career is central. A calculative attitude is taken toward one's own life. A passive and subordinated position in training programs is accepted in order to provide future protection from economic fluctuations. The life course is projected as if up a slope, with periods of achievement distinguished from plateaus of wasted time. The central themes of masculinity here are ratio-

nality and responsibility rather than pride and aggressiveness.

Young men from more privileged class backgrounds are likely to take this perspective from the start. Their families' collective practice is likely to be organized around credentials and careers from before they were born. For instance, I come from a family whose men have been in the professions—engineering, the church, medicine, education, law—for several generations. It never occurred to me that I would not go to university in my turn.

In such a milieu the practice of credentialing does not even require active consent, merely the nonoccurrence of a refusal. As Bill Lindeman, son of an administrator and an academic researcher, put it—

Because I'd had three siblings who'd gone ahead of me, so there was that sort of assumption there, that the opportunity was given to me to not question it, to not go to something else. And I didn't have strong interests: the strongest interest I had was surfing, in the Sixth Form. And there was nothing really to motivate me to go off and do anything else. So I went to Uni.

Here, very visibly, is a life course being constructed collectively and institutionally, through the education system and families' relationships to it. Of course, the young person has to do such things as sit in class and write exam answers: There is a personal practice involved. But to a marked degree it is a passive practice, following an external logic. The person's project is simply to become complicit in the functioning of an institutional system and the privileges it delivers. There is a painful contrast with the personal investments, and cost, involved in the hoods' doomed assaults on the same institutional system. One begins to feel the reason in all that anger.

DRY SCIENCES

What privileged young men find at the end of the educational conveyor belt is not necessarily to their taste. This becomes very clear in life histories from the environmental activists. Bill Lindeman went to university because there was nothing motivating him to go elsewhere. But after he had been there—and I hope it pleases his teachers—he began to think.

> When I chose science I chose zoology. My sister and my brother had done exactly the same and my other brother was doing physics, so we were all doing science. There was a strong analytical bent there. I chose life science because—that stemmed from my earlier childhood, enjoying natural places. It wasn't till I'd left Uni that I realized I was so bored with ninety-nine point nine percent of it. I just wasn't finding nature in laboratories, cutting up rats and dogfish. The vitality and change that you can learn from nature just isn't there. It was dry. I didn't relate it to the living world.

Bill's critique of the abstractness, the unlifelikeness, of biology is a familiar theme in critiques of other disciplines and of academic knowledge in general.[18] Bill's version is informed by his "green" politics. He began to resolve the problem in a research project involving long field trips to the Snowy Mountains, and then became deeply committed to environmental activism. In that context he also became concerned with the remaking of masculinity, though he has not specifically linked this theme back to his academic experience.

There is, nevertheless, a connection. The dry sciences of academic abstraction involve a particular institutionalization of masculinity. Masculinity shapes education, and education forms masculinity. This has become clear from work on the history and philosophy of science. It is not incidental that most of the people constructing Western science over the last four hundred years have been men. The view of the natural world that mainstream science embodies, the language and metaphors of scientific analysis—a discourse of uncovering, penetrating, controlling—have some of their deepest roots in the social relations between men and women. A different kind of knowledge could have been produced, and to some extent is produced, by people whose thinking is

shaped by experience of a different location in gender relations. For instance, a science constructed by women might be more likely to use metaphors of wholeness than metaphors of analysis, seek cooperation with nature rather than domination over it.

Some early work in this vein implied that the structure of science reflected masculinity in general, that the attitude of abstraction and domination over nature was based on something intrinsic to being male. This argument would hardly apply to the relation of men to nature in central Australian aboriginal society, where the ethic of humans caring for the land and the land's "ownership" of the people is traditional.[19] Western science is, rather, based on a culturally specific version of masculinity. Indeed, we may see it as a class-specific version. There is a wide gap between technocratic masculinity as embodied in science and the hot, loud, messy masculinity of the "hoods."

Yet the version of masculinity to which Bill Lindeman is pointing is important, even crucially important, in the contemporary world. Winter and Robert some time ago noted the importance of the changing scale and structure of the capitalist economy for the dynamics of masculinity—a theme much ignored by "men's studies" literature since.[20] The dry sciences are connected, on the one hand, to administration, whose importance is obvious in a world of enormous state apparatuses and multinational corporations. On the other hand, they are connected to professionalism, which is a synthesis of knowledge, power, and economic privilege. Professionalism is central both to the application of developing technologies and to the social administration of modern mass populations.

In both respects the sciences are connected to power, and they represent an *institutionalized* version of the claim to power that is central in hegemonic masculinity. But this is not the crude assertion of personal force that is all the power someone like Jack Harley can mobilize. Rather it is the organized, collective power embodied in large institutions like companies, the state, and property markets. This is power that delivers economic and cultural advantage to the relatively small number of people who can operate this machinery. A man who can command this power has no need for riding leathers and engine noise to assert masculinity. His masculinity is asserted and amplified on an immensely greater scale by the society itself.

READING FEMINISM

The men in the study who are involved in counter-sexist politics, or who have adopted some feminist principles, have almost all read feminist books. Indeed, some say this is their main source of feminist ideas, alongside personal relationships with feminist women. In contrast, mass media seem to be the main source of information about feminism (more exactly, misinformation about feminism) among men who have *not* moved toward feminism.

Contemporary feminism is a highly literate political movement. The mobilization of the "second wave" was accompanied by a vast outpouring of writing: new books, new magazines, special issues of old journals, and so on.[21] Students and teachers made up a high proportion of activists. Writers like Simone de Beauvoir, Betty Friedan, and Mary Daly occupy a central place in modern feminism. The conflict of texts is central to the definition of its various factions and currents.[22] To become a feminist does not absolutely require a higher degree in literature, but it is certainly usual that someone consciously becoming feminist will read a lot.

Many people cannot read. This is true absolutely for Mal Walton, whose alienation from school is described above. He was tipped out into the labor market at fifteen unable to read a job advertisement. He is desperately disadvantaged by illiteracy, tries to conceal it from the employment service as well as from employers, and is currently asking his girlfriend to teach him to read. Illiteracy in first-world countries tends to be concentrated among poor and marginalized groups.[23] In a case like Mal's it is easy to see its class-driven

connection with "getting into trouble," the war on school in which Mal's embattled masculinity was shaped.

More commonly in rich countries like the United States and Australia, young people do learn to read, in the sense that they can decode the letters and spell out the words, but do not put this skill to use for anything much beyond job advertisements and sports results. I think this is true for Eel and for Jack Harley. Patrick Vincent is in between, he can read reasonably well but has difficulty writing. None of these young men ever mention *ideas* they have got from print, only those that come from talk and television.

There is a level of *political literacy* where reading opens up new ideas, poses alternatives to existing reality, explains what forces are at work in the wider world. These young men have not entered this world. They are only likely to if there is a major politicization of the working class and a massive adult education initiative. Since the mass communication system that they are plugged into, commercial television, is totally opposed to radical reform, the strong likelihood is that they never will reach political literacy.

The men who do grapple with the textual politics of feminism are likely to be from privileged class backgrounds; Bill Lindeman's political literacy is an aspect of his easy insertion into higher education. Or they are men who, like Danny Taylor, have used the education system to escape a working-class milieu.

In neither case is the reading likely to be uplifting and enjoyable. The literature they are most likely to encounter, the "public face" of feminism, is—not to put too fine a point on it—hostile to men, and little is included to make distinctions between groups of men.[24] The reader is likely to encounter a lurid picture of men *en bloc* as rapists, batterers, pornographers, child abusers, militarists, exploiters—and women as victims. Titles like *Female Sexual Slavery, Women of Ideas and What Men Have Done to Them, Pornography: Men Possessing Women* set the tone. Young men who read much of this literature and take it seriously seem to have one major reaction: severe feelings of guilt. Barry Ryan sums it up:

> After university I was at the stage where I could understand academic literature, and I read some pretty heavy stuff, which made me feel terrible about being male for a long time.

Guilt is an emotion with social effects, but in this case they are likely to be disempowering rather than positive. A young man "feeling terrible about being male" will not easily join with other men in social action. Nor can he feel solidarity (except at some symbolic level) with women. Thus guilt implies that men's personalities must change but undermines the social conditions for changing them, an enterprise that requires substantial interpersonal support.

Nor is there any useful set of texts to turn to. In terms of what is widely available, there is little between popular feminism (which accuses men) and mass media (which ridicule feminism). A small literature of masculinity therapy exists, designed to assuage the guilt feelings of men affected by feminism.[25] This is almost as demobilizing as the guilt itself.

In such a situation, an educational effort in schools and tertiary institutions might bear rich fruit. Courses on sexual politics do exist at both levels. But they are few, especially in schools. Barry Ryan is the only one of the respondents to describe a school course of this kind, in a progressive private school:

> The teachers at that free school were the ones who decided to implement that sexism program and we [the students] were involved in it. I remember having to go and make a verbal submission. . . . We got this course together. I remember having all-male groups and the women having all-women groups, and talking about sexism, and that was basically it. We did a lot of discussion about sexism and how we communicated about women. I didn't learn that much in the course itself, it just taught me that it was something that I was going to have to think about. And so from then on I was always thinking about it.

On Barry's account the organizing framework of the course is "sexism," which would imply a focus on attitudes and perhaps a moralization of the issue.

Two respondents described meeting feminist content in tertiary courses, though not as focused as Barry's school course. Both had come back to education after a period in the workforce, with a project of personal change in mind. This may explain why they were in courses dealing with such issues. Material on sexual politics is rare in tertiary courses with high proportions of male students.

REFLECTIONS

In this paper I have been trying to give some articulation to two "voices" that are at best muted, at worst silenced, in the discourse of patriarchy. The interviews show an aspect of the formation of masculinity that is more conflictual and more contradictory than the older accounts of sex role socialization implied. The school is not necessarily in harmony with other major "agencies" like the family or the workplace. It is not necessarily in harmony with itself. Some masculinities are formed by battering against the school's authority structure, others by smooth insertion into its academic pathways, others again by a tortuous negotiation of possibilities. Teachers' own characters and sexual politics are not brought into focus in these interviews, but they are no less complex than the sexual politics of the pupils.[26]

Educational institutions sometimes explicitly address themes of masculinity, and examples are documented in these interviews. They range from the countersexist course described by Barry Ryan to the organized sports mentioned by many of the respondents. In most of these life stories, sport (Eel is the obvious exception) does not have the significance, either as symbol or as practice, that has been suggested in some other studies of the making of masculinity.[27] It may be that choosing two groups that are in various ways distanced from mainstream versions of masculinity has found life stories in which sport is less important than usual. Or it may be that we need to reconsider the role of sport more generally. It is culturally conspicuous as an arena of masculinity; but mundane institutional processes may be more broadly significant in the shaping of personality as practical being in the world.[28] Only a diminishing minority of men continue to practice team sports after mid-adolescence.

In the long perspective, I would argue, it is the inexplicit, indirect effects of the way schools work that are crucial. A stark case is the way streaming and "failure" push groups of working-class boys toward alienation, and state authority provides them a perfect foil for the construction of a combative, dominance-focused masculinity. Equally clear is the role of the academic curriculum and its machinery of assessment and selection in institutionalizing a rationalized masculinity in professions and administration.

To put the point in more familiar language, the "hidden curriculum" in sexual politics is more powerful than the explicit curriculum. This creates a dilemma for people concerned with democratizing gender relations in the schools. What the school acknowledges as its activity in relation to gender, and may therefore be willing to discuss under the heading of "equal opportunity" or "anti-discrimination," is less significant than what it does not acknowledge. A change of awareness, a bringing-effects-to-light, must happen before the full spectrum of the school's influence can even be debated.

The intractable situation in schools has a lot in common with the difficulty of formulating a progressive sexual politics for heterosexual men in other forums. Despite promising beginnings, it has proved difficult to find or create a base for a consistent countersexist practice.[29] The contrast with the political mobilization of gay men in gay liberation, and more recently around AIDS issues, is striking. The structural problem is obvious. Heterosexual men are the dominant group in the gender order of contemporary society; therefore, propping up patriarchy, rather than demolishing it,

will advantage them. In a quite basic way, trying to mobilize a countersexist politics is asking heterosexual men to act against their social interests.

Yet if recent research has shown anything, it is that heterosexual masculinity is not homogeneous; it is fissured, divergent, and stressed in many ways. The *possibility* of an educational politics of masculinity exists in these differences and tensions. Can this possibility be turned to practical account?

To the extent that learning depends on "interest," in the psychological sense, the omens are good. There is no lack of interest in questions of sexuality, gender, and sexual politics among boys and young men—as the topics of conversation in Mal Walton's toilet block illustrate. For many it is a matter of absorbing concern.[30]

At present the resources for responding to this interest are deployed in a way that makes them spectacularly difficult to use. Feminist textual politics are inaccessible to most men and require a teeth-gritting effort from the few who make contact. Courses on sexual politics are located mostly in higher education, which most men (like most women) do not reach. They are specifically located in sectors of higher education, (such as humanities courses) not entered by most of the men who do become students. School-level equity programs concerned with gender are mostly targeted on girls, as might be expected given their "equal opportunity" rationale.

The first task, then, is simply to frame programs that stand a chance of reaching large numbers of boys. Given the importance of the academic curriculum and selection process in the shaping of masculinities, it would be self-defeating to rely mainly on "extracurricular" special-purpose programs such as sex education. As Yates has forcefully argued, countersexist action in schools must be concerned with mainstream curriculum and school organization. It is a question of an effort *across the curriculum,* much as language development is now conceived.[31] Thus, a school trying to examine and reflect on masculinity with its pupils will do so in relation to sport, in relation to science, in relation to art and literature, in relation to personal interaction in the peer group and between teachers and pupils, and in relation to the school's own institutional practices such as examining, streaming, and the exercise of authority.

Such an approach is in fact adopted in schools that have had some success in countersexist work in a coeducational situation, such as Hugh Myddleton Junior School in London:

> Monitoring the classroom interactions and the use of social space by boys in the school has led to a firm, if understated, affirmative action policy at the school. For example, the arrival of the new micro-computer equipment led to a decision to prohibit the boys from using it until the girls got a head start. In classrooms traditional girls' activities are validated by granting more space to their discussion and activities. The girls are encouraged to be vocally demonstrative. Boys are encouraged to dance, and a good music-in-the-nursery program has been developed.... Changed relations between kids and teachers have been encouraged because Richard [the principal] refuses to be the discipline ogre of the school.... A slow deliberate building of gains made over the last ten years has produced a consensus on sexism that we'd all like to see. It also shows what can be done by a male teacher when he puts effort into the issue seriously.[32]

We are still far from having a well-reasoned overall strategy in gender education within which the countercurrents in masculinity could find a clear voice. Perhaps that is too much to expect at present. But there are some more limited rationales on which teachers can act.

For one thing, the sources of information about sexuality and gender available to boys are often narrow and reactionary. It is an appropriate purpose for schools to introduce their pupils to the *whole* truth about an important area of their lives. That means introducing them to gay sexuality as well as straight, to the range of gender patterns across the world, to issues of rape and domestic violence as well as happy families. To do this requires prioritizing the experiences of those who

are usually silenced or marginalized, especially women. This is not likely to be easy to do with many adolescent boys, but it is at least a coherent educational goal and one that may call on motives of curiosity and sympathy to expand horizons.

What this might mean is shown in Lees's splendid study of adolescent girls' experiences of sexuality. Lees argues for making "social education" the basis of sex education:

> Questions relating to the morality of sexual relations, domestic violence and the objectification of girls would be on the agenda. Instead of focusing purely on the mechanics of contraception, reasons for the fact that only a third of sexually active teenagers actually use contraception would be critically examined... It is by challenging the terms on which girls participate in social life that boys and girls can be encouraged to see their relationships not in sexist stereotypical ways or as sex objects, but in terms of their human attributes.[33]

It is the inclusion of girls' and women's experiences of sexuality that gives the possibility of challenging sexist and abusive discourse among boys.

The life histories document a good many blocked paths, cases where the development of a patriarchal masculinity follows from a sense of being trapped, or where an attempt at reconstruction peters out in frustration, doubts, or confusion. In my teaching on issues of gender at university level, I have often seen men starting out with good will; then, confronted with the endless facts of gender inequality, and feeling themselves under an increasing fire of blame, turn away because they had no method for dealing with this and saw nothing but more blame and guilt coming down the pipeline.

Developing a sense of agency, a confidence in being able to accomplish something on these issues, is needed. Here cooperative work with feminist women is essential. Educators may get very useful cues from people working on problems about adult masculinity, such as counselors working with battering husbands and unionists taking countersexist action in workplaces.[34] Politics was once defined as "slow boring through hard boards," and no one should expect quick results in this corner of sexual politics. But we now have enough leads, from practice and research, to make the effort worth undertaking.

GLOSSARY FOR OVERSEAS READERS

Hoods: Toughs, delinquents.
Dunnies: Outdoor toilets, so called from being traditionally painted a dun color.
Perve: The Male Gaze, looking at women as sex objects; or at women's underclothes, a couple having intercourse, etc.
Mob: Group (e.g., a flock of sheep, a peer group of people)—no overtone of Mafia.
Forms I–VI: The six years of high school in the New South Wales system. Form VI leads to the Higher School Certificate at matriculation level. Most working-class boys leave at Form IV.
Swots: Enthusiastic students, or simply those who "succeed" at academic work.
Slag off: To verbally abuse.

NOTES

1. P. Sexton, *The Feminized Male: Classrooms, White Collars, and the Decisions of Manliness* (New York: Random House, 1969).
2. J. P. Hantover, "The Boy Scouts and the Validation of Masculinity," *Journal of Social Issues* 34 (1) (1978): 184–95.
3. A. Rich, *On Lies, Secrets, and Silence* (New York: Norton, 1979).
4. R. W. Connell, *Gender and Power* (Stanford: Stanford University Press, 1987); B. B. Hess and M. M. Ferree, *Analyzing Gender* (Newbury Park, California: Sage, 1987).
5. T. Carrigan, R. W. Connell, and J. Lee, "Toward a New Sociology of Masculinity," *Theory and Society* 14 (5) (1985): 551–604.
6. G. W. Dowsett, *Boys Own* (Sydney: Inner City Education Centre, 1985); C. Thompson, "Education and Masculinity," in A. O. Carelli, ed., *Sex Equity in Education* (Springfield, Illinois: Thomas, 1988), 47–54.
7. E. Hansot and D. Tyack, "Gender in Public Schools: Thinking Institutionally," *Signs* 13 (4) (1988): 741–60.
8. B. Thorne, "Girls and Boys Together...But Mostly Apart: Gender Arrangements in Elementary Schools," in *Relationships and Development*, ed. W. W. Hartup and Z. Rubin (Hillsdale, Erlbaum, 1986), 167–84.
9. M. Messner, "Boyhood, Organized Sports, and the Construction of Masculinities," *Journal of Contemporary Ethnography* 18 (4) (1990): 416–44.
10. S. Kessler, D. J. Ashenton, R. W. Connell, and G. W. Dowsett, "Gender Relations in Secondary Schooling," *Sociology of Education* 58 (1) (1985): 34–48.
11. C. Heward, *Making a Man of Him* (London: Routledge, 1988).
12. J. C. Walker, *Louts and Legends* (Sydney: Allen & Unwin, 1988).
13. M. Donaldson, "Labouring Men: Love, Sex and Strife," *Australian and New Zealand Journal of Sociology* 23 (3) (1987): 165–84. R. W. Connell, "Live Fast and Die Young: The Construction of Masculinity among Young Working-Class Men on the Margin of the Labour Market," submitted for publication.
14. R. W. Connell, "Remaking Masculinity in the Context of the Environmental Movement," *Gender & Society*, 4 (4), in press.
15. D. H. Hargreaves, Social Relations in a Secondary School (London: Routledge & Kegan Paul, 1967); P. Willis, *Learning to Labour* (Farnborough, England: Saxon House, 1977); J. C. Walker, *Louts and Legends*.
16. R. W. Connell, *Teachers' Work* (Sydney: Allen & Unwin, 1985).
17. R. W. Connell, "An Iron Man: The Body and Some Contradictions of Hegemonic Masculinity," in *Sport, Men, and the Gender Order: Critical Feminist Perspectives* M. A. Messner and D. F. Sabo, eds. (Champaign, Illinois: Human Kinetics Books, 1990).

18. P. Lafitte, *The Person in Psychology* (London: Routledge & Kegan Paul, 1957); L. Johnson, *Free U.* (Sydney: Free University, 1968); A. Rich, *On Lies, Secrets, and Silence*.

19. K. Maddock, *The Australian Aborigines*, 2d ed. (Ringwood: Australia: Penguin, 1982): 29–36.

20. M. F. Winter and E. R. Robert, "Male Dominance, Late Capitalism, and the Growth of Instrumental Reason," *Berkeley Journal of Sociology* 24 (25) (1980): 249–80.

21. C. Ehrlich, "The Woman Book Industry," *American Journal of Sociology* 78 (1973): 1031–44.

22. H. Eisenstein, *Contemporary Feminist Thought* (London: Unwin Paperbacks, 1984); L. Segal, *Is the Future Female?* (London: Virago, 1987).

23. C. St. J. Hunter and D. Harman, *Adult Illiteracy in the United States* (New York: McGraw-Hill, 1979).

24. L. Segal, *Is the Future Female?*

25. H. Goldberg, *The Inner Male* (New York: Signet, 1987); W. Farrell, *Why Men Are the Way They Are* (New York: Berkeley, 1988).

26. R. W. Connell, *Teachers' Work*.

27. M. Messner, "Boyhood, Organized Sports, and the Construction of Masculinities"; R. W. Connell, "An Iron Man."

28. R. W. Connell, *Gender and Power*.

29. A. Tolson, *The Limits of Masculinity* (London: Tavistock, 1977); J. Snodgrass, *For Men against Sexism* (Albion, CA.: Times Change Press, 1977).

30. D. C. Holland and M. A. Eisenhart, *Educated in Romance* (Chicago: University of Chicago Press, 1990).

31. L. Yates, "The Theory and Practice of Counter-Sexist Education in Schools," *Discourse* 3 (2) (1983): 33–44.

32. G. W. Dowsett, *Boys Own*.

33. S. Lees, *Losing Out: Sexuality and Adolescent Girls* (London: Hutchinson, 1986): 149–50.

34. J. Ptacek, "Why Do Men Batter Their Wives?" in *Feminist Perspectives on Wife Abuse*, ed. K. Yllo and M. Bograd (Newbury Park, California: Sage, 1988), 133–57; D. Adams, "Treatment Models of Men Who Batter: A Profeminist Analysis" in Yllo and Bograd, *Feminist Perspectives on Wife Abuse*, 176–99; S. Gray, "Sharing the Shop Floor," in *Beyond Patriarchy*, ed. M. Kaufman (Toronto: Oxford University Press, 1987).

45

"Becoming Somebody"

Aspirations, Opportunities, and Womanhood

WENDY LUTTRELL

My parents they sit down and tell us, you going to be a school teacher. You know how they think. They told us what they wanted us to do, you know, so we wouldn't have to work as hard as them. But we knowed we weren't going to be. 'Cause we didn't have too many school teachers no way. The two schools we went to weren't but one school teacher.

So is that what you wanted to do—to be a school teacher?

I don't know, I guess a school teacher. That's the only thing we knowed. We didn't think about anything else.

When I was in grade school they asked us what we wanted to be when we grew up. I wrote that I wanted to be a judge. The nuns got very upset with this and asked me if I had copied it from somewhere. I mean, what little kid from the neighborhood ever thought about being a judge?

Despite their distinct backgrounds and experiences, these two women share similar stories about childhood aspirations. Ola, born and raised in a southern rural community, recalls her parents' hopes that one of their eight children would become a schoolteacher, yet as a child she knew that such a possibility was a dream, not a reality. Throughout the rest of her interview Ola elaborates on and accounts for this gap between her and her dreams and her realities as a Black woman growing up in the rural south. Joanne, born and raised in a northeastern, urban, industrialized neighborhood, describes how she first learned about the gap between her dreams and her destiny

as a White, working-class woman. Having revealed her longings to be a judge, Joanne remembers the force with which she was challenged by school officials. For the remainder of her interview, Joanne explains how she came to take on her teachers' views as her own.

This chapter is about what two groups of women remember about their childhood aspirations and what we learn from their accounts about how gender, race and class shaped what they "knew" about their futures. Their stories are part of a comparative ethnographic study which analyzes the past and present schooling experiences of women learners in two adult basic-education programs to show the effect of social differences on women's knowledge and power. A number of compelling mobility studies document the statistical reality of the part played by social differences in people's life trajectories and chances. Yet, we know little about the narrative realities of these patterns or how social differences and inequalities come into being and are sustained. This chapter focuses on women's aspirational stories as windows into these narrative realities and suggests new ways to theorize issues of gender, race and class. . . .

THE WOMEN IN THE STUDY

I provide here a brief sketch of each group of women. My intention is to discuss the similarities and differences in how the women interpreted their lives and projected their futures, rather than to generalize about either group. The women will be referred to by locality as the Philadelphia and North Carolina women. In the past I have identified the women by race and class (Luttrell 1989). However, these labels can serve to fix the women's identities and make it difficult for the reader to focus on how gender, race and class are produced and negotiated, which is the subject of this chapter (Ginsberg and Tsing 1990).

All the Philadelphia women were White and had been raised in the same neighborhood, which, when the study began, was in flux and disarray because of industrial relocation and massive social-service cutbacks. They had all attended neighborhood schools during the late 1940s, 1950s and early 1960s; only 20 percent had finished high school. They had moved in and out of the workforce as clerical workers, factory hands, waitresses, hospital or teachers' aides; two women were displaced homemakers when the study began in 1980.

All the North Carolina women were Black and had grown up in southern, rural communities where they had experience doing farm work; most had picked cotton or tended tobacco during their youth. They had attended segregated rural schools, but because of the demands of farm life, lack of transportation, and racial discrimination their school attendance had been sporadic. Only two of the Black women had graduated from high school, one of whom had completed one year at a local Black college. During the study all were employed at a university but shared similar work histories which included domestic work in White people's homes.

There were significant differences in the two groups of women. While equal numbers had gotten pregnant as teenagers, a higher proportion of the Philadelphia women had married as a result. More of the North Carolina than the Philadelphia women had been single heads of households, although during the course of the study this difference declined. The North Carolina women had lower incomes, earning no more than $8,000 a year; the Philadelphia women's income averaged $10,000. The women all shared one basic charac-

teristic: they were all mothers ranging in age between twenty-five and fifty with children still living at home.

There are many contrasting experiences to consider including race, region, ethnicity, religion, schooling, levels of economic deprivation, political participation all of which give rise to the different voices and dialogues about childhood aspirations presented in this chapter....

ASPIRATIONAL STORIES

Central to the women's aspirational stories is what each group of women "knew" about their futures:

> *The time I was coming along you could do housework, you could baby-sit, work jobs in the back of a kitchen, you know, or you could clean up outside.*

> *When I got grown up you couldn't find no job nowhere but tending to somebody's babies or cleaning somebody's house.*

> *If you were lucky you could end up like well, out there like where I'm working.*

In the neighborhood there were four choices: you could either be a secretary, nurse, mother, or nun (if you were Catholic).

> *When I grew up the choices were clear—either a nurse, nun, secretary or mother. We didn't think about other things, we didn't know anything different.*

Both groups of women shared the view that certain kinds of work awaited them and recalled that as children they had dreamed of escaping its most arduous demands. For example, Lilly, while explaining that she had wanted to be a nurse, remembered that "mostly I knew I didn't want to farm":

> *But I really liked going to school, and I said a million times I wished that I could have stayed in school like other kids did cause I wanted to be a nurse, but that didn't work out. Mostly I knew I didn't went to farm because we got tired of farming. Whenever we farmed on half we always wind up with nothing. We farmed one year and ended up*

with one hundred dollars apiece, and I bought our first refrigerator and record player. But mostly we ended up with nothing. It was hard work—my sister and I we was just working with children, the man wouldn't hire nobody else. We had to go out in the field and prime tobacco; we had to get up on the barn and get on those tills and hang it. We had to set up at night, you know, so the tobacco could dry out in the barn. We had to do all that stuff and, well, we had a hard time then. I knew I didn't want to do that all the time.

Helen explained that her desire to become a secretary was a way to avoid factory work:

I knew I wanted to be a secretary—which I am and I wish I weren't. I didn't know how crummy some secretarial jobs could be. But my sister was a secretary. I used to see her in the morning go to work, and she was all dressed up—she looked real nice. It was either that—and then I had another sister who worked in a factory. She always look like she was overtired, looked like a bum. I didn't want to do what that one did, I'd rather do what the other one did.

Lilly's and Helen's accounts are typical in that all the women's stories about aspirations were narrated "in the voice" and "in the image" of people they knew and valued (Holland 1988). What they "knew" about the future and how they learned not to "think about anything else" was inextricably linked and confounded with their feelings about and affiliations with those people who shared their destinies. Equally striking was how the women narrated their aspirations as part of an unfolding story about social differences and struggles within schools and workplaces. It was both within and against these two institutional settings that the women projected their futures and accounted for the gaps between childhood dreams and adult realities. But whereas the North Carolina women emphasized the organization of work, the Philadelphia women emphasized the organization of school in telling their aspirational stories. The contrasts in the telling of their stories enable us to explore the variable meaning and salience of gender, race and class in shaping aspirations.

NORTH CAROLINA WOMEN'S ASPIRATIONS

The North Carolina women knew of limited options beyond life on the farm. If lucky, they could "end up" doing domestic work in an institutional setting rather than in a private home, entitling them to benefits, such as vacation, sick leave and health insurance. Their view about the futility of education was as persistent as their knowledge about limited work options. In the telling of their aspirations, all but two of the North Carolina women told stories about people they knew who had gotten a "good education" only to find themselves working in laundries, banks, motels or schools as housekeepers:

I know a lot of educated ones doing work no better than I'm doing now. Then a job is a job. It's nothin' against the job but when you got a little education I think you most likely will try to find somethin' better than cleanin'. My niece, she has herself a Masters, I was there at her graduation. But she's working at a laundry, she's been there some five years. She kept going to one interview after another, and she never would get a job. Maybe it was somethin' she said, but you would think that she could be workin' in a place better than a laundry with a Master's degree.

Beyond this recurring theme about the limited social mobility of Blacks, what tied all the North Carolina women's aspirational stories together was a focus on work. Woven into every account were detailed descriptions of the racial organization of work, which included the difficulties Blacks had finding anything but menial jobs, the working conditions of the jobs they could find and, most important, the social relations between Blacks and Whites that characterized the jobs they had held.

Lilly's story illustrates the typical sequence of how the North Carolina women narrated their childhood aspirations:

I was wanting to be a nurse, but then we stopped school to help mama out and when she got straightened out then I didn't want to go back. I felt like all the kids that we went to school with had moved on.

And then when we went back we went back with a younger group. I was ashamed to be so big so I started to work in my first job that I had in a restaurant. And the Blacks had to be in the back, had to work in the back. Nobody could see you in the front unless they run short, unless the lunch hour would get busy and they couldn't keep up. Then they would pull somebody black from the back. I started as a dishwasher and helped the lady cook who was in the back. And then one day at lunch time when they couldn't keep up they would pull me out of the kitchen to make hotdogs. I still didn't get out on the floor to clean up, nothing like that. I had to stay behind the counter making hotdogs. All the White peoples was in the front and all the Black was in the back. And you didn't see the Blacks out until it was time for us to leave or if they needed some help. But I really liked going to school and I wished that I could have stayed in school cause I wanted to be a nurse.

Lilly's story begins with her dream of becoming a nurse, interrupted not only by family and work demands, but also by the shame she felt for having been left behind by others in school. Her story then shifts to a description of her first job working in a restaurant. Lilly describes the world of work in terms that were repeated throughout the North Carolina women's interviews. Her story highlights the marked divisions between Blacks who were relegated to the "back" and Whites who occupied positions in "front." Such divisions not only rendered the work of Blacks invisible, but also devalued Blacks in the eyes of the public. . . .

Charged memories of being invisible and worth less than Whites (and lighter-skinned Blacks) were persistent throughout the North Carolina women's descriptions of work as well as schools (Luttrell 1993). Their stories stress the profound effects of racial segregation and violence (as threats or as actual incidents) on what the women "knew" and how they learned not to think about anything else. Their anecdotes also speak to the risks attached to "knowing anything different, anything better than farming" (a familiar story told by Black women authors).

Betty's desire to "be somebody" illustrates the risks as well as the social-psychological costs that at once fueled and constrained her aspirations to become a social worker:

You can't imagine what people got beat out of in those days, how they had to answer to White people. It could make you ashamed to see them take it. But as my mother always say, that kindness don't hurt anybody. You can get more by being easy and kind than you can by being harsh and ugly. She would say you can get right next to a person being nice, but you can't by being ugly. As ugly as that person talks to you the nicer you be, that really does something to them. But I didn't see it like that. I wanted my mother to talk ugly to the teachers or to the man whose land we farmed. But she didn't do it. She took whatever it was and went on. And that's why I got mad with her. And I regret it. I reckon I'll regret it till I die. But I wanted to do it so—so much so that I wanted to talk for everyone, you know take up everybody's battle. I didn't want nobody thinking I was a coward. But I seen a lot of people made to be cowards and some of them are just afraid they might say the wrong things. They're afraid they will say something that will hurt their own self or get someone else hurt. So that's why I wanted to be a social worker. I wanted to be somebody, that's why I always tried in school and was interested in learning.

Told as an unfolding drama about how best to understand and negotiate social differences and inequalities, Betty's account echoes the fears, shame, and rage that persisted throughout the North Carolina women's aspirational stories. Still, while their stories reveal what the North Carolina women "knew " about gender, race and class as barriers to social mobility, their explanations about their own "problem" or "downfall," which they attributed to individual traits of "stubbornness," "temper," and "lack of motivation," suggest yet another version of the past. Indeed, it would be a mistake to categorize the women's stories in dualistic terms, as simply oppositional or compliant. But in order to appreciate more fully what the North Carolina women blamed themselves for, it is useful to turn to the Philadelphia women's stories.

THE PHILADELPHIA WOMEN'S ASPIRATIONAL STORIES

Whereas the North Carolina women's aspirational stories cohered around work themes, the Philadelphia women's stories cohered around school themes. All the Philadelphia women described their aspirations in the context of explaining school decisions and actions, particularly why they had not pursued a college education. Doris's account is typical of how the Philadelphia women narrated their aspirations:

> *I always wanted to be a secretary. No let me backtrack. I guess I always preferred to go to college, but the idea that there was no money to go made it that you was going to be a secretary. You knew their just wasn't an option to pick something else. There was one thing definite; I wasn't going to work in the factory.*

In telling their stories, all the Philadelphia women made a point of emphasizing that it was not that they did not *think* about going to college; the problem was that finances did not permit them to pursue this course:

> *It wasn't that I never thought about college—it was just that nobody around me ever went. We all knew that college was for kids whose parents had the money to send them. So we just didn't even discuss it.*
>
> *I remember thinking about college in eleventh grade, but it wasn't feasible. You could sit around and think about it, but it just wasn't feasible.*

Some women, like Peggy, provided insights into how schools "tracked" working-class students into working-class jobs (Bowles and Gintis 1976):

> *In high school I had signed up for commercial, but I got sent to kitchen practice.*

What was kitchen practice?

> *Being a waitress, cook, chef. That was the worst course in school. There was really the low life in that course.*

How did people get placed into kitchen practice?

> *I think they just went down and said, well this is a poor one and she's not going to do good; she probably doesn't have the mentality. Look at the income, look where she lives, she's not going to amount to anything so stick her in there. Once you got into ninth grade you ran into a lot of problems. It didn't matter how smart you were anymore, they didn't take that into consideration. It was where you lived and how much money you had backing you. There were academic courses where I went to high school, you know English and history and all. Only some of us were put into academic—I wasn't one of them.*

Even though you were a really good student in junior high? [She had made the honor roll every semester.]

> *That's right. You know at the time I just didn't think anything of it. I accepted it. Then afterwards I thought about it, why did that happen? I could have been put into academic. If only I had pushed harder I remember that I had wanted to become something professional, like a lawyer maybe. I did, I wanted to be somebody when I was younger.*

Yet, despite these insights about how schools reproduce class inequalities, Peggy goes on to blame herself for "accepting it." Moreover, she disclaims her insights by explaining that she could not have envisioned herself in college because she "would not have been comfortable" with people she perceived as "different." College represented the unknown, an unfamiliar and potentially unfriendly territory that had not been explored by people the women knew or could identify with. Students who attended college were not only viewed as unfamiliar but as having unique characteristics which several of the Philadelphia women referred to as "college material." As Pam explained:

> *Even though I was in the advanced track, the academic track, I really didn't think about being anything except a secretary. I wanted to stick to something I knew I could do.*

And what was that?

> *I knew I could do all the things a secretary does—I had seen my older sister do it. She was great at it,*

and I knew I'd be good at it, too. I wasn't sure I was college material, I guess mostly I didn't know anyone else who was.

The Philadelphia women's talk about college could be interpreted as a way to protect themselves from feeling like failures for not having achieved class mobility, what Sennett and Cobb refer to as one of the "hidden injuries of class" (1973). However, this interpretation misses the ways in which the Philadelphia women's stories highlight shared values about what "really matters" in life for working-class women. Anne makes this point as she tells about her childhood aspirations:

> *I wasn't interested in the academic track. I didn't know why I needed to study history and all. I was interested in learning what I needed for a job like typing, bookkeeping, and the commercial courses. I couldn't wait to get out of school where I could be on my own, where I could be myself and do what I wanted to do. Some of it was to have my own money so I could buy what I wanted for myself, but we all, all the girls I hung with, all of us were in commercial and we knew what we wanted. We knew what we needed to do too, you know, about life, we knew about life even if we didn't know what they were teaching us about in school.*

Anne's account draws on the images and voices of people she knew and valued to confirm and validate her school decision. She grounds her actions in the knowledge and judgments of "the girls I hung with." Sounding much like the low-income high school girls (White, Black and Hispanic) in Michelle Fine's (1991) ethnographic study, the Philadelphia women recalled feeling trapped by dominant school values and traditions which did not apply to their own experiences or desires. To account for why they had dropped out of school, the Philadelphia women emphasized the role and value of "common sense" or "streetwise" as opposed to "schoolwise" knowledge in a successful future (Luttrell 1989 and 1993). Again it would be a mistake to characterize the Philadelphia women's aspirational stories as either oppositional or compliant. Rather, their stories are complex cul-

tural texts which at once reveal and disguise how gender, race and class differences and inequalities are reproduced.

Ironically, while accepting a view of school as a vehicle that could move them up the social ladder, the Philadelphia women persistently gave reasons for rejecting the ride. Their acceptance of the ideology of meritocracy served both to validate and undermine their working-class identities and interests. Joanne's story illustrates this paradox. Recall that Joanne began her aspirational account with her dream of becoming a judge, for which she had been reprimanded in school. She continues her account by describing her career in school, including her decision to dropout in response to family demands, and then shifts to a discussion of how she had traveled around Europe, and returned to work as a receptionist in a doctor's office and in a law firm. Joanne concludes her discussion of childhood aspirations in the following way:

> *You know I think a lot of working-class people put professional people with educations on a pedestal. It is like with Blacks—if all you see of Blacks is that they are trash men, then you think they must all be like that. But I met a lot of professional people—people with more knowledge than me, and maybe more ambition, but they weren't really any better than me. They weren't really any different, even if they were somebody. You know, the thing is, with all the people I met I still married the boy on the corner. I just always felt most comfortable with him. Maybe I had a strong homing instinct, but that's just who I am.*

On one level, Joanne's story reveals an acceptance of the deeply ingrained, yet implicit value of upward mobility within American culture, best captured by Lillian Rubin's observation that we judge people according to how well they "move up or down, not just through" the class structure (1976: 8–9). Joanne's description of "professional people with educations" being put on a "pedestal" and Blacks being viewed as "trash men" exposes the inseparability and simultaneity of gender, race and class relations as the matrix of this value. Historically, it is upper-class, White women who are put on pedestals as cultural and symbolic figures of purity, moral superiority, virginity and domesticity. Having been relegated to manual, unskilled labor, Blacks have been culturally and symbolically associated with "dirty" and undesirable work, thus justifying their lowest position in the class hierarchy. These gender- and race-based images promote and sustain the class differences and inequalities which Joanne is critiquing, and yet she borrows the same images and ideologies to make her point.

On another level, Joanne's description of marrying the "boy on the corner" could also be interpreted as a rejection of the value of upward mobility. Joanne contends that professional people are not better than she is and that she could have married one if she had chosen to. Instead, she chose to marry the boy she felt most "comfortable with," rejecting marriage as a vehicle of upward mobility. Joanne's decisions regarding both school and marriage illuminate the avenues of upward mobility she viewed were open to her. Ironically, however, the language and logic of her "homing instinct" masks the oppositional nature of her actions, actions which appear to her as "natural" rather than "social," as inherited rather than made. Reminiscent of the North Carolina women's concept of being "treated as part of the family," the Philadelphia women's concept of being "comfortable with" reveals as it disguises the class and gender relations which conspired to shape their aspirations.

DISCUSSION

By juxtaposing how the North Carolina and Philadelphia women narrated their aspirational stories, we learn that both groups felt compelled to answer for their lack of social mobility, but with different emphases, implications and consequences. First, let us consider the thematic contrasts between the women's stories. Whereas the North Carolina women stressed the organization of work, the Philadelphia women stressed the organization of

school to explain their failed mobility. I would argue that these distinct views are produced by institutional elements, such as the goals, structure and modes of control that are found within rural community vs. urban bureaucratic schools and within domestic vs. "pink collar" (that is, clerical and waitressing) work. For example, in contrast to the one-room rural schools attended by the North Carolina women, the comprehensive urban high school attended by the Philadelphia women was large, differentiated in its instruction, and bureaucratic; it was not analogous in structure and operation to either family or church as was the rural school. Moreover, the urban school, unlike the rural school, was isolated from other institutions and required its students to negotiate between class, race and gender practices round in schools and those found in families and workplaces (Hansot and Tyak 1988)....

Second, let us consider what these thematic contrasts suggest about the women's acceptance and rejection of dominant ideologies about upward mobility. For the Philadelphia women, the ideology of opportunity and mobility promoted in school made it appear that they had and could make individual "choices" about their futures. In contrast, the North Carolina women did not fully embrace this dominant ideology and thus could see their destinies as part of a collective journey. Put another way, whereas the Philadelphia women's versions account for why they, as individuals, had rejected upward mobility, the North Carolina women's version account for why they, as a group, had been rejected by white society. Both versions reject the official, authorized interpretation of their social situation.

Split Images of Womanhood: Behind the Official Version of Social Mobility

An underlying coherence that tied all the women's stories together was an emphasis on women's work, particularly in terms of idealized but split images of womanhood.... The Philadelphia women anticipated doing "women's work" as "secretaries, nurses, mothers, or nuns." These options (which they understood as both constraints and possibilities) charted a traditional, subservient and culturally sanctioned view of, and pathway through, womanhood. This path offered them an opportunity to achieve idealized images of femininity as clean, good, domestic, nurturing and selfless beings. Regardless of whether they anticipated doing "women's work" in the paid labor force (as secretaries or nurses) or in the home/church (as mothers or nuns), they learned to view their work and authority in dualistic and contradictory ways.

Ironically, the Philadelphia women's so-called opportunities worked for and against them. On the one hand, as "secretaries, nurses, mothers and nuns," they could look forward to establishing female bonds with each other through shared work, family, and religious rituals. Through the creation of a working-class female culture, they could expect to acquire and exercise their own distinct knowledge and authority, albeit in a separate sphere. Their common experience and camaraderie with girlfriends, sisters, or other female family members generated shared values and views of the work world and a confidence that they "knew what they were good at." As part of their work as women they could exercise their judgments, making choices based on these distinct values and views. Their stories about why they dropped out of school, chose the "commercial track," rejected college as an option, and married the "neighborhood" boy illustrate not only their working-class affiliation but also their claims to knowledge and authority as women.

Yet, these opportunities also *undermined* their claims to knowledge and authority as women. In anticipating their work as secretaries, nurses, mothers and nuns, the Philadelphia women learned to focus on what Dorothy Smith (1987: 81) calls the "concrete, the particular, the bodily" aspects of daily life which characterize "women's work." In the patriarchal division of labor, men (whether as bosses, doctors, husbands, or clergy) are freed from a concern about main-

taining their daily existence which allows them to concentrate solely on the "abstracted conceptual mode of ruling." At the same time that women's work" produces the conditions of men's ruling, it also produces the conditions of its own undermining, suppression and invisibility. As the Philadelphia women learned to concentrate on the "concrete, the particular, the bodily," they also learned to suppress their own knowledge in favor of patriarchal authority and knowledge. Such suppression was expressed by their aspirations. First, when aspiring beyond their "choices" as secretaries, nurses, mothers and nuns, the Philadelphia women projected themselves outside their working-class world (as "college material" or as "professionals"). Second, these aspirations were set outside what has traditionally been considered a women's" sphere or domain (for example, Joanne's dream to be a judge and Peggy's dream to be a lawyer).

As domestics "working for White people," the North Carolina women anticipated a different path through womanhood. They were afforded fewer opportunities for achieving idealized images of womanhood but a greater chance to claim their own knowledge and authority as Black women. First, race-based lines of authority in domestic jobs required that the Black women answer not only to White men, but also to White women and children. And yet, these power relationships were mixed with the intimacies and interdependencies which come from doing domestic service work, the blurring of lines between who cares for whom, who depends on whom and who knows about whom (Tucker 1988; Rollins 1985). In such a division of labor, White people need not attend to certain aspects of daily maintenance and thus are freed to attend to the conceptual modes of ruling. Consequently, the North Carolina women, who saw themselves destined for the "concrete" and "bodily" work of White society, learned to anticipate their invisibility in its workings and in dominant conceptions of power and knowledge.

Yet, at the same time, when it came to preserving their own families and communities, an

act historically and currently viewed as outright resistance (hooks 1990; Davis 1971), the North Carolina women's attention to the "concrete, the particular, and the bodily" work of survival could not be ignored or minimized. In contrast to the Philadelphia women they could expect to acquire knowledge and exercise their authority because of, rather than in spite of, their work as women. Indeed, the North Carolina women's aspirations illuminated their ability to resist the suppression of their own knowledge and authority as women. When dreaming of their destinies beyond "working for White people," they most often imagined themselves as teachers and social workers. While still viewed as "women's work," these jobs offered them an opportunity to contest dominant racist authority relations by advocating for Black men, women and children. Thus, for the North Carolina women "being somebody" was projected in opposition to White society, but not in opposition to what is culturally expected from women....

Nonetheless, the North Carolina women was subject to what Pat Hill Collins calls "controlling images" of Black women, as "mammys" and "matriarchs," which divide Black women against each other as "good" and "bad" women (1990: 67–90). These split images surfaced in several ways. First, more than half of the North Carolina women told stories about how skin color had shaped their aspirations, and all offered examples of how the color line had affected their school achievement (Luttrell 1993). Eloise's aspiration to be a majorette is one such example:

> I wanted to be a majorette, you know those girls who represent the school. I wanted to be a majorette in the worst way. But at that particular time they wasn't takin' Black girls in there. We, all of us were Black, but I'm just saying they were not for the colored, you know. But that's what I wanted to be, a majorette, I wanted that in the worst way.

Second, split images of womanhood persisted throughout the North Carolina women's descriptions of work. The hard, dirty, and tiresome jobs they sought to avoid, their explanations of and emotions about who cared for their children while they were at work, their recurring references to why marriage had not occurred or worked out in their lives, and their persistent descriptions of typical interactions between themselves and the white "ladies" for whom they worked, were all told as counterpoints to idealized images of women as clean, domestic, married—that is, "good"—women. Third, whereas motherhood was mentioned as one of four "options" by the Philadelphia women, it was never once mentioned in that way by the North Carolina women....

...The North Carolina women's discussion of motherhood was woven into their descriptions of work and interdependence on kin relations, predominantly other Black women, wherein they reflected on their feelings about being "good" or "good enough" mothers. Geraldine explained that in order to support her children she had been forced to live apart from them:

> I'll never forgive myself for that. Only one of my children I kept for any length of time. That one there (she points to the picture on her television). That is my biggest grief.

The North Carolina women who had been able to raise their children alone or in nuclear families did not view this outcome as either expected or ideal, but rather as the result of "luck" or chance. More important, it was an aspect of their womanhood for which they felt compelled to account. Indeed, historically grounded and emotionally charged split images of womanhood were woven throughout all the women's aspirational stories....

In light of these split images of womanhood, it is not surprising, then, that both groups of women mentioned nursing as a childhood aspiration. No doubt the history of nursing and the varied avenues through which poor and working-class women have been able to enter the profession (as hospital aides, LPNS, RNs, midwives, and so on) provide a clue to this common aspiration. Just as important, nursing is a role that builds on symbolic and idealized images of women as clean, White (as in their uniforms), nurturing, and subservient, while simultaneously promising professionalization and better pay than other types of women's work. Moreover, the gender-based divisions between what women as nurses are allowed to know and make judgments about and what men as doctors are allowed to know and make judgments about, take precedence over race- and class-based differences between women. Indeed all of these factors may have converged in making nursing an aspiration within which women from varied class and race backgrounds could bridge available opportunity structures and ideologies about what a "good" or "ideal" woman should be.

Finally, these split images of womanhood undermined how both groups of women projected their futures. The women's shared images of good vs. bad, clean vs. dirty, Black vs. White antagonists in the struggle for upward mobility served to mediate the effects of class- and race-based barriers; these false antagonists also served to mask the female subordination that all the women shared (Palmer 1983). Indeed, idealized but split images direct our attention away from what poses a threat to society: the collective agency of "bad" women, whether Black or White, lower or upper class, married or single who refuse to accept patriarchal structures of family, work, or school. . . .

REFERENCES

Bowles, Samuel, and Herbert Gintis. 1976. *Schooling in Capitalist America.* New York: Basic Books.

Collins, Patricia Hill. 1990 *Black Feminist Thought: Knowledge, Consciousness and The Politics of Empowerment.* Boston: Unwin Hyman.

Davis, A. 1971. "Reflections on the Black Women's Role in the Community of Slaves." *The Black Scholar* 3: 3–15.

Fine, Michelle. 1991. *Framing Dropouts: Notes on the Politics of an Urban Public High School.* Albany: State University of New York Press.

Ginsberg, Faye, and Anna Tsing. 1990. *Uncertain Terms: Negotiating Gender in American Culture.* Boston: Beacon Press.

Holland, Dorothy. 1988. "In the Voice of, in the Image Of: Socially Situated Presentations of Attractiveness." IPA *Papers in Pragmatics* 2 (1/2).

hooks, bell. 1984. *From Margin to Center.* Boston: South End Press.

hooks, bell. 1990. *Yearning: Race, Gender and Cultural Politics.* Boston: South End Press.

Luttrell, Wendy. 1989. "Working-Class Women's Ways of Knowing: Effects of Gender, Race, and Class." *Sociology of Education* 62 (January): 33–46.

Luttrell, Wendy. 1993. "The Teachers They All Had Their Pets: Concepts of Gender, Knowledge and Power." *Signs: Journal of Women in Culture and Society* 18 (3): 505–46.

McRobbie, Angela. 1978. "Working Class Girls and the Culture of Femininity." In *Women Take Issue: Aspects of Women's Subordination,* edited by Women Studies Group CCCS, 96–108 London: Hutchinson.

Ogbu, John U. 1988. "Class Stratification, Racial Stratification, and Schooling." In *Class, Race and Gender in American Education*, edited by Lois Weis, pp. 163–82. Albany, New York: SUNY Press.

Palmer, Phyllis Marynick, 1983. "White Women/Black Women: The Dualism of Female Identity and Experience in the United States." *Feminist Studies* 9 (1): 151–70.

Rollins, Judith. 1985. *Between Women: Domestics and Their Employers.* Philadelphia: Temple University Press.

Rubin, Lillian. 1976. *Worlds of Pain: Life in the Working-Class Family.* New York: Basic Books.

Sennett, Richard, and Jonathon Cobb. 1973. *The Hidden Injuries of Class.* New York: Vintage Books.

Smith, Dorothy. 1987. *The Everyday World As Problematic: A Feminist Sociology.* Boston: Northeastern University Press.

Tucker, Susan. 1998. *Telling Memories Among Southern Women: Domestic Workers and their Employers in the Segregated South.* New York: Schocken Books.

PART SEVEN

Ideology

Chapter 13   Competing Ideas and Images

Most of the preceding readings in this book examine gender and other relations of inequality primarily in terms of peoples' lived experiences within social institutions such as families, workplaces, and schools. This reflects, in our minds, the importance of examining gender, race, class, and sexual orientation within a social structural perspective. However, an examination of peoples' lived experiences within institutions does not tell the whole story about gender relations. The arena of ideas, beliefs, and values is also of crucial importance. Take, for example, the recent legal debates about sexual violence in media, educational debates about sex education, and political debates about "family values." To be sure, the results of these debates will have a real impact on peoples' lives within social institutions. But the terrain of these debates is largely ideological. That is to say, the major players in these debates aim to manipulate cultural symbols and images—largely through the media—with the goal of influencing public opinion about issues such as sexual violence, "safer sex," and welfare.

Dominant ideas are often imposed on subordinate groups to control them. Sometimes, subordinate groups of people internalize these dominant ideas, essentially accepting the definition of the dominant group that they are, indeed, naturally inferior. However, the existence of social movements, such as the civil rights movement, the labor movement, feminism, and anti-colonial movements, demonstrates that subjugated people have the ability to resist dominant ideologies, at times even forging their own, oppositional system of beliefs and values. The first article in Part Seven illustrates this struggle to confront the damaging internalization of negative cultural beliefs. Manning Marable examines the impact of negative racial stereotypes, with the hope of helping Black men "comprehend the critical difference between the myths about ourselves and the harsh reality of being Black men." After outlining the history of conflict between Black and White men in the United States and examining recent socioeconomic data, Marable urges Black males to come to terms with Black women by recognizing how, together, they have been "imprisoned by images of the past, false distortions that seldom if ever capture the essence of our being."

In recent years, it has become commonplace among those who study popular culture to debate whether or not, for instance, Madonna represents "resistance" to culturally imposed narrow definitions of femininity and compulsory heterosexuality. More important, probably, than whether or not we decide to proclaim Madonna a "feminist" is the observation that symbolic "resistance" against the dominant group's ideologies is often highly paradoxical. The next article in this section, Stan Denski and David Sholle's examination of gender performance and symbolism in heavy metal music, illustrates this paradox. On the one hand, Denski and Sholle point out, heavy metal (like rock and roll and other youth musical forms that preceded it) is clearly a rebellion against the sexual, moral, and stylistic norms of adult culture. And on the surface, the appearance of male performers wearing long hair, makeup, and other signifiers of "femininity" appears to challenge culturally imposed dichotomies of gender. But, Denski and Sholle argue, we should not confuse "metal men" with feminists. Instead, rather than putting them into solidarity with feminism and gay rights, metal men's flamboyant styles incorporate aspects of "the feminine" into an aggressive masculinity that "offers a response to female power" and ultimately "disavows the need for women."

In recent years, the popular Disney film *Pocahontas*—and the seemingly endless number of products with which the film was successfully cross-marketed—entertained tens of millions of children. But in addition to entertainment, children were learning a particular historical version of the role of gender, race, and culture in the colonization of what became the United States of America. In the final article of Part Seven, Clara Sue Kidwell shows how the actual woman Pocahontas and other Native American women such as Sacagawea "were the first cultural mediators of meaning between the cultures of two worlds." It is through the reconstructions of the lives of these women, rather than through the ideology of Disney, that we may come to understand the complex ways that gender, sexuality, and race shaped—and in turn were shaped by—the process of colonization of the North American continent.

46

The Black Male
Searching beyond Stereotypes

MANNING MARABLE

What is a Black man? Husband and father. Son and brother. Lover and boyfriend. Uncle and grandfather. Construction worker and sharecropper. Minister and ghetto hustler. Doctor and mineworker. Auto mechanic and presidential candidate.

What is a Black man in an institutionally racist society, in the social system of modern capitalist America? The essential tragedy of being Black and male is our inability, as men and as people of African descent, to define ourselves without the stereotypes the larger society imposes upon us, and through various institutional means perpetuates and permeates within our entire culture. Our relations with our sisters, our parents and children, and indeed across the entire spectrum of human relations are imprisoned by images of the past, false distortions that seldom if ever capture the essence of our being. We cannot come to terms with Black women until we understand the half-hidden stereotypes that have crippled our development and social consciousness. We cannot challenge racial and sexual inequality, both within the Black community and across the larger American society, unless we comprehend the critical difference between the myths about ourselves and the harsh reality of being Black men.

CONFRONTATION WITH WHITE HISTORY

The conflicts between Black and White men in contemporary American culture can be traced directly through history to the earliest days of chattel slavery. White males entering the New World were ill adapted to make the difficult transition from Europe to the American frontier. As recent historical research indicates, the development of what was to become the United States was accomplished largely, if not primarily, by African slaves, men and women alike. Africans were the first to cultivate wheat on the continent; they showed their illiterate masters how to grow indigo, rice, and cotton; their extensive knowledge of herbs and roots provided colonists with medicines and preservatives for food supplies. It was the Black man, wielding his sturdy axe, who cut down most of the virgin forest across the southern colonies. And in times of war, the White man reluctantly looked to his Black slave to protect him and his property. As early as 1715, during the Yemassee Indian war, Black troops led British regulars in a campaign to exterminate Indian tribes. After another such campaign in 1747, the all-White South Carolina legislature issued a public vote of gratitude to Black men, who "in times of war, behaved themselves with great faithfulness and courage, in repelling the attacks of his Majesty's enemies." During the American Revolution, over two thousand Black men volunteered to join the beleaguered Continental Army of George Washington, a slaveholder. A generation later, two thousand Blacks from New York joined the state militia's segregated units during the War of 1812, and Blacks fought bravely under Andrew Jackson at the Battle of New Orleans. From Crispus Attucks to the 180,000 Blacks who fought in the Union Army during the Civil War, Black men gave their lives to preserve the liberties of their White male masters.

The response of White men to the many sacrifices of their sable counterparts was, in a word, contemptuous. Their point of view of Black males was conditioned by three basic beliefs. Black men were only a step above the animals—possessing awesome physical power but lacking in intellectual ability. As such, their proper role in White society was as laborers, not as the managers of labor. Second, the Black male represented a potential political threat to the entire system of slavery. And third, but by no means last, the Black male symbolized a lusty sexual potency that threatened White women. This uneven mixture of political fears and sexual anxieties was reinforced by the White males' crimes committed against Black women, the routine rape and sexual abuse that all slave societies permit between the oppressed and the oppressor. Another dilemma, seldom discussed publicly, was the historical fact that some White women of social classes were not reluctant to request the sexual favors of their male slaves. These inherent tensions produced a racial model of conduct and social context that survived the colonial period and continued into the twentieth century. The White male–dominated system dictated that the only acceptable social behavior of any Black male was that of subservience—the loyal slave, the proverbial Uncle Tom, the ever-cheerful and infantile Sambo. It was not enough that Black men must cringe before their White masters; they must express open devotion to the system of slavery itself. Politically, the Black male was unfit to play even a minor role in the development of democracy. Supreme Court Chief Justice Roger B. Tawney spoke for his entire class in 1857: "Negroes [are] beings of an inferior order, and altogether unfit to associate with the White race, either by social or political relations; and so far inferior that they have no rights which the White man was bound to respect." Finally, Black males disciplined for various crimes against White supremacy—such as escaping from the plantation, or murdering their masters—were often punished

in a sexual manner. On this point, the historical record is clear. In the colonial era, castration of Black males was required by the legislatures of North and South Carolina, Virginia, Pennsylvania, and New Jersey. Black men were castrated simply for striking a white man or for attempting to learn to read and write. In the late nineteenth century, hundreds of Black male victims of lynching were first sexually mutilated before being executed. The impulse to castrate Black males was popularized in White literature and folklore, and even today, instances of such crimes are not entirely unknown in the rural South.

The relations between Black males and White women were infinitely more complex. Generally, the vast majority of White females viewed Black men through the eyes of their fathers and husbands. The Black man was simply a beast of burden, a worker who gave his life to create a more comfortable environment for her and her children. And yet, in truth, he was still a man. Instances of interracial marriage were few and were prohibited by law even as late as the 1960s. But the fear of sexual union did not prohibit many White females, particularly indentured servants and working-class women, from soliciting favors from Black men. In the 1840s, however, a small group of white middle-class women became actively involved in the campaign to abolish slavery. The founders of modern American feminism—Susan B. Anthony, Elizabeth Cady Stanton, and Lucretia Mott—championed the cause of emancipation and defended Blacks' civil rights. In gratitude for their devotion to Black freedom, the leading Black abolitionist of the period, Frederick Douglass, actively promoted the rights of White women against the White male power structure. In 1848, at the Seneca Falls, New York, women's rights convention, Douglass was the only man, Black or White, to support the extension of voting rights to all women. White women looked to Douglass for leadership in the battle against sexual and racial discrimination. Yet curiously, they were frequently hostile to the continued contributions of Black women to the cause of freedom. When the brilliant orator Sojourner Truth, second only to Douglass as a leading figure in the abolitionist movement, rose to lecture before an 1851 women's convention in Akron, Ohio, White women cried out, "Don't let her speak!" For these White liberals, the destruction of slavery was simply a means to expand democratic rights to White women: the goal was defined in racist terms. Black men like Douglass were useful allies only so far as they promoted White middle-class women's political interests.

The moment of truth came immediately following the Civil War, when Congress passed the Fifteenth Amendment, which gave Black males the right to vote. For Douglass and most Black leaders, both men and women, suffrage was absolutely essential to preserve their new freedoms. While the Fifteenth Amendment excluded females from the electoral franchise, it nevertheless represented a great democratic victory for all oppressed groups.

For most White suffragists, however, it symbolized the political advancement of the Black male over White middle-class women. Quickly their liberal rhetoric gave way to racist diatribes. "So long as the Negro was lowest in the scale of being, we were willing to press his claims," wrote Elizabeth Cady Stanton in 1865. "But now, as the celestial gate to civil rights is slowly moving on its hinges, it becomes a serious question whether we had better stand aside and see 'Sambo' walk into the kingdom first." Most White women reformists concluded that "it is better to be the slave of an educated White man than of a degraded, ignorant black one." They warned Whites that giving the vote to the Black male would lead to widespread rape and sexual assaults against White women of the upper classes. Susan B. Anthony vowed "I will cut off this right arm of mine before I will ever work for or demand the ballot for the Negro and not the [White] woman." In contrast, Black women leaders like Sojourner Truth and Frances E. Watkins Harper understood that the enfranchisement of Black men was an essential step for the democratic rights of all people.

The division between White middle-class feminists and the civil rights movement of Blacks, beginning over a century ago, has continued today in debates over affirmative action and job quotas. White liberal feminists frequently use the rhetoric of racial equality but often find it difficult to support public policies that will advance Black males over their own social group. Even in the 1970s, such liberal women writers as Susan Brownmiller continued to resurrect the myth of the "Black male-as-rapist" and sought to define White women in crudely racist terms. The weight of White history, from White women and men alike, has been an endless series of stereotypes used to frustrate the Black man's images of himself and to blunt his constant quest for freedom.

CONFRONTING THE BLACK WOMAN

Images of our suffering—as slaves, sharecroppers, industrial workers, and standing in unemployment lines—have been intermingled in our relationship with the Black woman. We have seen her straining under the hot southern sun, chopping cotton row upon row and nursing our children on the side. We have witnessed her come home, tired and weary after working as a nurse, cook, or maid in White men's houses. We have seen her love of her children, her commitment to the church, her beauty and dignity in the face of political and economic exploitation. And yet, so much is left unsaid. All too often the Black male, in his own silent suffering, fails to communicate his love and deep respect for the mother, sister, grandmother, and wife who gave him the courage and commitment to strive for freedom. The veils of oppression, and the illusions of racial stereotypes, limit our ability to speak the inner truths about ourselves and our relationships to Black women.

The Black man's image of the past is, in most respects, a distortion of social reality. All of us can feel the anguish of our great-grandfathers as they witnessed their wives and daughters being raped by their White masters, or as they wept when their families were sold apart. But do we feel the double bondage of the Black woman, trying desperately to keep her family together and yet at times distrusted by her own Black man? Less than a generation ago, most Black male social scientists argued that the Black family was effectively destroyed by slavery; that the Black man was much less than a husband or father; and that the result was a "Black matriarchy" that crippled the economic, social, and political development of the Black community. Back in 1965, Black scholar C. Eric Lincoln declared that the slavery experience had "stripped the Negro male of his masculinity" and "condemned him to a eunuch-like existence in a culture that venerates masculine primacy." The rigid rules of Jim Crow applied more to Black men than to their women, according to Lincoln: "Because she was frequently the White man's mistress, the Negro woman occasionally flaunted the rules of segregation.... The Negro [male] did not earn rewards for being manly, courageous, or assertive, but for being accommodating—for fulfilling the stereotype of what he has been forced to be." The social by-product of Black demasculinization, concluded Lincoln, was the rise of Black matriarchs, who psychologically castrated their husbands and sons. "The Negro female has had the responsibility of the Negro family for so many generations that she accepts it, or assumes it, as second nature. Many older women have forgotten why the responsibility developed upon the Negro woman in the first place, or why it later became institutionalized," Lincoln argues. "And young Negro women do not think it absurd to reduce the relationship to a matter of money, since many of them probably grew up in families where the only income was earned by the mothers: the fathers may not have been in evidence at all." Other Black sociologists perpetuated these stereotypes, which only served to turn Black women and men against each other instead of focusing their energies and talents in the struggle for freedom.

Today's social science research on Black female–male relations tells us what our common sense should have indicated long ago—that the essence of Black family and community life has been a positive, constructive, and even heroic experience. Andrew Billingsley's *Black Families in White America* illustrates that the Black "extended family" is part of our African heritage that was never eradicated by slavery or segregation. The Black tradition of racial cooperation, the collectivist rather than individualistic ethos, is an outgrowth of the unique African heritage that we still maintain. It is clear that the Black woman was the primary transmitter and repositor of the cultural heritage of our people and played a central role in the socialization and guidance of Black male and female children. But this fact does not by any way justify the myth of a "Black matriarchy." Black women suffered from the economic exploitation and racism Black males experienced—but they also were trapped by institutional sexism and all of the various means of violence that have been used to oppress all women, such as rape, "wife beating," and sterilization. The majority of the Black poor throughout history have been overwhelmingly female; the lowest paid major group within the labor force in America is black women, not men.

In politics, the sense of the Black man's relations with Black women are again distorted by stereotypes. Most of us can cite the achievement of the great Black men who contributed to the freedom of our people: Frederick Douglass, W. E. B. DuBois, Marcus Garvey, Martin Luther King, Jr., Malcolm X, Paul Robeson, Medgar Evers, A. Philip Randolph. Why then are we often forgetful of Harriet Tubman, the fearless conductor on the Underground Railroad, who spirited over 350 slaves into the North? What of Ida B. Wells, newspaper editor and antilynching activist; Mary Church Terrell, educator, member of the Washington, D.C., Board of Education from 1895 to 1906, and civil rights leader; Mary McLeod Bethune, college president and director of the Division of Negro Affairs for the National Youth Administration; and Fannie Lou Hamer, courageous desegregation leader in the South during the 1960s? In simple truth, the cause of Black freedom has been pursued by Black women and men equally. In Black literature, the eloquent appeals to racial equality penned by Richard Wright, James Baldwin, and Du Bois are paralleled in the works of Zora Neale Hurston, Alice Walker, and Toni Morrison. Martin Luther King, Jr., may have expressed for all of us our collective vision of equality in his "I Have a Dream" speech at the 1963 March on Washington—but it was the solitary act of defiance by the Black woman, Rosa Parks, that initiated the great Montgomery bus boycott in 1955 and gave birth to the modern civil rights movement. The struggle of our foremothers and forefathers transcends the barrier of gender, as Black women have tried to tell their men for generations. Beyond the stereotypes, we find a common heritage of suffering, and a common will to be free.

THE BLACK MAN CONFRONTS HIMSELF

The search for reality begins and ends with an assessment of the actual socioeconomic condition of Black males within the general context of the larger society. Beginning in the economic sphere, one finds that the illusion of Black male achievement in the marketplace is undermined by statistical evidence. Of the thousands of small businesses initiated by Black entrepreneurs each year, over 90 percent go bankrupt within thirty-six months. The Black businessman suffers from redlining policies of banks, which keep capital outside his hands. Only one out of two hundred Black businessmen have more than twenty paid employees, and over 80 percent of all Black men who start their own firms must hold a second job, working sixteen hours and more each day to provide greater opportunities for their families and communities. In terms of actual income, the gap between the Black man and the White man has increased in the past decade. According to the Bureau of Labor Statistics, in 1979 only forty-six thousand Black men earned salaries between $35,000 and $50,000 annually. Fourteen thousand Black men (and only two thousand Black women) earned $50,000 to $75,000 that year. And in the

highest income level, $75,000 and above, there were four thousand Black males compared to five hundred and forty-eight thousand White males. This racial stratification is even sharper at the lower end of the income scale. Using 1978 poverty statistics, only 11.3 percent of all White males under fourteen years old live in poverty, while the figure for young Black males is 42 percent. Between the ages of fourteen and seventeen, 9.6 percent of White males and 38.6 percent of Black males are poor. In the age group eighteen to twenty-one years, 7.5 percent of White males and 26.1 percent of all Black males are poor. In virtually every occupational category, Black men with identical or superior qualifications earn less than their White male counterparts. Black male furniture workers, for example, earn only 69 percent of White males' average wages; in printing and publishing, 68 percent; in all nonunion jobs, 62 percent.

Advances in high-technology leave Black males particularly vulnerable to even higher unemployment rates over the next decades. Millions of Black men are located either in the "old line" industries such as steel, automobiles, rubber, and textiles, or in the public sector—both of which have experienced severe job contractions. In agriculture, to cite one typical instance, the disappearance of Black male workers is striking. As late as forty years ago, two out of every five Black men were either farmers or farm workers. In 1960, roughly 5 percent of all Black men were still employed in agriculture, and another 3 percent owned their own farms. By 1983, however, less than 130,000 Black men worked in agriculture. From 1959 to 1974, the number of Black-operated cotton farms in the South dropped from 87,074 to 1,569. Black tobacco farmers declined in number from 40,670 to barely 7,000 during the same period. About three out of four Black men involved in farming today are not self-employed.

From both rural and urban environments, the numbers of jobless Black adult males have soared since the late 1960s. In 1969, for example, only 2.5 percent of all Black married males with families were unemployed. This percentage increased to about 10 percent in the mid-1970s, and with the recession of 1982–1984 exceeded 15 percent. The total percentage of all Black families without a single income earner jumped from 10 percent in 1968 to 18.5 percent in 1977—and continued to climb into the 1990s.

These statistics fail to convey the human dimensions of the economic chaos of Black male joblessness. Thousands of jobless men are driven into petty crime annually, just to feed their families; others find temporary solace in drugs or alcohol. The collapse of thousands of black households and the steady proliferation of female-headed, single-parent households is a social consequence of the systematic economic injustice inflicted upon Black males.

Racism also underscores the plight of Black males within the criminal justice system. Every year in this country there are over 2 million arrests of Black males. About three hundred thousand Black men are currently incarcerated in federal and state prisons or other penal institutions. At least half of the Black prisoners are less than thirty years of age, and over one thousand are not even old enough to vote. Most Black male prisoners were unemployed at the time of their arrests; the others averaged less than $8,000 annual incomes during the year before they were jailed. And about 45 percent of the thirteen hundred men currently awaiting capital punishment on death row are Afro-Americans. As Lennox S. Hinds, former National Director of the National Conference of Black Lawyers has stated, "Someone Black and poor tried for stealing a few hundred dollars has a 90 percent likelihood of being convicted of robbery with a sentence averaging between 94 to 138 months. A White business executive who embezzled hundreds of thousands of dollars has only a 20 percent likelihood of conviction with a sentence averaging about 20 to 48 months." Justice is not "color blind" when Black males are the accused.

What does the economic and social destruction of Black males mean for the Black commu-

nity as a whole? Dr. Robert Staples, associate professor of sociology at the University of California–San Francisco, cites some devastating statistics of the current plight of younger Black males:

Less than twenty percent of all Black college graduates in the early 1980s are males. The vast majority of young Black men who enter college drop out within two years.

At least one-fourth of all Black male teenagers never complete high school.

Since 1960, Black males between the ages of 15 to 20 have committed suicide at rates higher than that of the general White population. Suicide is currently the third leading cause of death, after homicides, and accidents, for Black males aged 15 to 24.

About half of all Black men over age 18 have never been married [or are] separated, divorced or widowed.

Despite the fact that several million Black male youths identify a career in professional athletics as a desirable career, the statistical probability of any Black man making it to the pros exceeds 20,000 to one.

One half of all homicides in America today are committed by Black men—whose victims are other Black men.

The typical Black adult male dies almost three years before he can even begin to collect Social Security.

Fred Clark, a staff psychologist for the California Youth Authority, states that the social devastation of an entire generation of Black males has made it extremely difficult for eligible Black women to locate partners. "In Washington, D.C., it is estimated that there is a one to twelve ratio of Black [single] males to eligible females," Clark observes. "Some research indicates that the female is better suited for surviving alone than the male. There are more widowed and single Black females than males. Males die earlier and more quickly than females when single. Single Black welfare mothers seem to live longer than single unemployed Black males."

Every socioeconomic and political indicator illustrates that the Black male in America is facing an unprecedented crisis. Despite singular examples of successful males in electoral politics, business, labor unions, and the professions, the overwhelming majority of Black men find it difficult to acquire self-confidence and self-esteem within the chaos of modern economic and social life. The stereotypes imposed by White history and by the lack of knowledge of our own past often convince many younger Black males that their struggle is too overwhelming. Black women have a responsibility to comprehend the forces that destroy the lives of thousands of their brothers, sons, and husbands. But Black men must understand that they, too, must overcome their own inherent and deeply ingrained sexism, recognizing that Black women must be equal partners in the battle to uproot injustice at every level of the society. The strongest ally Black men have in their battle to achieve Black freedom is the Black woman. Together, without illusions and false accusations, without racist and sexist stereotypes, they can achieve far more than they can ever accomplish alone.

REFERENCES

Clark, K. 1965. *Dark Ghetto.* New York: Harper and Row.

Davis, A. Y. 1981. *Women, Race and Class.* New York: Random House.

Billingsley, A. 1968. *Black Families in White America.* Englewood Cliffs, NJ: Prentice-Hall.

Lincoln, C. E. 1965. "The Absent Father Haunts the Negro Family." *New York Times Magazine,* Nov. 28.

Marable, M. 1983. *How Capitalism Underdeveloped Black America.* Boston: South End Press.

47

Metal Men and Glamour Boys

Gender Performance in Heavy Metal

STAN DENSKI
DAVID SHOLLE

...Efforts toward locating the origins of any musical form will unavoidably involve a rich blend of ambiguity and uncertainty; history, in other words, always blurs at the edges. Locating the origins of contemporary heavy metal is no different. In general, we would point to the hard rock styles of bands like The Who; blues-based rock bands like The Rolling Stones; volume- and performance-based psychedelic bands like Cream and The Jimi Hendrix Experience; and the hard-rock-influenced Southern rock sounds of bands like The Allman Brothers, throughout the middle and late 1960s, and, perhaps, culminating with the appearance of Led Zeppelin, the most popular and influential hard rock band of the 1970s. Hibbard and Kaleialoha (1983) describe Led Zeppelin as the primary inspiration for a new style of 1970s hard rock (epitomized in the music of bands like Aerosmith, Alice Cooper, Foreigner, Journey, Thin Lizzie, Heart, and others), and place heavy metal as a genre within this particular stylistic locale.

Heavy metal, as a distinct genre, may be differentiated from its origins in the more general style of hard rock by an emphasis upon four- and eight-bar phrases rather than blues or pop structures. For example, groups like Black Sabbath, Uriah Heep, Judas Priest, AC/DC, The Scorpions, and Iron Maiden differ from their hard rock counterparts in their use of simplistic "very rudimentary harmonies and melodies [and] through the endless repetition of simple chords with extremely short progressions" (1983, p. 413). Throughout the middle- and late-1980s, heavy metal underwent ultra-

generic transformations, splintering into a variety of subgenres, in some cases openly hostile to one another. The influence of the punk rock movement of the late seventies resulted in the emergence of a genre described by its listeners as "speed metal" or "thrash metal." Characterized by high volume, the absence of ballads, a decrease in the presence of a blues-based influence, and very fast and often intricate rhythms, bands like Metallica and Megadeath eschew the theatrical complexities of costume and stage props associated with other metal varieties. The fans of "speed/thrash" metal define their terrain, in part, through their openly hostile attitude to the genre of "pop" or "glam" metal (exemplified by bands like Bon Jovi and Poison).

Where speed/thrash is influenced by punk, "glam metal" bears the influences of the glitter rock movement of the 1970s and performers like the New York Dolls and early David Bowie. Characterized by an elaborate emphasis upon theatrics, expansive staging, and costume, glam seems to, in its preference for slower, more ballad-like composition (for example, Poison's "Every Rose Has Its Thorn"), attracted a wider and more gender-mixed audience. In doing so, the popularity of heavy metal in terms of album sales, and an increased acceptance by radio and music television, has reached record highs, and, ironically, threatened its hardcore base of followers. The marginality of heavy metal and its audience, the lack of acceptance by the popular music mainstream throughout its development and emergence as a distinct genre, created a cult-like status that its fans could participate in and take pleasure in. An increased popularity and wider acceptance of pop and glam metal forms undermines a key use of the music in the establishment of difference and identity in many of its adolescent male fans. The cult-like status of contemporary speed or thrash metal bands like Slayer or Anthrax (and the resultant further delineation of heavy metal into these intra-generic forms) may represent one response to this development.

Until this intra-generic fragmentation of the 1980s, heavy metal enjoyed a certain marginal status in contrast to its mainstream pop music counterparts. Characterized by a general lack of interest on the part of pop radio programmers and a near blanket critical dismissal, this marginality could be understood as partially the result of its almost exclusively White male audience. While gender preferences continue to be exhibited in recent studies (e.g., Christenson & Peterson, 1988; Denski, 1990), there is growing evidence in the results of radio station call-out research (in which potential listeners are played fragments of records over the phone and asked to rate their listenability) to suggest a significant change in the preference of female listeners toward hard-rock and heavy metal genres. For example, under the headline "Fems Take to Hard Rock" in the October 8, 1988, issue of *Billboard* magazine, various call-out research attributes a flourishing of hard-rock and heavy metal acts in the Top 40 to a growing female audience, a phenomenon that has continued into the 1990s.

Heavy metal is often cited as the most straightforwardly coded example of masculine, macho posing in rock 'n' roll (thus the genre of "cockrock"). Yet heavy metal style is, at the same time, increasingly blurred. Heavily marked with feminine elements, glam metal in particular is increasingly attracting a female audience through its emphasis on more nurturing and romantic themes in the context of ballad-like composition and performance. This makes heavy metal an interesting, contradictory phenomenon in terms of its representation of masculinity, and it allows us to examine a number of multilayered relationships in popular culture's play with gender identity.

Throughout the development of heavy metal a distinctive aspect of its internal subculture of followers has been the different expectations that exist for male and female fans. In a recent participant observation study Friesen (1989) observed that males and females conform to a variety of social expectations in order to maintain peer acceptance. Failure to conform to these expectations resulted in a range of sanctions from ridicule to ostracism. The expectations for males, for the most part, represented the conformance to extremely rigid roles:

> *Males were expected to emulate certain characteristics (e.g., aggressiveness, independence) in their image, demeanor and argot, and were also expected to practice behaviors that would disassociate themselves from anything feminine. Females, on the other hand, were allowed the option at times to display certain male qualities in addition to female characteristics. (1989, p. 8)*

Heavy metal (as music and as cultural style) has undergone various changes. The music and the fans have splintered into subgroups, often around some notion of which "metal" is "really metal." Some fans argue that the music itself has progressed and is capable of making "important" statements (the political themes in the recent music of bands like Metallica and Megadeath are frequently cited as examples). But, nevertheless, a general heavy metal style can be discussed at the level of American mass media audiences. For our purposes, "heavy metal" will be applied to performers who proclaim themselves to be heavy metal and who generally fit into the genres of hard rock or glam metal. The discussion focuses on the situation in the United States, where the issue of working-class identity is of minimal importance for heavy metal fandom. Additionally, through all of this runs further disruptions and tensions across the terrain of masculinity and gender identity. It is to these tensions that the analysis now turns.

MASCULINITY AND THE PERFORMANCE OF GENDER

On the back cover of Hurricane's "Slave to the Thrill" (an album whose front cover features a naked woman strapped into a frightening-looking machine), the band members appear with teased hair, exposed belly buttons, low-slung pants, and jewelry—various stylistic marks that many rock critics and fans interpret as feminine. This example points to a number of contradictions in the representations of sexual identity that surface in heavy metal style. While male band members take up styles that imply female or homosexual identity, they are identified by most audiences as masculine/macho. What is at question here is the supposed "maleness" of rock 'n' roll and the manner in which it constructs gender, both for its performers and for its audiences. Our primary concern is with the question of what it is that constitutes sexual identity. This is particularly significant for the examination of the performative character of heavy metal: How is it that an adolescent heterosexual male audience identifies with performers who appear to take up the stylistic marks of the feminine? How is that young heterosexual female audiences fantasize over aggressive males in feminine clothes?...

Looking at heavy metal's taking up of various styles as expressive of an underlying male/female sex, or expressive of an underlying interpretation of sex, leads to two opposed viewpoints. On one hand, we might approach heavy metal as straightforwardly misogynist by simply reading off its surface images and statements. While, on the other hand, we might consider heavy metal (glam metal in particular) as expressive of a resistant parody of straight heterosexuality. Both views, however, simplify the phenomenon in that each assumes an essential truth to sex. Butler (1990) contends that this view is rooted in a *metaphysics of substance*; that is, in taking up either approach, it is assumed that there is, at the center of notions of sexuality/gender, some abiding substance that establishes the self as either man or woman.... But the reality of gender is created through sustained social per-

formances, so the idea of a true or essential maculinity or femininity is an illusion.... The representations of sexuality within heavy metal will be examined, using this notion of *gender as performance.*

HEAVY METAL: STYLE AND IMAGE

As heavy metal has evolved, the music itself has become expressive of an aggressive sexual prowess (Chambers, 1985). This is most evident in the cult of the guitar hero, where technical mastery of the instrument in conjunction with intense volume create a close link between the performer and the (male) audience. The technological power used and represented in heavy metal is one of the primary ways in which the male audience identifies with the masculine pose of the band. The improvisatory pretensions of the heavy metal musician are read as direct signs of mastery and aggressive "attack." As Klaus Meine of The Scorpions describes it: "This music is not played from the head, it's played from here (touches his heart) and here (ditto his groin)" (Drozdowski, 1990, p. 49).

The technological power of heavy metal slides easily into sexual power via a physical mastery of machine by man and the deployment of machine against women. The traditional male dominance of the heavy metal audience may be partly due to this emphasis on technical prowess (especially the guitar solo). Young males identify strongly with the *producerly* role in music as evidenced in concert settings where the audience participate as "air" guitarist, playing imaginary guitar runs in homage to their alter egos performing on the stage. The amplitude of the music and its sheer noise level enhance the connective link between the hero/performer and the imitative fans (Reist & Casey, 1989).

In keeping with these themes of futuristic machines and the warrior hero, heavy metal has acquired curious connections to a variety of visual images and narrative (particularly those associated with heroic sci-fi genres). An entire undercurrent of publication and artistic design has sprung up around these images. Examples can be found in the comic book *Heavy Metal,* heavy metal fanzines, iconography on clothing and tattoos on the body, and in the design of pinball machines, video games, and so on. Within heavy metal it is the heroic and masculine features of science fiction that are emphasized, and, along with this worship of the warrior/hero, technology again is emphasized in the form of machines of great power and destruction. The animated film *Heavy Metal* provides interesting examples of this machine-dominated world. The vignettes that compose the film all rely on young or weak males taking up or conquering machines on their way to sexual initiation with large-breasted women.

These themes are particularly foregrounded in a "Heavy Metal Special Issue" of *Musician* magazine (No. 71, September 1984), the cover of which features Rob Halford, lead singer for Judas Priest, in which his arm is replaced with the massive green illustrated arm of Marvel comics' Incredible Hulk. In the same issue, Bill Flanagan, with tongue planted partially in cheek, asks: "Why do adolescent boys like heavy metal music so much? Wrong. It has nothing to do with sexual frustration or adolescent rebellion, tendencies toward vandalism or the desire to show off. It has to do with comic books" (p. 58). Borrowing primarily from the Marvel inventory, Flanagan provides a list of comparisons that includes: David Bowie as Chameleon Boy; Elvis Costello as Clark Kent; Marshall Crenshaw as Peter Parker; Ozzy Osbourne as the Hulk; Ted Nugent as Wolverine; Joan Jett as Wonder Woman; Dave Lee Roth as Conan; Meat Loaf as The Thing; and Cheap Trick as The Archies. More recently, connections drawn between heavy metal, comic and sci-fi characters, and the spectacle of professional wrestling are suggestive of the collapse of categories and play of signification, the pastiches and bricolage of postmodern popular culture.

Machines of power and desire function as pivotal images in heavy metal performance and iconography, from hot rods and Hogs to cyborgs and robotic dozers. The *power of the machine* and the *power of the hero* are present in the production of the music itself. The heavy metal sound actually requires little in the way of sophisticated equip-

ment, yet every heavy metal band (with the exception of those in the speed/thrash metal genre) will have a drum kit of immense proportions, stacks of amplifiers and processing equipment, and the elaborate theatrical machinery of lighting and pyrotechnics. The band members themselves emulate the heroic gestures and even the narrative moves of the fantasy heroes of sci-fi (and backward sci-fi, e.g., the Conan fantasies). In larger stadium shows, the band members enter a scene of pandemonium and, taking up and taming an immense technological machinery, they physically take up the heroic posture, literally "destroying and tearing up" as they move about the stage with "heavy metal thunder."

These performative aspects of heavy metal lead to what Butler calls the *heterosexualization of desire* (1990, p. 141). This requires and institutes the production of discrete and asymmetrical oppositions between "masculine" and "feminine," where these are understood as expressive attributes of male and female. Thus, the practices of desire are made to follow from sex and gender. This is the domain of "intelligible" genders that heavy metal is heavily invested in maintaining. This is further offered as evidence in support of our assertion that, regardless of a certain level of play with gender signification, heavy metal does not bend gender outside of a dominant view of heterosexual definitions.

The physical look and gesture of the prototypical hard rock heavy metal band is at root an overblown adolescent macho pose. The heavy metal hard rock band is "bad," from the late-night routine of endless groupies, trashed hotel rooms, cases of hard liquor, and drugs (including a preference for heroin, which is not normative outside of hard-rock genres, and, as some players suggest, "separates the men from the boys"), to the onstage prancing and taunting behavior.

The performative/bodily gestures of heavy metal are stereotyped and exaggerated reproductions of aggressive masculine behaviors—fighting and/or protective fear gestures, such as jutting lips, fists forward in the air, back tilted forward, lower pelvis thrust out, and so on; aggressive sexual gestures, such as sticking out the tongue in mock cunnilingus, hoisting of the guitar from the crotch, grabbing and/or stuffing the crotch, mock coitus (usually depicting the man on top and from behind). More important, the heavy metal band carries on this erotic aggression in the context of "being with the boys." The physical contact of band members, the gestures to one another, and the visual gaze and exchange of looks, all signal an attachment to the male gang. Heavy metal band members are individuals, but typically are "band first"; that is, they are identified by male fans as members of a group with an image that defines the group as "bad" in a particular way (whether as hyper-drunks, super-studs, mega-musicians, and such).

The "badness as maleness" of the heavy metal band is expressed then both in the music itself, and in the language used to describe the sound and the making of the sound—for example, thunder, axe, attitude, outlaw, fast and mean, ball-busting, attack, crunch, cook, pump, and so on. One quintessential musical element of heavy metal is the power chord, which conceptually mirrors the entire style of heavy metal. The power chord is not more of a chord, but actually less of one in that it typically uses only the bottom three strings of the guitar. This reduction of the chord to its elemental triad is what creates the type of power that heavy metal has—elemental, singular, direct—the hyper-amplification of simplicity.

Heavy metal has increasingly appropriated elements of style that are traditionally regarded as feminine. Originally, the so-called hippie or long-hair culture blurred gender definitions through its disregard for dominant fashion definitions. This was, of course, primarily expressed in hairstyle, and heavy metal has retained the rebellious "long hair" of the original rock 'n' roll bad-boy bands. But this hairstyle is not directly symbolic of or reflected upon as a gender-blurring operation; instead, it seems to express a general rebelliousness, particularly toward parental authority. As heavy metal promoter Tom Zutat suggests: "That's what the 'heavy metal' bands are now. They're the rebellious kids who say 'fuck you' to the police, to the parents. That's what Elvis did" (Considine, 1990, p. 62).

However, in heavy metal in general and glam metal in particular, the feminine (or what is taken as feminine) has been taken up in a much stronger style. Heavy metal hair is not simply long, it is moussed, teased, dyed, or streaked in a manner that is much more directly gender-coded. In addition, many bands use makeup, particularly lipstick and mascara, not simply for emphasis (as in theatrical makeup), but to soften the face and emphasize the eyes and cheek bones. Makeup use reaches an extreme of masquerade in bands like Kiss and Twisted Sister, where the makeup loses its gendered coding and becomes a means for the creation of another species (tied again to the codes of comics and sci-fi).

Glam styles exaggerate the clothing styles of early heavy metal and progressive rock, adding gender-blurring elements inherited partly from the chameleon traditions of earlier glitter music styles (e.g., Bowie, New York Dolls, and so on). Low-slung denim jeans, leather pants and accessories, open skirts, scarves, jewelry, and such, all blur gender-coded styles. Heavy metal bands extend a curiously macho image, while stylistically feminizing the "male body" (or perhaps "masculinizing the feminine"). As R. Bolan, of the band Skid Row, notes: "Facial hair and heavy metal don't jive" (Raso, 1990, p. 39)....

The emergent question then is: Does heavy metal fit into an imitative parody, or does it fall short of such a subversive discourse? This is a key question for the fans and performers of heavy metal in addressing questions of signifying practices and gender construction as possible sites of struggle across the cultural terrain. Our description thus far leads to a tentative answer.

Contradictorily, heavy metal holds up a model of masculine power and sexual prowess, but not under the rubric of traditional masculine "muscled" power. The "new male" body is an object of desire, an object to be possessed, but in heavy metal's terms, only if one is willing to be possessed. Thus, the glam-styled body is seductive, but seduction is used to seduce the female and control her desire. For the male audience, the feminization of the body marks out a quite different discourse—one that overcomes fear of the feminine by incorporating it.

HEAVY METAL: AUDIENCE IDENTIFICATION

As noted, a large aspect of heavy metal is its emphasis on "producing rock," and the rock 'n' roll life-style (i.e., the identifications established are between star virtuosos and teenage, male, "would-be" guitar heroes). But as recent analyses have suggested, a growing female audience also exists for this music. Before dealing directly with the gender identification involved in this new division of the audience, a brief look at the social milieu of the heavy metal fans must be undertaken. Straw (1989) has noted that heavy metal tends not to define a subculture in the way that musical movements such as punk or rap do. It is consumed, and lived as consumed, rather then generating a productive subcultural body of fans. Thus heavy metal in the past tended not to generate local band scenes, underground magazines, or serious collectors. It was a *stadium culture*, a music consumed with a minimum of involvement. However, heavy metal has generated a powerful sense of commitment among its fans, who endlessly debate the authenticity of heavy metal and its existence as the "true" form of rock 'n' roll in the age of Madonna, corporate rock, dance music, and New Age.

Heavy metal has tended to be a working-class phenomenon, and there appears to be some correlation between low levels of educational performance and heavy metal fandom. We would suggest, however, that the implication is not that heavy metal is made by and produced for low-class, low-taste audiences, but that it is widely popular with alienated (rather than underprivileged) youth, who view the future as under-opportunitied. It should be emphasized that heavy metal is predominantly White music. Not that it is racist, it simply does not acknowledge difference—that is, rock 'n' rollers are White boys.

As Cashmore (1984) notes, "it would be unfair to call heavy metal conservative: inert would be more accurate" (p. 37). In general, heavy metal does not support the status quo, nor does it want to change it, it just wants to retreat into a world where one can sleep all day and rock all night. Given the male, White, suburban, inert world of heavy metal; how is it that fans—male and female—identify with heavy metal performers in terms of gender? Particularly, how can the contradictions surrounding gender identity be explained in heavy metal? For the male fan, how is it that young, heterosexual, White boys come to identify with performers who border on transvestism? For the female fan, how is it that young heterosexual White girls come to desire macho males styled in gay and female dress who act out adolescent fantasies of misogynist conquest? We have already laid out a basic description that points to one possible answer to each of these questions. At this point we will direct our focus only toward the male audience, leaving the newer female audience to a later examination.

HEAVY METAL: MALE, SELF, OTHER

The exaggerated male techno-power of heavy metal, along with its obsession with de(re)-romanticizing sexual relations with women, is the key aspect of our description thus far. This seems to point to an adolescent fear of "woman" (growing up) at the core of heavy metal. Young male adolescents remain the primary audience for heavy metal. For young male fans, adolescence is a time of sexual awakening, but a space where fear and loathing mix with desire. These boys are confronted by girls who may be larger, stronger, and smarter than they are, while at the same time these boys are being socialized into the dominant masculine cultural position of pursuer of the female, thus generating a fear of the feminine.

These contradictions and tensions, developed between feelings of powerlessness while wanting to exercise one's growing power, are the elements of the male adolescent experience that heavy metal has traditionally addressed. Faced with intimidating females, the heavy metal fan finds fantasy escape in the aggressive, powerful figures of heavy metal, who sing about and seem to act out an extreme control of woman. The fear and loathing of women expressed in heavy metal music would be merely paranoid and destructive, if it were not for the manner in which desire for women is set within the greater pleasures of male bonding in the gang—rock 'n' roll (and at times even beer) comes before sex in the heavy metal pleasure hierarchy. As Slash, lead guitarist for Guns N' Roses, recalls, "When I was 14 I was over at this girl's house I'd been trying to pick up for months, and she played 'Aerosmith Rocks'; I listened to it eight times and forgot all about her" (Rowland, 1990, p. 32). . . .

A repressed and, hence, disparaged sexuality (a relationship between men and bonds between men) takes place through the heterosexual exchange and distribution of women. This is particularly evident in the movie, *Heavy Metal,* and in music videos where groups of men divide the spoils, that is, the women. This is especially evident in the Motley Crüe video for their song, "Girls, Girls, Girls." In it, the women exotic dancers are obvious targets for exchange, yet function only as visual pleasure. The only physical, bodily

pleasure in the video takes place in the exchanges between the male band members.

The feminized appearance of heavy metal bands seems then to not stand as signification of solidarity with feminism and gay rights (a possible "resistant" reading); rather, it is, at the simplest level, a way for straight White performers to inject an element of flamboyance into their performance. At a deeper level, it is a complex practice that at once expresses both a rebellion against straight societal and parental rules, and offers a response to feminine power. By taking the feminine into itself, heavy metal disavows the need for women, thus overcoming the fear of exercising desire. . . .

It seems then that heavy metal's use of the feminine is neither simply a misogynist aggression nor an intentional playing with the boundaries of sexual identity. . . . Our review of fanzines, and interviews with musicians and fans, seem to point toward the latter conclusion: *Heavy metal may shift some outward signs of gender, but it leaves untouched the constructed core identity of binary sex, and unchallenged the asymmetrical dominant power relations of gender. . . .*

REFERENCES

Butler, J. (1990). *Gender trouble: Feminism and the subversion of identity.* New York: Routledge.

Cashmore, B.B. (1984). *No future: Youth and society.* London: Heinemann.

Chambers, J. (1985). *Urban rhythms: Pop music and popular culture.* New York: St. Martin's Press.

Christenson, P. G., & Peterson, J. B. (1988). Genre and gender in the structure of music preference. *Communication Research 15*(3), 282–302.

Considine, J. D. (1990, April). The sons of Aerosmith. *Metal Musician,* p. 62.

Denski, S. (1990). *An examination of popular music preference and functions by the contemporary popular music audience.* Unpublished doctoral dissertation, Ohio University.

Drozdowski, T. (1990, April). Monsters of guitar. *Metal Musician,* p. 49.

Friesen, B. (1989, August). *Functional aspects of adolescent socialization through deviant subcultures:*

Field research in heavy metal. Paper presented at a meeting of the American Sociological Association, San Francisco.

Hibbard, D. J., & Kaleialoha, C. (1983). *The role of rock.* Englewood Cliffs, NJ: Prentice-Hall.

Raso, A. (1990, May 31). Despite the headaches, Skid Row's not complaining. *Circus,* p. 39.

Reist, N., & Casey, B. C. (1989, May). *Where have all the heros gone? An analysis of the role of myth in speed metal and the Grateful Dead.* Paper presented at a meeting of the International Communication Association, San Francisco.

Rowland, M. (1990, April). If Guns N' Roses are outlawed. *Metal Musician,* p. 32.

Straw, W. (1989). Characterizing rock music culture: The case of heavy metal. In S. Frith & A. Goodwin (Eds.), *On record: Rock, pop, & the written word* (pp. 97–111). New York: Pantheon.

48

Indian Women as Cultural Mediators

CLARA SUE KIDWELL

Wherever Europeans and native people encountered each other in the New World, cultural ideas and perceptions were at work, and processes of cultural change began to take place. Hernando de Soto and his men encountered the "Lady of Cofitachequi" near the present site of Augusta, Georgia. She arrived for their meeting in a litter draped in white cloth and "borne on the shoulders of men," and she gave de Soto her own string of pearls as a sign of goodwill.[1] Did she intend to welcome him? To appease him with gifts? To encourage him to move on? We have no words from the lady herself about her motives and intentions.

There is an important Indian woman in virtually every major encounter between Europeans and Indians in the New World. As mistresses or wives, they counseled, translated, and guided White men who were entering new territory. While men made treaties and carried on negotiations and waged war, Indian women lived with White men, translated their words, and bore their children. Theirs was the more sustained and enduring contact with new cultural ways, and they gave their men an entrée into the cultures and communities of their own people. In this way, Indian women were the first important mediators of meaning between the cultures of two worlds.

Some of these women have entered the mythology of American history, and the myths have obscured the reality of their situations. Pocahontas continues to lay down her body if not her life to save John Smith and assure the survival of the Jamestown colony. Sacagawea stands pointing west, the leader of the Lewis and Clark expedition.[2] Explicitly, their actions led finally to the loss of Indian land and to destructive changes in Indian culture. But implicitly, they acted from motives that were determined by their own cultures.

The mythology of Indian women has overwhelmed the complexity of their roles in the history of Indian and White contact. Indian women stand in history as stereotypes such as the hot-blooded Indian princess, à la Pocahontas, or the stolid drudge, the Indian squaw plodding behind her man. They are not real people. The myths of colonialism and manifest destiny raise questions about their associations with European men. Their roles must be interpreted in two cultures. If American history portrays them as saviors and guides of White men and agents of European colonial expansion, were they explicitly or implicitly betraying their own people? Were they driven by passion, or were they victims of fate, forced to submit to men of a dominant society?[3]

The voices of Indian women are not heard in the written documents or in the history books. They did not write their own accounts to analyze their own actions. They were, nevertheless, actors in history, and their actions affected its course. But how, if at all, can we ever understand their actions and intentions in what they did?

The notion of authorial intention is currently fashionable in literary theory, and it has spilled over into history. At its heart, it questions how or whether we can understand the intentions of the author of any historical document when cultural context changes over time. Intentionality is particularly problematic when the sources are not written. Native people have written little in their own words, and what there is has been written primarily by men. Women's words are not the stuff of history.[4]

If we are to discover women's intentions in their actions, then the methods of ethnohistorians are particularly appropriate to the study of their history. If women did not explain their actions in documents, we must attempt to recreate the cultural context of their actions and to move beyond the myths that have been woven around their lives. We can discover some clues to intention by examining the cultural context of women's lives. Women, perceived as powerless by European men and voiceless in the historical records, are nevertheless powerful in the roles that they play in their own cultures, and even more powerful in the impact that they have on their husbands or consorts and on the children of those liaisons. We can examine some of the myths surrounding the roles of Indian women to see how complex their roles in intercultural contacts were.

The Indian woman Dona Marina, La Malinche, was crucial in Hernando Cortez's conquest of the Aztec empire. She was presented to Cortez as a captive, one of twenty women the Tabascan people gave him along with other tribute as he was on his march toward the Aztec capital of Tenochtitlan. The Tabascan people had obtained her originally as a slave from merchants in Xicalango. She had been given away or sold by her own people in Oluta. She was evidently of high rank in Aztec society, but not high enough to escape a condition akin to slavery. Her value to Cortez was that she spoke Nahuatl and a dialect of Mayan, and she could communicate with Jeronimo de Aguilar, a Spaniard who had been abandoned in the Yucatan by a previous expedition. He spoke Mayan and Spanish. In a triadic relationship, Marina communicated to Aguilar in Mayan, and he in turn spoke Spanish to Cortez.

Marina also advised Cortez in his overtures to the subject peoples of the Aztec empire, whose alliances ultimately led to his conquest of Tenochtitlan and the fall of the Aztec empire. She learned that the Cholulans intended not to assist but to kill Cortez and his men. This timely warning saved his expedition. Through Marina's linguistic skills, Cortez was able to exploit the fractures among tribes held together only by the military might of the Aztecs.

Did Marina indeed deliberately betray her people and contribute finally to the European conquest of the Indians of the New World? As a woman who had spent her life as a slave, she probably had no sense of place or loyalty to her captors. If she perceived Moctozuma as a cruel emperor, as the subject tribes largely did, then she had reason to aid Cortez in his overthrow of the empire.

If La Malinche acted out of passion (she was also Cortez's mistress), she was never his wife. Cortez gave her in marriage successively to two of his subordinates, although she bore him a son during one of these marriages. If we accept that she was virtually a slave in a state under military subjection to the Aztecs at Tenochtitlan, her actions become clearer. Whatever personal passions drove her we can never know. She was, however, an essential intermediary between Spaniards and native communities. To contemporary Mexican people, her role is particularly problematic, since she is both betrayer of their ancestors and mother, by Cortez, of a new mixed-blood people, From the historical accounts she emerges as an intelligent and articulate woman whose actions, whatever their motivation, had a significant impact on the history of the Americas.[5]

The story of Pocahontas, daughter of Powhatan, is taught to every schoolchild. The perplexing question is, did it really happen? The account of her dramatic rescue of John Smith, leader of the Jamestown colony, comes from his *General History*, published in 1624 and embroidered with many details not present in his earlier writings. Smith, who had been taken captive after killing two members of Powhatan's confederacy, was brought before the chief and feasted; then his head was laid on a large rock, where the Indians prepared to smash it with their clubs. Smith was rescued from this predicament when Pocahontas got his "head in her armes, and laid her owne upon his to save him from death."[6]

Why? Was she overcome by passion? Smith described her as a girlchild about twelve or thirteen years old; given the nature of hormones, passion was a possible motive. (Might we say that she had a crush on him?) Was she moved by compassion? That option is unlikely, since she came from a culture where torture of captives was accepted and carried out by men and women.[7] Or was she exercising a prerogative of women in her tribe to choose captives to be adopted into the tribe? The later history of the Southeast is replete with accounts of women who were recognized as leaders.[8] If "queens" or "squaw sachems" were recognized as rulers, could not Pocahontas as a woman (albeit a very young one) decide the life of a captive, particularly if it was to test her own newly emerging power?

Pocahontas certainly does not disappear from history after this dramatic episode with Smith. She continued to visit the Jamestown colony. In one particularly vivid English account of such a visit, she is described as cartwheeling naked through the town square with the ship's boys. In another, she and a group of young women, dressed only in paint and feathers, entertained Smith with a dance.[9]

Pocahontas also became an intermediary between her own people and the English. Powhatan sent her with one of his senior advisors to intercede for the return of some of his men, whom Smith had captured. The episode was evidence of the increasingly tense relations between Powhatan's people and the Jamestown colonists. Meanwhile, Pocahontas continued to visit the colony and to bring it food and supplies. Smith did not understand her motivation. "Were it the policies of her father thus to employ her, or the ordinance of God thus to make her his instrument, or her extraordinarie affection for our nation, I know not."[10]

Taken in the cultural context of women's power in coastal Algonquian societies, Pocahontas's actions make sense. Having saved Smith's life, she simply continued to take responsibility for it. She was not acting out her father's will, since she would not take presents from Smith for fear

that her father would discover her. She was acting out her own power as a woman in her society.[11]

Pocahontas could not escape the consequences of the cultural contact that was happening around her. The English made her their instrument in 1613 when Samuel Argall, an English captain, lured her aboard his ship and held her hostage pending her father's return of stolen goods, weapons, and runaway servants. Powhatan finally sent back seven men with broken muskets, at which Pocahontas complained that he valued weapons more than her.

Pocahontas did not return to her father. The English sent her to school to be educated as a Christian. They gave her a new name, Rebecca. Soon after, she was married to John Rolfe, an English tobacco planter. Rolfe described the union as one of love, not lust, as a properly restrained Englishman should do. Powhatan consented to the marriage, as an Indian father should do. But beyond the personal feelings of the participants, the marriage was part of a deliberate English strategy to promote the intermixing of the Indian and white populations and to establish peaceful relations. Although Pocahontas and Rolfe consummated the most famous interracial marriage in American history, there were probably forty or fifty others in this period.[12]

The final encounter between Pocahontas and John Smith was in England, where she had gone with Rolfe after their marriage. It is revealing of her thoughts and values, even after some time spent in her husband's world. She declared that she would consider herself Smith's daughter now that she was in his land, as he had declared himself the son of Powhatan when he had entered her father's land. This declaration of kinship is telling. Among her own people, Pocahontas could exercise certain prerogatives toward Smith because he was a stranger. She could take responsibility for his life. In England, where she was the stranger, she offered her life to Smith's care, as she had taken care of him. However much she might have moved in white society, she still saw her relationships in very Indian terms.

The life that Pocahontas offered Smith was a short one. She died at the start of a voyage back to Virginia, leaving behind her a son by John Rolfe and an enduring myth in American history.[13]

Sacagawea is another mythic heroine in American history. She was one of two (or perhaps three) Indian wives of Toussaint Charbonneau, who joined the Lewis and Clark expedition in Montana in 1805.[14] Shoshone by birth, she was captured by Minatarees in her youth, and Charbonneau bought or traded for her and another woman. She gave birth to a son and carried him with her on the expedition. She did not lead it. She recognized certain landmarks in the Bitterroot Mountains and was able to indicate what might lie ahead. When Lewis and Clark encountered a band of Shoshones, she was brought forward to interpret and recognized her brother Cameahwait, their leader. Cameahwait and his people gave the expedition horses and led it part of the way over the mountains to the west.[15]

Although Sacagawea returned to her own people, she did not stay with them. She learned at the meeting with the Shoshones that most of her relatives were dead. She went on with the expedition. As a captive and the wife of a White man, she no longer had a place within the social structure of her own tribe, and indeed that structure was largely destroyed. Charbonneau was evidently an abusive husband, but he and the expedition were now Sacagawea's main reference points. Having been removed from her tribe, she could not go back; indeed, she may have chosen freely not to go back.

Sacagawea's role in American history may be symbolic of westward expansion, but her presence in the expedition was important for what it told Indian people. Since Indian tribes did not take women on war parties, she was a sign that Lewis and Clark came in peace. Indeed, Clark wrote that her presence assured the Indians that the expedition's intentions were peaceful. Her importance in history is to show us how she was valued by two cultures: Lewis and Clark needed her as a translator, but the Indian people whom the expedition encountered saw her as a sign of peace.[16]

Sacagawea has entered not only the mythology of American history but also the history of one contemporary American Indian reservation. She left the expedition with Charbonneau, and the later historical record notes the death of "Charbonneau's squaw" from "putrid fever" in 1812. John Luttig praised her in death as the most honorable woman at Fort Mandan. Most historians have accepted that statement as a record of Sacagawea's death, but the record also shows that Charbonneau had more than one wife, and it is not clear which one died.

There are stories told on the Wind River Shoshone reservation today that Sacagawea left Charbonneau, went her own way through the West, and finally returned to her people. According to this tradition, she died on the reservation in 1884.[17] If her symbolic role as guide and translator is problematic in its consequences for American Indian people today, her myth lives on in American history and has become an important source of identity for contemporary Shoshones.

Nancy Ward, "beloved woman" of the Cherokees, played most dramatically the role of mediator during the period of turbulent relations between Cherokees and colonists in the latter part of the eighteenth century. She was with her husband when he was killed in a battle against the Creeks at Taliwa in 1755. Picking up his rifle, she fought in his place, and the Cherokees prevailed. Not only was she valiant, she was also the grandniece of Old Hop, a leading man of the Cherokee nation, and niece of Attakullakulla, a skillful Cherokee diplomat and leader. By personal valor and lineage she was an extraordinary woman.

After her demonstration of bravery, Ward was appointed to the office of Ghighau, the head beloved woman, in which role she exercised ceremonial and ritual powers and served as a leader of the "white" (peace) town of Chota, also a "mother" town, a designation of the oldest Cherokee towns. In the traditional dichotomy between war (red) and peace (white), Nancy, in her role as a beloved of Chota—the oldest "white" town—stood as a symbol of peace. In that role she also mediated relations among the Overhill Cherokees, White settlers in the Watauga Valley, and the British and American governments during the Revolutionary War.

After her first husband's death, Nancy married Bryant Ward, an Irishman and a trader. Her daughter, Betsy Ward, married Joseph Martin, Indian agent for the Virginia colony. Martin, one of the first Whites in Cherokee territory, became important in upholding Cherokee land claims.[18] Ward's daughter Kate married Ellis Harlin, another trader. Joseph Martin maintained a trading post at the Long Island of Holston; it became the major depot for goods moving into the Cherokee country, as well as the site of several treaty negotiations. Martin, Harlin, Isaac Thomas, and other "countrymen" who married Cherokee women were integrated into the tribe. They moved between two worlds, and they gathered military intelligence on the actions of British troops and Cherokee war parties.

Recruited as intelligence agents by the British, Harlin and Thomas gave misleading information about Cherokee war intentions. Sent by Nancy Ward, Harlin warned the White people of the Watauga region about an impending Cherokee attack against them by the dissident Chickamaugas. Nancy intervened to save the life of one White captive, Mrs. Lydia Bean, taken during the Cherokee raid on the Watauga settlement. She also informed the British commander Joseph Campbell about the activities of the Chickamaugas.[19]

Nancy Ward was a powerful woman in her own right in Cherokee society, but the Cherokees were faced with the push of White colonists passing through the Cumberland Gap to settle a new land. The Cherokees had been decimated by disease and warfare with Whites and among themselves.

Was Nancy Ward a traitor to her people when she informed British military officers of the plans of Cherokee warriors? As a beloved woman and councillor at a traditional Cherokee peace town, she was committed to preserving peace. She spoke eloquently to her male kinsmen and to the Americans, who after 1785 pressed the Cherokees

for cessions of land. She played her role as it was defined in her own culture—advocate for peace. To that end she protected American settlers and informed British military agents of the hostile intentions of Cherokee men.

As a Cherokee woman, Nancy brought new resources into the Cherokee nation through her marriage and the marriages of her daughters. Betsy Ward's husband, Joseph Martin, acted as an advocate for Cherokee interests, but ultimately Nancy's efforts to maintain peace failed, and the White men who entered the Cherokee nation were agents of change rather than protectors of culture.

There are no dramatic women like Nancy Ward among the Choctaws, but they too were participants in cultural change. Levi Perry and Charles Durant married Choctaw women and introduced domesticated cattle into the nation. Nancy and Rebecca Cravat, daughters of a Frenchman and a Choctaw woman, together married Louis LeFlore, a French trader. They were reputedly the nieces of Mushulatubbee, one of the principal chiefs of the Choctaw nation. Greenwood LeFlore, son of one of these marriages, was the chief of the Choctaws who signed the removal treaty of 1830.[20]

There were many such marriages between Choctaw women and White traders and settlers. Nathaniel Folsom sired twenty-four children by two Choctaw wives. His son David became a leading man and ultimately a chief of the Choctaws in 1826. The mixed-blood leaders of the Choctaws struggled during the 1820s under pressure from the United States government for cessions of land in Mississippi. They encouraged missionaries to educate their children and represented forces of change in Choctaw culture, but they also wrote a constitution that they hoped would allow them to live peacefully with their White neighbors. They worked to preserve the Choctaw nation as they had come to know it, and they still considered themselves Choctaws.[21]

In this brief survey of history we can mention only some of the more problematic figures. Mary Musgrove Matthews Bosomsworth was crucial to

James Oglethorpe's establishment of the Georgia colony in 1733. She was the niece of Old Brim, chief of the Creeks, and, like Nancy Ward, was important because of her family connections, but since her father was White, she was sent away from the Creek nation to go to school. Mary persuaded her people to give Oglethorpe land for his colony, and she and her respective husbands, all White, became traders—colonial entrepreneurs of a peculiar sort.[22]

We cannot give full attention to Molly Brant, who became the mistress of William Johnson's household in 1759 and bore him eight children during a relationship that probably began in the early 1750s. Her presence in his household must have given him a special insight into Iroquois culture.[23]

There is a growing body of literature on the roles that Indian women played in relations between cultures. The studies of fur trade families by Jennifer S. H. Brown and Sylvia Van Kirk document the importance of Indian women both as laborers and as intermediaries between their own people and White men in the fur trade.[24] The offspring of mixed marriages are the next important mediators of cultural change. As products of two cultures, they must find their own places in history.[25]

If historians do not have the voices of Indian women to listen to, anthropologists have a sense of women's lives and positions in their own societies. If historians despair of intentionality, anthropologists may be able to re-create from historical sources and personal observation the continuity of women's roles and motivations in their own cultures. Out of this joint inquiry we may be able to understand how cultures meet, how they change, and the important role that women play in that process.

NOTES

1. Garcilaso de la Vega, *The Florida of the Inca*, trans. and ed. John Grief Varner and Jeannette Johnson Varner (Austin, TX, 1988), 298–99; John R. Swanton, *Final Report of the United States De Soto Expedition Commission*, 76th Cong., 1st sess., 1939, H. Doc. 76 (reissued, Washington, DC, 1985), 169–70, 182–83.
2. The supposed place of her birth is marked by a monument near Salmon in eastern Idaho. See Ella E. Clark and Margot Edmonds, *Sacagawea of the Lewis and Clark Expedition* (Berkeley and Los Angeles, 1979), 7.
3. A concise and perceptive overview of stereotypes of Indian women in American history is Rayna Green, "The Pocahontas Perplex: The Image of Indian Women in American Culture," *Massachusetts Review* 16 (1975): 698–714.
4. See David Harlan, "Intellectual History and the Return of Literature," *American Historical Review* 94, no. 2 (June 1989): 588, 608. James Axtell, in a session at a National Endowment for the Humanities Summer Institute entitled "Myth, Memory, and History," held at the Newberry Library, Chicago, in 1990, maintained that contemporary historians are as distant culturally from their eighteenth-century relatives as they might be from American Indian cultures. See also Kathleen Barry, "The New Historical Synthesis: Women's Biography," *Journal of Women's History* I, no. 3 (Winter 1990): 76.
5. Rachel Phillips provides a perceptive reading of Dona Marina's personal history and her role in the larger history of Spanish-Aztec contacts. See Phillips, "Marina/Malinche: Masks and Shadows," in *Women in Hispanic Literature: Icons and Fallen Idols*, ed. Beth Miller (Berkeley and Los Angeles, 1983), 97–114. Nigel Davies is one historian who questions Marina's actions, saying, for instance, that the warning about a Cholulan plot against Cortez was an "old wives' tale" and that she did nothing to prevent the death of certain native leaders who were condemned on false allegations. See Davies, *The Aztecs: A History* (New York, 1975), 238, 252, 288. The most sympathetic account of Marina is found in the accounts of Bernal Diaz del Castillo, *The Bernal Diaz Chronicles*, trans. and ed. Albert Idell (New York, 1956). Pictorial representations of Marina as a large figure positioned close to Cortez are found in Bernardino de Sahagún, *Florentine Codex: Manuscript in Nahuatl of Fray Bernardino de Sahagún*, trans. James O. Anderson and Charles E. Dibble, 12 vols. (Salt Lake City, UT, 1950), pt. 12, plates 22, 44, 51.

6. John Smith, *The Complete Works of Captain John Smith (1580–1631)*, ed. Philip L. Barbour, 3 vols. (Chapel Hill, NC, 1986), 2: 258–60.

7. Samuel Purchas, *Purchas His Pilgrimage; or, Relations of the World*, 2d ed. (London, 1614), 767. The account is of the Chickahominys' torturing and killing George Cassen, an Englishman. Given Smith's experience, such ritual killing was culturally accepted.

8. For examples of female leadership, see Robert Steven Grumet, "Sunksuaws, Shamans, and Tradeswomen: Middle Atlantic Coastal Algonkian Women during the Seventeenth and Eighteenth Centuries," in *Women and Colonization: Anthropological Perspectives*, ed. Mona Etienne and Eleanor Leacock (South Hadley, MA, 1980), 43–62; Martha W. McCartney, "Cockacoeske, Queen of Pamunkey: Diplomat and Suzeraine," in *Powhatan's Mantle: Indians in the Colonial Southeast*, ed. Peter H. Wood, Gregory A. Waselkov, and M. Thomas Hatley (Lincoln, NE, 1989), 173–95. The written accounts of women leaders are, of course, postcontact, which might suggest that disruption of traditional male leadership patterns put women into leadership roles because there were no male claimants. The strength of matrilineal kinship patterns, mythological traditions, and women's roles in subsistence activities militate against the idea that women assumed powerful roles simply because men had died off.

9. William Strachey, *The Historie of Travell into Virginia Britania*, ed. Louis B. Wright and Virginia Freund (London, 1953), 72. Strachey did not arrive at Jamestown until 1610, and it is unclear whether the cartwheel episode occurred before or after the famous rescue. John Smith includes the account of the entertainment. See Smith, *Complete Works* 2: 182–83.

10. Smith, *Complete Works* 2: 198–99.

11. Ibid.

12. Ralph Hamor, *A True Discourse of the Present State of Virginia* (1615; rpt., Richmond, Virginia State Library Publications, No. 3, 1957), 53–54.

13. Smith, *Complete Works* 2: 260–61; Samuel Purchas, *Hakluytus Posthumus; or, Purchas His Pilgrimes, Contayning a History of the World in Sea Voyages and Land Travells*, 20 vols. (Glasgow, 1905–7), 19: 104–6, 117–18; Philip L. Barbour, ed., *The Jamestown Voyages under the First Charter*, 1600–1609, Hakluyt Society Publications, 2d ser., Vol. 137 (Cambridge, 1969), 459–62. Stuart E. Brown, Jr., summarizes the primary literature in *Pocahontas* (Pocahontas Foundation, 1989).

14. Clark and Edmonds, *Sacagawea*, 13.

15. Elliott Coues, ed., *History of the Expedition under the Command of Lewis and Clark*, 3 vols. (New York, 1965), 2: 546–49.

16. Harold P. Howard, *Sacagawea* (Norman, OK, 1973), 34. See James P. Ronda, *Lewis and Clark among the Indians* (Lincoln, NE, 1984), for a succinct summary of the scholarship on Sacagawea.

17. Clark and Edmonds, *Sacagawea,* 106–7; John Luttig, *Journal of a Fur Trading Expedition on the Upper Missouri, 1812–1813*, ed. Stella M. Drumm (New York, 1964). I would like to thank Sally McBeth for her ideas expressed in "Metaphorical Transformations of the Myth, Memory, and History of Sacajawea," the manuscript of a presentation given at a National Endowment for the Humanities Summer Institute entitled "Myth, Memory, and History," held at the Newberry Library, Chicago, 1990.

18. Norma Tucker, "Nancy Ward, Ghighau of the Cherokees," *Georgia Historical Quarterly* 53 (June 1969): 192, 199. See also Ben Harris McClary. "Nancy Ward, Beloved Woman," *Tennessee Historical Quarterly* 21 (December 1962): 352–64.

19. Sara Parker, "The Transformation of Cherokee Apalachia" (Ph.D. diss., Department of Ethnic Studies, University of California, Berkeley, 1991). I would like to acknowledge Ms. Parker's insight that White men married to Indian women brought new resources into tribes rather than taking them away from them. The primary sources on Nancy Ward and Joseph Martin are found in the Draper Papers, Wisconsin Historical Society, Madison.

20. Horatio B. Cushman, *History of the Choctaw, Chickasaw, and Natchez Indians* (New York, 1972), 331–31; Samuel J. Wells, "Choctaw Indians and Jeffersonian Policy" (Ph.D. diss., Department of History, Southern Mississippi University, 1987), 66–67.

21. Cushman, *History of the Choctaw*, 331–32.; American Board of Commissioners for Foreign Missions, *Report of the American Board of Commissioners for Foreign Missions, Compiled from Documents Laid before the Board, at the Seventeenth Annual Meeting, Which Was Held in Middletown (Con.) Sept. 14, and 15, 1826* (Boston, 1826); Henry S. Halbert, "The Last Indian Council on Noxubee River," *Publications of the Mississippi Historical Society* 4 (1901): 271–81.

22. E. Merton Coulter, "Mary Musgrove, 'Queen of the Creeks': A Chapter of Early Georgia Troubles," *Georgia Historical Quarterly* 11, no. 1 (March 1927): 1–30.

23. Isabel Thompson Kelsay, *Joseph Brant, 1743–1807* (Syracuse, NY, 1984), 68–69; Milton W. Hamilton, *Sir*

William Johnson: Colonial American, 1715–1763 (Port Washington, NY, 1976), 35, 304–5; James Thomas Flexner, *Lord of the Mohawks: A Biography of Sir William Johnson* (Boston, 1959), 319–22.

24. Jennifer S. H. Brown, *Strangers in Blood: Fur Trade Company Families in Indian Country* (Vancouver, 1980); Sylvia Van Kirk, *Many Tender Ties: Women in Fur-Trade Society, 1670–1870* (Norman, OK, 1980).

25. See Jacqueline Peterson and Jennifer S. H. Brown, eds., *The New Peoples: Being and Becoming Metis in North America* (Lincoln, NE, 1985).

PART EIGHT

Change and Politics

Chapter 14   Patriarchal Bargains: The Contradictions of Cultural Changes

Chapter 15   Social Movements: Communities and the State

Chapter 16   Visions of the Future

A husband convicted of spousal rape contends that Catholicism and the U.S. Constitution protect him, while his wife argues that her wedding vows do not include vows of abuse. A group of mothers takes to the streets on behalf of their children, demanding that politicians invest in job creation and safe streets. Activities such as these challenge orthodox definitions of motherhood and marriage. The articles in Part Eight examine how social change is emerging in the daily practices of families, communities, and organized religions, through social movements, and in the forward-looking visions of the future.

Patriarchal systems are not monolithic, and neither are women's responses to these systems. The articles collected in Chapter 14 are organized under Deniz Kandiyoti's concept of "patriarchal bargains." According to Kandiyoti, taking into account women's daily lives within institutions reveals that women actively strategize, negotiate, and bargain within diverse patriarchal constructs. Pierrette Hondagneu-Sotelo suggests the malleability of patriarchy in the organization of Mexican immigration to the United States, and Bachrach Ehlers explores how women's economic dependence on men in Guatemala shapes their negotiations. Strong patriarchal beliefs are the basis of many organized religions, but the article by Judith Stacey and Susan Elizabeth Gerard on fundamentalist Christian women shows that these dictates are not static. From these articles we learn that women often take the raw materials of patriarchal religions and redefine their meanings in ways that allow them to negotiate greater power and influence in their daily lives. We also learn that men affected by these negotiations respond to the changes in various ways.

The articles in Chapter 15 challenge traditional assumptions about women's participation in social and political movements. Mary Pardo's article reveals how Mexican

American women's identities as mothers helped to fuel grassroots political mobilization, which in turn sparked political transformations and expanded meanings of motherhood. Cheryl Townsend Gilkes examines organizing strategies and social networks among Black women community workers, and Helen Safa explores how poor women in Latin America challenge public-private dichotomies by organizing around collective consumption issues. Poor women of color living in developed, industrial societies or in developing nations are not generally recognized as feminist activists, but the articles in this segment begin to suggest how the diversity of these women's experiences fuels a more expansive range of feminist political activities.

Finally, Chapter 16 brings together reflections on difference and social change. In the first article, Audre Lorde urges us to work for justice by confronting and reshaping the meanings attached to difference. It is not difference, Lorde observes, but the refusal to recognize differences and "the distortions which result from our misnaming them" that lead to institutionalized inequalities. Continuing with this theme of embracing difference, Walter Williams examines several non-Western cultures and points to some of the ways in which respect for sexual diversity and gender nonconformity might prove beneficial for our society. Last, the dialogue between bell hooks and Cornel West suggests that social change needs to encompass spirituality, love, respect, and a rejection of all exclusionary impulses toward difference. Together, these authors show us that embracing the prism of difference is a vital step toward building a more democratic future.

49

Bargaining with Patriarchy

DENIZ KANDIYOTI

Of all the concepts generated by contemporary feminist theory, patriarchy is probably the most overused and, in some respects, the most undertheorized. This state of affairs is not due to neglect, since there is a substantial volume of writing on the question, but rather to the specific conditions of development of contemporary feminist usages of the term. While radical feminists encouraged a very liberal usage, to apply to virtually any form or instance of male domination, socialist feminists have mainly restricted themselves to analyzing the relationships between patriarchy and class under capitalism. As a result, the term *patriarchy* often evokes an overly monolithic conception of male dominance, which is treated at a level of abstraction that obfuscates rather than reveals the intimate inner workings of culturally and historically distinct arrangements between the genders.

It is not my intention to provide a review of the theoretical debates around patriarchy (Barrett 1980; Beechey 1979; Delphy 1977; Eisenstein 1978; Hartmann 1981; McDonough and Harrison 1978; Mies 1986; Mitchell 1973; Young 1981). Instead, I would like to propose an important and relatively neglected point of entry for the identification of different forms of patriarchy through an analysis of women's strategies in dealing with them. I will argue that women strategize within a set of concrete constraints that reveal and define the blueprint of what I will term the *patriarchal bargain*[1] of any given society, which may exhibit variations according to class, caste, and ethnicity. These patriarchal bargains exert a powerful influence on the shaping of women's gendered subjectivity and determine the nature of gender ideology in different contexts. They also influence both the potential for and specific forms of women's active or passive resistance in the face of their oppression. Moreover, patriarchal bargains are not timeless or immutable entities, but are susceptible to historical transformations that open up new areas of struggle and renegotiation of the relations between genders.

By way of illustration, I will contrast two systems of male dominance, rendered ideal-typical for the purposes of discussing their implications for women. I use these ideal types as heuristic devices that have the potential of being expanded and fleshed out with systematic, comparative, empirical content, although this article makes no pretense at providing anything beyond a mere sketch of possible variations. The two types are based on examples from sub-Saharan Africa, on the one hand, and the Middle East, South Asia, and East Asia on the other. My aim is to highlight a continuum ranging from less corporate forms of householding, involving the relative autonomy of mother-child units evidenced in sub-Saharan polygyny, to the more corporate male-headed entities prevalent in the regions identified by Caldwell (1978) as the "patriarchal belt." In the final section, I analyze the breakdown and transformation of patriarchal bargains and their relationship to women's consciousness and struggles.

AUTONOMY AND PROTEST: SOME EXAMPLES FROM SUB-SAHARAN AFRICA

I had one of my purest experiences of culture shock in the process of reviewing the literature on women in agricultural development projects in sub-Saharan Africa (Kandiyoti 1985). Accustomed as I was to only one type of patriarchy (which I shall describe in some detail later, under the rubric of classic patriarchy), I was ill prepared for what I found. The literature was rife with instances of women's resistance to attempts to lower the value of their labor and, more important, women's refusal to allow the total appropriation of their production by their husbands. Let me give some examples.

Wherever new agricultural schemes provided men with inputs and credit, and the assumption was made that as heads of household they would have access to their wives' unremunerated labor, problems seemed to develop. In the Mwea irrigated rice settlement in Kenya, where women were deprived of access to their own plots, their lack of alternatives and their total lack of control over men's earnings made life so intolerable to them that wives commonly deserted their husbands (Hanger and Moris 1973). In Gambia, in yet another rice-growing scheme, the irrigated land and credit were made available to men only, even though it was the women who traditionally grew rice in tidal swamps, and there was a long-standing practice of men and women cultivating their own crops and controlling the produce. Women's customary duties with respect to labor allocation to common and individual plots protected them from demands by their husbands that they provide free labor on men's irrigated rice fields. Men had to pay their wives wages or lend them an irrigated plot to have access to their labor. In the rainy season, when women had the alternative of growing their own swamp rice, they created a labor bottleneck for the men, who simply had to wait for the days women did not go to their own fields (Dey 1981).

In Conti's (1979) account of a supervised smallholder settlement project in Upper Volta, again, the men were provided with land and credit, leaving the women no independent resource base and a very inadequate infrastructure to carry out their daily household chores. The result was vocal protest and refusal to cooperate.

Roberts (forthcoming) similarly illustrates the strategies used by women to maximize their autonomy in the African context. Yoruba women in Nigeria, for instance, negotiate the terms of their farm-labor services to their husbands while they aim to devote more time and energy to the trading activities that will enable them to support themselves and ultimately give up such services. Hausa women, whose observance of Islamic seclusion reduces the demands husbands can make for their services, allocate their labor to trade, mainly the sale of ready-cooked foodstuffs.

In short, the insecurities of African polygyny for women are matched by areas of relative autonomy that they clearly strive to maximize. Men's responsibility for their wives' support, while normative in some instances, is in actual fact relatively low. Typically, it is the woman who is primarily responsible for her own and her children's upkeep, including meeting the costs of their education, with variable degrees of assistance from her husband. Women have very little to gain and a lot to lose by becoming totally dependent on husbands, and hence they quite rightly resist projects that tilt the delicate balance they strive to maintain. In their protests, wives are safeguarding already existing spheres of autonomy.

Documentation of a genuine trade-off between women's autonomy and men's responsibility for their wives can be found in some historical examples. Mann (1985) suggests that despite the wifely dependence entailed by Christian marriage, Yoruba women in Lagos accepted it with enthusiasm because of the greater protection they thought they would receive. Conversely, men in contemporary Zambia resist the more modern ordinance marriage, as opposed to customary marriage, because it burdens them with greater obligations for their wives and children (Munachonga 1982). A form of conjugal union in which the partners may openly negotiate the exchange of sexual and labor services seems to lay the groundwork for more explicit forms of bargaining. Commenting on Ashanti marriage, Abu (1983, p. 156) singles out as its most striking feature "the separateness of spouses' resources and activities and the overtness of the bargaining element in the relationship." Polygyny and, in this case, the continuing obligations of both men and women to their own kin do not foster a notion of the family or household as a corporate entity.

Clearly, there are important variations in African kinship systems with respect to marriage forms, residence, descent, and inheritance rules (Guyer and Peters 1987). These variations are grounded in complete cultural and historical processes, including different modes of incorporation of African societies into the world economy (Mbilinyi 1982; Murray 1987; S. Young 1977). Nonetheless, it is within a broadly defined Afro-Caribbean pattern that we find some of the clearest instances of noncorporateness of the conjugal family both in ideology and practice, a fact that informs marital and marketplace strategies for women. Works on historical transformations (for example, Etienne and Leacock 1980) suggest that colonization eroded the material basis for women's relative autonomy (such as usufructary access to communal land or traditional craft production) without offering attenuating modifications in either marketplace or marital options. The more contemporary development projects discussed above also tend to assume or impose a male-headed corporate family model, which curtails women's options without opening up other avenues to security and well-being, The women perceive these changes, especially if they occur abruptly, as infractions that constitute a breach of their existing accommodations with the male-dominated order. Consequently, they openly resist them.

SUBSERVIENCE AND MANIPULATION: WOMEN UNDER CLASSIC PATRIARCHY

These examples of women's open resistance stand in stark contrast to women's accommodations to the system I will call *classic patriarchy*. The clearest instance of classic patriarchy may be found in a geographical area that includes North Africa, the Muslim Middle East (including Turkey, Pakistan, and Iran), and South and East Asia (specifically, India and China).[2]

The key to the reproduction of classic patriarchy lies in the operations of the patrilocally extended household, which is also commonly associated with the reproduction of the peasantry in agrarian societies (E. Wolf 1966). Even though demographic and other constraints may have curtailed the numerical predominance of three-generational patrilocal households, there is little doubt that they represent a powerful cultural ideal. It is plausible that the emergence of the patriarchal extended family, which gives the senior man authority over everyone else including younger men, is bound up in the incorporation a control of the family by the state (Ortner 1978), and in the transition from kin-based to tributary modes of surplus control (E. Wolf 1982). The implications of the patrilineal-patrilocal complex for women not only are remarkably uniform but also entail forms of control and subordination that cut across cultural and religious boundaries, such as those of Hinduism, Confucianism, and Islam.

Under classic patriarchy, girls are given away in marriage at a very young age into households headed by their husband's father. There, they are subordinate not only to all the men but also to the more senior women, especially their mother-in-law. The extent to which this represents a total break with their own kin group varies in relation to the degree of endogamy in marriage practices and different conceptions of honor. Among the Turks, there are lower rates of endogamy, and a husband is principally responsible for a woman's honor. Among the Arabs, there is much greater mutuality among affines, and a women's natal family retains both an interest and a say in protecting their married daughter's honor (Meeker 1976). As a result, a Turkish woman's traditional position more closely resembles the status of the "stranger-bride" typical of prerevolutionary China than that of an Arab woman whose position in the patriarchal household may be somewhat attenuated by endogamy and recourse to her natal kin.

Whether the prevalent marriage payment is dowry or bride-price, in classic patriarchy, women do not normally have any claim on their father's patrimony. Their dowries do not qualify as a form of premortem inheritance since they are transferred directly to the bridegroom's kin and do not take the form of productive property, such as land (Agarwal 1987; Sharma 1980). In Muslim communities, for a woman to press for her inheritance rights would be tantamount to losing her brothers' favor, her only recourse in case of severe ill-treatment by her husband or divorce. The young bride enters her husband's household as an effectively dispossessed individual who can establish her place in the patriliny only by producing male offspring.

The patrilineage totally appropriates both women's labor and progeny and renders their work and contribution to production invisible. Woman's life cycle in the patriarchally extended family is such that the deprivation and hardship she experiences as a young bride is eventually superseded by the control and authority she will have over her own subservient daughters-in-law. The cyclical nature of women's power in the household and their anticipation of inheriting the authority of senior women encourages a thorough internalization of this form of patriarchy by the women themselves. In classic patriarchy, subordination to men is offset by the control older women attain over younger women. However, women have access to the only type of labor power they can control, and to old-age security, through their married sons. Since sons are a woman's most critical resource, ensuring their life-long loyalty is an enduring preoccupation. Older women have a vested interest in the suppression of romantic love between youngsters to keep the conjugal bond secondary and to claim sons' primary allegiance. Young women have an interest in circumventing and possibly evading their mother-in-law's control. There are culturally specific examples of how this struggle works to the detriment of the heterosexual bond (Boudhiba 1985; Johnson 1983; Mernissi 1975; M. Wolf 1972), but the overall pattern is quite similar.

The class or caste impact on classic patriarchy creates additional complications. Among the wealthier strata, the withdrawal of women from nondomestic work is frequently a mark of status institutionalized in various seclusion and exclusion practices, such as the purdah system and veiling. The institution of purdah, and other similar status markers, further reinforces women's subordination and their economic dependence on men. However, the observance of restrictive practices is such a crucial element in the reproduction of family status that women will resist breaking the rules, even if observing them produces economic hardship. They forego economically advantageous options, such as the trading activities engaged in by women in parts of Africa, for alternatives that are perceived as in keeping with their respectable and protected domestic roles, and so they become more exploitable. In her study of Indian lacemakers in Narsapur, Mies (1982, p. 13) comments:

> Although domestication of women may be justified by the older forms of seclusion, it has definitely changed its character. The Kapu women are no longer gosha—women of a feudal warrior caste— but domesticated housewives and workers who produce for the world market. In the case of the lacemakers this ideology has become almost a material force. The whole system is built on the ideology that these women cannot work outside the house.

Thus, unlike women in sub-Saharan Africa who attempt to resist unfavorable labor relations in the household, women in areas of classic patriarchy often adhere as far and as long as they possibly can to rules that result in the unfailing devaluation of their labor. The cyclical fluctuations of their power position, combined with status considerations, result in their active collusion in the reproduction of their own subordination. They would rather adopt interpersonal strategies that maximize their security through manipulation of the affections of their sons and husband. As M. Wolf's (1972) insightful discussion of the Chinese uterine family suggests, this strategy can even result in the aging male patriarch losing power to his wife. Even though these individual power tactics do little to alter the structurally unfavorable terms of the overall patriarchal script, women become experts in maximizing their own life chances.

Commenting on "female conservatism" in China, Johnson (1983, p. 21) remarks: "Ironically, women through their actions to resist passivity and total male control, became participants with vested interests in the system that oppressed them." M. Wolf (1974) comments similarly on Chinese women's resistance to the 1950 Marriage Law, of which they were supposed to be the primary beneficiaries. She concludes, however, that despite their reluctance to totally transform the old family system, Chinese women will no longer be content with the limited security their manipulation of family relationships can provide.

In other areas of classic patriarchy, changes in material conditions have seriously undermined the normative order. As expressed succinctly by Cain et al. (1979, p. 410), the key to and the irony of this system reside in the fact that "male authority has a material base, while male responsibility is normatively controlled." Their study of a village in Bangladesh offers an excellent example of the strains placed by poverty on bonds of obligation between kin and, more specifically, on men's fulfillment of their normative obligations toward women. Almost a third of the widows in the villages were the heads of their own households, struggling to make a living through waged work. However, the labor-market segmentation created and bolstered by patriarchy meant that their options for work were extremely restricted, and they had to accept very low and uncertain wages.

Paradoxically, the risks and uncertainties that women are exposed to in classic patriarchy create a powerful incentive for higher fertility, which under conditions of deepening poverty will almost certainly fail to provide them with an economic shelter. Greeley (1983) also documents the growing dependence of landless households in Bangladesh on women's wage labor, including that of married women, and discusses the ways in which the stability of the patriarchal family is thereby undermined. Stacey's (1983) discussion of the crisis in the Chinese family before the revolution constitutes a classic account of the erosion of the material and ideological foundations of the traditional system. She goes on to explore how Confucian pa-

triarchy was superseded by and transformed into new democratic and socialist forms. In the next section, I will analyze some of the implications of such processes of transformation.

THE DEMISE OF PATRIARCHAL BARGAINS: RETREAT INTO CONSERVATISM OR RADICAL PROTEST?

The material bases of classic patriarchy crumble under the impact of new market forces, capital penetration in rural areas (Kandiyoti 1984), or processes of chronic immiseration. While there is no single path leading to the breakdown of this system, its consequences are fairly uniform. The domination of younger men by older men and the shelter of women in the domestic sphere were the hallmarks of a system in which men controlled some form of viable joint patrimony in land, animals, or commercial capital. Among the propertyless and the dispossessed, the necessity of every household member's contribution to survival turns men's economic protection of women into a myth.

The breakdown of classic patriarchy results in the earlier emancipation of younger men from their fathers and their earlier separation from the paternal household. While this process implies that women escape the control of mothers-in-law and head their own households at a much younger age, it also means that they themselves can no longer look forward to a future surrounded by subservient daughters-in-law. For the generation of women caught in between, this transformation may represent genuine personal tragedy, since they have paid the heavy price of an earlier patriarchal bargain, but are not able to cash in on its promised benefits. M. Wolf's (1975) statistics on suicide among women in China suggest a clear change in the trend since the 1930s, with a sharp increase in the suicide rates of women who are over 45, whereas previously the rates were highest among young women, especially new brides. She relates this change explicitly to the emancipation of sons and their new possibility of escaping familial control in the choice of their spouse, which robs the older woman of her power and respectability as mother-in-law.

Despite the obstacles that classic patriarchy puts in women's way, which may far outweigh any actual economic and emotional security, women often resist the process of transition because they see the old normative order slipping away from them without any empowering alternatives. In a broader discussion of women's interest, Molyneux (1985, p. 234) remarks:

> This is not just because of "false consciousness" as is frequently supposed—although this can be a factor—but because such changes realized in a piecemeal fashion could threaten the short-term practical interests of some women, or entail a cost in the loss of forms of protection that are not then compensated for in some way.

Thus, when classic patriarchy enters a crisis, many women may continue to use all the pressure that can muster to make men live up to their obligations and will not, except under the most extreme pressure, compromise the basis for their claims by stepping out of line and losing their respectability. Their passive resistance takes the form of claiming their half of this particular patriarchal bargain— protection in exchange for submissiveness and propriety.

The response of many women who have to work for wages in this context may be an intensification of traditional modesty markers, such as veiling. Often, through no choice of their own, they are working outside their home and are thus "exposed"; they must now use every symbolic means at their disposal to signify that they continue to be worthy of protection. It is significant that Khomeini's exhortations to keep women at home found enthusiastic support among many Iranian women despite the obvious elements of repression. The implicit promise of increased male responsibility restores the integrity of their original patriarchal bargain in an environment where the range of options available to women is extremely restricted. Younger women adopt the veil, Azari (1983, p. 68) suggests, because "the restriction imposed on them by an Islamic order was

therefore a small price that had to be paid in exchange for the security, stability and presumed respect this order promised them."

This analysis of female conservatism as a reaction to the breakdown of classic patriarchy does not by any means exhaust the range of possible responses available to women. It is merely intended to demonstrate the place of a particular strategy within the internal logic of a given system, parallels to which may be found in very different contexts, such as the industrialized societies of Western Europe and the United States. Historical and contemporary analyses of the transformation of the facts and ideologies of Western domesticity imply changes in patriarchal bargains. Gordon's (1982) study of changing feminist attitudes to birth control in the nineteenth and twentieth centuries describes the strategy of voluntary motherhood as part of a broader calculus to improve women's situation. Cott's (1978) analysis of the ideology of passionlessness among Victorian women also indicates the strategic nature of women's choices.

For the modern era, Ehrenreich (1983) provides an analysis of the breakdown of the White middle-class patriarchal bargain in the United States. She traces the progressive opting out of men from the breadwinner role starting in the 1950s, and suggests that women's demands for greater autonomy came at a time when men's conjugal responsibility was already much diminished and alternatives for men outside the conjugal union had gained considerable cultural legitimacy. Despite intense ideological mobilization, involving experts such as doctors, counselors, and psychologists who tried to reinforce the idea of the responsible male breadwinner and the domesticated housewife, alternative trends started to emerge and to challenge the dominant normative order. Against this background, Ehrenreich evaluates the feminist and the antifeminist movements and says, "It is as if, facing the age-old insecurity of the family wage system, women chose opposite strategies: either to get out (figuratively speaking) and fight for equality of income and opportunity, or to stay home and attempt to bind men more tightly to them" (1983, p. 151). The familism of the antifeminist movement could therefore be interpreted as an attempt to reinstate an older patriarchal bargain, with feminists providing a convenient scapegoat on whom to blame current disaffection and alienation among men (Chafetz and Dworkin 1987). Indeed, Stacey (1987, p. 11) suggests that "feminism serves as a symbolic lightning rod for the widespread nostalgia and longing for lost intimacy and security that presently pervade social and political culture in the United States."

However, the forms of consciousness and struggle that emerge in times of rapid social change require sympathetic and open-minded examination, rather than hasty categorization. Thus Ginsburg (1984) evaluates antiabortion activism among women in the United States as strategic rather than necessarily reactionary. She points out that disengaging sexuality from reproduction and domesticity is perceived by many women as inimical to their best interests, since, among other things, it weakens the social pressure on men to take responsibility for the reproductive consequences of sexual activity. This concern and the general anxiety it expresses are by no means unfounded (English 1984) and speak to the current lack of viable alternatives for the emotional and material support of women with children. Similarly, Stacey (1987) identifies diverse forms of "postfeminist" consciousness of the postindustrial era. She suggests that a complex and often contradictory merging of depoliticized feminist attitudes to work and family and of personal strategies to enhance stability and intimacy in marriage are currently taking place.

At the ideological level, broken bargains seem to instigate a search for culprits, a hankering for the certainties of a more traditional order, or a more diffuse feeling that change might have gone either too far or badly wrong. Rosenfelt and Stacey's (1987) reflections on postfeminism and Stacey's (1986) discussion of conservative profamily feminism, although they criticize the alarmist premises of neoconservative discourse, take some of the legitimate concerns it expresses seriously.

CONCLUSION

Systematic analyses of women's strategies and coping mechanisms can help to capture the nature of patriarchal systems in their cultural, class-specific, and temporal concreteness and reveal how men and women resist, accommodate, adapt, and conflict with each other over resources, rights, and responsibilities. Such analyses dissolve some of the artificial divisions apparent in theoretical discussions of the relationships among class, race, and gender, since participants' strategies are shaped by several levels of constraints. Women's strategies are always played out in the context of identifiable patriarchal bargains that act as implicit scripts that define, limit, and inflect their market and domestic options. The two ideal-typical systems of male dominance discussed in this article provide different baselines from which women negotiate and strategize, and each affects the forms and potentialities of their resistance and struggles. Patriarchal bargains do not merely inform women's rational choices but also shape the more unconscious aspects of their gendered subjectivity, since they permeate the context of their early socialization, as well as their adult cultural milieu (Kandiyoti 1987a, 1987b).

A focus on more narrowly defined patriarchal bargains, rather than on an unqualified notion of patriarchy, offers better prospects for the detailed analysis of processes of transformation. In her analysis of changes in sexual imagery and mores in Western societies, Janeway (1980) borrows Thomas Kuhn's (1970) terminology of scientific paradigms. She suggests, by analogy, that widely shared ideas and practices in the realm of sexuality may act as sexual paradigms, establishing the rules of normalcy at any given time, but also vulnerable to change when "existing rules fail to operate, when anomalies can no longer be evaded, when the real world of everyday experience challenges accepted causality" (1980, p. 582). However, sexual paradigms cannot be fully comprehended unless they are inscribed in the rules of more specifically defined patriarchal bargains, as Janeway herself demonstrates in her discussion of the connection between the ideal of female chastity in Western societies and the transmission of property to legitimate heirs before the advent of a generalized cash economy.

To stretch the Kuhnian analogy even further, patriarchal bargains can be shown to have a normal phase and a crisis phase, a concept that modifies our very interpretation of what is going on in the world. Thus, during the normal phase of classic patriarchy, there were large numbers of women who were in fact exposed to economic hardship and insecurity. They were infertile and had to be divorced, or orphaned and without recourse to their own natal family, or unprotected because they had no surviving sons or—even worse—had "ungrateful" sons. However, they were merely considered "unlucky," anomalies and accidental casualties of a system that made sense otherwise. It is only at the point of breakdown that every order reveals its systemic contradictions. The impact of contemporary socioeconomic transformations upon marriage and divorce, on household formation, and on the gendered division of labor inevitably lead to a questioning of the fundamental, implicit assumptions behind arrangements between women and men.

However, new strategies and forms of consciousness do not simply emerge from the ruins of the old and smoothly produce a new consensus, but are created through personal and political struggles, which are often complex and contradictory (see Strathern 1987). The breakdown of a particular patriarchal system may, in the short run, generate instances of passive resistance among women that take the paradoxical form of bids for increased responsibility and control by men. A better understanding of the short- and medium-term strategies of women in different social locations could provide a corrective influence to ethnocentric or class-bound definitions of what constitutes a feminist consciousness.

NOTES

1. Like all terms coined to convey a complex concept, the term *patriarchal bargain* represents a difficult compromise. It is intended to indicate the existence of set rules and scripts regulating gender relations, to which both genders accommodate and acquiesce, yet which may nonetheless be contested, redefined, and renegotiated. Some suggested alternatives were the terms *contract, deal,* or *scenario*; however, none of these fully captured the fluidity and tension implied by bargain. I am grateful to Cynthia Cockburn and Nels Johnson for pointing out that the term *bargain* commonly denotes a deal between more or less equal participants, so it does not accurately apply to my usage, which clearly indicates an asymmetrical exchange. However, women as a rule bargain from a weaker position.

2. I am excluding not only Southeast Asia but also the Northern Mediterranean, despite important similarities in the latter regarding codes of honor and the overall importance attached to the sexual purity of women, because I want to restrict myself to areas where the patrilocal-patrilineal complex is dominant. Thus societies with bilateral kinship systems, such as Greece, in which women do inherit and control property and receive dowries that constitute productive property, do not qualify despite important similarities in other ideological respects. This is not, however, to suggest that an unqualified homogeneity of ideology and practice exists within the geographical boundaries indicated. For example, there are critical variations within the Indian subcontinent that have demonstrably different implications for women (Dyson and Moore 1983). Conversely, even in areas of bilateral kinship, there may be instances in which all the facets of classic patriarchy, namely, property, residence, and descent through the male line, may coalesce under specified circumstances (Denich 1974). What I am suggesting is that the most clear-cut and easily identifiable examples of classic patriarchy may be found within the boundaries indicated in the text.

REFERENCES

Abu, K. 1983. "The Separateness of Spouses: Conjugal Resources in an Ashanti Town." Pp. 156–68 in *Female and Male in West Africa,* edited by C. Oppong. London: George Allen & Unwin.

Agarwal, B. 1987. "Women and Land Rights in India." Unpublished manuscript.

Azari, F. 1983. "Islam's Appeal to Women in Iran: Illusion and Reality." Pp. 1–71 in *Women of Iran: The*

Conflict with Fundamentalist Islam, edited by F. Azari. London: Ithaca Press.

Barrett, M. 1980. *Woman's Oppression Today*. London: Verso.

Beechey, V. 1979. "On Patriarchy." *Feminist Review* 3:66–82.

Boudhiba, A. 1985. *Sexuality in Islam*. London: Routledge & Kegan Paul.

Cain, M., S. R. Khanan, and S. Nahar. 1979. "Class, Patriarchy, and Women's Work in Bangladesh." *Population and Development Review* 5:408–16.

Caldwell, J. C. 1978. "A Theory of Fertility: From High Plateau to Destabilization." *Population and Development Review* 4:553–77.

Chafetz, J. S. and A. G. Dworkin. 1987. "In Face of Threat: Organized Antifeminism in Comparative Perspective." *Gender & Society* 1:33–60.

Conti, A. 1979. "Capitalist Organization of Production Through Non-capitalist Relations: Women's Role in a Pilot Resettlement Project in Upper Volta." *Review of African Political Economy* 15/16:75–91.

Cott, N. F. 1978. "Passionlessness: An Interpretation of Victorian Sexual Ideology, 1790–1850." *Signs: Journal of Women in Culture and Society* 4:219–36.

Delphy, C. 1977. *The Main Enemy*. London: Women's Research and Resource Centre.

Denich, B. S. 1974. "Sex and Power in the Balkans." Pp. 243–62 in *Women, Culture and Society*, edited by M. Z. Rosaldo and L. Lamphere. Palo Alto, CA: Stanford University Press.

Dey, J. 1981. "Gambian Women: Unequal Partners in Rice Development Projects." Pp. 109–22 in *African Women in the Development Process*, edited by N. Nelson. London: Frank Cass.

Dyson, T. and M. Moore. 1983. "On Kinship Structures, Female Autonomy and Demographic Behavior." *Population and Development Review* 9:35–60.

Ehrenreich, B. 1983. *The Hearts of Men*. London: Pluto Press.

Eisensten, Z. 1978. "Developing a Theory of Capitalist Patriarchy and Socialist Feminism." Pp. 5–40 in *Capitalist Patriarchy and the Case for Socialist Feminism*, edited by Z. Eisenstein. New York: Monthly Review Press.

English, D. 1984. "The Fear That Feminism Will Free Men First." Pp. 97–102 in *Powers of Desire: The Politics of Sexuality*, edited by A. Snitow, C. Stansell, and S. Thompson. New York: Monthly Review Press.

Etienne, M. and E. Leacock (eds.). 1980. *Women and Colonization*. New York: Praeger.

Ginsburg, F. 1984. "The Body Politic: The Defense of Sexual Restriction by Anti-Abortion Activists." Pp. 173–88 in *Pleasure and Danger: Exploring Female Sexuality*, edited by C. S. Vance. London: Routledge & Kegan Paul.

Gordon, L. 1982. "Why Nineteenth Century Feminists Did Not Support (Birth Control) and Twentieth Century Feminists Do: Feminism, Reproduction and the Family." Pp. 40–53 in *Rethinking the Family: Some Feminist Questions*, edited by B. Thorne and M. Yalom. New York: Longman.

Greeley, M. 1983. "Patriarchy and Poverty: A Bangladesh Case Study." *South Asia Research* 3:35–55.

Guyer, J. I. and P. E. Peters. 1987. "'Introduction' to Conceptualizing the Household: Issues of Theory and Policy in Africa." *Development and Change* 18:197–213.

Hanger, J. and J. Moris. 1973. "Women and the Household Economy." Pp. 209–44 in *Mwea: An Irrigated Rice Settlement in Kenya*, edited by R. Chambers and J. Moris. Munich: Weltforum Verlag.

Hartmann, H. 1981. "The Unhappy Marriage of Marxism and Feminism: Towards a More Progressive Union." Pp. 40–53 in *Women and Revolution*, edited by L. Sargent. London: Pluto Press.

Janeway, E. 1980. "Who Is Sylvia? On the Loss of Sexual Paradigms." *Signs: Journal in Women in Culture and Society* 5:573–89.

Johnson, K. A. 1983. *Women, the Family and Peasant Revolution in China*. Chicago: Chicago University Press.

Kandiyoti, D. 1984. "Rural Transformation in Turkey and Its Implications for Women's Studies." Pp. 17–29 in *Women on the Move: Contemporary Transformations in Family and Society*. Paris: UNESCO.

———. 1985. *Women in Rural Production Systems: Problems and Policies*. Paris: UNESCO.

———. 1987a. "Emancipated but Unliberated? Reflections on the Turkish Case." *Feminist Studies* 13:317–38.

———. 1987b. "The Problem of Subjectivity in Western Feminist Theory." Paper presented at the American Sociological Association Annual Meeting, Chicago.

Kuhn, T. 1970. *The Structure of Scientific Revolutions* (2nd ed.). Chicago: Chicago University Press.

Mann, K. 1985. *Marrying Well: Marriage, Status and Social Change Among the Educated Elite in Colonial Lagos*. Cambridge: Cambridge University Press.

Mbilinyi, M. J. 1982. "Wife, Slave and Subject of the King: The Oppression of Women in the Shambala Kingdom." *Tanzania Notes and Records* 88/89:1–13.

McDonough, R. and R. Harrison. 1978. "Patriarchy and Relations of Production." Pp. 11–41 in *Feminism and Materialism*, edited by A. Kuhn and A. M. Wolpe. London: Routledge & Kegan Paul.

Meeker, M. 1976. "Meaning and Society in the New East: Examples from the Black Sea Turks and the Levantine Arabs." *International Journal of Middle East Studies* 7:383–422.

Mernissi, F. 1975. *Beyond the Veil: Male-Female Dynamics in a Muslim Society.* New York: Wiley.

Mies, M. 1982. "The Dynamics of Sexual Division of Labour and the Integration of Women into the World Market." Pp. 1–28 in *Women and Development: The Sexual Division of Labour in Rural Societies*, edited by L. Beneria. New York: Praeger.

———. 1986. *Patriarchy and Accumulation on a World Scale: Women in the International Division of Labour.* London: Zed.

Mitchell, J. 1973. *Women's Estate.* New York: Vintage.

———. 1986. "Reflections on Twenty Years of Feminism." Pp. 34–48 in *What is Feminism?* edited by J. Mitchell and A. Oakley. Oxford: Basil Blackwell.

Molyneux, M. 1985. "Mobilization Without Emancipation? Women's Interests, the State and Revolution in Nicaragua." *Feminist Studies* 11:227–54.

Munachonga, M. L. 1982. "Income Allocation and Marriage Options in Urban Zambia: Wives Versus Extended Kin." Paper presented at the Conference on Women and Income Control in the Third World, New York.

Murray, C 1987. "Class, Gender and the Household: The Developmental Cycle in Southern Africa." *Development and Change* 18:235–50.

Ortner, S. 1978 "The Virgin and the State." *Feminist Studies* 4:19–36.

Roberts, P. Forthcoming. "Rural Women in Western Nigeria and Hausa Niger: A Comparative Analysis," in *Serving Two Masters*, edited by K. Young. New Delhi: Allied Publishers.

Rosenfelt, D. and J. Stacey. 1987. "Second Thoughts on the Second Wave." *Feminist Studies* 13:341–61.

Sharma, U. 1980. *Women, Work and Property in North West India.* London: Tavistock.

Stacey, J. 1983. *Patriarchy and Socialist Revolution in China.* Berkeley: University of California Press.

———. 1986. "Are Feminists Afraid to Leave Home? The Challenge of Conservative Pro-Family Feminism." Pp. 219–48 in *What is Feminism?* edited by J. Mitchell and A. Oakley. Oxford: Basil Blackwell.

———. 1987. "Sexism by a Subtler Name? Postindustrial Conditions and Postfeminist Consciousness in the Silicon Valley." *Socialist Review* (Nov.):7–28.

Strathern, M. 1987. "An Awkward Relationship: The Case of Feminism and Anthropology." *Signs: Journal of Women in Culture and Society* 12:276–92.

Wolf, E. 1966. *Peasants.* Englewood Cliffs, NJ: Prentice-Hall.

———. 1982. *Europe and the People Without History.* Berkeley: University of California Press.

Wolf, M. 1972. *Women and the Family in Rural Taiwan.* Palo Alto, CA: Stanford University Press.

———. 1974. "Chinese Women: Old Skills in a New Context." Pp. 157–72 in *Women, Culture and Society*, edited by M. Z. Rosaldo and L. Lamphere. Palo Alto, CA: Stanford University Press.

———. 1975. "Woman and Suicide in China." Pp. 111–41 in *Women in Chinese Society*, edited by M. Wolf and R. Witke. Palo Alto, CA: Stanford University Press.

Young, I. 1981. "Beyond the Unhappy Marriage: A Critique of the Dual Systems Theory." Pp. 43–69 in *Women and Revolution*, edited by L. Sargent. London: Pluto Press.

Young, S. 1977. "Fertility and Famine: Women's Agricultural History in Southern Mozambique." Pp. 66–81 in *The Roots of Rural Poverty in Central and Southern Africa*, edited by R. Palmer and N. Parsons. London: Heinemann.

50

Overcoming Patriarchal Constraints

The Reconstruction of Gender Relations among Mexican Immigrant Women and Men

PIERRETTE HONDAGNEU-SOTELO

...This article examines family stage migration from Mexico to the United States, whereby husbands precede the migration of their wives and children, and it highlights how patriarchal gender relations organize migration and how the migration process reconstructs patriarchy.

In family stage migration, patriarchal gender relations are embedded in normative practices and expectations that allow men and deny women the authority and the resources necessary to migrate independently. Men are expected to serve as good financial providers for their families, which they attempt to do through labor migration; patriarchal authority allows them to act autonomously in planning and carrying out migration. Married women must accept their husbands' migration decisions, remain chaste, and stay behind to care for the children and the daily operation of the domestic sphere. These normative patterns of behavior, however, are renegotiated when the departure of one family member, the husband, prompts rearrangements in conjugal social power and the gender division of labor in the household.

The process of family stage migration diminishes patriarchy, but it does not do so uniformly. In this case study, the time period of male migration and settlement distinguishes between two groups. ...Women and men do not enter the migration process equally, but given the diverse historical and social contexts in which migration occurs, women in the same culture and in similar circumstances may encounter different types of patriarchal obsta-

cles and, hence, improvise different responses to migration. Distinct migration trajectories culminate in the creation of different types of gender relations once the families settle in the United States. Patriarchy is neither a monolithic nor a static construct, even within a group sharing similar class and racial-ethnic characteristics....

Although gender relations in Mexican immigrant families become less patriarchal, they do so in a heterogeneous fashion.... The analysis developed in this article focuses on a dimension that is generally overlooked—behavioral changes initiated by the migration process itself. I argue that the partial dismantling of patriarchy arises from new patterns of behavior induced by the arrangements of family stage migration. In light of this analysis, migration becomes a gendering process. These changes do not occur uniformly, and the analysis contrasts two groups that are distinguished by the historical period of migration and by length of spousal separation due to migration. Once families were reunited, these spousal separations and the context in which they occur were fundamental in shaping new gender relations....

DESCRIPTION OF RESEARCH

This article is based on a case study encompassing 44 adult women and men in 26 families. I began research in a San Francisco Bay-area community in November 1986, just as the Immigration Reform and Control Act passed,[1] and I engaged in

18 months of continuous, intensive social interaction using participant observation and in-depth interviews. Whenever possible, I interviewed husbands and wives separately; interviews were tape-recorded and fully transcribed with nearly all 44 individuals. All interviews and interactions occurred in Spanish; the quotes appearing in this article are verbatim translations selected from the transcripts. . . .

FAMILY STAGE MIGRATION

Direct labor recruitment of Mexican men by U.S. employers, dating back to the nineteenth century, and the bracero program, a temporary contract labor program established by the United States and Mexico between 1942 and 1964, institutionalized family stage migration. Although these programs provide historical precedent, the interviews and the discussions that I conducted with husbands and wives reveal the significance of patriarchal gender relations and ideologies in shaping family stage migration.

In all of the families in which men preceded their wives, patriarchal forms of authority prevailed, so that migration decisions did not arise as part of a unified family or household strategy. Generally, husbands unilaterally decided to migrate with only token, superficial regard for their wives' concerns and opinions. Women were not active decision-making participants. When I asked the men about their initial departure and their wives' responses, they were generally reluctant to present information that implied family conflict over migration. While some men admitted that their wives reacted unenthusiastically, they claimed that their wives agreed or, at worst, were resigned to this situation because of economic need. Typical of their responses was one man's comment: "How could she disagree? My brother was here [in the United States], and things were going well for him."

When I asked the women to recall these scenarios, many of them reported having been vehemently opposed to their husbands' migration. The principal reason was fear of their husbands' desertion, of becoming a *mujer abandonada* (an abandoned woman). One woman, speaking of her home town in Mexico, estimated that "out of ten men who come here [United States], six return home. The others who come here just marry another woman and stay here, forgetting their wives and children in Mexico." Women feared that their husbands' migration would signal not a search for a better means of supporting the family but escape from supporting the family. Their husbands' migration promised an uncertain future for them and for the children who would remain behind; therefore, women tended to respond negatively to their husbands' departure.

Even so, few women were in a position to voice this opposition. Some of them were young—teen brides when their husbands began their long migration careers. In retrospect, these women recognized that they were not accustomed to disagreeing with or even questioning their husbands' judgment. Dolores Avila, who was initially left behind with an infant and who gave birth to a second child while her husband was in the United States, recalled: "I had to believe that he knew what was best for us, that he knew how to advance our situation." Other women expressed their opposition in silence, through prayer. Several women reported that they implored God to have the border patrol capture their husbands and send them back home. While their prayers were sometimes answered, the men stayed home only momentarily before departing once again. Other women initially supported their husbands' decision to migrate in the hope that U.S. remittances and savings would alleviate economic needs; as time passed, these women became opposed to their husbands' lengthy sojourns.

The husbands' departures initiated lengthy spousal separations, ranging from 1 year to 16 years. The 10 couples discussed in this article were separated an average of nearly 6 years. During these periods, the men usually returned to Mexico for visits. In many of the families, spousal separations induced significant transformations in conjugal relations. The following discussion examines the dynamics through which this occurred.

The Women Who Stay Behind: New Rewards and New Burdens

Remittances sent by migrant husbands arrived sporadically and in smaller amounts than anticipated. While store credit and loans from kin provided emergency relief, these sources could not be relied upon indefinitely. In response to extreme financial urgencies and in spite of structural limitations on employment, women devised income-earning activities compatible with their child-rearing responsibilities. The most common solution was informal sector employment, usually vending or the provision of personal services, such as washing and ironing, which they performed in their homes. These women, especially those with young children, worked intensively. Often, it was precisely these conditions that prompted women to migrate. . . .

Although these expanded activities and responsibilities were onerous, the women discovered unanticipated rewards during these spousal separations. Women provided a substantial portion of family resources, and they became more competent at performing multiple roles, as they honed new skills, such as budgeting or public negotiation. . . . As Teresa Ibarra, a woman whose husband migrated to California while she remained behind in a small town in Michoacan caring for five children, explained:

> When he came here [to the United States], everything changed. It was different. It was me who took the responsibility for putting food on the table, for keeping the children clothed, for tending the animals. I did all of these things alone, and in this way, I discovered my capacities. And do you know, these accomplishments gave me satisfaction.

Earning and administering an autonomous income did not automatically translate into greater power for women. These women administered budgets with negligible disposable income, an experience characterized more by the burden of stretching

scarce resources than by holding the reigns of economic power. Paradoxically, the men migrated north for economic reasons, to fulfill breadwinner responsibilities, and to save money to purchase a house, buy land, or pay debts. Yet in the United States the men encountered—especially in this particular metropolitan area of California—an extremely high cost of living and low wages, which their "illegal" status only exacerbated. This situation hindered the accumulation of savings and remittances, and over time, the women resented their husbands' shunning of familial responsibilities, especially with so few economic resources returning in the form of remittances.

REMITTANCES

I don't know whether they earned a little or nothing, but that was what they sent.

As the quote above suggests, the small amount of money that husbands sent home, and women's ignorance about where the entirety of men's U.S. income was spent, fueled women's discontent. Several women strongly suspected that their husbands squandered the money frivolously on other women and in bars. The husbands' migration aggravated a situation in which women performed a disproportionate share of household reproduction tasks and men controlled the greatest share of income. Although men migrated in order to support their families better, they were less accountable to their families while in the United States than if they had not gone north and less accountable than the women who stayed behind.

Men's absences from the home enhanced their ability to withhold from their wives information on the exact amount of their earnings, a practice not uncommon among poor, working-class families in Mexico. This meant that the men could spend a greater share of their earnings on personal pleasures, if they were so inclined. In informal conversations, many women and men, respondents as well as other immigrants in the community, insinuated that many men prefer the life of an independent migrant, free of the constraints and daily responsibilities imposed by a wife and children. Without admitting these motives as his own, Luis Bonilla, a husband and father who remained apart from his wife and six children for two years, explained why he believes men wish to defer their families' migration to the United States:

> For many husbands it's just not convenient for their wives to come here. Sometime they don't want their families to come here because they feel more liberated alone here. When a man is by himself, he can go anywhere he pleases, do anything he chooses. He can spend money as he wants. Instead of sending them $400, he can send them $300 and spend the other $100 on what he wants. He's much freer when the family is in Mexico.

Women resented both the extra burdens imposed on them by men's absence from family obligations and the small amount of remittances. As one woman remarked, "The entire burden falls on one, and that isn't fair." For women such as Isabel Barrios, whose husband's first departure in 1950 initiated a 14-year separation before she and their seven children joined him, this anger became an impetus for migration:

> He would leave and come back, and sometimes he would leave for three years, four years. Every time that he returned home to visit I became pregnant, and I had children, and more children, as they say, "fatherless children." The check that they (migrant husbands] send, that's very different than being a father. Because as the priest at San Cristobal Church says, they are fathers only by check. They are fathers who in reality have not helped raise the children until they [children] arrive here, something for which I fought hard.... Because in reality, I didn't want them to be raised only by myself. I had to work to earn money, and I had to raise the children alone. It was exhausting.

Women's desire to migrate rarely coincided with their migrant husbands' wishes. The majority of sojourning husbands remained opposed to their wives' desire to migrate; during their brief visits home or in letters sent from the United States, the men discouraged their wives from migrating. The

men told their wives that landlords in the United States would not rent to large families, that the jobs in the United States were too hard, and that adolescent children would be corrupted by drugs, gangs, and other bad influences. Migrant husbands who had not obtained legal status told their wives that crossing the border surreptitiously was too dangerous for women.

Most of the men remained steadfastly opposed to their wives' and families' migrating. Conjugal struggles, some lasting several years, ensued. How, then, did the women successfully challenge their husbands' authority to achieve family reunification and migration? The men who began their migrant careers prior to 1965 faced a set of circumstances very different from those faced by men who began migrating after 1965. Consequently, the wives of husbands who went north prior to 1965 faced patriarchal constraints different from those faced by the wives of a later cohort of migrant husbands, and the following section contrasts the experiences of these groups.

PERSUADING PATRIARCHY

Because of changing U.S. immigration legislation, many of the pre-1965 cohort of migrant men had obtained legal status by the 1970s. In order to do likewise, the women needed their husbands' cooperation and formal assistance. To legally migrate, then, the women needed first to persuade their husbands into helping them. Women accomplished this by using family—in-laws, kin, and especially teenage sons and daughters—to help convince the men. Raymundo Carbajal, for example, for years had resisted the migration of his wife and six children, but he finally conceded when their eldest daughter joined forces with her mother. The daughter pointed out that she and her older siblings were approaching 21, and after that age, they would not be eligible to obtain legal status through their father. In the Avila family, in which the children were still young, in-laws helped Dolores convince her husband Marcelino to reunite the family by telling him that the children needed to grow up with their father present. In families with sons, this was perceived as imperative; Arturo Barrios, the father of seven boys, conceded to his family's migration, and years later acknowledged that "boys need their fathers." Family members and kin pressured husbands into assisting with family migration; the wives and teenage children often agreed in advance that their employment earnings would contribute to family income in the United States.

The long separations fostered by the men's solo sojourns diminished the hegemony of the husbands' authority and increased women's autonomy and influence in the family. This enabled the women to develop their own migrant agendas. The women who endured these long spousal separations seemed to develop the greatest sense of autonomy and social power; they used this in advancing their goal of migration. Sidra Galvan, now 73, recalled how she had stubbornly persisted in convincing her husband over the years:

> A lot of time had passed, and he always gave excuses. But after he came back that time [after deportation], I saw no good reason why I should not go too.... He always said it was too dangerous for women to cross, but his boss was going to fix his papers, so now he had not one pretext.

These women pursued their personal goal of migration by persuading and urging their husbands to help them go north.

The wives of men who began their migrant careers before 1965 relied on a more limited range of resources than did the wives of the later post-1965 cohort. Specifically, the absence of a significant representation of Mexican immigrant women in the United States denied them access to assistance from other immigrant women, leaving them more or less dependent on male kin, especially spouses. It is also important to note that because the men could easily obtain legal status, their wives expected to obtain U.S. legal status through their husbands. These women were placed in a position of persuading or negotiating with their husbands in order to achieve migration. Until the mid-1970s, women gained leverage in these spousal negotiations with their husbands through the support of family members in Mexico and reliance on resources such as their jobs, their expected U.S. earnings, and in one case, even literacy skills.

SUBVERTING PATRIARCHY THROUGH WOMEN'S NETWORKS

For a more recent cohort of undocumented immigrant men, those who began their migrant sojourns after 1965, obtaining legal status easily was no longer a viable option. Consequently, their wives were not dependent on obtaining legal status through their husbands. This effectively removed the women's need to gain their husbands' approval for migration.

By the 1970s and 1980s, women who wanted to migrate to the United States after their husbands and against their husbands' wishes were more likely to rely on the direct assistance of other migrant women to subvert or challenge their husbands' opposition to migration. Women's migrant networks work much the same as the men's migrant networks, with one exception: They provide prospective migrant women assistance in persuading their husbands to allow them to go north or in achieving migration without the husbands' knowledge. Immigrant women already in the United States assisted their sisters, mothers, and friends in this manner, helping them to write letters to their husbands or helping them to formulate convincing arguments about their earning potential in the United States. Teresa Ibarra, for example, recalled that she initially migrated with the help of a friend who had U.S. migration experience:

> Well, I came with this friend, because for years I had suffered from that illness in the eyes [migraine headaches]. So my friend had gone back there [Mexico]. ... She would say to me, "They'll cure you in the United States, they'll cure you over there," and in that way, she encouraged me to go. And she told me to write to him so I could go. She stayed in Mexico for three months, and during those three months I kept writing him, to see if I could go, until he finally gave in.

When husbands resisted, women's networks made material forms of assistance available to circumvent men's power. Women lent each other money to cover travel costs and "coyote" or smuggler fees, sometimes unbeknownst to the men. In some cases, separate income funds covered spouses' migration costs; sometimes husbands, much to their chagrin, did not learn of their wives' and children's migration until after the fact.

A case in point is the Bonilla family. In 1974 Tola Bonilla, an illiterate woman, managed with the help of a friend, to write letters to her husband in California, asking that he either return home or bring her and the children to the United States. Luis Bonilla ignored his wife's pleas, so Tola secretly borrowed money from her mother and sister, both of whom worked in California, and after Luis had unexpectedly arrived home for a brief visit due to an expulsion by the Immigration and Naturalization Service (INS), she used these funds to go north. She accompanied him when he departed, yet separate income funds covered their migration costs. Tola was pregnant at the time, and at her insistence, they took the eldest son and youngest daughter. Once in the United States, she saved part of her earnings and borrowed money from a friend to bring the remaining four children. She did this secretly: "Luis didn't know they were coming. He became very angry when they called from Tijuana, but by then it was too late. They were practically here." Tola Bonilla's migration and accomplishment in bringing her children north against her husband's will depended on the encouragement and financial assistance that she received from her mother and sister, her teen daughter's support and willingness to stay behind and care for the younger children, and help from her new friend in California.

The experiences of these migrant women suggest that when women are not accorded legitimate or institutional power, they may resort to subversion of legitimate authority. Two conditions are necessary for women to challenge their husband's authority. One is a sense of social power and autonomy, derived from the processes induced by the lengthy spousal separations.... Without this transformative process, set in motion by the husbands' migration, it is unlikely that women would have developed and actively pursued their own migration intentions.

The other important factor, one that appears to have become increasingly important since the 1970s, is access to women's network resources. Migration, as noted earlier, depends on social resources, and these were less available to women in the 1950s and 1960s when as one woman recalled, "it wasn't customary for women to cross [the border] without papers." By the 1970s women were "illegally" migrating and joining undocumented migrant husbands, and they no longer relied exclusively on their husbands' formal cooperation and assistance, as did the wives of the bracero-era men who had obtained legal status. In this sense, the husbands' illegal status helped to further erode their patriarchal authority in the family. Since more women had migrated and settled in immigrant communities in California by the 1970s, there was a greater pool of social resources available to women than during the 1950s and 1960s....

CONJUGAL RELATIONS IN THE UNITED STATES: MEN'S EXPERIENCES AND DIMINISHING PATRIARCHY

The migration process discussed above affected relations between wives and husbands once families were reunited in the United States. Two indicators of patriarchy are considered here: the household division of labor and patterns of decision making and authority. In those families in which the husbands first migrated prior to 1965, an unorthodox, more egalitarian gender division of labor emerged when the families were reunited. In order to understand why this happened, we must examine the men's experiences during the spousal separations.

Many of these long-term sojourning migrant husbands lived in what we might call "bachelor communities." These consisted of all-male residences, usually small apartments, shared by a number of migrant men. As few as 2 or 3 men, and sometimes as many as 15 or 20, shared a residence. In this context, men learned to do household chores that traditionally in U.S. or Mexican culture, men are not supposed to do. Men learned to cook, clean, iron, and shop for groceries. Most of them also held restaurant jobs, where they worked busing tables, washing dishes, preparing food, and in one case, cooking; these work experiences also widened their repertoire of domestic kitchen skills.

Symbolically, tortillas perhaps best represent Mexican food, and their preparation is traditionally women's work. Yet in these bachelor residential quarters, many of the men in the United States during the 1950s and 1960s learned to make tortillas. As one man related: "There were no tortillas for sale then [1950s] as there are now. So I learned to make tortillas and to cook food too."

Most striking was how proud some of these men were about their newly acquired repertoire of domestic skills. Marcelino Avila, who first came north in 1957, four years before his wife and two children, recalled:

> Back in Mexico, I didn't know how to prepare food, iron a shirt or wash my clothes. I only knew how to work, how to harvest. But when I found myself with certain urgencies here, I learned how to cook, iron my clothes and everything. I learned how to do everything that a woman can do to keep a man comfortable. And the custom stayed with me.... I now know how to prepare American food and Mexican food, while back in my country I didn't know to cook at all. Necessity forced me to do things which I had previously ignored.

Once reunited with their spouses in the United States, the domestic skills that men were forced to learn in their wives' absence often continued to be exercised. Based on what I observed during my visits to their homes, what these couples told me, and in some cases, on what I heard from neighbors, these families appear to maintain a more nontraditional division of household labor than other Mexican immigrant families that I visited. Men did part of the cooking and housework,

they unself-consciously assumed the role of host in offering me food and beverages, and in some cases, men continue to make tortillas on weekends and special occasions. These changes are modest if we judge them by ideal standards of feminist egalitarianism, but they are significant if we compare them to normative patriarchal practices.

On Sunday afternoon, while I interviewed Rebecca Carbajal, she and I sat at the large dining table while her husband Raymundo made soup and flour tortillas from scratch. When the soup and tortillas were prepared, he joined us, and commenting on his activities, he said, without a touch of sarcasm, "This is exactly how we are, this is how we live, just as you see us." He even boasted that he was a more talented cook than his wife. Manuel Galvan, at age 73, rose to squeeze fresh orange juice for him and his wife before taking his morning walk to a nearby donut shop, where he met with a small group of men for coffee and gossip. The women also held higher expectations for their husbands' activities in the domestic sphere. Isabel Barrios, for example, complained that by comparison with her grown sons, her husband was deficient, as he had never changed dirty diapers, neither in the United States nor in Mexico. Dolores Avila testified that her husband had changed babies' diapers after the family migrated, and in the current Avila household, it is Marcelino who takes primary responsibility for household chores, such as washing and ironing clothes, vacuuming, and cooking.

In those families in which husbands began their migrant sojourn prior to 1965, these new arrangements arose as a result of the long spousal separations and the small, isolated settlement communities characterized by the relative scarcity of women who would typically perform domestic household chores. Meanwhile, the wives had grown more independent and assertive during the long spousal separations. They were no longer accustomed or always willing to act subserviently before their husbands.

In families in which the men began their migrant sojourns after 1965, daily housework arrangements were not radically transformed once the families were reconstituted in the United States. In these families, the men did not perform a significant amount of housework. Although most of the wives held jobs outside the home, the men still expected their wives to wait on them and to take primary responsibility for cooking and cleaning. Most of the women did so.

The Bonilla family arrangements illustrate this pattern. When Tola Bonilla returned home in the late afternoon from cleaning other people's houses, she set about cleaning her own home, laundering, and cooking. On two occasions when I was invited for dinner, Tola cooked and served the meals but did not eat, and she sat down with a glass of juice only after she had served us, claiming that eating heavy food at night made her ill. I felt awkward discussing community organizational tactics with Luis while Tola assumed a subordinate position on the sidelines. Although the Bonillas advocated, in my eyes, a progressive social agenda, their household division of labor remained conservative and patriarchal. Although both Luis and Tola adopted the rhetoric of gender equality—part of the curriculum they learned in church-sponsored weekend marriage encounters—in practice, their daily activities did not challenge women's subordination. Similar inequities were apparent in the Ibarra, Macias, Gandara, and Duarte families—all of whom had migrated since the mid-1960s.

The continuation of a traditional gender division of labor among this group is, I believe, rooted in the conditions of migration. The post-1965 migrant men migrated a fewer number of times and for shorter periods before their families joined them. In the United States, the post-1965 migrant men countered and lived in a flourishing Mexican immigrant community that included both men and women, as well as entire families. They were more likely to live with kin or, in some instances, in amorous relationships with other women than in an all-male dwelling. Despite the absence of their wives, the post-1965 group of migrant men were not impelled to learn traditional "women's work," because they lived in residences where other women—kin, wives of the men who invited them to stay, or in some cases, "girlfriends"—performed these tasks. Traditional expectations that delegate domestic tasks to women were often reinforced by kinship obligations.

When husbands and wives were reunited, an orthodox gender division of household labor was generally reinstated. Yet traditional forms of patriarchy were not reconstituted in precisely the same form as they had existed prior to migration. Women did not relinquish the decision-making power and authority that they had established during their husbands' sojourns. . . .

CONCLUSION

Patriarchal gender relations organize family stage migration, and migration reorganizes gender relations. Men's authority within families and men's access to migrant network resources favor husbands' initial departure. Yet their departure rearranges gender relations in the family; as women assume new tasks and responsibilities, they learn to act more assertively and autonomously. This new sense of social power and later, for another cohort of migrant wives, additional access to women's network resources enable the wives to migrate. . . .

Once the families are reunited in the United States, migration and resettlement processes elicit transformations in patriarchal gender relations. During the spousal separations, women often learn to act independently, and men, in some cases, learn to cook and wash dishes. In other instances, they learn to concede to their wives' challenges to their authority. These behaviors are not readily discarded when the spouses are reunited. Not only is migration shaped by gender relations, but perhaps more important, the migration process experienced by those who pursue family stage migration forges new gender relations. In this sense, migration is both gendered and gendering. . . .

NOTE

1. The Immigration Reform and Control Act (IRCA), enacted in November 1986, included major provisions in the areas of employment and legalization for undocumented immigrants in the United States.

REFERENCES

Baca Zinn, Maxine. 1980. Employment and education of Mexican American women: The interplay of modernity and ethnicity in eight families. *Harvard Educational Review* 50:47–62.

51

Debunking Marianismo
Economic Vulnerability and Survival Strategies among Guatemalan Wives

TRACY BACHRACH EHLERS

In highland Guatemala, an old riddle asks, "How is a husband like an avocado?" The answer, "A good one is hard to find," is well known to every woman. My fieldnotes are filled with stories testifying to the truth of this adage. Marcela's common-law husband gambles every night and refuses to marry her because he has another wife—and five children—in the next town. Dona Violeta is called a widow, but everyone knows she was abandoned by her husband after the birth of her third child. Carmen had to send her children to live with her mother since their father left her and her new husband refuses to raise another man's offspring. Dona Magdalena's husband drank up her wages, beat her when she complained about it, then spent the next two weeks with his lover, leaving Magdalena penniless. Rich or poor, in towns and villages across the highlands, rarely a day passes without another woeful tale of offenses, abuses, and bad habits of men.

The research on gender relations in Latin America is replete with descriptions of women tormented by unhappy marriages and with explanations of male behavior in this context.[1] As early as the seventeenth century, Fray Alonso called it *"la mala vida,"* or "the bad life" (Boyer 1989). Where analysis fails us is when we ask why women put up with persistent male abuse and irresponsibility. In trying to explain this pattern, authors have often turned to the *machismo/ marianismo* model of gender relations, which

suggests that women welcome abusive male behavior as the spiritual verification of their true womanhood. Men's wickedness, this argument claims, is the necessary precondition for women's superior status as semidivine figures, without whose intercession men would have little chance of obtaining forgiveness for their transgressions (Stevens 1973a).

There are several problems with this model. First, *marianismo* is often considered as a complement to machismo, where the passive, long-suffering woman acts in response to male irresponsibility; without *marianismo, machismo* could not exist. Second, it alleges that this pattern offers women a positive and private realm and that, relegated to a separate domestic sphere, they are content with their feminine power in the home, and do not wish to change the sexual balance of power. On both counts, *marianismo* blames the victim, suggesting wives accept callousness from men because they benefit from the status of wife/mother. In addition, *marianismo* has evolved into a nearly universal model of the behavior of Latin American women.[2]

Some see *marianismo* as a powerful positive stance,[3] but I maintain that in Guatemala's patriarchal society, the sexual division of labor excludes women from valuable income-producing activities, thus giving them no choice but to accept irresponsible male behavior. Among Mayas and ladinos, the prevailing ideology of male domination in the economy minimizes the contribution women make to family survival and their ability to manage without a resident man. In this system, men are valuable scarce resources who can misbehave with impunity, assured that their wives and mistresses need them for economic reasons. In this paper, I argue that:

1. While female subordination is present, it comes in many different forms and in varying degrees.
2. Women's behavior vis-a-vis men is not merely a response to *machismo*, but is a survival strategy emerging from female economic, social, and sexual dependence in a society where men hold economic, political, and legal power.
3. Gender relations are not a static construction of ideal roles, but evolve and change with the material conditions of women's lives, and over the life span of each woman.

This article focuses on two highland communities where women have distinctly different relations to production. San Pedro Sacatepequez, San Marcos, is a changing indigenous town (pop. 15,000) in highland Guatemala. San Pedro's rapidly developing economy has created a myriad of income-producing activities for both sexes, reflected in a diversity of male/female relations. In contrast to San Pedro's urbanity, I also examine material from San Antonio Palopó, a traditional Cakchiquel-speaking village on Lake Atitlán. San Antonio (pop. 2600) has a subsistence-based economy, largely dependent upon corn and onion production. In the last dozen years the rapid growth of commercial weaving has resulted in a dramatic change in the sexual division of labor. These contrasting communities have in common a shift in relations of production, i.e., development, albeit on vastly different scales. My discussion focuses on how each town's increasing market integration has changed the sexual division of labor, emphasizing and exacerbating patriarchal relations to the detriment of women.[4]

THE MARIANISMO MODEL

Latin American women are aware of the realities of marriage. Safa's (1976) interviews in Puerto Rico revealed that two-thirds of the women regarded marriage as an unhappy situation doomed from the start because of male vices. Similarly, female Mexican textile workers considered marriage to be problem-ridden and thought themselves better off alone (Piho 1975). Still, 92 percent of Latin American women marry (Youseff 1973), and continue to speak fatalistically about the state of marriage. Peasant women in the Dominican Republic also believe marriage to be a matter of luck, that one must suffer whatever comes and make the best of it (Brown 1975).

This fatalistic acceptance of women suffering at the hands of men has been traced to the colonial period, when women were taught to emulate the virtues of the Virgin Mary. The Spanish fostered a nontemporal, spiritual, and therefore secondary, role for women with laws and social codes limiting women's rights and defining women as subservient (Leahy 1986). This tradition relegates the unquestioning, obedient woman to the home, the church and the family.

Stevens (1973a) coined the term *marianismo* to suggest the sacred significance of women's subordinate posture in Latin America, and described the idealized belief that women are semidivine, morally superior, spiritually strong beings who manifest these attributes in personal abnegation, humility and sacrifice. These attributes she believes appropriate, given the tensions surrounding the exaggerated masculinity (*machismo*) of their spouses. Thus women must be patient with frivolous and intemperate husbands. When men are truly sinful, women, who are closer to God, will intervene and, by their prayers, guide men along the difficult road to salvation. Above all, women are submissive and resigned to their status as pure, long-suffering martyrs to the irresponsible but domineering men in their lives.

Women use their subordinate status to their own advantage in "having their *marianismo* cake and eating it too," (Stevens 1973b:98). The myth of Marian martyrdom is perpetuated in order to assure the "security blanket" which covers all women, giving them a strong sense of identity and historical continuity (Stevens 1973b:98). By this way of reasoning, female power emerges from the private, domestic domain where women rule and are as liberated as they wish to be, free from the pressures of the male-oriented business world. Women are satisfied with their domestic domain and will likely work hard to hold onto a system that supports it. However, the price for controlling this powerful resource can be a lifetime of suffering, both in childbearing and in the trials and humiliations of the marriage itself. Nonetheless, as Neuhouser (1989:690) notes, "the positive impact of marianismo as a resource for women increases over the life course," as a woman's accumulated pain is transformed into sainthood.

Critics of the *marianismo* concept take issue with the notion that women consciously place themselves within the domestic safety net of *la mala vida*. Bourque and Warren (1981) reject the idea that women enjoy parity with men through their control of the domestic sphere. They argue, that where female status is undercut by a hierarchy of men in the larger world, women cannot have power in the home no matter how much they are venerated. Nash (1989) adds that combining public isolation with the spiritual emulation of the Virgin acts to rationalize female powerlessness as it condones male superiority. Moreover, the ideal of the good woman reigning at home rarely corresponds to daily reality (Kinzer 1973; Browner and Lewin 1982). I suggest that as men move away from agricultural dependence, fatherhood becomes an expression of male virility or proof of masculine control over females, and the home becomes the realm of a tyrannical husband, not the idealized domain of women.

Where the *marianismo* model breaks down entirely is among the millions of poor women for whom work is a necessity. They are often underreported and underestimated, especially in subsistence or domestic production. Urban and rural women are rarely idle; their children might not eat if they do not work. Employed as maids, factory workers, in subsistence or export agriculture, as artisans, petty commodity producers, etc., Latin American women work and, when compared to men, occupy the more onerous, insecure, and unrewarding jobs. Female laborers have fewer productive opportunities than men (Deere and Leon de Leal 1981), are severely restricted in what choices they do have (Schminck 1977), and are often forced to accept oppressive conditions and physically taxing work (Piho 1975).

While the sexual division of labor in productive activities is mixed, reproductive responsibilities for Latin American women are relatively uniform. Women perform the bulk of household duties, which proscribes their potential productivity outside the home. Men can find wage labor while many women take up subsistence activities "almost as an extension of domestic work" (Deere and Leon de Leal 1981:360). Even cottage industry, which allows women to direct child labor and is compatible with housework, is usually an extension of labor-intensive domestic skills (Beuchler 1985) and can be a highly exploitative, low-profit endeavor (Ehlers 1982). Moreover, whether a woman works in the informal sector or in the home, she still works two shifts, juggling children, cooking, washing, and cleaning with income-production. Managing these two full-time jobs impinges upon female income potential and diminishes the seriousness with which women are treated in jobs and careers. In short, the *marianismo* model does not fully take into account Latin American male domination.

Male dominance over economic and political institutions limits female access to economic resources. Because it marginalizes women as economic actors, patriarchy does not have to dominate women physically, but can use indirect market control to limit female independence. This may vary by class, ethnicity, or geography, but any examination of gender relations in Latin America shows male dominance in economic control, access to critical roles in society, and in maintaining cultural stereotypes which reinforce male power. Women are therefore economically and socially vulnerable. Modernization and the accompanying elaboration of market relations usually make this situation worse.

Wolf (1966) and Adams (1960) argue that egalitarian relations among indigenous Mayan men and women emerge from a traditional culture that supports a strong, positive husband-father role. Bossen (1984) correctly observes that this argument underestimates the importance of economic roles in determining gender values. In peasant economies where the family productive system functions, as a cooperative unit, women's productive and reproductive labor is as valuable as men's work. Loucky's (1988:119) research in two Lake Atitlan towns convinced him that, "so indispensable is this partnership that individual accumulation and highly unequal distribution of goods is rare." Women are confident of their roles and have little reason to be submissive. Both sexes acknowledge the mutuality of their labor contributions within a flexible, supportive social system. This domestic balance would encourage a woman to leave an abusive husband and return to her natal home (Wagley 1949).

All this changes when individualized cash income enters the system, creating a redivision of labor that negatively affects women. The interdependency, cooperation, and equal distribution of labor characteristic of couples in small traditional communities breaks down when men work autonomously outside the home. Male accessibility to private income production establishes female dependency characteristic of nuclear families in a situation of industrialization (Bossen 1984).

The increasing value given to male income from outside employment is problematic for women in the two communities I examine. In each, women's economic status diminishes with the increasing occupational fortunes of their spouses. In one community, new male-dominated industry has begun to make complementary peasant production irrelevant. In the other, modernization has under-

mined women's independent businesses while it greatly enhanced male external trade opportunities. The evidence suggests that with increased autonomous income, men devalue their wives, who are no longer essential to them. The economic vulnerability of women from these two very different towns compels them to accept male callousness or irresponsibility because they have no alternative sources of economic security. Those middle-class women who are able to manage without a man do so through resources not available to the ordinary Guatemalan wife.

SAN ANTONIO PALOPÓ

San Antonio Palopó is a traditional, Cakchiquel-speaking community on the eastern shore of Lake Atitlán, whose people have depended upon *milpa* agriculture (small-scale corn agriculture) supplemented by small-scale cash crops (namely onions and previously, anise), and seasonal plantation labor. Families live in tiny, one-room houses, few of which have access to running water, and nearly half the households are landless. Harvested maize (corn) lasts about six months, after which cash must be generated to buy food. The precarious quality of life is perhaps best reflected in the poor diet and the high frequency of chronic illness.

Men and women share this impoverished life, but women carry a larger share of the burden. Half marry by age sixteen and 60 percent have their first child by eighteen. Families with six or seven children under twelve years old are common, although 43 percent have lost one or more children to illness associated with malnutrition. Beyond nursing and child care, women bear an arduous and repetitive domestic routine that takes up to nine hours each day, and which diminishes the time for income production.

Although both men and women are poor and socially marginalized, men have more familiarity with and access to the dominant ladino culture. Women are rarely educated (77 percent have no schooling), with only a 15 percent literacy rate, compared with 32 percent for men. Eighty-four percent of men are fluent in Spanish, while women speak Cakchiquel almost exclusively. All indigenous women wear the local costume, compared to three-quarters of men, a figure that will no doubt decrease since men are beginning to insist their sons wear Western dress.

Cultural, economic, and physical isolation handicap Tunecas[5] in many ways. Only a few women regularly travel beyond San Antonio to sell handweavings in the nearby tourist town of Panajachel, and their sales are sporadic at best. In fact, most Tunecas avoid Panajachel, preferring to do their shopping from itinerant traders who charge high prices when they pass through town. Women who choose the forty-minute bus ride to Panajachel to shop are uncomfortable and shy beyond the market, where Cakchiquel is spoken. They usually accomplish their errands quickly and go home on the next bus.

Female social vulnerability is clearest when women interact with outsiders—doctors, teachers, ladino traders—and must defer to men. In part this is because they do not speak Spanish, but also because of cultural prescriptions that deny respectability to those women who openly converse with strangers. Without men present, women can be outspoken about themselves. Tunecas visiting me needed little encouragement to talk about sex and contraception. They agreed that where children were concerned, women suffered on many counts: they did not like intercourse, they hated pregnancy, feared childbirth, and resented having to care for several small children because it made income production so difficult. Like the women of San Pedro la Laguna interviewed more than fifty years before (Paul 1974), my Tuneca informants characterized men as "curs" who wanted sex all the time, but had little consideration for their wives' needs.

While skewed gender relations have long existed in San Antonio, a clear pattern of male dominance is more evident now than in the past. Until recently, men and women worked together to survive. Men were responsible for agricultural pro-

duction, women for processing grains, preparing onions for market, and maintaining the home. Both sexes traveled to the coast to pick cotton on large plantations. There was little money to be made beyond this, and the cash generated from migratory labor was quickly absorbed in consumption or fertilizer for corn. In 1978, however, a handful of entrepreneurial men and women worked with the Peace Corps and the Catholic Church to establish a commercial weaving industry in the town. This innovation totally realigned the relations of production, creating a severe discrepancy in the contributions men and women make to the family income.

Today, 60 percent of Tuneco homes have looms. These families generate an average of nearly $50 a month, more than replacing plantation labor as a source of cash income. The average plantation income is approximately $25 a month, and few work for more than one month. Coastal weather is hot and extremely humid, the work is arduous and food and housing are abysmal. Weaving is home-based, often year-round, and clean. One man said he likes to weave because while he works he can listen to his new radio and look at his new watch. Moreover, instead of eating *frijoles* (beans) three times a day, his wife cooks various dishes for him, keeps his clothes clean, and generally provides domestic support services for his productive efforts.

In San Antonio in 1978, no men wove, but nearly all their wives did. Women used their backstrap looms to produce the blouses, shirts, and handcloths for the family and for a small tourist trade. It seemed obvious that women should lead in the introduction of four-harness footlooms since they understood the basic weaving system and could easily adapt to the new technology. In fact, women far outnumbered men at the early co-operative meetings, but later, when it was clear that the new production system was to be ongoing, men signed up in increasing numbers. As an indication of their incipient dominance of commercial weaving, a handful of entrepreneurial male leaders took over as officers of the co-operative, pushing women into peripheral organizational positions.

In a very short time, the sexual division of labor evolved to afford female weavers a small part in the town's new economic profile. Only five percent of commercial weavers are women, despite their prominent role in the establishment of the textile co-operative. Quite simply, with all the other (non-paying) labor they have to do, women do not have the time to weave. Men replace themselves in the fields with day laborers paid from their weaving earnings. The demand for local fieldhands to tend the corn fields has risen with the popularity of weaving and become a secondary occupation replacing plantation labor. In fact, so many men weave there is a scarcity of fieldhands. Women cannot do the same in their domestic work, and this compromises their effectiveness as weavers. While men can start weaving upon rising and work all day, female domestic responsibilities seriously diminish the number of hours available for commercial textile production. Weaving contractors admit they would rather not give work to women because of their longer delivery time compared to men. Despite their traditional skill as weavers, women's labor is now less valuable than their husbands'.

Men have readily taken advantage of the opportunity to weave, as evidenced by the cash purchases of new tape decks, watches, roofs, and cement block houses. Several men have invested their earnings in motorboats, bars, *tiendas* (stores), and other businesses. As soon as they learned how to market belts and table linens, a dozen or so enterprising men began their own weaving organizations as *contratistas* (middlemen), a system paralleling the co-operative, but with one distinction. Rather than putting the standard 20 percent of each order back into the co-operative, the *contratistas* keep it for themselves. Every few months, someone else decides to try being a middleman by drumming up new business. Since looms can produce only so much, new weavers regularly enter the labor pool. Thus, privatization of the weaving business enlarged the small existing bourgeoisie by infusing it with male entrepreneurs. The men of San Antonio Palopá have embraced a new productive activity affording them a better living.

It is too soon to state unequivocally how development has disrupted male-female interactions in San Antonio. However, given the new relations of production accompanying weaving, we might gain some insight by looking to those who have profited most from the individualization of income, the entrepreneurial class. The incidence of *casitas* (parallel marriages) is highest among the town's wealthier men. While few men have the opportunity for more than casual affairs, men with money can take second wives, and they tend to flaunt their behavior. In a flagrant case of polygyny, one of the new *contratistas* built a house for his second wife and their children next to his first wife's house. The families involved have complained to the local authorities about these arrangements, making the affair a public scandal. In another case, one of the town's well-to-do middlemen brought his parallel family to San Antonio's saint's day fiesta, an action so outrageous that his first wife tried to kill him. Both these wives took action to stop their husbands' infidelities, but neither has been successful.

San Antonio women are at a considerable disadvantage in maintaining themselves as partners in the family productive system. Like other rural Maya, they shared their impoverishment with the men in their lives. Currently, a discrepancy in income and control of earnings deprives them of that comfort, however small, and the security of knowing that their husbands need them as much as they need their husbands. It is clear that development has been beneficial to men, creating a large new job category (weaving), and expanding another (day laborer). Although men still require female domestic service, the traditional complementarity of peasant agricultural production has been replaced by individualization of income and concentration of business in the hands of men. At the same time, women's productive contribution has been devalued and marginalized, exacerbating female economic vulnerability and creating worrisome implications for gender relations in the future.

SAN PEDRO SACATEPEQUEZ

San Pedro Sacatepequez is a busy Indian commercial center in San Marcos, located between the high altiplano and the coastal towns and hotland plantations. The town has a heterogeneous, stratified population made even more diverse by the large hinterland comprising seventeen hamlets (*aldeas*), a favorable location for trade. Since World War II, expansion of commerce, cottage industry, transportation and education has placed San Pedro and several other large, enterprising Indian towns in stark contrast to the poverty of most highland communities.

The pace of business is such that townsfolk are fully employed, with few families relying entirely upon *milpa* production for food. Evidence of decades of entrepreneurial vigor are found in the town's educated children, handsome new houses, and imported automobiles. Although consumerism is rampant among the growing middle-class, poor townspeople and rural *aldeanos* also have disposable income. Few rural Sampedranos need to work on coastal plantations to feed their families. Those in the four or five nearest *aldeas* are well-integrated into the commercial activity of the town whose middle-class values they now emulate.

The creation of a middle-class (15 percent of the urban population) in a mere forty years is an indication of the potential for material gain in San Pedro. Since the late 1940s, business opportunities have multiplied with better transportation and the demand for more consumer goods, and many commercial families have dramatically expanded their earning power. Nowadays, grandchildren of itinerant textile peddlers have comfortable lives and successful careers as doctors, lawyers, architects, teachers, and engineers. Education has become a valuable and accessible commodity as the desire for learning and diploma-related employment has grown. Oddly enough, the local passion

for business often supersedes entering the positions that come with post-graduate training. There are several cases where new professionals postponed establishing a practice to return to their first love, the family store.

The good fortune of the middle-class is built upon the same strategy used by poorer Sampedranos, the family productive system. But middle-class families have been able to educate enough children to generate reliable salaries, thus providing capital for the commercial development of household-based businesses. Poorer families must continue to invest in labor-intensive enterprises and jobs. While the poor, too, are beginning to send their children to school, class differences handicap *aldeanos* as wage earners, making their material progress slower.

Women, more than men, exploit the available labor supply, depending upon the free labor of children working side-by-side with supervising mothers in what I have called the female family business (Ehlers 1982). Female members of the family cooperate in the home, store, or small workshop for the efficient running of both business and household. Domestic functions are undisturbed since daughters care for babies, cook meals, and run errands to free their older siblings and mothers for income production. The family productive system maximizes the potential for under-capitalized, labor-intensive work while socializing girls for the same occupations when they are mature.

Women must engage in several productive activities to survive, and it is the rare woman who has only one strategy for earning money. A teacher is an after-school knitter or shopkeeper or both. A weaver comes to the huge Thursday market to sell the week's *huipil* (a woven blouse or dress), but also stocks up on candies and breads for her little *aldea* store. When their live chicken market closes, three teenage girls help their mother make *piñatas* and paper floral decorations for graves. The woman who sells vegetables returns home at 7:00 P.M. to her knitting machine, and will bake several dozen breads for sale if she has time. The dedication to work is near-constant and Sunday mass provides the only respite most women have from productive activities.

To justify their workaholism, Sampedranas claim they live to work, but the opposite is equally true: they must work in order to live. The pace of commercial development in San Pedro is brisk enough and the new middle-class large enough, that it is an easy mistake to assume that the locals are doing well. They are better off than other highland communities, but in most cases their earnings are grossly insufficient. A growing population, competition, and unstable markets have kept profit margins for female cottage industry or trade only slightly above cost. Labor is never figured into the price of a handmade product since a woman's saleable work is considered part of her normal domestic responsibility. Accordingly, in ten day's time, a woman and her two daughters might produce a *huipil* in which they have invested $50 in thread, but for which they will garner only $60. Their profit of just over one dollar a day is standard.

Weaving and other female family businesses provide women with their own productive enterprises where they control family labor, manage money, and make creative decisions, but profits from female enterprises are so low that few can completely depend upon them to sustain the family. For the family to survive and flourish, men must do their part as well. The standard highland budgetary division of labor assumes men will contribute the household staples of corn and firewood, while their wives provide everything else through domestic manufacture or cash production. Until recently, women were able to fulfil their obligations by producing goods domestically. Today, women are buying more items because the demands of earning a living do not allow for the home manufacture of necessities like bread, soap, candies, or clothes. Budgets from nearby *aldeas* show that families require a cash minimum of $80 each month, far more than a woman can earn by herself.

An alliance with a male pays off for women in another way. Men father children and, most important, daughters. While boys are valuable for potential remittances from salaried jobs, girls are a necessary requirement for their mother's immediate security. In the poorest households, girls help with domestic chores or low-level cottage industry, and mothers benefit from the small income their teenage daughters provide as domestics. Artisan women use their daughters' labor through the female family business and keep up handicraft output. In both situations, women are keenly aware of the crucial productive and reproductive contributions of men.

Middle-class women are in a somewhat different situation, one complicated by the diversity of productive options among the socially mobile. Some middle-class women have jobs as teachers, but most who work are *comerciantes* (business operators). Rarely do they have their own businesses, however. Instead they function as the retail end of a commercial enterprise which their husbands own and manage. Few of these women control the money their stores take in, being little more than front office overseers. Other wives of this class do not work at all, in many cases because their husbands insist they remain at home as a visible sign of male affluence. In either situation, these women control little of their families' resources and are entirely reliant upon their husbands for money. Children in this case legitimate a woman's role as a mother, but require expensive outlays to outfit and educate, rather than being productive assistants. Nonetheless, children of the professional middle-class do contribute to household expenses and are often regarded as fiscal safety nets in the event that their mother is widowed or abandoned.

FEMALE VULNERABILITY AND DEVELOPMENT

Since World War II, men in San Pedro have been able to take advantage of their town's burgeoning commercial enterprises by establishing relatively lucrative commercial networks and artisanal occupations (Smith 1977). Men now control transportation, storefront retail businesses, and professions. Men have more tools for investment than women (among them better education, easier credit and, most important, exclusive control of the external market), and have done remarkably well in taking advantage of the bullish economy. Quite the opposite is true for their wives.

One by-product of modernization has been the undermining of women's traditional occupations in cottage industry and trade. For generations, woman-centered artisan shops satisfied indigenous consumer habits. Now, however, they are unable to compete with the cheaper, commercially manufactured modern products merchandized by local men, and their handiworks are no longer even minimally profitable. Identification with the national culture has also meant that hand-woven textiles and handmade household goods are now considered old-fashioned. Without their customary markets, independent female family businesses are dying out. They have been replaced by employment or piece-work jobs which transfer control of production from the woman to a male patron or supervisor. Overall, while most women in San Pedro have work if they want it, the relations of production are changing. Analysis of production data I collected in town and three *aldeas* shows the following:

1. Women's work is segregated into a handful of occupations, while male jobs are spread across a much wider spectrum.
2. Women's occupations were overwhelmingly labor-intensive and based on family production. Men do take advantage of their sons' labor to some extent, but they generally work in more solitary jobs.
3. Nearly half the women surveyed currently worked only in nonpaying household duties, compared to a small fraction of men primarily occupied with *milpa* production.
4. Female family business made an average of one dollar a day while solitary male workers made nearly three times as much for about the same hours worked per week.

In sum, women's work is narrowly confined to traditional production systems which are steadily declining as a viable part of the economy. Lacking the skills or capital to begin new businesses, many traditional producers have returned to being housewives, being able to do this because their husbands are making more money. As women's traditional enterprises fade, men's productive opportunities have expanded, particularly in solitary occupations and businesses. Education has afforded them more jobs and access to credit for start-up companies. The result of this transition in the sexual division of labor has been an increase in female economic vulnerability and, correspondingly, a greater dependence upon male wage earners for family survival.

The repercussions of decades of modernization are sizeable, and one clear problem for women is that diminishing economic responsibility translates directly into a loss in female status. Women who no longer manage a household productive system forfeit fiscal independence, supervision of child labor, business decision-making, and personal mobility. Instead they move toward a peripheral productive role in the family, where they are minor contributors to the household budget, dependent upon husbands' earnings, and thus more vulnerable to male domination.

MATING PATTERNS

Adult Sampedranas regard marriage and the bearing of children as the only way to fully legitimize their status as women. Emphasis on the domestic role is so pervasive that middle-aged *senoritas* are extremely rare. Women are invariably newly married, married with children, single but with children, abandoned with children, or widowed. Women understand that at some stage in their relationships with men they will become hapless victims of their *mal caracter* (bad character). Even the early stages of married life are seldom enjoyable for women. Sampedranas tend to marry or, more commonly, move in with a man before they know much about sexuality or the reproductive system. In most cases, girls marry when their parents discover they have been seduced and/or impregnated, and few of these *unido* marriages are legally binding. Thus women are mothers before they are out of their teens, often forced into marriages with boys they hardly know or care for. Patrilocal residence extracts them from their natal families and the female family business into which they were socialized. They come under the direction of an often hostile mother-in-law, who may oblige the new wife to work for her for no wages. Young wives begin their marriages lacking power, and remain that way until their daughters are old enough to provide a modicum of economic security.

These mating patterns and the alternatives to *la mala vida* have been disparately affected by developments in San Pedro. Lacking the resources for personal survival, poor unskilled women have little choice but to stay with abusive husbands. Artisans have traditional skills, but their declining market share is quickly rendering them obsolete as independent producers. They are becoming instead a cottage proletariat, dependent upon work orders from their husbands and other men, or they are unemployed. As the productive mobility and individualized incomes of their spouses rises, these women experience more seriously problematic relationships. What they have that unskilled women lack is a family productive system into which they were socialized as children. For the time being, abused artisans can still return to their natal homes and find a certain amount of economic security, however fragile.

Middle-class male infidelity is likely to increase with the advent of an affluent lifestyle and the status that accompanies it. Middle-class women are often powerless to rein in a wayward spouse since their welfare is entirely based upon a male breadwinner. However, middle-class women have more latitude than poor women when they are unmarried. Educated girls have begun to spurn irresponsible suitors, even if the young woman has become pregnant. With schooling, a job, and a family business for support, these young women are not obligated to marry. They can support themselves and their children without men, and can thus afford to be more selective in choosing a husband.

From late childhood, Sampedranas worry about being abandoned, mostly because of the money difficulties involved. They are taught to prepare themselves so that when and if their husbands leave them, they will be able to feed their children. Some women are able to do this better than others, but modernization has made single motherhood more troublesome for many Sampedranas who are forfeiting their traditional businesses and the personal status it provides. Moreover, in today's economy women are making less money and men more, further skewing the relations of production. Sampedranas are more economically vulnerable than ever, with less leverage to control male behavior, and fewer resources to retreat to if abandoned. Survival demands that women passively accept male irresponsibility or suffer the consequences.

CONCLUSIONS

Although *marianismo* has been widely accepted as an ideological explanation for why Latin American women endure abuse, this concept does not address the economic basis for gender relations. Instead, *marianismo* provides a rationale for female subordination and idealizes the harsh reality of women's lives. Women tolerate abusive husbands and continue in bad marriages because they have no alternatives. Most highland Guatemalan women rely upon male economic support and to a lesser extent their children, which men provide. The arrangement between men and women is simple. When men abandon the home, women rarely miss them as much as the money or the corn they supply. Deserted women repeatedly enter into temporary or fragile alliances with married men for the same reasons they originally wed: the money and the children that will result.

The basis for this dependence on men lies in the unprofitable and tangential connection women have to production. In two very different highland Guatemalan communities there exists a trend toward female economic degradation associated with accelerated male integration into entrepreneurial activities, cash income, and the external labor market. While this tendency has just begun

in San Antonio, if men continue to monopolize income production, female subordination will eventually come to resemble that of San Pedro, where parallel marriages and abandonment are common.

NOTES

1. See, for example, Basham (1976); Lewis (1959, 1961); Peñalosa (1968); Hewes (1954).
2. Some writers exclude traditional indigenous families who maintain their "cultural purity" (Stevens 1973b).
3. See, for example, Paul (1974); Neuhouser (1989); Stevens (1973c); Jacquette (1976).
4. Research in San Antonio began in 1988. In the summer of 1989, I administered a comprehensive sociode-

mographic survey of 80 Tuneco families from which the current analysis emerges. The study of San Pedro Sacatepequez began with a year's dissertation research (1976–1977) and research visits continued in the 1980s.
5. Female residents of San Antonio are called Tunecas; males are called Tunecos.

REFERENCES

Adams, R. N. 1960. "An Inquiry in the Nature of the Family," in G. Dole and R. Carneiro, eds., *Essays in the Science of Culture: In Honor of Leslie A. White.* New York: Thomas Y. Crowell.

Basham, R. 1976. "Machismo." *Frontiers,* 1:126–143.

Beuchler, J. M. 1985. "Women in Petty Commodity Production in La Paz, Bolivia," in J. Nash and H. Safa, eds., *Women and Change in Latin America.* South Hadley, MA: Bergin and Garvey.

Bossen, Laurel. 1984. *The Redivision of Labor: Women and Economic Change in Four Guatemalan Communities.* SUNY Series in the Anthropology of Work, June Nash, ed. Albany: State University of New York Press.

Bourque, S. C. and K. B. Warren. 1981. *Women of the Andes: Patriarchy and Social Change in Two Peruvian Towns.* Ann Arbor: University of Michigan Press.

Boyer, R. 1989. "Women, 'La Mala Vida' and the Politics of Marriage," in A. Lavrin, ed., *Sexuality and Marriage in Colonial Latin America.* Lincoln: University of Nebraska Press.

Browner, C. and E. Lewin. 1982. "Female Altruism Reconsidered: The Virgin Mary as Economic Woman." *American Enthologist,* 9:61–75.

Deere, C. D., and M. Leon de Leal. 1981. "Peasant Production, Proletarianization, and the Sexual Division of Labor in the Andes." *Signs,* 7:338–360.

Ehlers, T. B. 1982. "The Decline of Female Family Business: A Guatemalan Case Study." *Women and Politics,* 7:7–21.

Hewes, G. W. 1954. "Mexicans in Search of the 'Mexican': Notes on Mexican National Character." *American Journal of Economics and Sociology,* 13:209–305.

———. 1976. "Female Political Participation in Latin America," in L. B. Iglitzin and R. Ross, eds., *Women in the World, A Comparative Study.* Santa Barbara:ABC-Clio.

Kinzer, N. S. 1973. "Women Professionals in Buenos Aires," in A. Pescatello, ed., *Female and Male in Latin America.* Pittsburgh: University of Pittsburgh Press.

Leahy, M. E. 1986. *Development Strategies and the Status of Women. A Comparative Study of the United States, Mexico, the Soviet Union, and Cuba.* Boulder: Westview.

Lewis, O. 1959. *Five Families.* New York: Basic Books.

———. 1961. *Children of Sánchez.* New York: Random House.

Loucky, J. 1988. *Children's Work and Family Survival in Highland Guatemala.* Ph.D. dissertation, University of California, Los Angeles.

Nash, June. 1989. "Gender Studies in Latin American," in Sandra Morgen, ed. *Gender and Anthropology: Critical Reviews for Research and Teaching.* Washington, DC: American Anthropological Association.

Neuhouser, K. 1989. "Sources of Women's Power and Status among the Urban Poor in Contemporary Brazil." *Signs,* 14:685–702.

Paul, L. 1974. "The Mastery of Work and the Mystery of Sex in a Guatemalan Village," in Michelle

Zimbalist Rosaldo and Louise Lamphere, eds., *Women, Culture and Society.* Stanford: Stanford University Press.

Peñalosa, F. 1968. "Mexican Family Roles." *Journal of Marriage and the Family,* 30:681–689.

Piho, V. 1975. "Life and Labor of the Women Textile Worker in Mexico City," in Ruby Rohrlicht-Leavitt, ed., *Women Cross-Culturally: Change and Challenge.* The Hague: Mouton.

Safa, H. I. 1976. "Class Consciousness among Working Class Women in Latin America: A Case Study in Puerto Rico," in J. Nash and H. Safa, eds. *Sex and Class in Latin America.* New York: Praeger.

Wagley, Charles. 1949. *The Social and Religious Life of a Guatemalan Village.* Menosha, WI: American Anthropological Association.

Wolf, E. 1966. *Peasants.* Englewood Cliffs, NJ: Prentice-Hall.

Youseff, N. H. 1973. "Cultural Ideals, Feminine Behavior and Family Control." *Comparative Studies in Society and History,* 15: 326–347.

52

"We Are Not Doormats"

The Influence of Feminism on Contemporary Evangelicals in the United States

JUDITH STACEY
SUSAN ELIZABETH GERARD

We begin this essay by asking readers to indulge us by participating in a silent multiple-choice quiz. Please select the answer that best describes the author of the book from which the following excerpt is drawn:

> Feminism is a response to structural questions which will not go away. There is widespread injustice to women in our society. The same issue crops up in family life, education, the law, the Church and marriage: women are not respected as men's equals. They are frequently used and abused. Many women in fact experience not only frustration and discrimination but also real oppression at the hands of some men...the patriarchal emphasis of our society means that the unjust way many men behave towards women is legitimated in legal and economic structures. It is embedded in attitudes and stereotypes. Those women who object to all of this are frequently pilloried; their womanliness is challenged because they will not have it defined for them by a male-dominated culture. An individual response then can only work away at small areas. The problem is also an overall structural one, and as such needs a coherent structural response.

The author of this statement is: a) a feminist sociologist; b) an evangelical Christian; c) a married, heterosexual mother; d) an anti-abortion philosopher; e) none of the above; f) all of the above.

The best answer, as suspicious readers may have guessed, is (f) all of the above. The statement appears in *What's Right with Feminism*,[1] a book in which Elaine Storkey, a feminist sociologist and theologian, proposes and theorizes "a biblically rooted Christian feminism."

We imagine that most readers of this article will be as surprised as we were to discover the existence of the growing body of literature to which Storkey's book belongs, or to learn of the extensive diffusion of feminist ideas within contemporary evangelical discourse that it represents. Most secular feminists (and most feminists are secular), consider contemporary feminism and Christian evangelicalism to represent incompatible world views and social movements, and they interpret the gender ideology of the latter largely as a reactionary backlash response to the former. Certainly Phyllis Schlafly, Jerry Falwell, Beverly La Haye and other leaders of the most visible, politically organized segments of the Christian right wing have given feminists ample provocation for such a reading. But, as our introductory quiz implies, and the remainder of this paper demonstrates, the gender ideology and politics of born-again Christians in the United States today are far more diverse, complex and contradictory than widely held stereotypes allow.

We examine the diffusion of feminist ideas within Christian evangelicalism in order to contribute to assessments of the nature and status of feminism in the conservative 1980s and 1990s. Is feminism progressing, in retreat, or in a new mode of phase? In earlier articles, one of us argued that "postfeminism" was an apt term to capture the enormous influence of feminism on American culture in a period when overt feminist activism is less evident.[2] By postfeminism we mean the simultaneous incorporation, revision and depoliticization of some of the central goals of Second Wave feminism. Feminists who object to the term believe it sounds a premature death knell for the feminist movement.[3] We agree that feminist activism survives in the Reagan-Bush era, but believe it coexists with postfeminism, a consciousness that accepts many feminist convictions, while rejecting both the feminist label and feminist political engagement.

This essay depicts the presence of both feminism and postfeminist consciousness among contemporary Christian evangelicals. Like most feminists, we regard evangelicals as the vanguard of the anti-feminist backlash. If feminist ideology has permeated there, it suggests the magnitude of feminist influence upon American culture. Drawing upon national evangelical literature and media materials and from fieldwork conducted in a small evangelical Christian ministry in California's Silicon Valley, we show that contemporary evangelicalism in the United States is not a monolithic, patriarchal restorationist movement. Instead, evangelical theology and institutions are serving as remarkably flexible resources for renegotiating gender and family relationships, and not exclusively in reactionary or masculinist directions.[4]

CONTEMPORARY EVANGELICAL GENDER IDEOLOGY

Evangelical religions have flourished, while mainstream churches have declined during recent postindustrial decades; and women have swelled the burgeoning ranks of the former in proportions even greater than they outnumber men in the latter. Estimates of evangelicals range from 18% to 40% of the adult population, and more than 60% of the participants in this fastest growing variety of religious orientation in the United States today are women.[5] The growth in the numbers, visibility and respectability of evangelicals has alarmed feminists and other progressives, who have assumed that evangelicals are a politically cohesive, well-organized, conservative and anti-feminist constituency. But, as few besides those who study American religion recognize, evangelicals are remarkably diverse.

Evangelicals believe in the full truth and authority of the bible and in its usefulness as a practical guide to the conduct of everyday life. They have differing views, however, on the nature of biblical truth. While strict constructionists attempt to interpret the scriptures literally, many evangelicals incorporate metaphorical and contextual readings of the book that they all consider to be the inspired word of God. The most definitive characteristic of contemporary evangelicals is their conviction that a deeply personal relationship with Jesus Christ is the only path to a meaningful life and to salvation after death. Most have had a "born-again" or conversion experience, which led to an emotionally intimate relationship with Jesus, whom they view as a friend who intervenes personally in their lives. As his evangelicals, they commit themselves, in turn, to spread the "Good News" by bearing public witness to their faith.[6]

Born-again Christians do not share a unified political perspective. They hold views on most political issues almost as diverse as those affirmed by once-born Americans.[7] Most analysts characterize fundamentalism as the right wing of evangelicalism. Fundamentalism is a separatist movement that formed at the turn of the century in reaction to the adoption of the social gospel by mainstream Protestantism; in this separatist spirit many fundamentalists think of themselves as the only true evangelicals. Partly in response to fundamentalist insularity, a less separatist movement called neo-evangelicalism arose in the 1940s. It shares the conservative theology of fundamentalism, but is more ecumenical in spirit and more "in the world." Billy Graham, the most prominent neo-evangelist, brought the evangelical message to the ears of presidents and to the living rooms of middle-Americans. The respectability Graham brought to this movement paved the way for its explosive growth during the late 1960s and 1970s. A number of right wing televangelists built large ministries in this period, but evangelicalism also achieved an appeal to members of the urban middle-classes with middle-of-the-road and even liberal politics. In 1976 the United States elected its first evangelical president, Jimmy Carter.[8]

The secular new left that emerged in the same period inspired parallel political developments, not only within mainstream Christianity, but among evangelical Christians as well. A small, but vocal minority of leftwing evangelical Christians have formed communal living and working groups that publish an evangelical brand of liberation theology in such periodicals as *Sojourners, Radix,* and *The Other Side....*

In a similar fashion and period, the rise of evangelical feminism paralleled that of secular feminism. It had early ties with the evangelical left but soon developed as an autonomous movement. Evangelical women published critical feminist articles in Christian magazines as early as 1966.[9] In 1973 a meeting of the leftwing Evangelicals for Social Action was convened to discuss social issues; women struggled successfully to include in the meeting's final declaration: "We acknowledge that we have encouraged men to prideful domination and women to irresponsible passivity. So we call both men and women to mutual submission and active discipleship."[10] The organizational base that feminists established at this meeting enabled them the following year to found a feminist evangelical monthly, *Daughters of Sarah.* One year later, an evangelical feminist conference in Washington, D.C., attended by 360, endorsed the ERA and formed a lasting organization, the Evangelical Women's Caucus.[11]

Evangelical feminists are serious about both their evangelicalism and their feminism, and each belief system modifies the other. They bring feminist criticism to their Christian communities and theology; and their deeply-felt Christian commit-ment shapes their feminist ideology. "Biblical feminists" or simply "Christian feminists," as many often identify themselves, contend that the inspiration for the notion that women are the equals of men is not the affairs of the world, but the teachings of the New Testament. They devote most of their attention to dialogue with evangelicals in their confrontation with patriarchal church leaders, or toward efforts to win evangelical women and men to feminism. Consequently they scrupulously seek, and find, scriptural justification for their feminist beliefs. Evangelical feminists have focused most of their energies on three issues: claiming women's right to leadership roles in the church, including ordination; demonstrating the need for the Bible and its interpreters to employ "inclusive language" that presents God, not as male, but androgynous;[12] and challenging the scriptural basis for the subordinate role of women in marriage.

The third issue has been the arena in which biblical feminists have made their greatest impact on evangelical theology and gender ideology. To counter evangelicals' standard patriarchalist reading of the scriptural foundation for women's subordination to their husbands, Christian feminists have developed an ingenious, and perhaps somewhat forced, doctrine of mutual submission. Biblical feminists argue that the essence of Christ's message and practice was a radically egalitarian challenge to prevailing patriarchal society, a society so profoundly patriarchal that Jesus was compelled to couch his subversive and implicitly feminist teachings in terms comprehensible and tolerable to his compatriots. When read in this context, those troubling passages in the bible that direct wives to submit to their husbands, such as Paul's notorious message to the Ephesians, can be understood to mean instead mutual submission:

It is in the context of mutual submission that we must read the famous passages about the submission of Christian wives to their husbands, in particular Ephesians 5:22 and following... Therefore, when Paul speaks of wives' submitting themselves to their husbands, he is building upon the concept that every Christian is intended to submit to every other Christian, to serve every other Christian, to defer lovingly to every other Christian...The Christlike husband takes upon himself the form of a servant, humbles himself, and dies to himself by living for the best interests of his family. He loves his wife as he loves his own body, because he and his wife are one flesh.[13]

A doctrine of mutual submission leaves little room for feminist anger. Biblical feminists challenge unequal marriages as unChristian, and they take feminist positions on many issues unpopular with most fundamentalists, like their support for the ERA, for singlehood as a worthy option for women, and their (far from unanimous) acceptance of homosexuality and abortion as matters of personal conscience.[14] However, their writings lack the righteous anger that characterizes much of secular feminist literature....

Even James C. Dobson, a right wing evangelical who founded Focus on the Family, a multimedia ministry committed to combatting feminism's pernicious influence on American family life, shows postfeminist influences on his own family views. He advises women in troubled marriages that the Bible does not demand that they tolerate disrespect or abuse from their husbands:

> *Please understand that I believe firmly in the biblical concept of submission, as described in the book of Ephesians and elsewhere in scripture. But there is a vast difference between being a confident, spiritually submissive woman and being a doormat. People wipe their feet on doormats, as we know.[15]...*

As Barbara Ehrenreich, Elizabeth Hess, and Gloria Jacobs have pointed out, even elements of the sexual revolution have "penetrated" the Bible Belt,[16] but sexuality remains, we believe, the most conservative aspect of evangelical gender ideology. Even most biblical feminists find it difficult to overcome scriptural and personal antipathy to homosexuality and abortion, and the popular evangelical literature is almost uniformly reactionary on these issues. We personally believe that

this is the political arena in which the new Christian right has scored its most disturbing and significant ideological victory.[17] Nonetheless, the Metropolitan Community Church, one of the largest gay religious churches in the country, is evangelical, and Christian women's magazines show modest signs of recognizing moral complexities to anti-abortion politics.[18]

Secular feminists can find numerous other surprises in Christian women's magazines, including information on rape self-defense, a criticism of social pressures for thinness and youth, and reviews for books celebrating friendships between women. Such literature lends support to Hunter's provocative claim that despite the small numbers of evangelical feminists, "feminist sensibilities are, nevertheless, ingrained within substantial sectors of Evangelicalism."[19] In our view, however, postfeminism better characterizes the dominant gender ideology of contemporary evangelicals.

GLOBAL MINISTRIES OF LOVE

Fieldwork conducted between 1984 and 1987 among participants in a small, evangelical Christian ministry in the Silicon Valley illustrates some of the creative uses to which evangelical women apply postfeminist evangelical doctrines and institutions.[20] Global Ministries of Love[21] is a nondenominational, grassroots ministry that operates its own small church and evangelizes among youth, derelicts, the infirm, and the institutionalized in the Silicon Valley and in two other states, where it has established mission branches. Global Ministries was founded in the early 1970s, during the height of Second Wave feminism, by Eleanor Morrison, a divorced, White, single mother who supported her children by working as an electronics employee. Eleanor, and the male pastors whom she attracted to her ministry and continues to guide, advocate a marital doctrine of male headship and wifely submission. At the same time, however, they offer their female constituents considerable support for creative adaptations of Christian gender ideology towards more egalitarian family reform projects. Global's director and many of her followers selectively employ and revise Christian theology in order to reform and strengthen heterosexual marriages, as well as to forge a variety of viable alternatives to nuclear family life.

The *tabula rasa* premise of born-again theology, that one's life before conversion is morally irrelevant, may be its most seductive feature to new recruits. Global Ministries applies this second chance cosmology to marital relationships with some unexpected consequences. Those who regard evangelical Christians as the last bastion of stable marriages in an era of family turmoil should be as surprised as we were to note the prevalence of divorced and remarried individuals in Global Ministries. "I don't care what a person's done outside of Christ—rape, murder, the most awful things don't change it, if people completely repent," Bill Jensen, the senior pastor of the ministry explained when one of us expressed amazement at the number of divorced people she had encountered in this Christian community. This can be a deeply appealing message to those suffering the rejection, bitterness, or anxieties of marital rupture. Like its founder, many members of the ministry have found the Global community to be a supportive environment for recovering from a failed marriage.

Global Ministries does celebrate marital commitment, however, and it seems to provide a fruitful milieu for helping previously unsuccessful spouses to achieve it the second time around. Ministerial staff often assist cupid's labors towards this end. For example, after 15 years as a single mother, Eleanor fell in love with a new recruit to her ministry, Paul Garrett, a recently divorced man 13 years her junior. Pastor Jensen encouraged Eleanor to express her love to Paul and, when Paul responded with trepidation, the pastor spent a day helping him pray for release from his fears and for the ability to decide to commit himself to loving Eleanor. His prayers were answered, and delighted to have secured the male "covering" deemed proper by most evangelical Christians, Eleanor

appointed her self-selected head-of-household to co-direct the ministry. Still blissful newlyweds nearly four years later, the couple conduct seminars on love, sex, and marriage where they present themselves as a model of committed, Christian union.

Global ministers perceive no inconsistency in such advocacy of conjugal permanence, because they draw a sharp distinction between Christian and secular marriages. Pastor Jensen articulated the contrast while officiating over an unusual wedding ceremony. A secular marriage, he informed the bride, the groom, and gathered wellwishers, is based on a contract which, in turn, is based on a lack of trust. Secular marriages, as a result, do not last. Christian marriage, by contrast, "involves a covenant which is much deeper than a contract, a covenant based on trust in each other and in Jesus, and," he concluded, "that is why Christian marriage is permanent." These were reassuring words to the bride and groom, Pamela and Albert Gama, who both had divorced previous spouses, cohabited intermittently for five years, been legally married for four years and then separated and reunited before deciding to fortify their commitment with Christian nuptial vows. Three years later, Pam judged the pastor's analysis perceptive. Christian conversion enabled Al to make a deepened level of commitment to their marriage, and Pam identifies the security she derives from this as the most valuable outcome of the Christian nuptial ceremony.

Pam had been a feminist for more than a decade when her estranged second husband had the religious conversion experience that led him, through Pam's born-again daughter Katie, to the Global Ministries community. Like most feminists, Pam had deep reservations about the patriarchal character of Christian marital doctrine. Nonetheless, Pam was so impressed with profound emotional changes in Al that his conversion appeared to have inspired, that she had decided to suspend these reservations and to resume their marriage with the assistance of Christian marital counseling. Pastor Jensen had served as marriage counselor for the new recruits, guiding them to renew their conjugal commitment with a Christian gender ideology sufficiently revisionist to temper most of Pam's residual feminist objections.

"A ring is not a shackle, and marriage is not a relationship of domination, but of equality," Pastor Jensen gently reminded Al during the wedding ring ceremony, as he proceeded to lecture him on the responsibilities of a Christian husband. "You are the head of the household, Al," he continued, "and therefore, you have the larger responsibility, but that has nothing to do with dominating a wife." The pastor did advise Pam to submit to her "husband in all things as we all submit to Jesus," but, employing terms strikingly reminiscent of those found in Christian feminist literature, he attempted to rid the directive of its authoritarian connotations. Submitting to a husband is actually submitting to Jesus, Jensen explained, and thus a wife "does so with love and trust, knowing that the husband must love his wife as his own body and as Jesus loves us."

During an interview several months later, the pastor elaborated his revisionist understanding of the doctrine of submission. Feminists and other critics of evangelical marriage principles misunderstand this Christian concept, Jensen argued. They fail to recognize the "big difference between obedience and submission," or that authority is a burden and submission a privilege. "Rebellious humanity" resists humility, but "to be humbled is good." Just as Bill's role as pastor is to serve his congregation, "the person in authority should actually be the servant." Thus, "the husband's job is not to dominate, but to serve his wife." Although Pastor Jensen enjoyed defending the doctrine of submission, he thought it beside the point entirely to scrutinize Christian marriage through a judicial lens. He tried to teach the couples like Pam and Al whom he counseled that Christian marriage is "a total giving relationship," and thus,

> you don't look at fairness and unfairness, at what you get for yourself. In fact, it's ridiculous to apply standards of justice to marriage, because it's amaz-

> ing how little we know about justice. Christian marriage is no fifty-fifty, give-and-take affair; in marriage it's one hundred percent.

Pam found herself quite receptive to Jensen's views and impressed with their salutary effect on her marriage. Having failed in her past efforts to establish a committed, egalitarian, intimate relationship guided by democratic, feminist principles, she was willing to modify these in exchange for a marriage reform strategy she found more effective. Because the doctrine of love and marriage preached by Global Ministries seemed to demand and exact greater changes from Al than from her, Pam judged it "not so bad a deal" to accept nominal patriarchal authority in exchange for greater intimacy and security.

By all accounts, including his own, Al's religious conversion had profoundly transformed his approach to love and marriage. A rather taciturn, noncommittal man by disposition, Al had become much more committed to Pam, more open, loving, and expressive since joining the Global fold. He credited his Christian rebirth with releasing his previously truncated capacity for love, and the Christian marriage counseling with teaching him the means for expressing it.

Although Al was predictably more enthusiastic than Pam about the patriarchal principles of Christian marriage, he interpreted these, like Pastor Jensen, to mean he had the greater responsibility to make his marriage work:

> I'm not really an open person, and to be a truly loving person is not something you just get into being because somehow you get converted. I take most of the responsibility for our problems because it's up to me to make the difference, because I can't make her do anything, but I can make a change in myself...I don't consider myself an honest person. I don't always say anything. I don't always have that need to be talking like she does. But you know one thing good about being a Christian is that, I tell you, sometimes you can just open up like you never did before. There's a certain amount of love that comes into your heart that was not there before.

Few contemporary feminists would be likely to find fault with Al's description of his goals for his relationship with Pam:

I just hope that we can come closer together and be more honest with each other. Try to use God as a guideline. The goals are more openness, a closer relationship, be more loving both verbally and physically, have more concern for the other person's feelings.

The concept of male authority Global Ministries appears to disseminate might best be described as "patriarchy in the last instance."[22] Eleanor and her disciples, like Pastor Jensen, urge couples to talk over everything and to resolve their differences through mutual discussion. Only if a conflict proves to be irreconcilable should a wife submit to her husband's will. Such a circumstance is so rare, in fact, that neither Eleanor, Pam, nor Pam's young, married daughter Katie could provide a single illustration of it. "We never let the sun set on our anger," Katie explained. Eleanor's husband conceded that he was more likely to yield to his loquacious wife than the other way around: "I have the responsibility to listen to her, too, because she may just be the one with the answer." "That's really true," Eleanor affirmed. And Pam employed the principle only when she wished to enlist Al's assistance in resolving her ambivalence about decisions she found difficult to make on her own.

In Global Ministries' version of born-again theology, women find powerful resources for efforts to remake their husbands in their own images. The dominant discourse on desirable heterosexual relationships that the ministry propagates is a Christian version of what Francesca Cancian has aptly termed the "feminization of love."[23] Ironically, feminist Cancian is critical of the woman-centered ideology of love that evangelical Global Ministries celebrates. She criticizes current love ideals for celebrating emotional expressiveness and ignoring "the more instrumental and physical aspects of love that men prefer."[24] Pastor Jensen, however, urges men to develop their capacity for expressive love:

One of the greatest failures in marriage is communication. The husband is afraid to reveal his emotions. Women are generally much better at this. A man needs to learn to open up emotionally, to cry on his wife's shoulders. Now I realize how this might sound chauvinist, but most women, not all, but most still want a strong leader in a husband. But it's not weak to reveal your emotions. A lot of men have the wrong idea about how being emotional is being weak.... And sex has so much more meaning than just the physical act. It's an ultimate expression of a spiritual and emotional relationship. Often men abuse this. Men often just want sex for its own sake. Women want more from sex emotionally. Sex is a sacred thing; it's not just physical. It's holy. But a lot of men expect their wives to make love to them without even communicating or regardless of what's going on between them emotionally. And they don't realize how abusive that is to a woman, because a woman integrates the sexual and emotional more.

Although Global Ministries offers women effective resources for securing marital commitments and fostering emotional transformations of men, it exhibits far less nostalgia for the 1950s nuclear family ideal than feminists might expect. Perhaps Eleanor's personally traumatic experience with nuclear family life in that decade bred the more creative and pluralist pro-family strategies she encourages in her ministry. Having spent 15 years as a single, working mother, Eleanor has learned to appreciate the benefits of extended households. She treats her own domestic sites as accordion constructions whose membership regularly expands and contracts. Blood and marital ties determine some of the participants in Eleanor's matrilocal domiciles. Her divorced mother lived with her for several years, and later when her daughter married a young Chicano who joined the ministry, not only did Eleanor welcome her new son-in-law into her household, but she ordained him as well. Not all who have shared Eleanor's living quarters are formal relatives, however. Friends have lived with Eleanor, and she has been foster mother to 15 adolescents, a few of whom made her a foster grandmother also.

Indeed, Eleanor has achieved much more socio-spatial integration in her life than most feminists or other Progressives who decry the modern schisms between public and private worlds, between work and family life. Wherever she lives also becomes Global's organizational and social hub, the site of its staff meetings, its recording studio, and its public relations office. Global's matriarchal leader encourages her "sheepies" to form joint households also. The ministry purchased and leased several adjacent houses, which it subleases to Global staff and recruits so that they too can derive the benefits of "living in community." These Christian communes serve as a laboratory for Eleanor's attempts at social engineering, the experimental terrain for her activist approach to family reform. Eleanor points out the economic advantages of communal households. The ministry provides full support to four pastors and their families, all of whom live "in community" with others, like Katie and her husband, who subsidize the pastors' rent and food expenses at the same time that they reduce their own.

Eleanor is even more enthusiastic about the social benefits of cooperative living. The communes provide a means to integrate single people into Global family and community life. The long years Eleanor spent as a divorcee have made her unusually reflective about the social needs of single women and probably fueled her quite activist responses to the single woman "crisis." Eleanor herself and other Global women have reaped matrimonial benefits from the ministry's not-always-casual matchmaking services. But Eleanor does not rely on romantic attachments alone to extend kin ties and familial arrangements to the unmarried. She consciously seeks to maintain a balance of married and single members in the community and regards the communes as an opportunity to bridge the social gulf that might divide them. "In fact," Eleanor explains:

> there's a scripture that I love, that the single belongs in the family. And we feel, Paul and I both agree on this, that singles in the family of God are there to serve the family. And the families are also

> to serve the singles by providing that that they need. I think single people need to see married people, they need to be around them, because they need to see something good and positive in that kind of a relationship. So that's why we have singles living with all of our marrieds.

Since marrying Paul, Eleanor has made it Global policy to "yoke" singles to married couple-headed households. This, she believes, prevents social isolation for the singles and anti-social withdrawal by the marrieds....

Global Ministries gives more than rhetorical support to unwed mothers. It established a shelter for "girls in crisis" to help pregnant adolescents; and unlike other Christian homes for unwed mothers that offer adoption as the only alternative, the Global shelter supports teenage mothers who wish to keep and raise their children without husbands. Eleanor has always taken an activist approach to supporting pregnant teenagers. Perhaps it is her long years of experience in this work that makes her opposition to abortion less strident or rigid than we had anticipated. "It makes me sick to see people signing petitions about abortion and not doing anything for those pregnant girls," she volunteered. Eleanor regards abortion as tragic and sinful, but, unlike most born-again opponents of women's reproductive freedom, she concedes that, "In certain situations, I can't say in my heart it wouldn't be right."...

CONCLUSIONS

It has been challenging and painful for feminists to explain why many women who have been exposed to feminist ideas and values voluntarily embrace a Christian ideology of male headship and female submission, often attempting to convert their more secular husbands. For in postindustrial America, although male supremacy is alive and well, participation in a formally patriarchal marriage is a woman's choice. The social and material conditions that underwrote the Victorian family, the family many evangelicals portray erroneously as the biblical family, are long gone. Thus, as a recent ethnography of a fundamentalist community notes, no fundamentalist husband can dominate a wife who doesn't choose to submit today.[25] Julie Cabrera, coordinator of women's Bible study at Crossroads Bible Church in San Jose, California, asserts this more directly. Told that an evangelical feminist interprets submissive Christian women as fearful of divorce, Cabrera replies, "Nonsense. I am in submission to my husband by choice. I do this in order to please God. He has put our husbands in the head of us. We choose to be in this position. We are not doormats."[26]

We agree partially both with that evangelical feminist and with Cabrera. Women remain structurally disadvantaged in postindustrial society, but from that position they make their own choices and develop their own strategies (including patriarchal Christian marriage). Women's gender strategies are creative, resourceful, and often contradictory, and these in turn are always revising received institutional and cultural forms. The surprising emergence of postfeminist evangelicalism is just such a strategic and cultural phenomenon. A decidedly postmodern excrescence, it is difficult for secular feminists to appraise. Generated partly as a backlash against feminism, postfeminist evangelical gender ideology also selectively incorporates and adapts many feminist family reforms. Secular and biblical feminists alike, we believe, can take credit for the extraordinary diffusion of our ideological influence on even this most unlikely of constituencies.

Women's turn to evangelicalism represents a search not just for spirituality, but for stability and security in turbulent, contested times; but it is a strategy that refuses to forfeit, and even builds upon, the feminist critique of men and the "traditional" family. Acute "pro-family" and spiritual longings in this period comingle with an uncompleted, but far from repudiated feminist revolution. Part of the genius of the postfeminist evangelical strategy is its ability to straddle both sides of this ambivalent divide. To heterosexual women like Eleanor and Pam, more exhausted than outraged by the insecurities of contemporary family and work conditions, joining a community that promises love and affirmation can be deeply appealing, particularly when it provides effective strategies for reshaping husbands in their own image. And, ironically, one of the main places where the commune movement of the sixties still survives is in the evangelical world.[27]...

The gender views and strategies of contemporary evangelical women indicate the fluid and contradictory character of feminist politics in this period. Although feminist activism is far less visible or confrontational than it was in the militant late 1960s and early 1970s, it continues in new and often surprising guises. Such activism, however, coexists with postfeminism, the extraordinary diffusion of feminist principles in American culture discernible in even the most unlikely places and among people who shun the feminist label and avoid political engagement. Feminism appears to be advancing, retreating, and assuming new forms, all at once.

NOTES

1. Elaine Storkey, *What's Right with Feminism* (Grand Rapids: Eerdmans Publishing Company, 1985). Quotation is from p. 160.

2. Judith Stacey, "Sexism By a Subtler Name: Postindustrial Conditions and Postfeminist Consciousness in the Silicon Valley," *Socialist Review* 96 (November-December 1987): 7–28; Deborah Rosenfelt and Judith Stacey, "Second Thoughts on the Second Wave," *Feminist Studies* 13, no. 2 (Summer 1987): 341–61.

3. See Rayna Rapp, "Is the Legacy of Second Wave Feminism Postfeminism?" *Socialist Review* 97 (January-March 1988); Myra Marx Ferree, personal communication to author.

4. An important early exception to feminist treatment of evangelicals as monolithically submissive, antifeminist, and reactionary was Carol Virginia Pohli, "Church Closets and Back Doors: A Feminist View of Moral Majority Women," *Feminist Studies* 9, no. 3 (Fall 1983): 529–58.

Pohli argued that there were inherent tensions in evangelical world views and organizational structure that limited evangelical participation in reactionary politics and allowed limited opportunities for feminist dialogue with evangelical women. More recently, Susan D. Rose portrayed deeper conflicts about gender norms and power relationships among women in a charismatic Christian community; see her "Women Warriors: The Negotiation of Gender in a Charismatic Community," *Sociological Analysis* 48, no. 3 (Fall 1987): 245–58. The most dissident feminist interpretation of evangelicalism we have seen is Elizabeth Brusco's provocative analysis of the progressive and womanist effects of Protestant evangelicalism in Colombia, "Colombian Evangelicalism as a Strategic Form of Women's Collective Action," *Feminist Issues* 6, no. 2 (Fall 1986): 3–13. Brusco argues that growing numbers of Colombian women are using Protestant evangelicalism to combat machismo, reform their husbands, and improve their lives. She goes so far as to interpret Colombian evangelicalism as a radical challenge to gender inequality that "may have more practical results for women in terms of improving their condition (and surely for some men) than any feminist reform movements I know of" (p. 10). Brusco attributes the progressive effects of evangelicalism in Colombia to particular historical and cultural conditions. But in societies, "where there is less sex segregation, less female dependency, and a more individualistic orientation for both men and women," Brusco speculates, "such a movement would not be viable in terms of improving women's status but it would also probably never get off the ground anyway" (p. 11). As the rest of this article demonstrates, however, just such a movement is thriving in the highly individualistic United States today.

5. James Davison Hunter, *American Evangelicalism* (New Brunswick, NJ: Rutgers University Press, 1983), see esp. p. 50. Since 1965, evangelical denominations are reported to have increased their memberships at an average five-year rate of 8% while membership in liberal denominations declined at an average five-year rate of 4.6%. James Davison Hunter, *Evangelicalism: The Coming Generation* (Chicago: University of Chicago Press, 1987), 6. For estimates of numbers of evangelicals, see also Richard Quebedeaux, *The Wordly Evangelicals* (San Francisco: Harper & Row, 1978); R. Stephen Warner, *New Wine in Old Wineskins* (Berkeley: University of California Press, 1988); and Pohli.

6. For discussion of the characteristics of contemporary evangelicals, see Hunter, *American Evangelicalism;* Quebedeaux; and Warner.

7. For discussions of the political beliefs of evangelicals, see Richard Quebedeaux, *The Young Evangelicals* (New York: Harper & Row, 1974) and Quebedeaux, *The Worldly Evangelicals;* Hunter, *Evangelicalism* and *American Evangelicalism;* Nancy Tatom Ammerman, *Bible Believers: Fundamentalists in the Modern World* (New Brunswick, NJ: Rutgers University Press, 1987); and Warner.

8. For historical treatments of fundamentalism and evangelicalism, see George W. Dollar, *A History of Fundamentalism in America* (Greenville, SC: Bob Jones Univ. Press, 1973); George Marsden, ed., *Evangelicalism and Modern America* (Grand Rapids: Eerdmans Publishing Company, 1984); Richard Quebedeaux, *By What Authority: The Rise of Personality Cults in American Christianity* (San Francisco: Harper & Row, 1982); Quebedeaux, *Young Evangelicals;* and Quebedeaux, *Worldly Evangelicals.*

9. Quebedeaux identifies Letha Scanzoni's "Women's Place: Silence or Service?" in the February 1966 issue of *Eternity* as one of the earliest of these feminist essays. *The Worldly Evangelicals,* 121.

10. Chicago Declaration, cited in Letha Dawson Scanzoni and Nancy A. Hardesty, *All We're Meant to Be: Biblical Feminism for Today,* rev. ed. (Nashville, Abingdon Press, 1986), 18–19.

11. For histories of evangelical feminism, see Quebedeaux, *Worldly Evangelicals;* Scanzoni and Hardesty; and Margaret Bendroth, "The Search for 'Women's Role' in American Evangelicalism, 1930–1980," in Marsden, 122–34. The first edition of the Scanzoni and Hardesty book is described in *Christian History* magazine as "the 1973 classic that set in motion a substantial biblical feminism." *Christian History* VII, no. 1, issue 17 (1988): 36.

12. Virginia Mollenkott, a prominent biblical feminist, devotes one of her books to an androgynous reading of divine imagery, with such chapter titles as "God as Nursing Mother," "God as Midwife," "God as Mother Bear," "God as Female Homemaker," "God as Female Beloved," and "God as Dame Wisdom." In the chapter on God as homemaker, she argues that "Psalm 123:2 gives us permission to see in Proverbs 31 a full-scale description of Yahweh as the perfect female homemaker, the perfect wife to a humanity which is cast by this image into a masculine role." Virginia Ramey Mollenkott, *The Divine Feminine: The Biblical Imagery of God as Female* (New York: Crossroad, 1983), 62.

13. Virginia Ramey Mollenkott, *Women, Men and the Bible* (Nashville, TN: Abingdon Press, 1977), 23–24.

For other examples of this form of interpreting scripture, see Evelyn Stagg and Frank Stagg, "Jesus and Women," *Christian History* VII, no. 1, issue 17 (1988): 29–31; Alvera Mickelsen, *Women, Authority & the Bible* (Downers Grove, Illinois: InterVarsity Press, 1986); Scanzoni and Hardesty; Storkey.

14. Responding to feminist criticism of the first edition of *All We're Meant to Be,* Scanzoni and Hardesty revised the second edition of their book to take a more sympathetic stand on homosexuality. The Evangelical Women's Caucus International was split in July 1986 by approval of a resolution that recognized "the presence of the lesbian minority in EWCI" and called for "a firm stand in favor of civil-rights protection for homosexual persons." Beth Spring, "Gay Rights Resolution Divides Membership of Evangelical Women's Caucus," *Christianity Today* 30, no. 14 (Oct. 3, 1986): 40–43.

15. Jones C. Dubson, *Love Must Be Tough* (Waco, TX: Word Books, 1983), 25.

16. *Re-Making Love: The Feminization of Sex* (Garden City, New York: Anchor Press, 1986), chapter 5.

17. The 1980 Gallup Poll data reported by Hunter found 41% of evangelicals, compared with 29% of non-evangelicals, claiming to support a ban on abortion. Hunter, *Evangelicalism,* 126. Perhaps because of the wording of the poll, this seriously understates the sexual conservatism of evangelicals and their impact on the broader American populace. Confusingly, Wuthnow cites an essay by Hunter as his source for a 1978 Gallup Poll which found 97% of evangelicals opposed to premarital sex, 95% expressing "opposition to abortion," and 89% opposed to homosexuality. Wuthnow interprets these data as evidence that while evangelicals "remained deeply divided in many other ways...on questions of morality they were unified." Robert Wuthnow, "The Political Rebirth of American Evangelicals," in Robert C. Liebman & Robert Wuthnow, eds., *The New Christian Right: Mobilization and Legitimation* (New York: Aldine, 1983), 178. Although Wuthnow, we believe, slightly overstates the case, we share his view that this is the most distinctive feature of contemporary evangelical beliefs.

18. A recent *TCW* editorial, for example, concludes: "Aborting a baby is wrong, but simply stopping an abortion is not enough...And I pray that the next time someone needs help, God will give me the strength to go beyond my idealistic theology and live with the realities of commitment." Dale Hanson Bourke, "The Cost of Commitment," *Today's Christian Woman,* 7.

19. Hunter, *Evangelicalism,* 106.

20. Between 1984 and 1987, Judith Stacey conducted oral histories and participant observation fieldwork in this evangelical group as part of her study of changing family life in the Silicon Valley. For a full description of that study, see her *Brave New Families: Stories of Domestic Upheaval in Late Twentieth Century America* (New York: Basic Books, 1990).

21. We employ pseudonyms to refer to the ministry and to all participants in the field study.

22. Barbara Epstein first coined this apt descriptive phrase. (personal communication to author)

23. "The Feminization of Love," *Signs* 11, no. 4 (Summer 1986): 692. See also Francesca M. Cancian, *Love in America* (New York: Cambridge University Press, 1987).

24. "The Feminization of Love," 692.

25. See Ammerman, 141.

26. Quoted in David Early, "Equal Before God," *San Jose Mercury News,* March 1986.

27. Quebedeaux, *Worldly Evangelicals* describes the communes of left wing evangelicals. Warner's study of a Methodist church in Mendocino, California, recounts the wholesale conversion of The Land, a libertarian sixties commune, into The Holy Land, an ascetic evangelical Christian community. Brusco emphasizes the collective ethos of Colombian evangelicalism and stresses as most revolutionary its capacity to transform intimate relationships.

53

Mexican American Women
Grassroots Community Activists
"Mothers of East Los Angeles"

MARY PARDO

The following case study of Mexican American women activists in "Mothers of East Los Angeles" (MELA) contributes another dimension to the conception of grassroots politics. It illustrates how these Mexican American women transform "traditional" networks and resources based on family and culture into political assets to defend the quality of urban life. Far from unique, these patterns of activism are repeated in Latin America and elsewhere. Here as in other times and places, the women's activism arises out of seemingly "traditional" roles, addresses wider social and political issues, and capitalizes on informal associations sanctioned by the community. Religion, commonly viewed as a conservative force, is intertwined with politics. Often, women speak of their communities and their activism as extensions of their family and household responsibility. The central role of women in grass roots struggles around quality of life, in the Third World and in the United States, challenges conventional assumptions about the powerlessness of women and static definitions of culture and tradition.

In general, the women in MELA are long-time residents of East Los Angeles; some are bilingual and native born, others Mexican born and Spanish dominant. All the core activists are bilingual and have lived in the community over thirty years. All have been active in parish-sponsored groups and activities; some have had experience working in community-based groups arising from

schools, neighborhood watch associations, and labor support groups. To gain an appreciation of the group and the core activists, I used ethnographic field methods.... The following discussion briefly chronicles an intense and significant five-year segment of community history from which emerged MELA and the women's transformation of "traditional" resources and experiences into political assets for community mobilization.[1]

THE COMMUNITY CONTEXT: EAST LOS ANGELES RESISTING SIEGE

...MELA initially coalesced to oppose the state prison construction but has since organized opposition to several other projects detrimental to the quality of life in the central city.[2] Its second large target is a toxic waste incinerator proposed for Vernon, a small city adjacent to East Los Angeles. This incinerator would worsen the already debilitating air quality of the entire county and set a precedent dangerous for other communities throughout California.[3] When MELA took up the fight against the toxic waste incinerator, it became more than a single-issue group and began working with environmental groups around the state.[4] As a result of the community struggle, AB58 (Roybal-Allard), which provides all Californians with the minimum protection of an environmental impact report before the construction of hazardous waste incinerators, was signed into law. But the law's effectiveness relies on a watchful community network. Since its emergence, "Mothers of East Los Angeles" has become centrally important to just such a network of grassroots acitivists including a select number of Catholic priests and two Mexican American political representatives. Furthermore, the group's very formation, and its continued spirit and activism, fly in the face of the conventional political science beliefs regarding political participation....

. . . All the women live in a low-income community. Furthermore, they identify themselves as active and committed participants in the Catholic Church; they claim an ethnic identity—Mexican American; their ages range from forty to sixty; and they have attained at most high school educations. However, these women fail to conform to the predicted political apathy. Instead, they have transformed social identity—ethnic identity, class identity, and gender identity—into an impetus as well a basis for activism. And, in transforming their existing social networks into grassroots political networks, they have also transformed themselves.

TRANSFORMATION AS
A DOMINANT THEME

. . . First, women have transformed organizing experiences and social networks arising from gender-related responsibilities into political resources.[5] When I asked the women about the first community, not necessarily "political," involvement they could recall, they discussed experiences that pre-dated the formation of MELA. Juana Gutiérrez explained:

> Well, it didn't start with the prison, you know. It started when my kids went to school. I started by joining the Parents Club and we worked on different problems here in the area. Like the people who come to the parks to sell drugs to the kids. I got the neighbors to have meetings. I would go knock at the doors, house to house. And I told them that we should stick together with the Neighborhood Watch for the community and for the kids.[6]. . .

Part of a mother's "traditional" responsibility includes overseeing her child's progress in school, interacting with school staff, and supporting school activities. In these processes, women meet other mothers and begin developing a network of acquaintanceships and friendships based on mutual concern for the welfare of their children.

Although the women in MELA carried the greatest burden of participating in school activities, Erlinda Robles also spoke of strategies they used to draw men into the enterprise and into the networks:

> At the beginning, the priests used to say who the president of the mothers guild would be; they used to pick 'um. But, we wanted elections, so we got elections. Then we wanted the fathers to be involved, and the nuns suggested that a father should be president and a mother would be secretary or be involved there [at the school site].

Of course, this comment piqued my curiosity, so I asked how the mothers agreed on the nuns' suggestion. The answer was simple and instructive:

> At the time we thought it was a "natural" way to get the fathers involved because they weren't involved; it was just the mothers. Everybody [the women] agreed on them [the fathers] being president because they worked all day and they couldn't be involved in a lot of daily activities like food sales and whatever. During the week, a steering committee of mothers planned the group's activities. But now that I think about it, a woman could have done the job just as well!

So women got men into the group by giving them a position they could manage. The men may have held the title of "president," but they were not making day-to-day decisions about work, nor were they dictating the direction of the group. Erlinda Robles laughed as she recalled an occasion when the president insisted, against the wishes of the women, on scheduling a parents' group fundraiser—a breakfast—on Mother's Day. On that morning, only the president and his wife were present to prepare breakfast. This should alert researchers against measuring power and influence by looking solely at who holds titles.

Chapter 15: Social Movements: Communities and the State

Each of the cofounders had a history of working with groups arising out of the responsibilities usually assumed by "mothers"—the education of children and the safety of the surrounding community. From these groups, they gained valuable experiences and networks that facilitated the formation of "Mothers of East Los Angeles." ...

Second, the process of activism also transformed previously "invisible" women, making them not only visible but the center of public attention. From a conventional perspective, political activism assumes a kind of gender neutrality. This means that anyone can participate, but men are the expected key actors. In accordance with this pattern, in winter 1986 an informal group of concerned businessmen in the community began lobbying and testifying against the prison at hearings in Sacramento. Working in conjunction with Assemblywoman Molina, they made many trips to Sacramento at their own expense. Residents who did not have the income to travel were unable to join them. Finally, Molina, commonly recognized as a forceful advocate for Latinas and the community, asked Frank Villalobos, an urban planner in the group, why there were no women coming up to speak in Sacramento against the prison. As he phrased it, "I was getting some heat from her because no women were going up there."

In response to this comment, Veronica Gutiérrez, a law student who lived in the community, agreed to accompany him on the next trip to Sacramento.[7] He also mentioned the comment to Father John Moretta at Resurrection Catholic Parish. Meanwhile, representatives of the business sector of the community and of the 56th assembly district office were continuing to compile arguments and supportive data against the East Los Angeles prison site. Frank Villalobos stated one of the pressing problems:

We felt that the Senators whom we prepared all this for didn't even acknowledge that we existed. They kept calling it the "downtown" site, and they argued that there was no opposition in the community. So, I told Father Moretta, what we have to do is demonstrate that there is a link (proximity) between the Boyle Heights community and the prison.[8]

The next juncture illustrates how perceptions of gender-specific behavior set in motion a sequence of events that brought women into the political limelight. Father Moretta decided to ask all the women to meet after mass. He told them about the prison site and called for their support. When I asked him about his rationale for selecting the women, he replied:

I felt so strongly about the issue, and I knew in my heart what a terrible offense this was to the people. So, I was afraid that once we got into a demonstration situation we had to be very careful. I thought the women would be cooler and calmer than the men. The bottom line is that the men came anyway. The first times out the majority were women. Then they began to invite their husbands and their children, but originally it was just women.[9]

Father Moretta also named the group. Quite moved by a film, *The Official Story,* about the courageous Argentine women who demonstrated for the return of their children who disappeared during a repressive right-wing military dictatorship, he transformed the name "Las Madres de la Plaza de Mayo" into "Mothers of East Los Angeles."[10]

However, Aurora Castillo, one of the cofounders of the group, modified my emphasis on the predominance of women:

Of course the fathers work. We also have many, many grandmothers. And all this IS with the support of the fathers. They make the placards and the posters; they do the security and carry the signs; and they come to the marches when they can.

Although women played a key role in the mobilization, they emphasized the group's broad base of active supporters as well as the other organizations in the "Coalition Against the Prison." Their intent was to counter any notion that MELA was composed exclusively of women or mothers and to stress the "inclusiveness" of the group. All the women who assumed lead roles in the group had long histories of volunteer work in the Boyle Heights community; but formation of the group brought them out of the "private" margins and into "public" light.

Third, the women in "Mothers of East L.A." have transformed the definition of "mother" to include militant political opposition to state-proposed projects they see as adverse to the quality of life in the community. Explaining how she discovered the issue, Aurora Castillo said,

> You know if one of your children's safety is jeopardized, the mother turns into a lioness. That's why Father John got the mothers. We have to have a well-organized, strong group of mothers to protect the community and oppose things that are detrimental to us. You know the governor is in the wrong and the mothers are in the right. After all, the mothers have to be right. Mothers are for the children's interest, not for self-interest; the governor is for his own political interest.

The women also have expanded the boundaries of "motherhood" to include social and political community activism and redefined the word to include women who are not biological "mothers." At one meeting a young Latina expressed her solidarity with the group and, almost apologetically, qualified herself as a "resident," not a "mother," of East Los Angeles. Erlinda Robles replied:

> When you are fighting for a better life for children and "doing" for them, isn't that what mothers do? So we're all mothers. You don't have to have children to be a "mother."

At critical points, grassroots community activism requires attending many meetings, phone calling, and door-to-door communications—all very labor-intensive work. In order to keep harmony in the "domestic" sphere, the core activists must creatively integrate family members into their community activities. I asked Erlinda Robles how her husband felt about her activism, and she replied quite openly:

> My husband doesn't like getting involved, but he takes me because he knows I like it. Sometimes we would have two or three meetings a week. And my husband would say, "Why are you doing so much? It is really getting out of hand." But he is very supportive. Once he gets there, he enjoys it and he starts in arguing too! See, it's just that he is not used to it. He couldn't believe things happened the way that they do. He was in the Navy twenty years and they brainwashed him that none of the politicians could do wrong. So he has come a long way. Now he comes home and parks the car out front and asks me, "Well, where are we going tonight?"...

Working-class women activists seldom opt to separate themselves from men and their families. In this particular struggle for community quality of life, they are fighting for the family unit and thus are not competitive with men.[11] Of course, this fact does not preclude different alignments in other contexts and situations.[12]

Fourth, the story of MELA also shows the transformation of class and ethnic identity. Aurora Castillo told of an incident that illustrated her growing knowledge of the relationship of East Los Angeles to other communities and the basis necessary for coalition building:

> And do you know we have been approached by other groups? [She lowers her voice in emphasis.] You know that Pacific Palisades group asked for our backing. But what they did, they sent their powerful lobbyist that they pay thousands of dollars to get our support against the drilling in Pacific Palisades. So what we did was tell them to send their grassroots people, not their lobbyist. We're suspicious. We don't want to talk to a high-salaried lobbyist; we are humble people. We did our own lobbying. In one week we went to Sacramento twice.

The contrast between the often tedious and labor-intensive work of mobilizing people at the "grassroots" level and the paid work of a "high salaried lobbyist" represents a point of pride and integrity, not a deficiency or a source of shame. If the two groups were to construct a coalition, they must communicate on equal terms.

The women of MELA combine a willingness to assert opposition with a critical assessment of their own weaknesses. At one community meeting, for example, representatives of several oil companies attempted to gain support for placement of an oil pipeline through the center of East Los Angeles. The exchange between the women in the audience and the oil representative was heated, as women alternated asking questions about the chosen route for the pipeline:

> *"Is it going through Cielito Lindo [Reagan's ranch]?" The oil representative answered, "No." Another woman stood up and asked, "Why not place it along the coastline?" Without thinking of the implications, the representative responded, "Oh, no! If it burst, it would endanger the marine life." The woman retorted, "You value the marine life more than human beings?" His face reddened with anger and the hearing disintegrated into angry chanting.[13] . . .*

People living in Third World countries as well as in minority communities in the United States face an increasingly degraded environment.[14] Recognizing the threat to the well-being of their families, residents have mobilized at the neighborhood level to fight for "quality of life" issues. The common notion that environmental well-being is of concern solely to white middle-class and upper-class residents ignores the specific way working-class neighborhoods suffer from the fallout of the city "growth machine" geared for profit.[15] . . .

Mexican American women living east of downtown Los Angeles exemplify the tendency of women to enter into environmental struggles in defense of their community. Women have a rich historical legacy of community activism. . . .

But something new is also happening. The issues "traditionally" addressed by women—health, housing, sanitation, and the urban environment—have moved to center stage as capitalist urbanization progresses. Environmental issues now fuel the fires of many political campaigns and drive citizens beyond the rather restricted, perfunctory political act of voting. Instances of political mobilization at the grassroots level, where women often play a central role, allow us to "see" abstract concepts like participatory democracy and social change as dynamic processes.

The existence and activities of "Mothers of East Los Angeles" attest to the dynamic nature of participatory democracy, as well as to the dynamic nature of our gender, class, and ethnic identity. The story of MELA reveals, on the one hand, how individuals and groups can transform a seemingly "traditional" role such as "mother." On the other hand, it illustrates how such a role may also be a social agent drawing members of the community into the "political" arena. Studying women's contributions as well as men's will shed greater light on the networks dynamic of grassroots movements. . . .

NOTES

1. During the last five years, over 300 newspaper articles have appeared on the issue. Frank Villalobos generously shared his extensive newspaper archives with me. See Leo C. Wolinsky, "L.A. Prison Bill 'Locked Up' in New Clash," *Los Angeles Times,* 16 July 1987, sec. 1, p. 3; Rudy Acuña, "The Fate of East L.A.: One Big Jail," *Los Angeles Herald Examiner,* 28 April 1989, A15; Carolina Serna, "Eastside Residents Oppose Prison," *La Gente UCLA Student Newspaper* 17, no. 1 (October 1986): 5; Daniel M. Weintraub, "10,000 Fee Paid to Lawmaker Who Left Sickbed to Cast Vote," *Los Angeles Times,* 13 March 1988, sec. 1, p. 3.

2. MELA has also opposed the expansion of a county prison literally across the street from William Mead Housing Projects, home to 2,000 Latinos, Asians, and Afro-Americans, and a chemical treatment plant for toxic wastes.

3. The first of its kind in a metropolitan area, it would burn 125,000 pounds per day of hazardous wastes. For an excellent article that links recent struggles against hazardous waste dumps and incinerators in minority communities and features women in MELA, see Dick Russell, "Environmental Racism: Minority Communities and Their Battle against Toxics," *The Amicus Journal* 11, no. 2 (Spring 1989): 22–32.

4. Miguel G. Mendívil, field representative for Assemblywoman Lucille Roybal-Allard, 56th assembly district, Personal Interview, Los Angeles, 25 April 1989.

5. Karen Sacks, *Caring by the Hour.*

6. Juana Gutiérrez, Personal Interview, Boyle Heights, East Los Angeles, 15 January 1988.

7. The law student, Veronica Gutiérrez, is the daughter of Juana Gutiérrez, one of the cofounders of MELA. Martín Gutiérrez, one of her sons, was a field representative for Assemblywoman Lucille Roybal-Allard and also central to community mobilization. Ricardo Gutiérrez, Juana's husband, and almost all the other family members are community activists. They are a microcosm of the family networks that strengthened community mobilization and the Coalition Against the Prison. See Raymundo Reynoso, "Juana Beatrice Gutiérrez: La incansable lucha de una activista comunitaria," *La Opinion,* 6 Agosto de 1989, Acceso, p. 1, and Louis Sahagun, "The Mothers of East L.A. Transform Themselves and Their Community," *Los Angeles Times,* 13 August 1989, sec. 2, p. 1.

8. Frank Villalobos, Personal Interview.

9. Father John Moretta, Resurrection Parish, Personal Interview, Boyle Heights, Los Angeles, 24 May 1989.

10. The Plaza de Mayo mothers organized spontaneously to demand the return of their missing children, in open defiance of the Argentine military dictatorship. For a brief overview of the group and its relationship to other women's organizations in Argentina, and a synopsis of the criticism of the mothers that reveals ideological camps, see Gloria Bonder, "Women's Organizations in Argentina's Transition to Democracy," in *Women and Counter Power,* edited by Yolanda Cohen (New York: Black Rose Books, 1989): 65–85. There is no direct relationship between this group and MELA.

11. For historical examples, see Chris Marín, "La Asociación Hispano-Americana de Madres Y Esposas: Tucson's Mexican American Women in World War II," *Renato Rosaldo Lecture Series 1: 1983–1984* (Tucson, Ariz.: Mexican American Studies Center, University of Arizona, Tucson, 1985) and Judy Aulette and Trudy Mills, "Something Old, Something New: Auxiliary Work in the 1983–1986 Copper Strike," *Feminist Studies* 14, no. 2 (Summer 1988): 251–69.

12. Mina Davis Caulfield, "Imperialism, the Family and Cultures of Resistance."

13. As reconstructed by Juana Gutiérrez, Ricardo Gutiérrez, and Aurora Castillo.

14. For an overview of contemporary Third World struggles against environmental degradation, see Alan B. Durning, "Saving the Planet," *The Progressive* 53, no. 4 (April 1989): 35–59.

15. John Logan and Harvey Molotch, *Urban Fortunes* (Berkeley: University of California Press, 1988). Logan and Molotch use the term in reference to a coalition of business people, local politicians, and the media.

54

Building in Many Places

Multiple Commitments and Ideologies in Black Women's Community Work

CHERYL TOWNSEND GILKES

Popular perspectives on Black communities and their problems often fail to comprehend the tremendous efforts at internal transformation that exist alongside persistent efforts to combat racism. Historical struggles against diverse expressions of institutional racism such as slavery, Jim Crow, ghetto poverty, and political disenfranchisement, for example, have also addressed internal problems and conflicts that would impede participation, autonomy, self-reliance, and dignity. For instance, many Black abolitionists were also involved in educational and benevolent organizations that were working for the survival of Black communities. The legal and direct actions of the civil rights movement existed side by side with activities designed to educate and empower Black communities. The Urban League worked to transform external economic structures that peculiarly oppressed, exploited, and excluded Black people at the same time as it developed a corps of Black social workers whose efforts would enhance the success of Black women and men in the labor force. Historically, a struggle for social justice and institutional transformation never developed without a struggle for group survival. The struggle to transform White racist attitudes and intergroup antipathies was inextricably linked to concerted efforts to foster social uplift and self-esteem.

Women have been central to this work for social change in the wider society as well as survival and uplift within the Black community. Their con-sciousness highlights the strategic importance of women to the emergence and mobilization of what Mina Caulfield called "cultures of resistance."[1] Black women see the consequences of racism not only in their own lives as Black women but in the lives of their husbands and other male relatives, of their friends, and of their children. Even those community workers who had no children of their own were deeply involved in children's and young people's issues. Thus, these experiences provide three sources of anger to fuel the political consciousness of Black women. Their historical role as agents of social transformation and community uplift emerged during slavery, the rise of Jim Crow, and urban migration. In each period, this multifaceted perspective on racism has been evident in Black women's public activities.[2]

Within the historical traditions associated with a distinctive Black experience, working for "the Race" emerged as a central historical role and a highly esteemed social status. Formerly called "Race men" and "Race women," the men and women who do such work are often called community workers now. That term, arising during the late 1960s and early 1970s, focused emphasis on community control, group solidarity, and cultural pride. There was also a shift that included occupational settings (especially in the human services) as arenas in which to shape social change. Community workers are found in a wide variety of occupations and professions—they are nurses, teachers, lawyers, ministers, social workers—and are prominent within the Black community as people who have "worked hard for a long time for change in the Black community" and, less often, are prominent outside the Black community as "Black leaders." Although those men identified as community workers are usually, but not exclusively, clergy, the women are spread across a broad range of human service professions.

Black women's community work, with its duality of external and internal efforts, is a complex phenomenon. Certain aspects of community work demonstrate the manner in which these women define and execute their historical role in contemporary human service settings. As contemporary representatives of a historical tradition of Black women making social change, they decide for themselves and their community the appropriate objects of their efforts and the new goals to be achieved. The civil rights and Black power movements removed the more overt symbols of racial oppression and nurtured a militance that opened new pathways into predominantly White settings for "qualified" Black people. Such changes made it possible for community workers to discover the more subtle and complex realities of institutional racism and its pervasive consequences for their everyday lives and their futures. No longer did the healing of the wounds of racial oppression require simply an internal effort based in voluntary associations, nor could the elimination of oppressive domination be effected simply by concerted public and collective action. This newer era brought a need for complex, dynamic organizational approaches both to transform White institutions and to nurture and strengthen Black ones.

This study focuses on the activities, ideologies, and perspectives of prominent Black women community workers in a Northeast urban setting called Hamptonville.[3] The women see their social role as "building 'Black-oriented' institutions" in the many places they work. A Black-oriented institution is an organization or agency that responds to and cooperates with the needs and aspirations of individuals and groups in the Black

community. For community workers, the "Black community" encompasses not only the people in their ghetto in Hamptonville but also a national community, formerly called "the Race" and sometimes called "Black America"; there is also an international identification, "wherever Black people are." Not only do the Black-oriented institutions evince cooperation and responsiveness; these places also depict and advocate a "Black perspective" within the organizational setting. In order to produce these institutions, community workers utilize a wide variety of friendships, associations, and ideologies, and they maintain numerous memberships in organizations and on boards of directors. This strategy of diverse but pragmatic affiliations produces a connectedness and cohesion within a pluralistic Black community. It also provides a limited degree of empowerment and visibility beyond the ghetto walls, and an acceptance of ideological diversity. The honors community workers receive symbolize not only the admiration of their community and of their professional colleagues but also the importance of the women's networks.

THE STUDY

During 1976 and 1977, I interviewed twenty-five women who had been identified as women "who have worked hard for a long time for change in the Black community" by individuals and newspapers in Hamptonville. Twenty-three of the women were between thirty and sixty years old, and the two oldest women were in their eighties. The younger women were employed in human service settings and were members and directors of local and national agencies and organizations. The older women had long, distinguished careers in racial uplift and religious organizations and, although retired from the labor market, served on the boards of directors of human service organizations, some of which employed the twenty-three younger women. These younger women were human service professionals who managed agencies, projects, or programs that were in some way related to the social, educational, economic, or political life of Hamptonville's Black population. Their past and present positions—in employment training, teaching, child welfare, social welfare, civil rights enforcement, health care, electoral politics, and the ministry, to name a few—touched upon every conceivable area where the private troubles and public issues of surviving in a racist society merged and surfaced.

Although some observation was conducted at public events and meetings, the study relied primarily on interviews. The sampling procedure was reputational and emphasized the community's perception that these women performed a public, political role central to its collective needs—in spite of the women's occupational and political diversity. In crises, these women were the ones upon whom Hamptonville residents called in order to seek advice and to shape responses. Community workers were women who saw their own problems as public issues shared by their friends, neighbors, and relatives—other Black people. Beyond that, they also observed and understood the problems of others. Their attempts to engineer collective, rather than individual, responses brought them into the social world and historical tradition of community work.

BUILDING IN MANY PLACES

Nikki Giovanni's poetic insistence, "I mean it's my house . . . 'cause I run the kitchen and I *can* stand the heat . . . ," aptly describes the determination of community workers to strive for social change regardless of the "heat" in the places where they are employed.[4] They perceive that institutional racism takes the form of bureaucratic indifference and abuse, and this perspective shapes their strategies to promote change in their everyday lifestyles. Through their own daily confrontations with a variety of problems, they eventually learn that the institutions of the dominant society are not organized to "be responsive" to Black community needs. The older women had created pathways into these institutions, and the

younger women perceived their task as the making of these institutions into "Black-oriented" ones.

The places these women manage and administer reflect their attitudes toward the organizational practices of the dominant society. In order to fashion new organizational structures and practices and to transform old ones, the women become involved in two kinds of conflict. First, they rebel against traditional human service practices that appear to perpetuate institutional racism. Second, they restructure their own organizational settings to make them "Black-oriented."

By virtue of their positions, the women are members of the "helping professions" and they have "clients." Although they are not (with two exceptions) members of such established professions as law and medicine, they participate in occupational groups whose members espouse professional ideologies, exercise administrative and public authority, and hold more power than the people they ostensibly serve. Community workers judge certain of these professional ideologies and practices to be inimical to the interests of their community by reinforcing patterns of racist domination. Consequently, they rebel against aspects of this professionalism and seek to redefine the client–professional relationship. Since community workers are primarily political actors who view their client constituencies as peers, they do not see professional expertise and occupational status as legitimate bases for sociopolitical differentiation. Instead, professional expertise and training are aspects of their commitment to the community.

The women are also in a position where they are able to make demands upon White institutions to accommodate the needs of Black people. They use their positions to create a "Black orientation" or "Black presence" in these White institutions as a means for Black community empowerment. They work to force White institutions to "do right" by demanding that White officials and professionals do their jobs properly, by blocking opportunities for White institutional abuses, and by setting alternative examples for other White and Black professionals. This involves both teaching and confrontation. Although the women enunciate the need for total systemic change, they act on whatever level they happen to find themselves through employment, appointment, election, or simply membership.

Thus, the administrations of these women are consciously Black administrations. The alternatives they create reflect their critique of certain social relations that they perceive as contributing to the problem of institutional racism in the United States. Their strategy is to attack aspects of a multifaceted problem and to make a conscientious attempt to translate their images of community into the practices and procedures of dominant institutional settings. Wherever, whenever, and by almost any means community workers carefully build their alternative styles of administration in order to eliminate racism.

"DOING WITH": RESPONSIVENESS RATHER THAN PROFESSIONAL DISTANCE

Since the women live and work in the Black community, there is already a lack of physical distance between themselves and the people they serve. The early-morning and late-night phone calls, a permanent feature of their "typical day," are symptoms of their distaste for professional distance. Their places of employment represent one activity among a consistent line of activities. Their *work* extends beyond the boundaries of *a job*, eliminating the compartmentalization between professional, political, and social activities. Their specific jobs represent one place among the many political structures that govern Black people's lives. In the face of accusations that "you are being unprofessional," these women act to replace professional styles that reinforce dominance with something more responsive and humane.

Being "unprofessional" means a "laying on of hands." The women, thoroughly schooled in the textbook definitions of appropriate professional distance, physically reach out to do things

with (not *to* or *for*) the people they serve. One woman worked as an administrative assistant under a stream of social workers before being hired as the director of an occupational and family service program. While discussing the meaning of the term "qualified," she mentioned that her job normally required a Master of Social Work (M.S.W.) degree, which she did not have. She reflected:

> Somebody will say to me, "You have to have an M.S.W." If I tried to get this job today, I would have to have an M.S.W. I don't have that, yet I've been doing this job and no one's complaining.... We had one lady who came here who was technical about everybody that walked in that door.... I was the [assistant] then. I'd be sitting there and laughing and talking with someone...waiting to be interviewed by her, and she said that it was "naht professionalll" behavior [doing an exaggerated imitation of the social worker's proper behavior] because you don't do that unless...you know how to have a discussion with that person.

She described her own style of giving services as reflective of the wishes of a board of directors who were themselves Black women community workers. She said:

> One thing I think the [agency] can do, they can give you a personal service, not sit down and you come for a service. "I'm going to call you next week; a year from now I might look through my lists and say, 'I'll call you and see if you're still doing all right.'" And, you see, that's the kind of personal service we give. And so when we find out they have children, you say, "How are your children doing in school? Can we get them a tutor?" "Do you want...?" We try to think of the person as a whole human being with all their various needs....

A mental health program director minimized totally the distance between herself and her troubled clients. Her husband's reaction, when she approached him with her idea for starting an innovative outpatient program, was very supportive. She said, "He was worried but said, 'if you want to work with them all day, eat with them all day, and sleep with them all night, it's all right with me.'" However, he "put his foot down" in the area of arrests and insisted that she not go to police stations alone in the middle of the night. Another mental health worker also gave her phone number freely to patients and other community people.

Most women discussed the troubled people who came to their homes. For some problems, home meetings were better than office meetings. One woman said:

> *I had a person call me this morning, at six this morning, wanted me to give her a decision as to whether she should have an abortion...and I talked to her at length. [After a long, detailed recounting of the conversation] I told her I would meet with her tomorrow morning [at home].*

Since the women viewed their work as part of a total lifestyle, they rarely regarded their homes as inviolate sanctuaries from the troubles of the Black community. When they discussed the troubled neighbors who came to their doorsteps, it was not to complain. Instead, their descriptions of the home visits served to show how important their visitors' problems truly were. One woman took her role for young Black women so seriously that she "dressed for business" when she was at home in order to be a good role model when she answered the door.

This lack of social distance between the women and other members of the community paralleled their insistence that they and their organizations be accessible and flexible. One director of an educational services agency commented at length on the importance of this organizational style. She said:

> *We try to present an informal approach because most Black people...are kind of timid because of the way they have been dealt with by bureaucratic institutions.... We have a very good rapport with parents and the students; they walk in and out any time they feel like it.... I've had mothers come in here very excited and crying, and if she's got to stand there and explain her story to a receptionist*

> *first and then a secretary before she gets to see someone to talk to, by that time she feels as though "What's the use!" I know myself, as much as I've been through and as knowledgeable as I am about the system, that after three or four phone calls, and I have to keep repeating myself, I attempt to find some sort of alternative...because by then I'm totally disgusted.*

Sometimes the women were criticized by agency employees and board members committed to a more elitist and traditional style of professional helping. Such board members and employees had to be taught patiently but firmly that things should, to the minds of the community workers, be different. Some women were effective agents of change precisely because they had been trained in elite institutions of social work and had developed long and distinguished careers in traditional agencies as well as in national associations, both Black and white. One such professional, who managed a large agency, talked at length about her enforcement of her philosophy of service delivery. She said:

> *They [people from traditional agencies] had to learn to work with minority peoples, which many of them had not had that experience before, and particularly minority people who were calling the shots. They had to learn to use their agencies in a positive way because we were making demands on them.... It gave them a different view of how to treat a client. We firmly believed that human beings had a certain dignity. And we didn't care whether they came in dirty, whether they came in drunk, whether they came in high—and, by the way, there wasn't too much drug use in our community at that time—whether they tried to manipulate us or not. We were there to provide on-site services and we did it....*

The importance of accessibility and flexibility as expressions of responsiveness is illustrated by the manner in which community workers use their agencies when a community crisis arises. Sometimes it is a crisis involving the total community. At other times it is something involving only those having a direct relationship with the agency, its program, or the related public politics. An agency director who is also a community worker will open her agency at night or keep it open past closing time in order to accommodate meetings. Several times I arrived for interviews and observed offices showing the telltale signs of late-night meetings—coffee cups, chairs, and full ashtrays. My observations were always confirmed.

Such responsiveness means that these women never expect to leave their offices on time. Those who do not control their own buildings must usually close their offices at five o'clock. Those who do not have to leave their offices make use of the public time for people in need of services and use time after their agencies close to complete paperwork, answer mail, and return phone calls. Because one women's program depended upon other agencies' being open for services, her efforts to be flexible placed additional burdens upon her. She said:

> We've even had to take somebody home with us. Other agencies, they work with a client until it gets to be four o'clock, and then, "Oh my goodness, I haven't got a place for you; go to the [agency]." Five o'clock, here comes somebody—no home, no money, no anything, no references, no job experience. So you take them home!—until you find a place for them. That is not required of the job, but, on the other hand, what do you do with a sister?! Do you say [in a sweetly sarcastic and exaggeratedly professional tone], "Sorry about that. It's five o'clock."

Not shutting their doors in the faces of "sisters" and "brothers" is part of the personal commitment that makes community workers' agencies and programs responsive, "unprofessional," and, therefore, different.

OUR HOUSE: ENFORCING A BLACK PERSPECTIVE

…When community workers have the power, they want to build "Black-oriented" organizations. A Black-oriented organization, according to these women, is one that starts from the promise that competent Black people can be found to manage

and provide services flexibly and accessibly, without compromising legitimate professional standards. Over and over again community workers said, "The word *qualified* has racist connotations." Some said, "I don't use that word [*qualified*]." One woman said, "Qualifications don't mean a thing. Can the person actually *do* the job?" Their experiences in predominantly white institutions of higher education cause them to question the realistic meaning of credentials. One program director, who was still working on her graduate management degree, said:

> The schools…can't give you the feeling for people. I don't think there's a course in it…. There could be. There could be just a little old playing thing on the days you don't feel too well; have somebody come who's blowing alcohol in your face, and see how you feel about it, and how you overcome that without giving the person a bad feeling.

For some women, the experience of succeeding at a job without the traditional credentials gives them a realistic basis for criticizing the obsession with credentials. A veteran social worker highlighted the contrast between credentials and experience that contributed to her critical stance. She declared:

> That's a sore point in terms of overestimating what an earned degree means. And yet I'm not saying people shouldn't have them. All I'm saying is don't make this a hard, fast criterion that opts out the value [of] somebody's life experience, which in the long run,… if that person is a capable person, will enable that person to move much faster into whatever the job than a person who is fresh out of school with a degree.

If these views were expressed by unsuccessful people, it would be easy to dismiss them as rationales for failure. Instead, these community workers have performed well enough to maintain their own organizations. They have received awards not only from members of their community but, oddly enough, from their professional peers. The women write well enough to obtain funding for their programs, and they negotiate the bureaucracies of government and foundations to acquire funds in difficult circumstances. Several women had conducted demonstration projects and programs that were later cited by their funding agencies as models for both Black *and White* communities. One woman's project had become part of a national funding policy package from which other cities could obtain funds to start an agency like the one she had founded.

Ideally, Black-oriented organizations should be full of people, both Black and White, who understand the legacy of institutional racism in the United States, the ways by which the dominant society historically has excluded Black people from decision making and economic opportunity, and how such powerlessness has shaped troublesome conditions in the lives of Black people. If service agencies hired only community workers who shared the women's sense of mission and identity, there would be fewer problems for the women who manage them. Rather, the size and complexity of their agencies and programs require that they hire both Black and White professionals who subscribe to the dominant societal values and who protest and complain about an alternative professional style. Consequently, the women are accused of nationalism, particularism, and reverse racism. It is then that community workers must carefully articulate and enforce their ideals. Sometimes they must attempt to enforce their values in White organizations serving predominantly but not exclusively Black people. Besides other people of color, there are White clients living in or near Black neighborhoods who confront similar economic and political problems and come seeking help.

The women are sympathetic to the disorientation of their employees, but they continue to advocate the importance of Black empowerment. One director of a large, racially mixed agency expressed her feelings quite plainly. She stated:

> I think that I am bent on self-government, meaning that Black people are able to govern themselves, are able to efficiently handle the various programs, and so forth. I am not sympathetic to those White people who work in the community and feel that forever and a day they will be in charge of things. I

am more inclined to let them know in one way or another that they will be moving over as we move in. And I don't find that a problem because I still hold to a human relations approach as far as people are concerned, so I tend not to challenge them. For example, I don't ever use the word racist. I don't find it necessary to call a White person a racist. I consider that a cultural "given"—that in the United States it is a fact that this particular group does see itself as the group that consciously or unconsciously feels it is due certain things, that they as a people are due certain things.... I work around the offensive approaches, but I think I do it in such a way that people feel it. I let them know that it is my intention to move people up; that job mobility is important and that what I would do within programming is look for those opportunities for Black people, Hispanic people, et cetera.

Another agency director, who employed quite a few White professionals, insisted upon educating her staff to new attitudes and organizational order. As part of her administrative tasks, she said, "I see myself as an educator." She explained her administrative style:

> The way I like to function around here with my staff is that this whole thing is a learning process and that the only way we can have a good running operation is for us to learn from each other and to recognize that we all have something to offer the goals of the organization.

She then described an incident in which conflict among her staff members had erupted around a newly hired Black professional who was perceived as "militant." "I mean," said the director, "she's got 'UJIMA' on her license plate."[5] When the White staff members labeled this woman a racist, the director called a meeting. She said:

> This was just a couple of weeks ago, and if I closed my eyes I would have thought I was in a White middle-class establishment. I mean that's how upset I really then became—very concerned! And I said to the people who were sitting there, "This is a Black health center, it serves predominantly Black patients, and it's got a Black administration, and that's what we're going to be about. Now we're going to have to learn what that means."...

Several women had worked in child welfare. The issue of adopting across racial lines was quite explosive at the time of my research. One woman felt the need to reeducate her central agency. She said, "I call it the 'Big House.'" The agency, she claimed, perpetuated the distortion that Black families would not take in Black foster children. She described her own professional priorities as a child welfare worker in a predominantly White agency.

> Now I do have a problem when it comes to a choice as to who will I service first; it's going to be the Black girl; it's going to be the Black community...because it's harder to place our Black kids. And I show them. They said you couldn't place black kids in Black homes, because you couldn't get Black homes. I've shown them just the opposite. I have a lot more Black homes than I have White homes.

Her ability to recruit Black foster parents created an unusual situation where during several emergencies she was forced to place White children in Black homes.

> That's the reason we have to place some of our White girls in Black homes for the same reason that we didn't have enough White homes. [Visiting professionals] asked whether I was placing them across racial lines. I said, "Well, I try not to because [the teenagers] are under stress as it is, and I don't want to add another problem to their situation. But I haven't had as many White homes as I've had Black homes, and I have placed White girls in Black homes as long as they can get along with it." And they reacted [imitating the visitors' shocked surprised]: "How has that worked out?!" I said, "Extremely well. Black folks have been taking care of White folks' children since we've been here!"...

The opportunity for successful confrontation is not always available. Community workers in large, White-controlled and predominantly White organizations are limited to more modest goals. A Black perspective may be advocated, but it cannot be enforced. One woman occupied an appointive position whose tenure was limited. There were limits to the impact she was able to have through direct confrontation. While maintaining her desire to build a Black-oriented institution, she used other strategies and maintained her idealism. She said:

> I still do some of the things that slaves did. I don't always say to them what I'm thinking. I've learned at points to keep a blank face. There are times when I feel great anger, but I have learned to control it if the controlling of that anger means that I can advance, whatever I'm about doing, better by controlling it. There are other times when I don't bother to control it.... I'm determined by the time I leave the [agency]...that there will be a salt-and-pepper kind of combination of workers here as opposed to what there was when I came a few years back. I'm determined that Hispanic and Black [clients] will be better understood and better treated. And I hope that the quality of [service] for all people, Black, White, green, purple—any color—will be improved by the time I leave.

Teaching the politically unaware is a task that extends for these women beyond the boundaries of their own organizations or "houses." The heat generated within their administrations prepares them for the problems that stem from political confrontations in other settings such as the boards of directors, boards of trustees, and membership meetings of the interracial, political, economic, educational, cultural, and health organizations in which they participate. These positions are also part of the role of community worker. They are what one woman called the "small pieces" that make up, along with their full-time jobs, the total lifestyle and role set of the contemporary community worker.

"LOTS OF SMALL PIECES": THE DYNAMICS OF MULTIPLE COMMITMENTS

Community workers assumed that if the agencies were responsive to the most oppressed and deprived, they were by definition responsive to everyone. Simply changing professional ideologies and practices and reshaping White attitudes toward Black professionals and clients was only one part of the struggle. The women also found ways to confront the larger power structure of which their "Black-oriented institutions" were a part. Beyond their full-time human-service positions, the twenty-three younger women participated in a wide variety of organizations aimed at interracial cooperation, political empowerment, economic advancement, education, cultural enhancement, and community endurance—"lots of small pieces." While attempting to summarize her style of life in community work, the woman who had coined this phrase captured the complexity and multiplicity of all the women's activities and the diversity of the community and its problems. She said, "You see, there are lots of small pieces that I'm involved in, and [they] take very specific actions at very specific times.... It's hard to explain!"

Black community politics revolve around the web of intragroup and intergroup affiliations of community workers. As they build Black-oriented institutions in many places, their web of affiliations expands, and they are recruited to join a variety of boards and organizations. As new problems and crises arise, these diverse activities contribute to the duality of community work—overall social transformation along side everyday community survival. From the outside, an urban Black community can appear divided as debates between competing ideologies and organizations proceed. The organizational ties among community workers act as a cohesive force in spite of this diversity. These pragmatic affiliations of individual community workers provide the social basis of unity in spite of diversity, something that James Blackwell identified as characteristic of the Black community.[6]

It is through these pragmatic affiliations that the women contribute to the full range of tasks comprised by community work. The network of community workers extends a web of support through various boards of directors. The women sit on one anothers' boards and provide the kind of support they have in the past received. Besides administration, they perform the tasks of advocacy, community organizing, planning policy, political strategizing, raising funds, and managing confrontations. Through participation in "lots of small pieces," they attempt to change what one woman called "the big picture"—the social, economic, and political position of the total Black community and the systemic context in which this position is embedded.

"BY ANY MEANS NECESSARY": PRAGMATIC AFFILIATIONS

The variety of these affiliations often makes no ideological sense. Rather, the affiliations are reflections of the locations and types of problems in the community. Although a community worker may have a well-articulated political ideology, her affiliations are not always a reflection of her choice between sides of an ideological debate such as integration versus separatism or radical political strategies versus traditional party politics. The women's affiliations with White-controlled institutions are a reflection of where they feel Black folks need to be in order to exert some control over their lives and futures. They may find certain organizations objectionable, but if the quality of life for Black people is affected by one of these organizations, they will accept a position.

A community worker involved with the Red Cross commented on such an incongruous affiliation. She said, "I know, to Blacks, when they hear the words 'Red Cross,' I know a lot of people had bad experiences with the Red Cross." She then referred to its history of racism and to the differences among local chapters. She talked about other organizations that seemed antithetical to the Black experience, finally saying, "You know, it's all good and well to sit back and criticize these organizations, but if you don't sit in with them and become part of them, how are you ever going to bring about a change?"

Another woman discussed her "deviant" affiliations more bluntly: "It's like being properly dressed. You do something you don't want to do [like emphasizing that she is Catholic by birth], so you can come back and fight." I replied to her statement with my own analysis: "So you can manage to get your weapons to the line of battle?" She responded eagerly, "Right!"

Several of the women were Republicans. They had long histories of working for Republican candidates and had occasionally run for local office on the Republican Party ticket. One woman discussed her political affiliation in contrast to her other affiliations, which were "responses to community needs, the needs of Black people." She said, "Certainly being a Black Republican would not be considered a response by the Black community to a need.... But, yet and still, I am able to do some things *because* I am a Black Republican." Another woman recalled her recruitment as a lobbyist by the national office of the NAACP during the debates on the Civil Rights Act. Because of her position in the state party, senators and representatives welcomed her to their offices. Other women's affiliations created ties between White conservative religious organizations and radical protest groups and between traditional interracial service organizations and Black nationalist ones.

Often affiliations with cultural institutions, such as museums, fine arts organizations, scientific associations, and zoological societies, serve two purposes: Black children from various agencies administered by these women or other community workers gain free admission to public programs, *and* the women develop talking relationships with powerful representatives of White economic, political, and educational institutions. Though they often learn that their potential impact on the social structure is more limited than they had hoped, community workers use these talking relationships to chip away at some of the attitudes and assumptions related to the maintenance of the status quo. Since these community workers are often *the* Black trustee or *the* Black board member, they try to represent sincerely a Black perspective on policies.

These affiliations with White organizations are never isolated from women's more numerous affiliations within the Black community; these are the Black interests that they represent elsewhere. Their affiliations with boards governing a variety of Black community activities are broadly pragmatic, placing them in direct relationships with particular social problems and needs and with diverse ideological perspectives. The woman whom Whites may consider to be the most cooperative interracial worker may be intimately linked with some other community worker whom Whites consider to be "too radical" and "hard to get along with."...

The women's descriptions of their processes of self-criticism and evaluation imply that an element of community work is the constant fitting together of talents and actions in order to develop appropriate and effective political strategies. The ethic "by any means necessary," although associated with the radical revolutionary style of the late 1960s, adequately describes the women's multiple commitments and pragmatic affiliations. These diverse activities are the collective action through which community workers exert pressure against the broadest possible variety of dominating institutions and bind together the widest possible array of constituencies within the Black community. Rather than perceiving their differences in style and opinion as impediments, community workers utilize the differences among themselves as resources to be used in the most strategically productive manner. Community workers evaluate each other in terms of their contribution to all of the "small pieces" that could possibly change "the big picture."

HONORS AND AWARDS: SYMBOLS OF CONNECTEDNESS AND MISSION

Members of the Black community recruit the community workers because they trust these women to act in their interests. The community then reinforces and rewards with honors their activities on its behalf. These honors symbolize the importance of community work and increase the public exposure and visibility of the community worker. Consequently, she is more vulnerable to recruitment to higher positions and more intense commitment to service. The awards also highlight her role in unifying the community by publicizing her pragmatic affiliations. Her determination "to set my people free" is acknowledged and honored by members of the community.

Awards are an expression of the mandate that Black people have given to these community workers to represent the community. As spokeswomen, administrators, trustees, and directors, they are, through these awards, reminded of the faith and trust being offered to them....

The awards and honors are important at another level as well. The women experience a community-sponsored upward mobility precisely because of their reasoned and pragmatic dedication to the cause and the struggle. Since their professional experiences are augmented by their trustee positions, board memberships, and organizational participation, their human capital, in orthodox economic terms, increases. Paradoxically, the women become upwardly mobile in the very same occupational structure and political economy they are trying to change. Awards and honors, and the public ceremonies associated with them, serve to remind the women of their purpose in increasingly difficult circumstances. Whatever opportunities they seek or are offered they evaluate with reference to their role as a community worker.

Over the years, organizations have seen some women and men acquire skills and, according to one worker, "let go of us as a community, as a people." Another worker vividly described the attempt of a White institution to lure her away from community work and her highly vocal, visible, and effective activism. The community culture recognizes—"everybody knows"—that the potential for co-optation exists. The community counters this with its only weapon and resource—public admiration, honor, and awards. Through these awards the community openly encourages the building process that transforms institutions, represents the Black perspective, creates a presence beyond the ghetto walls, and maintains unity in the context of the community's diversity.

CONCLUSION: THE POWER OF POWERLESSNESS

This study focused singularly on women. In spite of the overwhelming visibility of male leaders in the civil rights and Black power movements, women outnumber men in the local world of community work. The women are aware of the fact that they do the bulk of the community work. Many men openly acknowledge this fact as well. The most visible male community workers are usually ministers, and their sudden moves to new congregations can disrupt coalitions and projects. Moreover, their primary allegiance is to their congregation, and occasionally they must represent that constituency in conflicts and disputes. The fact that White politicians invariably approach the minister before they approach the women produces occasional hostility. Thus, men may at times be a problem in the world of community work.

The position of Black women at the bottom of both the status and income hierarchies produces an interesting paradox in their politics of liberation. They have a better and more comprehensive view of the dynamics of oppression. As the mothers who, like many Black women workers, depend upon older friends and relatives for child care, Black women community workers participate in the intergenerational network of women simply to survive. As mothers and friends of mothers, they apprehend more sharply the consequences of racism for the total life course and for both boys and girls. They also suffer the consequences of Black men's oppression as their limited work lives, criminal justice encounters, and other humiliations place additional burdens upon the women. From such a deprived position, Black women have advanced some of the most powerful critiques of the racist society in which they live....

Beyond the folklore, the collective recognition of this power of the powerless women emerged in the "larger share" of public power Black women were granted within their communities in organizations and movements.[7] Drake and Cayton observed that "Bronzeville" residents—both men and women—were able to name prominent women as local and national heroines who represented their interests. Furthermore, they suggested that Bronzeville *trusted* its "Race women" more than it trusted its "Race men." Perceiving the limits of women's opportunities, the community noted that the women could not capitalize on their activities in the same way as men could.[8] Thus, while men—ministers moving to new congregations and politicians seeking public office—were a suspicious source of instability, women were perceived as more committed to the everyday life, troubles, and interests of the community.

This trust can be an important constraint and a source of anguish for the women. The less skilled and more deprived members of the community see the middle-class trappings of their work and lifestyle and assume the women have more power than they actually possess. The women, on the other hand, because of their upward mobility, perceive more clearly the depths of the crisis confronting the community and the all-too-real limits of power. Excessive trust in the women's ability to get things done may sometimes undercut their ability to organize massive community participation before a problem reaches crisis proportions. Among the most powerless in the larger society, Black women community workers have moral power and prestige because they are women who represent the total community's interests and who build carefully a culture of resistance through community work in many critical places.

Katie G. Cannon has described four basic struggles that shape the consciousness of Black women—the struggle for human dignity, the struggle against white hypocrisy, the struggle for justice, and the struggle for survival. As a result of the historical constancy of those struggles, she argues, Black women "articulate possibilities for decisions and actions which address forthrightly the circumstances that inescapably color and shape black life."[9] The historical tradition and contemporary practice of community work is a predominantly female social institution[10] that demonstrates the powerful way in which consciousness is shaped and an alternative history is forged. No matter how high they rise, and no matter how diverse and many the places they go to build, Black women community workers are the ones who will come home to the community.

ACKNOWLEDGMENTS

An earlier version of this study was presented in 1982 at the Kirsch Center for Marxist Studies of the University of Massachusetts–Boston. Support for various stages of the research and writing was provided by the National Fellowships Fund, the Minority Fellowship program of the American Sociological Association, and the Center for Research on Women at Memphis State University, Memphis.

NOTES

1. M. Caulfield, "Imperialism, the Family, and Cultures of Resistance," *Socialist Revolution* 4, No. 2 (1974): 67–85.

2. Several old and new works describe this complexity and historical depth: Angela Davis, *Women, Race, and Class* (New York: Random House, 1981); Elizabeth Lindsey Davis, *Lifting As They Climb: A History of the National Association of Colored Women* (Washington, D.C.: Moorland Spingarn Research Center, 1933); St. Clare Drake and Horace Cayton, *Black Metropolis: A Study of Negro Life in a Northern City* (Chicago: University of Chicago Press, 1970); Sharon Harley and Rosalyn Terborg-Penn, *The Afro-American Woman: Struggles and Images* (Port Washington, N.Y.: Kennikat Press, 1978); Paula Giddings, *When and Where I Enter: The Impact of Black Women on Race and Sex in America* (New York: Morrow, 1984); Alfreda Duster, ed., *The Autobiography of Ida B. Wells* (Chicago: University of Chicago Press, 1970).

3. All of the names of persons and places in this study are pseudonyms. Unattributed and uncited quotations are from the interviews and field notes.

4. Nikki Giovanni, *My House* (New York: Morrow, 1972).

5. *Ujima,* meaning collective work and responsibility, is one of the seven principles of *Kwanza* outlined in Ron Karenga's doctrine of *Kawaida.* The other six are *Umoja* (unity), *Kujichagalia* (self-determination), *Ujamaa* (cooperative economics), *Nia* (purpose), *Kuumba* (creativity), and *Imani* (faith). These are described in detail in Alphonso Pinckney, *Red, Black and Green: Black Nationalism in the United States* (New York: Cambridge University Press, 1976), esp. 129 and 140–143.

6. James E. Blackwell, *The Black Community: Diversity and Unity* (New York: Harper & Row, 1985).

7. Drake and Cayton, *Black Metropolis.*

8. *Ibid.*

9. Katie G. Cannon, "The Emergence of Black Feminist Consciousness," in Letty M. Russell, ed., *Feminist Interpretation of the Bible* (Philadelphia: Westminster, 1985), 30–40, esp. 40.

10. Deborah Grey White, in the most comprehensive and scholarly analysis of women's experience during slavery, argues persuasively that "the female slave network" stood with the slave family and slave religion as a social institution that facilitated survival and selfhood. See Deborah Gray White, *Ar'n't I a Woman?: Female Slaves in the Plantation South* (New York: Norton, 1985), 119–141.

55

Women's Social Movements in Latin America

HELEN ICKEN SAFA

The past decade has witnessed a marked increase in participation by women in social movements in Latin America. Latin American women are participating in organizations led by and for women, struggling for their rights as workers in trade unions, as housewives in squatter settlements, and as mothers defending human rights against state repression. While undoubtedly influenced by the feminist movements that developed earlier and were largely middle class in origin, these social movements are distinguished by the widespread participation by poor women, who focus their demands on the state in their struggle for basic survival and against repression.

While many studies trace the origin of these movements to the current economic and political crisis in the region, I believe they are indicative of a broader historical trend toward the breakdown of the traditional division between the private and public spheres in Latin America.[1] The private sphere of the family has always been considered the domain of women, but it is increasingly threatened by economic and political forces. Industrialization and urbanization have reduced the role of the family and strengthened the role of the state. There have been marked occupational changes, including an increasing incorporation of women into the labor force. The importance of women as wage earners has been made even more acute by the economic crisis now gripping Latin America, while state services upon which women have come to depend have been reduced or curtailed. Authoritarian military regimes have invaded the very heart of the family by taking the lives of children and other loved ones and subjecting them to terror and state repression.

However, women in Latin America are not just defending the private domain of the family against increasing state and market intervention. They are also demanding incorporation into the state, so that their rights as citizens will be fully recognized. In this sense, these movements not only are symptomatic of the breakdown between the public and private spheres in Latin America but are themselves furthering this process. Women are demanding to be recognized as full participants in the public world and no longer wish to have their interests represented solely by men, whether as heads of household, *barrio* leaders, politicians, or union officials.

At the same time, as Jelin notes (1987), Latin American women are insisting upon distinct forms of incorporation that reaffirm their identity as women, and particularly as wives and mothers. This form of incorporation differs from the contemporary U.S. and Western European expedience, in which women seek a gender-neutral participation in the public sphere. Latin American women, in contrast, think that their roles as wives and mothers legitimize their sense of injustice and outrage, since they are protesting their inability to effectively carry out these roles, as military governments take away their children or the rising cost of living prevents them from feeding their families adequately. In short, they are redefining and transforming their domestic role from one of private nurturance to one of collective, public protest, and in this way challenging the traditional seclusion of women into the private sphere of the family.

The prominence of women in these new social movements challenges Marxist theory in at least two fundamental ways. In the first place, participation in these women's movements is based primarily on gender rather than on class, which Marxists have emphasized as the principal avenue for collective action. Most of the poor women who participate in these movements are conscious of both class and gender exploitation, but they tend to legitimize their concerns over issues such as human rights or the cost of living primarily in terms of their roles as wives and mothers rather than as members of a subordinated class. This tendency points out the weakness of Marxist theory in addressing the importance of gender, racial, or religious differences within the working class. Second, and as a consequence of their gender emphasis, the primary arena of confrontation for women's social movements in Latin America has not been with capital but with the state, largely in terms of their reproductive role as wives, mothers, and consumers of both state services and private consumer goods. The state has assumed a major role in social reproduction in Latin America, particularly in terms of the provision of basic services, such as health, education, and transportation. At the same time, the need for these services has grown with the rapid increase in urbanization and industrialization in the post-World War II period.

Women are not the only subordinated group to challenge the state, and social movements have arisen as well among youth, peasants, the urban poor, and broader-based human rights groups. Latin American women have also demanded greater participation in labor unions, political parties, and peasant movements that have attempted to make the state more responsive to their needs. They have worked with feminists in establishing day-care centers or in developing ways to cope with sexual violence and other problems. However, this article focuses on Latin American women's movements for human rights and those centering around consumer issues. It explores the factors that contributed to the increased participation of women in social movements in Latin America and why women have chosen the state as the principal arena of confrontation rather than capital, as in workplace-related issues of collective action. It also discusses how successful these social movements have been in bringing about fundamental changes in gender roles in Latin America.

THE BASES OF WOMEN'S SOCIAL MOVEMENTS IN LATIN AMERICA

Women's social movements in Latin America are commonly seen as a response to military authoritarian rule and the current economic crisis, both of which create particular hardships for the working class. In an attempt to address the growing debt crisis, many Latin American governments have set up structural adjustment programs designed by the International Monetary Fund. These programs have had a devastating impact on women and children, since they have resulted in increased unemployment and underemployment, a decline in real wages coupled with accelerated inflation, the elimination of state subsidies for basic foods, as well as cuts in government expenditures for social services, such as health and education (Cornia 1987). The economic crisis has reinforced the need for collective action, particularly among poor urban women who organize primarily on a neighborhood basis.

The urban poor in Latin America have a long history of collective action, as demonstrated by the squatter settlements and other neighborhood actions to improve urban services (e.g., Safa 1974). Women have always played a prominent role in these neighborhood forms of collective action, though their importance has seldom been explicitly acknowledged (Caldeira 1987, 77). At the same time, women commonly resort to informal networks of mutual aid, including extended family and neighbors, to help stretch the family income and resolve community problems. Women also add to the family income through participation in the informal economy as domestic servants, street vendors, industrial homeworkers, and other forms of self-employment. With the economic crisis, these survival strategies have been intensified and institutionalized into formal organizations, such as the *comedores populares* or *ollas comunes* (communal kitchens) for food distribution or *talleres productivos* (workshops) for making garments or doing other types of piecework. In Santiago, Chile, in 1986, there were 768 organizations dedicated to collective consumption, including consumer cooperatives (Arteaga 1988, 577).

The participation of women in social movements in Latin America is also a product of the changes in women's roles in Latin America in the past two decades. Fertility has been declining steadily in most countries of the region, so that by 1980–85, only three Latin American countries registered average fertility rates in excess of six children per woman, while eight countries had rates of fewer than four children per woman (ECLAC 1988a, 2). Fertility decline was associated with women's higher educational levels and increased labor-force participation, as well as with greater access to contraceptives and the promotion of family-planning programs in several Latin American countries. Women's educational levels rose at a faster rate than men's as part of the enormous expansion in primary and, in particular, secondary education between 1950 and 1970. The number of women in higher education rose from 35 percent to 45 percent from 1970 to 1985 (ECLAC 1988a, 3–4). As a result, the female labor force increased threefold in Latin America between 1950 and 1980, with overall participation rates rising from almost 18 percent to over 26 percent in the same period (ECLAC 1988b, 15). Work-force participation rates for women grew faster than those for men, and while all age groups experienced growth, single women between the ages of 20 and 29 continued to have the highest level of paid employment among women.

Women industrial workers in the Caribbean are now making a major contribution to their household economies, which has resulted in a shift toward more egalitarian conjugal relationships (Safa 1990). In contrast to the assumptions of some feminist theorists (e.g., Barrett 1980),

women in Latin America and the Caribbean seem to have been more successful in negotiating change within the home than at the level of the workplace or the state, where their needs are still not given legitimacy.

The increased educational and occupational levels of Latin American women also contributed to the growth of a feminist movement among middle-class women, who felt their exclusion from the public sphere even more sharply than poor women did. These feminists have devoted much attention to the poor through research and involvement in action projects, such as day care, health services, and centers for raped and battered women. These programs helped to transmit feminist concerns for greater gender equality and have stimulated poor women to challenge their traditional role. The visibility these gender issues received during the U.N. Decade for the Equality of Women through numerous conferences, publications, and projects reinforced their appeal.

Poor women in Latin America also received considerable support from the church (Alvarez 1989, 20–26). Women played a major role in the Catholic church's organization of ecclesiastic base communities (CEBs) in Brazil and other Latin American countries. The CEBs were part of the church's efforts to give more support to social justice for the poor in Latin America, emanating from liberation theology, which is now under increasing attack from the Vatican. The CEBs were also an attempt by the church to reinforce grassroots support, which was weakening with the growth of Protestantism and the church's elitist stance. Women were organized into mothers' clubs for the provision of food, sewing classes, and other traditional domestic tasks. Many of women's collective consumption strategies, such as communal kitchens, have received church support. While based on traditional women's roles, these clubs provided an additional organizational base from which women could challenge the existing order.

Under military rule, the church often provided the only legitimate umbrella under which women and other groups could organize, since all other forms of mobilization were prohibited. In some Latin American countries, such as Chile and Brazil, women from all class levels, with church support, organized into human rights groups to protest the disappearance or killing of their loved ones, or to seek amnesty for political prisoners or exiles. Catholic doctrine played an important role in these women's self-definition and quest for legitimacy, and they rarely questioned traditional gender roles. On the contrary, these women often appealed to Catholic symbols of motherhood and the family in legitimizing their protest—values that these authoritarian states also proclaimed but destroyed in the name of national security. Women themselves were often victims of this repression: They were systematically sought out for violent sexual torture designed to destroy their femininity and human dignity (Bunster-Burotto 1986).

In sum, many factors have contributed to the recent increased participation of women in social movements in Latin America. Women had long been active at the neighborhood level, both through informal networks and more organized forms of collective action, such as squatter settlements and *barrio* committees. With economic crisis and military rule, these activities took on added importance and also received the support of important groups, such as the Catholic church and nongovernmental agencies. Increased educational and occupational opportunities made women more aware of previous restrictions and more vocal in protesting them. Poor women became more receptive to the largely middle-class feminist movement in Latin America and began to redefine their traditional role, including their relationship to the state.

WOMEN'S SOCIAL MOVEMENTS AND THE STATE

Women's social movements have been described as a new form of doing politics (*nueva forma de hacer política*) in Latin America, but the impetus

for most of these movements has not come from traditional political parties and labor unions in the region. Most women's movements have consciously avoided partisan political connections, in part because of the weakness of these traditional avenues of political action during the period of authoritarian military rule when most of these movements arose. The attempt of these regimes to limit legitimate political action contributed to the politicization of women and other groups who had not been participating actively in the public arena (Jelin 1987).

The other reason women's social movements took place largely outside the realm of traditional political parties is that politics is seen as men's sphere, particularly by poor women. Latin American political parties traditionally have been dominated by men and have been seen as engaged in struggles for power in which the poor are essentially clients. Poor people's loyalty to the party is exchanged for favors, such as paving a road, providing state services, guaranteeing title to land, or getting jobs. The Centros de Madres in Chile, which had begun to acquire some autonomy under the governments of Frei and Allende, were, under the military dictatorship of Pinochet, completely subverted to the needs of the state for the control and co-optation of poor women (Valdes et al. 1989). Although the Centros de Madres were privatized, they were run by a staff of volunteers appointed by the government and headed by Pinochet's wife, who offered to both rural and urban women such services as training courses that focused largely on improving their domestic role. Political participation was discouraged as "unfeminine," although members were often called upon to display their loyalty to the regime by participating in rallies and other activities. As a result, membership in the Centros de Madres declined drastically from the premilitary period, and new nonofficial women's groups arose, in the areas of both human rights and collective survival strategies, in response to Chile's severe economic crisis and rising rates of unemployment (Arteaga 1988, 573). These nonofficial groups provided the base for the women's movement against Pinochet starting in 1983.

Latin American women appear to have chosen the state as the principal arena of their collective action rather than the workplace as men traditionally have, partly because industrial capitalism transformed the organization and social relations of production and the gendered division of labor. While industrial capitalism initially drew women into the paid labor force in many areas, they were never as fully incorporated as men, who became the chief breadwinners. Women were relegated to a role as supplementary wage earners, while their reproductive role as housewives and consumers assumed new importance. Despite recent significant increases in women's labor-force participation in Latin America, this image of women as supplementary workers persists and helps explain women's comparatively low level of consciousness as workers. Most poor women are relatively recent and less-stable entrants to the formal labor force in Latin America and work primarily to support themselves and their families, obtaining little gratification or self-fulfillment from their jobs. Their primary identification, even when they are working, is as wives and mothers.

The gendered division of labor in the workplace may reinforce gender hierarchies rather than weaken them, by relegating women to inferior jobs. Even in São Paulo, Brazil, where the spectacular industrial boom of the 1970s led to a 181 percent increase in women's employment in manufacturing between 1970 and 1980, women workers were largely concentrated in exclusively women's jobs at the bottom of the job hierarchy (Humphrey 1987). These gender asymmetries in the workplace were reflected in the conflict between male-dominated unions and working women. Souza-Lobo's study (forthcoming) of the metallurgy industry found that although women formed union committees, and some individually active women were integrated into the union structure, women continued to see the union as a men's sphere that remained largely unresponsive to their demands.

As a result of their frustration in working through political parties and labor unions, the recognized channels for collective action, Latin American women presented their demands to the state directly. One of the principal demands was for the provision of public services, such as running water, electricity, and transportation, all of which are sorely lacking in the squatter settlements in which most of these poor women live. Women's reproductive role as housewives and mothers has tended to push them into the foreground as champions of these collective consumption issues, and they have been in the forefront of protests against the cost of living and for demands for programs to provide day care, health services, and even food.

One of the most successful and unique collective consumption strategies to combat the growing economic crisis is the *comedores populares* or communal kitchens organized by women in Lima, Santiago, and other Latin American cities. Groups of 15 to 50 households buy and prepare food collectively for the neighborhood, with each family paying according to the number of meals requested. Many of these *comedores* sprang up spontaneously, while others have been started or at least supported by the church, the state, and other local and international agencies. UNICEF-Peru in 1985 estimated that there were 300 in Lima (Cornia 1987, 99), while Blondet (1989) recently estimated their number at 1,000–1,200. Their growing number is evidence of women's collective response to the increasing severity of the economic crisis in Peru and other Latin American countries in the past decade.

In Lima, popular organizations may be the only alternative to acquire basic services, such as health, education, and food, yet the *asistencialismo* (welfare dependency) that this policy encourages may be exploited by the government, political parties, and other agencies (Blondet 1989). Traditional district and neighborhood organizations are controlled by male leaders, who attempt to usurp the popular support enjoyed by women's groups for their own partisan ends.

Blondet (1989) recounts, for example, how the popular women's federation in Villa El Salvador, a large shanty town in Lima, split and was partially absorbed through pressure brought by the traditional men's organization. The political fragmentation then occurring among leftist political parties in Peru was reproduced within the women's organizations, further weakening their base of support.

Some feminists have been critical of these women's self-help organizations because they focus almost exclusively on traditional women's tasks and do not challenge the traditional division of labor. I would argue that the collectivization of private tasks, such as food preparation and child care, is transforming women's roles, even though they are not undertaken as conscious challenges to gender subordination. These women never reject their domestic role but use it as a base to give them strength and legitimacy in their demands on the state (Alvarez 1989, 20; Caldeira 1987, 97). In moving their domestic concerns into the public arena, they are redefining the meaning associated with domesticity to include participation and struggle rather than obedience and passivity.

Nowhere is their militancy more apparent than in the demands Latin American women have placed on the state for the recognition of human rights. One of the best-known cases in contemporary Latin America is Las Madres del Plaza de Mayo, who played a decisive role in the defeat of the military dictatorship that ruled Argentina from 1976 to 1983. Composed mostly of older women with no political experience, Las Madres take their name from the Plaza de Mayo, the principal seat of government power in Buenos Aires, in which they march every Thursday, wearing a white kerchief and carrying photographs of their missing children as a symbol of protest. Although the military government attempted to discredit them as mad women or mothers of subversives, they continued to march, publish petitions in the newspaper, organize trips abroad, and seek cooperation with other human rights groups and youth movements, with whom they organized larger demonstrations in 1981 and 1982. The publicity they received from the foreign media and the support given them by some European countries and the United States during the Carter administration contributed to their popular support (Reimers 1989). In order to maintain their legitimacy during the military regime, they refused any identification with political parties or feminism. They maintained, "*Nosotros no defendemos ideologías, defendemos la vida*" ("We don't defend ideologies, we defend life"; Feijoo and Gogna 1987, 155). Their demands were not political power for themselves, but that the state guarantee the return of their loved ones and punish the military who had violated the sanctity of the home and family. These demands remain largely unfulfilled. Though the top military were prosecuted, most officers were granted amnesty, and even some of those imprisoned were later released.

After the end of military rule, Las Madres were weakened by internal struggles that reflected a split between those who wished to remain aloof from partisan politics and those who sought alliances with political parties, chiefly the Peronists, to achieve their goals. Although women's human rights groups similar to Las Madres del Plaza de Mayo have arisen in Uruguay, Chile, Brazil, Honduras, El Salvador, Guatemala, and other Latin American countries subject to military rule, the decline in popular support for Las Madres reflects the difficulty women's social movements have in converting political mobilization into institutional representation (cf. Jaquette 1989, 194).

THE TRANSFORMATIVE POTENTIAL OF WOMEN'S SOCIAL MOVEMENTS IN LATIN AMERICA

Most participation by women in social movements arises out of women's immediate perceived needs and experiences, or out of what Molyneux (1986) terms women's "practical gender interests." Molyneux claims these practical gender interests do not challenge gender subordination directly, whereas strategic gender interests question or transform the division of labor. As we have seen, women's social movements are often based on their roles as wives and mothers and may reinforce or defend women's domestic role. However, as these practical gender interests are collectivized and politicized, they may also lead to a greater consciousness of gender subordination and the transformation of practical into strategic gender interests.

Although neither women's movements for human rights not collective consumption were designed as challenges to gender subordination, participation in those movements has apparently led to greater self-esteem and recognition by women of their rights, as the following statement by a Brazilian woman, leader of a neighborhood organization, underlines:

> Within the Women's Movement, as a woman, I discovered myself, as a person, as a human being. I had not discovered that the woman…always was oppressed. But it never came to my mind that the woman was oppressed, although she had rights. The woman had to obey because she was a woman.… It was in the Women's Movement that I came to identify myself as a woman, and to understand the rights I have as a woman, from which I have knowledge to pass on as well to other companions. (Caldeira 1987, 95–96, my translation)

As this statement exemplifies, women's participation in social movements has produced changes in Latin American women's self-definition. Such changes are the best guarantee that these women will resist any attempt to reestablish the old order and will continue to press for their rights. They imply a redefinition of women's roles from a purely domestic image as guardians of the private sphere into equal participants as citizens in a democratic state. However, this redefinition must occur not only in the minds of women themselves but in the society at large, so that women are no longer treated as supplementary wage earners and pawns in the political process. To achieve such goals, there must be unity within the women's movement, across class, ethnic, and ideological lines; and women must also gain sup-

port from other groups in the society, such as political parties and labor unions, whom we have seen often try to utilize women's movements for their own ends.

A glaring example of co-optation comes from an earlier period in Bolivia, when women's committees within the party then in power and the housewives' committee of the miners' union were used for partisan politics, and neither the party nor the union ever addressed demands specific to women (Ardaya 1986). Neither of these women's committees had sought autonomy, since they saw themselves serving class rather than gender interests.

Tension between the primacy of class and gender interests in women's organizations throughout Latin America produces differences between women who are feminists and those who are *políticas* (party militants of the left) (Kirkwood 1986, 196). While feminists view politics as a way of furthering their own interests, *políticas* subordinate women's needs to a political program in the hope of their future incorporation. Those who profess to uphold both feminist and partisan political goals are said to be practicing *doble militancia* or double militancy.

This tension between feminists and *políticas* has become more apparent with the end of military rule in Latin America and the reemergence of political parties, which reactivate divisions within the women's movement formerly united in the opposition. The women's movement in Chile suffered less partisan fragmentation than other social sectors opposing the military dictatorship and was an important force in the plebiscite to oust General Pinochet. A group of 12 women's organizations were able to draft the Demands of Women for Democracy, which were presented to the opposition shortly before the plebiscite, and which included the constitutional guarantee of equality between men and women; the reform of civil, penal, and labor legislation that discriminates against women; and an affirmative action policy to reserve 30 percent of government posts for women. However, although the military and the opposition political parties have recognized the importance of women's electoral support, few have given women access to power (Valenzuela 1989). Since the newly elected democratic government in Chile has only recently taken power, it is too early at this writing to see whether women's demands will be implemented, but the small number of women elected or appointed to government office does not augur well for the future.

The Brazilian liberal, democratic state that supplanted military rule has been more successful in addressing women's needs and electing women to public office, including 26 women in the 1986 congressional elections (Alvarez 1989, 58). The initial impetus given by the church through the development of base communities (CEBs) and by feminist groups for the women's movement was critical in building a wider base of support, even though these groups remain divided on some issues, such as family planning. Women also gained greater representation within the state through the government-appointed Council on the Status of Women in São Paulo, which was subsequently established in 23 other states and municipalities, and through the National Council on Women's Rights, which played a critical role in developing women's proposals for the new Brazilian constitution. Pressure put on the council, particularly in São Paulo, by an active grass-roots constituency operating outside the state has kept it responsive to women's needs (Alvarez 1989, 53). However, in Brazil as in Chile, the increased importance of elections rekindled old political divisions between rival political parties formerly united in the opposition. The recent election of a conservative president and the continuing economic crisis weakens the possibility of implementing women's demands, because of budgetary constraints and because of the election and appointment of women with less identification with women's interests.

Women's organizations under socialism have been accused of being imposed from above and of being instruments of state policy. Molyneux (1986) claims that although women's emancipation is officially recognized and supported by the socialist state, it is contained within defined limits. Both Cuba and Nicaragua have been eminently successful in the incorporation of women into the labor force, which is considered a key to women's emancipation, and have supported working women with education and training programs, day-care centers, ample maternity leaves, and other measures. Women's employment has helped the state to meet its labor needs but has also been costly because of the support services women require, which make women considerably more expensive to employ than men (Safa 1989). Therefore, it is hard to argue, as some critics have, that socialist states have simply taken advantage of women's labor power.

Perhaps the most controversial issue for socialist feminists is continued state support of the family, embodied in legal reforms such as the Family Code in Cuba and the Provision Law in Nicaragua. While both reforms aim at greater sharing of responsibility in the household and financial support for women and children, they are also attempts by the state to make the family responsible for needs the state at present cannot meet, given its limited resources (Molyneux 1989). Thus, the goal of these socialist states is to modify the family, to make it more egalitarian rather than to do away with it. This does not differ radically from the goal of most women's social movements in capitalist Latin American countries.

The tenacity of the family in Latin American socialist or capitalist societies derives not only from the needs of the state, or Catholic doctrine, but from the strong identification and emotional gratification women feel in their roles as wives and especially mothers (Safa 1990). The family fulfills their emotional needs for giving and receiving affection, needs that men tend to deny or undervalue. Women continue to value the family because their role within it is never questioned, while they continue to seek legitimacy in the public sphere. As Jaquette (1989, 193) notes, "The feminist perception of the family as an arena of conflict between men and women directly contradicts how women in urban poor neighborhoods understand and justify their politicization—*for* the family." The strong attachment to the family may be one reason why the distinction between the public and private spheres is still more prevalent in Latin America than in more advanced industrial countries like the United States.

CONCLUSION

What is the future of women's social movements in Latin America? Are we to conclude with Jelin (1987) that Latin American women participate more frequently in short-term, sporadic protest movements than in long-term, formalized institutional settings? Or does women's political mobilization represent part of a progressive longer-term trend that may suffer setbacks but not total eclipse?

I would argue for the latter perspective. Latin American women have been too incorporated into the public sphere to retreat back into the private domestic sphere. They have become increasingly important members of the labor force and contributors to the household economy; they have organized social movements for human rights and social welfare; and they are trying to voice their demands in labor unions and political parties. Even if these activities are not undertaken as conscious challenges to gender subordination, they show that women have broken out of the domestic sphere and that gender roles are changing. Latin American women's emergence into the public sphere is both cause and effect of profound cultural changes in the private sphere, in which women are demanding more "democracy in the home" as well as in the state. These changes in Latin American women's self-definition are most likely to endure and to give women the confidence to continue bringing pressure on public authorities for greater recognition of women's rights.

Despite the political and economic problems Latin American countries are facing in the transition to democracy, important gains in women's rights have been made as a result of these social movements. The new Brazilian constitution adopted in 1988 guarantees women equality before the law, including right to property ownership, equal rights in marriage, maternity leave, and the prohibition of salary differences based on sex, age, or civil status (*Debate Sindical* 1989, 24). Argentina has legalized divorce and modified *patria potestad* to give women joint custody of children and equality in other family matters (Jaquette 1989, 199–200). Despite concerted efforts by the Pinochet dictatorship to court women's support in the 1988 plebiscite, 52 percent of Chilean women rejected the continuation in power of the military government, reflecting in part the effectiveness of opposition women's groups.[2] Whether current governments in power in these countries will continue to support women's needs depends on the importance of their electoral support and on the strength and unity of the women's movement in each country.

When women's demands are confined to domestic issues like child care, communal kitchens, or even human rights, they pose less of a threat than when women attempt to gain leverage in men's power structures, such as political parties or labor unions. In short, as women move away from practical to strategic gender interests, they are likely to encounter more opposition on both gender and class lines from established interest groups who are unwilling to grant them the same legitimacy as men in the public arena.

Latin American women are attempting to establish a new relationship to the state, one based not on subordination, control, and dependency but on rights, autonomy, and equality (Valdes and Weinstein 1989). They have passed beyond the stage in which women's needs were largely invisible and ignored, to where women are now heard, even if some may be co-opted for partisan political ends. By politicizing the private sphere, women have redefined rather than rejected their domestic role and extended the struggle against the state beyond the workplace into the home and community. This shift does not invalidate the Marxist theory of class struggle but calls for its reinterpretation to accommodate these new political voices. As Kirkwood (1986, 65) reminds us, the issue is not simply one of women's incorporation into a male-defined world but of transforming this world to do away with the hierarchies of class, gender, race, and ethnicity that have so long subordinated much of the Latin American population, men as well as women.

NOTES

1. While the concept of public-private spheres have been criticized by many feminists and has been largely replaced by the notion of production and reproduction, it has validity for Latin America, the Caribbean, and Mediterranean Europe, where it has been widely used in the study of gender roles. While the reasons for its usefulness for this region lie beyond the scope of this article, it should be noted that I am using the concept of public-private spheres as poles of a continuum rather than as a dichotomy between mutually exclusive cate-gories (cf. Tiano 1988, 40). It is this fluidity that makes possible the domination of the private by the public sphere.

2. The importance of women's labor-force participation in arousing political consciousness can be seen in a study conducted two months prior to the plebiscite, according to which a greater percentage of housewives supported Pinochet than working women (Valenzuela 1989).

REFERENCES

Alvarez, Sonia. 1989. Women's movements and gender politics in the Brazilian transition. In *The women's movement in Latin America: Feminism and the transition to democracy,* edited by Jane Jaquette. Winchester, MA: Unwin Hyman.

Ardaya, Gloria. 1986. The Barzolas and the housewives committee. In *Women and change in Latin America,* edited by J. Nash and H. Safa. Westport, CT: Bergin & Garvey/Greenwood.

Arteaga, Ana María. 1988. Politización de lo privado y subversión de lo cotidiano (Politicization of the private and subversion of everyday life). In *Mundo de Mujer: Continuida y Cambio* (Woman's world: Continuity and change). Santiago: Centro de Estudios de la Mujer.

Barrett, Michèle. 1980. *Women's oppression today.* London: Verso.

Blondet, Cecilia. 1989. Women's organizations and politics in a time of crisis. Paper presented at the Helen Kellogg Institute for International Studies, University of Notre Dame, Notre Dame, IN.

Bunster-Burotto, Ximena. 1986. Surviving beyond fear: Women and torture in Latin America. In *Women and changes in Latin America,* edited by J. Nash and H. Safa. Westport, CT: Bergin & Garvey/Greenwood.

Caldeira, Teresa. 1987. Mujeres, cotidianidad y política (Women, everyday life & politics). In *Ciudadanía e Identidad: Las Mujeres en los Movimientos Sociales Latino-Americanos* (Citizenship and identity: Women and Latin American social movements), edited by E. Jelin. Geneva: UNRISD (United Nations Research Institute for Social Development).

Cornia, Giovanni. 1987. Adjustment at the household level: Potentials and limitations of survival strategies. In *Adjustment with a human face,* edited by G. Cornia, R. Jolly, and F. Stewart. New York: UNICEF/Oxford: Clarendon Press.

Debate Sindical. 1989. *A mujer trabalhadora* (The woman worker). São Paulo: Depanamento de Estudos Socio-Económicos, Central Unicas dos Trabalhadores (Department of Socioeconomic Studies, Central Workers Federation).

ECLAC (Economic Commission for Latin America and the Caribbean). 1988a. *Women, work and crisis.* LC/L. 458 (CRM. 4/6). Santiago, Chile.

———. 1988b. *Latin American and Caribbean women: Between change and crisis.* LC/L. 464 (CRM. 4/2). Santiago, Chile.

Feijoo, María del Carmen and Monica Gogna. 1987. Las mujeres en la transición a la democrácia (Women in the transition to democracy). In *Ciudadanía e Identidad. Las Mujeres en los Movimientos Sociales Latino-Americanos* (Citizenship and identity: Women and Latin American social movements), edited by E. Jelin. Geneva: UNRISD (United Nations Research Institute for Social Development).

Humphrey, John. 1987. *Gender and work in the Third World.* London: Tavistock.

Jaquette, Jane. 1989. Conclusion: Women and the new democratic politics. In *The women's movement in Latin America: Feminism and the transition to democracy,* edited by J. Jaquette. Winchester, MA: Unwin Hyman.

Jelin, Elizabeth. 1987. Introduction. In *Ciudadanía e Identidad: Las Mujeres en los Movimientos Sociales Latino-Americanos* (Citizenship and identity: Women and Latin American social movements), edited by E. Jelin. Geneva: UNRISD (United Nations Research Institute for Social Development).

Kirkwood, Julieta. 1986. *Ser política en Chile: Las feministas y los partidos (To be political in Chile: Feminists and parties).* Santiago: FLACSO (Latin American Faculty of Social Science).

Molyneux, Maxine. 1986. Mobilization without emancipation? Women's interests, state, and revolution. In *Transition and development: Problems of Third World socialism,* edited by R. Fagen, C. D. Deere, and J. L. Corragio. New York: Monthly Review Press.

———. 1989. Women's role in the Nicaraguan revolutionary process: The early years. In *Promissory notes: Women in the transition to socialism,* edited by S. Kruks, R. Rapp, and M. Young. New York: Monthly Review Press.

Reimers, Isolde. 1989. *The decline of a social movement: The Mothers of the Plaza de Mayo.* Master's thesis, Center for Latin American Studies, University of Florida, Gainesville.

Safa, Helen I. 1974. *The urban poor of Puerto Rico: A study in development and inequality.* New York: Holt, Rinehart & Winston.

———. 1989. Women, industrialization and state policy in Cuba. Working Paper no. 133. Helen Kellogg Institute for International Studies, University of Notre Dame, Notre Dame, IN.

———. 1990. Women and industrialization in the Caribbean. In *Women, employment and the family in the international division of labor,* edited by S. Stichter and J. Parpart. London: Macmillan.

Souza-Lobo, Elizabeth. Forthcoming. Brazilian social movements, feminism and women worker's struggle in the São Paulo trade unions. In *Strength in diversity: Anthropological perspectives on women's collective action,* edited by Constance Sutton.

Tiano, Susan. 1988. Women's work in the public and private spheres: A critique and reformulation. In *Women, development and change: The Third World experience,* edited by M. F. Abraham and P. S. Abraham. Bristol, IN: Wyndham Hall Press.

Valdés, Teresa, and Marisa Weinstein. 1989. *Organizaciones de pobladoras y construción en Chile* (Organizations of squatter settlements and democratic reconstruction in Chile). Documento de Trabajo 434 (Working Paper 434), Santiago: FLACSO-CHILE.

Valdés, Teresa, Marisa Weinstein, M. Isabel Toledo, and Lilian Letelier. 1989. *Centros de Madres 1973–1989: Sólo disciplinamiento? (Mothers' Centers 1973–1989: Only imposed discipline?).* Documento de Trabajo 416 (Working Paper 416). Santiago: FLACSO-CHILE.

Valenzuela, María Elena. 1989. Los nuevos roles de las mujeres y la transición democrática en Chile (The new roles of women and the democratic transition in Chile). Paper presented at Conference on Transformation and Transition in Chile, 1982–89, University of California, San Diego.

56

Age, Race, Class, and Sex
Women Redefining Difference

AUDRE LORDE

Much of western European history conditions us to see human differences in simplistic opposition to each other: dominant/subordinate, good/bad, up/down, superior/inferior. In a society where the good is defined in terms of profit rather than in terms of human need, there must always be some group of people who, through systematized oppression, can be made to feel surplus, to occupy the place of the dehumanized inferior. Within this society, that group is made up of Black and Third World people, working-class people, older people, and women.

As a forty-nine-year-old Black lesbian feminist socialist mother of two, including one boy, and a member of an interracial couple, I usually find myself a part of some group defined as other, deviant, inferior, or just plain wrong. Traditionally, in american society, it is the members of oppressed, objectified groups who are expected to stretch out and bridge the gap between the actualities of our lives and the consciousness of our oppressor. For in order to survive, those of us for whom oppression is as american as apple pie have always had to be watchers, to become familiar with the language and manners of the oppressor, even sometimes adopting them for some illusion of protection. Whenever the need for some pretense of communication arises, those who profit from our oppression call upon us to share our knowledge with them. In other words, it is the responsibility of the oppressed to teach the oppressors their mistakes. I am responsible for educating teachers who dismiss my children's culture in school. Black and Third World people are expected to educate white people as to our humanity. Women are expected to educate men. Lesbians and gay men are expected to educate the heterosexual world. The oppressors maintain their position and evade responsibility for their own actions. There is a constant drain of energy which might be better used in redefining ourselves and devising realistic scenarios for altering the present and constructing the future.

Institutionalized rejection of difference is an absolute necessity in a profit economy which needs outsiders as surplus people. As members of such an economy, we have all been programmed to respond to the human differences between us with fear and loathing and to handle that difference in one of three ways: ignore it, and if that is not possible, copy it if we think it is dominant, or destroy it if we think it is subordinate. But we have no patterns for relating across our human differences as equals. As a result, those differences have been misnamed and misused in the service of separation and confusion.

Certainly there are very real differences between us of race, age, and sex. But it is not those differences between us that are separating us. It is rather our refusal to recognize those differences, and to examine the distortions which result from our misnaming them and their effects upon human behavior and expectation.

Racism, the belief in the inherent superiority of one race over all others and thereby the right to dominance. Sexism, the belief in the inherent su-

periority of one sex over the other and thereby the right to dominance. Ageism. Heterosexism. Elitism. Classism.

It is a lifetime pursuit for each one of us to extract these distortions from our living at the same time as we recognize, reclaim, and define those differences upon which they are imposed. For we have all been raised in a society where those distortions were endemic within our living. Too often, we pour the energy needed for recognizing and exploring difference into pretending those differences are insurmountable barriers, or that they do not exist at all. This results in a voluntary isolation, or false and treacherous connections. Either way, we do not develop tools for using human difference as a springboard for creative change within our lives. We speak not of human difference, but of human deviance.

Somewhere, on the edge of consciousness, there is what I call a *mythical norm*, which each one of us within our hearts knows "that is not me." In America, this norm is usually defined as White, thin, male, young, heterosexual, Christian, and financially secure. It is with this mythical norm that the trappings of power reside within this society. Those of us who stand outside that power often identify one way in which we are different, and we assume that to be the primary cause of all oppression, forgetting other distortions around difference, some of which we ourselves may be practicing. By and large within the women's movement today, White women focus upon their oppression as women and ignore differences of race, sexual preference, class, and age. There is a pretense to a homogeneity of experience covered by the word *sisterhood* that does not in fact exist.

Unacknowledged class differences rob women of each others' energy and creative insight. Recently a women's magazine collective made the decision for one issue to print only prose, saying poetry was a less "rigorous" or "serious" art form. Yet even the form our creativity takes is often a class issue. Of all the art forms, poetry is the most economical. It is the one which is the most secret, which requires the least physical labor, the

least material, and the one which can be done between shifts, in the hospital pantry, on the subway, and on scraps of surplus paper. Over the last few years, writing a novel on tight finances, I came to appreciate the enormous differences in the material demands between poetry and prose. As we reclaim our literature, poetry has been the major voice of poor, working class, and Colored women. A room of one's own may be a necessity for writing prose, but so are reams of paper, a typewriter, and plenty of time. The actual requirements to produce the visual arts also help determine, along class lines, whose art is whose. In this day of inflated prices for material, who are our sculptors, our painters, our photographers? When we speak of a broadly based women's culture, we need to be aware of the effect of class and economic differences on the supplies available for producing art.

As we move toward creating a society within which we can each flourish, ageism is another distortion of relationship which interferes without vision. By ignoring the past, we are encouraged to repeat its mistakes. The "generation gap" is an important social tool for any repressive society. If the younger members of a community view the older members as contemptible or suspect or excess, they will never be able to join hands and examine the living memories of the community, nor ask the all important question, "Why?" This gives rise to a historical amnesia that keeps us working to invent the wheel every time we have to go to the store for bread.

We find ourselves having to repeat and relearn the same old lessons over and over that our mothers did because we do not pass on what we have learned, or because we are unable to listen. For instance, how many times has this all been said before? For another, who would have believed that once again our daughters are allowing their bodies to be hampered and purgatoried by girdles and high heels and hobble skirts?

Ignoring the differences of race between women and the implications of those differences presents the most serious threat to the mobilization of women's joint power.

As White women ignore their built-in privilege of Whiteness and define *woman* in terms of their own experience alone, then women of Color become "other," the outsider whose experience and tradition is too "alien" to comprehend. An example of this is the signal absence of the experience of women of Color as a resource for women's studies courses. The literature of women of Color is seldom included in women's literature courses and almost never in other literature courses, nor in women's studies as a whole. All too often, the excuse given is that the literatures of women of Color can only be taught by Colored women, or that they are too difficult to understand, or that classes cannot "get into" them because they come out of experiences that are "too different." I have heard this argument presented by White women of otherwise quite clear intelligence, women who seem to have no trouble at all teaching and reviewing work that comes out of the vastly different experiences of Shakespeare, Molière, Dostoyefsky, and Aristophanes. Surely there must be some other explanation.

This is a very complex question, but I believe one of the reasons White women have such difficulty reading Black women's work is because of their reluctance to see Black women as women and different from themselves. To examine Black women's literature effectively requires that we be seen as whole people in our actual complexities—as individuals, as women, as human—rather than as one of those problematic but familiar stereotypes provided in this society in place of genunine images of Black women. And I believe this holds true for the literatures of other women of Color who are not Black.

The literatures of all women of Color recreate the textures of our lives, and many White women are heavily invested in ignoring the real differences. For as long as any difference between us means one of us must be inferior, then the recognition of any difference must be fraught with guilt. To allow women of Color to step out of stereotypes is too guilt provoking, for it threatens the complacency of those women who view oppression only in terms of sex.

Refusing to recognize difference makes it impossible to see the different problems and pitfalls facing us as women.

Thus, in a patriarchal power system where Whiteskin privilege is a major prop, the entrapments used to neutralize Black women and White women are not the same. For example, it is easy for Black women to be used by the power structure against Black men, not because they are men, but because they are Black. Therefore, for Black women, it is necessary at all times to separate the needs of the oppressor from our own legitimate conflicts within our communities. This same problem does not exist for White women. Black women and men have shared racist oppression and still share it, although in different ways. Out of that shared oppression we have developed joint defenses and joint vulnerabilities to each other that are not duplicated in the white community, with the exception of the relationship between Jewish women and Jewish men.

On the other hand, White women face the pitfall of being seduced into joining the oppressor under the pretense of sharing power. This possibility does not exist in the same way for women of Color. The tokenism that is sometimes extended to us is not an invitation to join power; our racial "otherness" is a visible reality that makes that quite clear. For White women there is a wider range of pretended choices and rewards for identifying with patriarchal power and its tools.

Today, with the defeat of ERA, the tightening economy, and increased conservatism, it is easier once again for White women to believe the dangerous fantasy that if you are good enough, pretty enough, sweet enough, quiet enough, teach the children to behave, hate the right people, and marry the right men, then you will be allowed to co-exist with patriarchy in relative peace, at least until a man needs your job or the neighborhood rapist happens along. And true, unless one lives and loves in the trenches it is difficult to remember that the war against dehumanization is ceaseless.

But Black women and our children know the fabric of our lives is stitched with violence and with hatred, that there is no rest. We do not deal with it only on the picket lines, or in dark midnight alleys, or in the places where we dare to verbalize our resistance. For us, increasingly, violence weaves through the daily tissues of our living—in the supermarket, in the classroom, in the elevator, in the clinic and the schoolyard, from the plumber, the baker, the saleswoman, the bus driver, the bank teller, the waitress who does not serve us.

Some problems we share as women, some we do not. You fear your children will grow up to join the patriarchy and testify against you, we fear our children will be dragged from a car and shot down in the street, and you will turn your backs upon the reasons they are dying.

The threat of difference has been no less blinding to people of Color. Those of us who are Black must see that the reality of our lives and our struggle does not make us immune to the errors of ignoring and misnaming difference. Within Black communities where racism is a living reality, differences among us often seem dangerous and suspect. The need for unity is often misnamed as a need for homogeneity, and a Black feminist vision mistaken for betrayal of our common interests as a people. Because of the continuous battle against racial erasure that Black women and Black men share, some Black women still refuse to recognize that we are also oppressed as women, and that sexual hostility against Black women is practiced not only by the White racist society, but implemented within our Black communities as well. It is a disease striking the heart of Black nationhood, and silence will not make it disappear. Exacerbated by racism and the pressures of powerlessness, violence against Black women and children often becomes a standard within our communities, one by which manliness can be measured. But these woman-hating acts are rarely discussed as crimes against Black women.

As a group, women of Color are the lowest paid wage earners in America. We are the primary targets of abortion and sterilization abuse, here and abroad. In certain parts of Africa, small girls are still being sewed shut between their legs to keep them docile and for men's pleasure. This is known as female circumcision, and it is not a cultural affair as the late Jomo Kenyatta insisted, it is a crime against Black women.

Black women's literature is full of the pain of frequent assault, not only by a racist patriarchy, but also by Black men. Yet the necessity for and history of shared battle have made us, Black women, particularly vulnerable to the false accusation that anti-sexist is anti-Black. Meanwhile, womanhating as a recourse of the powerless is sapping strength from Black communities, and our very lives. Rape is on the increase, reported and unreported, and rape is not aggressive sexuality, it is sexualized aggression. As Kalamu ya Salaam, a Black male writer points out, "As long as male domination exists, rape will exist. Only women revolting and men made conscious of their responsibility to fight sexism can collectively stop rape."[*]

Differences between ourselves as Black women are also being misnamed and used to separate us from one another. As a Black lesbian feminist comfortable with the many different ingredients of my identity, and a woman committed to racial and sexual freedom from oppression, I find I am constantly being encouraged to pluck out some one aspect of myself and present this as the meaningful whole, eclipsing or denying the other parts of self. But this is a destructive and fragmenting way to live. My fullest concentration of energy is available to me only when I integrate all the parts of who I am, openly, allowing power from particular sources of my living to flow back and forth freely through all my different selves, without the restrictions of externally imposed definition. Only then can I bring myself and my energies as a whole to the service of those struggles which I embrace as part of my living.

A fear of lesbians, or of being accused of being a lesbian, has led many Black women into tes-

---

[*]From "Rape: A Radical Analysis, An African-American Perspective" by Kalamu ya Salaam in *Black Books Bulletin*, vol. 6, no. 4 (1980).

tifying against themselves. It has led some of us into destructive alliances, and others into despair and isolation. In the White women's communities, heterosexism is sometimes a result of identifying with the White patriarchy, a rejection of that interdependence between women-identified women which allows the self to be, rather than to be used in the service of men. Sometimes it reflects a diehard belief in the protective coloration of heterosexual relationships, sometimes a self-hate which all women have to fight against, taught us from birth.

Although elements of these attitudes exist for all women, there are particular resonances of heterosexism and homophobia among Black women. Despite the fact that woman-bonding has a long and honorable history in the African and Africanamerican communities, and despite the knowledge and accomplishments of many strong and creative women-identified Black women in the political, social and cultural fields, heterosexual Black women often tend to ignore or discount the existence and work of Black lesbians. Part of this attitude has come from an understandable terror of Black male attack within the close confines of Black society, where the punishment for any female self-assertion is still to be accused of being a lesbian and therefore unworthy of the attention or support of the scarce Black male. But part of this need to misname and ignore Black lesbians comes from a very real fear that openly women-identified Black women who are no longer dependent upon men for their self-definition may well reorder our whole concept of social relationships.

Black women who once insisted that lesbianism was a White woman's problem now insist that Black lesbians are a threat to Black nationhood, are consorting with the enemy, are basically un-Black. These accusations, coming from the very women to whom we look for deep and real understanding, have served to keep many Black lesbians in hiding, caught between the racism of White women and the homophobia of their sisters. Often, their work has been ignored, trivialized, or misnamed, as with the work of Angelina Grimke, Alice Dunbar-

Nelson, Lorraine Hansberry. Yet women-bonded women have always been some part of the power of Black communities, from our unmarried aunts to the amazons of Dahomey.

And it is certainly not Black lesbians who are assaulting women and raping children and grandmothers on the streets of our communities.

Across this country, as in Boston during the spring of 1979 following the unsolved murders of twelve Black women, Black lesbians are spearheading movements against violence against Black women.

What are the particular details within each of our lives that can be scrutinized and altered to help bring about change? How do we redefine difference for all women? It is not our differences which separate women, but our reluctance to recognize those differences and to deal effectively with the distortions which have resulted from the ignoring and misnaming of those differences.

As a tool of social control, women have been encouraged to recognize only one area of human difference as legitimate, those differences which exist between women and men. And we have learned to deal across those differences with the urgency of all oppressed subordinates. All of us have had to learn to live or work or coexist with men, from our fathers on. We have recognized and negotiated these differences, even when this recognition only continued the old dominant/subordinate mode of human relationship, where the oppressed must recognize the masters' difference in order to survive.

But our future survival is predicated upon our ability to relate within equality. As women, we must root out internalized patterns of oppression within ourselves if we are to move beyond the most superficial aspects of social change. Now we must recognize differences among women who are our equals, neither inferior nor superior, and devise ways to use each others' difference to enrich our visions and our joint struggles.

The future of our earth may depend upon the ability of all women to identify and develop new definitions of power and new patterns of relating across difference. The old definitions have not served us, nor the earth that supports us. The old patterns, no matter how cleverly rearranged to imitate progress, still condemn us to cosmetically altered repetitions of the same old exchanges, the same old guilt, hatred, recrimination, lamentation, and suspicion.

For we have, built into all of us, old blueprints of expectation and response, old structures of oppression, and these must be altered at the same time as we alter the living conditions which are a result of those structures. For the master's tools will never dismantle the master's house.

As Paulo Freire shows so well in *The Pedagogy of the Oppressed,** the true focus of revolutionary change is never merely the oppressive situations which we seek to escape, but that piece of the oppressor which is planted deep within each of us, and which knows only the oppressors' tactics, the oppressors' relationships.

Change means growth, and growth can be painful. But we sharpen self-definition by exposing the self in work and struggle together with those whom we define as different from ourselves, although sharing the same goals. For Black and White, old and young, lesbian and heterosexual women alike, this can mean new paths to our survival.

> *We have chosen each other*
> *and the edge of each others battles*
> *the war is the same*
> *if we lose*
> *someday women's blood will congeal*
> *upon a dead planet*
> *if we win*
> *there is no telling*
> *we seek beyond history*
> *for a new and more possible meeting.***

** From "Outlines," unpublished poem.

* Seabury Press, New York, 1970.

57

Benefits for Nonhomophobic Societies
An Anthropological Perspective

WALTER L. WILLIAMS

In a recent publication of the Coalition for Traditional Values, the Reverend Lou Sheldon commits himself to "open warfare with the gay and lesbian community.... [This is] a battle with one of the most pernicious evils in our society: homosexuality."[1] What does the Christian Right think is so bad about homosexuality? We are all familiar with the litany: homosexuals are seen as evil because they are said to be a threat to children, the family, religion, and society in general.

In sharp contrast to the heterosexist views of some people in Western society, the majority of other cultures that have been studied by anthropologists condone at least some forms of same-sex eroticism as socially acceptable behavior.[2] Beyond that, quite a number of societies provide honored and respected places for people who are roughly comparable to what we in Western culture would call gay men and lesbians. One example is the Navajo people of Arizona and New Mexico, the largest American Indian group in North America. *Nadle*, a Navajo word meaning "one who is transformed," is applied to androgynous male or female individuals who combine elements of both masculinity and feminity in their personalities. The rare case of a person who is born hermaphroditic, with ambiguous genitalia or with the sexual organs of both the male and the female, is also considered to be a *nadle*, but most *nadle* are individuals whom Western society would characterize as effeminate men or masculine women. While each society of course constructs its own categories of sexuality in different ways, Navajo people

traditionally accepted the fact that such androgynous people almost always have inclinations to be sexually active with people of the same biological sex.

Today's Navajos, like other Native Americans, have been significantly affected by Christian attitudes condemning homosexuality, but among those who value their traditions, there still continues a strong respect for *nadle*. We can see traditional Navajo attitudes more clearly by reading the testimony of an anthropologist who lived among the Navajos in the 1930s, before they had been so affected by Western values. This anthropologist documented the extremely reverential attitudes toward *nadle*. He wrote that traditional Navajo families who had a child who behaved androgynously were "considered by themselves and everyone else as very fortunate. The success and wealth of such a family was believed to be assured. Special care was taken in the raising of such children and they were afforded favoritism not shown to other children of the family. As they grew older and assumed the character of *nadle,* this solicitude and respect increased.... This respect verges almost on reverence in many cases."[3]

To illustrate these attitudes, this anthropologist quoted what the Navajo people told him about *nadle:*

> *They know everything. They can do both the work of a man and a woman. I think when all the nadle are gone, that will be the end of the Navajo.*
>
> *If there were no nadle, the country would change. They are responsible for all the wealth in the coun-*

try. If there were no more left, the horses, the sheep, and Navajo would all go. They are leaders, just like President Roosevelt. A nadle around the hogan will bring good luck and riches. They have charge of all the riches. It does a great deal for the country if you have a nadle around.

You must respect a nadle. They are, somehow, sacred and holy.[4]

On reading such quotations, the insight that immediately springs to mind is how attitudes toward similar phenomenon may differ widely from one culture to another. Presented above are opposing views of homosexually oriented people, condemned by Christian fundamentalist as "one of the most pernicious evils in society," but seen by the Navajo as something "sacred and holy." Why the difference?

My research in societies that do not discriminate against homosexuals suggests that the main reason for nonprejudicial attitudes is that those societies have figured out specific ways that homosexuality can contribute positively to the good of society as a whole. In other words, acceptance of sexual diversity is due not so much to "toleration" on the part of the heterosexual majority as it is to distinct advantages perceived by the general populace in having a certain proportion of the population homosexually inclined.

In Western culture, where only heterosexuality is valued, it occurs to few people that homosexuality might enrich society. From over a decade of research on this topic, I have come to have a different perspective than most Americans. The knowledge that I have gained has come primarily from fieldwork with native people of North American, Pacific, and Southeast Asian cultures. After three years of documentary research in many libraries, I lived among the American Indians of the Great Plains and the Southwest (1982), the Mayas of Yucatan (1983), and Native Alaskans (1989). I also did field research among the peoples of Hawaii (1984, 1985, 1990), Thailand (1987), and Indonesia (1987–88).[5] This essay will refer to the results of my fieldwork among these indigenous peoples. Much more ethnographic fieldwork certainly needs to be conducted in these and other societies

before we can draw firm conclusions, but I have formulated some tentative points that I outline below.

BENEFITS TO RELIGION

In Western writings about homosexuality, the emphasis has usually been on its "cause," with the implication that homosexuality is an "abnormality" that must be prevented. In contrast, among American Indians the reaction is usually acceptance, based on the notion that all things are "caused" by the spirits and therefore have some, spiritual purpose. It is left to them only to discover each individual's spiritual purpose.

Traditional American Indians seem more interested in finding a useful social role for those who are different than in trying to force people to change character. One's basic character is a reflection of one's spirit, and to interfere with that is dangerously to disrupt the instructions from the spirit world. Many native North American religions are of a type called "animistic"; they emphasize not one creator god but a multiplicity of spirits in the universe. Everything that exists has a spirit; all things that exist are due equal respect because they are part of the spiritual order of the universe. The world cannot be complete without them.

In this religious view, there is no hierarchy among the beings—the humans, animals, and plants—that populate the earth. Humans are not considered to be any more spiritual or any more important than the other beings. Neither is the spirit of man more important than the spirit of woman. Each spirit may be different, but all are of equal value. However, American Indian religions see an androgynous individual as evidence that that person has been blessed by being bestowed with *two* spirits. Because both women and men are respected for their equal but distinct qualities, a person who combines attributes of both is considered as higher, as above the regular person—who only has one spirit.

In contrast to Western sexist views, where a male who acts like a woman is considered to be "lowering himself" to the subordinate female status, in the egalitarian American Indian religions feminine roles are accorded equal respect with men's roles. Therefore, a male who acts like a woman is not "lowering himself"; rather, he is indicating that he has been favored with an extra gift of spirituality. He is respected as a "double person." Such an individual is considered to be not entirely man and not entirely woman but a mixture of both masculine and feminine elements with additional unique characteristics. Such a distinctive personality is respected as a different gender, distinct from either man or woman.

This concept of respect for gender nonconformity is quite foreign to mainstream American society today. Despite the gains made in recent decades by the women's movement, our culture still does not respect the social contributions of anyone other than masculine men. Perhaps the best way to see this is to look at attitudes toward androgynous males. On American schoolyards today, the worst insult that can be thrown at a boy is to call him a *sissy*. What does it say about a society's gender values when the worst insult that can be directed toward a man is to say that he is like a woman?

While androgyny among males is seldom defended in mainstream American culture, it can be argued that many men need social permission to express those aspects of their personalities that in our society are more commonly associated with women. American men in particular are under constant pressure to conform, to maximize their masculine side—to "be tough," not to show emotion. Seldom verbalized are the dangers to society of excessive masculinity, even though the evidence appears daily in newspaper headlines. Violence is preponderantly a characteristic of masculine personalities: physical and sexual violence by men against women, children, and other men is a major social problem. Not only are men's tempers not conducive to cooperation in the workplace, but they also lead to stress-related health problems for hot-headed men themselves.

In contrast, American Indian cultures that are not prejudiced against androgynous persons allow more flexibility among personality types. A major reason for this flexibility is the basic respect that their religions accord human diversity. According to these religions, since everything that exists comes from the spirit world, people who are different have been made that way by the spirits and therefore maintain an especially close connection to the spirit world. Accordingly, androgynous people are often seen as sacred, as spiritually gifted individuals who can minister to the spiritual needs of others. In many tribes, such androgynous men—called *berdache* by the early explorers and by modern anthropologists—were often shamans or sacred people who work closely with shamans. Females who were inclined to take the traditional masculine role of hunter and warrior were called *amazons* by the early explorers, after the ancient Greek legend of warrior women.

Nonprejudiced Native American societies recognized that the berdache and the amazon were almost always homosexual, but an androgynous personality, not sexual behavior, was the defining characteristic. Many tribes had special career roles for berdache and amazons. Many Indian tribes, believing that sickness can be cured by the intervention of the spirits, will turn to the spiritually powerful as healers. While conducting my fieldwork on a Lakota reservation in South Dakota, I often observed people who were ill calling on *winkte* (the word in the Lakota language meaning "half man/half woman") to perform healing ceremonies for them. *Winktes* spend much of their time helping others, visiting the ill and infirm, comforting those in distress, and drawing on their spiritual connections to help people get well.

With a spiritual justification provided by the culture, berdache and amazons are not seen as a threat to religion. Instead, they are often considered sacred. Sexuality—indeed bodily pleasure—is seen not as sinful but as a gift from the spirit world. Both the spirit and the flesh are sacred. The homosexual inclinations of such berdache and amazons are accepted as a reflection of their spiritual nature. The American Indian example shows that it is not enough for a religion to "tolerate" sexual diversity; it must also provide a specific religious explanation for such diversity.

Some worldviews see reality as pairs of opposites: everything is viewed as good versus evil, black versus white, the spiritual versus the physical. The latter derides the needs and desires of the physical body as "temptations of the flesh," in contrast to the devotions of the spirit. The American Indian religions take a different view, seeing both the body and the spirit as good, as reflections of each other. As a consequence, sexual behavior—the epitome of the physical body—may be seen as something positively good, as something spiritual in and of itself, at the same time as it is physical.

The conceptualization by Native American societies of the berdache and the amazons as sacred has its practical applications. Those male berdache whom I have met and read about are uniformly gentle, peaceful people who would simply not fill the traditional Indian man's role of hunter and warrior effectively. By recognizing that they are special and encouraging them to become religious leaders and healers, Indian cultures give such people a means by which to contribute constructively to society. Rather than wasting time and energy trying to suppress their true nature or assuming an unsuitable role, they are encouraged to see their uniqueness as a special spiritual gift and to maximize their capabilities to help others. A Crow elder told me, "We don't waste people, the way White society does. Every person has their gift, every person has their contributions to make."[6]

BENEFITS TO THE FAMILY

This emphasis on the social usefulness of the person who is different can be seen especially clearly in the contributions of such people to their families. Because most pre-Columbian Native Americans lived in extended families, with wide networks of kin who depended on one other, it was not necessary for everyone to have children. In contrast to a society with only nuclear families (father-mother-children), where all must reproduce to have someone take care of them in old age, an extended family offers some adults the opportunity not to reproduce. Childless people have nephews

and nieces care for them. It is actually economically advantageous to the extended family for one or two adults *not* to reproduce because then there is a higher ratio of food-producing adults to food-consuming children. Also, by assuming gender roles that mix both the masculine and the feminine, the berdache and the amazon can do both women's and men's work. Not being burdened with their own childcare responsibilities, they can care for others' children or for their aged parents and grandparents.

The same pattern occurs in Polynesian culture, where an androgynous role similar to that of the berdache exists. Called *mahu* in Hawaii and Tahiti and *fa'afafine* among Samoans, such alternatively gendered people were traditionally those who took care of elderly relatives while their heterosexual siblings were busy raising their own children. With this kind of gender flexibility, and with their families holding high expectations for them (since they are spiritual people), berdache and amazons are often renowned for being hard workers, productive, and intelligent.

Since they are not stigmatized or alienated, berdache and amazons are free to make positive contributions to family life. Today, they often allow adolescent nieces and nephews to move in with them when the parents' home gets overcrowded and also help them finance schooling. A Navajo woman whose cousin is a respected *nadle* healer told me,

> They are seen as very compassionate people, who care for their family a lot and help people. That's why they are healers. Nadles are also seen as being great with children, real Pied Pipers. Children love nadles, so parents are pleased if a nadle takes an interest in their child. One that I know is now a principal of a school on the reservation. . . . Nadles are not seen as an abstract group, like "gay people," but as a specific person, like "my relative so-and-so." People who help their family a lot are considered valuable members of the community.[7]

It is thus in the context of individual family relations that much of the high status of the berdache and amazon must be evaluated. When such people play a positive and valued role in their societies, and when no outside interference disrupts the normal workings of those societies, unprejudiced family love can exert itself.

In most Western cultures, such people are often considered misfits, an embarrassment to the family. They often leave the family in shame or are thrown out by homophobic relatives, the family thereby losing the benefit of their productive labor. In contrast, traditional Native American families will often make such people central to the family. Since other relatives do not feel threatened by them, family disunity and conflict are avoided. The male berdache is not pressured to suppress his feminine behavior, nor is the female amazon pressured to suppress her masculine inclinations. Neither are they expected to deny their same-sex erotic feelings. Berdache and amazons thereby avoid the tendency of those considered deviant in Western culture to harbor a low self-esteem and to engage in self-destructive behavior. Because they are valued by their families, few become alcoholic or suicidal, even in tribes where such problems are common.

Male berdache are often highly productive at women's work. Unlike biological females, who must take time away from farming or foraging when they are menstruating, pregnant, or nursing children, the berdache is always available to gather or prepare food. Anthropologists have often commented on the way in which berdache willingly take on the hardest work. Many berdache are also renowned for the high quality of their craftswork, whether pottery, beadwork, weaving, or tanning. In many tribes, berdache are known as the best cooks in the community and are often called on to prepare feasts for ceremonies and funerals. Women in particular seem to appreciate the help provided by berdache. An elderly Papago woman for example, spoke fondly of a berdache she had known in her youth (referring to him as *she*): "The man-woman was very pleasant, always laughing and talking, and a good worker. She was so strong! She did not get tired

grinding corn....I found the man-woman very convenient."[8]

The female amazon is often appreciated for her prowess at hunting and fighting. In the Crow tribe of the Great Plains, one of the most famous warriors of the nineteenth century was an amazon called "Woman Chief." Edward Denig, a White frontier trader who lived with the Crows for over twelve years, wrote that Woman Chief "was equal if not superior to any of the men in hunting, both on horseback and foot." After single-handedly warding off an attack by an enemy tribe, she developed a reputation as a brave fighter. She easily attracted male warriors to follow her in battle, where she always distinguished herself by her bravery. According to Denig, the Crows believed that she had "a charmed life which, with her daring feats, elevated her to a point of honor and respect not often reached by male warriors." Crow singers composed special songs to commemorate her gallantry, and she eventually became the third highest ranked chief in the entire tribe. Her status was so high, in fact, that she easily attracted women to marry her. By 1850, she had four wives, which also gave her additional status in the tribe. Denig concluded his biography of Woman Chief by saying in amazement, "Strange country this, where [berdache] males assume the dress and perform the duties of females, while women turn [like] men and mate with their own sex!"[9]

Whether attaining status as a warrior, a hunter, a healer, or an artist or simply by being hard working and generous, most amazons and berdache share an urge for success and prestige. They might not be good at doing the kinds of things that are typically expected of their sex, but instead of feeling deviant, they merely redirect their efforts into other kinds of prestigious activities. Moreover, berdache and amazons can gain notable material prosperity by selling their craftwork. Since they are considered sacred, their work is highly valued for its magical power as well as for its beauty.

The economic opportunities open to berdache and amazons are especially evident among the

Navajo. Whereas average men and women are restricted to certain economic activities, *nadle* know no such constraints. Goods produced by them are much in demand. Also, because they are believed to be lucky, they usually act as the head of the family and make decisions about family property. They supervise the family's farming, sheepherding, and selling or trading. With such opportunities, talented *nadle* are valued and respected for their contributions to the family's prosperity.

More than economic success is involved in such people's striving for excellence, however. Atypical children soon recognize their difference from other people. Psychological theory suggests that, if a family does not love and support such children, they will quickly internalize a negative self-image. Severe damage call result from feelings of deviance or inferiority. The way out of such self-hatred is either to deny any meaningful difference or to appreciate uniqueness. Difference is transformed—from *deviant* to *exceptional*— becoming a basis for respect rather than stigma. American Indian cultures deal with such atypical children by offering them prestige and rewards beyond what is available to the average person.

Masculine females and effeminate males in Western culture are often equally productive and successful, but they are so in the face of overwhelming odds. They may eventually come to appreciate their difference, but such self-acceptance comes more easily when one is considered "special" rather than "deviant." Few Western families show such youths more than grudging tolerance. If American families would adopt an appreciative attitude when faced with difference, much conflict and strife could be avoided when a family member turns out to be gay, lesbian, or bisexual. Such children could be nurtured and supported, and such nonprejudiced treatment would ultimately rebound to the family's great benefit.

BENEFITS FOR CHILDREN

From the Native American and Polynesian viewpoints, then, homosexuality and gender noncon-
formity do not threaten the family. An unusual phenomenon is instead incorporated into the kinship system in a productive and nondisruptive manner. Similarly, berdache and amazons are not seen as a threat to children. In fact, because they often have the reputation for intelligence, they are encouraged in some tribes to become teachers. In my fieldwork on Indian reservations and in the Yucatan, Alaska, Hawaii, and Thailand, I met a number of gender nonconformists who are highly respected teachers. Many of the venerated teachers of the sacred traditional hula ceremony among native Hawaiians are *mahus*.

Native American amazons also have the opportunity to become fathers. Among the Mohave, for example, the last person to have sex with the mother before she gives birth is considered to be the true father of the child. This allows an amazon to choose a male to impregnate her wife yet still claim paternity. The child is thus socially recognized as having an amazon father, who is thus able to fulfill all social roles that any other father would do.

Berdache have the opportunity to become parents through adoption. In fact, since they have a reputation for intelligence and generosity, they are often the first choice to become adoptive parents when there is a homeless child. For example, a Lakota berdache with whom I lived while conducting my 1982 fieldwork had adopted and raised four boys and three girls in his lifetime. The youngest boy was still living with him at the time, a typical teenager who was doing well in school. The household consisted of the berdache, his adopted son, the berdache's widowed mother, a number of nephews and nieces, and an elderly aunt.

Such an extended family contrasts sharply with contemporary American society, where gays, lesbians, and bisexuals are often alienated from their families, have trouble becoming adoptive or foster parents, and are often denied custody of their own children. Whereas American Indian communities can remedy the tragedy of a homeless child quickly and easily, foster and adoptive families are not so easy to come by in mainstream American society. As a result, the costs that Americans pay are high—in terms of both tax dollars and crimes committed by homeless youths.

Of course, the main reason for preventing gays and lesbians from becoming adoptive or foster parents—or even Big Brothers or Big Sisters—is the often expressed fear that the youths will be sexually molested. Since recent statistics show that well over 90 percent of child molesters are heterosexual men and their victims young girls, sexual orientation by itself is not a valid criterion on which to base adoption decisions. If it were, heterosexual men would not be allowed to adopt. The fact that homophobic leaders continue to oppose gay and lesbian adoptions when they know the statistics suggests that this issue is merely a rhetorical ploy. The real issue emerges most clearly in custody cases. Children are taken away from lesbian mothers or gay fathers, not because of molestation, but because they will provide "bad role models."

To consider an adult lesbian, gay man, or bisexual a bad role model is simple heterosexism. Children growing up in America today, no matter who their parents are, will see plenty of heterosexual role models—on television, at school, among neighbors and the parents of friends. Why not have a few gay and lesbian role models as an alternative? The answer is simple: American culture still regards it as a tragedy if a youth turns out to be lesbian, gay, or bisexual.

Nonheterosexist cultures, by contrast, emphasize an individual's freedom to decide his or her own fate. Paradoxically, those cultures often see sexual variance or gender nonconformity not as matters of choice but as inborn or as determined by the spirit world. Ironically, while the professed American ideal is "freedom of choice," in reality every child is subjected to extreme social pressures to conform. Despite the omnipresent American rhetoric of freedom, mainstream American culture continues to deny lesbian, gay, and bisexual youths the freedom to choose their own lifestyles. Ever since Freud, however, research has

made it abundantly clear that many psychological problems arise when childhood sexual desires are repressed. In fact, a greater incidence and severity of mental illness has been documented among more repressive cultures.[10]

BENEFITS FOR FRIENDSHIP

In America today, many men are prevented from expressing their feelings or developing close friendships with other men by the fear that others will think them homosexual. Men can be coworkers, sports buddies, even social companions, but nothing more personal. Consequently, many American men are left with only one legitimate, socially sanctioned intimate relationship in their lives—that with their wives. Is it therefore surprising that most men equate intimacy with sex or that, starved for intimacy, many elect to keep a mistress? To expect marriage to meet all a person's needs—to expect a spouse or significant other to be sexual playmate, economic partner, and best friend—places too heavy a burden on what today is an infirm institution.

During my fieldwork in Indonesia, by contrast, I was struck by the intensity of friendships between men (friendships that reminded me of the intense "blood brother" relationships between Native American men). In Indonesia, the highly structured mixed-sex marriage and kinship system is balanced and strengthened by unstructured same-sex friendship networks. The one complements the other, and both provide men with the support that they need to get through their lives.

Once gay men, lesbians, and bisexuals have transcended the fear of being thought homosexual, they open themselves to whole new possibilities for more satisfying same-sex friendships. In nonhomophobic societies, heterosexual men are free to develop same-sex friendships and nurture their same-sex friends. Because no stigma is attached to same-sex friendship, no pressure exists to choose between an exclusively homosexual or heterosexual orientation. In contemporary America, by contrast, where men are socialized to equate intimacy with a sexual relationship, some may feel forced to abandon an exclusively heterosexual identity for an exclusively homosexual one. Homophobia creates two distinct classes of men, self-identified "heterosexuals" and self-identified "homosexuals." More flexible notions of same-sex friendship in nonhomophobic societies mean less of a need to compartmentalize people on the basis of sexual behavior and less social consternation should the relationship between same-sex friends become erotic.

BENEFITS FOR SOCIETY AT LARGE

A culture that does not try to suppress the same-sex desires of its people can focus instead on the contributions that can be made by those who are different. We have already seen that American Indian berdache and amazons are honored for their spirituality, their artistic skills, and their hard work, all of which benefit the entire community. They are also often called on to mediate disputes between men and women. Married couples in particular turn to them since, as "half men/half women," they can see things from the perspective of both sexes. Their roles as go-betweens is integral to the smooth functioning of Native American communities.

Although there is not as much information on the social roles of amazons, the historical documents suggest that berdache performed their go-between function in traditional Indian cultures for males and females on joyous occasions as well. A number of tribes were noted to have employed berdache to facilitate budding romances between young women and men, a role that reached its highest development among the Cheyenne tribe of the Great Plains. One Cheyenne informant reported that berdache "were very popular and special favorites of young people, whether married or not, for they were noted matchmakers. They were fine love talkers. . . . When a young man wanted to send gifts for a young woman, one of these half-men-halfwomen was sent to the girl's relatives to do the talking in making the marriage."[11] Because of their spiritual connection, berdache were be-

lieved to possess the most potent love medicines. A Cheyenne bachelor who gained the assistance of a berdache was believed to be fortunate indeed since the berdache could often persuade the young woman and her family to accept the gift-laden horses that a man offered when he made a marriage proposal.

Whereas American Indian societies recognize and incorporate sexual diversity, others simply ignore it. When I was in Southeast Asia in 1987 and 1988, I learned that it was commonly known in both Thailand and Indonesia that some major government figures were homosexual. Although those men did not publicly broadcast their homosexuality, neither did they make any attempt to hide their same-sex lovers from public view. Such tolerance benefits both the individuals, who are allowed to live their lives as they choose, and the nation, which utilized their leadership skills.

In my research, I have found that those societies with accepted homosexual roles ironically do not emphasize the sexual activities of homosexuals. Everyone knows their sexual preferences, but those preferences are considered matters for private, not public, concern. Homosexuality is therefore not politicized. In America, however, the homophobic Right has made such an issue of what it considers to be deviant sexuality that it has stimulated the development of a politically active gay community.

The suppression of sexual diversity *inevitably* results in social turmoil. Families and communities are divided by the issue. Suicides are occasioned by the discovery, or the fear of discovery, of secret sex lives. When the individuals whose secrets are uncovered are public figures, the ensuing media scandal can bring a community to the point of hysteria—witness Boise, Idaho, in the 1950s and schoolteacher firings in countless communities.

The persecution of gays, lesbians, and bisexuals also endangers the freedom of other groups—indeed, any group. For persecution rarely confines itself to one group. For example, Adolf Hitler tried to rid Germany of Jews, but also extended his campaign to include homosexuals. The Ayatollah Khomeini similarly exterminated infidels and beheaded homosexuals. The point here is that no one group is safe until all groups are safe.

By continuing to discriminate against lesbians, gay men, and bisexuals, the United States is losing the respect of many in the world community—the Dutch and other progressive governments have already made formal diplomatic protests against discriminatory U.S. policies. Sodomy laws remain on the books and are enforced in many states, homosexuals are excluded from the military, sexual minorities are denied equal protection under the law—all this in a nation devoted to "life, liberty, and the pursuit of happiness." The situation today is similar to that in the early 1960s, when progressive governments in Europe, Asia, and especially the newly independent African nations voiced their support for African-American civil rights protestors. Such diplomatic action helped pressure the Kennedy administration to take action against racial segregation. For how could America champion its ideals of freedom and expect to maintain its position as the leader of the "free" world when people of color were treated so unequally?

Acceptance of people's right to be different is the certain hallmark of democracy and freedom. This is why the New Right's attempt to suppress homosexuality is so dangerous for the larger society. The dominant message propounded by the New Right in the 1980s has been that everyone should be the same. That desire for sameness has a strong attraction for people living in a diverse and changing society. Instead, we should be thankful that we are *not* all the same. If we were, society would lose the creativity and vitality that comes from difference. Faced with the new global competitiveness of the 1990s, we as Americans are hardly in a position *not* to promote independent thinking and creativity. Mindless conformity is an economic and emotional and intellectual dead end.

An appreciation of diversity, not just a tolerance of minorities, is what will promote future American progress. As the American Indian example illustrates so well, far from being a threat to religion, to the family, to children, and to society in general, homosexuality can benefit both men and women as well as bring freedom to all.

NOTES

1. Quoted in *Project 10 Newsletter* (March 1989), 1.
2. Clellan Ford and Frank Beach, *Patterns of Sexual Behavior* (New York: Harper, 1951).
3. W. W. Hill, "The Status of the Hermaphrodite and Transvestite in Navaho Culture," *American Anthropologist* 37 (1935): 274.
4. Ibid.
5. The results of my 1979–84 fieldwork are reported in Walter L. Williams, *The Spirit and the Flesh: Sexual Diversity in American Indian Culture* (Boston: Beacon, 1986). Part of my Indonesian research is contained in Walter L. Williams, *Javanese Lives: Women and Men in Modern Indonesian Society* (New Brunswick, N.J.: Rutgers University Press, 1991). My research among Polynesians and Native Alaskans has not yet been written up. I express my gratitude to the Council for the International Exchange of Scholars, for a Fulbright research grant to Indonesia (with a side trip to Thailand and Malaysia), to the University of Southern California faculty research fund for trips to conduct research in Hawaii, and to the Institute for the Study of Women and Men for a travel grant to go to Alaska. My main work there was among Aleuts and Yupik Eskimos.
6. Quoted in Williams, *Spirit and Flesh*, 57.
7. Ibid., 54.
8. Ibid., 58–59.
9. Ibid., 245–46,
10. George Devereux, Mohave Ethnopsychiatry (Washington, D.C.: Smithsonian Institution, 1969), viii–ix, xii–xiii, and "Institutionalized Homosexuality of the Mohave Indians," *Human Biology* 9 (1937): 498–499, 518. For examples of other sexually free societies, see Williams, *Spirit and Flesh*, chap. 12.
11. Quoted in Williams, *Spirit and Flesh*, 70–71.

58

Breaking Bread

BELL HOOKS
CORNEL WEST

bh: In the past you have talked about "combative spirituality" that seeks to, as you put it, "develop a mode of community that sustains people in their humanity." What do you feel is eroding that kind of dynamic spirituality in Black life?

CW: Well, there's no doubt about it, what is eroding it is market forces. What is eroding it is consumerism, hedonism, narcissism, privatism, and careerism of Americans in general, and Black Americans in particular. You cannot have a tradition of resistance and critique along with pervasive hedonism. It means then that we must have spokesmen for genuine love, care, sacrifice, and risk in the face of market forces that highlight buying, selling, and profit making. And poor communities of course have been so thoroughly inundated and saturated with the more pernicious forms of buying and selling, especially drugs and women's bodies and so forth, that these traditions of care and respect have almost completely broken down.

When our grandmothers are not respected, so that mothers are not respected, fathers have no respect, preachers have no respect—no one has respect. Respect is externalized, given to those who exercise the most brutal forms of power. Respect goes to the gun; that's what market forces lead to....

CW: ...I want to suggest that there are only three ways out. All of them are forms of conversion. There is either personal conversion by means of love of another, love of a mother, fa-

ther, a mate, a spouse, that's strong enough to convince one to shift from a nihilistic mode to a meaningful mode. The second is political conversion, in which an ideology or a cause becomes strong enough to shift from a nihilistic mode to a meaningful mode.

And the third form of conversion is that of religious conversion, be it Christianity or Islam, or any faith that convinces you that there are, in fact, reasons to live and serve, so that one sidesteps the nihilistic traps, be it drugs, alcoholism, or any of the various forms of addiction that are so deeply ingrained in our society. Without some form of conversion, we will simply lose thousands of people, especially Black people. This will have serious repercussions for the next generation.

bh: When people talk about the growing popularity of Black women writers, or when they try to contrast that and say somehow Black male writers are receiving less attention, I always find that problematic, because people often don't go on to talk about what it is in these works that are giving them the quality of appeal that we may not see in many works by Black male writers.

And I would say that one of the things that's in all these works is a concern with spiritual well-being. Toni Cade Bambara begins her novel *The Salt Eaters* with the question, "are you sure that you want to be well?" And she is not just talking about physical well-being, she is talking about a well-being of the spirit.

CW: That's right. Of the spirit and the soul.

bh: Certainly a novel like Paule Marshall's *Praise Song for the Widow* has to do with a politicized spiritual reawakening.

CW: I think something else is going on, too. And I think, for example, of Toni Morrison's *Beloved*, in which the love ethic sits at the center. You don't see that kind of self-love affirmed in many works by Black male writers.

bh: When I think about *Beloved* I remember that the person who brings the prophetic message of redemptive love, it is the grandmother, in her role of preacher—she goes into the field —and preaches that sermon about the necessity of love.

CW: That sermon is one of the great moments in American literature. One of the great moments in modern literature. And you don't find that kind of sermon in a Richard Wright or a James Baldwin or even Ralph Ellison. You just don't find it. There is a depth of love for Black humanity which is both affirmed and enacted that, I think, speaks very deeply to these spiritual issues. And I think this relates precisely to the controversy in the relations between Black men and women.

bh: That is exactly what I was going to ask you. What does it mean for a progressive Black male on the Left to ally himself with the critique of patriarchy and sexism, to be supportive of feminist movement?

CW: We have to recognize that there cannot be relationships unless there is commitment, unless there is loyalty, unless there is love, patience, persistence. Now, the degree to which these values are eroding is the degree to which there cannot be healthy relationships. And if there are no relationships then there is only the joining of people for the purposes of bodily stimulation.

   And if we live in a society in which these very values are eroding, then it's no accident that we are going to see less and less qualitative relations between Black men and women.

   At the same time, and this is one reason why I think many Black men and women are

at each other's throats, is because there is tremendous rage in Black men.

bh: Talk about it.

CW: Just as there is a tremendous sense of inadequacy and rage in Black women. That feeling of inadequacy and rage is also in Black men.

bh: But this rage takes a different form.

CW: That's right. The rage takes a different form, the sense of inadequacy takes a different form.

bh: You are one of the few men who's talked about the fact that often suppressed rage takes the form of Black male violence against Black women.

CW: That's right, it is one of the most insidious manifestations imaginable. This rage and this inadequacy, when they come up in their raw form in a violent culture means combat. We have always had the rage—don't get me wrong. We have always felt the inadequacy, but we've also had traditions that were able to channel it in such a way that we could remain in that boat with the tension, with the hostility, because there was also love, care, loyalty, and solidarity.

bh: Well, one of the things that you talked about earlier and I think you can link that rage to is the whole question of fear and failure.

CW: That's right. That's the fundamental problem. This is what Marcus Garvey understood. In many ways he was the first one to understand it. He understood the fact that Black people could only be fully human when they were free enough from the fear and failure which is imposed upon them by a larger racist society, but it would not be a matter of blaming that society, it would be a matter of understanding that society and asserting themselves boldly and defiantly as human beings. Very few Black folk ever reach that level, and more must.

bh: I think we also have to break away from the bourgeois tradition of romantic love which isn't necessarily about creating the conditions for what you call critical affirmation. And I think this produces a lot of the tensions between heterosexual Black men and Black women, and between gays. We must think of not just romantic love, but of love in general as being about people mutually meeting each other's needs and giving and receiving critical feedback.

CW: That's so, so very true. We actually see some of the best of this in the traditions of contemporary Africa that has a more deromanticized, or less romanticized, conception of relationship, talking more about partnership. I know this from my loving Ethiopian wife.

bh: That's where, as Black people, we have much to learn from looking at global revolutionary struggles, looking at, for example, the work of Nicaraguans. There has to be a re-conceptualization of what it means to be engaged in a primary liberation struggle as we also try to alter issues of gender.

That's what we haven't done enough of yet, theoretically, as African Americans, to begin to conceptualize how we re-envision Black liberation struggle in ways that allow us to look at gender and the pain that we feel negotiating gender politics.

CW: Sexuality in general must be discussed. There is a reluctance in the Black community to talk seriously about sexuality. We've got significant numbers of gays and lesbians who often-times are rendered invisible, as if their humanity somehow ought to be hidden and concealed.

bh: It's interesting when you think about the kind of compassion, love, and openness that many of us remember in the traditional Black church, because in fact we don't remember those Black gay folk as going off to set up a separate sub-culture that alienates and estranges them from Black community. But in fact we remember them vitally engaged in the maintenance and sustaining of Black culture.

CW: There's no doubt, good God almighty, if you look Black music in the Black church and the crucial role that Black gays and lesbi-

ans have played there, this is the grand example. And it's the failure of the Black religious leadership to come to terms with these issues of sexuality, but it's also a fear on behalf of the congregation that talking about this may undermine some of the consensus in other areas and thereby render the community less able to confront other issues.

bh: So the people won't think I'm stereotyping, when we talk about the roles people play musically, I think that we have to remember that there has always been in the realm of Black cultural production an acceptance of certain forms of radical behavior, behavior that, within the status quo of everyday life, people might object to, but certainly when we look at the tradition of blues singers, the Black women who were cross-dressing, if we look at the career of someone like Josephine Baker, I mean, we see an openness, a tolerance within the sphere of cultural production that may not have made itself known in other spheres of Black life.

CW: That is so very true.

bh: Well, Cornel, as we bring this discussion to a close, are there any last words that you want to give us? Will we have a renewed Black liberation struggle? Will the struggle take another form? Will it be a more inclusive struggle? Or will we have simultaneous movements?

CW: It's hard to say, but, I think the important thing is that we must never give up hope. Black people have always been in a very difficult predicament, we must always preserve our subversive memory, which is to say our attempt to stay in tune with the best of our history. And at the same time we must always be explicitly moral in an all-inclusive manner so that we resist all forms of xenophobia.

bh: How do you define xenophobia?

CW: Xenophobia is a hatred of the other, be it a hatred of individuals different from one's self, be it a Black, White, Jewish, or Korean person.

All forms of racism must be rejected directly and openly.

I have hope for the next generation. I think that they're up against a lot. Market forces are stronger now than they've been in American history. But I also believe in the ingenuity, in the intelligence, the beauty, the laughter and the love that Black people can give both themselves and to others. And that is the raw stuff out of which any major movement for justice is made.

bh: When you talked about the need for a politics that deals with death, dread, despair, disappointment, you talked about the fact that even as we identify strategic conflicts and problems, we also have to identify the location of our joys.

CW: That's right.

bh: You certainly identified that one way cultural production functions in Black communities is to awaken our joy. And I was thinking, as we close, of the impact of Anita Baker's song, "You Bring Me Joy."

CW: Yes.

bh: Which returns us to that notion of redemptive care, reciprocal, mutual sharing, that brings about a sense of joy. It's the kind of joy and fellowship I feel always in talking with you. Thank you.

CW: Thank you.

CREDITS

15. Matthews, Nancy A. *Gender & Society,* 3(4), pp. 518–532. Copyright © 1989 by Sociologists for Women in Society. Reprinted by permission of Sage Publications, Inc.
16. Messner, Mike. "When Bodies Are Weapons." *Changing Men: Issues in Gender, Sex and Politics,* 21: 89–98, 1990.
17. "Abortion Stories on the Border" by Debbie Nathan. Copyright © Debbie Nathan, 1991. Originally published in *Women and Other Aliens: Essays from the U.S.–Mexican Border.* Reprinted by permission of Cinco Puntos Press.
18. Rapp, Rayna. "Constructing Amniocentesis: Maternal and Medical Discourses." From *Uncertain Terms* by Faye Ginsburg and Anna Lowenhaupt Tsing. Copyright © 1990 by Faye Ginsburg and Anna Lowenhaupt Tsing. Reprinted by permission of Beacon Press.
19. Rothman, Barbara Katz. On "Surrogacy." From *Recreating Motherhood: Ideology and Technology in a Patriarchal Society* by Barbara Katz Rothman. Copyright © 1989 by Barbara Katz Rothman. Reprinted by permission of W. W. Norton & Company, Inc.
20. Tolman, Deborah L. *Gender & Society,* 8(3), pp. 324–342. Copyright © 1994 by Sociologists for Women in Society. Reprinted by permission of Sage Publications, Inc.
21. Staples, Robert. "Anita Hill, Sexual Harassment, and Gender Politics in the Black Community." From *The Black Family,* 5th ed., Robert Staples (ed.), pp. 45–51. Copyright © 1993 Wadsworth Publishing Co.
22. Enloe, Cynthia. *The Morning After: Sexual Politics at the End of the Cold War,* pp. 152–160. Copyright © 1993 University of California Press.
23. Frye, Marilyn. "Lesbian 'Sex.'" In *Willful Virgin: Essays In Feminism,* The Crossing Press, 1992. pp. 109–119.
24. From *Gay Culture in America* by Gilbert Herdt. Copyright © 1992 by Beacon Press. Reprinted by permission of Beacon Press.
25. Accad, Evelyne. "Sexuality and Sexual Politics: Conflicts and Contradictions for Contemporary Women in the Middle East," in Chandra Talpade Mohanty, Ann Russo, and Lourdes Torres (eds.), *Third World Women and the Politics of Feminism.* Bloomington, IN: Indiana University Press, 1991.
26. From *How We Survived Communism and Even Laughed* by Slavenka Drakulic. Copyright © 1991 by Slavenka Drakulic. Reprinted by permission of W. W. Norton & Company, Inc.
27. Kimmel, Michael S. "Judaism, Masculinity and Feminism." *Changing Men,* Summer/Fall 1987, pp. 77–80.
28. From *Borderlands/La Frontera: The New Mestiza,* copyright © 1987 by Gloria Anzaldúa. Reprinted with permission from Aunt Lute Books.
29. Higginbotham, Anastasia. "Chicks Goin' at It," in *Listen Up: Voices from the Next Feminist Generation,* pp. 3–11. Barbara Findler (ed.), Seattle: Seal Press, 1995.
30. Scheper-Huges, Nancy. *Death Without Weeping: Mother Love and Child Death in Northeast Brazil,* pp. 340–365. Berkeley: University of California Press, 1992.
31. Collins, Patricia Hill. "The Meaning of Motherhood in Black Culture and Black Mother–Daughter Relationships." In *Double Stitch,* pp. 42–60, Patricia Bell-Scott et al. (eds.) Beacon Press, 1991.
32. Reprinted from *Mothering: Ideology, Experience and Agency,* edited by Evelyn Na-

kano Glenn, Grace Chang and Linda Rennie Forcey. New York: Routledge, 1994. Reprinted by permission of Routledge, New York.

33. LaRossa, Ralph. "Fatherhood and Social Change." *Family Relations,* 37: 451–457. Copyright © 1988 by the National Council on Family Relations, 3989 Central Ave. NE, Suite 550, Minneapolis, MN 55421. Reprinted by permission.

34. Gilmore, David D. "Men and Women in Southern Spain: 'Domestic Power' Revisited." *American Anthropologist,* 92:4, December 1990.

35. From *Uncertain Terms* by Faye Ginsburg and Anna Lowenhaupt Tsing. Copyright © 1990 by Faye Ginsburg and Anna Lowenhaupt Tsing. Reprinted by permission of Beacon Press.

36. Kibria, Nazli. *Gender & Society,* 9(3), pp. 289–309. Copyright © 1995 by Sociologists for Women in Society. Reprinted by permission of Sage Publications, Inc.

37. Higginbotham, Elizabeth and Lynn Weber. *Gender and Society,* 6(3), pp. 416–440 (edited). Copyright © 1992 by Sociologists for Women in Society. Reprinted by permission of Sage Publications, Inc.

38. Nardi, Peter M. "The Social World of Magicians: Gender and Conjuring." *Sex Roles,* 19(11/12): 759–770, 1988.

39. Williams, Christine. *Doing Women's Work,* pp. 128–151. Copyright © 1993 by Sage Publications. Reprinted by permissions of Sage Publications, Inc.

40. Giuffre, Patti A., and Christine L. Williams, *Gender & Society,* 8(3), pp. 378–401. Copyright © 1994 by Sociologists for Women in Society. Reprinted by permission of Sage Publications, Inc.

41. Reprinted from Karen J. Hossfeld "Their Logic against Them: Contradictions in Sex, Race, and Class in Silicon Valley" in *Women Workers and Global Restructuring,* edited by Kathryn Ward. Copyright © 1990 by Cornell University. Used by permission of the publisher, Cornell University Press. An ILR Press book.

42. Copyright © 1993 by Teresa Amott. Reprinted by permission of Monthly Review Foundation.

43. Reprinted from Esther Ngan-Ling Chow, "Asian-American Women at Work" in *Women of Color in U.S. Society,* edited by Maxine Baca Zinn and Bonnie Thorton Dill, pp. 203–227. Copyright © 1994 by Temple University. Reprinted by permission of Temple University Press.

44. Reprinted from *Beyond Silence Voices,* edited by Lois Weis and Michelle Fine by permission of the State University of New York Press. Copyright © 1993 by State University of New York Press.

45. *Color, Class, and Country,* Gay Young and Bette J. Dickerson (eds.). London: Zed Books, 1994.

46. From *The American Black Male,* R. Majors and J. V. Gordon (eds.). Chicago: Nelson-Hall, 1993.

47. Denski, Stan and Sholle, David, "Metal Men and Glamour Boys: Gender Performance in Heavy Metal" in Craig, (ed.), *Men, Masculinity and the Media,* pp. 41–60. Copyright © 1991 by Sage Publications. Reprinted by permission of Sage Publications, Inc.

48. Clara Sue Kidwell, "Indian Women as Cultural Mediators," *Ethnohistory,* 39:2 (Spring 1992), pp. 97–107. Copyright © 1992 American Society for Ethnohistory. Reprinted with permission.